SOCIOLOGY

A BRIEF INTRODUCTION

Third Canadian Edition

SOCIOLOGY'S GLOBAL VIEW

Sociology: A Brief Introduction explores key sociological issues from the viewpoints of many global cultures. This map serves as a quick guide to a *sample* of passages related to globalization topics.

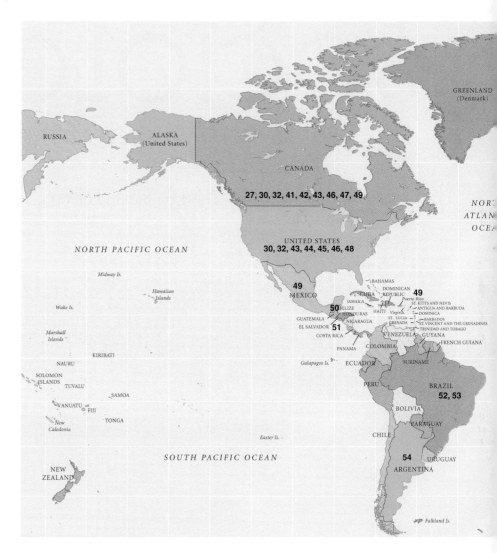

Africa

1. International MTV (Africa) p. 141
2. Strategies to eradicate poverty (sub-Saharan Africa) p. 223
3. AIDS crisis p. 400
4. Infant mortality (Sierra Leone) p. 385
5. Rites of passage (Congo) p. 86
6. Women in politics (South Africa, Uganda) p. 354

Asia / Oceania

7. Media impact (Bhutan) p. 151
8. Female beauty and tribal identity (Thailand) p. 165
9. Disability as master status (China) p. 376
10. Cloning of cows (Japan) p. 418
11. Internal stratification (Japan) p. 226
12. Respect for elders (South Korea) p. 87
13. Cultural insensitivity (Japan) p. 142
14. Oligarchy (China) p. 350
15. Capitalism (China) p. 346
16. Media censorship (China) p. 417
17. Population policy (China) p. 376
18. Nike and Reebok factories in Indonesia p. 213

Central Asia

19. Western media in India p. 70
20. Collapse of communism (U.S.S.R.) p. 4
21. Effects of globalization (India) p. 213
22. Caste system (India) p. 187
23. Outsourcing (India) p. 364
24. Opium trade (Afghanistan), p. 158
25. Global off-shoring (India/Romania/ Japan/China/Africa) p. 363
26. New social movements in rural villages (India) p. 411

Europe

27. Child care policy (Western Europe, Canada) p. 93
28. Iris scanning (Netherlands) p. 164

SOCIOLOGY

A BRIEF INTRODUCTION

Third Canadian Edition

RICHARD T. SCHAEFER
DePaul University

BONNIE HAALAND
Kwantlen Polytechnic University

McGraw-Hill
Ryerson

Toronto   Montréal   Boston   Burr Ridge, IL   Dubuque, IA   Madison, WI   New York
San Francisco   St. Louis   Bangkok   Bogotá   Caracas   Kuala Lumpur   Lisbon   London
Madrid   Mexico City   Milan   New Delhi   Santiago   Seoul   Singapore   Sydney   Taipei

The McGraw·Hill Companies

McGraw-Hill Ryerson

Sociology: A Brief Introduction
Third Canadian Edition

ISBN-13: 978-0-07-076420-0
ISBN-10: 0-07-076420-4

1 2 3 4 5 6 7 8 9 10   TCP   0 9

Printed and bound in Canada.

Vice-President and Editor-in-Chief: Joanna Cotton
Publisher: Cara Yarzab
Sponsoring Editor: Nick Durie
Marketing Manager: Michele Peach
Managing Editor, Development: Kelly Dickson
Developmental Editors: Su Mei Ku & Kelly Cochrane
Editorial Associate: Marina Seguin
Photo/Permission Research: Cynthia Howard
Supervising Editor: Kara Stahl
Copy Editors: Joe Zingrone & Elspeth McFadden
Team Lead, Production: Jennifer Hall
Cover Design: Dianna Little
Interior Design: Brett Miller
Cover Image Credit: © Mike Powell/Getty Images
Page Layout: Aptara, Inc.
Printer: Transcontinental Printing Group—Interglobe

Library and Archives Canada Cataloguing in Publication

Schaefer, Richard T.
    Sociology : a brief introduction / Richard T. Schaefer, Bonnie
Haaland. – 3rd Canadian ed.

Includes bibliographical references and index.
ISBN 978-0-07-076420-0

    1. Sociology.   2. Sociology–Textbooks.   I. Haaland, Bonnie   II. Title.

HM586.S32 2009   301   C2008-907154-9

DEDICATION

To my son, Peter
— Richard T. Schaefer

In memory of Patrick Kennedy Dooley
1991–2008
— Bonnie Haaland

ABOUT THE AUTHORS

RICHARD T. SCHAEFER

Growing up in Chicago at a time when neighbourhoods were going through transitions in ethnic and racial composition, Richard T. Schaefer found himself increasingly intrigued by what was happening, how people were reacting, and how these changes were affecting neighbourhoods and people's jobs. His interest in social issues caused him to gravitate to sociology courses at Northwestern University, where he eventually received a B.A. in sociology.

"Originally as an undergraduate, I thought I would go on to law school and become a lawyer. But after taking a few sociology courses, I found myself wanting to learn more about what sociologists studied and fascinated by the kinds of questions they raised." This fascination led him to obtain his M.A. and Ph.D. in sociology from the University of Chicago. Dr. Schaefer's continuing interest in race relations led him to write his master's thesis on the membership of the Ku Klux Klan and his doctoral thesis on racial prejudice and race relations in Britain.

Dr. Schaefer went on to become a professor of sociology. He has taught introductory sociology for over 35 years to students in colleges, adult education programs, nursing programs, and even a maximum-security prison. Dr. Schaefer's love of teaching is apparent in his interaction with his students. "I find myself constantly learning from the students who are in my classes and from reading what they write. Their insights into the material we read or current events that we discuss often become part of future course material and sometimes even find their way into my writing."

Dr. Schaefer is author of the 10th edition of *Sociology* (McGraw-Hill, 2008) and the 3rd edition of *Sociology Matters* (McGraw-Hill, 2008). He is also the author of *Racial and Ethnic Groups*, now in its 10th edition, and *Race and Ethnicity in the United States*, 4th edition. Dr. Schaefer is the general editor of the three-volume *Encyclopedia of Race, Ethnicity, and Society* (2008). His articles and book reviews have appeared in many journals, including *American Journal of Sociology*; *Phylon: A Review of Race and Culture*; *Contemporary Sociology*; *Sociology and Social Research; Sociological Quarterly*; and *Teaching Sociology*. He served as president of the Midwest Sociological Society in 1994–1995.

Dr. Schaefer's advice to students is to "look at the material and make connections to your own life and experiences. Sociology will make you a more attentive observer of how people in groups interact and function. It will also make you more aware of people's different needs and interests—and perhaps more ready to work for the common good, while still recognizing the individuality of each person."

BONNIE HAALAND

Bonnie Haaland has been teaching sociology for more than 25 years, to teachers, bankers, and nurses, to new high school graduates, and senior undergraduates. She has taught classes with as many as 350 students and as few as nine, and she has used various modes of instruction. Bonnie was one of the first instructors at the University of Western Ontario to teach courses by using distance education technology, which simultaneously connected clusters of students in smaller cities and towns throughout southwestern Ontario. At Western, she later coordinated a program involving distance education, overseeing the delivery of courses in such fields as chemistry, nursing, psychology, anthropology, and English. During this time, Bonnie has also been actively involved in research related to distance and continuing education, and presenting papers at conferences, such as the International Congress on Distance Education in Melbourne, Australia.

In addition to teaching at the University of Western Ontario, Bonnie has taught at the University of Regina and is currently at Kwantlen Polytechnic University, where she teaches introductory sociology and other undergraduate courses.

Bonnie is the author of *Emma Goldman: Sexuality and the Impurity of the State*; a co-author of *Sociology: A Brief Introduction*, First Canadian Edition, Census Update Edition, and Second Canadian Edition; and author of articles published in Canadian and U.S. academic journals. She is the recipient of the Canadian Association for University Continuing Education's Award of Excellence for her article "In Pursuit of Self: The Values of the Post-War Baby Boom Generation and the Implications for Continuing Education."

Bonnie grew up in Saskatchewan and graduated with distinction from the University of Saskatchewan with a B.A., from the University of Western Ontario with an M.A., and from the University of Toronto with a Ph.D. She currently lives in South Surrey/White Rock, British Columbia.

CONTENTS IN BRIEF

CONTENTS

15

POPULATION, HEALTH, AND COMMUNITIES 368

16

GLOBALIZATION, THE ENVIRONMENT, AND SOCIAL CHANGE 405

LIST OF BOXES

LIST OF SOCIAL POLICY SECTIONS

SOCIOLOGY
MAKE THE CONNECTION

These days, students like you are required to meet ever-increasing and often conflicting demands on both your academic and personal time. Your technological savvy allows you to navigate through social worlds from what seems like a never-ending set of possibilities. In how many ways can your friends contact you? Can you even remember a time, in the past year, when you turned off *all* your MP3 players, cellphones, PDAs, laptops, and other communication devices? (Maybe when on an airplane?)

To survive this new age and rise to the challenges it sets for us, we are becoming more and more "connected." Your own social networks, shaped and maintained fundamentally by newer communication technologies, are larger and more wide-reaching than those of other age groups. To be successful, both professionally and personally, you need to learn to connect the dots which represent your networks.

Sociology, A Brief Introduction is your guide. After all, sociology is the study of social worlds. This text offers you the opportunity to learn how to see yourselves as part of a larger entity—a friendship, a university community, a national community, a global community—and to explore diverse and often contradictory interpretations of those relationships.

The ability to draw parallels between the forces shaping your own lives and those shaping a friendship, a university, a nation, or the globe, is the first step in developing your own sociological imagination, and thus, making the connection.

PREFACE

As I leave the classroom each day, I am struck by how my students' lives have changed since I taught my first sociology class in the late 1970s. I can't help but notice how "connected" students seem today; how technologically savvy they appear; how their social networks, shaped and maintained fundamentally by newer communication technologies, are larger and more wide-reaching than those of other age groups. The rapidity of technological change and the diverse—and often conflicting—demands for undergraduates' time and attention are challenges with which students must contend on a daily basis. The dramatic increases in tuition costs and the increased need to hold a job while studying, the need for Internet access and currency in computer skills, the ubiquitous intrusion of the mass media and consumer culture, environmental issues and the building of "green" communities, and the global financial crisis—these are just a few of the concerns that preoccupy students. By implication, of course, my students' challenges, to a large degree, become my challenges. Increasingly, I see my role, and more specifically the role of my discipline, as instrumental in helping undergraduates process and navigate the content of their social worlds. In this way, sociology is a dynamic discipline with great potential to engage learners in their social worlds, not solely as actors but also as observers and interpreters. Sociology offers the opportunity to see ourselves as part of a larger entity—a friendship, a university community, a national community, a global community—and to explore diverse and often contradictory interpretations of those relationships.

To see Mills's *sociological imagination* actualized through students' ability to make the connections among the forces shaping their own lives and those shaping a friendship, a university, a nation, or the globe is a challenge and accomplishment for student and instructor alike. *Sociology: A Brief Introduction, Third Canadian Edition,* is written with that goal in mind. This text strengthens the foundation laid in the first and second Canadian editions, providing compelling and relevant topics and examples that resonate with students, that are situated in a global context, and that are consistently interpreted through the lens of four theoretical perspectives. Key features of this third Canadian edition include the following:

- **A new chapter and restructured chapters.** The third Canadian edition contains a new chapter on the mass media (Chapter 6); a stand-alone chapter on global inequality (Chapter 9); a chapter (Chapter 5) amalgamating former Chapters 5 ("Social Interaction and Social Structure") and 6 ("Groups and Organizations"); a restructured chapter that combines population, health, and communities (Chapter 15); and an amalgamated and expanded chapter (Chapter 16) that now includes the topic of globalization and contains former Chapters 15 ("Communities and the Environment") and 16 ("Social Movements, Social Change, and Technology").

- **Hot topics of Canadian interest with a strengthened global focus.** The third Canadian edition covers such topics as Africentric schools in Toronto, the role of religion in accessing the labour market in Canada, the growth of "knowledge workers" in Canada, the views of Muslim Canadians on their treatment by fellow Canadians, media racism, the increase in the percentage of families without children in Canada, the global "McDonaldization" of society, the global reach of media, transnational crime, global immigration, the brain drain, the economic effects of globalization, global social movements, the impact of globalization on the environment, global poverty, consumer culture and global patterns of consumption, global disparities in computer access, and gender and global rates of literacy and educational access.

- **Extensive updates to statistics, research, and visuals.** This edition uses the latest data and reports from Statistics Canada (the 2006 census in particular), data from the Canadian

Council on Learning, Human Resources and Social Development Canada, the International Institute for Democracy and Electoral Assistance, Elections Canada, the Inter-Parliamentary Union, the United Nations, the results of polls conducted by such groups as Environics, Decima Research, and the Pew Research Center. New research findings have been incorporated, drawing on the work of Canadian researchers whenever possible. In terms of pedagogical features, roughly half of the boxes, 25 percent of the Social Policy sections, and 43 percent of the chapter-opening excerpts are new. Furthermore, the photo program has been revised to include current and relevant examples and illustrations for students.

- **Continued focus on providing student applications and fostering the sociological imagination.** Each chapter of *Sociology: A Brief Introduction, Third Canadian Edition*, contains Use Your Sociological Imagination critical thinking sections, appropriately positioned, which foster critical thinking about the material covered in the chapter. In addition, as part of the theoretical foundation of this edition, Applying Theory questions have been retained as well as revised, placed in the popular boxed features, Research in Action and Sociology in the Global Community. Think About It captions accompany some figures, encouraging students' critical engagement with sociological data. Updated end-of-chapter Social Policy sections continue to help students forge links between sociological theory and the world around them. Additional Social Policy readings have been revised and updated.
- **Comprehensive and balanced coverage of sociological perspectives throughout the text.** Chapter 1 introduces, defines, and contrasts the functionalist, conflict, interactionist, and feminist perspectives. The postmodern perspective is also introduced in Chapter 1. We explore the distinctive views of the four major perspectives as they relate to such topics as social institutions (Chapter 5), deviance (Chapter 7), families (Chapter 12), education (Chapter 13) and health (Chapter 15).
- **An integrated learning system.** The text, iStudy Sociology, Online Learning Centre Web site, and *Reel Society* video clips work together as an integrated learning system to bring the theories, research findings, and basic concepts of sociology to life for students. Offering a combination of print, multimedia, and Web-based materials, this comprehensive system meets the needs of instructors and students who have a variety of teaching and learning styles.

The Plan for this Book

Sociology: A Brief Introduction, Third Canadian Edition, is divided into 16 chapters that study human behaviour concisely from the perspective of sociologists. The opening chapter ("Understanding Sociology") presents a brief history of the discipline, introduces key Canadian sociologists, and explains the four basic theories and perspectives used in sociology. Chapter 2 ("Sociological Research") describes the major quantitative and qualitative research methods.

The next five chapters focus on key sociological concepts: Chapter 3 ("Culture") illustrates how sociologists study people's behaviour. Chapter 4 ("Socialization") reveals how humans are most distinctively social animals who learn the attitudes and behaviour viewed as appropriate in their particular cultures. We examine "Social Interaction, Groups, and Social Structure" in Chapter 5, and "The Mass Media" in Chapter 6. Chapter 7 ("Deviance and Social Control") reviews how we conform to and deviate from established norms.

The next four chapters consider various aspects of social inequality. Chapter 8 ("Stratification in Canada") introduces us to the presence of social inequality in this country, while Chapter 9 ("Global Inequality") examines inequality within, between, and among countries and regions of the world. Chapter 10 ("Racial and Ethnic Inequality") and Chapter 11 ("Gender Relations") analyze specific and ubiquitous types of inequality.

The next three chapters examine the major social institutions of human society. Marriage, family diversity, and divorce are some of the topics discussed in Chapter 12 ("Families and Intimate Relationships"). Other social institutions are considered in Chapter 13 ("Religion and Education") and Chapter 14 ("Politics and the Economy").

The final chapters of the text introduce major themes in our changing world. Chapter 15 helps us understand "Population, Health, and Communities" in Canadian society and around the world. In Chapter 16, we examine the importance of "Globalization, the Environment, and Social Change" in our lives.

The third Canadian edition has been fully updated to reflect the most recent developments in sociology both in Canada and around the globe. It provides the most relevant and meaningful applications for students, including the Use Your Sociological Imagination sections, the updated Applying Theory questions that appear in each boxed feature and Social Policy section, and the new tables that help to sum up the theory discussed. Following is a summary of just some of the content changes in the third Canadian edition.

☐ CHAPTER-BY-CHAPTER CHANGES

CHAPTER 1 Understanding Sociology

- Updated feminist theories
- Expanded discussion on early women sociologists
- New Research in Action box: "Looking at Sports from Four Perspectives"
- New table on the major sociological perspectives

CHAPTER 2 Sociological Research

- Reorganized chapter topics: ethics of research is moved to the outset of the chapter to give this topic greater emphasis
- The differences between qualitative and quantitative research are clarified
- Discussion on technology and sociological research is expanded
- New table of Major Research Designs

CHAPTER 3 Culture

- Updated statistics and examples throughout
- Postmodernism is discussed in more detail
- Updated and expanded "Social Policy and Culture: Multiculturalism"

CHAPTER 4 Socialization

- New chapter-opening vignette from "The Residential School Impact" in *Healing Words* by the Aboriginal Healing Foundation
- Reorganized order of topics
- Discussion of aging is moved from a later chapter to this chapter
- Updated section on teens in the workforce, with more international examples
- New table on theoretical approaches to the development of the self
- Expanded and updated "Social Policy: Day Care Around the World"

CHAPTER 5 Social Interaction, Groups, and Social Structure

- Merging of Chapters 5 and 6 from the Second Canadian Edition
- New table on the comparison of primary and secondary groups
- New table on comparison of *Gemeinschaft* and *Gesellschaft*
- New box: "Sociology in the Global Community: McDonald's and the Worldwide Bureaucratization of Society"

CHAPTER 6 The Mass Media

- Brand new chapter focuses on why the media are so influential, who benefits from media influence and why, and who maintains cultural and ethical standards

CHAPTER 7 Deviance and Social Control

- New chapter-opening vignette from "A World Awash in Heroin" from *The Economist*
- Updated Research in Action box on street kids
- New table covering sociological perspectives on deviance
- New box: "Research in Action: Labelling a Behaviour as a Crime: *Road Rage*"
- Updated data on crime in Canada
- New section on transnational crime
- Expanded box: "Social Policy and Social Control: Illicit Drug Use in Canada"

CHAPTER 8 Stratification in Canada

- Shortened chapter focuses on national stratification
- New chapter–opening vignette: "No New Year's Hangover for Top CEOs" from the Canadian Centre for Policy Alternatives
- New section on stratification entitled "Anti-colonial Views"
- Updated box: "Social Policy and Stratification: Rethinking Social Assistance in North America and Europe"

CHAPTER 9 Global Inequality

- Discussion of global inequality from Chapter 8 of the Second Canadian Edition is moved and expanded further to create a new chapter

CHAPTER 10 Racial and Ethnic Inequality

- New box: "Sociology in the Global Community: Cultural Survival in Brazil"
- New section entitled "The Privileges of the Dominant"
- Updated box: "Social Policy and Race and Ethnicity: Global Immigration"

CHAPTER 11 Gender Relations

- New chapter-opening vignette: "Boys Trail Girls by Age 15 in Preparing for University" by Janice Tibbetts from *The Vancouver Sun*
- New table on sociological perspectives on gender
- New box: "Research in Action: Differences in Male and Female Physicians' Communication with Patients"

CHAPTER 12 Families and Intimate Relationships

- Updated statistics and examples throughout
- New table on sociological perspectives of the family
- Updated and expanded discussion entitled "Social Policy and the Family: Reproductive Technology"

CHAPTER 13 Religion and Education

- New section called "What are the Major World Religions?"
- New table on major world religions
- New Research in Action boxes: "Islam in Canada" and "Income and Education, Religiously Speaking"
- New table covering sociological perspectives on education
- Expanded discussion entitled "Social Policy and Religion: Religion in the Schools"

CHAPTER 14 Politics and the Economy

- New chapter-opening vignette called "More Media Consumed, More Civic Engagement: Study" by Brodie Fenlon from *The Globe and Mail*
- New table on characteristics of the three major economic systems
- New Sociology in the Global Community boxes: "Capitalism in China" and "Gender Quotas in the Ballot Box"
- New section: "How do Sociologists Conceptualize War and Peace?"
- New section: "How is the Economy Changing?"
- New end-of-chapter discussion: "Social Policy and the Economy: Global Offshoring"

CHAPTER 15 Population, Health, and Communities

- Restructured chapter: the section on aging is moved to Chapter 4 of this edition and a new discussion on communities is added
- New table on sociological perspectives on health and illness

CHAPTER 16 Globalization, the Environment, and Social Change

- Amalgamated topics from Chapters 15 and 16 of the second Canadian edition
- New table covering sociological perspectives on social change
- New table on contributions to social movement theory
- Greater emphasis on globalization, with an expanded discussion of global social change and

a new section entitled "What Impact does Social Change have on the Environment?"
- New box: "Sociology in the Global Community: A New Social Movement in Rural India"
- New box: "Research in Action: The Human Genome Project"
- New end-of-chapter discussion: "Social Policy and Globalization: Transnationals"

☐ INSTRUCTOR SUPPLEMENTS

Instructor Online Learning Centre (OLC)

The Online Learning Centre (OLC) at www.mcgrawhill.ca/olc/schaefer includes a password-protected Web site for instructors. The site offers downloadable supplements, including an Instructor's Manual, Microsoft® PowerPoint® slides, professional resources, and more.

- Instructor's Manual. The Instructor's Manual contains lecture ideas, class discussion topics, essay questions, topics for student research, and lists of audiovisual materials, additional readings, and Web sites. New to the third Canadian edition are in-class activities to promote student engagement.
- Test Bank in Rich Text Format. The Test Bank features short-answer, multiple-choice, and essay questions. Each question is accompanied by an answer and a page reference in the text. Multiple-choice questions are categorized by question type.
- Computerized Test Bank. This flexible and easy-to-use electronic testing program allows instructors to create tests from book-specific items. It accommodates a wide range of question types, and instructors may add their own questions. Multiple versions of the test can be created and printed.
- Microsoft® PowerPoint® Slides. These robust presentations offer high quality visuals to bring key sociological concepts to life.

CBC Videos

CBC CBC videos are available to adopters of this textbook. As well, they are posted as streaming video on the Online Learning Centre (www.mcgrawhill.ca/olc/schaefer).

The Integrator

Keyed to the chapters and topics of *Sociology: A Brief Introduction, Third Canadian Edition,* the Integrator ties together all the elements in your resource package, guiding you to where you'll find corresponding coverage in each of the related support package components–be it the Instructor's Manual, Computerized Test Bank, PowerPoint slides, Online Learning Centre, or Online Study Guide. The Integrator is presented at www.mcgrawhill.ca/olc/schaefer.

Superior Service

Service takes on a whole new meaning with McGraw-Hill Ryerson and *Sociology: A Brief Introduction, Third Canadian Edition*. More than just bringing you the textbook, we have raised the bar for innovation and educational research. These investments in learning and the academic community have helped us understand the needs of students and educators across the country, and allowed us to foster the growth of integrated learning.

iLearning Sales Specialist

 Your Integrated Learning Sales Specialist is a McGraw-Hill Ryerson representative who has the experience, product knowledge, training, and support to help you assess and integrate any of our products, technology, and services into your course for optimum teaching and learning performance. Whether it's using our test banks software, helping students improve their grades, or putting your entire course online, your iLearning Sales Specialist is there to help you do it.

Teaching, Technology and Learning Conference Series

The educational environment has changed tremendously in recent years, and McGraw-Hill Ryerson continues to be committed to helping you acquire the skills you need to succeed in this new milieu. Our innovative Teaching, Technology and Learning Conference Series brings faculty together from across Canada with 3M Teaching Excellence Award winners to share teaching strategies and learn best practices in a collaborative and stimulating environment. Pre-conference workshops on general topics, such as teaching large classes and technology integration, are also offered. We will also work with you at your own institution to customize workshops that best suit the needs of the faculty at your institution.

CPS is a student response system using wireless connectivity. It gives instructors and students immediate feedback from the entire class. The response pads are remote controls that are easy to use and engage students. Please contact your iLearning Sales Specialist for more information on how you can integrate CPS into your sociology classroom.

Course Management

 Content cartridges are available for course management systems such as WebCT and Blackboard. These platforms provide instructors with user-friendly, flexible teaching tools. Please contact your iLearning Sales Specialist for details.

Student Supplements

iStudy Sociology

 This innovative online study space was developed in partnership with Youthography, a Canadian youth research company, and hundreds of students from across Canada. It helps students master the concepts with all of the learning tools they've come to expect, including multiple-choice and true/false quizzes, chapter-by-chapter learning objectives, and key term reviews, plus interactivities, videos, and pre- and post-diagnostic assessments that point them to the concepts they need to focus on to improve their grades. Students can choose from all of these features to create their own personalized study plan—iStudy offers the best, most convenient way to Learn, Interact, and Succeed!

Student Online Learning Centre

Improve your grades! Visit the Online Learning Centre at www.mcgrawhill.ca/olc/schaefer to access learning and study tools, such as

- Chapter Outlines
- Multiple-choice questions
- True–false questions
- E-STAT
- Information about Career Opportunities
- Web resources
- A primer on Statistics

E-Stat

Σ-STAT E-Stat is an educational resource designed by Statistics Canada and made available to Canadian educational institutions. Using 450 000 current CANSIM (Canadian Socio-economic Information Management System) Time series and the most recent—as well as historical—census data, E-Stat lets you bring data to life in colourful graphs and maps. Access to E-Stats is made available to purchasers of this book, via the Schaefer Online Learning Centre, by special agreement between McGraw-Hill Ryerson and Statistics Canada. Visit the Online Learning Centre at www.mcgrawhilll.ca/olc/schaefer for access.

☐ ACKNOWLEDGEMENTS FROM BONNIE HAALAND

I am deeply indebted to a number of individuals at McGraw-Hill Ryerson who provided support, encouragement, and technical expertise throughout the development of this project. I wish to express my sincere thanks and appreciation to Nick Durie, sponsoring editor; Kara Stahl, supervising editor; Jennifer Hall, team head, Production; and Joe Zingrone and Elspeth McFadden, copy editors.

Special words of thanks are owing to Kelly Cochrane and Su Mei Ku, developmental editors. Kelly provided invaluable technical support while Su Mei was my daily working partner, providing direction and guidance, always with care, kindness, and the utmost of professionalism. Thank you, Su Mei.

I would also like to extend sincere thanks to those instructors across Canada whose painstaking reviews helped to inform and strengthen this edition:

Seema Ahluwalia, Kwantlen Polytechnic University

Penny Biles, Sheridan College

Jennifer Brayton, Ryerson University

Karen Chandler, George Brown College

Catherine Chiappetta-Swanson, McMaster University

Naomi Couto, York University

Barry Green, University of Toronto

Renée Ferguson, Georgian College

Marissa Fleming, Georgian College

Augie Fleras, University of Waterloo

Cindy Gervais, Fleming College

Lynn Hanley, Seneca College

Camille Hernandez-Ramdwar, Ryerson University

Gail Hunter, George Brown College

Mark Ihnat, Humber College

Rita Isola, Capilano University

Neil Jamieson-Williams, Mohawk College

Jill Esmonde Moore, Georgian College

Margot Murray, Durham College

Mary Louise Noce, Sheridan College

John Patterson, Canadore College

Daniel Popowich, Mohawk College

Charles Quist-Adade, Kwantlen Polytechnic University

Allan Warnke, Vancouver Island University (formerly Malaspina University College)

Carolyne Willoughby, Durham College

Sandy Yorke, Durham College

I am also indebted to many departmental colleagues at Kwantlen Polytechnic University for their generosity and support. Special thanks are owing to Steve Dooley, director of the National Institute for Sustainable Community Development, and to Dr. Frances Chiang, Department of Sociology for their letters of support in applying for research funding. I wish also to acknowledge the support provided by the Office of Research and Scholarship, Kwantlen Polytechnic University, which assisted me during the early stages of this project. To Dr. Rob Adamoski, dean of social science at Kwantlen Polytechnic University, I offer sincere thanks for his encouragement throughout the course of completing this edition and for his understanding, compassion, and patience.

Thank you to Jordie Haaland and Caitlin Spelliscy for providing invaluable assistance in compiling the bibliography of this text.

To Jay and Jordie, I wish to convey my heartfelt gratitude for your patience and encouragement throughout the completion of another edition.

With Saska, who sat patiently at my feet awaiting her daily walk, through what amounted to hundreds of hours, I share the completion of this edition.

And, finally, to my students, this book is ultimately for you, in appreciation for helping me see the world through your eyes.

Teaching Students to Think Sociologically

The third Canadian edition of *Sociology: A Brief Introduction* continues its tradition of teaching students how to think critically about society and their own lives from a wide range of sociological perspectives.

Intriguing Excerpts

Chapter-opening excerpts convey the excitement and relevance of sociological inquiry by means of lively excerpts from the writings of sociologists and others who explore sociological topics. Forty-three percent are new to this edition, including selections on the Canadian consumption of news media, the salaries of Canadian CEOs, and the poppy crop in Afghanistan.

Use Your Sociological Imagination Sections

Use Your Sociological Imagination sections within each chapter pose questions designed to stimulate students' sociological imagination and help them connect major concepts and issues to their own lives. Students can respond to the questions in these sections on the Online Learning Centre and email their answers to their instructors.

Excerpt Links to Chapters

Chapter overviews provide a bridge between each chapter-opening excerpt and the content of the following chapter.

diffusion via the media is discussed in more detail in Chapter 4.)

Use Your Sociological Imagination

If you had grown up in your parents' generation—without computers, email, the Internet, text-messaging, and cellphones—how would your daily life differ from the one you lead today?

☐ WHAT ARE THE ELEMENTS OF CULTURE?

Each culture considers its own distinctive ways of handling basic societal tasks as "natural." But, in fact, methods of education, marital ceremonies, religious doctrines,

Unique Social Policy Sections

The Social Policy sections, highly praised by reviewers of this text, provide a sociological perspective on contemporary social issues, such as the HIV/AIDS crisis, union membership and activity, and financing health care. Providing a global view of the issues, these sections are organized around a consistent heading structure and include Applying Theory questions designed to stimulate critical thinking about the issues being explored.

These Bhutanese householders are watching the Oprah Winfrey Show on their brand-new television set. The Bhutanese were introduced to television in 1999. Since then, Canadian communications guru Marshall McLuhan's global village has become a reality in their remote Asian kingdom, where rulers have become concerned about the cultural impact of Western media.

the promotion of a world music that is not clearly identifiable with any single culture. Even the most future-oriented thinker would find the growth in the reach of the mass media in post-industrial and postmodern societies remarkable (Castells 2000, 2001; Croteau and Hoynes 2001, 2003).

The lack of one national home for the various forms of mass media raises a potential dilemma for media consumers. People worry that unhealthy influences and even crime pervade today's electronic global village, and that few if any controls prevent them. For example, the leaders of Bhutan worry about the impact of newly introduced television programming on their culture and their people. Similarly, in industrial countries, including Canada, officials are concerned about everything from online pornography to the menace posed by hackers. In the social policy section that follows, we'll discuss media violence and its influences.

The Internet has also facilitated other forms of communication. Reference materials and data banks can now be made accessible across national boundaries. Information related to international finance, marketing, trade, and manufacturing is literally just a keystroke away. We have seen the emergence of truly world news outlets and

Social Policy and the Mass Media
Media Violence

The Issue

Imagine a forensic expert in blood patterns working for a major city's police department, who is also a serial killer and who hides his double life from his sister, girlfriend, and co-workers. This is the premise of the popular television series, *Dexter*.

Scenes of violence are not limited to television; they are also common on the Internet, in motion pictures, and in video games. The video game, *Grand Theft Auto III: Vice City*, was a virtual urban war game. Companion Internet sites encouraged players to run over pedes-

trians, shoot the paramedics who show up, and loot the bodies for spare change. *Vice City* sold 1.4 million copies in the first three days of its release in 2002. Its 2004 sequel, *San Andreas*, featured crooked cops, rival gangs, and attackers kicking victims as they lay in pools of blood (*The Economist* 2005b; Houghton County 2005; Rainey 2004).

What effects do such violent scenes have on an audience? Will viewers engage in violent acts themselves? The idea for the electrical maze used in *Fear Factor* came from the Web site of a college student who

Sociology in the Global Community   5-1
Disability as a Master Status

When the Canadian Transportation Agency ordered VIA Rail to make the passenger rail cars it had purchased several years ago accessible to people with disabilities, VIA responded by mounting a legal challenge. After a number of lower court decisions, in 2007, the Supreme Court of Canada—guided by the Canadian Charter of Rights and Freedoms—ruled that the rail service must be usable to people with and without disabilities.

Throughout history and around the world, people with disabilities have often been subjected to cruel and inhuman treatment. For example, in the early twentieth century, people with disabilities were frequently viewed as subhuman creatures who were a menace to society. In Alberta, between 1928 and 1972, over 2800 individuals were sterilized because they were deemed to be mentally "unfit." In Japan, more than 16 000 women with disabilities were involuntarily sterilized with government approval from 1945 to 1995. Sweden recently apologized for the same action taken against 62 000 of its citizens in the 1970s.

Such blatantly hostile treatment of people with disabilities generally gave way to a medical model that views people with disabilities as chronic patients. Increasingly, however, those concerned with the rights of people with disabilities have criticized this model as well. In their view, it is the unnecessary and discriminatory barriers present in the environment—both physical and attitudinal—that stand in the way of people with disabilities more than any biological limitations do. Apply-

of studies of people with disabilities disclosed that most academic research on the subject does not differentiate gender, thereby perpetuating the view that a disability overrides other personal characteristics. Consequently, disability serves as a master status.

Without question, people with disabilities occupy a subordinate position in Canadian society. The first International Day of Persons with Disabilities was declared by the United Nations in 1992, and advocates from around the world continue to lobby for the adoption of an international convention on disability rights. Women and men involved in this movement are working to challenge negative views of disabled people and to modify the social structure by reshaping laws, institutions, and environments so that people with disabilities can be fully integrated into mainstream society.

The effort to overcome disability's master status is global in nature. Despite a regulation in China that universities may not reject students because of a physical disability, many universities do just that. In fact, in the last five years, the dozens of universities in Beijing alone have accepted only 236 students with any kind of disability, however minor. It appears that bias against those with disabilities runs deep in China, and many universities use a mandate to nurture physical development as an excuse to keep them out.

Kenya's constitution outlaws discrimination on the basis of many characteristics, including race, sex, tribe, place

Sociology in the Global Community Boxes

The Sociology in the Global Community boxes provide a global perspective on topics such as poverty, domestic violence, and terrorism, and feature Applying Theory questions. Four boxes are completely new to the third Canadian edition of *Sociology: A Brief Introduction*.

Research in Action Boxes

Research in Action boxes present sociological findings on relevant topics, such as the relationship between students' grades and hard work, immigrant women's social networks, and the impact of Wal-Mart on communities. They also feature Applying Theory questions. Five boxes are completely new to the third Canadian edition.

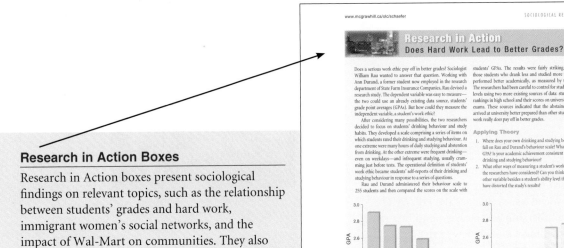

Research in Action   **2-2**
Does Hard Work Lead to Better Grades?

Does a serious work ethic pay off in better grades? Sociologist William Rau wanted to answer that question. Working with Ann Durand, a former student now employed in the research department of State Farm Insurance Companies, Rau devised a research study. The dependent variable was easy to measure—the two could use an already existing data source, students' grade point averages (GPAs). But how could they measure the independent variable, a student's work ethic?

After considering many possibilities, the two researchers decided to focus on students' drinking behaviour and study habits. They developed a scale comprising a series of items on which students rated their drinking behaviour. At one extreme were many hours of daily studying and abstention from drinking. At the other extreme were frequent drinking—even on weekdays—and infrequent studying, usually cramming just before tests. The operational definition of students' work ethic became students' self-reports of their drinking and studying behaviour in response to a series of questions.

Rau and Durand administered their behaviour scale to 255 students and then compared the scores on the scale with students' GPAs. The results were fairly striking. Generally, those students who drank less and studied more than others performed better academically, as measured by their GPAs. The researchers had been careful to control for students' ability levels using two more existing sources of data: students' class rankings in high school and their scores on university entrance exams. These sources indicated that the abstainers had not arrived at university better prepared than other students. Hard work really *does* pay off in better grades.

Applying Theory

1. Where does your own drinking and studying behaviour fall on Rau and Durand's behaviour scale? What is your GPA? Is your academic achievement consistent with your drinking and studying behaviour?

2. What other ways of measuring a student's work ethic could the researchers have considered? Can you think of any other variable besides a student's ability level that might have distorted the study's results?

Source: Rau and Durand 2000.

Cross-Reference Icons

When the text discussion refers to a concept introduced earlier in the book, an icon points the reader to the page where it first appeared.

family. On the microlevel, these changes affect the nature of social interactions. Each individual takes on multiple social roles, and people come to rely more on social networks and less on kinship ties. As the social structure becomes more complex, people's relationships become more impersonal, transient, and fragmented.

☐ HOW ARE ORGANIZATIONS STRUCTURED?

Formal Organizations and Bureaucracies

As contemporary societies have shifted to more advanced forms of technology and their social structures have become more complex, our lives have become increasingly dominated by large secondary groups referred to as *formal organizations.* A **formal organization** is a group designed for a special purpose and structured for maximum efficiency. Canada Post, McDonald's, and the Vancouver Symphony are examples of formal organizations. Though organizations vary in their size, specificity of goals, and degree of efficiency, they are all structured to facilitate the management of large-scale operations. They also have a bureaucratic form of organization, which we describe in the next section.

In our society, formal organizations fulfil an enormous variety of personal and societal needs, shaping the lives of every one of us. In fact, formal organizations have become such a dominant force that we must create organizations to supervise other organizations, such as the

Characteristics of a Bureaucracy

A **bureaucracy** is a component of formal organization that uses rules and hierarchical ranking to achieve efficiency. Rows of desks staffed by seemingly faceless people, endless lines and forms, impossibly complex language, and frustrating encounters with red tape—all these unpleasant images have combined to make *bureaucracy* a dirty word and an easy target in political campaigns. As a result, few people want to identify their occupation as "bureaucrat," despite the fact that all of us perform various bureaucratic tasks. In an industrial society, elements of bureaucracy enter into almost every occupation.

Max Weber ([1913–1922] 1947) first directed researchers to the significance of bureaucratic structure. He developed an *ideal type* of bureaucracy that would reflect the most characteristic aspects of all human organizations. By **ideal type**, Weber meant a construct or model for evaluating specific cases. In actuality, perfect bureaucracies do not exist; no real-world organization corresponds exactly to Weber's ideal type.

Weber proposed that whether the purpose is to run a temple, a corporation, or an army, the ideal bureaucracy displays five basic characteristics. A discussion of those characteristics, as well as the dysfunctions of a bureaucracy, follows.

1. **Division of labour.** Specialized experts perform specific tasks. In your college or university bureaucracy, the admissions officer does not do the job of registrar; the guidance counsellor doesn't see to the maintenance of buildings. By working at a specific task, people are more likely to become

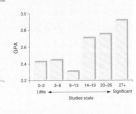

Demographic Map Program

"Mapping Life Worldwide" maps are featured throughout the text.

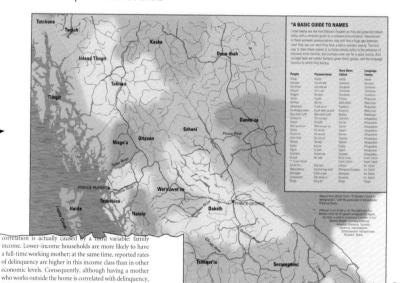

▶ **FIGURE 10-2**

First Nations People of British Columbia

---

suggest how one aspect of human behaviour influences or affects another. The variable hypothesized to cause or influence another is called the **independent variable**. The second variable is termed the **dependent variable** because its action "depends" on the influence of the independent variable.

Our hypothesis is that the higher their parents' income, the more likely it is that children go to university or college. The independent variable to be measured is parents' income levels. The variable thought to depend on it—attendance at a postsecondary institution—must also be measured.

Identifying independent and dependent variables is a critical step in clarifying cause-and-effect relationships in society. As shown in Figure 2-2, **causal logic** involves the relationship between a condition or variable and a particular consequence, with one event leading to the other. Under causal logic, being less integrated into society may

▶ **FIGURE 2-2**

Causal Logic

In causal logic, an independent variable (often designated by the symbol x) influences a dependent variable (generally designated as y); thus, x leads to y. For example, parents who attend church regularly (x) are more likely to have children who are churchgoers (y).

Independent variable		Dependent variable
x	→	y
Level of educational	→	Level of income

---

correlation is actually caused by a third variable: family income. Lower-income households are more likely to have a full-time working mother; at the same time, reported rates of delinquency are higher in this income class than in other economic levels. Consequently, although having a mother who works outside the home is correlated with delinquency, it does not *cause* delinquency. Sociologists seek to identify the *causal* link between variables; this causal link is generally described by researchers in their hypotheses.

Think about It

Identify two or three variables that might "depend" on this independent variable: number of alcoholic drinks ingested.

Collecting and Analyzing Data

How do you test a hypothesis to determine whether it is supported or refuted? You need to collect information, using one of the research designs described later in the chapter. The research design guides the researcher incollecting and analyzing data.

Selecting the Sample

In most studies, social scientists must carefully select what is known as a *sample*. A **sample** is a selection from a larger population that is statistically representative of that population. There are many kinds of samples, but the one social scientists most frequently use is the random sample. In a **random sample**, every member of an entire population being studied has the same chance of being selected. Thus, if researchers wish to examine the opinions of people

"Think about It" Caption Feature

The "Think about It" captions, which accompany many of the book's maps, graphs, and tables, encourage students to think critically about information presented in illustrative materials.

Table 1-1 Comparing Major Theoretical Perspectives

	Functionalist	Conflict	Interactionist	Feminist
View of society	Stable, well-integrated	Characterized by tension and struggle between and among groups	Active in influencing and affecting everyday social interaction	Characterized by gender and inequality; causes and solutions vary
Level of analysis emphasized	Macro	Macro	Micro-analysis as a way of understanding the larger macro phenomena	Both macro- and microlevels of analysis
Key concepts	Manifest functions Latent functions Dysfunction	Inequality Capitalism Stratification	Symbols Nonverbal communication Face to face	Standpoint of women Political action Gender inequality Oppression
View of the individual	People are socialized to perform societal functions	People are shaped by power, coercion, and authority	People manipulate symbols and create their social worlds through interaction	Differs according to social class, race, ethnicity, age, sexual orientation, and physical ability
View of the social order	Maintained through cooperation and consensus	Maintained through force and coercion	Maintained by shared understanding of everyday behaviour	Maintained through standpoints that do not include those of women
View of social	Predictable	Change takes place	Reflected in people's	Essential in order

NEW! Tables recap coverage of the major theoretical perspectives on key topics.

CHAPTER RESOURCES

Summary

What are the Theoretical Perspectives on the Mass Media?

- The **mass media** (p. 133) are print and electronic instruments of communication that carry messages to often-widespread audiences. They pervade all social institutions, from entertainment to education to politics.
- From the functionalist perspective, the media entertain, socialize, enforce social norms, confer status, and promote consumption. They can be dysfunctional to the extent that they desensitize us to serious events and issues (the **narcotizing dysfunction**) (p. 137).
- Conflict theorists think the media reflect and even deepen the divisions in society through **gatekeeping** (p. 137), or control over which material reaches the public; **media monitoring** (p. 138), the covert observation of people's media usage and choices; imposed **hegemony** (p. 140), which is the process of creating acceptance of the views of the ruling class so that they are seen as "normal" by the exploited classes; and support of the **dominant ideology** (p. 138), which defines reality and overwhelms local cultures.
- Some feminist theorists point out that media images of the sexes communicate unrealistic, stereotypical, limiting, and sometimes violent perceptions of women.
- Interactionists examine the media on the micro level to see how they shape day-to-day social

behaviour. Interactionists have studied shared TV viewing and staged public appearances intended to convey self-serving definitions of reality.

Who are the Media's Audiences?

- The mass media require the presence of an audience—whether it is small and well defined or large and amorphous. With the ever-increasing number of media outlets come more and more targeting of segmented (or niche) audiences.
- Social researchers have studied the role of **opinion leaders** (p. 149) in influencing audiences.

What does the Media Industry Look Like?

- The media industry is becoming more and more concentrated, creating media conglomerates. This concentration raises concerns about how innovative and independent the media can be. In some countries, governments own and control the media.
- The Internet is the one significant exception to the trend toward centralization, allowing millions of people to produce their own media content.
- The media have a global reach thanks to new communications technologies, especially the Internet. Some people are concerned that the media's global reach will spread unhealthy influences to other cultures.

Critical Thinking Questions

1. What kind of audience is targeted by the producers of televised professional wrestling? By the creators of an animated film? By a rap group? What factors determine who makes up a particular audience?
2. Trace the production process for a new television situation comedy (sitcom). Who do you imagine are the gatekeepers in the process?
3. Use the functionalist, conflict, interactionist, and feminist perspectives to assess the effects of global TV programming on developing countries.

www.mcgrawhill.ca/olc/schaefer

Key Terms

Gatekeeping The process by which a relatively small number of people in the media industry control what material eventually reaches the audience. (p. 137)

Hegemony The process through which the views of the ruling class are accepted and seen as "normal" by the exploited classes. (p. 140)

Mass media Print and electronic means of communication that carry messages to widespread audiences. (p. 133)

Narcotizing dysfunction The phenomenon in which the media provide such massive amounts of coverage that the audience becomes numb and fails to act

on the information, regardless of how compelling the issue. (p. 137)

Opinion leader Someone who influences the opinions and decisions of others through day-to-day personal contact and communication (e.g., a film or theatre critic). (p. 149)

Stereotype An unreliable generalization about all members of a group that does not recognize individual differences within the group. (p. 140)

Additional Readings

Chomsky, Noam. 2002. *Media Control: The Spectacular Achievements of Propaganda*, Second Edition. New York: Seven Stories Press.

Gant, Scott. 2007. *We're All Journalists Now: The Transformation of the Press and Reshaping of the Law in the Internet Age*. Toronto: Simon and Schuster Canada.

Lorimer, Rowland. 2007. *Mass Communication in Canada*, Sixth Edition. Don Mills, ON: Oxford University Press.

Online Learning Centre

Visit the *Sociology: A Brief Introduction* Online Learning Centre at www.mcgrawhill.ca/olc/schaefer to access quizzes,

interactive exercises, video clips, and other research and study tools related to this chapter.

Reel Society Video Clips

Reel Society video clips can be used to spark discussion about the following topics from this chapter:
- Sociological Perspectives on the Media
- The Media Industry

End-of-Chapter Resources

Each chapter concludes with a Summary, Critical Thinking Questions, a list of Key Terms with definitions, and Additional Readings to help students review and extend their knowledge.

chapter 1

UNDERSTANDING SOCIOLOGY

Sociology places people, groups, cultures, and societies in a global context. Live Earth symbolized these four aspects of sociology, as citizens from around the world gathered in concerts across the globe, unified in one cause—bringing attention to Earth's climate crisis.

☐ **What is Sociology?**

☐ **What is Sociological Theory?**

☐ **How did Sociology Develop?**

☐ **What are the Major Theoretical Perspectives?**

☐ **How did the Sociological Imagination Develop?**

☐ **Social Policy throughout the World**

| Boxes |

RESEARCH IN ACTION: Looking at Sports from Four Perspectives

SOCIOLOGY IN THE GLOBAL COMMUNITY: Women in Public Places Worldwide

In the terrible days after September 11, 2001, U.S. President George W. Bush exhorted his compatriots to shop for their country. "I ask your continued participation and confidence in the American economy," he said in an address before a joint session of Congress on September 20. About six weeks later, in a speech in Atlanta, he noted with approval that despite the terrorist threat, "People are going about their daily lives, working and shopping and playing, worshiping at churches and synagogues and mosques, going to movies and to baseball games." Put this way, shopping was as noble a pursuit as praying, as much a part of American life as baseball. Shopping, it appeared, would save the U.S.A.

The sentiment was widely derided at the time, and it did seem a rather facile response to a cataclysmic attack. But in a way—and it pains me to admit this—Dubya was right. Love it or hate it, shopping makes the modern western economy go round.

Here's a sobering fact: in the United States, "personal consumption expenditures"—the economist's phrase for the money that individuals, not companies, spend on goods and services—is equal to roughly two thirds of the gross domestic product. If we stopped shopping, the economy as we know it really would collapse.

However, most of us probably aren't thinking about improving the country's bottom line when we head to the mall. At the most basic level, we shop because we need things: bread, a warm blanket, shingles to fix the hole in the roof.

But once we've bought the minimum number of clothes we need to protect us from the elements, and enough food to sustain us through another day in the salt mines, what keeps us going back to the cash register? When we have sensible loafers, why do we want Manolo Blahnik stilettos? Don't we realize that if we just stopped shopping, we'd have more money, more free time, less stress, and less debt?

Well, sure. But there are many reasons we shop, and very few of them have much to do with either supporting the economy or keeping ourselves fed and warm. Daniel Miller, an anthropology professor at University College London, believes that we—particularly women—shop as a way of showing love to others, particularly our families. According to *Shopping, Place and Identity*, a book he co-authored, "shopping is an investment in social relationships, often within a relatively narrowly defined household or domestic context, as much as it is an economic activity devoted to the acquisition of particular commodities."

… Two researchers—Cele Otnes of the University of Illinois and Mary Ann McGrath of Loyola University—have countered the "shopping as affiliation" theories with one of their own, based on their study of male shopping habits. They contend that, among men at least, shopping is all about making the best decision and getting the best deal. "Men who profess to enjoy shopping still typically do so in order to fulfill one entrenched tenet of the masculine code—achievement," they wrote in the *Journal of Retailing*. "We argue that in contrast to Daniel Miller's theory that women shop to express love to their families and social networks, men shop to win."

Meanwhile, medical researchers are trying to figure out whether the physical act of plunking down a credit card and carting off a new pair of shoes gives some of us an addictive rush, similar to the high that hooks gamblers and alcoholics.

There are countless other theories…. But the theory that appeals to me most is perhaps naively simplistic: we shop because, in most cultures, shopping has always been part of the way we experience the world. From the patrician haggling for pottery in the marketplaces of ancient Rome to the teenager shopping for CDs on the Internet, we have always liked to acquire things. The sentiment has stayed the same in western societies for several millennia. Only the trappings of the process have changed.

☐ *(Paquet 2003)*

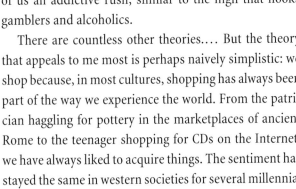
Laura Byrne Paquet

THE URGE TO SPLURGE
A Social History of Shopping

What makes shopping an appropriate subject to study in sociology? Uniting all sociological studies is their focus on patterns of human behaviour. Laura Byrne Paquet's book *The Urge to Splurge: A Social History of Shopping* discusses the social history of shopping and how today, particularly in developed countries, shopping has become an activity that goes far beyond the need to acquire the daily necessities of life. Beginning her book with the words from a bumper sticker of the late twentieth century, "Veni, Vidi, VISA: I came, I saw, I shopped," Paquet covers such topics as fashion victims, shopaholics, the politics of shopping, and the conflicting attitudes to shopping among consumers in Canada and the United States.

Sociologists are not concerned with what one individual does or does not do, but with what people do as members of a group or while interacting with one another, and with what that means for the individuals and for society as a whole. Shopping is, in fact, a subject that sociologists can study in any number of ways. They might, as Paquet does, examine shopping's history or its uses in different groups, regions, and cultures.

Sociology is extremely broad in scope. You will see throughout this book the range of topics sociologists investigate—from suicide to TV viewing habits, from Amish society to global economic patterns, from peer pressure to pickpocketing techniques. Sociologists look at how others influence our behaviour and how major social institutions, like the government, religion, and the economy, affect us.

In this chapter, we will explore the nature of sociology as a field of inquiry and as an exercise of the *sociological imagination*. We'll look at the discipline as a science and consider its relationship to other social sciences. We will evaluate the contributions of pioneering thinkers— Émile Durkheim, Max Weber, Karl Marx, and others— to the development of sociology. Next we will discuss a number of important theoretical perspectives used by sociologists. Finally, we will consider the ways sociology helps us to develop our sociological imagination.

Use Your Sociological Imagination

Why do you think so much emphasis is placed on material possessions in Canadian society? What do you think the slogan "shop till you drop" says about our society? Do you shop for reasons other than to buy necessities, such as food?

☐ WHAT IS SOCIOLOGY?

Sociology is the systematic study of social behaviour and human groups. It focuses primarily on the influence of social relationships on people's attitudes and behaviour and on how societies are established and change. In this textbook, we deal with such varied topics as families, workplaces, street gangs, business firms, political parties, genetic engineering, schools, religions, and labour unions. Here, we are concerned with love, poverty, conformity, discrimination, illness, technology, and community.

The Sociological Imagination

In attempting to understand social behaviour, sociologists rely on an unusual type of creative thinking. C. Wright Mills (1956) described such thinking as the **sociological imagination**—an awareness of the relationship between an individual and the wider society. This awareness allows all of us (not just sociologists) to comprehend the links between our immediate, personal social settings and the remote, impersonal social world that surrounds us and helps to shape us.

A key element in the sociological imagination is the ability to view our own society as an outsider would, rather than only from the perspective of personal experiences and cultural biases. Consider something as simple as the practice of eating while walking. In Canada, we think nothing of seeing people consuming coffee or candy bars as they walk along. Sociologists see this as a pattern of acceptable behaviour because others regard it as acceptable. Yet sociologists need to go beyond one culture to place the practice in perspective. This behaviour is quite unacceptable elsewhere. For example, in Japan people do not eat while walking. Streetside sellers and vending machines dispense food everywhere, but the Japanese will stop to eat or drink whatever they buy before they continue on their way. In their eyes, to engage in another activity while eating shows disrespect for the food preparation, even if the food comes out of a vending machine.

The sociological imagination allows us to go beyond personal experiences and observations to understand broader public issues; it involves critical thinking and questioning what otherwise may simply be taken for granted or assumed to be "natural." Unemployment, for example, is unquestionably a personal hardship for a person without a job. However, C. Wright Mills pointed out that when unemployment is a social problem shared by millions of people, it is appropriate to question the way that a society is structured or organized. Similarly, Mills advocated using the sociological imagination to view divorce not simply as the personal problem of a particular man or woman, but rather as a societal problem, since it is the outcome of many marriages. And he was writing this in the 1950s, when the divorce rate was but a fraction of what it is today (I. Horowitz 1983).

The sociological imagination can bring new understanding to daily life. For example, in Canada, growing numbers of families are turning to food banks to provide them with daily necessities. A 1999 report on hunger, homelessness, and food bank use published by Edmonton's Food Bank and the Edmonton Social Planning Council found that 54 percent of Edmonton families using food banks were living on less than $1000 per month. The majority of these families (71 percent) reported that they turn to food banks because of ongoing money shortages. Most of the families utilizing food banks (55 percent) were led by female single parents who had children under 12.

Many observers would uncritically applaud the distribution of food to the needy, but let's look deeper to offer a more probing view of these activities. In Canada, food and consumer manufacturers have joined in charitable food-distribution arrangements. For example, Food and Consumer Products of Canada (FCPC), which represents 150 Canadian corporations, formed an alliance with the Canadian Association of Food Banks (CAFB) to create the ShareGoods program. In 2004, FCPC donated $33 million to charitable causes and more than five million bags of groceries to Canadian families in need. Perhaps as a result, the focus of such relief programs is too restricted. The homeless are to be fed, not housed; the unemployed are to be given meals, not jobs. Relief efforts assist hungry individuals and families without challenging the existing social order (for example, by demanding a redistribution of wealth). Of course, without these limited successes in distributing food, starving people might assault patrons of restaurants, loot grocery stores, or literally die of starvation on the steps of city halls. Such critical thinking is typical of sociologists, as they draw on the sociological imagination to study a social issue—in this case, hunger in North America (Vladimiroff 1998).

Use Your Sociological Imagination

You attend a rock concert one night and a religious service the next morning. What differences would you see in how the two audiences behave and in how they respond to the leader? What might account for these differences?

Sociology and the Social Sciences

Is sociology a science? The term **science** refers to the body of knowledge obtained by methods based on systematic observation. Just like other scientific disciplines, sociology engages in the organized, systematic study of phenomena (in this case, human behaviour) in order to enhance understanding. All scientists, whether studying mushrooms or murderers, attempt to collect precise information through methods of study that are as objective as possible. These researchers rely on careful recording of observations and accumulation of data.

Of course, there is a great difference between sociology and physics, between psychology and astronomy. For this reason, the sciences are commonly divided into natural and social sciences. **Natural science** is the study of the physical features of nature and the ways in which they interact and change. Astronomy, biology, chemistry, geology, and physics are all natural sciences. **Social science** is the study of various aspects of human society. The social sciences include sociology, anthropology, economics, history, psychology, and political science.

The social sciences have a common focus on the social behaviour of people, yet each has a particular orientation. Anthropologists usually study past cultures and pre-industrial societies that continue today, as well as the origins of men and women; this knowledge is used to examine contemporary societies, including industrial societies. Economists explore the ways in which people produce and exchange goods and services, along with money and other resources. Historians are concerned with the peoples and events of the past and their significance for us today. Political scientists study international relations, the workings of government, and the exercise of power and authority. Psychologists investigate personality and individual behaviour. So what does sociology focus on? It emphasizes the influence that society has on people's attitudes and behaviour and the ways in which people shape society. Humans are social animals; therefore, sociologists scientifically examine our social relationships with people.

Let's consider how the different social sciences might approach the issue of gun control. This issue began to receive increased public attention in Canada after December 6, 1989, when Marc Lepine systematically shot and killed 14 female engineering students at l'École Polytechnique in Montreal. The event became known as the Montreal Massacre and eventually led to stricter gun control laws in Canada in the form of registration requirements under the Firearms Act. Political scientists would look at the impact of political action groups, such as the National Firearms Association, on lawmakers. Historians would examine how guns were used over time in our country and elsewhere. Anthropologists would focus on the use of weapons in a variety of cultures as means of protection and as symbols of power. Psychologists would look at individual cases and assess the impact guns have on their owners as well as on individual victims of gunfire. Economists would be interested in how firearms manufacture and sales affect communities. Sociologists would examine the social, economic, and political factors influencing gun laws and gather data to inform policymakers. For example, they would examine data from different regions to evaluate the effect of gun restrictions on the incidence of firearm accidents or violent crimes involving firearms. They would ask, "What explanations can be offered for the gender, income, age, rural–urban, and geographic differences in gun ownership? How do these differences affect the formulation of a government policy?" Sociologists might also look at data that show how Canada compares with other nations, particularly the United States, in gun ownership and use.

Sociologists put their imaginations to work in a variety of areas—including aging, criminal justice, the family, human ecology, religion, health, and gender. Canadian sociologist Michael Atkinson, for example, has studied why men undergo cosmetic surgery procedures. After interviewing 44 men who had had such procedures done, as well as 12 cosmetic surgeons, Atkinson concluded, "Men are doing it more to maintain a position, to hold on to a sense of power or masculinity. For some women, it's about staying pretty. That's a disempowering image. That's not the same as a guy trying to keep his job" (Schmidt 2004:A8). Throughout this book, the sociological imagination will be used to examine Canada (and other societies) from the viewpoint of respectful but questioning outsiders.

Sociology and Common Sense

Sociologists focus on the study of human behaviour. We all have experience with human behaviour and at least some knowledge of it. All of us might well have theories about why people get tattoos, for example, or why people become homeless. Our theories and opinions typically come from "common sense"—that is, from our experiences and conversations, from what we read, from what we see on television, and so forth.

In our daily lives, we rely on common sense to get us through many unfamiliar situations. However, this common-sense knowledge, although sometimes accurate, is not always reliable, because it rests on commonly held beliefs rather than on a systematic analysis of facts. It was once considered common sense to accept that Earth was flat—a view rightly questioned by Pythagoras

and Aristotle. Incorrect common-sense notions are not just a part of the distant past; they remain with us today.

Common sense, for example, tells us that people panic when faced with natural disasters, such as floods, earthquakes, or ice storms. However, these particular common-sense notions—such as that Earth is flat—are untrue; they are not supported by sociological research. Natural disasters do not generally produce panic. In the aftermath of disasters and even explosions, greater social organization and structure emerge to deal with a community's problems. In Canada, for example, emergency response teams often coordinate public services and even certain services normally performed by the private sector, such as food distribution. Decision making becomes more centralized in times of disaster.

Like other social scientists, sociologists do not accept something as a fact because "everyone knows it." Instead, each piece of information must be tested, recorded, and

Do disasters produce panic or an organized, structured response? Common sense might tell us the former, but, in fact, disasters bring out a great deal of structure and organization to deal with their aftermath. Pictured, students evacuate Dawson College in Montreal on September 13, 2006, as police help during a shooting incident at the school.

then analyzed in relation to other data. Sociologists rely on scientific studies in order to describe and understand a social environment. At times, the findings of sociologists may seem like common sense because they deal with facets of everyday life. The difference is that such findings have been *tested* by researchers. Common sense now tells us that Earth is round. But this particular common-sense notion is based on centuries of scientific work upholding the breakthrough made by Pythagoras and Aristotle.

☐ WHAT IS SOCIOLOGICAL THEORY?

Why do people commit suicide? One traditional common-sense answer is that people inherit the desire to kill themselves. Another view is that sunspots drive people to take their own lives. These explanations may not seem especially convincing to contemporary researchers, but they represent beliefs widely held as recently as 1900.

Sociologists are not particularly interested in why any one individual commits suicide; they are more concerned with the social forces that systematically cause some people to take their own lives. In order to undertake this research, sociologists develop a theory that offers a general explanation of suicidal behaviour.

We can think of theories as attempts to explain events, forces, materials, ideas, or behaviour in a comprehensive manner. Within sociology, a **theory** is a template containing definitions and relationships used to organize and understand the social world. A theory may have explanatory power, predictive power, or both. That is, it may help us to see the relationships among seemingly isolated phenomena and to understand how one type of change in an environment leads to others.

Émile Durkheim (1951, original edition 1897) looked into suicide data in great detail and developed a highly original theory about the relationship between suicide and social factors. He was primarily concerned not with the personalities of individual suicide victims, but rather with suicide *rates* and how they varied from country to country. As a result, when he looked at the number of reported suicides in France, England, and Denmark in 1869, he also examined the populations of these nations to determine their rates of suicide. He found that whereas England had only 67 reported suicides per million inhabitants, France had 135 per million, and Denmark had 277 per million. The question then became, "Why did Denmark have a comparatively high rate of reported suicides?"

Durkheim went much deeper into his investigation of suicide rates, and the result was his landmark work, *Suicide*, published in 1897. Durkheim refused to automatically accept unproven explanations regarding suicide, including the beliefs that cosmic forces or inherited tendencies caused such deaths. Instead, he focused on such problems as the cohesiveness or lack of cohesiveness of religious, social, and occupational groups.

Durkheim's research suggested that suicide, although a solitary act, is related to group life. Protestants had much higher suicide rates than Catholics did; the unmarried had much higher rates than married people did; soldiers were more likely to take their lives than civilians were. In addition, it appeared that there were higher rates of suicide in times of peace than in times of war and revolution, and in times of economic instability and recession rather than in times of prosperity. Durkheim concluded that the suicide rates of a society reflected the extent to which people were or were not integrated into the group life of the society.

Émile Durkheim, like many other social scientists, developed a theory to explain how individual behaviour can be understood within a social context. He pointed out the influence of groups and societal forces on what had always been viewed as a highly personal act. Clearly, Durkheim offered a more *scientific* explanation for the causes of suicide than that of sunspots or inherited tendencies. His theory has predictive power, since it suggests that suicide rates will rise or fall in conjunction with certain social and economic changes.

Of course, a theory—even the best of theories—is not a final statement about human behaviour. Durkheim's theory of suicide is no exception; sociologists continue to examine factors that contribute to differences in suicide rates around the world and to a particular society's rate of suicide, or differences in rates between and among various groups in a single country. For example, for over a decade, rates of suicide for young people in First Nations communities in Canada have been five or more times greater than the rates for other Canadians (Health Canada 2003a). First Nations communities, at the same time, experience marked differences in their rates of suicide among provinces, regions, and even within the same geographic region (Kral 2003; White and Jodoin 2003). "Community wellness" strategies may have the best hope of providing young Aboriginal people with cultural continuity, buffering them somewhat from social changes that may have affected their integration within the community (for a critique of Durkheim's work, see Douglas 1967).

Use Your Sociological Imagination

If you were Durkheim's successor in his research on suicide, how would you investigate the factors that may explain the suicide rates in Canada today?

☐ HOW DID SOCIOLOGY DEVELOP?

People have always been curious about sociological matters—such as how we get along, what we do, and whom we select as our leaders. Philosophers and religious authorities of ancient and medieval societies made countless observations about human behaviour. They did not test or verify these observations scientifically; nevertheless, these observations often became the foundation for moral codes. Several of the early social philosophers predicted that a systematic study of human behaviour would one day emerge. Beginning in the nineteenth century, European theorists made pioneering contributions to the development of a science of human behaviour.

Early Thinkers: Comte, Martineau, and Spencer

The nineteenth century was an unsettling time in France. The French monarchy had been deposed in the Revolution of 1789, and Napoleon had subsequently suffered defeat in his effort to conquer Europe. Amid this chaos, philosophers considered how society might be improved. Auguste Comte (1798–1857), credited with being the most influential of these philosophers of the early nineteenth century, believed that a theoretical science of society and systematic investigation of behaviour were needed to improve society. He coined the term *sociology* to apply to the science of human behaviour.

Writing in the nineteenth century, Comte feared that the excesses of the French Revolution had permanently impaired France's stability. Yet he hoped that the systematic study of social behaviour would eventually lead to more rational human interactions. In Comte's hierarchy of sciences, sociology was at the top. He called it the "queen" and its practitioners "scientist-priests." This French theorist did not simply give sociology its name; he also presented a rather ambitious challenge to the fledgling discipline.

Scholars were able to learn of Comte's works largely through translations by the English sociologist Harriet Martineau (1802–1876). But Martineau was a trailblazer in her own right as a sociologist. She offered insightful observations of the customs and social practices of both her native Britain and North America. Martineau's book, *Society in America* (1962, original edition 1837), examines religion, politics, child rearing, and immigration in the United States. She gave special attention to social class distinctions and to such factors as gender and race.

Martineau's writings emphasized the impact that the economy, law, trade, and population could have on the social problems of contemporary society. She spoke out in favour of the rights of women, the emancipation of slaves, and religious tolerance. In Martineau's view (1896), intellectuals and scholars should not simply offer observations of social conditions; they should act on their convictions in a manner that will benefit society. In line with this view, Martineau conducted research on the nature of female employment and pointed to the need for further investigation of this important issue (Lengermann and Niebrugge-Brantley 1996).

Another important contributor to the discipline of sociology was Herbert Spencer (1820–1903). A relatively prosperous Victorian Englishman, Spencer (unlike Martineau) did not feel compelled to correct or improve society; instead, he merely hoped to understand it better. Spencer applied the concept of evolution of the species to societies in order to explain how societies change, or evolve, over time. In 1852, in the *Westminister Review*, Spencer's article, "A Theory of Population, Deduced from the General Law of Animal Fertility," presented the evolutionary view of the "survival of the fittest." Charles Darwin, in later editions of *The Origins of the Species*, adopted this last phrase to describe struggle between competing life forms (McIntyre 2006).

Harriet Martineau was an early pioneer of sociology who studied social behaviour both in her native England and in North America.

Spencer's approach to societal change was extremely popular in his own lifetime. Unlike Comte, Spencer suggested that societies are bound to change eventually; therefore, no one need be highly critical of present social arrangements or work actively for social change. This position appealed to many influential people in England and North America who had a vested interest in the status quo and were suspicious of change-endorsing social thinkers.

Émile Durkheim

Émile Durkheim made many pioneering contributions to sociology, including his important theoretical work on suicide. The son of a rabbi, Durkheim (1858–1917) was educated in France and Germany. He established an impressive academic reputation and was appointed as one of the first professors of sociology in France. Above all, Durkheim will be remembered for his insistence that behaviour must be understood within a larger social context, not just in individualistic terms.

As one example of this emphasis, Durkheim (1947, original edition 1912) developed a fundamental thesis to help understand all forms of society through intensive study of the Arunta, an Australian tribe. He focused on the functions that religion performed for the Arunta and underscored the role that group life plays in defining what we consider religious. Durkheim concluded that, like other forms of group behaviour, religion reinforces a group's solidarity.

Another of Durkheim's main interests was the consequences of work in modern societies. In his view, the growing division of labour found in industrial societies as workers became much more specialized in their tasks led to what he called *anomie*. **Anomie** refers to the loss of direction that a society feels when social control of individual behaviour has become ineffective. The state of anomie occurs when people have lost their sense of purpose or direction, often during a time of profound social change. In a period of anomie, people are so confused and unable to cope with the new social environment that they may resort to taking their own lives.

Durkheim was concerned about the dangers that alienation, loneliness, and isolation might pose for modern industrial societies. He shared Comte's belief that sociology should provide direction for social change. As a result, he advocated the creation of new social groups—between the individual's family and the state—which would ideally provide a sense of belonging for members of huge, impersonal societies. Unions would be an example of such a group.

Like many other sociologists, Durkheim did not limit his interests to one aspect of social behaviour. Later in this book, we will consider his thinking on crime and punishment, religion, and the workplace. Few sociologists have had such a dramatic impact on so many different areas within the discipline.

Max Weber

Another important early theorist was Max Weber (pronounced "vay-ber"). Born in Germany in 1864, Weber took his early academic training in legal and economic history, but he gradually developed an interest in sociology. Eventually, he became a professor at various German universities. Weber taught his students that they should employ *Verstehen* (pronounced "fehr—SHTEH—ehn), the German word for "understanding" or "insight," in their intellectual work. He pointed out that we cannot analyze much of our social behaviour by the kinds of objective criteria we use to measure weight or temperature. To fully comprehend behaviour, we must learn the subjective meanings people attach to their actions—how they themselves view and explain their behaviour.

For example, suppose that a sociologist was studying the social ranking of students at a high school. Weber would expect the researcher to employ *Verstehen* to determine the significance of the school's social hierarchy for its members. The researcher might examine the effects of athleticism or grades or social skills or physical appearance in the school. She would seek to learn how students relate to other students of higher or lower status. While investigating these questions, the researcher would take into account people's emotions, thoughts, beliefs, and attitudes (Coser 1977).

We also owe credit to Weber for a key conceptual tool: the ideal type. An **ideal type** is a construct, a made-up model that serves as a measuring rod against which actual cases can be evaluated. In his own works, Weber identified various characteristics of bureaucracy as an ideal type (discussed in detail in Chapter 5). In presenting this model of bureaucracy, Weber was not describing any particular business, nor was he using the term *ideal* in a way that suggested a positive evaluation. Instead, his purpose was to provide a useful standard for measuring just how bureaucratic an actual organization is (Gerth and Mills 1958). Later in this textbook, we use the concept of ideal type to study family, religion, authority, and economic systems and to analyze bureaucracy.

Although their professional careers coincided, Émile Durkheim and Max Weber never met and had little or no impact on each other's ideas. This was certainly not true of the work of Karl Marx. Durkheim's thinking about the impact of the division of labour in industrial societies was related to Marx's writings, while Weber's concern for a value-free, objective sociology was a direct response to Marx's deeply held convictions. Thus, it is not surprising that Karl Marx is viewed as a major figure in the

▶ **FIGURE 1-1**

Early Social Thinkers

	Émile Durkheim 1858–1917	Max Weber 1864–1920	Karl Marx 1818–1883
Academic training	Philosophy	Law, economics, history, philosophy	Philosophy, law
Key works	1893—*The Division of Labor in Society* 1897—*Suicide: A Study in Sociology* 1912—*Elementary Forms of Religious Life*	1904–1905—*The Protestant Ethic and the Spirit of Capitalism* 1922—*Wirtschaft und Gesellschaft*	1848—*The Communist Manifesto* 1867—*Das Kapital*

development of sociology as well as several other social sciences (see Figure 1-1).

Karl Marx

Karl Marx (1818–1883) shared with Durkheim and Weber a dual interest in abstract philosophical issues and the concrete reality of everyday life. Unlike the others, Marx was so critical of existing institutions that a conventional academic career was impossible, and although he was born and educated in Germany, he spent most of his life in exile.

Marx's personal life was a difficult struggle. When a paper that he had written was suppressed, he fled his native land for France. In Paris, he met Friedrich Engels (1820–1895), with whom he formed a lifelong friendship. They lived at a time when European and North American economic life was increasingly being dominated by the factory rather than the farm.

In 1847, Marx and Engels attended the secret meetings in London of an illegal coalition of labour unions known as the Communist League. The following year, they wrote a platform called *The Communist Manifesto*. Here, they argued that the masses of people who had no resources other than their labour (whom they referred to as the *proletariat*) should unite to fight the owners of the means of production (whom they referred to as the

bourgeoisie) for the overthrow of capitalist societies. In the words of Marx and Engels,

> The history of all hitherto existing society is the history of class struggles. ... The proletarians have nothing to lose but their chains. They have a world to win. WORKING MEN OF ALL COUNTRIES UNITE! (Feuer 1959:7, 41)

After completing *The Communist Manifesto*, Marx returned to Germany, only to be expelled. He then moved to England, where he continued to write books and essays. Marx lived there in extreme poverty—he pawned most of his possessions, and several of his children died of malnutrition and disease. Marx clearly was an outsider in British society, a fact that may well have affected his view of Western cultures.

In Marx's analysis, society is fundamentally divided between classes, which clash in pursuit of their own class interests. When he examined the industrial societies of his time, such as Germany, England, and the United States, he saw the factory as the centre of conflict between the exploiters (the owners of the means of production) and the exploited (the workers). Marx viewed these relationships in systematic terms; that is, he believed that an entire system of economic, social, and political relationships maintained the power and dominance of the owners over the workers. Consequently, Marx and Engels argued that the working class needed to overthrow the existing class system. Marx's influence on contemporary thinking has been dramatic—his writings inspired those who were later to lead communist revolutions in Russia, China, Cuba, Vietnam, and elsewhere.

Even apart from the political revolutions that his work fostered, Marx's influence on contemporary thinking has been dramatic. Marx emphasized the *group* identifications and associations that influence an individual's place in society. This area of study is the major focus of contemporary sociology. Throughout this textbook, we consider how membership in a particular gender classification, age group, racial or ethnic group, or economic class affects a person's attitudes and behaviour. In an important sense, we can trace this way of understanding society back to the pioneering work of Karl Marx.

Modern Developments

Sociology today builds on the firm foundation developed by Émile Durkheim, Max Weber, and Karl Marx. However, the discipline of sociology has certainly not remained stagnant over the last century. Although Europeans have continued to make contributions to the discipline, sociologists from throughout the world have advanced sociological theory and research. Their new insights have helped them to better understand the workings of society.

Today, some of the most exciting developments in sociology are taking place outside of the traditional Eurocentric (meaning "centred on European thought") framework. We now find numerous non-Western developments in sociological theory, such as indigenous or indigenist perspectives. These perspectives highlight the degree to which Western views—through centuries of colonization—define, shape, and name the world (Tuhiwai Smith 2005). Indigenous/indigenist perspectives challenge the domination and control of sociology by Western ideas and methods through the use of decolonizing frameworks.

Charles Horton Cooley (1864–1929) was typical of the sociologists who came to prominence in the early 1900s. Cooley received his graduate training in economics but later became a sociology professor at the University of Michigan. Like other early sociologists, he had become interested in this "new" discipline while pursuing a related area of study.

Cooley shared the desire of Durkheim, Weber, and Marx to learn more about society. But to do so effectively, Cooley preferred to use the sociological perspective to look first at smaller units—intimate, face-to-face groups, such as families, gangs, and friendship networks. He saw these groups as the seedbeds of society in the sense that they shape people's ideals, beliefs, values, and social nature. Cooley's work increased our understanding of groups of relatively small size.

In the early twentieth century, many leading sociologists in the United States saw themselves as social reformers dedicated to systematically studying and then improving what they saw as a corrupt society. They were genuinely concerned about the lives of newcomers to the nation's growing cities, whether these people came from Europe or the rural American south. Early female sociologists, in particular, often took active roles in poor urban areas as leaders of community centres known as *settlement houses*. For example, Jane Addams (1860–1935), an active member of the American Sociological Society, co-founded the famous Chicago settlement, Hull House. Addams and other pioneering female sociologists commonly combined intellectual inquiry, social service work, and political activism—all with the goal of assisting the underprivileged and creating a more egalitarian society. For example, working with the black journalist and educator Ida B. Wells, Addams successfully prevented the implementation of a racial segregation policy in the Chicago public schools. Addams's efforts to establish a juvenile court system and a women's trade union also reflect the practical focus of her work (Addams 1910, 1930; Deegan 1991; Lengermann and Niebrugge-Brantley 1998).

By the middle of the twentieth century, however, the focus of the discipline had shifted. Sociologists for the most part restricted themselves to theorizing and gathering information; the aim of transforming society was left to social workers and others. This shift away from social reform was accompanied by a growing commitment to

In a photograph taken around 1930, social reformer Jane Addams reads to children at the Mary Crane Nursery. Addams was an early pioneer both in sociology and in the settlement house movement.

scientific methods of research and to value-free interpretation of data. Not all sociologists were happy with this emphasis. A new organization, the Society for the Study of Social Problems, was created in 1950 to deal more directly with social inequality and other related problems.

Sociologist Robert Merton (1968) made an important contribution to the discipline by successfully combining theory and research. Born in 1910 of Slavic immigrant parents in Philadelphia, Merton's teaching career has been based at Columbia University in New York.

Merton produced a theory that is one of the most frequently cited explanations of deviant behaviour. He noted different ways in which people attempt to achieve success in life. In his view, some may not share the socially agreed-on goal of accumulating material goods or the accepted means of achieving this goal. For example, in Merton's classification scheme, "innovators" are people who accept the goal of pursuing material wealth but use illegal means to do so, including robbery, burglary, and extortion. Merton bases his explanation of crime on individual behaviour—influenced by society's approved goals and means, yet it has wider applications. It helps to account for the high crime rates among the nation's poor, who may see no hope of advancing themselves through traditional roads to success. In Chapter 7, we discuss Merton's theory in greater detail.

Merton also emphasized that sociology should strive to bring together the "macro-level" and "micro-level" approaches to the study of society. **Macrosociology** concentrates on large-scale phenomena or entire civilizations. Thus, Émile Durkheim's cross-cultural study of suicide is an example of macrolevel research. More recently, macrosociologists have examined international crime rates (see Chapter 7), the stereotype of Asians as a "model minority" (see Chapter 10), and the population patterns of Islamic countries (see Chapter 15). By contrast, **microsociology** stresses study of small groups and often uses experimental study in laboratories. Sociological research on the micro level has included studies of how divorced men and women, for example, disengage from significant social roles (see Chapter 5); of how conformity can influence the expression of prejudiced attitudes (see Chapter 7); and of how a teacher's expectations can affect a student's academic performance (see Chapter 13).

In Canada, the work of sociologists Harold A. Innis (1894–1952) and S.D. Clark (1910–2003) established a strong foundation for the examination of Canada from a political economy perspective. Innis rejected existing interpretations of Canadian society and theorized about the relationship between the extraction of products, such as fish, timber, wheat, and hydroelectric power, and the development of the Canadian state. Innis's works, such as *A History of the Canadian Pacific Railway* (1923), *The Fur Trade in Canada: An Introduction to Canadian Economic History* (1930), *The Cod Fisheries: The History of an International Economy* (1942), and *Political Economy in the Modern State* (1946), took a historical perspective on the production of staple goods (e.g., fish, fur, and forest products) in the young Canadian economy, emphasizing the importance of communication and transportation to the development of political and economic systems. Innis's later research at the University of Toronto also included an examination of modern communication theory: *The Bias of Communication* (1951). In addressing the influence of the media on society, Innis made yet another contribution to the development of Canadian sociology.

S.D. Clark studied under Innis at the University of Toronto, completing his PhD in 1938. At that time, Clark began his academic career teaching in the political science department at the University of Toronto, as no department of sociology had yet been formed. Clark's books, such as *The Social Development of Canada* (1942), *Church and Sect in Canada* (1948), and *Movements of Political Protest* (1959), depict the struggle between the hinterlands and the cultural and financial power centres of Canada, which results in regional conflicts, the emergence of new political parties and religions, and social movements. His body of work helped to win increasing respect for sociology as a discipline in Canada, and he is credited with establishing the Department of Sociology at the University of Toronto in 1963.

Later, John Porter's *The Vertical Mosaic* (1965) provided a formative examination of social inequality as it relates to race, ethnicity, social class, and gender in Canada. Porter's depiction of Canadian society as a "mosaic" continues to be used in contrast to the U.S. metaphor of the "melting pot." (These concepts will be discussed in more detail in Chapter 3). Using Canadian census data before 1961, Porter revealed the existence of a hierarchy among ethnic groups in which the charter groups—the French and British—occupied the top socioeconomic positions. The charter groups were followed by other northern Europeans (e.g., Norwegians, Swedes, Dutch, Belgians), who were then followed by southern and Eastern Europeans (e.g., Ukrainians, Hungarians, Italians, Greeks). At the bottom of this socioeconomic hierarchy were visible minority groups, such as Chinese, blacks, and Aboriginals. Porter referred to groups that were not charter groups as *entrance groups*. These groups typically were assigned to lower-status jobs, according to the stereotypical preferences of the dominant charter groups. According to sociologist Richard Wanner (1998), "*The Vertical Mosaic* set the agenda for several streams of research, including studies of elites and the structure of power, social mobility and the role of education in the occupational attainment process, and immigrant integration and ethnic inequality."

The work of Patricia Marchak, which examined the ways in which Canadians make sense of their social world, contributed to the building of the foundation of Canadian society.

In 1975, Patricia Marchak contributed to the foundation of Canadian sociology through the publication of *Ideological Perspectives on Canada*. In this work, Marchak examines the way in which Canadians perceive and make sense of their social world.

Marchak's work is helpful in understanding why inequality exists, why tension exists between the police and a particular ethnic group, why a labour dispute results in a lockout, or why young people demonstrate at World Trade Organization meetings. In *Ideological Perspectives on Canada*, Marchak claims that people interpret such events according to ideologies, which act as "screens" through which they perceive the world. Ideologies, according to Marchak, are rarely taught explicitly; they are learned through observation, casual conversation, and example. Children learn an ideology by listening to and internalizing their parents' responses to questions, such as "Why is that family poor?" or "Why do doctors make more money than police officers?" In many cases, children receive responses that, according to Marchak, represent a dominant Canadian ideology—an ideology that supports the prevailing order.

Counter-ideologies, according to Marchak, challenge the assumptions of the dominant ideology, providing

alternative interpretations to views that simply reflect the interests of the dominant ruling class.

Contemporary sociology reflects the diverse contributions of earlier theorists. As sociologists approach such topics as divorce, drug addiction, and religious cults, they can draw on the theoretical insights of the discipline's pioneers. A careful reader can hear Comte, Durkheim, Weber, Marx, Cooley, and many others speaking through the pages of current research. Sociology has also broadened beyond the intellectual confines of North America and Europe. Contributions to the discipline now come from sociologists studying and researching human behaviour in other parts of the world. In describing the work of today's sociologists, it is helpful to examine a number of influential theoretical approaches (also known as *perspectives*).

☐ WHAT ARE THE MAJOR THEORETICAL PERSPECTIVES?

Students studying sociology for the first time may be surprised to learn that sociologists view society in different ways. Some see the world basically as a stable and ongoing entity. They are impressed with the endurance of the family, organized religion, and other social institutions. Some sociologists see society as composed of many groups in conflict, competing for scarce resources. To other sociologists, the most fascinating aspects of the social world are the everyday, routine interactions among individuals that we sometimes take for granted. Others see the world in terms of how gender is socially constructed. These four views, the ones most widely used by sociologists, are the functionalist, conflict, feminist, and interactionist perspectives. They will provide an introductory look at the discipline. One way to think about the theoretical perspectives used by sociologists is to compare them to the wearing of a lens. A sociologist explains the social world according to the assumptions and emphases of his or her theoretical perspective, just as the wearer of a lens sees the world according to the lens's size, shape, colour, and other characteristics.

Functionalist Perspective

Think of society as a living organism in which each part of the organism contributes to its survival. This view is the **functionalist perspective**, which emphasizes the way that parts of a society are structured to maintain its stability.

Let's examine prostitution as an example of the functionalist perspective. Why is it that a practice so widely condemned continues to display such persistence and vitality? Functionalists suggest that prostitution satisfies needs of patrons that may not be readily met through more socially acceptable forms, such as courtship or marriage. The "buyer" receives sex without any responsibility for procreation or sentimental attachment; at the same time, the "seller" makes a living through this exchange.

Such an examination leads us to conclude that prostitution does perform certain functions that society seems to need. However, this is not to suggest that prostitution is a desirable or legitimate form of social behaviour. Functionalists do not make such judgments. Rather, advocates of the functionalist perspective hope to explain how an aspect of society that is so frequently attacked can nevertheless manage to survive (K. Davis 1937).

Talcott Parsons

Talcott Parsons (1902–1979), a Harvard University sociologist, was a key figure in the development of functionalist theory. Parsons had been greatly influenced by the work of Émile Durkheim, Max Weber, and other European sociologists. For more than four decades, Parsons dominated sociology in the United States with his advocacy of functionalism. He saw any society as a vast network of connected parts, each of which helps to maintain the system as a whole. The functionalist approach holds that if an aspect of social life does not contribute to a society's stability or survival—if it does not serve some identifiably useful function or promote value consensus among members of a society, it will not be passed on from one generation to the next. Parsons viewed society as naturally being in a state of equilibrium. By "equilibrium," he meant that society tends toward a state of stability or balance. Parsons would view even prolonged labour strikes or civilian riots as temporary disruptions in the status quo rather than as significant alterations in social structure. Therefore, according to his **equilibrium model**, as changes occur in one part of society, there must be adjustments in other parts. If this does not take place, the society's equilibrium will be threatened and strains will occur.

Reflecting an evolutionary approach, Parsons (1966) maintained that four processes of social change are inevitable. The first, *differentiation*, refers to the increasing complexity of social organization. A change from "medicine man" to physician, nurse, and pharmacist is an illustration of differentiation in the field of health. This process is accompanied by the second process, *adaptive upgrading*, whereby social institutions become more specialized in their purposes. The division of labour among physicians into obstetricians, internists, surgeons, and so forth, is an example of adaptive upgrading.

The third process identified by Parsons is the *inclusion* of groups into society that were previously excluded because of such factors as gender, race, and social class

background. Medical schools have practised inclusion by admitting increasing numbers of women and visible minorities. Finally, Parsons contends that societies experience *value generalization*, the development of new values that tolerate and legitimate a greater range of activities. The acceptance of preventive and alternative medicine is an example of value generalization; our society has broadened its view of health care. All four processes identified by Parsons stress consensus—societal agreement on the nature of social organization and values (B. Johnson 1975; R. Wallace and Wolf 1980).

Manifest and Latent Functions

Your college or university calendar typically states various functions of the institution. It may inform you, for example, that the university intends to offer each student a broad education in classical and contemporary thought, in the humanities, in the sciences, and in the arts. However, it would be quite a surprise to find a calendar that declared, "This university was founded in 1895 to keep people between the ages of 18 and 22 out of the job market, thus reducing unemployment." No postsecondary institution would declare that this is the purpose of postsecondary education. Yet societal institutions serve many functions, some of them quite subtle. Postsecondary education, in fact, *does* delay people's entry into the job market.

Robert Merton (1968) made an important distinction between manifest and latent functions. **Manifest functions** of institutions are open, stated, conscious functions. They involve the intended, recognized consequences of an aspect of society, such as the college or university's role in certifying academic competence and excellence. By contrast, **latent functions** are unconscious or unintended functions and may reflect hidden purposes of an institution. One latent function of colleges and universities is to hold down unemployment. Another is to serve as a meeting ground for people seeking marital partners.

Dysfunctions

Functionalists acknowledge that not all parts of a society contribute to its stability all the time. A **dysfunction** refers to an element or a process of society that may actually disrupt a social system or lead to a decrease in stability.

We consider many dysfunctional behaviour patterns, such as homicide, to be undesirable. Yet we should not automatically interpret dysfunctions as negative. The evaluation of a dysfunction depends on a person's own values or, as the saying goes, on "where you sit." For example, the official view in prisons in the United States is that inmate gangs should be eradicated because they are dysfunctional to smooth operations. Yet some guards have actually come to view the presence of prison gangs as functional for their jobs. The danger posed by gangs creates a "threat to security," requiring increased surveillance and more overtime work for guards (Hunt et al. 1993:400).

Conflict Perspective

In contrast to functionalists' emphasis on stability and consensus, conflict sociologists see the social world as being in continual struggle. The **conflict perspective** assumes that social behaviour is best understood in terms of conflict or tension between competing groups. Such conflict and change need not be violent; they can take the form of labour negotiations, gender relations, party politics, competition between religious groups for members, or disputes over the federal budget. Conflict theorists contend that social institutions and practices persist because powerful groups have the ability to maintain them. Change has crucial significance, because it is needed to correct social injustices and inequalities.

Throughout most of the twentieth century, the functionalist perspective had the upper hand in sociology in North America. However, the conflict approach has become increasingly persuasive since the late 1960s. The rise of the feminist and gay rights movements, First Nations land claims, and confrontations at abortion clinics offered support for the conflict approach—the view that our social world is characterized by continual struggle between competing groups. Currently, the discipline of sociology views conflict theory as one way, among many others, to gain insight into a society.

The Marxist View

Karl Marx accepted the evolutionary argument that societies develop along a particular path. However, unlike Comte and Spencer, he did not view each successive stage as an inevitable improvement over the previous one. History, according to Marx, proceeds through a series of stages, each of which exploits a class of people. Ancient society exploited slaves; the estate system of feudalism exploited serfs; modern capitalist society exploits the working class. Ultimately, through a socialist revolution led by the proletariat, human society will move toward the final stage of development: a classless communist society, or "community of free individuals," as Marx described it in *Das Kapital* in 1867 (see Bottomore and Rubel 1956:250).

Karl Marx viewed struggle as inevitable, given the exploitation of workers under capitalism. Marx had an important influence on the development of sociology. His thinking offered insights into such institutions as the economy, the family, religion, and government. The Marxist view of social change is appealing because it does not restrict people to a passive role in responding to inevitable cycles or changes in material culture. Rather, Marxist theory offers a tool for those who want to seize control of the historical process and gain their freedom from injustice. In contrast to functionalists' emphasis on stability, Marx argues that conflict is a normal and desirable aspect of social change. In fact, change must be encouraged as a means of eliminating social inequality (Lauer 1982).

Expanding on Marx's work, sociologists and other social scientists have come to see conflict not merely as a class phenomenon but as a part of everyday life in all societies. Thus, in studying any culture, organization, or social group, sociologists want to know who benefits, who suffers, and who dominates at the expense of others. They are concerned with the conflicts between women and men, parents and children, and urban and rural areas, to name only a few. Conflict theorists are interested in how society's institutions—including the family, government, religion, education, and the media—may help to maintain the privileges of some groups and keep others in a subservient position. Their emphasis on social change and redistribution of resources makes conflict theorists more "radical" and "activist" than functionalists (Dahrendorf 1958).

Feminist Perspectives

Feminist perspectives attempt to explain, understand, and change the ways in which gender socially organizes our public and private lives in such a way as to produce inequality between men and women.

There are as many feminist perspectives as there are social and political philosophies; they run the gamut from liberal feminism to Marxist feminism and from anarchist feminism to eco-feminism. There is no *one* feminist perspective. Feminist perspectives, which can be macro or micro, have been a major contributor to contemporary sociological theory, providing frameworks within which gender inequality can be examined, understood, and changed. The following sections provide a sample of various feminist theories, highlighting the vast diversity among them.

Liberal Feminism

Liberal feminism advocates that women's equality can be obtained through the extension of the principles of equality of opportunity and freedom. Rather than advocating structural change to the capitalist economy or attempting to eliminate patriarchy (the system and practice of male domination in society), liberal feminist approaches assume that extending women's opportunities for education and employment, for example, will result in greater gender equality.

Marxist Feminism

Marxist feminism places the system of capitalism at fault for the oppression of women. Marxist feminists believe that women are not oppressed by sexism or patriarchy, but rather by a system of economic production that is based on unequal gender relations in the capitalist economy (Tong 1989).

Socialist Feminism

Gender relations, according to **socialist feminism**, are shaped by both patriarchy and capitalism. Socialist feminists, unlike Marxist feminists, who believe that the elimination of class distinctions will bring about gender equality, see patriarchy's grip in the home as well as in the public sphere (Luxton 1980).

Radical Feminism

The root of all oppression, according to **radical feminism**, is embedded in patriarchy (Code 1993). Some radical feminists (Firestone 1970) have based their view of women's oppression on reproduction, arguing that women's freedom from reproduction (i.e., through technological developments) will lead to their overall emancipation.

Transnational Feminism

Transnational feminism recognizes that capitalism and systems of political power have severe consequences and oppress women around the world. This form of feminism embraces the multiplicity of cultures, languages, geographies, and experiences that shape the lives of women and highlights the Western/non-Western hierarchy that continues to exist in thought and practice (Talpade Mohanty 2003; Grewal 2005).

Despite their differences, according to Patricia Madoo Lengermann and Gillian Niebrugge, contemporary feminist theories ask the following questions:

1. "And what about women?"
2. "Why is all this as it is?"
3. "How can we change and improve the social world so as to make it a more just place for all people?" (2008:451)

Dorothy Smith (1926–) is a Canadian sociologist whose contributions to sociology in general and feminist sociology in particular have been influential worldwide. Smith argues for a sociology that is built on the everyday experiences of women, and she points out how sociology used to ignore these experiences. Smith's groundbreaking work, *The Everyday World as Problematic* (1987), has helped students of sociology see the everyday world from the standpoint of women.

Margrit Eichler (1942–), also a Canadian sociologist, was among the first sociologists in this country to examine the ways in which sexism can influence research in social science (Nelson and Robinson 1999). Eichler examined sexist language and concepts, the androcentric perspective, and sexist methodology and interpretations of results (Eichler 1984:20).

The work of such sociologists as Smith and Eichler addresses the long-standing exclusion of women's standpoint in sociology, as well as sexist biases in the way in which sociological research has been conducted.

Interactionist Perspective

Workers interacting on the job, encounters in public places like bus stops and parks, behaviour in small groups—these are all aspects of microsociology that catch the attention of interactionists. Whereas functionalist and conflict theorists both analyze large-scale society-wide patterns of behaviour, the **interactionist perspective** generalizes about everyday forms of social interaction in order to understand society as a whole. Canadian interactionist sociologist Robert Prus, for example, studies the social world according to how people make sense out of their day-to-day lived experiences (1996). Employing an interactionist perspective, Prus has studied business, not as a strictly economic activity, but as a social activity based on lived experiences (1989). In the 1990s, for example, the workings of juries became a subject of public scrutiny. High-profile trials ended in verdicts that left some people shaking their heads. Long before jury members in the United States were being interviewed on their front lawns following trials, interactionists tried to better understand behaviour in the small-group setting of a jury deliberation room.

Interactionism is a sociological framework for viewing human beings as living in a world of meaningful objects. These "objects" may include material things, actions, other people, relationships, and even symbols.

Although functionalist and conflict approaches were initiated in Europe, interactionism developed first at the University of Chicago in the early 1900s. Interactionism became prominent when the Department of Sociology at the University of Chicago (known as the Chicago School) came to dominate North American sociology during the first four decades of the twentieth century (Marshall 1998). George Herbert Mead (1863–1931) is widely regarded as the founder of the interactionist perspective. Mead taught at the University of Chicago from 1893 until his death. His sociological analysis, like that of Charles Horton Cooley, often focused on human interactions within one-to-one situations and small groups. Mead was interested in observing the most minute forms of communication—smiles, frowns, nodding of the head—and in understanding how such individual behaviour was influenced by the larger context of a group or society. Despite his innovative views, Mead only occasionally wrote articles and never a book. He was an extremely popular teacher, and most of his insights have come to us through edited volumes of lectures that his students published after his death. Mead continued Cooley's exploration of interactionist theory (1934, 1964a), developing a useful model of the process by which the self emerges. According to Mead, this process was defined by three distinct stages, which he called the preparatory stage, the play stage, and the game stage.

Mead is best known for his theory of the self. According to Mead (1964b), the self begins as a privileged, central position in a person's world. Young children picture themselves as the focus of everything around them and find it difficult to consider the perspectives of others. For example, when shown a mountain scene and asked to describe what an observer on the opposite side of the mountain might see (such as a lake or hikers), young children describe only objects visible from their own perspective. As people mature, the self changes and begins to show greater concern about the reactions of others. Parents, friends, teachers, coaches, and co-workers are often among those who play a major role in shaping a person's self. Mead used the term **significant others** to refer to those individuals who are the most important in the development of the self. Many young people, for example, find themselves drawn to the same kind of work as their parents engage in (Schlenker 1985).

Mead uses the term **generalized other** to refer to the attitudes, viewpoints, and expectations of society that a child takes into account. Simply put, this concept suggests that when an individual acts, he or she considers an entire group of people. For example, a child will not act courteously merely to please a particular parent. Rather, the child comes to understand that courtesy is a widespread social value endorsed by parents, teachers, and religious leaders.

Erving Goffman (1922–1982) popularized a particular type of interactionist method known as the **dramaturgical approach**. The dramaturgist compares everyday life to the setting of the theatre and stage. Just as actors project certain images, all of us seek to present particular features of our personalities while we hide other qualities. Thus, in a class, we may feel the need to project a serious image; at a party, we want to look relaxed and friendly.

The Postmodern Critique

More recently, sociologists have expanded their thinking to reflect the conditions of postmodern society. A **postmodern society** is a technologically sophisticated society that is preoccupied with consumer goods and media images (Brannigan 1992). Such societies consume goods and information on a mass scale. Postmodern theorists take a global perspective and note the ways that aspects of culture cross national boundaries (Lyotard 1993). For example, residents of Yellowknife may listen to reggae music from Jamaica, eat sushi and other types of Japanese food, and wear clogs from the Netherlands.

Postmodern theorists point to this diversity in their rejection of the notion that the social world can be explained by a single paradigm. The intermingling of cultures and ideologies that characterizes the modern, electronically connected planet has led to a relativist approach. As part of just one of the debates taking place among sociologists, postmodernists reject science as a panacea, arguing that no single theory can accurately explain the causes and consequences of postmodern global society. For example, postmodern theorists suggest that there is no objective way of differentiating true beliefs from false ones, since there is a plurality of claims to truth. As well, postmodern perspectives reject rigid boundaries or distinctions between and among academic disciplines, such as art, philosophy, and sociology, arguing that much can be gained through sharing ideas of many disciplines.

The emphasis of postmodern theorists is on describing emerging cultural forms and patterns of social interaction. Within sociology, the postmodern view offers support for integrating the insights of various theoretical perspectives—functionalism, conflict theory, interactionism, labelling theory, and feminist theories. Some feminist sociologists argue optimistically that, with its indifference to hierarchies and distinctions, postmodernism will discard traditional values of male dominance in favour of gender equality. Yet others contend that despite new technology, postindustrial and postmodern societies can be expected to experience the problems of inequality that have plagued industrial societies (Ritzer 1995a; Sale 1996; Smart 1990; Turner 1990; van Vucht Tijssen 1990).

Contemporary debates in sociological theory may consist of two opposing views: (1) one advocates the presence of a pre-existing social structure (i.e., a "society") in which reality is represented in social institutions and culture; (2) another advocates that reality is socially constructed, locally, on a micro level.

Postmodernism as a sociological approach, for example, focuses on individual action in which reality is socially constructed through a process of negotiated interaction with other individuals. In contrast, sociologists who offer the view that a social structure exists before an individual's entry into the world proceed from a macro rather than a micro perspective; consequently, they focus on how, for example, social institutions, such as the mass media, the education system, and religious organizations, have an impact on individuals. Although the debate may appear to be irreconcilably polarized between the social constructionist view of reality and the idea of a pre-existing social structure, human history may be viewed dialectically—that is, individuals are creators of and, at the same time, creations of their social worlds.

The Sociological Approach

Which perspective should a sociologist use in studying human behaviour? functionalist? conflict? interactionist? feminist?

Sociology makes use of all four perspectives (see Table 1-1), since each offers unique insights into the

same issue. Box 1-1 shows how sports might look from the functionalist, conflict, interactionist, and feminist points of view.

No one approach to a particular issue is "correct." In this book, we assume that sociologists can gain the broadest understanding of our society by drawing on all four perspectives in the study of human behaviour and institutions. These perspectives overlap as their interests coincide but can diverge according to the dictates of each approach and of the issue being studied. A sociologist's theoretical orientation influences her approach to a research problem in important ways.

Table 1-1 Comparing Major Theoretical Perspectives

	Functionalist	**Conflict**	**Interactionist**	**Feminist**
View of society	Stable, well-integrated	Characterized by tension and struggle between and among groups	Active in influencing and affecting everyday social interaction	Characterized by gender and inequality; causes and solutions vary
Level of analysis emphasized	Macro	Macro	Micro-analysis as a way of understanding the larger macro phenomena	Both macro and micro levels of analysis
Key concepts	Manifest functions Latent functions Dysfunction	Inequality Capitalism Stratification	Symbols Nonverbal communication Face to face	Standpoint of women Political action Gender inequality Oppression
View of the individual	People are socialized to perform societal functions	People are shaped by power, coercion, and authority	People manipulate symbols and create their social worlds through interaction	Differs according to social class, race, ethnicity, age, sexual orientation, and physical ability
View of the social order	Maintained through cooperation and consensus	Maintained through force and coercion	Maintained by shared understanding of everyday behaviour	Maintained through standpoints that do not include those of women
View of social change	Predictable, reinforcing	Change takes place all the time and may have positive consequences	Reflected in people's social positions and their communications with others	Essential in order to bring about equality
Example	Public punishments reinforce the social order	Laws reinforce the positions of those in power	People respect laws or disobey them based on their own past experience	Spousal violence, date rape, and economic inequality need to be eliminated
Proponents	Émile Durkheim Talcott Parsons Robert Merton	Karl Marx C. Wright Mills	George Herbert Mead Charles Horton Cooley Erving Goffman	Dorothy Smith Margrit Eichler

Research in Action 1-1
Looking at Sports from Four Perspectives

We watch sports. Talk sports. Spend money on sports. Some of us live and breathe sports. Because sports occupy much of our time and directly or indirectly consume and generate a great deal of money, it should not be surprising that sports have sociological components that can be analyzed from the various theoretical perspectives.

Functionalist View

In examining any aspect of society, functionalists emphasize the contribution it makes to overall social stability. Functionalists regard sports as a quasi-religious institution that uses ritual and ceremony to reinforce the common values of a society:

- Sports socialize young people into such values as competition and patriotism.
- Sports help to maintain people's physical well-being.
- Sports serve as a safety valve for both participants and spectators, who are allowed to shed tension and aggressive energy in a socially acceptable way.
- Sports bring together members of a community (supporting local athletes and teams) or even a nation (as seen during World Cup soccer matches and the Olympics) and promote an overall feeling of unity and social solidarity.

Conflict View

Conflict theorists argue that the social order is based on coercion and exploitation. They emphasize that sports reflect and even exacerbate many of the divisions in society:

- Sports are a form of big business in which profits are more important than the health and safety of the workers (athletes).
- Sports perpetuate the false idea that success can be achieved simply through hard work, while failure should be blamed on the individual alone (rather than on injustices in the larger social system). Sports also serve as an "opiate" that encourages people to seek a "fix" or temporary "high" rather than focus on personal problems and social issues.
- Gender expectations encourage female athletes to be passive and gentle, qualities that do not support the emphasis on competitiveness in sports. As a result, women find it difficult to enter sports traditionally dominated by men, such as ice hockey or boxing.

Interactionist View

In studying the social order, interactionists are especially interested in shared understandings of everyday behaviour. Interactionists examine sports on the micro level by focusing on how day-to-day social behaviour is shaped by the distinctive norms, values, and demands of the world of sports:

- Sports often heighten parent–child involvement; they may lead to parental expectations for participation and (sometimes unrealistically) for success.
- Participation in sports provides friendship networks that can permeate everyday life.

☐ HOW DID THE SOCIOLOGICAL IMAGINATION DEVELOP?

Throughout the book, we will be illustrating the sociological imagination in several different ways—by showing theory in practice and research in action; by speaking across race, gender, class, and national boundaries; and by highlighting social policy throughout the world.

Theory in Practice

We will illustrate how the four sociological perspectives—functionalist, conflict, interactionist, and feminist—are helpful in understanding today's issues. Sociologists do not necessarily declare "we are using functionalism," but their research and approaches do tend to draw on one or more theoretical frameworks, as will become clear in the pages that follow.

Research in Action

Sociologists actively investigate a variety of issues and social behaviour. We have already seen that such research might involve the meaning of sports and decision making in the jury box. Often, the research has direct applications for improving people's lives, as in the case of increasing the participation of blacks in Canada and the United States in diabetes testing. Throughout the rest of the book, the research done by sociologists and other

- Despite class, racial, and religious differences, teammates may work together harmoniously and may even abandon old stereotypes and prejudices.
- Relationships in the sports world are defined by people's social positions as players, coaches, and referees—as well as by the high or low status that individuals hold as a result of their performances and reputations.

Feminist Views

Feminist theorists believe that gender is constructed by society; thus, sports play a major role not only in reflecting society's ideas about gender but also in constructing their own images:

- Girls' and boys' bodies are gendered through sporting activities.
- Different patterns of participation in sports are produced through the intersection of gender, social class, race, and age.
- Male athletes are paid more than female athletes; the general public considers male teams and leagues more important than female ones.
- Masculinity is socially constructed in such a way as to stress athletic prowess and success.

Despite their differences, functionalists, conflict theorists, interactionists, and feminist theorists would all agree that there is much more to sports than exercise or recreation. They would also agree that sports and other popular forms of culture are worthy subjects of serious study by sociologists.

Sources: Acosta and Carpenter 2001; H. Edwards 1973; Eitzen 2003; Fine 1987.

Women often have difficulty entering what are considered men's sports. However, in recent years, numerous international successes have brought more attention to women's hockey in Canada. In this photo, members of Canada's women's hockey team celebrate their gold medal victory in the 2006 Winter Olympic Games at Turin, Italy.

Applying Theory

1. How would functionalist thinkers interpret discrimination in sports based on gender or race?
2. Which perspective do you think is most useful in looking at the sociology of sports? Why?

---

social scientists that we present will shed light on group behaviour of all types.

Speaking Across Race, Gender, Class, and National Boundaries

Sociologists include both men and women, people from a variety of socioeconomic backgrounds (some privileged and many not), and individuals from a wealth of ethnic, racial, national, and religious origins. In their work, sociologists seek to draw conclusions that speak to all people—not just the affluent or powerful. This is not always easy. Insights into how a corporation can increase its profits tend to attract more attention and financial support than do, say, the merits of a needle-exchange

program for drug addicts in urban centres. More than ever, though, sociology today seeks to better understand the experiences of *all* people. In Box 1-2 on page 20, we take a look at how a woman's role in various public spheres is defined differently from that of a man's in different parts of the world.

☐ SOCIAL POLICY THROUGHOUT THE WORLD

One important way we can use the sociological imagination is to enhance our understanding of current social issues throughout the world. Beginning with Chapter 2, which focuses on research, each chapter will conclude

Sociology in the Global Community 1-2
Women in Public Places Worldwide

By definition, a public place, such as a sidewalk or a park, is open to all persons. Even some private establishments, such as restaurants, are intended to belong to people as a whole. Yet sociologists and other social scientists have found that societies define access to these places differently for women and men.

In some Middle Eastern societies, women are prohibited from public spaces and are restricted to certain places in households. Shirin Ebadi, the first Muslim woman and first Iranian to win the Nobel Peace Prize, says that once a woman in Iran steps out onto the street, "she cannot be a traditional woman any more" (Ebadi in de Luce 2003). In Iran, young women are engaging in a quiet revolution by wearing wispy (transparent) coloured head scarves in public (as opposed to the traditional hijab). This has caused the authorities to call for an end of the sale of such products, the success of which is yet to be determined (de Luce 2003). In many societies, the coffeehouse and the market are considered male domains. Some other societies, such as Malagasy, strictly limit the presence of women in "public places" yet allow women to conduct the haggling that is a part of shopping in open-air markets. In some West African societies, women actually control the marketplace. In various Eastern European countries and Turkey, women appear to be free to move about in public places, but the coffeehouse remains the exclusive preserve of males. Contrast this with coffeehouses in North America, where women and men mingle freely and even engage each other in conversation as total strangers.

Although casual observers may view both private and public space in North America as gender-neutral, private all-male clubs do persist, and even in public spaces women experience some inequality. Erving Goffman, an interactionist, conducted classic studies of public spaces, which he found to be settings for routine interactions, such as "helping" encounters when a person is lost and asks for directions. But sociologist Carol Brooks Gardner has offered a feminist critique of Goffman's work: "Rarely does Goffman emphasize the habitual disproportionate fear that women can come to feel in public toward men, much less the routine trepidation that ethnic and racial minorities and the disabled can experience" (1989:45). Women are well aware that a casual helping encounter with a man in a public place can too easily lead to undesired sexual queries or advances.

Whereas Goffman suggests that street remarks about women occur rarely—and that they generally hold no unpleasant or threatening implications—Gardner (1989:49) counters that "for young women especially ... appearing in public places carries with it the constant possibility of evaluation, compliments that are not really so complimentary after all, and harsh or vulgar insults if the woman is found wanting." She adds that these remarks are sometimes accompanied by tweaks, pinches, or even blows, unmasking the latent hostility of many male-to-female street remarks.

Many women have well-founded fears for their safety in public places (DeKeseredy and Schwartz 1998). Gardner concludes that "public places are arenas for the enactment of inequality in everyday life for women and for many others" (1989:56). The intersection of gender with race and ethnicity produce varying degrees of visibility and invisibility for women, resulting in different treatment—among and between women—on the street (England 2004).

Unlike in many countries in the developing world, the inequality experienced by breastfeeding mothers in public spaces in Canada has long been a topic of debate. In 2000, after court challenges regarding the activity, most provincial and territorial human rights commissions supported women's right to breastfeed their babies in public places as a human right, allowing them to breastfeed, openly, in hockey rinks, restaurants, schools, shopping malls, and so on. A "Breastfeeding Friendly" logo was created in Canada to be placed on the doors and walls of various public places to indicate that women are welcome to breastfeed their babies on the premises.

Applying Theory

1. How might women be treated in a coffeehouse in Turkey? in Vancouver, British Columbia? What might account for these differences?
2. Do you know a woman who has encountered sexual harassment in a public place? How do the various feminist perspectives account for the prevalence of this harassment?

Sources: DeKeseredy and Schwartz, 1998; England 2004; Gardner 1989, 1990, 1995; Goffman 1963b, 1971.

with a discussion of a contemporary social policy issue. In some cases, we will examine a specific issue facing national governments. For example, government funding of child-care centres will be discussed in Chapter 4, "Socialization"; sexual harassment in Chapter 5, "Social Interaction, Groups, and Social Structure"; and the search for shelters in Chapter 15, "Population, Communities, and Health." These social policy sections will demonstrate how fundamental sociological concepts can enhance our critical-thinking skills and help us to better understand current public policy debates taking place around the world.

Sociologists expect the next quarter-century to be perhaps the most exciting and critical period in the history of the discipline. This is because of a growing recognition—both in Canada and around the world—that current social problems *must* be addressed before their magnitude overwhelms human societies. We can expect sociologists to play an increasing role in the government sector by researching and developing public policy alternatives. It seems only natural for this textbook to focus on the connection between the work of sociologists and the difficult questions confronting the policymakers and people of Canada.

CHAPTER RESOURCES

Summary

What is Sociology?
- **Sociology** (p. 3) is the systematic study of social behaviour and human groups.

What is the Sociological Imagination?
- The **sociological imagination** (p. 3) is an awareness of the relationship between an individual and the wider society. It is the ability to view our own society as an outsider might, rather than from the perspective of our limited experiences and cultural biases.

What is Sociological Theory?
- Sociologists employ **theories** (p. 6) to examine the relationships between or among observations/data that may seem completely unrelated.

How did Sociology Develop?
- Nineteenth-century thinkers who contributed sociological insights included Auguste Comte, a French philosopher; Harriet Martineau, an English sociologist; and Herbert Spencer, an English scholar.
- Other important figures in the development of sociology were Émile Durkheim, who pioneered work on suicide; Max Weber, who taught the need for "insight" in intellectual work; and Karl Marx, who emphasized the importance of the economy and of conflict in society.
- The discipline of sociology is indebted to such twentieth century sociologists as Charles Horton Cooley, Robert Merton, Harold A. Innis, S.D. Clark, John Porter, and Patricia Marchak.

What are the Major Sociological Perspectives?
- The **functionalist perspective** (p. 12) of sociology emphasizes the way that parts of a society are structured to maintain its stability. Social change should be slow and evolutionary.
- The **conflict perspective** (p. 14) assumes that social behaviour is best understood in terms of conflict or tension between and among competing groups. Social change, spurred by conflict and competition, is viewed as desirable.
- The **interactionist perspective** (p. 15) is primarily concerned with fundamental or everyday forms of interaction, including symbols and other types of nonverbal communication. Social change is ongoing, as individuals are shaped by society and in turn shape it.
- **Feminist perspectives** (p. 14) are varied and diverse; however, they argue that women's inequality is constructed by our society. Feminist perspectives include both micro and macro levels of analysis.

How is the Sociological Imagination Developed?
- Sociologists make use of all four perspectives, since each offers unique insights into the same issue.
- In this textbook, we make use of the **sociological imagination** by showing theory in practice and research in action; by speaking across race, gender, class, and national boundaries; and by highlighting aspects of social policy around the world.

Critical Thinking Questions

1. What aspects of the social and work environment in a fast-food restaurant would be of particular interest to a sociologist because of his or her "sociological imagination"?
2. What are the manifest and latent functions of shopping?
3. How might the interactionist perspective be applied to a place where you have been employed or to an organization you joined?
4. How could the sociological imagination be used to study the practice of shopping in North America?

Key Terms

Anomie The loss of direction felt in a society when social control of individual behaviour has become ineffective. (p. 8)

Conflict perspective A sociological approach that assumes that social behaviour is best understood in terms of conflict or tension between competing groups. (p. 14)

Dramaturgical approach A view of social interaction that examines people as if they were theatrical performers. (p. 16)

Dysfunction An element or a process of society that may disrupt a social system or lead to a decrease in stability. (p. 13)

Equilibrium model Talcott Parsons's functionalist view of society as tending toward a state of stability or balance. (p. 13)

Feminist perspectives Sociological approaches that attempt to explain, understand, and change the ways in which gender socially organizes our public and private lives in such a way as to produce inequality between men and women. (p. 14)

Functionalist perspective A sociological approach that emphasizes the way that parts of a society are structured to maintain its stability. (p. 12)

Generalized others A term used by George Herbert Mead to refer to the attitudes, viewpoints, and expectations of society as a whole that a child takes into account in his or her behaviour. (p. 16)

Ideal type A construct or model that serves as a measuring rod against which actual cases can be evaluated. (p. 8)

Interactionist perspective A sociological approach that generalizes about fundamental or everyday forms of social interaction. (p. 15)

Latent functions Unconscious or unintended functions; hidden purposes. (p. 13)

Liberal feminism The stream of feminism asserting that women's equality can be obtained through the extension of the principles of equality of opportunity and freedom. (p. 14)

Macrosociology Sociological investigation that concentrates on large-scale phenomena or entire civilizations. (p. 11)

Manifest functions Open, stated, and conscious functions. (p. 13)

Marxist feminism The stream of feminist sociological approaches that place the system of capitalism at fault for the oppression of women and hold that women are not oppressed by sexism or patriarchy, but rather by a system of economic production that is based on unequal gender relations in the capitalist economy. (p. 15)

Microsociology Sociological investigation that stresses study of small groups and often uses laboratory experimental studies. (p. 11)

Natural science The study of the physical features of nature and the ways in which they interact and change. (p. 4)

Postmodern society A technologically sophisticated society that is preoccupied with consumer goods and media images. (p. 16)

Radical feminism The stream of feminism maintaining that the root of all oppression of women is embedded in patriarchy. (p. 15)

Science The body of knowledge obtained by methods based on systematic observation. (p. 4)

Significant others A term used by George Herbert Mead to refer to those individuals who are most important in the development of the self, such as parents, friends, and teachers. (p. 16)

Socialist feminism The stream of feminism that maintains that gender relations are shaped by both patriarchy and capitalism, and thus equality for women implies that both the system of capitalism and the ideology of patriarchy must be challenged and eliminated. (p. 15)

Social science The study of various aspects of human society. (p. 4)

Sociological imagination An awareness of the relationship between an individual and the wider society. (p. 3)

Sociology The systematic study of social behaviour and human groups. (p. 3)

Theory A template through which to organize a way to view the world. (p. 6)

Transnational feminism Transnational feminism recognizes that capitalism and systems of political power have severe consequences and oppress women around the world. This form of feminism embraces the multiplicity of cultures, languages, geographies, and experiences which shape the lives of women and highlights the Western/non-Western hierarchy that continues to exist in thought and practice. (p. 15)

Verstehen The German word for "understanding" or "insight"; used to stress the need for sociologists to take into account people's emotions, thoughts, beliefs, and attitudes. (p. 8)

Additional Readings

Glasser, Barry, Rosanna Hertz, and Herbert J. Gans (eds.). 2003. *Our Studies, Our Selves: Sociologists' Lives and Work*. Oxford, UK: Oxford University Press. This is a collection of 22 autobiographical essays by 12 women and 10 men from Canada and the United States, all contributing to the field of sociology.

McDonald, Lynn. 1994. *Women Founders of the Social Sciences*. Ottawa: Carlton University Press. The author examines the important but often overlooked contributions of such pioneers as Mary Wollstonecraft, Harriet Martineau, Beatrice Webb, Jane Addams, and many more.

Ritzer, George. 2007. *Contemporary Sociological Theory and Its Classical Roots: The Basics*, 2nd edition. New York: McGraw-Hill. This book provides coverage of all the major sociological theorists and theoretical traditions.

Thomson, Anthony. 2005. *The Making of Social Theory— Order, Reason, and Desire*. Don Mills, ON: Oxford University Press. This introduction to social thought is organized thematically and places intellectual history in a social, political, and economic context.

 ## Online Learning Centre

Visit the *Sociology: A Brief Introduction* Online Learning Centre at www.mcgrawhill.ca/olc/schaefer to access quizzes, interactive exercises, video clips, and other research and study tools related to this chapter.

 ## Reel Society CD and Video Clips

Exercise your imagination and step into the world of *Reel Society*, a professionally produced movie on CD-ROM that demonstrates the sociological imagination through typical scenarios drawn from campus life. In this movie, you will become part of the exploits of several students and will influence the plot by making key choices for them. Through it all, you'll learn to relate sociological thought to real life through a variety of issues and perspectives. In addition to the interactive movie, *Reel Society* includes explanatory text screens and a glossary, as well as quizzes and discussion questions to test your knowledge of sociology. The CD also includes a link to the Online Learning Centre Web site for *Reel Society*.

Reel Society video clips can be used to spark discussion about the following topics from this chapter:

- The sociological imagination
- Major theoretical perspectives
- Speaking across race, gender, and national boundaries

chapter 2

SOCIOLOGICAL RESEARCH

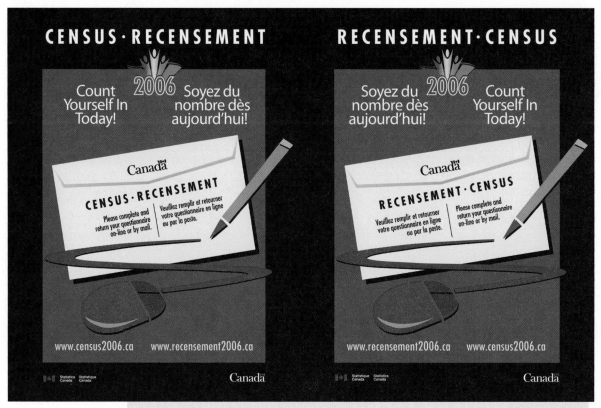

In Canada, the census is the primary mechanism for collecting information about citizens. The questions asked on the census reflect changing social and political patterns that reveal the dynamic nature of Canadian society.

☐ **What are the Ethics of Research?**

☐ **What is the Scientific Method?**

☐ **What are the Major Research Designs?**

☐ **How does Technology Influence Sociological Research?**

> **Boxes**

SOCIOLOGY IN THE GLOBAL COMMUNITY: Polling in Baghdad

RESEARCH IN ACTION: Does Hard Work Lead to Better Grades?

SOCIAL POLICY AND SOCIOLOGICAL RESEARCH: Studying Human Sexuality

The lost status of the distinguished older man and the emerging clout of the power woman are driving men to cosmetic surgeons at a record rate, new research suggests.

Sociologist Michael Atkinson tracks this drive to regain power in his study of Canadian men who have undergone cosmetic surgery. He said many men believed they could not compete with younger men and increasingly couldn't compete with women in the workplace without surgical enhancement.

"Traditionally, we've said to men, 'You can get away with aging.' That's quickly changing," Atkinson said. "Now, the older form isn't culturally revered at all."

The McMaster University professor conducted interviews with 44 men who have undergone cosmetic surgery procedures once considered the exclusive domain of women, including Botox injections and eye lifts. Atkinson also interviewed 12 surgeons and found a clear fault line in the motivating factors for men and women.

"Men are doing it more to maintain a position rather than attain a position, to hold on to a sense of power or masculinity. For some women, it's about staying pretty. That's a disempowering image. That's not the same as a guy trying to keep their job," said Atkinson, who will present the results of the study . . . at the Technology and Body conference in Ottawa.

. . . The Social Sciences and Humanities Research Council (SSHRC), a federal government agency that funds university-based research, awarded Atkinson its Aurora Prize for his groundbreaking research on the emerging cosmetic surgery phenomenon.

The prize, valued at $25,000, honours an outstanding new researcher who has demonstrated particular originality and insight in social science and humanities research. Atkinson has also studied tattooing, extreme exercising and ticket scalping.

The first survey of Canadian cosmetic surgeons and dermatologists about cosmetic enhancement, undertaken earlier this year, shows Atkinson is on to something.

Toronto-based Medicard Finance Inc., which provides financing for elective medical procedures, found that male clients now account for 14.5 per cent of cosmetic procedures in Canada. The top services requested by men are liposuction, rhinoplasty, eye lifts and Botox injections, according to the survey of 2650 cosmetic surgeons.

Overall, the number of cosmetic surgeries increased 16 per cent from 2002 to 2003, the survey showed. The number of Botox injections jumped an estimated 19 per cent and the number of Canadians who used injectable wrinkle fillers increased by 23 per cent.

Medicard CEO Ann Kaplan says men's acceptance of eye laser surgery in recent years has opened up the possibility of other cosmetic procedures to preserve or enhance their looks.

"You could almost chart it. I believe the eventual acceptance of laser eye surgery allowed men to say, 'This surgery worked for me. These procedures do work.' It has helped them accept other procedures," says Kaplan.

Today, men represent 21 per cent of Medicard's business.

Atkinson said the male cosmetic surgery phenomenon speaks to a fundamental shift in how men see themselves. "Men's roles and responsibilities have already shifted, and we've been slow to notice," he said.

☐ *(Schmidt 2004)*

This article by Sarah Schmidt discusses the research of McMaster University sociologist Michael Atkinson documenting the growing number of Canadian men currently undergoing cosmetic procedures, such as rhinoplasty, eye lifts, and Botox injections—an increase of 16 percent from 2002 to 2003. After interviewing 44 men and 12 surgeons, Atkinson studied the motivating factors that propelled men to undergo cosmetic surgery procedures.

Much has been researched about the "beauty myth" as a societal control mechanism that is meant to keep women in their place—as subordinates to men at home and on the job. But some men are now captive to unrealistic expectations regarding their physical appearance. In hopes of regaining a younger look and maintaining their power in the workplace, more and more men, as Michael Atkinson's research revealed, are now having Botox injections or electing to undergo cosmetic surgery.

Effective sociological research can be quite thought-provoking. It may suggest many new questions about social interactions that require further study, such as why we make assumptions about people's intentions based merely on their gender or age. In some cases, rather than raising additional questions, a study will simply confirm previous beliefs and findings.

In this chapter, we will examine the research process used in conducting sociological studies. First, we'll pay particular attention to the ethical challenges sociologists face in studying human behaviour and the debate raised by Max Weber's call for "value neutrality" in social science research. We will then look at the steps that make up the scientific method in doing research. Next, we will take a look at various techniques commonly used in sociological research, such as experiments, observations, and surveys. We will also examine the role that technology plays in research today. The social policy section considers the difficulties in researching human sexuality.

Whatever the area of sociological inquiry and whatever the perspective of the sociologist—whether functionalist, conflict, interactionist, feminist, or any other—there is one crucial requirement: imaginative, responsible research that meets the highest ethical standards.

Use Your Sociological Imagination

Have you ever thought about how your perception of beauty is influenced by the gender or age of others? Have you ever thought about how the perception of youthful appearance might influence one's chances of advancing in the workplace?

□ WHAT ARE THE ETHICS OF RESEARCH?

A biochemist cannot inject a drug into a human being unless the drug has been thoroughly tested and the subject agrees to the shot. To do otherwise would be both unethical and illegal. Sociologists must also abide by certain specific standards in conducting research—a **code of ethics**.

The professional society of the discipline, the Canadian Sociology and Anthropology Association (CSAA), published a code of ethics in 1994. The following is a short excerpt from the CSA's *Statement of Professional Ethics*. The complete statement is available online at www.csaa.ca/structure/Code.htm:

Organizing and initiating research

4.   Codes of professional ethics arise from the need to protect vulnerable or subordinate populations from harm incurred, knowingly or unknowingly, by the intervention of researchers into their lives and cultures. Sociologists and anthropologists have a responsibility to respect the rights, and be concerned with the welfare, of all the vulnerable and subordinate populations affected by their work. . . .

Protecting people in the research environment

12.   Researchers must respect the rights of citizens to privacy, confidentiality and anonymity, and not to be studied. Researchers should make every effort to determine whether those providing information wish to remain anonymous or to receive recognition and then respect their wishes. . . .

Informed consent

15.   Researchers must not expose respondents to risk of personal harm. Informed consent must be obtained when the risks of research are greater than the risks of everyday life. . . .

Covert research and deception

20. Subjects should not be deceived if there is any reasonably anticipated risk to the subjects or if the harm cannot be offset or the extent of the harm be reasonably predicted.

On the surface, these and the rest of the basic principles of the CSAA's *Statement of Professional Ethics* probably seem clear-cut. How could they lead to any disagreement or controversy? However, many delicate ethical questions cannot be resolved simply by reading the points above. For example, should a sociologist engaged in participant-observation research *always* protect the confidentiality of subjects? What if the subjects are members of a religious cult allegedly engaged in unethical and possibly illegal activities? What if the sociologist is interviewing political activists and is questioned by government authorities about the research?

Most sociological research uses *people* as sources of information—as respondents to survey questions, subjects of observation, or participants in experiments. In all cases, sociologists need to be certain that they are not invading the privacy of their subjects. Generally, they handle this by ensuring anonymity and by guaranteeing the confidentiality of personal information. However, a study by William Zellner raised important questions about the extent to which sociologists can threaten people's right to privacy.

The Right to Know versus the Right to Privacy

A car lies at the bottom of a cliff, its driver dead. Was this an accident or a suicide? Sociologist William Zellner (1978) wanted to learn whether fatal car crashes are sometimes suicides disguised as accidents in order to protect family and friends (and perhaps to collect otherwise unredeemable insurance benefits). These acts of "autocide" are by nature covert. Zellner found that research on automobile accidents in which fatalities occur poses an ethical issue—the right to know against the right to privacy.

In his efforts to assess the frequency of such suicides, Zellner sought to interview the friends, co-workers, and family members of the deceased. He hoped to obtain information that would allow him to ascertain whether the deaths were accidental or deliberate. Zellner told the people approached for interviews that his goal was to contribute to a reduction of future accidents by learning about the emotional characteristics of accident victims. He made no mention of his suspicions of autocide, out of fear that potential respondents would refuse to meet with him.

Zellner eventually concluded that at least 12 percent of all fatal single-occupant crashes are suicides. This information could be valuable for society, particularly since some of the probable suicides actually killed or critically injured innocent bystanders in the process of taking their own lives. Yet the ethical questions still must be faced. Was Zellner's research unethical because he misrepresented the motives of his study and failed to obtain his subjects' informed consent? Or was his deception justified by the social value of his findings?

The answers to these questions are not immediately apparent. Zellner appeared to have admirable motives and took great care in protecting confidentiality. He did not reveal names of suspected suicides to insurance companies, though Zellner did recommend that the insurance industry drop double indemnity (payment of twice the person's life insurance benefits in the event of accidental death) in the future.

Zellner's study raised an additional ethical issue: the possibility of harm to those who were interviewed. Subjects were asked if the deceased had "talked about suicide" and if they had spoken of how "bad or useless" they were. Could these questions have led people to guess the true intentions of the researcher? Perhaps, but according to Zellner, none of the informants voiced such suspicions. More seriously, might the study have caused the bereaved to *suspect* suicide—when before the survey they had accepted the deaths as accidental? Again, there is no evidence to suggest this, but we cannot be sure.

Given our uncertainty about this last question, was the research justified? Was Zellner taking too big a risk in asking the friends and families if the deceased victims had spoken of suicide before their death? Does the right to know outweigh the right to privacy in this type of situation? And who has the right to make such a judgment? In practice, as in Zellner's study, it is the *researcher*, not the subjects of inquiry, who makes the critical ethical

Are some people who die in single-occupant car crashes actually suicides? One sociological study of possible "autocides" concluded that at least 12 percent of such accident victims had, in fact, committed suicide. But the study also raised some ethical questions concerning the right to know and the right to privacy.

decisions. Therefore, sociologists and other investigators bear the responsibility for establishing clear and sensitive boundaries for ethical scientific investigation.

Preserving Confidentiality

Like journalists, sociologists occasionally find themselves subject to questions from law enforcement authorities or to legal threats because of knowledge they have gained in conducting research and maintaining confidentiality. This situation raises profound ethical questions.

In 1994, Russel Ogden was a graduate student at Simon Fraser University (SFU) in British Columbia. In his research, Ogden conducted interviews with people involved in assisted suicide or euthanasia among people with AIDS. A newspaper report about the study came to the attention of the Vancouver coroner, who was already holding an inquest into the death of an "unknown female." Ogden's thesis reported that two research participants had knowledge about her death. The coroner subpoenaed Ogden to identify his sources, but he cited a promise of "absolute confidentiality" and refused to name them. This promise had been authorized by SFU's Research Ethics Board.

The coroner initially found Ogden to be in contempt of court but later accepted a common law argument that the communications between Ogden and his participants were privileged. In doing so, the coroner released Ogden from "any stain or suggestion of contempt." But Ogden's battle in coroner's court was fought without the support of his university. He sued SFU, unsuccessfully, to recover his legal costs. However, the judge condemned SFU for failing to protect academic freedom and urged the university to remedy the situation. Simon Fraser's president responded with a written apology to Ogden, compensation for legal costs and lost wages, and a guarantee that the university would assist "any researchers who find themselves in the position of having to challenge a subpoena" (Lowman and Palys 2000).

This case points to the delicate balance researchers and sponsoring institutions must maintain between the value of research and the confidentiality of the subjects, and the threat of litigation.

Neutrality and Politics in Research

The ethical considerations of sociologists lie not only in the methods they use but also in the way they interpret results. Max Weber ([1904] 1949) recognized that personal values would influence the questions that sociologists select for research. In his view, that was perfectly acceptable, but under no conditions could a researcher allow his or her personal feelings to influence the *interpretation* of data. In Weber's phrase, sociologists must practise **value neutrality** in their research. Weber's use

of the concept *verstehen* is "one of his best-known and most controversial contributions to the methodology of contemporary sociology" (Ritzer 2008:117).

As part of this neutrality, investigators have an ethical obligation to accept research findings even when the data run counter to their own personal views, to theoretically based explanations, or to widely accepted beliefs. For example, Émile Durkheim challenged popular conceptions when he reported that social (rather than supernatural) forces were an important factor in suicide.

Some sociologists believe that neutrality is impossible. At the same time, Weber's insistence on value-free sociology may lead the public to accept sociological conclusions without exploring the biases of the researchers. As we have seen, Weber was quite clear that sociologists may bring values to their subject matter. In his view, however, they must not confuse their own values with the social reality under study (Bendix 1968).

Let's consider what might happen when researchers bring their own biases to the investigation. A person investigating the impact of intercollegiate sports on alumni contributions, for example, may focus only on the highly visible revenue-generating sports of football and basketball and neglect the so-called minor sports, such as tennis or soccer, which are more likely to involve female athletes. Despite the work of Dorothy Smith and Margrit Eichler, sociologists still need to be reminded that the discipline often fails to adequately consider *all* people's social behaviour.

☐ WHAT IS THE SCIENTIFIC METHOD?

Like all of us, sociologists are interested in the central questions of our time. Is the family falling apart? Why is there so much crime? Is the world failing in its ability to feed the population? Such issues concern most people, whether or not they have academic training. However, unlike the typical citizen, some sociologists have a commitment to the use of the **scientific method** in studying society. The scientific method is a systematic, organized series of steps that ensures maximum objectivity and consistency in researching a problem.

Many of us will never actually conduct scientific research. Why, then, is it important that we understand the scientific method? Because it plays a major role in the workings of our society. Residents of Canada are constantly being bombarded with "facts" or "data." Almost daily, advertisers cite supposedly scientific studies to prove that their products are superior. Such claims may be accurate or exaggerated. We can make better evaluations of such information—and will not be fooled so easily—if we are familiar with the standards of scientific research. These standards are quite stringent and demand as strict adherence as possible.

▶**FIGURE 2-1**

The Scientific Method

The scientific method allows sociologists to objectively and logically evaluate data they collect. Their findings can prompt further ideas for sociological research.

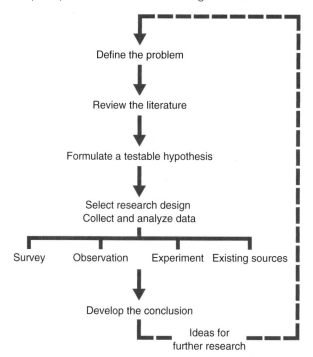

It seems reasonable to assume that parents' income relates to whether their children pursue postsecondary education. But how would you go about researching this hypothesis?

The scientific method requires precise preparation in developing useful research. Otherwise, the research data collected may not prove accurate. Sociologists and other researchers follow five basic steps in the scientific method: (1) defining the problem, (2) reviewing the literature, (3) formulating the hypothesis, (4) selecting the research design and then collecting and analyzing data, and (5) developing the conclusion (see Figure 2-1). We'll use an actual example to illustrate the workings of the scientific method.

Defining the Problem

Some people make great sacrifices and work hard to get a postsecondary education. Some parents borrow money for their children's tuition. Some students work part-time jobs or even take full-time positions while attending evening or weekend classes. But are these students and parents typical? Or do people whose parents have higher incomes have higher rates of university attendance?

The first step in any research project is to state as clearly as possible what you hope to investigate, that is, *define the problem*. In this instance, we are interested in knowing how parents' income relates to their children's postsecondary education. Early on, any social science

researcher must develop an **operational definition** of each concept being studied. An operational definition is an explanation of an abstract concept that is specific enough to allow a researcher to assess the concept. For example, a sociologist interested in status might use membership in exclusive social clubs as an operational definition of status. Someone studying prejudice might consider a person's unwillingness to hire or work with members of minority groups as an operational definition of prejudice. In our example, we need to develop two operational definitions—education and income—in order to study whether parents with higher incomes have children who are more likely to attend a postsecondary institution.

Initially, we take a functionalist perspective (although we may end up incorporating other approaches). We argue that opportunities for postsecondary education are related to parents' income.

Reviewing the Literature

By conducting a *review of the literature*—the relevant scholarly studies and information—researchers define the problem under study, clarify possible techniques to be used in collecting data, and eliminate or reduce avoidable mistakes. For our example, we would examine information about the income of the parents of students in university.

The review of the literature would soon tell us that many other factors besides parents' income influence whether people attend university. And if we learn that the children of richer parents are more likely to go to college or university than are those from modest backgrounds, we might consider the possibility that these parents may also help their children secure better-paying jobs after their children get their degrees.

Formulating the Hypothesis

After reviewing earlier research and drawing on the contributions of sociological theorists, the researchers may then *formulate the hypothesis*. A **hypothesis** is a speculative statement about the relationship between two or more factors known as variables. Income, religion, occupation, and gender can all serve as variables in a study. We can define a **variable** as a measurable trait or characteristic that is subject to change under different conditions.

Researchers who formulate a hypothesis generally must suggest how one aspect of human behaviour influences or affects another. The variable hypothesized to cause or influence another is called the **independent variable**. The second variable is termed the **dependent variable** because its action "depends" on the influence of the independent variable.

Our hypothesis is that the higher their parents' income, the more likely it is that children go to university or college. The independent variable to be measured is parents' income levels. The variable thought to depend on it—attendance at a postsecondary institution—must also be measured.

Identifying independent and dependent variables is a critical step in clarifying cause-and-effect relationships in society. As shown in Figure 2-2, **causal logic** involves the relationship between a condition or variable and a particular consequence, with one event leading to the other. Under causal logic, being less integrated into society may

▶ FIGURE 2-2

Causal Logic

In *causal logic*, an independent variable (often designated by the symbol *x*) influences a dependent variable (generally designated as *y*); thus, *x* leads to *y*. For example, parents who attend church regularly (*x*) are more likely to have children who are churchgoers (*y*).

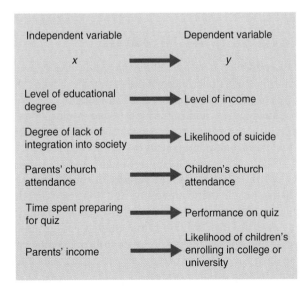

be directly related to or produce a greater likelihood of suicide. Similarly, the time students spend reviewing material for a quiz may be directly related to or produce a greater likelihood of getting a high score on the quiz.

A **correlation** exists when a change in one variable coincides with a change in the other. Correlations are an indication that causality *may* be present; they do not necessarily indicate causation. For example, data indicate that working mothers are more likely to have delinquent children than are mothers who do not work outside the home. But this correlation is actually caused by a third variable: family income. Lower-income households are more likely to have a full-time working mother; at the same time, reported rates of delinquency are higher in this income class than in other economic levels. Consequently, although having a mother who works outside the home is correlated with delinquency, it does not *cause* delinquency. Sociologists seek to identify the *causal* link between variables; this causal link is generally described by researchers in their hypotheses.

Think about It

Identify two or three variables that might "depend" on this independent variable: number of alcoholic drinks ingested.

Collecting and Analyzing Data

How do you test a hypothesis to determine whether it is supported or refuted? You need to collect information, using one of the research designs described later in the chapter. The research design guides the researcher incollecting and analyzing data.

Selecting the Sample

In most studies, social scientists must carefully select what is known as a *sample*. A **sample** is a selection from a larger population that is statistically representative of that population. There are many kinds of samples, but the one social scientists most frequently use is the random sample. In a **random sample**, every member of an entire population being studied has the same chance of being selected. Thus, if researchers want to examine the opinions of people listed in a city directory (a book that, unlike the telephone directory, lists all households), they might use a computer to randomly select names from the directory. This would constitute a random sample. The advantage of using specialized sampling techniques is that sociologists do not need to question everyone in a population.

Sampling is a complex aspect of research design. In Box 2-1 on page 31, we consider the approach some researchers took when trying to create an appropriate sample of people during the U.S. occupation of Baghdad in 2003. Before this time, polling of public opinion had

Sociology in the Global Community

Polling in Baghdad

2-1

In 2003, as the White House launched the war in Iraq, pollsters watched President George W. Bush's approval rating carefully. Such periodic measures of the public pulse have become routine in the United States, an accepted part of presidential politics. But in Iraq, a totalitarian state ruled for 24 years by dictator Saddam Hussein, polling of public opinion on political and social issues was unknown until August 2003, when representatives of the Gallup Organization began regular surveys of the residents of Baghdad. Later in the occupation, Gallup extended its survey to other areas in Iraq.

Needless to say, conducting a scientific survey in the war-torn city presented unusual challenges. Planners began by assuming that no census statistics would be available, so they used satellite imagery to estimate the population in each of Baghdad's neighbourhoods. They later located detailed statistics for much of Baghdad, which they updated for use in their sampling procedure. Gallup's planners also expected that they would need to hire trained interviewers from outside Iraq, but they were fortunate to find some government employees who had become familiar with Baghdad's neighbourhoods while conducting consumer surveys. To train and supervise these interviewers, Gallup hired two seasoned executives from the Pan Arab Research Center in Dubai.

To administer the survey, Gallup chose the time-tested method of private, face-to-face interviews in people's homes. This method not only put respondents at ease, but it also allowed women to participate in the survey at a time when venturing out in public may have been dangerous for them. In all, Gallup employees conducted more than 3400 person-to-person interviews in the privacy of Iraqis' homes. Respondents, they found, were eager to offer opinions and would talk with them at length. Only 3 percent of those who were sampled declined to be interviewed.

The survey's results are significant, since the more than six million people who live in Baghdad constitute one-fourth of Iraq's population. Asked which of several forms of government would be acceptable to them, equal numbers of respondents chose (1) a multiparty parliamentary democracy and (2) a system of governance that includes consultations with Islamic leaders. Fewer respondents

Sources: China Daily 2005; Gallup 2003; Saad 2003.

A Gallup employee interviews an Iraqi army veteran at his home in Baghdad. Pollsters had to carefully estimate the population of Baghdad's many districts, subdistricts, and neighbourhoods to obtain a statistically representative sample of respondents.

endorsed a constitutional democracy or an Islamic kingdom. At a time when representatives of the Iraqi people had convened to establish a new form of government for the nation, this kind of information was invaluable.

In 2005, building on its experience in Iraq, Gallup began to expand its overseas polling operations. Gallup employees completed work on a public opinion survey in China in which they surveyed the attitiudes of the "new rich." Fang Xiaoguang, vice-chair of Gallup China, reported that this group of affluent families, which makes up 27 percent of China's urban households, is not concerned about saving money and want to express their individuality through consumer purchases.

Applying Theory

1. The 97 percent response rate interviewers obtained in this survey was extremely high. Why do you think the response rate was so high, and what do you think it tells political analysts about the residents of Baghdad?
2. What might be some limitations of this survey?

never happened. We'll also see how Gallup made use of data from the sample.

It is easy to confuse the careful scientific techniques used in representative sampling with the many *nonscientific* polls that receive much more media attention. For example, television viewers and radio listeners are encouraged to email their views on today's headlines or on political contests. Such polls reflect nothing more than the views of those who happened to see the television program (or hear the radio broadcast) and took the time, perhaps at some cost, to register their opinions. These data do not necessarily reflect (and indeed may distort) the views of the broader population. Not everyone has access to a television or radio, has the time to watch or listen to a program, or has the means or inclination to send email. Similar problems are raised by "mail-back" questionnaires found in many magazines and by "mall intercepts" where shoppers are asked about some issue. Even when these techniques include answers from tens of thousands of people, their accuracy will be far less than that of a carefully selected representative sample of 1500 respondents.

In our research example, we will use information collected in the General Social Survey (GSS) and the Survey of Consumer Finances (SCF) to examine the relationship between family income and participation in postsecondary education in Canada (Statistics Canada 2005h). The study set out to examine whether the relationship between family income and university attendance for 18- to 24-year-olds changed from 1979 to 1997. The GSS gathers data on Canadian social trends and provides information on specific policy issues. The SCF provides data on the income of Canadians and information on labour market activities.

Ensuring Validity and Reliability

The scientific method requires that research results be both valid and reliable. **Validity** refers to the degree to which a measure or scale truly reflects the phenomenon under study. **Reliability** refers to the extent to which a measure produces consistent results. A valid measure of income depends on gathering accurate data. Various studies show that people are reasonably accurate in knowing how much money they earned in the most recent year. One problem of reliability is that some people may not *disclose* accurate information, but most do.

Developing the Conclusion

Scientific studies, including those conducted by sociologists, do not aim to answer all the questions that can be raised about a particular subject. Therefore, the conclusion of a research study represents both an end and a beginning. It terminates a specific phase of the investigation, but it should also generate ideas for future study.

Supporting Hypotheses

In our example, we find that the data support our hypothesis: People whose parents have higher incomes have higher rates of postsecondary attendance.

The relationship is not perfect. Obviously, some people from families of lower incomes do attend university, as shown in Figure 2-3. A student might earn a

▶ **FIGURE 2-3**

University Participation Rates of 18- to 24-Year-Olds by Parental Income

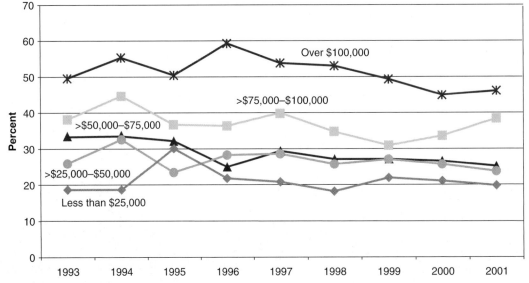

Source: Statistics Canada 2005h.

master's degree, for example, even though his or her parents' income was considered low.

Sociological studies do not always generate data that support the original hypothesis. In many instances, a hypothesis is refuted, and researchers must reformulate their conclusions. Unexpected results may also lead sociologists to reexamine their methodology and make changes in the research design.

Controlling for Other Factors

A **control variable** is a factor held constant to test the relative impact of the independent variable. For example, if researchers wanted to know how adults in Ontario feel about restrictions on smoking in public places, they would probably attempt to use a respondent's smoking behaviour as a control variable. That is, how do smokers versus nonsmokers feel about smoking in public places? The researchers would compile separate statistics on how smokers and nonsmokers feel about antismoking regulations.

> ### Think about It
> What would constitute an unbiased question for a survey on smoking?

Our study of the influence of parental income on education suggests that not everyone enjoys equal educational opportunities, a disparity that is one of the causes of social inequality. Since education affects a person's income, we may want to call on the conflict perspective to explore this topic further. What impact does a person's race or gender have? Do the occupations of the parents have an impact on the advanced education of their children? Do parents' occupations have an impact on their children's levels of education? Later in the text, we will more fully explore the relationship between family income and educational achievement of children, accounting for variables of gender, race, and other factors.

In Summary: The Scientific Method

Let us briefly summarize the process of the scientific method through a review of the example. We *defined a problem* (the question of whether parental income affects educational attainment). We *reviewed the literature* (other studies of the relationship between parental income and education) and *formulated a hypothesis* (the higher the parents' income the more likely their children will go to university). We *collected and analyzed the data,* making sure the sample was representative and the data were valid and reliable. Finally, we *developed the conclusion:* The data do support our hypothesis about the influence of parental income on children's attendance at a postsecondary education.

☐ WHAT ARE THE MAJOR RESEARCH DESIGNS?

An important aspect of sociological research is deciding *how* to collect the data. A **research design** is a detailed plan or method for obtaining data scientifically. Selection of a research design requires creativity and ingenuity. This choice will directly influence both the cost of the project and the amount of time needed to collect the results of the research. Research designs that sociologists regularly use to generate data include surveys, field research, experiments, and use of existing sources.

Surveys

Almost all of us have responded to surveys of one kind or another. We may have been asked what kind of detergent we use, which political candidate we intend to vote for, or what our favourite television program is. A **survey** is a study, generally in the form of an interview or questionnaire, that provides researchers with information about how people think and act. Among Canada's

Doonesbury

BY GARRY TRUDEAU

best-known surveys of opinion are those by Ipsos-Reid and Environics. As anyone who watches the news during election campaigns knows, polls have become a staple of political life.

When you think of surveys, you may recall seeing many "person on the street" interviews on local television news programs. Although such interviews can be highly entertaining, they are not necessarily an accurate indication of public opinion. First, they reflect the opinions of only those people who happen to be at a certain location. Such a sample can be biased in favour of commuters, middle-class shoppers, or factory workers, depending on which street or area the newspeople select. Second, television interviews tend to attract outgoing people who are willing to appear on the air, while they frighten away others who may feel intimidated by a camera. As we've seen, a survey must utilize precise, representative sampling if it is to genuinely reflect a broad range of the population.

In preparing to conduct a survey, sociologists must not only develop representative samples, but they must also exercise great care in the wording of questions. An effective survey question must be simple and clear enough for people to understand it. It must also be specific enough so that there are no problems in interpreting the results. Open-ended questions ("What do you think of educational programming on television?") must be carefully phrased to solicit the type of information desired. Surveys can be indispensable sources of information, but only if the sampling is done properly and the questions are worded accurately and without bias.

There are two main forms of surveys: the **interview**, in which a researcher obtains information through face-to-face or telephone questioning, and the **questionnaire**, which uses a printed or written form to obtain information from a respondent. Each of these has its own advantages. An interviewer can obtain a high response rate because people find it more difficult to turn down a personal request for an interview than to throw away a written questionnaire. In addition, a skilful interviewer can go beyond written questions and "probe" for a subject's underlying feelings and reasons. However, questionnaires have the advantage of being cheaper, especially in large samples. See Box 2-2 on page 35 for a discussion of one study that successfully used interviews.

Studies have shown that characteristics of the interviewer have an impact on survey data. For example, female interviewers tend to receive more feminist responses from female subjects than do male researchers, and black interviewers tend to receive more detailed responses about race-related issues from black subjects than do white interviewers. The possible impact of gender and race only indicates again how much care social research requires (D. Davis 1997; Huddy et al. 1997).

The survey is an example of **quantitative research**, which collects and reports data primarily in numerical form.

Field Research

Although quantitative research may make use of large samples, it can't look at a topic in great depth and detail. Many researchers prefer to use **qualitative research**, which relies on what is seen in field and naturalistic settings and often focuses on small groups and communities rather than on large groups or whole nations. Forms of qualitative research may include in-depth interviews.

While qualitative research cannot answer questions posed in quantitative research—questions such as "how many" and "what are the causes," it can help to reveal how people make, and act upon, decisions in their daily lives:

> Qualitative research is particularly well suited to studying context. It also excels at illuminating *process*, whether this is organizational change or individual decision-making, since it allows us to examine how changes affect daily procedures and interactions. This may lead to us uncovering unintended as well as intended consequences of new arrangements (Barbour 2007:13).

While those sociologists who employ a scientific or positivist methodology, using quantitative data, believe it is important to remove or minimize *bias* from the research agenda, thoughts and feelings—considered by science to be bias—are central elements of qualitiative research (Neuman 2000). Thus, it may be argued, in the context of the differences between qualitiative and quantitative approaches, that research is rarely boring. Debate, argument, and controversy influence and inform what is considered to be *evidence* in the realm of sociological research.

Observation

Investigators who collect information through direct participation or by closely watching a group or community under study are engaged in **observation**. This method allows sociologists to examine certain behaviours and communities that could not be investigated through other research techniques.

An increasingly popular form of qualitative research in sociology today is ethnography. **Ethnography** refers to efforts to describe an entire social setting through extended, systematic observation. Typically, this description emphasizes how the subjects themselves view their social setting. Some anthropologists rely heavily on ethnography. Much as an anthropologist may seek to understand the people of some Polynesian island, the sociologist as an ethnographer seeks to understand and present to us an entire way of life in some setting.

Research in Action   2-2
Does Hard Work Lead to Better Grades?

Does a serious work ethic pay off in better grades? Sociologist William Rau wanted to answer that question. Working with Ann Durand, a former student now employed in the research department of State Farm Insurance Companies, Rau devised a research study. The dependent variable was easy to measure—the two could use an already existing data source, students' grade point averages (GPAs). But how could they measure the independent variable, a student's work ethic?

After considering many possibilities, the two researchers decided to focus on students' drinking behaviour and study habits. They developed a scale comprising a series of items on which students rated their drinking and studying behaviour. At one extreme were many hours of daily studying and abstention from drinking. At the other extreme were frequent drinking—even on weekdays—and infrequent studying, usually cramming just before tests. The operational definition of students' work ethic became students' self-reports of their drinking and studying behaviour in response to a series of questions.

Rau and Durand administered their behaviour scale to 255 students and then compared the scores on the scale with students' GPAs. The results were fairly striking. Generally, those students who drank less and studied more than others performed better academically, as measured by their GPAs. The researchers had been careful to control for students' ability levels using two more existing sources of data: students' class rankings in high school and their scores on university entrance exams. These sources indicated that the abstainers had not arrived at university better prepared than other students. Hard work really *does* pay off in better grades.

Applying Theory

1. Where does your own drinking and studying behaviour fall on Rau and Durand's behaviour scale? What is your GPA? Is your academic achievement consistent with your drinking and studying behaviour?

2. What other ways of measuring a student's work ethic could the researchers have considered? Can you think of any other variable besides a student's ability level that might have distorted the study's results?

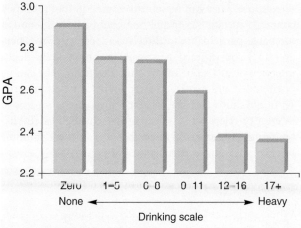

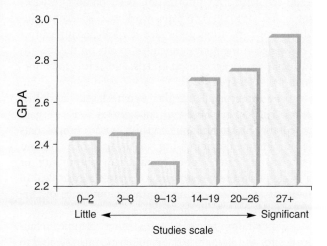

Source: Rau and Durand 2000.

In some cases, the sociologist actually joins a group for a time to get an accurate sense of how it operates. This is called *participant observation*.

Robert Park, of the University of Chicago, had a career as a reporter before becoming a sociologist, which gave him a sense of the importance of personal observation, particularly in relation to urban problems. During the early decades of the twentieth century, Park was instrumental in guiding his students' work in participant observation research related to homelessness and many other social problems of urban life.

During the late 1930s, in a classic example of participant-observation research, William F. Whyte moved into a low-income Italian neighbourhood in Boston. For nearly four years, he was a member of the social circle of "corner boys" that he describes in *Street Corner Society*.

This street in Bangkok provides a rich setting for observation research. An ethnographer would take note of the interplay of cultures in the everyday street life.

Whyte revealed his identity to these men and joined in their conversations, bowling, and other leisure-time activities. His goal was to gain greater insight into the community that these men had established. As Whyte listened to Doc, the leader of the group, he "learned the answers to questions I would not even have had the sense to ask if I had been getting my information solely on an interviewing basis" (1981:303). Whyte's work was especially valuable, since, at the time, the academic world had little direct knowledge of the poor and tended to rely on the records of social service agencies, hospitals, and courts for information (Adler et al. 1992).

The initial challenge that Whyte faced—and that every participant observer encounters—was to gain acceptance into an unfamiliar group. It is no simple matter for a trained sociologist to win the trust of a religious cult, a youth gang, a poor Appalachian community, or a circle of skid row residents. It requires a great deal of patience and an accepting, nonthreatening type of personality on the part of the observer.

Observation research poses other complex challenges for the investigator. Sociologists must be able to fully understand what they are observing. In a sense, then, researchers must learn to see the world as the group sees it in order to fully comprehend the events taking place around them.

This raises a delicate issue: If the research is to be successful, the observer cannot allow the close associations or even friendships that inevitably develop to influence the subjects' behaviour or the conclusions of the study. Anson Shupe and David Bromley (1980), two sociologists who have used participant observation, have likened this challenge to that of "walking a tightrope." Even while working hard to gain acceptance from the group being studied, the participant observer *must* maintain some degree of detachment.

Feminist perspectives in sociology have drawn attention to a shortcoming in ethnographic research as well as other forms of sociological research. For most of the history of sociology, studies were conducted on male subjects or about male-led groups and organizations, and the findings were generalized to all people. For example, for many decades, studies of urban life focused on street corners, neighbourhood taverns, and bowling alleys—places where men typically congregated. Although the insights were valuable, they did not give a true impression of city life because they overlooked the areas where women were likely to gather. Feminist perspectives attempt to redress this bias in the way in which ethnographic research is conducted. Feminist researchers also tend to involve and consult their subjects more than other types of researchers do, and they are more oriented to seeking change, raising consciousness, or trying to affect policy. In addition, feminist research is particularly open to a multidisciplinary approach, such as making use of historical evidence or legal studies as well as feminist theory (Baker 1999; Lofland 1975; Reinharz 1992).

In-Depth Interviews

In-depth interviews have the advantage of possibly revealing more than the observer or researcher can observe from the outside. They can be semistructured in that they may contain a specific set of questions but be flexible enough to enable participants to direct their responses to wherever they are deemed personally meaningful. In-depth interviews can also be unstructured in form; they can be open-ended and may, therefore, not be confined to a core set of questions that the observer or researcher deems of interest or relevance. The key is that, through careful listening, the observer or researcher can uncover multiple layers of meaning in participants' responses.

Experiments

When sociologists want to study a possible cause-and-effect relationship, they may conduct experiments. An **experiment** is an artificially created situation that allows the researcher to manipulate variables.

In the classic method of conducting an experiment, two groups of people are selected and matched for similar characteristics, such as age or education. The researchers then assign the subjects to one of two groups: the experimental or the control group. The **experimental group** is exposed to an independent variable; the **control group** is not. Thus, if scientists were testing a new type of antibiotic drug, they would administer that drug to an experimental group but not to a control group.

Stacey.

McGraw-Hill

SOCIOLOGY — net (before bookstore)
$83.95
prob 100.

Brief intro — $71. ≈

... that an arrest ...
... ...e suspect was employed. Pate and Hamilton concluded that although an arrest may be a sobering experience for any individual, the impact of being taken to a police station is greater if a person is employed and is forced to explain what is happening in his or her personal life to a boss.

In some experiments, just as in observation research, the presence of a social scientist or other observer may affect the behaviour of people being studied. The recognition of this phenomenon grew out of an experiment conducted during the 1920s and 1930s at the Hawthorne plant of the Western Electric Company. A group of researchers set out to determine how to improve the productivity of workers at the plant. The investigators manipulated such variables as the lighting and working hours to see what impact changes in them had on productivity. To their surprise, they found that *every* step they took seemed to increase productivity. Even measures that seemed likely to have the opposite effect, such as reducing the amount of lighting in the plant, led to higher productivity.

Why did the plant's employees work harder even under less favourable conditions? Their behaviour apparently was influenced by the greater attention being paid to them in the course of the research and by the novelty of being subjects in an experiment. Since that time, sociologists have used the term **Hawthorne effect** to refer to subjects of research who deviate from their typical behaviour because they realize that they are under observation (Jones 1992; Lang 1992; Pelton 1994).

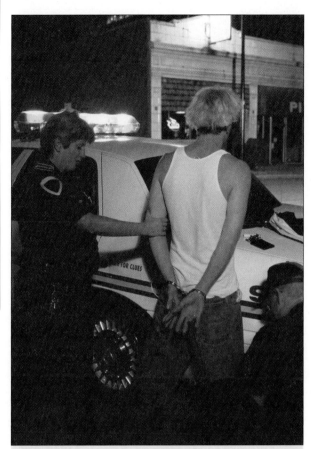

Does arresting someone for domestic assault deter future incidents of violence? An experiment in Miami, Florida, studied this question by making use of control and experimental groups.

How do people respond to being observed? Evidently, these employees at the Hawthorne plant enjoyed the attention paid them when researchers observed them at work. No matter what variables were changed, the workers increased their productivity every time, including when the level of lighting was reduced.

Content analysis of popular song lyrics shows that over the last 50 years, female artists such as Beyoncé Knowles have used fewer sexually explicit words, while male artists have used more.

Use Your Sociological Imagination

You are a researcher interested in the effect of TV-watching on the grades of school children. How would you go about setting up an experiment to measure this?

Use of Existing Sources

Sociologists do not necessarily have to collect new data in order to conduct research and test hypotheses. The term **secondary analysis** refers to a variety of research techniques that make use of previously collected and publicly accessible information and data. Generally, in conducting secondary analysis, researchers utilize data in ways unintended by the initial collectors of information. For example, census data are compiled for specific uses by the federal government but are also valuable for marketing specialists in locating everything from bicycle stores to nursing homes.

Sociologists consider secondary analysis to be *nonreactive*, since it does not influence people's behaviour. As an example, Émile Durkheim's statistical analysis of suicide neither increased nor decreased human self-destruction. Researchers, then, can avoid the Hawthorne effect by using secondary analysis.

There is one inherent problem, however: the researcher who relies on data collected by someone else may not find exactly what is needed. Social scientists studying family violence can use statistics from police and social service agencies on *reported* cases of spouse abuse and child abuse. But how many cases are not reported? Government bodies have no precise data on *all* cases of abuse.

Many social scientists find it useful to study cultural, economic, and political documents, including newspapers, periodicals, radio and television tapes, the Internet, scripts, diaries, songs, folklore, and legal papers, to name some examples (see Table 2.1). In examining these sources, researchers employ a technique known as **content analysis**, which is the systematic coding and objective recording of data, guided by some rationale.

Table 2-1 Existing Sources Used in Sociological Research

Most Frequently Used Sources

Statistics Canada
Polls, such as Ipsos-Reid and Environics
Birth, death, marriage, and divorce statistics

Other Sources

Newspapers and periodicals
Personal journals, diaries, email, and letters
Records and archival material of religious
    organizations, corporations, and other organizations
Transcripts of radio programs
Videos of motion pictures and television programs
Web pages
Song lyrics
Scientific records (such as patent applications)
Speeches of public figures (such as politicians)
Votes cast in elections or by elected officials on
    specific legislative proposals
Attendance records for public events
Videotapes of social protests and rallies
Literature, including folklore

Using content analysis, Erving Goffman (1979) conducted a pioneering exploration of how advertisements portrayed women as inferior to men. The ads typically showed women being subordinate to or dependent on others or being instructed by men. They used caressing and touching gestures more than men. Even when presented in leadership-type roles, women were likely to be shown in seductive poses or gazing out into space.

Researchers today are analyzing the content of films to look at the increase in smoking in motion pictures, despite major public health concerns. This type of content analysis can have clear social policy implications if it draws the attention of the motion picture industry to the message it may be delivering (especially to young people) that smoking is acceptable, even desirable. For example, a 1999 content analysis found that tobacco use appeared in 89 percent of the two hundred most popular movie rentals (Kang 1997; Roberts et al. 1999).

Table 2-2 summarizes the major research designs.

Theoretical Perspectives and Research Methods

The research methods that researchers choose to employ in their study of social phenomena are informed and guided by the theoretical perspectives they hold. Functionalist thinkers, for example, tend to value neutrality and objectivity, thus leaning toward quantitative methods, such as surveys, experiments, and secondary data analysis. Their focus is on uncovering the truth or the facts about the relationships among specified variables, according to the researchers' interpretation of the data. In response to this approach, conflict thinkers, such

as Alvin Gouldner (1970) and others, have suggested that sociologists may use objectivity as a sacred justification for remaining uncritical of the dominant institutions and ruling classes of society. Unlike functionalists, conflict thinkers might employ historical analysis or engage in field research to uncover the hidden economic and political interests of a society. Again, unlike functionalists, conflict thinkers view their research as a basis for action and change.

Such research methods as ethnography and participant observation may be guided by interactionist perspectives, in which the goal of the researcher is to describe the meanings and to understand the definitions that people give to their own situations. As for feminist perspectives, no *single* research method is employed by feminist researchers, just as no *single* feminist theory exists. However, feminist researchers, like conflict thinkers, are guided by the common desire to bring about action or change through their research.

Feminist sociologist Shulamit Reinharz (1992) has argued that sociological research should not only be inclusive but should also be open to bringing about social change and drawing on relevant research by nonsociologists. Reinharz maintains that research should always analyze whether women's unequal social status has affected the study in any way. For example, a researcher might broaden the study of the impact of family income on education participation to consider the implications of participation according to gender, class, and race. The issue of the importance of value neutrality, which is often emphasized in mainstream or functional sociology, can be contrasted to feminist research, in which researchers integrate their own experiences into the research process.

Table 2-2   Major Research Designs

Method	Examples	Advantages	Limitations
Survey	Questionnaires Interviews	Yields information about specific issues	Can be expensive and time consuming
Observation	Ethnography	Yields detailed information about specific groups or organizations	Involves months if not yet years of labour-intensive data collection
Experiment	Deliberate manipulation of people's social behaviour	Yields direct measures of people's behaviour	Ethical limitations on the degree to which subjects' behaviour can be manipulated
Existing sources/ Secondary analysis	Analysis of census or health data Analysis of films or TV commercials	Cost-efficiency	Limited to data collected for some other purpose

Reinharz contends that feminist researchers may use their own experiences to inform their research questions and to guide the research process; at the same time, however, feminist researchers are discussing the ways in which to "work out the tension between objectivity and subjectivity" (1992:262).

☐ HOW DOES TECHNOLOGY INFLUENCE SOCIOLOGICAL RESEARCH?

Advances in technology have affected all aspects of life, and sociological research is no exception. The increased speed and capacity of computers enable sociologists to handle larger and larger sets of data. In the recent past, only people with grants or major institutional support could easily work with census data. Now anyone with a desktop computer and modem can access census information to learn more about social behaviour. Moreover, data from other countries concerning crime statistics and health care are sometimes as available as information from Canada.

Researchers usually rely on computers to deal with quantitative data, that is, numerical measures, but electronic technology is also assisting us with qualitative data, such as information obtained in observation research. Numerous software programs, such as Ethnograph and NUD*IST, allow the researcher not only to record observations, as a word processing program does, but also to identify common behavioural patterns or similar concerns expressed in interviews. For example, after observing students in a cafeteria over several weeks and putting your observations into the computer, you could then group all your observations related to certain variables, such as "club" or "study group."

Internet-based research presents many of the same ethical considerations as traditional fields of research, as well as some special considerations. A central consideration is the degree to which researchers treat discussion from virtual communities as unproblematically in the "public domain." Barbara Scharf, who has done research based on time spent with a breast cancer discussion group, states that there is an obligation on the part of the researcher to "maintain and demonstrate a respectful sensitivity toward the psychological boundaries, purposes, vulnerabilities, and privacy of the individual members of a self-defined virtual community, even though its discourse is publicly accessible" (1999:255).

The Internet affords an excellent opportunity to communicate with fellow researchers as well as to locate useful information on social issues posted on Web sites. It would be impossible to calculate all the sociological

Computers have tremendously extended the range and capability of sociological research, from allowing large amounts of data to be stored and analyzed to facilitating communication with other researchers via websites, newsgroups, and email.

postings on Internet mailing lists or Web sites. Of course, you need to apply the same critical scrutiny to Internet material that you would use on any printed resource.

How useful is the Internet for conducting survey research? That's unclear as yet. It is relatively easy to send out or post on an electronic bulletin board a questionnaire and solicit responses. It is an inexpensive way to reach large numbers of potential respondents and get a quick return of responses. However, there are some obvious dilemmas. How do you protect a respondent's anonymity? Second, how do you define the potential audience? Even if you know to whom you sent the questionnaire, the respondents may forward it on to others.

Web-based surveys are still in their early stages. Even so, the initial results are promising. For example, InterSurvey has created a pool of Internet respondents, initially selected by telephone to be a diverse and representative sample. Using similar methods to locate

50 000 adult respondents in 33 nations, the National Geographic Society conducted an online survey that focused on migration and regional culture. Social scientists are closely monitoring these new approaches to gauge how they might revolutionize one type of research design (Bainbridge 1999; Morin 2000).

This new technology is exciting, but there is one basic limitation to the methodology: Internet surveying works only with those who have access to the Internet. For some market researchers, such a limitation is acceptable. For example, if you were interested in the willingness of Internet users to order books or make travel reservations online, limiting the sample population to those already

online makes sense. However, if you were surveying the general public about plans to buy a computer or iPod in the coming year or about their views on a particular political candidate, your online research would need to be supplemented by more traditional sampling procedures, such as mailed questionnaires.

Sociological research relies on a number of tools—from observation research and use of existing sources of data to considering how the latest technology can help inform the sociological imagination. We turn now to Box 2–3, about a research study that used a survey of the general population to learn more about a particular social behaviour—human sexuality.

Social Policy and Sociological Research
Studying Human Sexuality

The Issue

The Kaiser Family Foundation conducts a study of sexual content on U.S. television every two years. The latest report, released in 2005, shows that more than two-thirds of all shows on TV include some sexual content, up from about half of all shows seven years earlier (see Figure 2.4). Media representations of sexual behaviour are important because surveys of teens and young adults tell us that television is a top source of information and ideas about sex for them; it has more influence than school, parents, or peers (Kunkel et al. 2001). A study on Canadian broadcasting, tabled in the House of Commons in June 2003,

demonstrated that the vast majority of English-language programs viewed by Canadians (aged two and older) during prime time are "foreign" (meaning, for the most part, from the United States). Thus, it could be extrapolated that Canadians' exposure to sexual content on television would be roughly equivalent to that of their U.S. neighbours.

In this age of sexually transmitted diseases, it is important to increase our understanding of human sexuality. However, it can be a difficult topic to research because of all the preconceptions, myths, and beliefs that may accompany the subject of sexuality. How can we

FIGURE 2-4

Percentage of Television Shows that Contain Sexual Content

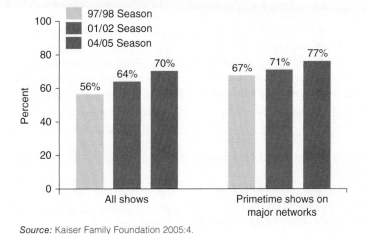

Source: Kaiser Family Foundation 2005:4.

Table 2-3 Percentage of Young Canadian Females who had Sexual Intercourse without a Condom, According to Age of First Sexual Activity

Age at Which Became Sexually Active	Percentage Not Using Condom during Last Sexual Intercourse
13	60
14–17	46
20–24	37

Source: Statistics Canada 2005a.

carry out research of what might be considered a controversial and personal topic?

The Setting

Perhaps the most comprehensive study of sexual behaviour was the famous two-volume Kinsey Report prepared in the 1940s (Kinsey, Pomeroy, and Martin 1948; Kinsey, Pomeroy, and Gebhard 1953). Although the Kinsey Report is still widely quoted, the volunteers interviewed for the report were not representative of the adult population. The Kinsey Report revealed the wide range of sexual behaviours among U.S. citizens, including that 70 percent of men in the United States had patronized prostitutes, that 92 percent of men and 58 percent of women had masturbated, and that 60 percent of men had had some form of homosexual experience before adulthood (Nelson and Fleras 1998). Also revealed in the report was the greater tendency for women to be bisexual (having sexual relations with both male and female partners) than exclusively lesbian.

In Canada, statistics on Canadians' sexual behaviour are collected by Statistics Canada, the primary statistical information source of the Canadian government and a major employer of sociologists. The agency's mandate is to collect, analyze, and disseminate statistical information on a broad range of subjects, including employment, health, education, agriculture, and sexual behaviour. Much of the statistical information collected by Statistics Canada about the sex lives of Canadians comes from the National Public Health Survey, the Canadian Community Health Survey, and the Canadian census. For instance, Table 2-3 shows that about 60 percent of young Canadian females who did not use a condom during their last act of sexual intercourse were sexually active by age 13 (Statistics Canada 2005a). The table illustrates that as the age

of becoming sexually active increases, the percentage of condom use during last sexual encounter also increases.

Most of the studies that have been done on sexuality in North America over the past two decades have not included ethnicity as a variable (Kennedy and Gorzalka 2002). Recent studies have revealed, however, that the length of time spent in Canada is a significant factor in influencing some, but not all, sexual attitiudes and behaviours of Asian-Canadians.

Sociological Insights

The controversy surrounding research on human sexual behaviour raises the issue of value neutrality. And this becomes especially delicate when we consider the relationship of sociology to the government. Canada's federal government has become the major source of funding for sociological research. Yet Max Weber urged that sociology remain an autonomous discipline and not become unduly influenced by any one segment of society. According to his ideal of value neutrality, sociologists must remain free to reveal information that is embarrassing to government or, for that matter, is supportive of government institutions. Thus, researchers investigating a prison riot must be ready to examine objectively not only the behaviour of inmates but also the conduct of prison officials before and during the riot.

Conflict theorists and feminists, among others, are critical of some research that claims to be objective. In turn, their research is occasionally criticized for not sufficiently addressing Weber's concern for value neutrality. In any case, maintaining objectivity may be difficult if sociologists fear that findings critical of government institutions will jeopardize their chances of obtaining federal support for new research projects.

In the United States, although the American Sociological Association's code of ethics expects sociologists to disclose all funding sources, the code does not address the issue of whether sociologists who accept funding from a particular agency may also accept their perspective on what needs to be studied. Lewis Coser has argued that as sociologists in the United States have increasingly turned from basic sociological research to research with application for government agencies and the private sector, "they have relinquished to a large extent the freedom to choose their own problems, substituting the problems of their clients for those which might have interested them on purely theoretical grounds" (1956:27). Viewed in this light, the importance of government funding for sociological studies raises troubling questions for those who cherish Weber's ideal of value neutrality in research. In Canada, the code of ethics set out by the Canadian Sociology and Anthropology Association (CSAA) states,

> Researchers must guard against the uncritical promotion of research, which in design, execution, or results, furthers the power of states, corporations, churches, or other institutions, over the lives and cultures of research subjects.... Researchers should be sensitive to the possible exploitation of individuals and groups.

In the funding of sociological research, the CSAA's code of ethics directly warns its members to guard against the promotion of research that furthers the power of a corporation, a government, or a church over the lives of those being studied. In addition, the code prompts sociologists to be mindful of the implications of their research and the potential for exploitation of particular individuals and groups. As we'll see in the next section, applied sociological research on human sexuality has run into barriers constructed by government funding agencies.

Policy Initiatives

In Canada, there has been willingness to research and openness toward research on such topics as same-sex relationships, condom use among teens, bisexuality, and number of sexual partners, as demonstrated by the vast number and variety of reports published by Statistics Canada. The 2001 census results, for example, were the first to provide data on same-sex relationships. It is a different story in the United States, where conservative voices in government have made government-sponsored research on the topic of sexual behaviour more difficult.

In 1987, the federal National Institute of Child Health and Human Development sought proposals for a national survey of sexual behaviour. Sociologists responded with various proposals that a review panel of scientists approved for funding. However, in 1991, led by Senator Jesse Helms and other conservatives, the U.S. Senate voted 66–34 to forbid funding any survey on adult sexual practices. Helms appealed to popular fears by arguing that such surveys of sexual behaviour were intended to "legitimize homosexual lifestyles" and to support "sexual decadence." Two years earlier, a similar debate in Great Britain had led to the denial of government funding for a national sex survey (A. Johnson et al. 1994; Laumann, Gagnon, and Michael 1994a:36).

Despite the vote by the U.S. Senate, sociologists Edward Laumann, John Gagnon, Stuart Michaels, and Robert Michael developed the National Health and Social Life Survey (NHSLS) to better understand the sexual practices of adults in the United States. The researchers raised $1.6 million of private funding to make their study possible (Laumann et al. 1994a, 1994b).

The researchers made great efforts to ensure privacy during the NHSLS interviews, as well as confidentiality of responses and security in maintaining data files. Perhaps because of this careful effort, the interviewers did not typically experience problems getting responses, even though they were asking people about their sexual behaviour. All interviews were conducted in person, although there was also a confidential form that included questions about such sensitive subjects as family income and masturbation. The researchers used several techniques to test the accuracy of subjects' responses, such as asking redundant questions at different times in different ways during the 90-minute interview. These careful procedures helped establish the validity of the NHSLS findings.

Today, research on human sexuality is not the only target of policymakers. Congress began in 1995 considering passage of the Family Privacy Protection Act, which would force all federally funded researchers to obtain written consent from parents before surveying young people on such issues as drug use, antisocial behaviour, and emotional difficulties, as well as sexual behaviour. Researchers around the country suggest that this legal requirement will make it impossible to survey representative samples of young people. They note that when parents are asked to return consent forms, only about half do so, even though no more than 1 percent to 2 percent actually object to the survey. Moreover, the additional effort required to get all the forms returned raises research costs by twenty-five-fold (Elias 1996; Levine 2001).

Despite the political battles, the authors of the NHSLS believe that their research was important. These researchers argue that using data from their survey allows us to more easily address such public policy issues as AIDS, sexual harassment, rape, welfare reform, sex discrimination, abortion, teenage pregnancy, and family planning. Moreover, the research findings help to counter some "common-sense" notions. For instance, contrary to the popular belief that women regularly use abortion for birth control and that poor teens are the most likely socioeconomic group to have abortions, the researchers found that three-fourths of all abortions are the first for the woman and that well-educated and affluent women are more likely to have abortions than are poor teens (Sweet 2001).

The NHSLS researchers have lately moved on to other topics. One is studying adolescent behaviour in general and another is studying sexuality in China and Chicago, adding health care, jealousy, and violence to the mix of issues. The researchers hope to update the NHSLS data before too much time passes, especially now that the environment for conducting research on human sexuality has improved, and people have proved that they are more comfortable talking about sexual issues. As one of the researchers noted, "people aren't as uptight about sex as their politicians and their funders. That's good news" (Sweet 2001:13).

Applying Theory

1. When studying human sexuality, what theoretical perspective(s) would advocate high levels of objectivity and neutrality?
2. Would you be willing to participate in a study related to sexuality if you were asked?
3. For feminist researchers, what might be a major goal or purpose of any study on human sexuality?

CHAPTER RESOURCES

Summary

What are the Ethics of Research?
- The **code of ethics** (p. 26) of the Canadian Sociology and Anthropology Association calls for objectivity and integrity in research, respect for the subject's privacy, and confidentiality.

What is the Scientific Method?
- There are five basic steps in the **scientific method** (p. 28): defining the problem, reviewing the literature, formulating the hypothesis, selecting the research design and then collecting and analyzing data, and developing the conclusion.
- Whenever researchers want to study abstract concepts, such as intelligence or prejudice, they must develop workable **operational definitions** (p. 29).
- A **hypothesis** (p. 30) usually states a possible relationship between two or more variables.
- By using a **sample** (p. 30), sociologists avoid having to test everyone in a population.

- According to the scientific method, research results must possess both **validity** (p. 32) and **reliability** (p. 32).

What are the Major Research Designs?
- Sociologists use four major research designs in their work: **survey** (p. 33) research of a population, utilizing the **interview** (p. 34) and the **questionnaire** (p. 34); **observation** (p. 34) and in-depth interviews, focusing on small groups and communities; **experiments** (p. 36) that test cause-and-effect relationships; **secondary analysis** (p. 38) or the analysis of existing sources.

How does Technology Influence Sociological Research?
- Technology today plays an important role in sociological research, whether it be a computer database or information from the Internet.

Critical Thinking Questions

1. Suppose that your sociology instructor has asked you to do a study of the issues facing Canadians today. Which research technique would you find most useful? How would you use that approach to complete your assignment?
2. Do you think you or any sociologist can maintain value neutrality while studying any group of people, such as younger Canadians?
3. Why is it important for sociologists to have a code of ethics?
4. What research method(s) do you think would produce the best results when studying the views and attitudes of the under-30 age group? Why?

Key Terms

Causal logic The relationship between a condition or variable and a particular consequence, with one event leading to the other. (p. 30)

Code of ethics The standards of acceptable behaviour developed by and for members of a profession. (p. 26)

Content analysis The systematic coding and objective recording of data, guided by some rationale. (p. 38)

Control group Subjects in an experiment who are not introduced to the independent variable by the researcher. (p. 36)

Control variable A factor held constant to test the relative impact of an independent variable. (p. 33)

Correlation A relationship between two variables whereby a change in one coincides with a change in the other. (p. 30)

Dependent variable The variable in a causal relationship that is subject to the influence of another variable. (p. 30)

Ethnography The study of an entire social setting through extended, systematic observation. (p. 34)

Experiment An artificially created situation that allows the researcher to manipulate variables. (p. 36)

Experimental group Subjects in an experiment who are exposed to an independent variable introduced by a researcher. (p. 36)

Hawthorne effect The unintended influence that observers or experimenters can have on their subjects. (p. 37)

Hypothesis A speculative statement about the relationship between two or more variables. (p. 30)

Independent variable The variable in a causal relationship that causes or influences a change in a second variable. (p. 30)

Interview A face-to-face or telephone questioning of a respondent to obtain desired information. (p. 34)

Observation A research technique in which an investigator collects information through direct participation or by closely watching a group or community. (p. 34)

Operational definition An explanation of an abstract concept that is specific enough to allow a researcher to assess the concept. (p. 29)

Qualitative research Research that relies on what is seen in field or naturalistic settings more than on statistical data. (p. 34)

Quantitative research Research that collects and reports data primarily in numerical form. (p. 34)

Questionnaire A printed or written form used to obtain desired information from a respondent. (p. 34)

Random sample A sample for which every member of the entire population has the same chance of being selected. (p. 30)

Reliability The extent to which a measure provides consistent results. (p. 32)

Research design A detailed plan or method for obtaining data scientifically. (p. 33)

Sample A selection from a larger population that is statistically representative of that population. (p. 30)

Scientific method A systematic, organized series of steps that ensures maximum objectivity and consistency in researching a problem. (p. 28)

Secondary analysis A variety of research techniques that make use of previously existing and publicly accessible information and data. (p. 38)

Survey A study, generally in the form of interviews or questionnaires, that provides researchers with information concerning how people think and act. (p. 33)

Validity The degree to which a scale or measure truly reflects the phenomenon under study. (p. 32)

Value neutrality Objectivity of sociologists in the interpretation of data. (p. 28)

Variable A measurable trait or characteristic that is subject to change under different conditions. (p. 30)

Additional Readings

Babbie, Earl. 2003. *The Practice of Social Research,* 10th ed. Belmont, CA: Wadsworth. Covers inquiry and social research, the structuring of inquiry, types of observation, and analysis of data in qualitative and quantitative research methods.

Brown, Leslie and Susan Strega. 2005. *Research As Resistance: Critical, Indigenous and Anti-Oppressive Approaches.* Toronto: CSPI/WS. This book brings together the theory and practice of critical, Indigenous, and anti-oppressive approaches to social science research.

Canadian Sociology and Anthropology Association. *Canadian Review of Sociology and Anthropology.* Montreal: CSAA. Since its inception in 1964, the *Review* has provided peer-reviewed articles and critiques on topics of sociology and anthropology. This journal provides an excellent scholarly source for research about social issues in Canada.

 ## Online Learning Centre

Visit the *Sociology: A Brief Introduction* Online Learning Centre at www.mcgrawhill.ca/olc/schaefer to access quizzes, interactive exercises, video clips, and other research and study tools related to this chapter.

 ## Reel Society Video Clips

Reel Society video clips can be used to spark discussion about the following topics from this chapter:

- The scientific method
- Neutrality and politics in research

chapter 3

CULTURE

This Canada Day winning poster by teenager Sharon Huang of Richmond, British Columbia, depicts some of the symbols and people that reflect the multicultural character of Canada.

☐ **How do Culture and Society Compare?**

☐ **How do Cultures Develop around the World?**

☐ **What are the Elements of Culture?**

☐ **How does Culture Relate to the Dominant Ideology?**

☐ **What Forms does Cultural Diversity Take?**

> **Boxes**

RESEARCH IN ACTION: Dominant Ideology and Poverty
SOCIAL POLICY AND CULTURE: Multiculturalism

Nacirema culture is characterized by a highly developed market economy which has evolved in a rich natural habitat. While much of the people's time is devoted to economic pursuits, a large part of the fruits of these labors and a considerable portion of the day are spent in ritual activity. The focus of this activity is the human body, the appearance and health of which loom as a dominant concern in the ethos of the people. While such concern is certainly not unusual, its ceremonial aspects and associated philosophy are unique.

The fundamental belief underlying the whole system appears to be that the human body is ugly and that its natural tendency is to debility and disease. Incarcerated in such a body, man's only hope is to avert these characteristics through the use of the powerful influences of ritual and ceremony. Every household has one or more shrines devoted to this purpose. The more powerful individuals in this society have several shrines in their houses, and, in fact, the opulence of a house is often referred to in terms of the number of such ritual centers it possesses. . . .

While each family has at least one such shrine, the rituals associated with it are not family ceremonies but are private and secret. The rites are normally only discussed with children, and then only during the period when they are being initiated into these mysteries. I was able, however, to establish sufficient rapport with the natives to examine these shrines and to have the rituals described to me.

The focal point of the shrine is a box or chest which is built into the wall. In this chest are kept the many charms and magical potions without which no native believes he could live. These preparations are secured from a variety of specialized practitioners. The most powerful of these are the medicine men, whose assistance must be rewarded with substantial gifts. However, the medicine men do not provide the curative potions for their clients, but decide what the ingredients should be and then write them down in an ancient and secret language. This writing is understood only by the medicine men and by the herbalists who, for another gift, provide the required charm.

☐ *(Miner 1956)*

Anthropologist Horace Miner cast his observant eyes on the intriguing behaviour of the Nacirema. If we look a bit closer, however, some aspects of this culture may seem familiar, for what Miner is describing is actually the culture of the United States ("Nacirema" is "American" spelled backwards). The "shrine" is the bathroom, and we are correctly informed that in this culture a measure of wealth is often how many bathrooms are in a person's house. The bathroom rituals make use of charms and magical potions (beauty products and prescription drugs) obtained from specialized practitioners (such as hair stylists), herbalists (pharmacists), and medicine men (physicians). Using our sociological imagination, we could update the Nacirema "shrine" by describing blow-dryers, mint-flavoured dental floss, electric toothbrushes, and hair gel.

We begin to appreciate how to understand behaviour when we step back and examine it thoughtfully, objectively—whether it is "Nacirema" culture or another one. Take the case of Fiji, an island nation in the South Pacific Ocean. A recent study showed that eating disorders were showing up for the first time among young people there. Fiji was a society where, traditionally, "you've gained weight" was a compliment and "your legs are skinny" was a major insult. Having a robust, nicely rounded body was the expectation for both men and women. What happened to change this cultural ideal? Since the introduction of cable television in 1995, many Fiji islanders, especially girls, have come to want to look like the thin-waisted stars of *Desperate Housewives* and *Gossip Girl*, not their full-bodied mothers and aunts. By understanding life in Fiji, we can also come to understand our own society much better (Becker 1995; Becker and Burwell 1999).

The study of culture is basic to sociology. In this chapter, we will examine the meaning of culture and society as well as the development of culture from its roots in the prehistoric human experience to the technological advances of today. The major aspects of culture—including language, norms, sanctions, and values—will be defined and explored. We will see how cultures develop a dominant ideology, and how functionalist, conflict, interactionist, and feminist theorists view culture. The discussion will focus both on general cultural practices found in all societies and on the wide variations that can distinguish one society from another. The social policy section will look at the conflicts in cultural values that underlie current debates about multiculturalism.

Use Your Sociological Imagination

What do you think the contents of your "shrine" symbolize? Who benefits from a culture preoccupied with filling up the shrine with "charms and magical potions"?

☐ HOW DO CULTURE AND SOCIETY COMPARE?

Culture is the totality of learned, socially transmitted customs, knowledge, material objects, and behaviour. It includes the ideas, values, customs, and artifacts (for example, iPods, comic books, and birth control devices) of groups of people. Patriotic attachment to the game of ice hockey in Canada is an aspect of culture, as is the widespread passion for the tango in Argentina.

Sometimes, people refer to a particular person as "very cultured" or to a city as having "lots of culture." That use of the term *culture* is different from our use in this book. In sociological terms, *culture* does not refer solely to the fine arts and refined intellectual taste. It consists of all objects and ideas within a society, including ice cream cones, rock music, and slang words. Sociologists consider both a portrait by Rembrandt and a portrait by

a billboard painter to be aspects of a culture. A tribe that cultivates soil by hand has just as much of a culture as a people that relies on computer-operated machinery. Each people has a distinctive culture with its own characteristic ways of gathering and preparing food, constructing homes, structuring the family, and promoting standards of right and wrong.

Sharing a similar culture may help to define the group or society to which we belong. A fairly large number of people are said to constitute a **society** when they live in the same territory, are relatively independent of people outside their area, and participate in a culture. Mexico City is more populous than many nations of the world, yet sociologists do not consider it a society in its own right. Rather, it is seen as part of—and dependent on—the larger society of Mexico.

A society is the largest form of human group. It consists of people who share a culture. Members of the society learn a culture and transmit it from one generation to the next. They even preserve their culture through literature, art, video recordings, and other means of expression. If it were not for the social transmission of culture, each generation would have to reinvent television, not to mention the wheel.

Sharing aspects of a common culture may simplify many day-to-day interactions. For example, when you buy an airline ticket, you know you don't have to bring along hundreds of dollars in cash. You can pay with a credit card. When you are part of a society, there are many small, as well as many important, cultural patterns that you take for granted. You assume that theatres will provide seats for the audience, that physicians will not disclose confidential information, and that parents will be careful when crossing the street with young children. All these assumptions reflect the basic values, beliefs, and customs of the culture of Canada.

Language is a critical element of culture that sets humans apart from other species. Members of a society generally share a common language, which facilitates day-to-day exchanges with others. When you ask a hardware store clerk for a flashlight, you don't need to draw a picture of the product. You share the same cultural term for a small, battery-operated, portable light. However, if you were in Britain and needed the same item, you would have to ask for an "electric torch." Of course, even within the same society, a term can have a number of different meanings. In Canada, *grass* signifies both a plant eaten by grazing animals and an intoxicating drug.

☐ HOW DO CULTURES DEVELOP AROUND THE WORLD?

We've come a long way from our prehistoric heritage. We can transmit an entire book anywhere in the world via the Internet; we can clone cells; and we can prolong lives through organ transplants. The human species has produced achievements in music, poetry, painting, novels, and films. We can peer into the outermost reaches of the universe, and we can analyze our innermost feelings. In all these ways, we are remarkably different from other species of the animal kingdom.

The process of expanding culture has been under way for thousands of years. The first archaeological evidence of human-like primates places our ancestors back many millions of years. About 700 000 years ago, people built hearths to harness fire. Archaeologists have uncovered tools that date back over 100 000 years. From 35 000 years ago, we have evidence of paintings, jewellery, and statues. By that time, elaborate ceremonies had already been developed for marriages, births, and deaths (M. Harris 1997; Haviland 1999).

Tracing the development of culture is not easy. Archaeologists cannot "dig up" weddings, laws, or governments, but they are able to locate items that point to the emergence of cultural traditions. Our early ancestors were primates that had characteristics of human beings; they made important advances in the use of tools. Recent studies of chimpanzees in the wild have revealed that they frequently use sticks and other natural objects in ways learned from other members of the group. However, unlike chimpanzees, our ancestors gradually made tools from increasingly durable materials. As a result, the items could be reused and later refined into more effective implements.

Cultural Universals

Despite their differences, all societies have developed certain common practices and beliefs, known as **cultural universals**. Many cultural universals are, in fact, adaptations to meet essential human needs, such as people's need for food, shelter, and clothing. Anthropologist George Murdock (1945:124) compiled a list of cultural universals. Some of these include athletic sports, cooking, funeral ceremonies, medicine, and sexual restrictions.

The cultural practices listed by Murdock may be universal, but the manner in which they are expressed varies from culture to culture. For example, one society may let its members choose their own marriage partners. Another may encourage marriages arranged by the parents.

Not only does the expression of cultural universals vary from one society to another, but it also may change dramatically over time within a society. Thus, the most popular styles of dancing in North America today are sure to be different from the styles dominant in the 1950s or the 1970s. Each generation, and each year for that matter, most human cultures change and expand through the processes of innovation and diffusion.

Innovation

The process of introducing an idea or object that is new to a culture is known as **innovation**. Innovation interests sociologists because of the social consequences that introducing something new can have in any society. There are two forms of innovation: discovery and invention. A **discovery** involves making known or sharing the existence of an aspect of reality. The finding of the DNA molecule and the identification of a new moon of Saturn are both acts of discovery. A significant factor in the process of discovery is the sharing of new-found knowledge with others. By contrast, an **invention** results when existing cultural items are combined into a form that did not exist before. The bow and arrow, the automobile, and the television are all examples of inventions, as are Protestantism and democracy.

Diffusion and Technology

You don't have to sample gourmet food to eat "foreign" foods. Breakfast cereal comes originally from Germany, candy from the Netherlands, and chewing gum from Mexico. The United States has also "exported" foods to other lands. Residents of many nations enjoy pizza, which was popularized in the United States. However, in Japan, they add squid; in Australia, it is eaten with pineapple; and in England, people like kernels of corn with the cheese.

Just as a culture does not always discover or invent its foods, it may also adopt ideas, technology, and customs from other cultures. Sociologists use the term **diffusion** to refer to the process by which a cultural item is spread from group to group or society to society. Diffusion can occur through a variety of means, among them exploration, military conquest, missionary work, the influence of the mass media, tourism, and the Internet. In recent decades, international trade and the exchange of ideas have accelerated cultural diffusion. Sociologists use the term **globalization** to refer to the worldwide integration of government policies, cultures, social movements, and financial markets.

Early in human history, culture changed rather slowly through discovery. Then, as the number of discoveries in a culture increased, inventions became possible. The more inventions there were, the more rapidly additional inventions could be created. In addition, as diverse cultures came into contact with one another, they could each take advantage of the other's innovations. Thus, when people in Canada read a newspaper, we look at characters invented by the ancient Semites, printed by a process invented in Germany, on a material invented in China (Linton 1936).

Citizens of nations may tend to feel a loss of identity when they are bombarded with culture from outside. Postmodern theorists such as Jean Baudrillard (1983) suggest that reality is simulated through media, cyberspace, and Disney-like theme parks in which the United States is idealized as "heaven." As Stephen M. Fjellman—who studied the worldview of Disney World—suggests, "how nice if they all could be like us—with kids, a dog, and General Electric appliances . . ."(1992:317). We have already mentioned in Chapter 1 that postmodern theorists take a global perspective and note how aspects of culture cross national boundaries, contributing to an intermingling of ideologies and cultures typical of an electronically connected planet. People throughout the world decry U.S. cultural exports, from films to language to Bart Simpson. Movies produced in the United States account for 65 percent of the global box office. Magazines as diverse as *Cosmopolitan* and *Reader's Digest* sell two issues abroad for every one they sell in the United States. *CSI: Crime Scene Investigation* airs in roughly 60 countries. These examples of canned culture all facilitate the diffusion of cultural practices (Farhi and Rosenfeld 1998).

Many societies try to protect themselves from the invasion of too much culture from other countries, especially the economically dominant United States. Canada's federal government, for example, requires that 35 percent of a radio station's daytime programming be Canadian songs or artists. Among private televison networks in Canada in 2006, however, more money was spent on foreign (primarily U.S.) programs than on Canadian programs—12 percent more than the previous

Starbucks opened its first outlet in China in 2000 and today has more than 200 shops in 21 mainland cities. In 2008, however, a Starbucks shop in the top tourist destination—the Forbidden City—was "under review" by the administrators of the museum due to concerns about Western presence in such a culturally sensitive location.

year (CRTC 2007; see Figure 3-1). In Brazil, a toy manufacturer has eclipsed Barbie's popularity by designing a doll named Susi that looks more like Brazilian girls. Susi has a slightly smaller chest, much wider thighs, and darker skin than Barbie. Her wardrobe includes the skimpy bikinis favoured on Brazilian beaches as well as a soccer shirt honouring the great Brazilian men's and women's national teams. According to the toy company's marketing director, "we wanted Susi to be more Latin, more voluptuous. We Latins appreciate those attributes." Brazilians seem to agree: before Christmas in 1999, five Susi dolls were sold for every two Barbies (DePalma 1999; Downie 2000).

Technology in its many forms has now increased the speed by which aspects of culture are shared and has broadened the distribution of cultural elements. Sociologist Gerhard Lenski has defined **technology** as "information about how to use the material resources of the environment to satisfy human needs and desires" (Nolan and Lenski 1999:41). Today's technological developments no longer have to await publication in journals with limited circulation. Press conferences, often simultaneously carried on the Internet, now trumpet new developments.

Technology not only accelerates the diffusion of scientific innovations but also transmits culture. Later, in Chapter 16, we will discuss the widespread concern in many parts of the world that the English language and North American culture dominate the Internet and World Wide Web. Control, or at least dominance, of technology influences the direction of diffusion of culture. Web sites abound with the most superficial aspects of Canadian and U.S. culture but little information about the pressing issues faced by citizens of other nations. People all over the world find it easier to visit electronic chat rooms about daytime television soap operas like *All My Children* than to learn about their own government's policies on daycare or infant nutrition programs.

Sociologist William F. Ogburn (1922) made a useful distinction between the elements of material and nonmaterial culture. **Material culture** refers to the physical or technological aspects of our daily lives, including food items, houses, factories, and raw materials. **Nonmaterial culture** refers to ways of using material objects and also to customs, beliefs, philosophies, governments, and patterns of communication. Generally, the nonmaterial culture is more resistant to change than the material culture. Consequently, Ogburn introduced the term **culture lag** to refer to the period of maladjustment when the nonmaterial culture is still adapting to new material conditions. For example, the ethics of using the Internet, particularly privacy and censorship issues, have not yet caught up with the explosion in Internet use and technology. Technology has a globalizing effect as diverse cultures become interconnected through the material and nonmaterial elements of its use. Technological applications, such as the Internet, provide a shared element of material culture, while the behaviours employed and attitudes acquired during participation in an online chat room contribute to shared nonmaterial culture.

▶ FIGURE 3-1

Foreign Content by Private Broadcasters in Canada

In 2006, private television networks spent $688 million on foreign (primarily U.S.) programming and $624 million on Canadian shows.

The competitors of TV reality show *Survivor* from the season *Panama: Exile Island.*

Foreign Content by Private Broadcasters in Canada	
$71 million CDN $479 million foreign	**Dramas**
$101 million CDN $120 million foreign	**Human Interest** (including reality and talk shows)
$35 million CDN $21 million foreign	**Music/Variety**
$5 million CDN $35 million foreign	**Game Shows**

Canadian TV sitcom *Da Kink in My Hair.*

Source: CRTC, 2007.

Diffusion can involve a single word, like "cyber," or an entirely new orientation toward living, which may be transmitted through advances in electronic communication. Sociologist George Ritzer (1995b) coined the term "McDonaldization of society" to describe how the principles of fast-food restaurants developed in the United States have come to dominate more and more sectors of societies throughout the world. For example, hair salons and medical clinics now take walk-in appointments. In Hong Kong, sex selection clinics offer a menu of items—from fertility enhancement to methods of increasing the likelihood of producing a child of the desired sex. Religious groups—from evangelical preachers on local stations or Web sites to priests at the Vatican Television Center—use marketing techniques similar to those that sell Happy Meals.

McDonaldization is associated with the melding of cultures, so that we see more and more similarities in cultural expression. In Japan, for example, African entrepreneurs have found a thriving market for hip-hop fashions popularized by teens in the United States. In Austria, the McDonald's organization itself has drawn on Austrians' love of coffee, cake, and conversation to create the McCafe as part of its fast-food chain. Many observers believe that McDonaldization and the use of technology to spread elements of culture through diffusion both serve to dilute the distinctive aspects of a society's culture (Alfino, Carpeto, and Wyngard 1998; Clark 1994; Ritzer 1995b; Rocks 1999). (Cultural diffusion via the media is discussed in more detail in Chapter 4.)

> ### Use Your Sociological Imagination
> If you had grown up in your parents' generation—without computers, email, the Internet, text-messaging, and cellphones—how would your daily life differ from the one you lead today?

☐ WHAT ARE THE ELEMENTS OF CULTURE?

Each culture considers its own distinctive ways of handling basic societal tasks as "natural." But, in fact, methods of education, marital ceremonies, religious doctrines, and other aspects of culture are learned and transmitted through human interactions within specific societies. Parents in India are accustomed to arranging marriages for their children, whereas most parents in Canada leave marital decisions up to their offspring. Lifelong residents of Naples consider it natural to speak Italian, whereas lifelong residents of Buenos Aires feel the same way about Spanish. We'll now take a look at the major aspects of culture that shape the way the members of a society live—language, norms, sanctions, and values.

Language

The English language makes extensive use of words dealing with war. We speak of *conquering* space, *fighting* the *battle* of the bulge, *waging a war* on drugs, making a *killing* on the stock market, and *bombing* an examination; something monumental or great is *the bomb*. An observer from an entirely different and warless culture could gauge the importance that war and the military have had on our lives simply by recognizing the prominence that militaristic terms have in our language. In the Old West, words such as *gelding*, *stallion*, *mare*, *piebald*, and *sorrel* were all used to describe one animal—the horse. Even if we knew little of this period of history, we could conclude from the list of terms that horses were quite important in this culture. The Slavey First Nations people, who live in the Northwest Territories, have 14 terms to describe ice, including 8 for different kinds of solid ice and others for seamed ice, cracked ice, and floating ice. Clearly, language reflects the priorities of a culture (Basso 1972; Haviland 1999).

Language is, in fact, the foundation of every culture. **Language** is an abstract system of word meanings and symbols for all aspects of culture. It includes speech, written characters, numerals, symbols, and gestures and expressions of nonverbal communication. Figure 3-2 shows the number of languages spoken in the 10 countries with the highest and the 10 countries with the lowest number of different spoken languages.

Although many different languages are spoken in Canada, English and French are recognized as the country's official languages.

▶ **FIGURE 3-2**

Languages of the World: How Many do You Speak?

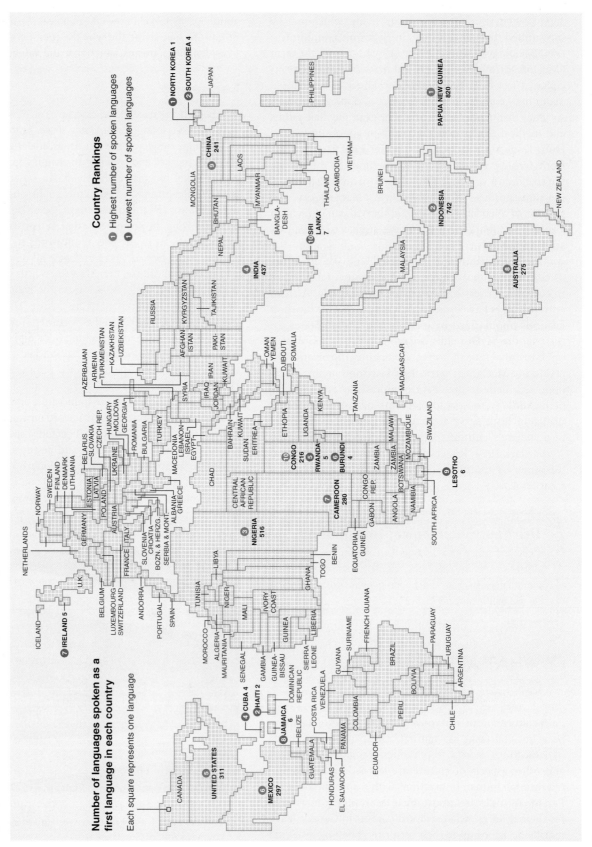

Number of languages spoken as a first language in each country

Each square represents one language

Country Rankings

❶ Highest number of spoken languages

❶ Lowest number of spoken languages

Source: Erard 2005; R. Gordon 2005.

Language is not an exclusively human attribute. Although they are incapable of human speech, primates, such as chimpanzees, have been able to use symbols to communicate. However, even at their most advanced level, other animals operate with essentially a fixed set of signs that have fixed meanings. By contrast, humans can manipulate symbols in order to express abstract concepts and rules and to expand human cultures.

Unlike some other elements of culture, language permeates all parts of society. Certain cultural skills, such as cooking or carpentry, can be learned without the use of language through the process of imitation. However, is it possible to transmit complex legal and religious systems to the next generation simply by showing how they are performed? You could put on a black robe and sit behind a bench as a judge does, but would you ever be able to understand legal reasoning without language? People invariably depend on language for the use and transmission of the complex aspects of a culture.

Although language is a cultural universal, striking differences in the use of language are evident around the world. This is the case even when two countries use the same spoken language. For example, an English-speaking person from Canada who is visiting London may be puzzled the first time an English friend says, "I'll ring you up." The friend means, "I'll call you on the telephone." Similarly, the meanings of nonverbal gestures vary from one culture to another. Whereas residents of North America attach positive meanings to the commonly used thumbs-up gesture, the same action carries only vulgar connotations in Greece and other places (Ekman, Friesen, and Bear 1984).

Sapir-Whorf Hypothesis

Language does more than simply describe reality; it also serves to *shape* the reality of a culture. For example, most people in the southern parts of Canada cannot easily make the verbal distinctions about ice that are possible in the Slavey First Nations culture. As a result, they are less likely to notice such differences.

The **Sapir-Whorf hypothesis**, named for two linguists, describes the role of language in interpreting our world. According to Sapir and Whorf, since people can conceptualize the world only through language, language *precedes* thought. Thus, the word symbols and grammar of a language organize the world for us. The Sapir-Whorf hypothesis also holds that language is not a "given." Rather, it is culturally determined and leads to different interpretations of reality by focusing our attention on certain phenomena.

In a literal sense, language may colour how we see the world. Berlin and Kay (1991) have noted that humans possess the physical ability to make millions of colour distinctions, yet languages differ in the number of colours

that are recognized. The English language distinguishes between yellow and orange, but some other languages do not. In the Dugum Dani language of New Guinea's West Highlands, there are only two basic colour terms—*modla* for "white" and *mili* for "black." By contrast, there are 11 basic colour terms in English. Russian and Hungarian, though, have 12 colour terms. Russians have terms for light blue and dark blue, while Hungarians have terms for two different shades of red.

Gender-related language can reflect—although in itself it will not determine—the traditional acceptance of men and women in certain occupations. Each time we use such a term as *mailman*, *policeman*, or *fireman*, we are implying (especially to young children) that these occupations can be filled only by males. Yet many women work as *letter carriers*, *police officers*, and *firefighters*—a fact that is being increasingly recognized and legitimized through the use of such nonsexist language (Henley, Hamilton, and Thorne 1985; Martyna 1983).

Language can also transmit stereotypes related to race. Look up the meanings of the adjective *black* in dictionaries. You will find *dismal*, *gloomy*, *forbidding*, *destitute of moral light or goodness*, *atrocious*, *evil*, *threatening*, *clouded with anger*. By contrast, dictionaries list *pure* and *innocent* among the meanings of the adjective *white*. Through such patterns of language, our culture reinforces positive associations with the term (and skin colour) *white* and a negative association with *black*. Is it surprising, then, that a list preventing people from working in a profession is called a *blacklist*, while a lie that we think of as somewhat acceptable is called a *white lie*?

Language can shape how we use our senses, how we see, taste, smell, feel, and hear. It also influences the way we think about the people, ideas, and objects around us. Language communicates a culture's most important norms, values, and sanctions to people. That's why the introduction of a new language into a society is such a sensitive issue in many parts of the world.

Non-verbal Communication

You know the appropriate distance to stand from someone when you talk informally. You know the circumstances under which it is appropriate to touch others, with a pat on the back or by taking someone's hand. If you are in the midst of a friendly meeting and one member suddenly sits back, folds his arms, and turns down the corners of his mouth, you know at once that trouble has arrived. These are all examples of non-verbal communication, the use of gestures, facial expressions, and other visual images to communicate.

We are not born with these expressions. We learn them, just as we learn other forms of language, from people who share our culture. This is as true for the basic expressions of smiling, laughter, and crying as it

Many people in North America found the sight of former U.S. President George W. Bush holding hands with Saudi Arabian Crown Prince Abdullah a bit odd. Actually, the two leaders were using nonverbal language common in the Middle East, where holding hands is a sign of friendship and mutual respect. While people in North America may have been startled or amused, Arab observers were impressed.

is for more complex emotions such as shame or distress (Fridlund, Erkman, and Oster 1987).

Like other forms of language, nonverbal communication is not the same in all cultures. For example, sociological research at the micro level documents that people from various cultures differ in the degree to which they touch others during the course of normal social interaction.

Norms

"Wash your hands before dinner." "Thou shalt not kill." "Respect your elders." All societies have ways of encouraging and enforcing what they view as appropriate behaviour while discouraging and punishing what they consider to be improper behaviour. **Norms** are established standards of behaviour maintained by a society.

For a norm to become significant, it must be widely shared and understood. For example, in movie theatres in Canada, we typically expect that people will be quiet while the film is shown. Because of this norm, an usher can tell a member of the audience to stop talking so loudly. Of course, the application of this norm can vary, depending on the particular film and type of audience. People attending a serious art film will be more likely to insist on the norm of silence than those attending a slapstick

comedy or horror movie. Norms involving certain activities, such as the online downloading of music, may be murky and their application may also vary.

Types of Norms

Sociologists distinguish between norms in two ways. First, norms are classified as either formal or informal. **Formal norms** generally have been written down and specify strict rules for punishment of violators. In North America, we often formalize norms into laws, which must be very precise in defining proper and improper behaviour. Sociologist Donald Black (1995) has termed **law** to be "governmental social control," establishing laws as formal norms enforced by the state. Laws are just one example of formal norms. The requirements for a college or university major and the rules of a card game are also considered formal norms.

By contrast, **informal norms** are generally understood but they are not precisely recorded. Standards of proper dress are a common example of informal norms. Our society has no specific punishment or sanction for a person who comes to school, say, wearing a monkey suit. Making fun of the nonconforming student is usually the most likely response.

Norms are also classified by their relative importance to society. When classified in this way, they are known as *mores* and *folkways*.

Mores (pronounced "MOR-ays") are norms deemed highly necessary to the welfare of a society, often because they embody the most cherished principles of a people. Each society demands obedience to its mores; violation can lead to severe penalties. Thus, Canada has strong mores against murder and child abuse, which have been institutionalized into formal norms.

Folkways are norms governing everyday behaviour. Folkways play an important role in shaping the daily behaviour of members of a culture. Consider, for example, something as simple as footwear. In Japan, it is a folkway for youngsters to wear flip-flop sandals while learning to walk. A study of Japanese adults has found that, even barefoot, they walk as if wearing flip-flops—braking their thigh muscles and leaning forward as they step. This folkway may even explain why Japan produces so few competitive track and field runners (Stedman 1998).

Society is less likely to formalize folkways than mores, and their violation raises comparatively little concern. For example, walking up a "down" escalator in a department store challenges our standards of appropriate behaviour, but it will not result in a fine or a jail sentence.

In many societies around the world, folkways exist to reinforce patterns of male dominance. Various folkways reveal men's hierarchical position above women within the traditional Buddhist areas of Southeast Asia. In the sleeping cars of trains, women do not sleep in upper berths above men. Hospitals that house men on the first floor do not place women patients on the second floor. Even on clotheslines, folkways dictate male dominance: women's attire is hung lower than that of men (Bulle 1987).

Use Your Sociological Imagination

You are a high school principal. What norms would you want to govern the students' behaviour? How might these norms differ from those appropriate for university students?

Acceptance of Norms

People do not follow norms, whether mores or folkways, in all situations. In some cases, they can evade a norm because they know it is weakly enforced. It is illegal for young Canadian teenagers to drink alcoholic beverages, yet drinking by minors is common throughout the nation.

In some instances, behaviour that appears to violate society's norms may actually represent adherence to the norms of a particular group. Teenage drinkers conform to the standards of a peer group. Conformity to group norms also governed the behaviour of the members of a religious cult associated with the Branch Davidians. In 1993, after a deadly gun battle with United States federal officials, nearly 100 members of the cult defied government orders to abandon their compound near Waco, Texas. After a 51-day standoff, the United States Department of Justice ordered an assault on the compound and 86 cult members died.

Norms are violated in some instances because one norm conflicts with another. For example, suppose that you live in an apartment building and one night hear the screams of the woman next door, who is being beaten by her husband. If you decide to intervene by ringing their doorbell or calling the police, you are violating the norm of "minding your own business" while, at the same time, following the norm of assisting a victim of violence.

Even when norms do not conflict, there are always exceptions to any norm. The same action, under different circumstances, can cause a person to be viewed either as a hero or as a villain. Secretly taping telephone conversations is normally considered illegal and abhorrent. However, it can be done with a court order to obtain valid evidence for a criminal trial.

Acceptance of norms is subject to change as the political, economic, and social conditions of a culture are transformed. For example, under traditional norms in Canada, a woman was expected to marry, rear children, and remain at home if her husband could support the family without her assistance. However, these norms have changed hugely in recent decades, in part as a result of the contemporary feminist movement (see Chapter 11). As support for traditional norms weakens, people feel free

to violate them more frequently and openly and are less likely to be punished for doing so.

Sanctions

Suppose that a hockey coach sends a seventh player onto the ice. Or imagine a business school graduate showing up in shorts for a job interview at a large bank. Or consider a driver who neglects to put any money into a parking meter. These people have violated widely shared and understood norms. So what happens? In each of these situations, the person will receive sanctions if his or her behaviour is detected.

Sanctions are penalties and rewards for conduct concerning a social norm. Note that the concept of *reward* is included in this definition. Conformity to a norm can lead to positive sanctions, such as a pay raise, a medal, a word of gratitude, or a pat on the back. Negative sanctions include fines, threats, imprisonment, and stares of contempt.

Table 3-1 summarizes the relationship between norms and sanctions. As you can see, the sanctions that are associated with formal norms (those written down and codified) tend to be formalized as well. If a hockey coach sends too many players onto the ice, the team will be called for a two-minute minor penalty. The driver who fails to put money in the parking meter will be given a ticket and expected to pay a fine. But sanctions for violations of informal norms can vary. The business school graduate who comes to the bank interview in shorts will probably lose any chance of getting the job; however, he or she might be so brilliant that the bank officials will overlook the unconventional attire.

Applying sanctions entails first *detecting* violations of norms or obedience to norms. A person cannot be penalized or rewarded unless someone with the power to

Table 3-1 Norms and Sanctions

Norms	Sanctions Positive	Negative
Formal	Salary bonus	Demotion
	Testimonial dinner	Firing from a job
	Medal	Jail sentence
	Diploma	Expulsion
Informal	Smile	Frown
	Compliment	Humiliation
	Cheers	Belittling

provide sanctions is aware of the person's actions. Therefore, if none of the referees in the hockey game realizes that there is an extra player on the ice, there will be no penalty. If the police do not check the parking meter, there will be no fine or ticket. Furthermore, there can be *improper* application of sanctions in certain situations. The referee may make an error in counting the number of hockey players and levy an undeserved penalty on one team for too many players on the ice.

The entire fabric of norms and sanctions in a culture reflects that culture's values and priorities. The most cherished values will be most heavily sanctioned; matters regarded as less critical will carry light and informal sanctions.

Values

We each have our own personal set of standards—which may include such things as caring or fitness or success in business—but we also share a general set of objectives as members of a society. Cultural **values** are these collective conceptions of what is considered good, desirable, and proper—or bad, undesirable, and improper—in a culture. They indicate what people in a given culture prefer as well as what they find important and morally right (or wrong). Values may be specific, such as honouring our parents and owning a home, or they may be more general, such as health, love, and democracy. Of course, the members of a society do not uniformly share its values. Angry political debates and billboards promoting conflicting causes tell us that much.

Values influence people's behaviour and serve as criteria for evaluating the actions of others. There is often a direct relationship among the values, norms, and sanctions of a culture. For example, if a culture highly values the institution of marriage, it may have norms (and strict sanctions) that prohibit the act of adultery. If a culture views private property as a basic value, it will probably have stiff laws against theft and vandalism.

Do you think that there is such a thing as Canadian values? Sociologists disagree about whether or not certain values can be representative as those shared by Canadians. When asked the following question in an Environics Research survey (2007a), "What is it about Canada that gives you the greatest source of pride?", a representative sample of 2045 Canadians over the age of 18 gave the following responses (in descending order of frequency):

> freedom/democracy
> multiculturalism
> humanitarianism/kind/caring
> peaceful country
> beauty of land/geography
> quality of life

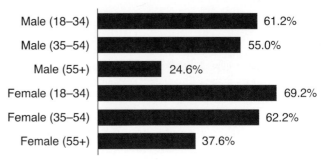

FIGURE 3-3

Support for Gay Marriage by Age and Sex, 2003

Male (18–34)	61.2%
Male (35–54)	55.0%
Male (55+)	24.6%
Female (18–34)	69.2%
Female (35–54)	62.2%
Female (55+)	37.6%

Source: Anderssen, Valpy, et al. 2004.

People's values may differ according to such factors as their age, gender, region, ethnic background, and language. For example, a major study by Erin Anderssen, Michael Valpy, and others (2004) found that, in 2003, both older (those over 30 years of age) and younger (those 18 to 30 years of age) Canadians valued security over salary and valued more free time over more money. When asked about choosing a spouse, however, younger people placed far less importance on similar ethnic background than did older Canadians.

Figure 3-3 shows the difference in support for gay marriage according to the age and sex of respondents among Canadians in 2003. The influence of technology, particularly computers and the Internet, may be weakening the connection between demographic characteristics (gender, ethnic background, religion, region, etc.) and values, contributing to less consensus and greater diversity of values (Adams 1998).

☐ HOW DOES CULTURE RELATE TO THE DOMINANT IDEOLOGY?

Functionalist Perspective

Functionalists (see Chapter 1, p. 12) maintain that stability requires a consensus and the support of society's members; consequently, there are strong central values and common norms. This view of culture became popular in sociology beginning in the 1950s. It was borrowed from British anthropologists who saw cultural traits as all working toward stabilizing a culture. From a functionalist perspective, a cultural trait or practice will persist if it performs functions that society seems to need or it contributes to overall social stability and consensus. This view helps explain why widely condemned social practices, such as prostitution, continue to survive. Both functionalist and conflict theorists agree that culture and society are in harmony with each other, but for different reasons.

Conflict Perspective

Conflict theorists (see Chapter 1, p. 14) agree that a common culture may exist, but they argue that it serves to maintain the privileges of certain groups. Moreover, while protecting their own self-interests, powerful groups may keep others in a subservient position. The term **dominant ideology** describes the set of cultural beliefs and practices that helps to maintain powerful social, economic, and political interests. This concept was first used by Hungarian Marxist Georg Lukacs (1923) and Italian Marxist Antonio Gramsci (1929). In Karl Marx's view, a capitalist society has a dominant ideology that serves the interests of the ruling class. Box 3-1 illustrates that

there is a dominant ideology about poverty that derives its strength from the more powerful segments of society.

From a conflict perspective, the dominant ideology has major social significance. Not only do a society's most powerful groups and institutions control wealth and property, but they also control the means of producing beliefs about reality through religion, education, and the media. For example, if society's message, as communicated by the mass media, is to tell us that we should be consumers, this dominant ideology will help to control us and keep us in a subordinate position (while maximizing the profits of the powerful economic groups).

Neither the functionalist nor the conflict perspective alone can explain all aspects of a culture. Nevertheless, certain cultural practices in our society and others clearly benefit some to the detriment of many. These practices may indeed promote social stability and consensus—but at whose expense?

Research in Action 3-1
Dominant Ideology and Poverty

What causes poverty? *Individualistic* explanations emphasize personal responsibility: Poor people haven't the proper work ethic, lack ability, or are unsuited to the workplace because of problems such as drinking or drug abuse. *Structural* explanations lay the blame for poverty on such external factors as inferior educational opportunities, prejudice, and low wages in some industries. Research documents that people in Canada and the United States generally go along with the individualistic explanation. The dominant ideology in North America holds that people are poor largely because of their own shortcomings.

In a world survey assessing the causes of poverty, Canadians were asked, "Why are there people in this country who live in need?" (Institute for Social Research 1994). Respondents stated with equal frequency that personal laziness and societal injustice caused poverty (31.8 percent for each reason). Such countries as Sweden, where individualistic beliefs are not as strong as in North America, responded that societal injustice far outweighed personal laziness as being the cause of poverty.

How pervasive is this individualistic view? Do the poor and rich alike subscribe to it? In seeking answers, sociologists have conducted studies of how various groups of people view poverty. The research has shown

that people with lower incomes are more likely than the wealthy to see the larger socioeconomic system as the cause of poverty. In part, this structural view, focusing on the larger job market, relieves them of some personal responsibility for their plight, but it also reflects the social reality that they are close to. The wealthy tend to embrace the dominant individualistic view because continuation of the socioeconomic status quo is in their best interest. Affluent people also tend to regard their own success as the result of their own accomplishments, with little or no help from external factors.

Is the dominant ideology on poverty widespread? Yes, but it appears that the individualist ideology is dominant in Canadian society not because of a lack of alternatives, but because those who see things differently lack the political influence and status needed to get the ear of the mainstream media and the culture at large (Francis 1986).

Applying Theory

1. Do you think support for the dominant ideology about poverty divides along income lines among racial and ethnic minority groups? Why or why not?
2. Does your university or college administration have a dominant ideology? How is it manifested? Are there any groups that challenge it? On what basis?

Sources: Bobo 1991; Institute for Social Research 1994.

Interactionist Perspective

Using the example of consumerism as a dominant ideology found in Canadian culture, an analysis by interactionist (see Chapter 1, p. 15) thinkers on the topic would differ from those of conflict thinkers and of functional thinkers. Interactionist sociologists would examine shopping, or consumer practices, from a micro perspective in order to understand the larger macro phenomenon of consumerism. Interactionists might probe consumers to discover what meaning shopping has for them or what value they attach to the activity. For example, could shopping be viewed as an activity that contributes to the economic and social well-being of Canada? Or is shopping seen as an activity that creates a bond between child and parent as they spend time together at the supermarket selecting groceries? Someone using Goffman's dramaturgical approach (1959, 1963b, 1971) might study particular features of people's personalities that they disclose to fellow shoppers while concealing the same features from the store manager or sales assistant.

Feminist Perspectives

Some feminist thinkers would argue that the mass media, acting as mouthpieces for the dominant ideology, contribute to the control and marginalization of women (see Chapter 1, p. 14). The mass media communicate to their readers, viewers, and listeners the message that women's value in society is based on their sexual attractiveness, their domestic skills, their roles as mothers and wives, their adeptness at staying fit and appearing youthful, and their abilities to provide support and comfort to others (e.g., men, children, the elderly). Some feminist perspectives advocate that the mass media's portrayal of women as powerless, child-like sex objects contributes to cultural norms, beliefs, and values that reinforce and perpetuate patriarchy as a dominant ideology (Graydon 2001).

☐ WHAT FORMS DOES CULTURAL DIVERSITY TAKE?

Each culture has a unique character. The Inuit people of Canada have little in common with farmers in Southeast Asia. Cultures adapt to meet specific sets of circumstances, such as climate, level of technology, population, and geography. This adaptation to different conditions shows up in differences in all elements of culture, including norms, sanctions, values, and language. Thus, despite the presence of cultural universals, such as courtship and religion, there is still great diversity among the world's many cultures. Moreover, even within a single nation, certain segments of the populace develop cultural patterns that differ from the patterns of the dominant society.

Aspects of Cultural Diversity

Subcultures

Residents of a retirement community, workers on an offshore oil rig, rodeo performers, street gangs, goth music fans—all are examples of what sociologists refer to as *subcultures*. A **subculture** is a segment of society that shares a distinctive pattern of mores, folkways, and values that differs from the pattern of the larger society. In a sense, a subculture can be thought of as a culture existing within a larger, dominant culture. The existence of many subcultures is characteristic of complex and diverse societies, such as Canada.

You can get an idea of the impact of subcultures within Canada by considering the variety of seasonal traditions in December. The religious and commercial celebration of the Christmas holiday is an event well entrenched in the dominant culture of our society. However, the Jewish subculture observes Hanukkah, Muslims observe Ramadan (which falls at different times during the year, but at present is occurring during the winter months), and others join in rituals celebrating the winter solstice.

Members of a subculture participate in the dominant culture, while at the same time engaging in unique and distinctive forms of behaviour. Frequently, a subculture will develop an **argot**, or specialized language, that distinguishes it from the wider society. For example, if you were to join a band of pickpockets, you would need to learn what the *dip*, *dish*, and *tailpipe* are expected to do (see Figure 3-4).

An argot allows insiders, the members of the subculture, to understand words with special meanings. It also establishes patterns of communication that outsiders can't understand. Sociologists associated with the interactionist perspective emphasize that language and symbols offer a powerful way for a subculture to feel cohesive and maintain its identity.

Subcultures develop in a number of ways. Often a subculture emerges because a segment of society faces problems or even privileges unique to its position. Subcultures may be based on common age (teenagers or old people), region (Newfoundlanders), ethnic heritage (Indo-Canadians), occupation (firefighters), or beliefs (environmentalists). Certain subcultures, such as computer hackers, develop because of a shared interest or hobby. In still other subcultures, such as that of prison inmates, members have been excluded from conventional society and are forced to develop alternative ways of living.

▶**FIGURE 3-4**

The Argot of Pickpockets

Source: Gearty 1996.

Interactionists contend that individuals confer meaning differently: what it means to be a successful surfer living out of a van in Tofino, British Columbia, may be quite different from what it means to be a successful Bay Street lawyer living in Toronto. Feminist perspectives might point to cultural diversity as contributing to the perpetuation of multiple layers and degrees of inequality based on gender, ethnicity, race, and class. The greater the deviation from the norms of the dominant culture, the greater the impact of inequality experienced by various subcultures.

Functionalist and conflict theorists agree that variation exists within a culture. Functionalists view subcultures as variations of particular social environments and as evidence that differences can exist within a common culture. However, conflict theorists suggest that variation often reflects the inequality of social arrangements within a society. A conflict perspective would view the challenge to dominant social norms by Quebec separatists, the feminist movement, and groups representing people with disabilities as a reflection of inequity based on ethnicity, gender, and disability status. Conflict theorists also argue that subcultures sometimes emerge when the dominant society unsuccessfully tries to suppress a practice, such as the use of illegal drugs.

Countercultures

By the end of the 1960s, an extensive subculture had emerged in North America comprising young people turned off by a society they believed was too materialistic and technological. This group primarily included political radicals and "hippies" who had "dropped out" of mainstream social institutions. Hippies rejected societal pressures to accumulate more and more cars, larger and larger homes, and an endless array of material goods. Instead, they expressed a desire to live in a culture based on more humanistic values, such as sharing, love, and coexistence with the environment.

When a subculture conspicuously and deliberately *opposes* certain aspects of the larger culture, it is known as a **counterculture**. Countercultures typically thrive among the young, who have the least investment in the existing culture. In most cases, a 20-year-old can adjust to new cultural standards more easily than can someone who has spent 60 years following the patterns of the dominant culture (Zellner 1995).

An example of a Canadian counterculture is the Front de libération du Québec (FLQ). In 1970, the FLQ opposed the social, economic, political, and educational institutions of the dominant culture of Quebec. Its activities included the murder of a prominent Quebec politician and the kidnapping of a British

"IT'S ENDLESS. WE JOIN A COUNTER-CULTURE; IT BECOMES THE CULTURE. WE JOIN ANOTHER COUNTER-CULTURE; IT BECOMES THE CULTURE..."

Cultures change. Aspects we once regarded as unacceptable—such as men wearing earrings and people wearing jeans in the workplace—and associated with fringe groups are now widely accepted. Countercultural practices are often absorbed by the mainstream culture.

trade commissioner posted in Quebec. The FLQ produced a manifesto containing all of its demands, which was broadcast through public media.

Culture Shock

Anyone who feels disoriented, uncertain, out of place, or even fearful when immersed in an unfamiliar culture may be experiencing **culture shock**. For example, a resident of Canada who visits certain areas in China and wants a local dinner may be stunned to learn that the specialty is scorpion. Similarly, someone from a strict Islamic culture may be shocked on first seeing the comparatively provocative dress styles and open displays of affection that are common in North American and many European cultures. Culture shock can also occur within the larger confines of a person's own culture. For example, a 14-year-old boy from a small town in northern Saskatchewan might feel the effects of culture shock while visiting Toronto for the first time. The speed of the traffic, the level of the street noise, and the intensity and variation of external stimuli may cause him to feel disoriented and uncomfortable within his surroundings.

All of us, to some extent, take for granted the cultural practices of our society. As a result, it can be surprising and even disturbing to realize that other cultures do not follow our way of life. In fact, customs that seem strange to us are considered normal and proper in other cultures, which may in turn see *our* mores and folkways as odd.

Cultural Diversity in Canada

If a tourist were to travel across Canada for the first time, he or she would most certainly be struck by the country's diversity—of region, ethnicity, race, and language. Cultural diversity, as the traveller would observe, is greatest in Canada's metropolitan areas, where the largest number of cultural and visible minorities reside. On the basis of his or her observations of cultural diversity, the traveller might conclude that Canada is a "multicultural" society. But what does multiculturalism really mean? Does it simply describe (numerically) the variety of cultures represented in Canada?

Multiculturalism is not only a description of the reality of Canada's cultural makeup—"what is" (Fleras and Kunz 2001)—but, in Canada, it is an explicit policy set out by the federal government. **Multiculturalism** is a policy that promotes cultural and racial diversity and full and equal participation of individuals and communities of all origins as a fundamental characteristic of Canadian identity. The federal Multiculturalism Program of 1997 set three main goals (Communications Canada 2001):

1. *Identity*—fostering a society where people of all backgrounds feel a sense of attachment and belonging to Canada
2. *Civic participation*—developing citizens who are actively involved in their communities and country
3. *Social justice*—building a country that ensures fair and equitable treatment of people of all origins

Multiculturalism can also take the form of an ideology—a set of beliefs, goals, ideals, and attitudes about what multiculturalism *should be*. In embracing multiculturalism as an ideology, Canadians often compare their society's way of expressing cultural diversity with the way it is expressed in the United States (Fleras and Kunz 2001). The analogy of the "mosaic" is commonly used to describe Canada's cultural diversity, where various tiles represent distinct cultural groups that collectively form the whole. In the United States, the "melting pot" analogy represents the model of assimilation, in which U.S. citizens become more like one another, rather than distinct from one another.

Support for the mosaic version of Canada has been declining and shifting toward the melting pot. Across region, age, and education levels, in 1985, 56 percent of Canadians said they preferred the mosaic and 28 percent the melting pot. In 1995, only 44 percent preferred the mosaic, while 40 percent preferred the melting pot (Bibby 1995).

The ideal of multiculturalism in Canada has two desirable outcomes: the survival of ethnic groups and their cultures, and tolerance of this diversity as reflected by an absence of prejudice toward ethnic minorities (Weinfeld 1994). Multiculturalism, however, is not without its critics. Some argue that it is a divisive rather than unifying force in Canada, while others claim that it is only "window dressing," diverting attention from the real problems of ethnic and racial prejudice and discrimination (A. Nelson and Fleras 1998). The domination of European cultural patterns in Canada—known as **Eurocentrism**—contributes to discrimination and prejudice toward those who are seen as non-European and, thus, the "other."

The American Influence   One of the original purposes of multiculturalism was to establish a national uniqueness that would make Canadians distinct from their U.S. counterparts (Bibby 1990). In 1972, Prime Minister Pierre Elliott Trudeau stated that with this policy, "we become less like others; we become less susceptible to

cultural, social, or political envelopment by others" (Bibby 1990:49).

The Americanization of Canada (as well as of many other countries) has lead to **cultural imperialism**—the influence or imposition of the material or nonmaterial elements of a culture on another culture or cultures. This phenomenon is particularly relevant in the context of the global export of U.S. culture through various forms of that country's mass media. Canadians have been, and continue to be, particularly susceptible to cultural imperialism because of geographic, economic, social, and political ties with the United States. Some organizations, such as the Council of Canadians, have an explicit mandate to protect and preserve Canada's national interests and sovereignty from forces of globalization, in which U.S. cultural imperialism looms large.

Even though Canadians generally hold the view that the United States does not have "too much power" in our society (Bibby 1995), Canadians frequently consider people south of the border to be their favourite authors, TV personalities, and screen stars (Bibby 1995). Given Canadians' (particularly those outside Quebec) reliance on U.S. culture, our heroes may be those that are defined stateside (Bibby 1995). A Pew Global Attitudes Project—focusing on the global influence of superpowers—in 2007 surveyed people in 46 countries around the world, including Canada (see Table 3-2). When asked their views of U.S. movies,

Table 3-2 Selected Countries' Views of U.S. Exports, 2007

	Positive Views of . . .		
	U.S. Movies, TV, and Music (%)	**U.S. Science and Technology (%)**	**Spread of U.S. Ideas* (%)**
Canada	73	74	22
Peru	50	78	29
Germany	62	65	17
China	42	80	38
Japan	70	81	42
Mali	68	88	45
Turkey	22	37	4
Sweden	77	73	28

*"Good that American customs are spreading here."

Source: Adapted from Pew Global Attitudes Project, 2007a.

television, and music, the vast majority of Canadians (73 percent) reported a positive response; Canada was among the top—of 46 countries—in its favourable response to these U.S. pop culture exports. However, in contrast and seeming contradiction, Canadians' views on the statement, "good that American values are spreading here," were considerably lower (22 percent), dropping 13 percent since 2002. Israel, Ethiopia, Ivory Coast, and Nigeria were the only countries outside of the United States, where a majority of the population had a favourable view of the spread of U.S. culture (Pew Global Attitudes Project, 2007b). The report states, "Despite near universal admiration for U.S. technology and a strong appetite for its culture in most parts of the world, large proportions in most countries think it is bad that American ideas and customs are spreading to their countries" (2007b:5).

Attitudes toward Cultural Diversity

Ethnocentrism

Many everyday statements reflect our attitude that our culture is best. We use terms such as *underdeveloped*, *backward*, and *primitive* to refer to other societies. What "we" believe is a religion; what "they" believe is superstition and mythology (Johnson 2000).

It is tempting to evaluate the practices of other cultures on the basis of our own perspectives. Sociologist William Graham Sumner (1906) coined the term **ethnocentrism** to refer to the tendency to assume that our own culture and way of life constitute the norm or are superior to all others. The ethnocentric person sees his or her own group as the centre or defining point of culture and views all other cultures as deviations from what is "normal."

Those westerners who are contemptuous of India's Hindu religion and culture because of its view of cattle as sacred are engaged in ethnocentrism. Another manifestation of ethnocentrism occurs when people in one culture may dismiss as unthinkable the mate-selection or child-rearing practices of another culture. We might, in fact, be tempted to view the Nacirema culture from an ethnocentric point of view—until we learn it is a culture similar to our own that Horace Miner describes (see the chapter-opening vignette).

Conflict theorists point out that ethnocentric value judgments serve to devalue diversity and to deny equal opportunities. The treatment of Aboriginal children in Christian-based residential schools in the middle of the last century is an example of ethnocentrism that conflict theorists might point to in Canadian history. Church authorities were so convinced of the cultural superiority of their own beliefs that they set out to deny Aboriginal children the expression of theirs.

Functionalists note that ethnocentrism serves to maintain a sense of solidarity by promoting group pride. Canadians' view of their country as peaceful, safe, and relatively free from violence may create a feeling of national solidarity when comparing themselves with their U.S. neighbours.

The importance of the problem of ethnocentrism for students of sociology is particularly relevant. Students must understand that their membership in the social world—and a particular social world at that—is not an advantage in the practice of sociology (Harris 1974).

Cultural Relativism

Although ethnocentrism evaluates foreign cultures by using the familiar culture of the observer as a standard of correct behaviour, **cultural relativism** views people's behaviour from the perspective of their own culture. It places a priority on understanding other cultures, rather than on dismissing them as strange or exotic. Unlike ethnocentrism, cultural relativism employs the kind of value neutrality in scientific study that Max Weber saw as so important.

Cultural relativism stresses that different social contexts give rise to different norms and values. Thus, we must examine such practices as polygamy, bullfighting, and monarchy within the particular contexts of the cultures in which they are found. Although cultural relativism does not suggest that we must unquestionably *accept* every cultural variation, it does require a serious and unbiased effort to evaluate norms, values, and customs in light of their distinctive culture.

There is an interesting extension of cultural relativism, referred to as *xenocentrism*. **Xenocentrism** is the belief that the products, styles, or ideas of our own society are inferior to those that originate elsewhere (W. Wilson, Dennis, and Wadsworth 1976). In a sense, it is a reverse ethnocentrism. For example, people in Canada often assume that French wine or Japanese electronic devices are superior to their domestic versions. Are they? Or are people unduly charmed by the lure of goods from exotic places? Such fascination with overseas products can be damaging to competitors in Canada. Conflict theorists are most likely to consider the economic impact of xenocentrism in the developing world. Consumers in developing nations frequently turn their backs on locally produced goods and instead purchase items imported from Europe or North America.

How people view their culture—whether from an ethnocentric point of view or through the lens of cultural relativism—has important consequences in the area of social policy concerned with multiculturalism. We'll take a close look at this issue in the Social Policy box on page 65.

Social Policy and Culture
Multiculturalism

The Issue

In 1971, multiculturalism became official government policy in Canada. It was a policy established to promote tolerance for cultural minorities, or in the words of then Prime Minister Pierre Trudeau, to "explore the delights of many cultures." Although the Canadian policy on multiculturalism provides an alternative to the U.S. melting pot approach to cultural diversity, it has generated a great deal of conflict and faced a great deal of opposition (A. Nelson and Fleras 1998).

Much of the conflict surrounding multiculturalism stems from the variety of meanings or definitions Canadians have for the concept. The term *multiculturalism* can be used to refer to (1) the fact (what *is*; i.e., the existing complexion of Canadian society); (2) an ideology (what should be); (3) policy (what is proposed); (4) a process (what really happens); (5) a critical discussion (what is being challenged); and (6) a social movement (collective resistance) (Fleras and Elliott 1999). In general, multiculturalism can be defined as a process through which Canadians come to be engaged in their society as different from one another yet equal to one another (Fleras and Kunz 2001).

The Setting

According to Citizenship and Immigration Canada, the government accepts more immigrants, proportional to the size of the country's population, than any other nation in the world. One in every five residents in Canada was born outside the country. The top five sources for immigration between 2001 and 2006 were countries in Asia and the Middle East (Statistics Canada 2007f). According to the 2006 census, most foreign-born immigrants who came to Canada between 2001 and 2006 were from China, followed by India, the Philippines, and Pakistan. Overall, multicultural minorities tend to live in Canada's large urban centres, making Toronto, Vancouver, and Montreal the most culturally diverse regions of the country. Over 60 percent of all immigrants in Canada settled in one of these three places (Statistics Canada 2007f).

From the standpoint of the two major sociological perspectives—conflict theory and structural-functional theory—the implementation of multiculturalism as a social policy has two distinct interpretations. Conflict sociologists view multiculturalism as an attempt to empower minorities to pursue the goals of ethnic identification and equality. It is seen as an attempt to nurture, preserve, and protect different cultural traditions in the midst of domination by one

cultural group. Multiculturalism policies also aim to make diversity, and the inevitable struggles that result, an accepted and welcome element of the cultural fabric of Canadian life.

Functional sociologists view culture as something that all Canadians share. It is the common values that unite and integrate us, resulting in a shared sense of identity. Therefore, according to functional thinkers, the more we diversify Canadian culture, the less we share in common; the more we hyphenate our identities (e.g., Indo-Canadian, Chinese-Canadian, Italian-Canadian, etc.), the

Policies on multiculturalism attempt to preserve, protect, and nurture different cultural traditions in the midst of the domnation of one cultural group. This boy sits outside a court hearing to decide whether he has the right to wear his kirpan, a sikh ceremonial dagger, to school.

less Canadian we actually become. However, both functionalist and conflict theorists have criticized multiculturalism for a number of reasons. Sociologists Augie Fleras and Jean Elliott (1999) argue that criticisms regarding multiculturalism can be classified into four categories:

1. Those claiming that multiculturalism is divisive and serves to weaken Canadian society
2. Those that see multicultural programs and policies as regressive, as a tool to pacify the needs and legitimate claims of the minority cultural groups
3. Those that consider the efforts of multiculturalism to be ornamental or superficial, with much form and little substance
4. Those that consider multiculturalism as a policy impractical in a capitalist society such as Canada, where the principles of individualism, private property, profit, and consumerism prevail

Policy Initiatives

Official multiculturalism in Canada currently is a portfolio in the federal Canadian Heritage Department. According to Fleras and Kunz (2001), policies on multiculturalism have evolved from those in the 1970s, which celebrated Canadians' differences (e.g., cultural sensitivity training programs), through those in the 1980s, which managed diversity through policies on employment equity and race relations, to those of the 1990s, with the objectives of inclusion and integration of cultural minorities. The current policies on multiculturalism encourage the full participation of all cultural groups, based on the goals of social justice. As Fleras and Kunz (2001:16) state, "emphasis is on what we have in common as rights-bearing and equality-seeking individuals rather than on what separates or divides us." Special activities, such as Black History Month and the "Racism: Stop It!" campaign, which focus on the promotion of social justice, have been created by the federal government's multicultural programs.

Fleras and Elliott (1999) state that multiculturalism is not what divides Canada but is rather what unites us, separating us and making us distinct from the United States. They claim that multiculturalism policies focus on institutional barriers for minority groups and therefore attempt to break down the patterns of inequality. A recent study by Jeffery Reitz and Rupa Banerjee from the University of Toronto suggests that the policy of multiculturalism is not working for many people—particularly for newer immigrants and their children who come from East Asia, South Asia, and the Caribbean (Jimenez 2007). These groups face discrimination and marginalization and, thus, are not able to enjoy equal participation in mainstream institutions—this is a setback to the central tenet of multiculturalism. These immigrants often feel excluded and vulnerable, and fearful of racial attacks in Canadian society. Ratna Omidvar, director of a Canadian organization that works with immigrants, says that "good multicultural policy must not only protect our rights to equality, but it must also create real opportunities" (Jimenez 2007).

Applying Theory

1. What functions do you think the policy of multiculturalism serves? Do you think these functions are manifest or latent?
2. According to the assumptions of conflict thinking, how might the ideology of multiculturalism differ from the reality of living in a multicultural country?

CHAPTER RESOURCES

Summary

How do Culture and Society Compare?
- **Culture** (p. 49) is the totality of learned, socially transmitted customs, knowledge, material objects, and behaviour. In this chapter, we examined the basic elements that make up a culture, social practices common to all cultures, and variations that distinguish one culture from another.

- Sharing a similar culture helps to define the group or society to which we belong.

How do Cultures Develop around the World?
- **Cultural universals** (p. 50) are general practices found in every culture, including courtship, family, games, language, medicine, religion, and sexual restrictions.
- In recent decades, international trade and the exchange of ideas have accelerated cultural change.
- Sociologists use the term **globalization** (p. 51) to refer to the resulting worldwide integration of government policies, cultures, social movements, and financial markets.

What are the Elements of Culture?
- **Langua**ge (p. 53) is an important element of culture, and includes speech, written characters, numerals, symbols, and gestures and other forms of non-verbal communication. Language both describes culture and shapes it for us.
- **Norms** (p. 56) are established standards of behaviour maintained by society. Sociologists distinguish between **formal norms** (p. 56)—those which are written down—and **informal** norms (p. 56)—those which are generally understood.
- **Sanctions** (p. 57) are penalties and rewards for conduct concerning a social norm.

How does Culture Relate to the Dominant Ideology?
- The **dominant ideology** (p. 59) of a culture describes the set of cultural beliefs and practices that help to maintain powerful social, economic, and political interests.
- **Subcultures** (p. 60) can be thought of as cultures existing within a larger, dominant culture.
- **Countercultures** (p. 61) are subcultures that deliberately oppose aspects of the larger culture.

What Forms does Cultural Diversity Take?
- People who measure other cultures by the standard of their own, engage in **ethnocentrism** (p. 64). Using **cultural relativism** (p. 64) allows us to view people from the perspective of *their* culture.
- **Multiculturalism** (p. 62) is a process through which citizens come to be engaged in their society as different from one another, yet equal to one another.

Critical Thinking Questions

1. Who do you think promotes the dominant culture most rigorously?
2. Drawing on the theories and concepts presented in the chapter, apply sociological analysis to one subculture with which you are familiar. Describe the norms, values, argot, and sanctions evident in that subculture.
3. In what ways is the dominant ideology of Canada evident in the nation's literature, music, movies, theatre, television programs, and sporting events?
4. Given your understanding of culture after reading this chapter, in what way do you think the contents of bathrooms, and the activities carried out in them, reflect the culture of a given group?

Key Terms

Argot Specialized language used by members of a group or subculture. (p. 60)

Counterculture A subculture that deliberately opposes certain aspects of the larger culture. (p. 61)

Cultural imperialism The influence or imposition of the material or non-material elements of a culture on another culture or cultures. (p. 63)

Cultural relativism The viewing of people's behaviour from the perspective of their own culture. (p. 64)

Cultural universals General practices found in every culture. (p. 50)

Culture The totality of learned, socially transmitted customs, knowledge, material objects, and behaviour. (p. 49)

Culture lag Ogburn's term for a period of maladjustment during which the nonmaterial culture is still adapting to new material conditions. (p. 52)

Culture shock The feeling of surprise and disorientation that is experienced when people witness cultural practices different from their own. (p. 62)

Diffusion The process by which a cultural item is spread from group to group or society to society. (p. 51)

Discovery The process of making known or sharing the existence of an aspect of reality. (p. 50)

Dominant ideology A set of cultural beliefs and practices that helps to maintain powerful social, economic, and political interests. (p. 59)

Ethnocentrism The tendency to assume that our own culture and way of life represent the norm or are superior to all others. (p. 64)

Eurocentrism The dominance of European cultural patterns which contribute to the view of non-European people and cultural patterns as being "other" (p. 63).

Folkways Norms governing everyday social behaviour whose violation raises comparatively little concern. (p. 56)

Formal norms Norms that generally have been written down and that specify strict rules for punishment of violators. (p. 56)

Globalization The worldwide integration of government policies, cultures, social movements, and financial markets. (p. 51)

Informal norms Norms that generally are understood but are not precisely recorded. (p. 56)

Innovation The process of introducing new elements into a culture through either discovery or invention. (p. 50)

Invention The combination of existing cultural items into a form that did not previously exist. (p. 50)

Language An abstract system of word meanings and symbols for all aspects of culture. It also includes gestures and other nonverbal communication. (p. 53)

Law Governmental social control. (p. 56)

Material culture The physical or technological aspects of our daily lives. (p. 52)

Mores Norms deemed highly necessary to the welfare of a society. (p. 56)

Multiculturalism A policy that promotes cultural and racial diversity and full and equal participation of individuals and communities of all origins as a fundamental characteristic of Canadian identity. (p. 62)

Nonmaterial culture Cultural adjustments to material conditions, such as customs, beliefs, patterns of communication, and ways of using material objects. (p. 52)

Norms Established standards of behaviour maintained by a society. (p. 56)

Sanctions Penalties and rewards for conduct concerning a social norm. (p. 57)

Sapir-Whorf hypothesis A hypothesis concerning the role of language in shaping cultures. It holds that language is culturally determined and serves to influence our mode of thought. (p. 55)

Society A fairly large number of people who live in the same territory, are relatively independent of people outside it, and participate in a common culture. (p. 49)

Subculture A segment of society that shares a distinctive pattern of mores, folkways, and values that differs from the pattern of the larger society. (p. 60)

Technology Information about how to use the material resources of the environment to satisfy human needs and desires. (p. 52)

Values Collective conceptions of what is considered good, desirable, and proper—or bad, undesirable, and improper—in a culture. (p. 58)

Xenocentrism The belief that the products, styles, or ideas of our own society are inferior to those that originate elsewhere. (p. 64)

Additional Readings

Anderssen, Erin, Michael Valpy, et al. 2004. *The New Canada: A Globe and Mail Report on the Next Generation*. Toronto: Globe and Mail/McClelland & Stewart Ltd. A portrait of a "new" Canada that is urban, ethnically diverse, secular, and media-savvy, focusing on Canadians between 20 and 29 years of age.

Dunk, Thomas W. 2003. *It's a Working Man's Town*, 2nd ed. Montreal: McGill-Queen's University Press. An examination of leisure activities of working-class males in Thunder Bay, Ontario, illustrating the importance of these activities for understanding the link between culture and consciousness.

Fleras, Augie, and Jean Lock Kunz. 2001. *Media and Minorities: Representing Diversity in Multicultural Canada*. Scarborough, ON: Thomson Educational Publishing. Fleras and Kunz analyze and assess the representation of minority groups in the mass media against a backdrop of Canada's commitment to multiculturalism.

O'Brien, Susie, and Imre Szeman. 2004. *Popular Culture: A User's Perspective*. Toronto: Thomson Educational Publishing. This book introduces students to the concept of popular culture and covers such topics as the history of popular culture, identity and the body, and globalization and popular culture.

Online Learning Centre

Visit the *Sociology: A Brief Introduction* Online Learning Centre at www.mcgrawhill.ca/olc/schaefer to access quizzes, interactive exercises, video clips, and other research and study tools related to this chapter.

Reel Society Video Clips

Reel Society video clips can be used to spark discussion about the following topics from this chapter:

- Cultural universals
- Norms

SOCIALIZATION

chapter 4

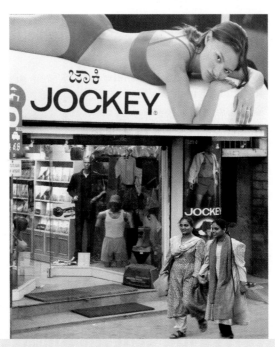

On a busy commercial street in Bangalore, India, pedestrians dressed in traditional garb stroll past a shop and billboard advertising Western fashions. Socialization comes from corporate influences as well as from those who are closest to us, such as family and friends. In today's globalized world, Western media expose children to cultural values their parents and other authorities may not embrace.

☐ **What is the Role of Socialization?**

☐ **What are some Major Theoretical Perspectives on Socialization?**

☐ **What are some Agents of Socialization?**

☐ **How does Socialization Occur throughout the Life Course?**

Boxes

RESEARCH IN ACTION: Impression Management by Students after Exams

SOCIOLOGY IN THE GLOBAL COMMUNITY: Raising Amish Children

SOCIOLOGY IN THE GLOBAL COMMUNITY: Aging Worldwide: Issues and Consequences

SOCIAL POLICY AND SOCIALIZATION: Child Care around the World

The following excerpt is an account of how the Canadian residential school system for Aboriginal people made an impact on one person's life. This story could be told by almost any person who attended residential school in any part of Canada.

As a child of six, I remember being loaded on the back of a cattle truck with stock racks and taken to a residential school. I remember getting to the school and feeling so lonely. I was so far from home. I wanted my parents; instead a stern nun told me something in a harsh voice. I did not understand a word of English. No one ever called me by my name—I was just a number.

I had lost my identity. I was no longer an individual. I was part of a group that was all dressed the same with the same haircut. We were expected to act the same as everyone else and to eat the same food. For breakfast we had rolled oats (porridge) with crumbs on top. Most of the time those crumbs were blue from mold.

Since that time, I have been scared of abandonment and hate standing in line for anything. There are deep psychological scars that remain today. Some residential school survivors have been abused physically, emotionally, mentally, sexually and spiritually. There was no compassion shown; no parental skills were taught.

There was loss of culture and cultural teachings. In fact, we were taught that if we went to any ceremony we were committing a sin and therefore we would go to hell. Hell was a place where we would burn forever in eternal damnation.

We were brainwashed into believing that the white race was superior. Women were inferior to men. Indians were heathens, savages and pagans, and if we listened to our parents and grandparents, we would go to hell.

One of the results of these residential school teachings was the lack of trust for parents, grandparents and other Elders—a loss of trust for anyone in authority, any adult or anyone with any power, especially over you. The loss of respect for parents and Elders was due to the brainwashing. We were forbidden to speak our native language and forced to speak English. We could no longer communicate with our Elders. As a child, no one ever told you that the Elders had the wisdom, knowledge and experience to guide you through the turbulent times of your life.

☐ *(Aboriginal Healing Foundation 2000)*

This personal story of how the residential school system scarred the life of a First Nations person reveals how the dominant culture used education as a justification to separate families and to socialize "savage," "heathen," "pagan" children with non-Aboriginal culture.

Sociologists, in general, are interested in the patterns of behaviour and attitudes that emerge throughout the life course, from infancy to old age. These patterns are part of the process of **socialization**, whereby people learn the attitudes, values, and behaviours appropriate for members of a particular culture. Socialization occurs through human interactions. We learn a great deal from those people most important in our lives—immediate family members, best friends, and teachers. But we also learn from people we see on the street, on television, on the Internet, and in films and magazines. From a microsociological perspective, socialization helps us to discover how to behave "properly" and what to expect from others if we follow (or challenge) society's norms and values. From a macrosociological perspective, socialization provides for the transmission of a culture from one generation to the next and thereby for the long-term continuance of a society.

Socialization affects the overall cultural practices of a society, and it also shapes our self-image. For example, in North America, a person who is viewed as "too heavy" or "too short" does not conform to the ideal cultural standard of physical attractiveness. More seriously, First Nations children in residential schools were taught that their culture was inferior and that the white race was superior. These kinds of unfavourable evaluations can significantly influence a person's self-esteem. In this sense, socialization experiences can help shape our personalities. In everyday speech, the term **personality** is used to refer to a person's typical patterns of attitudes, needs, characteristics, and behaviour.

In this chapter, we will examine the role of socialization in human development. We begin by analyzing the interaction of heredity and environmental factors. We pay particular attention to how people develop perceptions, feelings, and beliefs about themselves. We will also explore important agents of socialization, among them family, schools, peers, and the media, as well as the lifelong nature of the socialization process. Finally, the social policy section covers the socialization experience of group child care for infants and toddlers.

Use Your Sociological Imagination

What do you think the impact has been, is, and will be for former students of residential schools? How might the traumatic experiences in these schools affect one's ability to relate to other family members, be they tribal elders or children?

☐ WHAT IS THE ROLE OF SOCIALIZATION?

What makes us who we are? Is it the genes we are born with? Or the environment in which we grow up? Researchers have traditionally clashed over the relative importance of biological inheritance and environmental factors in human development—a conflict called the *nature versus nurture* (or *heredity versus environment*) debate. Today, most social scientists have moved beyond this debate, acknowledging instead the interaction of these variables in shaping human development. However, we can better appreciate how heredity and environmental factors interact and influence the socialization process if we first examine situations in which one factor operates almost entirely without the other (Homans 1979).

Environment: The Impact of Isolation

In the 1994 movie, *Nell*, Jodie Foster played a young woman hidden from birth by her mother in a backwoods cabin. Raised without normal human contact, Nell crouches like an animal, screams wildly, and speaks or sings in a language all her own. This movie was drawn from the actual account of an emaciated 16-year-old boy who mysteriously appeared in 1828 in the town square of Nuremberg, Germany (Lipson 1994).

The Case of Isabelle

Some viewers may have found the story of Nell difficult to believe, but the painful childhood of Isabelle was all too real. For the first six years of her life, Isabelle lived in almost total seclusion in a darkened room. She had little contact with other people, with the exception of her mother, who could neither speak nor hear. Isabelle's mother's parents had been so deeply ashamed of Isabelle's illegitimate birth that they kept her hidden away from the world. Ohio authorities finally discovered the child in 1938, when Isabelle's mother escaped from her parents' home, taking her daughter with her.

When she was discovered at age 6, Isabelle could not speak. She could merely make various croaking sounds. Her only communications with her mother were simple gestures. Isabelle had been largely deprived of the typical interactions and socialization experiences of childhood. Since she had actually seen few people, she initially showed a strong fear of strangers and reacted almost like a wild animal when confronted with an unfamiliar person. As she became accustomed to seeing certain individuals, her reaction changed to one of extreme apathy. At first, it was believed that Isabelle was deaf, but she soon began to react to nearby sounds. On tests of maturity, she scored at the level of an infant rather than a 6-year-old.

Specialists developed a systematic training program to help Isabelle adapt to human relationships and socialization. After a few days of training, she made her first attempt to verbalize. Although she started slowly, Isabelle quickly passed through six years of development. In a little over two months, she was speaking in complete sentences. Nine months later, she could identify both words and sentences. Before Isabelle reached the age of 9, she was ready to attend school with other children. By her fourteenth year, she was in sixth grade, doing well in school, and emotionally well-adjusted.

Yet, without an opportunity to experience socialization in her first six years, Isabelle had been hardly human in the social sense when she was first discovered. Her inability to communicate at the time of her discovery—despite her physical and cognitive potential to learn—and her remarkable progress over the next few years underscore the impact of socialization on human development (K. Davis 1940, 1947).

Isabelle's experience is important for researchers because it is one of few cases of children reared in total isolation. Unfortunately, however, there are many cases of children raised in extremely neglectful social circumstances. Recently, attention has focused on infants and young children in orphanages in the formerly communist countries of Eastern Europe. For example, in Romanian orphanages, babies lie in their cribs for 18 or 20 hours a day, curled against their feeding bottles and receiving little adult care. Such minimal attention continues for the first five years of their lives. Many of the Romanian orphans are fearful of human contact and prone to unpredictable antisocial behaviour. This situation came to light as families in North America and Europe began adopting thousands of these children. The adjustment

problems for about 20 percent of them were often so dramatic that the adopting families suffered guilty fears of being unfit adoptive parents. Many of them have asked for assistance in dealing with the children. Slowly, efforts are being made to introduce the deprived youngsters to feelings of attachment that they have never experienced before (Groza, Ilena, and Irwin 1999; Talbot 1998).

Increasingly, researchers are emphasizing the importance of early socialization experiences for children who grow up in more normal environments. We know that it is not enough to care for an infant's physical needs; parents must also concern themselves with children's social development. If, for example, children are discouraged from having friends, they will miss out on social interactions with peers that are critical for emotional growth.

Use Your Sociological Imagination
What events in your life have had a strong influence on who you are?

Primate Studies

Studies of animals raised in isolation also support the importance of socialization in development. Harry Harlow (1971), a researcher at the primate laboratory of the University of Wisconsin, conducted tests with rhesus monkeys that had been raised away from their mothers and away from contact with other monkeys. As was the case with Isabelle, the rhesus monkeys raised in isolation were fearful and easily frightened. They did not mate, and the females who were artificially inseminated became abusive mothers. Apparently, isolation had had a damaging effect on the monkeys.

A creative aspect of Harlow's experimentation was his use of "artificial mothers." In one such experiment, Harlow presented monkeys raised in isolation with two substitute mothers—one cloth-covered replica and one covered with wire that had the ability to offer milk. Monkey after monkey went to the wire mother for the life-giving milk, yet spent much more time clinging to the more mother-like cloth model. In this study, the monkeys valued the artificial mothers that provided a comforting physical sensation (conveyed by the terry cloth) more highly than those that provided food. It appears that the infant monkeys developed greater social attachments from their need for warmth, comfort, and intimacy than from their need for milk.

Although the isolation studies discussed above may seem to suggest that inheritance can be dismissed as a factor in the social development of humans and animals, studies of twins provide insight into a fascinating interplay between hereditary and environmental factors.

The Influence of Heredity

Oskar Stohr and Jack Yufe were identical twins who were separated soon after their birth and raised on different continents in very different cultural settings. Oskar was reared as a strict Catholic by his maternal grandmother in the Sudetenland of the former Czechoslovakia. As a member of the Hitler Youth movement in Nazi Germany, Oskar learned to hate Jews. By contrast, his brother Jack was reared in Trinidad by the twins' Jewish father. Jack joined an Israeli kibbutz (a collective settlement) at age 17 and later served in the Israeli army. But when they were reunited in middle age, some startling similarities emerged:

> Both were wearing wire-rimmed glasses and moustaches, both sported two pocket shirts with epaulets. They share idiosyncrasies galore: they like spicy foods and sweet liqueurs, are absent-minded, have a habit of falling asleep in front of the television, think it's funny to sneeze in a crowd of strangers, flush the toilet before using it, store rubber bands on their wrists, read magazines from back to front, dip buttered toast in their coffee. (Holden 1980)

The twins also were found to differ in many important respects: as adults, Jack was a workaholic; Oskar enjoyed leisure-time activities. Whereas Oskar was a traditionalist who was domineering toward women, Jack was a political liberal who was much more accepting of feminism. Finally, Jack was extremely proud of being Jewish, while Oskar never mentioned his Jewish heritage (Holden 1987).

Oskar and Jack are prime examples of the interplay of heredity and environment. For a number of years, researchers at the Minnesota Center for Twin and Adoption Research have been studying pairs of identical twins reared apart to determine what similarities, if any, they show in personality traits, behaviour, and intelligence. Thus far, the preliminary results from the available twin studies indicate that both genetic factors and socialization experiences are influential in human development. Certain characteristics, such as temperaments, voice patterns, and nervous habits, appear to be strikingly similar even in twins reared apart, suggesting that these qualities may be linked to hereditary causes. However, identical twins reared apart differ far more in their attitudes, values, types of mates chosen, and even drinking habits; these qualities, it would seem, are influenced by environmental patterns. In examining clusters of personality traits among such twins, the Minnesota studies have found marked similarities in their tendency toward leadership or dominance, but significant differences in their need for intimacy, comfort, and assistance.

Researchers have also been impressed with the similar scores on intelligence tests of twins reared apart in *roughly similar* social settings. Most of the identical twins register scores even closer than those that would be expected if the same person took a test twice. At the same time, however, identical twins brought up in *dramatically different* social environments score quite differently on intelligence tests—a finding that supports the impact of socialization on human development (McGue and Bouchard 1998).

We need to be cautious when reviewing the studies of twin pairs and other relevant research. Widely broadcast findings have often been based on extremely small samples and preliminary analyses. For example, one study (not involving twin pairs) was frequently cited as confirming genetic links with behaviour. Yet the researchers had to retract their conclusions after they increased the sample from 81 to 91 cases and reclassified 2 of the original 81 cases. After these changes, the initial findings were no longer valid. Critics add that the studies on twin pairs have not provided satisfactory information concerning the extent to which these separated identical twins may have had contact with each other, even though they were raised apart. Such interactions—especially if they were extensive—could call into question the validity of the twin studies (Kelsoe et al. 1989).

Psychologist Leon Kamin fears that overgeneralizing from the Minnesota Center's twin results—and granting too much importance to the impact of heredity—may

Two twins celebrate their special identity at the annual Twins Day Festival in Twinsburg, Ohio. Every year, social scientists descend on Twinsburg to study the 3000 pairs of twins who gather at the festival. Research points to some behavioural similarities between twins, but little beyond the likenesses found among non-twin siblings.

lead to blaming the poor and downtrodden for their unfortunate condition. As this debate continues, we can certainly anticipate numerous efforts to replicate the research and clarify the interplay between hereditary and environmental factors in human development (Horgan 1993; Leo 1987; Plomin 1989; Wallis 1987).

Sociobiology

Do the *social* traits that human groups display have biological origins? As part of the continuing debate on the relative influences of heredity and the environment, there has been renewed interest in sociobiology in recent years. **Sociobiology** is the systematic study of the biological bases of social behaviour. Sociobiologists basically apply naturalist Charles Darwin's principles of natural selection to the study of social behaviour. They assume that particular forms of behaviour become genetically linked to a species if they contribute to its fitness to survive (van den Berghe 1978). In its extreme form, sociobiology suggests that *all* behaviour is the result of genetic or biological factors and that social interactions play no role in shaping people's conduct.

Sociobiology does not seek to describe individual behaviour on the level of, "Why is Fred more aggressive than Jim?" Rather, sociobiologists focus on how human nature is affected by the genetic composition of a *group* of people who share certain characteristics (such as men or women, or members of isolated tribal bands). Many sociologists are highly critical of sociobiologists' tendency to explain, or seemingly justify, human behaviour on the basis of nature and ignore its cultural and social basis.

Some researchers insist that intellectual interest in sociobiology will merely deflect serious study of the more significant factor influencing human behaviour—socialization. Yet Lois Wladis Hoffman (1985), in her presidential address to the Society for the Psychological Study of Social Issues, argued that sociobiology poses a valuable challenge to social scientists to better document their own research. Interactionists, for example, could show how social behaviour is not programmed by human biology but instead adjusts continually to the attitudes and responses of others.

Conflict theorists (like functionalists and interactionists) believe that people's behaviour rather than their genetic structure defines social reality. Conflict theorists fear that the sociobiological approach could be used as an argument against efforts to assist disadvantaged people, such as schoolchildren who are not learning successfully (M. Harris 1997).

Edward O. Wilson, a zoologist at Harvard University, has argued that there should be parallel studies of human behaviour with a focus on both genetic and social causes. Certainly, most social scientists would agree that there is a biological basis for social behaviour. But there is less support for the most extreme positions taken by certain advocates of sociobiology (Begley 1998; Gove 1987; Wilson 1975, 1978; see also Guterman 2000; Segerstråle 2000).

☐ WHAT ARE SOME MAJOR THEORETICAL PERSPECTIVES ON SOCIALIZATION?

Social Psychological Perspectives

We all have various perceptions, feelings, and beliefs about who we are and what we are like. How do we come to develop these? Do they change as we age?

We were not born with these understandings. Building on the work of George Herbert Mead (1964b), sociologists recognize that we create our own designation: the self. The **self** is a distinct identity that sets us apart from others. It is not a static phenomenon but continues to develop and change throughout our lives.

Sociologists and psychologists alike have expressed interest in how the individual develops and modifies the sense of self as a result of social interaction. The work of sociologists Charles Horton Cooley and George Herbert Mead, contributors to the development of the interactionist approach (see Chapter 1, p. 15), has been especially useful in furthering our understanding of these important issues (Gecas 1982).

Cooley: Looking-Glass Self

In the early 1900s, Charles Horton Cooley advanced the belief that we learn who we are by interacting with others. Our view of ourselves, then, comes not only from direct contemplation of our personal qualities but also from our impressions of how others perceive us. Cooley used the phrase **looking-glass self** to emphasize that the self is the product of our social interactions with other people.

The process of developing a self-identity or self-concept has three phases: First, we imagine how we present ourselves to others—to relatives, friends, even strangers on the street. Second, we imagine how others evaluate us (attractive, intelligent, shy, or strange). Finally, we develop some sort of feeling about ourselves, such as respect or shame, as a result of these impressions (Cooley 1902; M. Howard 1989).

A subtle but critical aspect of Cooley's looking-glass self is that the self results from an individual's "imagination" of how others view him or her. As a result, we can develop self-identities based on *incorrect* perceptions of how others see us. A student may react strongly to a teacher's criticism and decide (wrongly) that the instructor views the student as stupid. This misperception can easily be converted into a negative self-identity through the following process: (1) *the teacher criticized me*, (2) *the teacher must think that I'm stupid*, (3) *I am stupid*. Yet self-identities are also subject to change. If the student receives an "A" at the end of the course, he or she will probably no longer feel stupid.

Mead: Stages of the Self

As we mentioned in Chapter 1, George Herbert Mead continued Cooley's work in social psychology, developing a useful model of the process by which the self emerges. His model was defined by three distinct stages: the *preparatory stage*, the *play stage*, and the *game stage*.

During the **preparatory stage**, children merely imitate the people around them, especially family members with whom they continually interact. Thus, a small child will bang on a piece of wood while a parent is engaged in carpentry work or will try to throw a ball if an older sibling is doing so nearby.

As they grow older, children become more adept at using symbols to communicate with others. **Symbols** are the gestures, objects, and language that form the basis of human communication. By interacting with relatives and friends, as well as by watching cartoons on television and looking at picture books, children in the preparatory stage begin to understand the use of symbols. Like spoken languages, symbols vary from culture to culture and even between subcultures. Raising an eyebrow may mean astonishment in North America, but in Peru it means "money" or "pay me," while in the Pacific island nation of Tonga it means "yes" or "I agree" (Axtell 1990).

Mead was among the first to analyze the relationship of symbols to socialization. As children develop skill in communicating through symbols, they gradually become more aware of social relationships. As a result, during the **play stage**, the child learns to pretend to be other people. Just as an actor "becomes" a character, a child becomes a doctor, parent, superhero, or ship captain.

Mead, in fact, noted that an important aspect of the play stage is role-playing. **Role taking** is the process of mentally assuming the perspective of another, thereby enabling the person to respond from that imagined viewpoint. For example, through this process, a young child will gradually learn when it is best to ask a parent for favours. If the parent usually comes home from work in a bad mood, the child will wait until after dinner when the parent is more relaxed and approachable.

In Mead's third stage, the **game stage**, the child of about 8 or 9 years old no longer just plays roles but begins to consider several actual tasks and relationships simultaneously. At this point in development, children grasp not only their own social positions but also those of others around them—just as in a hockey game the players must understand their own and everyone else's positions. Consider a girl or boy who is part of a scout troop out on a weekend hike in the mountains. The child

must understand what he or she is expected to do but also must recognize the responsibilities of other scouts as well as of the leaders. This is the final stage of development under Mead's model; the child can now respond to numerous members of the social environment.

Again as we discussed in Chapter 1, Mead uses the term *generalized other* (See p. 16) to refer to the attitudes, viewpoints, and expectations of society as a whole that a child takes into account.

At the game stage, children can take a more sophisticated view of people and the social environment. They now understand what specific occupations and social positions are and no longer equate Mr. Sahota only with the role of "librarian" or Ms. La Haigue only with "principal." It has become clear to the child that Mr. Sahota can be a librarian, a parent, and a marathon runner at the same time and that Ms. La Haigue is one of many principals in our society. Thus, the child has reached a new level of sophistication in his or her observations of individuals and institutions.

Use Your Sociological Imagination

How has the *generalized other* influenced the decisions you've made?

Goffman: Presentation of the Self

How do we manage our self? How do we display to others who we are? Erving Goffman, a sociologist associated with the interactionist perspective, suggested that many of our daily activities involve attempts to convey impressions of who we are.

Early in life, the individual learns to slant his or her presentation of the self in order to create distinctive appearances and satisfy particular audiences. Goffman (1959) refers to this altering of the presentation of the self as **impression management**. Box 4-1 provides an everyday example of this concept by describing how students engage in impression management after getting their examination grades.

In examining such everyday social interactions, Goffman makes so many explicit parallels to the theatre that his view has been termed the *dramaturgical approach* (see Chapter 1, p. 16). According to this perspective, people resemble performers in action. For example, a clerk may try to appear busier than he or she actually is if a supervisor happens to be watching. A customer in a singles' bar may try to look as if he or she is waiting for a particular person to arrive.

Goffman (1959) has also drawn attention to another aspect of the self: **face-work**. How often do you initiate some kind of face-saving behaviour when you feel embarrassed or rejected? In response to a rejection at the singles' bar, a person may engage in face-work by saying

Research in Action   4-1
Impression Management by Students after Exams

When you get an exam back, you probably react differently with fellow classmates, depending on the grades that you and they earned. This is all part of impression management, as sociologists Daniel Albas and Cheryl Albas (1988) demonstrated. They explored the strategies that postsecondary students use to create desired appearances after receiving their grades on exams. Albas and Albas divide these encounters into three categories: those between students who have all received high grades (Ace–Ace encounters), those between students who have received high grades and those who have received low or even failing grades (Ace–Bomber encounters), and those between students who have all received low grades (Bomber–Bomber encounters).

Ace–Ace encounters occur in a rather open atmosphere because there is comfort in sharing a high mark with another high achiever. It is even acceptable to violate the norm of modesty and brag when among other Aces since, as one student admitted, "It's much easier to admit a high mark to someone who has done better than you, or at least as well."

Ace–Bomber encounters are often sensitive. Bombers generally attempt to avoid such exchanges because "you . . . emerge looking like the dumb one" or "feel like you are lazy or unreliable." When forced into interactions with Aces, Bombers work to appear gracious and congratulatory. For their part, Aces offer sympathy and support for the dissatisfied Bombers and even rationalize their own "lucky" high scores. To help Bombers save

face, Aces may emphasize the difficulty and unfairness of the examination.

Bomber–Bomber encounters tend to be closed, reflecting the group effort to wall off the feared disdain of others. Yet, within the safety of these encounters, Bombers openly share their disappointment and engage in expressions of mutual self-pity that they themselves call "pity parties." They devise face-saving excuses for their poor performances, such as, "I wasn't feeling well all week" or "I had four exams and two papers due that week." If the grade distribution in a class included particularly low scores, Bombers may blame the instructor, who will be attacked as a sadist, a slave driver, or simply an incompetent.

As is evident from these descriptions, students' impression management strategies conform to society's informal norms regarding modesty and consideration for less successful peers. In classroom settings, as in the workplace and in other types of human interactions, efforts at impression management are most intense when status differentials are more pronounced, as in encounters between the high-scoring Aces and the low-scoring Bombers.

Applying Theory

1. What theoretical perspective would most likely be employed in the study of students' impression management strategies?
2. How do you think some feminist sociologists might approach the study of impression management on the part of their students?

Source: Albas and Albas 1988.

---

to a friend, "There really isn't an interesting person in this entire crowd." We feel the need to maintain a proper image of the self if we are to continue social interaction.

Goffman's approach is generally regarded as an insightful perspective on everyday life, but it is not without its critics. Writing from a conflict perspective, sociologist Alvin Gouldner (1970) sees Goffman's work as implicitly reaffirming the status quo, including social class inequalities. Using Gouldner's critique, we might ask whether women and members of minority groups are expected to deceive both themselves and others while paying homage to those with power. In considering impression management and other concepts developed by Goffman, sociologists must remember that by describing social reality, a person is not necessarily endorsing its harsh impact on many individuals and groups (S. Williams 1986).

Goffman's work represents a logical progression of the sociological efforts begun by Cooley and Mead on how personality is acquired through socialization and how we manage the presentation of our self to others. Cooley stressed the process by which we come to create a self; Mead focused on how the self develops as we learn to interact with others; Goffman emphasized the ways in which we consciously create images of ourselves for others.

Feminist Perspectives

Given the vast variety of feminist theories and the differences among them, it is not surprising that they do not all stress the importance of socialization as a key element in explaining the condition of women's lives. Some feminist theorists believe that what a society believes to be "masculine" and "feminine" is culturally imposed through systematic socialization of girls and boys, as well as women and men, according to sex. This systematic socialization takes place in the family, among peers, in the school, in the workplace, in religious organizations, and through the mass media. Liberal feminists are one such group of feminist theorists who stress the importance of avoiding this type of socialization in order to achieve equality of the sexes. Liberal feminists, who are sometimes called **equality feminists**, endorse individual freedom and equality of opportunity, which for them takes place in the public or economic sphere, not the private or domestic sphere.

Thus, according to liberal feminists, institutions that socialize children and adults according to a division of labour based on gender deprive girls and women of individual achievement, success, and freedom (as defined by the male-dominated public sphere).

Functionalist Perspectives

Functionalist perspectives stress the importance of consensus, stability, and equilibrium in society; therefore, socialization of society's members is essential to meet these goals (see Chapter 1, p. 12). Socialization, according to functionalists, serves to ensure that the members of a given society share or buy into the basic values of that society in order to promote consensus or agreement and stability. Without high levels of agreement on the core values of society, functionalists argue that the society will become destabilized and its survival may be threatened.

Since functionalist theorists maintain that a society is analogous to a human body in which the various organs—heart, lungs, kidney, liver, and so on—work as a system to maintain the health or balance of the entire body, so must the parts of society. Such institutions as the family, schools, the state, the mass media, the legal system, and religion must function as an integrated system in which each part contributes to the functioning of the others and to that of the whole society. Here, the function of the socialization of society's members concerning basic values and goals is key, as it provides cohesion and coordination among various institutions, creating equilibrium. For example, Canada's economy, and those of many other countries, is a capitalist one based on the value of competition and individual achievement. For it to function effectively and efficiently, workers must buy into the value, goal, and means of success as defined by the capitalist economy. Therefore, it becomes imperative, according to functionalists, that the family, for example, socialize its children according to the values of hard work, individual effort, and achievement; this socialization will ensure the provision of a workforce that is properly primed, ready to meet the challenges of a capitalist economy. Similarly, the education system must socialize its students with these values, as well as with the specific skills and training necessary to meet the demands of the economy.

Overall, functionalist perspectives stress the importance of maintaining the status quo. Socialization, therefore, is viewed as a way to ensure that a society's members share values, beliefs, and goals that contribute to the maintenance of society as a whole.

Conflict Perspectives

Like the functionalist theorists, conflict thinkers agree that the socialization of a society's members by the major institutions (e.g., the economy, the state, the mass media) contributes to the perpetuation of the status quo. For conflict thinkers, however, this is not viewed as desirable, given the inherent inequalities of the capitalist society.

Since the capitalist society is based on the unequal distribution of power and resources, conflict thinkers advocate that the messages communicated through various forms of socialization will reflect this inequity. Karl Marx, for example, believed that the dominant ideas of a society at any given point in history will be the ideas of the dominant ruling class. Marx argued that the economic base of society (i.e., capitalism) determined the nature of the other institutions, such as the family, the education system, and the mass media, causing them also to reflect the ideas of the ruling class. For example, the mass media has often been considered by conflict thinkers as the mouthpiece of the ruling class, socializing all members of society with values and goals that reflect the economic interests of the ruling class. In this way, socialization serves to ensure that the working classes continue to buy into an economic system based on the dominance and control of the ruling class. According to conflict thinkers Edward Herman and Noam Chomsky (1988), the mass media represent a propaganda model that acts to "manufacture consent" by "generating compliance" on the part of the mass population, which works for and consumes the products produced by the dominant ruling class.

Psychological Approaches

Psychologists have shared the interest of Cooley, Mead, and other sociologists in the development of the self. Early work in psychology, such as that of Sigmund Freud (1856–1939), stressed the role of inborn drives—among them the drive for sexual gratification—in channelling human behaviour. In more recent times, such psychologists as Jean Piaget have emphasized the stages through which human beings progress as the self develops.

Like Charles Horton Cooley and George Herbert Mead, Freud believed that the self is a social product and that aspects of personality are influenced by other people (especially parents). However, unlike Cooley and Mead, he suggested that the self has components that are always fighting with each other. According to Freud, our natural impulsive instincts such as sex and aggression—which he referred to as the *id*—are in constant conflict with societal constraints or the *superego*. The *ego*, according to Freud, is the part of the personality which mediates between the id and the superego. Both the ego and the superego are shaped through the process of socialization: "One of Freud's central theses is that society forces people to suppress basic human impulses such as sex and aggression, so that they must find expression in indirect and often distorted ways" (Collier, Minton, and Reynolds 1991:105).

Research on newborn babies by the Swiss child psychologist Jean Piaget (1896–1980) has underscored the importance of social interactions in developing a sense of self. Piaget found that newborns have no self in the sense of a looking-glass image. Ironically, though, they are quite self-centred; they demand that all attention be directed toward them. Newborns have not yet separated themselves from the universe of which they are a part. For these babies, the phrase "you and me" has no meaning; they understand only "me." However, as they mature, children are gradually socialized into social relationships even within their rather self-centred world.

In his well-known **cognitive theory of development**, Piaget (1954) identifies four stages in the development of children's thought processes. In the first, or **sensorimotor**, stage, young children use their senses to make discoveries. For example, through touching, they discover that their hands are actually a part of themselves. During the second, or **preoperational**, stage, children begin to use words and symbols to distinguish objects and ideas. The milestone in the third, or **concrete operational**, stage is that children engage in more logical thinking. They learn that even when a formless lump of clay is shaped into a snake, it is still the same clay. Finally, in the fourth, or **formal operational**, stage, adolescents are capable of sophisticated abstract thought and can deal with ideas and values in a logical manner.

Piaget has suggested that moral development becomes an important part of socialization as children develop the ability to think more abstractly. When children learn the rules of a game, such as checkers or jacks, they are learning to obey societal norms. Those under 8 years old display a basic level of morality: rules are rules, and there is no concept of "extenuating circumstances." However, as they mature, children become capable of greater autonomy and begin to experience moral dilemmas as to what constitutes proper behaviour.

According to Jean Piaget, social interaction is the key to development. As they grow older, children give increasing attention to how other people think and why they act in particular ways. To develop a distinct personality, each of us needs opportunities to interact with others. As we saw earlier, Isabelle was deprived of the chance for normal social interactions, and the consequences were severe (Kitchener 1991).

Table 4-1 shows a summary of the rich literature on the development of the self.

Table 4-1 Theoretical Approaches to Development of the Self

Scholar	Key Concepts and Contributions	Main Points of Theory
Sigmund Freud 1856–1939 psychotherapist (Austria)	Psychoanalysis	Self influenced by parents and by inborn drives, such as the drive for sexual gratification
George Herbert Mead 1863–1931 sociologist (U.S.A.)	The self Generalized other	Three distinct stages of development; self develops as children grasp the roles of others in their lives
Charles Horton Cooley 1864–1929 sociologist (U.S.A.)	Looking-glass self	Stages of development not distinct; feelings toward ourselves developed through interaction with others
Jean Piaget 1896–1980 child psychologist (Switzerland)	Cognitive theory of development	Four stages of cognitive development; moral development linked to socialization
Erving Goffman 1922–1982 sociologist (U.S.A.)	Impression management Dramaturgical approach Face-work	Self developed through the impressions we convey to others and to groups

☐ WHAT ARE SOME AGENTS OF SOCIALIZATION?

The continuing and lifelong socialization process involves many different social forces that influence our lives and alter our self-image.

The family is the most important agent of socialization in Canada, especially for children. But we also want to give particular attention in this chapter to five other agents of socialization: the school, the peer group, the mass media, the workplace, and the state. The role of religion in socializing young people into society's norms and values will be explored in Chapter 13.

Family

Children in Amish communities are raised in a highly structured and disciplined manner. But they are not immune to the temptations posed by their peers in the non-Amish world—"rebellious" acts such as dancing, drinking, and riding in cars. Still, Amish families don't get too concerned; they know the strong influence they ultimately exert over their offspring (see Box 4-2 on page 81). The same is true for the family in general. It is tempting to say that the peer group or even the media really raise kids these days, especially when the spotlight falls on young people involved in shooting sprees and hate crimes. Almost all available research, however, shows that the role of the family in socializing a child cannot be underestimated (W. Williams 1998; for a different view, see J. Harris 1998).

The lifelong process of learning begins shortly after birth. Since newborns can hear, see, smell, taste, and feel heat, cold, and pain, they are constantly orienting themselves to the surrounding world. Human beings, especially family members, constitute an important part of their social environment. People minister to the baby's needs by feeding, cleansing, carrying, and comforting the baby.

The caretakers of a newborn are not concerned with teaching social skills per se. Nevertheless, babies are hardly asocial. An infant enters an organized society, becomes part of a generation, and typically joins a family. Depending on how they are treated, infants can develop strong social attachments and dependency on others.

Most infants go through a relatively formal period of socialization generally called **habit training**. Caregivers impose schedules for eating and sleeping, for terminating breast- or bottle-feeding, and for introducing new foods. In these and other ways, infants can be viewed as objects of socialization. Yet they also function as socializers. Even as the behaviour of a baby is being modified by interactions with people and the environment, the baby

is causing others to change their behaviour patterns. He or she converts adults into mothers and fathers, who, in turn, assist the baby in progressing into childhood (Rheingold 1969).

As both Charles Horton Cooley and George Herbert Mead noted, the development of the self is a critical aspect of the early years of life. But how children develop this sense of self can vary from one society to another. For example, many parents in Canada would never think of sending 6-year-olds to school unsupervised. But this is the norm in Japan, where parents push their children to commute to school on their own from an early age. In cities like Tokyo, first-graders must learn to negotiate buses, subways, and long walks. To ensure their safety, parents carefully lay out rules: never talk to strangers; check with a station attendant if you get off at the wrong stop; if you miss your stop, stay on to the end of the line, then call; take stairs, not escalators; don't fall asleep. Some parents equip the children with cellphones or pagers. One parent acknowledges that she worries, "but after they are 6, children are supposed to start being independent from the mother. If you're still taking your child to school after the first month, everyone looks at you funny" (Tolbert 2000:17).

In Canada, social development includes exposure to cultural assumptions regarding gender, class, and race. Augie Fleras and Jean Kunz (2001) argue that the news media tend to undermine the contributions of minority groups in Canadian society, emphasizing "their status as athletes, entertainers, or criminals, while the occasional fawning reference to minorities in [a] position of political or economic power represents an exception that simply proves the rule" (Fleras and Kunz 2001:83). Since children are watching television at an increasingly younger age, they are, more and more, susceptible to absorbing the images packaged for and by the dominant culture.

Family and Gender Socialization

Have you ever noticed when parents mention their newborn babies, they may describe their daughters as "pretty," "sweet," or "angelic" and their sons as "tough," "rugged," or "strong"? Although newborn babies look much the same regardless of sex (with one noticeable exception), parents often apply cultural and social assumptions about femininity and masculinity to their children from the moment of birth. With the development of technologies, such as ultrasound and amniocentesis, that can reveal the sex of the fetus, parents may well begin to apply these assumptions before birth. This pattern begins a lifelong process of **gender socialization**—an aspect of socialization through which we learn the attitudes, behaviours, and practices associated with being male or female (called **gender roles**) according to our society and social groups within it. Our society (and various social groups,

Sociology in the Global Community

Raising Amish Children

4-2

Jacob is a typical teenager in his Amish community near Aylmer, Ontario. At 14, he is in his final year of schooling. Over the next few years, he will become a full-time worker on the family farm, taking breaks only for a three-hour religious service each morning. When he is a bit older, Jacob may bring a date in his family's horse-drawn buggy to a community "singing." But he will be forbidden to date outside his own community and can marry only with the deacon's consent. Jacob is well aware of the starkly different way of life of non-Amish people who live close to him. One summer, he and his friends hitchhiked late at night to a nearby town to see a movie, breaking several Amish taboos. Jacob's parents learned of his adventure, but, like most Amish, they are confident that their son will choose the Amish way of life. What is this way of life and how can the parents be so sure of its appeal?

Jacob and his family live in a manner very similar to that of their ancestors, members of the conservative Mennonite church who migrated to North America from Europe in the eighteenth and nineteenth centuries. Schisms in the church after 1850 led to a division between those who wanted to preserve the "old order" and those who favoured a "new order" with more progressive methods and organization. Today, the old-order Amish live in about 50 communities in Canada (primarily southern Ontario) and the United States. Estimates put their number at about 80 000 with approximately 75 percent living in three American states—Ohio, Pennsylvania, and Indiana.

The old-order Amish live a "simple" life and reject most aspects of modernization and contemporary technology. That's why they spurn such conveniences as electricity, automobiles, radio, and television. The Amish maintain their own schools and traditions, and they do not want their children socialized into many norms and values of the dominant cultures of the United States and Canada. Those who stray too far from Amish mores may

be excommunicated and shunned by all other members of the community—a practice of social control called *Meiding*. Sociologists sometimes use the term "secessionist minorities" to refer to groups like the Amish and the Hutterites of Western Canada and the United States, who reject assimilation and coexist with the rest of society primarily on their own terms.

Life for Amish youth attracts particular attention since their socialization pushes them to forgo movies, radio, television, cosmetics, jewellery, musical instruments of any kind, and motorized vehicles. Yet, as Jacob did, Amish youth often test their subculture's boundaries during a period of discovery called *rumspringe*, a term that literally means "running around." Amish young people attend barn dances where taboos like drinking, smoking, and driving cars are commonly broken. Parents often react by looking the other way, sometimes literally. For example, when they hear radio sounds from a barn or a motorcycle entering the property in the middle of the night, often, they don't immediately investigate and punish their offspring. Instead, parents will pretend not to notice, secure in the comfort that their children almost always return to the traditions of the Amish lifestyle. Research shows that only about 20 percent of Amish youth leave the fold, generally to join a more liberal Mennonite group; and rarely does a baptized adult ever leave. The socialization of Amish youth moves them gently but firmly into becoming Amish adults.

Applying Theory

1. What makes Amish parents so sure that their children will choose to remain in the Amish community? How does the growing presence of technology make this more difficult?

2. If you lived in an Amish community, how would your life differ from the way it is now? In your opinion, what advantages and disadvantages would that way of life have?

Source: Meyers 1992; Remnick 1998; Zellner 2001.

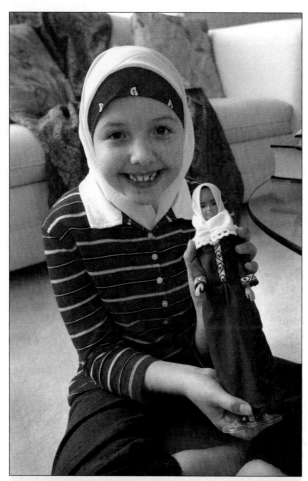

A young girl displays Razanne, a modestly dressed doll made especially for Muslim children. Because children learn about themselves and their social roles by playing with toys such as dolls, having a doll that represents their own heritage is important to them.

such as social classes and ethnic groups) produces ideals and expectations about gender roles, reinforcing these ideals and expectations at each stage of the life course. As we will see in Chapter 11, other cultures do not necessarily assign these qualities to each gender in the way that our culture does.

As the primary agents of childhood socialization, parents play a critical role in guiding children into those gender roles deemed appropriate in a society. Other adults, older siblings, the mass media, and religious and educational institutions also have a noticeable impact on a child's socialization into feminine and masculine norms. A culture or subculture may require that one sex or the other take primary responsibility for socialization of children, economic support of the family, or religious or intellectual leadership.

Social class may also play a role in gender socialization. Members of certain social classes may be more or less likely to engage in socialization patterns geared to traditional gender roles. Tuck et al. (1994), for example, studied gender socialization in middle-class homes with career-oriented mothers. They found these homes to be less stereotypical in terms of behaviour expectations than working-class homes. Other studies have found that working-class homes are more likely to conform to traditional or stereotypical notions of masculinity and femininity and socialize their children accordingly (A. Nelson and Robinson 2002). Daughters in a working-class family might, for example, be called on more often to help with domestic chores, such as cooking or attending to the needs of younger siblings. Sons might not be expected to help out with chores or younger children and instead might be encouraged to pursue independent activities outside the home.

Some feminists support the view that the socio-economic situation of a child's family, commingled with that child's gender, sexual orientation, race, and ethnicity, produce nongeneralizable experiences in which family contributes to the child's overall situation.

The differential gender roles absorbed in early childhood often help define a child's popularity later on. A qualitative study on norms surrounding beauty and thinness for adolescent girls found that girls who were successful with a peer group were more likely to judge themselves by the appearance norms of the group (Matthews 2000).

Like other elements of culture, socialization patterns are not fixed. The last 30 years, for example, have witnessed a sustained challenge to traditional gender-role socialization in North America, in good part because of the efforts of the feminist movement (see Chapter 11). Nevertheless, despite such changes, children growing up today are hardly free of traditional gender roles.

Interactionists remind us that socialization concerning not only masculinity and femininity but also marriage and parenthood begins in childhood as a part of family life. Children observe their parents as they express affection, deal with finances, quarrel, complain about in-laws, and so forth. This represents an informal process of anticipatory socialization. The child develops a tentative model of what being married and being a parent are like. (We will explore socialization for marriage and parenthood more fully in Chapter 12.)

School

Where did you learn the national anthem? Who taught you about the early Canadian explorers? Where were you first tested on your knowledge of your culture? Like the family, schools have an explicit mandate to socialize people in Canada—and especially children—into the norms and values of the dominant culture.

As conflict theorists Samuel Bowles and Herbert Gintis (1976) have observed, schools foster competition through built-in systems of reward and punishment, such as grades and evaluations by teachers. Consequently, a child who is working intently to learn a new skill can sometimes come to feel stupid and unsuccessful. However, as the self matures, children become capable of increasingly realistic assessments of their intellectual, physical, and social abilities.

Functionalists point out that, as agents of socialization, schools fulfil the function of teaching children the values and customs of the larger society. Conflict theorists agree but add that schools can reinforce the divisive aspects of society, especially those of social class. For example, higher education in Canada is quite costly despite the existence of student-aid programs. Students from affluent backgrounds have an advantage in gaining access to universities and professional training. At the same time, less affluent young people may never receive the preparation that would qualify them for the best-paying and most prestigious jobs. Moreover, conflict sociologists argue that schools tend to socialize students to emulate the dominant values of society, in preparation for them to assume their places as workers in an appropriate social class. According to conflict sociologists, students are socialized by the school system to value hard work and effort, based on the belief that the most deserving students will invariably rise to the top positions. The contrast between the functionalist and conflict views of education will be discussed in more detail in Chapter 13.

In other cultures as well, schools serve socialization functions. During the 1980s, for example, Japanese parents and educators were distressed to realize that children were gradually losing the knack of eating with chopsticks. This became a national issue in 1997 when school lunch programs introduced plastic "sporks" (combined fork and spoon). National leaders, responding to the public outcry, banished sporks in favour of *hashi* (chopsticks). On a more serious note, Japanese schools came under increasing pressure in recent years as working parents abdicated more and more responsibility to educational institutions. To rectify the imbalance, the Japanese government in 1998 promoted a guide to better parenting, calling on parents to read more with their children, allow for more playtime, limit TV watching, and plan family activities, among other things (Gauette 1998).

School and Gender Socialization

In teaching students the values and customs of the larger society, schools in Canada have traditionally socialized children into conventional gender roles. Professors of education Myra Sadker and David Sadker (1985:54, 1995)

note that "although many believe that classroom sexism disappeared in the early '70s, it hasn't."

Sadker and Sadker's research points to a gender bias in terms of the time, effort, and attention that is given to boys in the classroom, as opposed to that given to girls. For example, boys were called on more frequently by teachers to answer questions and, even when they were not directly asked to participate, boys tended to call out in class (Sadker and Sadker 1994). A study carried out by researchers from Memorial University in Newfoundland and Labrador found that high school teachers—in their classrooms—had a tendency to interact more with their male students than with their female students (Duffy, Warren and Walsh 2001).

Despite the apparent gender bias that exists in classroom participation, educators in Canada are becoming concerned that boys are lagging behind girls in academic achievement, as demonstrated by girls' overrepresentation on the high school honour rolls in Ontario and British Columbia (Galt 1998). Patricia Clarke, former president of the B.C. Teachers' Federation, suggests that boys are immersed in a gender-specific culture that undervalues academic achievement and that greater attention needs to be paid to dispelling the myth that "the coolest thing to do is be stupid" (T. Holmes 2000:11). Similar gender gaps in academic performance are being experienced in other countries, such as Britain, where girls are also academically outperforming their male classmates (Galt 1998).

Peer Group

Ask 13-year-olds who matters most in their lives and they are likely to answer "friends." As a child grows older, the family becomes somewhat less important in social development. Instead, peer groups increasingly assume the role of Mead's significant others. Within the peer group, young people associate with others who are approximately their own age and who often enjoy a similar social status.

Peer groups can ease the transition to adult responsibilities. At home, parents tend to dominate; at school, the teenager must contend with teachers and administrators. But within the peer group, each member can assert himself or herself in a way that may not be possible elsewhere. Nevertheless, almost all adolescents in our culture remain economically dependent on their parents, and most are emotionally dependent as well.

Teenagers imitate their friends in part because the peer group maintains a meaningful system of rewards and punishments. The group may encourage a young person to follow pursuits that society considers admirable, as in a school club engaged in volunteer work in hospitals and nursing homes. However, the group may encourage someone to violate the culture's norms and values by driving recklessly, shoplifting, engaging in acts of vandalism, taking drugs, and the like.

Peers can be the source of harassment as well as support. This problem has received considerable attention in Japan, where bullying in school is a constant fact of life. Groups of students act together to humiliate, disgrace, or torment a specific student, a practice known in Japan as *ijime*. Most students go along with the bullying out of fear that they might be the target some time. In some cases, the *ijime* has led to a child's suicide. In 1998, the situation became so desperate that a volunteer association set up a 24-hour telephone hotline in Tokyo just for children. The success of this effort convinced the government to sponsor a nationwide hotline system (Matsushita 1999; Sugimoto 1997).

Peer Group and Gender Socialization

A study done in British Columbia schools points to the prevalence of bullying and some of the gender-related patterns of the activity. Approximately 10 percent to 15 percent of British Columbia students are bullies, while approximately 8 percent to 10 percent are victims (*Vancouver Sun* 2000). Researchers Debra Pepler of York University and Wendy Craig of Queen's University found that girls do more of the verbal and social bullying while boys' bullying behaviour tends to be more physical. Girls bullied boys approximately half the time, while boys primarily bullied other boys. Bullies of both sexes tended to be perceived as popular and powerful by their peer groups while victims were perceived as lacking humour, having a tendency to cry easily, and deserving to be picked on. Pepler and Craig's research also showed that families of bullies tend to be permissive and display more positive attitudes toward aggression and that other students who have not yet been victimized may want to align with bullies to avoid possible bullying in the future.

Gender differences are noteworthy in the social world of adolescents. Males are more likely to spend time in groups of males, while females are more likely to interact with a *single* other female. This pattern reflects differences in levels of emotional intimacy; teenage males are less likely to develop strong emotional ties than are females. Instead, males are more inclined to share in group activities. These patterns are evident among adolescents in many societies around the world (Dornbusch 1989).

Mass Media and Technology

In the last 75 years, media innovations—radio, motion pictures, television, downloadable music, the Internet, and cellphones—have become important agents of socialization. Television, in particular, is a critical force in the socialization of children in North America. In Canada, for example, virtually all households own at least one television set (Canadian Media Research 2006). In addition, in 2005, an estimated 87 percent of Canadians lived in households with cable or satellite TV service (Canadian Media Research 2006); during the same year, 61 percent of Canadian households were connected to the Internet (Statistics Canada, 2006a).

According to Statistics Canada, Canadians watched an average of 21.4 hours of television per week during the fall of 2004 (the survey period). Women who were 60 years and older were the heaviest viewers (35.6 hours per week), while children aged 2 to 11 viewed an average of 14.1 hours per week and teens aged 12 to 17 viewed an average of 12.9 hours per week (2006h). A Canadian feminist organization called MediaWatch was established in 1981 to identify and monitor trends in the mass media (particularly in advertising) as they relate to the portrayal of women. Table 4-2 shows some of the ways the mass media present a distorted view of women.

Television has certain characteristics that distinguish it from other agents of socialization. It permits imitation and role-playing but does not encourage more complex forms of learning. Watching television is, above all, a passive

Table 4-2 Distorted Viewing: The Mass Media's Treatment of Women	
Objectification	Portraying women as objects that can be manipulated, bought, and sold
Irrelevant sexualization	Portraying women's bodies in a sexual way in order to attract attention and perpetuate the attitude that women's primary role is to attract male attention
Infantilization	Presenting women as childlike, coy, silly, and powerless
Domestication	Defining women in relation to their children, husbands, and family in a domestic environment
Victimization	Portraying women as victims of male brutality, inside and outside their homes

Source: Based on Graydon 2001.

experience; we sit back and wait to be entertained. Critics of television are further alarmed by the programming that children view as they sit for hours in front of a television set. It is generally agreed that children (as well as adults) are exposed to a great deal of violence on television. Despite much attention paid to the issue, a 1998 study showed that the situation had not changed over the previous two years. Of particular concern was the fact that 40 percent of violent incidents on television were initiated by "good" characters, who were likely to be perceived as positive role models (J. Federman 1998; L. Mifflin 1999).

Although we have focused on television as an agent of socialization, it is important to note that similar issues have been raised regarding the content of popular music (especially rock music and rap), music videos, motion pictures, video games, and various kinds of Internet Web sites. These forms of entertainment, like television, serve as powerful agents of socialization for many young people around the globe. For many years, controversies have raged over the content of music, music videos, and films—this has sometimes led to celebrated court battles, as certain parents' organizations and religious groups have challenged the intrusion of these media into the lives of children and adolescents. In recent years, people have expressed concern about the type of material that children can access on the Internet, especially pornography.

Finally, sociologists and other social scientists have begun to consider the impact of technology on socialization, especially as it applies to family life. The Silicon Valley Cultures Project studied families in California's Silicon Valley (a technological corridor) for ten years beginning in 1991. Although these families may not have been typical, they probably represented a lifestyle that more and more households will approximate. This study found that technology in the form of email, Web pages, cellular phones, voice mail, digital organizers, and pagers has allowed householders to let outsiders do everything from grocery shopping to soccer pools. Researchers also found that families were socialized into multi-tasking (doing more than one task at a time) as the social norm; devoting our full attention to one task—even eating or driving—is less and less common on a typical day (Silicon Valley Cultures Project 1999).

Workplace

Learning to behave appropriately within an occupation is a fundamental aspect of human socialization. In North America, working full-time confirms adult status; it is an indication to all that a person has passed out of adolescence. In a sense, socialization into an occupation can represent both a harsh reality ("I have to work in order to buy food and pay the rent") and the realization of an ambition ("I've always wanted to be an airline pilot") (W. Moore 1968:862).

Some observers feel that the increasing number of teenagers who are working earlier in life and for longer hours are now finding the workplace almost as important an agent of socialization as is school. In fact, a number of educators complain that student time at work is adversely affecting schoolwork. Will Boyce, a professor of education at Queen's University, found that the number of working high school students in Ontario is increasing (Philip 2001). Boyce discovered that 46.3 percent of high school students in the province were working, while, in 1996, the number was 31 percent. Researchers are trying to gauge the impact of employment on students' lives and have found that those students who work fewer than 20 hours per week often do better academically and are more involved in hobbies and sports than those students without jobs (Philip 2001). A more recent study conducted by Statistics Canada showed that Canadian young people, aged 15 to 19, ranked first among 10 industrialized countries—Belgium, United States, Australia, Netherlands, United Kingdom, France, Norway, Germany, and Finland—in terms of

This young woman's day doesn't end when school lets out. Because so many teenagers have jobs after school, the workplace has become another important agent of socialization for that age group.

hours spent on paid and unpaid work in 2005 (Statistics Canada 2007o). Averaged over a full week (school and non-school days), Canadians aged 15 to 19 performed 7.1 hours of labour per week in 2005.

Socialization in the workplace changes when it involves a more permanent shift from an after-school job to full-time employment. Wilbert Moore (1968:871–880) has divided occupational socialization into four phases. The first phase is **career choice**, which involves selection of academic or vocational training appropriate for the desired job. The second phase, **anticipatory socialization**, may last only a few months or may extend for a period of years. In a sense, young people experience anticipatory socialization through-out childhood and adolescence as they observe their parents at work.

The third phase of occupational socialization—conditioning and commitment—occurs in the work-related role. **Conditioning** consists of reluctantly adjust-ing to the more unpleasant aspects of one's job. Most people find that the novelty of a new daily schedule quickly wears off and then realize that parts of the work experience are rather tedious. **Commitment** refers to the enthusiastic acceptance of pleasurable duties that comes with recognition of the positive tasks of an occupation.

In Moore's view, if a job proves to be satisfactory, the person will enter a fourth stage of socialization, which Moore calls continuous commitment. At this point, the job becomes an indistinguishable part of the person's self-identity. Violation of proper conduct becomes unthinkable. A person may choose to join professional associations, unions, or other groups that represent the occupation in the larger society.

Occupational socialization can be most intense dur-ing the transition from school to job, but it continues through a person's work history. Technological advances may alter the requirements of the position and neces-sitate some degree of resocialization. Many men and women today change occupations, employers, or places of work many times during their adult years. Therefore, occupational socialization continues throughout a per-son's years in the labour market.

The State

Social scientists have increasingly recognized the impor-tance of the state as an agent of socialization because of its growing impact on the life course. Traditionally, family members have served as the primary caregivers in our culture, but in the twenty-first century, the family's protective function has steadily been transferred to out-side agencies, such as hospitals, mental health clinics, and insurance companies. The state runs many of these agencies or licenses and regulates them.

In the past, heads of households and local groups, such as religious organizations, influenced the life course most significantly. However, today national interests are increasingly influencing the individual as a citizen and an economic actor. For example, labour unions and political parties serve as intermediaries between the individual and the state.

The state has had a noteworthy impact on the life course by reinstituting the rites of passage that had dis-appeared in agricultural societies and in periods of early industrialization. For example, government regulations stipulate the ages at which a person may drive a car, drink alcohol, vote in elections, marry without parental permis-sion, work overtime, and retire. These regulations do not constitute strict rites of passage: most 18-year-olds choose not to vote, and most people choose their age of retire-ment without reference to government dictates. Still, the state shapes the socialization process by regulating the life course to some degree and by influencing our views of appropriate behaviour at particular ages (Mayer and Schoepflin 1989).

In the social policy section that appears at the end of this chapter, we will see that the state is under pressure to become a provider of child care, which would give it a new and direct role in the socialization of infants and young children.

☐ HOW DOES SOCIALIZATION OCCUR THROUGHOUT THE LIFE COURSE?

The Life Course

Adolescents among the Kota people of the Congo in Africa paint themselves blue, Mexican American girls go on a daylong religious retreat before dancing the night away, Egyptian mothers step over their newborn infants seven times, and graduating North American students may throw hats in the air. These are all ways of celebrating **rites of passage**, a means of dramatizing and validating changes in a person's status. The Kota rite marks the pas-sage to adulthood. The colour blue, viewed as the colour of death, symbolizes the death of childhood. Hispanic girls in the United States celebrate reaching woman-hood with a *quinceañera* ceremony at age 15. In Miami, Florida, the popularity of the *quinceañera* supports a network of party planners, caterers, dress designers, and the Miss Quinceañera Latina pageant. For thousands of years, Egyptian mothers have welcomed their newborns to the world in the Soboa ceremony by stepping over the seven-day-old infant seven times. North American graduates may celebrate their graduation from college or university by hurling their caps skyward (D. Cohen 1991; Garza 1993; McLane 1995; Quadagno 1999).

These specific ceremonies mark stages of development in the life course. They indicate that the socialization process continues throughout all stages of the human life cycle. Sociologists and other social scientists use the life-course approach in recognition that biological changes mould but do not dictate human behaviour from birth until death.

Within the cultural diversity of Canada, each individual has a "personal biography" that is influenced by events both in the family and in the larger society. Although the completion of religious confirmations, school graduations, marriage, and parenthood can all be regarded as rites of passage in our society, people do not necessarily experience them at the same time. The timing of these events depends on such factors as gender, economic background, region (urban or rural area), and even when a person was born.

Sociologists and other social scientists have moved away from identifying specific life stages that we are all expected to pass through at some point. Indeed, people today are much less likely to follow an "orderly" progression of life events (leaving school, then obtaining their first job, then getting married) than they were in the past. For example, an increasing number of women in Canada are beginning or returning to postsecondary education after marrying and having children. With such changes in mind, researchers are increasingly reluctant to offer sweeping generalizations about stages in the life course.

We encounter some of the most difficult socialization challenges (and rites of passage) in the later years of life. Assessing our accomplishments, coping with declining physical abilities, experiencing retirement, and facing the inevitability of death may lead to painful adjustments. Old age is further complicated by the negative way that many societies view and treat the elderly. The common stereotypes of the elderly as helpless and dependent may well weaken an older person's self-image. However, as we will explore more fully in the next section, many older people continue to lead active, productive, fulfilled lives—whether within the paid labour force or as retirees.

Use Your Sociological Imagination

What was the last rite of passage you participated in? Was it formal or informal?

Aging and Society

Aging is one important aspect of socialization—the life-long process through which an individual learns the cultural norms and values of a particular society. There are no clear-cut definitions for different periods of the aging cycle in Canada. *Old age* has typically been regarded as beginning at 65, which corresponds to the retirement age for many workers, but not everyone in our society accepts this definition. With life expectancy being extended, writers are beginning to refer to people in their 60s as the "young old" to distinguish them from those in their 80s and beyond (the "old old").

The particular problems of the elderly have become the focus for a specialized area of research and inquiry known as gerontology. **Gerontology** is the scientific study of the sociological and psychological aspects of aging and the problems of the aged. It originally developed in the 1930s, as an increasing number of social scientists became aware of the plight of the elderly.

Gerontologists rely heavily on sociological principles and theories

In Korea, certain birthdays are celebrated as milestones, complete with formal feasts. At a 60th birthday, for example, all the younger family members bow before the fortunate elder one by one, in order of their ages, and offer gifts. Later, they compete with one another in composing poetry and singing songs to mark the occasion. Unfortunately, not all older people are so lucky; in many other cultures, being old is considered next to being dead.

to explain the impact of aging on the individual and society. They also draw on the disciplines of psychology, anthropology, physical education, counselling, and medicine in their study of the aging process. Two influential views of aging—disengagement theory and activity theory—can be best understood in terms of the sociological perspectives of functionalism and interactionism, respectively. The conflict and feminist perspectives also contribute to our sociological understanding of aging.

Functionalist Approach: Disengagement Theory

Elaine Cumming and William Henry (1961) introduced **disengagement theory** to explain the impact of aging during the life course. This theory, based on a study of elderly people in good health and relatively comfortable economic circumstances, contends that society and the aging individual mutually sever many of their relationships. In keeping with the functionalist perspective, disengagement theory emphasizes that passing social roles on from one generation to another ensures social stability.

According to this theory, the approach of death forces people to drop most of their social roles—including those of worker, volunteer, spouse, hobby enthusiast, and even reader. Younger members of society then take on these functions. The aging person, it is held, withdraws into an increasing state of inactivity while preparing for death. At the same time, society withdraws from the elderly by segregating them residentially (retirement homes and communities), educationally (programs designed solely for senior citizens), and recreationally (senior citizens' social centres). Implicit in disengagement theory is the view that society should *help* older people to withdraw from their accustomed social roles.

Since it was first outlined more than three decades ago, disengagement theory has generated considerable controversy. Some gerontologists have objected to the implication that older people want to be ignored and "put away"—and even more to the idea that they should be encouraged to withdraw from meaningful social roles. Critics of disengagement theory insist that society *forces* the elderly into an involuntary and painful withdrawal from the paid labour force and from meaningful social relationships. Rather than voluntarily seeking to disengage, older employees find themselves pushed out of their jobs—in many instances, even before they are entitled to maximum retirement benefits (Boaz 1987).

Although functionalist in its approach, disengagement theory ignores the fact that post-retirement employment has been *increasing* in recent decades. Some employees move into a "bridge job"—employment that bridges the period between the end of a person's career and his or her retire-

ment. Unfortunately, the elderly can easily be victimized in such "bridge jobs." Psychologist Kathleen Christensen (1990), warning of "bridges over troubled water," emphasizes that older employees do not want to end their working days as minimum-wage job holders engaged in activities unrelated to their career jobs (Doeringer 1990; Hayward, Grady, and McLaughlin 1987).

Interactionist Approach: Activity Theory

Often seen as an opposing approach to disengagement theory, **activity theory** argues that the elderly person who remains active and socially involved will be best adjusted. Proponents of this perspective acknowledge that a 70-year-old person may not have the ability or desire to perform the various social roles that he or she had at age 40. Yet they contend that old people have essentially the same need for social interaction as any other group.

The improved health of older people—sometimes overlooked by social scientists—has strengthened the arguments of activity theorists. Illness and chronic disease are no longer quite the scourge of the elderly that they once were (see Box 4-3 on page 90). The recent emphasis on fitness, the availability of better medical care, greater control of infectious diseases, and the reduction of fatal strokes and heart attacks have combined to mitigate the traumas of growing old. Accumulating medical research also points to the importance of remaining socially involved. Among those who decline in their mental capacities later in life, deterioration is most rapid in older people who withdraw from social relationships and activities (Liao et al. 2000; National Institute on Aging 1999).

The Raging Grannies—shown here protesting on the steps of Parliament Hill in Ottawa—counteract the stereotype of older women being passive and politically inactive.

Admittedly, many activities open to the elderly involve unpaid labour, for which younger adults may receive salaries. Such unpaid workers include hospital volunteers (versus aides and orderlies), drivers for charitable organizations (versus chauffeurs), tutors (as opposed to teachers), and craftspeople for charity bazaars (as opposed to carpenters and dressmakers). However, some companies have initiated programs to hire retirees for full-time or part-time work. For example, about 130 of the 600 reservationists at the Days Inn motel chain are over 60 years of age.

Disengagement theory suggests that older people find satisfaction in withdrawal from society. Functionally speaking, they conveniently recede into the background and allow the next generation to take over. Proponents of activity theory view such withdrawal as harmful for both the elderly and society; they focus on the potential contributions of older people to the maintenance of society. In their opinion, aging citizens will feel satisfied only when they can be useful and productive in society's terms—primarily by working for wages (Civic Ventures 1999; Dowd 1980; Quadagno 1999).

The Conflict Approach

Conflict theorists have criticized both disengagement theory and activity theory for failing to consider the impact of social structure on patterns of aging. Neither approach, they say, attempts to question why social interaction "must" change or decrease in old age. In addition, these perspectives, in contrast to the conflict perspective, often ignore the impact of social class on the lives of the elderly.

The privileged position of the upper class generally leads to better health and vigour and to a lower likelihood of dependency in old age. Affluence cannot forestall aging indefinitely, but it can soften the economic hardships faced in later years. Although pension plans, retirement packages, and insurance benefits may be developed to assist older people, those whose wealth allows them access to investment funds can generate the greatest income for their later years.

By contrast, working-class jobs often carry greater hazards to health and a greater risk of disability; aging will be particularly difficult for those who suffer job-related injuries or illnesses. Working-class people also depend more heavily on government and private pension programs. During inflationary times, their relatively fixed incomes from these sources barely keep pace with escalating costs of food, housing, utilities, and other necessities (Atchley 1985).

Conflict theorists have noted that the transition from agricultural economies to industrialization and capitalism has not always been beneficial for the elderly. As a society's production methods change, the traditionally valued role of older people within the economy tends to erode. Their wisdom is no longer relevant.

According to the conflict approach, the treatment of older people in Canada reflects the many divisions in our society. The low status of older people is seen in prejudice and discrimination against them, age segregation, and unfair job practices—none of which is directly addressed by either disengagement or activity theory.

Feminist Approaches

Feminist frameworks view aging in women from a variety of perspectives. However, feminist researchers have frequently challenged two biases in the study of women's aging: (1) an androcentricity in the discussion of the life course (assuming that generalizations on the male life course can be applied to women) and (2) a lack of diversity in identifying the stages and central issues that mark women's lives (C. Jones, Marsden, and Tepperman 1990). In sociological research in previous decades, women's aging was seen almost exclusively in the context of marriage and family development (A. Nelson and Robinson 1999). This perspective, to a large degree, implies women's biological determinism; that is, that their life course is largely shaped by reproduction and nurturing of children. Moreover, studies on family life often contain an *ageist* bias: they adopt the perspective of middle-aged adults while regarding the aged as passive members of families (Eichler 2001). This bias also results in a failure to recognize that aging family members, particularly women, not only receive care but also give care to the younger members. Thus, they are not solely dependent but are interdependent members of the family (Connidis 1989).

Perhaps most importantly, feminist perspectives have drawn attention to how aging affects women of diverse backgrounds and characteristics. Aging does not manifest itself in all women in a universal, uniform manner, but rather intersects with class, race and ethnicity, and sexual orientation to produce diverse patterns and conditions.

The four perspectives considered here take different views of the elderly. Functionalists portray them as socially isolated with reduced social roles; interactionists see older people as involved in new networks of people in a change of social roles; conflict theorists regard older people as victimized by social structure, with their social roles relatively unchanged but devalued; and feminist perspectives have challenged the androcentricity and biological determinism implicit in many explanations of women's aging. Feminist perspectives also draw attention

Sociology in the Global Community
Aging Worldwide: Issues and Consequences

4-3

An electric water kettle is wired so that people in another location can determine if it has been used in the previous 24 hours. This may seem a zany use of modern technology, but it symbolizes a change taking place around the globe—the growing needs of an aging population. The Japanese Welfare Network Ikebukuro Honcho has installed these wired hot pots so that volunteers can monitor whether the elderly have used the devices to prepare their morning tea. An unused pot will trigger personal contact to see if the older person needs help. This

of Europe and North America—now have increasingly higher proportions of older citizens.

The overall population of Europe is older than that of any other continent. As the proportion of older people in Europe continues to rise, many governments that have long prided themselves on their pension programs have reduced benefits and raised the age at which retired workers can receive benefits.

In most developing countries, people over the age of 60 are likely to be in poorer health than their counter-

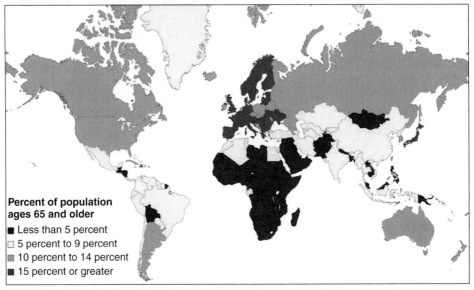

Percent of population ages 65 and older

- ■ Less than 5 percent
- □ 5 percent to 9 percent
- ▨ 10 percent to 14 percent
- ■ 15 percent or greater

Source: Population Reference Bureau, 2007.

technological monitoring system is an indication of the tremendous growth of Japan's elderly population, and particularly significant, the increasing numbers who live *alone.*

Around the world, there are more than 453 million people aged 65 or over, representing about 7 percent of the world's population. By 2050, 1 in 3 people will be over 65. In an important sense, the aging of the world's population represents a major success story that unfolded during the latter years of the twentieth century. Through the efforts of both national governments and international agencies, many societies have drastically reduced the incidence of disease and the rate of death. Consequently, these nations—especially the industrialized countries

parts in industrialized nations. Yet, few of those countries are in a position to offer extensive financial support to the elderly. Ironically, modernization of the developing world, while bringing with it many social and economic advances, has undercut the traditionally high status of the elderly. In many cultures, the earning power of younger adults now exceeds that of older family members.

Applying Theory

1. For an older person, how might life in Pakistan differ from life in France?
2. Do you know an elderly person who lives alone? What arrangements have been made (or should be made) for the person's care in case of emergency?

Sources: Hani 1998; Haub 2005; He et al. 2005; Kinsella and Phillips 2005; R. Samuelson 2004.

Table 4-3   Theories of Aging

Sociological Perspective	View of Aging	Social Roles	Portrayal of Elderly
Functionalist	Disengagement	Reduced	Socially isolated
Interactionist	Activity	Changed	Involved in new networks
Conflict	Competition	Relatively unchanged	Victimized, organized to confront victimization
Feminist	Challenges androcentric bias and assumptions of homogeneity	Socially constructed, diverse according to class, race and ethnicity, sexual orientation	Caught in a double-standard, men gain status and women lose status

to how aging intersects with class, race and ethnicity, and sexual orientation. Table 4-3 summarizes these perspectives.

Ageism

It "knows no one century, nor culture, and is not likely to go away any time soon." This is how physician Robert Butler (1990:178) described prejudice and discrimination against the elderly, which he called **ageism**. Ageism reflects a deep uneasiness among young and middle-aged people about growing old. For many people, old age symbolizes disease, disability, and death; seeing the elderly serves as a reminder that *they* may someday become old and infirm. The notion of ageism was popularized by Maggie Kuhn, a U.S. senior citizen who took up the cause of elder rights after she was forced to retire from her position at the United Presbyterian Church. Kuhn formed the Gray Panthers in 1971, a national organization dedicated to the fight against age discrimination (R. Thomas 1995).

With ageism pervasive in North America, it is hardly surprising that older people are barely visible on television. A content analysis of 1446 U.S. fictional television characters in the early 1990s revealed that only 2 percent were age 65 and over—even though this age group accounted for roughly 13 percent of the nation's population. A second study found older women particularly under-represented on television (J. Robinson and Skill 1993; J. Vernon et al. 1990).

Feminist perspectives have drawn attention to the social construction of gender as it relates to ageism in North American society. Although men's aging is seen as a sign of wisdom and experience, women's aging is seen as a sign of decline and diminishing status. Standards of beauty in our society are based on women's youth and sexual attractiveness and are often narrowly defined and frequently impossible to achieve (Abu-Laban and

McDaniel 1995). Aging women are, therefore, seen as a departure from our culture's norms of physical beauty and sexual attractiveness. The culture, through messages transmitted by mass media, encourages us to "steal beauty back from the ravages of time" (A. Nelson and Robinson 1999:464). Thus, a multibillion-dollar beauty industry of cosmetics, fashion, fitness, and cosmetic surgery is flourishing (N. Wolf 1991) among an aging population in the midst of an anti-aging culture.

Use Your Sociological Imagination

How might women be portrayed by the mass media if society's dominant culture revered age rather than youth?

Anticipatory Socialization and Resocialization

The development of a social self is literally a lifelong transformation that begins in the crib and continues until a person prepares for death. Two types of socialization occur at many points throughout the life course: anticipatory socialization and resocialization.

Anticipatory socialization refers to the processes of socialization in which a person "rehearses" for future positions, occupations, and social relationships. A culture can function more efficiently and smoothly if members become acquainted with the norms, values, and behaviour associated with a social position before actually assuming that status. Preparation for many aspects of adult life begins with anticipatory socialization during childhood and adolescence and continues throughout our lives as we prepare for new responsibilities.

You can see the process of anticipatory socialization take place when high school students start to consider which postsecondary institutions they may attend. Traditionally, this meant looking at publications received in the mail or making campus visits. However, in this era of new technologies, more and more students are using the Internet to begin their educational experience. Institutions are investing more time and money in developing attractive Web sites where students can take virtual campus walks and hear audio clips of everything from a school cheer to a sample zoology lecture.

Occasionally, assuming new social and occupational positions or moving to a new region or country requires us to *unlearn* a previous orientation. **Resocialization** refers to the process of discarding former behaviour patterns and accepting new ones as part of a transition in life. Often, resocialization occurs when there is an explicit effort to transform an individual, as happens in therapy groups, prisons, religious conversion settings, and political indoctrination camps. The process of resocialization typically involves considerable stress for the individual, much more so than socialization in general or even anticipatory socialization (Gecas 1992).

Resocialization is particularly effective when it occurs within a total institution. Erving Goffman (1961) coined the term **total institutions** to refer to institutions, such as prisons, the military, mental hospitals, and convents, that regulate all aspects of a person's life under a single authority. Because the total institution is generally cut off from the rest of society, it provides for all the needs of its members. Quite literally, the crew of a merchant vessel at sea becomes part of a total institution. So elaborate are its requirements, and so all-encompassing are its activities, that a total institution often represents a miniature society.

Goffman (1961) has identified four common traits of total institutions:

1. All aspects of life are conducted in the same place and are under the control of a single authority.
2. Any activities within the institution are conducted in the company of others in the same circumstances—for example, novices in a convent or army recruits.
3. The authorities devise rules and schedule activities without consulting the participants.
4. All aspects of life within a total institution are designed to fulfil the purpose of the organization. Thus, all activities in a monastery might be centred on prayer and communion with God (Davies 1989; P. Rose et al. 1979).

People often lose their individuality within total institutions. For example, a person entering prison may experience the humiliation of a **degradation ceremony** as he or she is stripped of clothing, jewellery, and other personal possessions. Even the person's self is taken away to some extent; the prison inmate loses a name and becomes known to authorities as a number. From this point on, scheduled daily routines allow for little or no personal initiative. The individual becomes secondary and nearly invisible in the overbearing social environment (Garfinkel 1956).

In 1934, the world was enthralled by the birth of quintuplets to Olivia and Elzire Dionne in Ontario. In the midst of the Depression, people wanted to hear and see all they could about these five girls, born generations before fertility drugs made multiple births more common. What seemed like a heartwarming story turned out to be a tragic case of Goffman's total institutionalization. The government of Ontario soon took the quintuplets from their home and set them up in a facility complete with an observation gallery overlooking their playground. Each month, 10 000 tourists paid an entry fee to view the five little "Cinderellas." When the girls left the nine-room compound, it was almost always to raise money for a worthwhile cause or to flog merchandise. Within their compound, even the Dionne girls' parents and older siblings had to make appointments to see them. A child psychiatrist responsible for their child-rearing ordered they never be spanked—or hugged (to prevent the chance of infection).

After nine years, the quintuplets were reunited with their family. But the legacy of total institutionalization persisted. Sharp divisions and jealousies had developed among the five girls and the other siblings. The parents were caught up in charges of doing too much or too little for all their children. In 1997, the three surviving quintuplets made public a poignant letter to the parents of recently born septuplets in Iowa:

> We three would like you to know we feel a natural affinity and tenderness for your children. We hope your children receive more respect than we did. Their fate should be no different from that of other children. Multiple births should not be confused with entertainment, nor should they be an opportunity to sell products. . . .
>
> Our lives have been ruined by the exploitation we suffered at the hands of the government of Ontario, our place of birth. We were displayed as a curiosity three times a day for millions of tourists. . . .
>
> We sincerely hope a lesson will be learned from examining how our lives were forever altered by our childhood experiences. If this letter changes the course of events for these newborns, then perhaps our lives will have served a higher purpose. (Dionne et al. 1997:39)

It is to be hoped that the Iowa septuplets won't find themselves in the position of the Dionne women in 1998, waging a lawsuit against the government for the way they were raised in an institutional environment.

Social Policy and Socialization
Child Care around the World

The Issue

The rise in the number of single-parent families, increased job opportunities for women, and the need for additional family income have all propelled an increasing number of mothers of young children into the paid labour force of Canada. In 2006, 73 percent of women with children under the age of 16 were in the paid labour force (Statistics Canada 2007m). Who, then, is responsible for children during work hours?

For 25 percent of all preschoolers with employed parents, the solution has become daycare programs. Daycare centres have in many ways become the functional equivalent of the nuclear family, performing some of the nurturing and socialization functions previously handled only by family members. But how does daycare compare with other forms of child care? And what is the state's responsibility to ensure high-quality care (Fields 2003; K. Smith 2000)?

The Setting

Few people in Canada or elsewhere can afford the luxury of having a parent stay at home or of paying for high-quality live-in child care. For millions of working mothers and fathers, finding the right kind of child care is a challenge to parenting and to their financial responsibilities.

Researchers have found that high-quality daycare benefits children. The value of preschool programs was documented in a series of studies conducted in Canada by the Childcare Resource and Research Unit at the University of Toronto. Researchers found no significant differences in infants who had received extensive non-maternal care compared with those who had been cared for solely by their parents. They also reported that more and more infants in Canada are being placed in child care outside the home and that, overall, the quality of daycare centres is mixed, depending on whether they are non-profit or commercial. It is difficult, therefore, to generalize about child care. But daycares that are non-profit have been found to be of higher quality than those that are run to make money (Cleveland and Krashinsky 1998).

Sociological Insights

Studies that assess the quality of child care outside the home reflect the micro level of analysis and the interest of interactionists in the impact of face-to-face interaction.

These studies also explore macro-level implications for the functioning of social institutions like the family. But some of the issues surrounding daycare have also been of interest to those who take the conflict perspective.

In Canada, high-quality daycare is not equally available to all families. Parents in wealthy neighbourhoods have an easier time finding daycare than do those in poor or working-class communities. Finding affordable child care is also a problem. Parents in Quebec have more accessible and affordable child care, as the government currently sponsors a program costing $7 per day.

Viewed from a conflict perspective, child-care costs are an especially serious burden for lower-income families. The poorest families spend 25 percent of their earnings on preschool child care, while families who are not poor pay only 6 percent or less of their income for daycare.

Feminists echo the concern of conflict theorists that high-quality child care has received little government support because it is regarded as a private or personal issue rather than a social one. Nearly all child-care workers are women; many find themselves in low-status, minimum-wage jobs. The average salary of a child-care worker in Canada is among the lowest of all occupational groups, and the job has few fringe benefits. Although parents may complain about child-care costs, the staff members, in effect, subsidize that cost by working for low wages.

Policy Initiatives

Policies regarding child care outside the home vary throughout the world. Most developing nations do not have the economic base to provide subsidized child care. Working mothers rely largely on relatives, or they take their children to work. In the comparatively wealthy industrialized countries of Western Europe, government provides child care as a basic service, at little or no expense to parents.

When policymakers decide that child care is desirable, they must determine the degree to which taxpayers should subsidize it. In Sweden and Denmark, one-third to one-half of children under age 3 were in government-subsidized child care full-time in 2001. By contrast, in Canada, the total cost of child care typically falls to the family unit, and although the costs and options vary from urban to rural communities, informal care by friends, neighbours, relatives, and paid babysitters is most prevalent among parents who work for pay and whose children are under 6 years old (Baker 2001). According to the Childcare Resource and Research Unit, licensed or regulated family daycare accounted for less than 14 percent of all regulated spaces in Canada in 1998 (Childcare Resource and Research Unit 2000).

There is a long way to go in making quality child care more affordable and more accessible, not just in Canada, but throughout the world. Government daycare facilities in Mexico have lengthy waiting lists. In an attempt to reduce government spending, the French government is considering cutting back the budgets of subsidized nurseries, even though waiting lists already exist and citizens heartily disapprove of any cutbacks (L. King 1998; Simons 1997; Women's International Network 1995).

Margrit Eichler, a Canadian feminist and sociologist, proposes a "social responsibility model" for family life, endorsing the establishment and support of public daycare centres (Eichler 1997). Eichler argues that the establishment and support of such centres would make good economic sense, generating jobs for daycare workers and enabling mothers to work for pay. In addition, children would benefit from the social setting of the daycare as well as the more individualized setting of the home. Eichler states,

> Financing does not have to come from the federal government alone. Part of it can come from municipalities, from employers, and from parents according to the ability to pay. (Eichler 1997:159–160)

A report on child care released in 2004 by the Organisation for Economic Co-operation and Development (OECD) was highly critical of the Canadian government's efforts in the area of daycare. The OECD stated that the overall funding for Canadian child care programs needs to be increased. Canada has enough regulated child-care spaces for less than 20 percent of children under age 6 with working parents, while Denmark and the United Kingdom, for example, have 78 percent and 60 percent, respectively (OECD 2004). Forty percent of all regulated

Educational planners in Latin America are beginning to view preschool classes—such as this one in Bolivia—as a means to improving the quality of the early primary school years.

child care spaces in Canada are currently in Quebec. After years of promising funding, in late 2004, the federal government pledged $5 billion over five years for the establishment of a national child care program.

Experts in child development view such reports as a vivid reminder of the need for greater government and private-sector support for child care. A 2007 study by SOMS Surveys suggests that although family matters are of top priority to Canadians, only 29 percent feel their employer cares about their work–life balance (*The Province* 2007). Glenn Thompson, CEO of the Canadian Mental Health Association, states, "Usually, these employees are looking for ways to help a lifestyle that is now encumbered with their senior parents and child care" (*The Province* 2007:A41).

Applying Theory

1. What importance would liberal feminist thinkers place on the establishment of a national child care program for Canada? What about radical feminist thinkers?
2. If you were a conflict sociologist, how would you view the establishment of such a program in light of the overall belief in the need to eliminate social inequality?
3. What role do you think a national child care program might serve in terms of the socialization of Canadian children?

CHAPTER RESOURCES

Summary

What is the Role of Socialization?

- **Socialization** (p. 72) is the process whereby people learn the attitudes, values, and actions appropriate for members of a particular culture.
- Socialization affects the overall cultural practices of a society, and it also shapes the images that we hold of ourselves.
- Heredity and environmental factors interact in influencing the socialization process. **Sociobiology** (p. 75) is the systematic study of the biological bases of social behaviour.

What are some Major Theoretical Perspectives on Socialization?

- In the early 1900s, Charles Horton Cooley advanced the belief that we learn who we are by interacting with others, a phenomenon he called the **looking-glass self** (p. 75).
- George Herbert Mead, best known for his theory of the **self** (p. 75), proposed that as people mature, their selves begin to reflect their concern about reactions from others—both generalized others and significant others.
- Erving Goffman has shown that many of our daily activities involve attempts to convey distinct impressions of who we are, a process called **impression management** (p. 76).

What are some Agents of Socialization?

- The major agents in this lifelong process are the family, schools, peer groups, the mass media and technology, the workplace, and the state.

How does Socialization Occur throughout the Life Course?

- Sociologists who study socialization throughout the life course are interested in the social factors that influence people throughout their lives, from birth to death.
- The particular problems of the aged have become the focus for a specialized area of research and inquiry known as **gerontology** (p. 87).
- **Disengagement theory** (p. 88) implicitly suggests that society should help older people withdraw from their accustomed social roles, whereas **activity theory** (p. 88) argues that the elderly person who remains active and socially involved will be best adjusted.
- From a conflict perspective, the low status of older people is reflected in prejudice and discrimination against them in unfair job practices.
- The Greying of Canada: An increasing proportion of the population of Canada comprises older people.

Critical Thinking Questions

1. Should social research in such areas as sociobiology be conducted even though many investigators believe that this analysis is potentially detrimental to particular groups of people?
2. Drawing on Erving Goffman's dramaturgical approach, discuss how the following groups engage in impression management: athletes, students, university instructors, parents, physicians, politicians.
3. How would functionalists and conflict theorists differ in their analyses of socialization by the mass media? How would they be similar?
4. Do you think that media socialize the members of our society to be consumers, first and foremost? Why?

Key Terms

Activity theory   An interactionist theory of aging that argues that elderly people who remain active and socially involved will be best adjusted. (p. 88)

Ageism   Prejudice and discrimination against the elderly. (p. 91)

Anticipatory socialization   Processes of socialization in which a person "rehearses" for future positions, occupations, and social relationships. (p. 91)

Career choice   The first phase of occupational socialization. (p. 86)

Cognitive theory of development   Jean Piaget's theory explaining how children's thought progresses through four stages. (p. 79)

Commitment   Part of the third phase of occupational socialization, it involves a worker enthusiastically accepting the pleasurable duties; this acceptance comes with the recognition by the person of the positive tasks of an occupation. (p. 86)

Concrete operational   The third stage in Piaget's theory of cognitive development. (p. 79)

Conditioning   Part of the third phase of occupational socialization, it involves a worker reluctantly adjusting to the more unpleasant aspects of a job. (p. 86)

Degradation ceremony   An aspect of the socialization process within total institutions, in which people are subjected to humiliating rituals. (p. 92)

Disengagement theory   A functionalist theory of aging that contends that society and the aging individual mutually sever many of their relationships. (p. 88)

Equality feminists   Another term for liberal feminists, who endorse individual freedom and equality of opportunity in the public and economic spheres. (p. 78)

Face-work   The efforts of people to maintain the proper image and avoid embarrassment in public. (p. 76)

Formal operational   The fourth stage in Piaget's theory of cognitive development. (p. 79)

Game stage   In interactionist theory, the third stage of Mead's three-stage model for the emergence of self. (p. 76)

Gender roles   Expectations regarding the proper behaviour, attitudes, and activities of males and females. (p 80)

Gender socialization   An aspect of socialization through which we learn the attitudes, behaviours, and practices associated with being male and female according to our society and social groups within it. (p 80)

Gerontology   The scientific study of the sociological and psychological aspects of aging and the problems of the aged. (p. 87)

Habit training   A relatively formal period of infant socialization, during which caregivers impose routines on the infant. (p. 80)

Impression management   The altering of the presentation of the self to create distinctive appearances and satisfy particular audiences. (p. 76)

Looking-glass self   A concept that emphasizes the self as the product of our social interactions with others. (p. 75)

Personality   In everyday speech, a person's typical patterns of attitudes, needs, characteristics, and behaviour. (p. 72)

Play stage   In interactionist theory, the second stage of Mead's three-stage model for the emergence of self. (p. 76)

Preoperational   The second stage in Piaget's theory of cognitive development. (p. 79)

Preparatory stage   In interactionist theory, the first stage of Mead's three-stage model for the emergence of self. (p. 76)

Resocialization   The process of discarding former behaviour patterns and accepting new ones as part of a transition in life. (p. 92)

Rites of passage   Rituals marking the symbolic transition from one social position to another. (p. 86)

Role taking   The process of mentally assuming the perspective of another, thereby enabling a person to respond from that imagined viewpoint. (p. 76)

Self   A distinct identity that sets us apart from others. (p. 75)

Sensorimotor   The first stage in Piaget's theory of cognitive development. (p. 79)

Socialization   The process whereby people learn the attitudes, values, and behaviours appropriate for members of a particular culture. (p. 72)

Sociobiology   The systematic study of biological bases of social behaviour. (p. 75)

Symbols   The gestures, objects, and language that form the basis of human communication. (p. 76)

Total institutions   Institutions that regulate all aspects of a person's life under a single authority, such as prisons, the military, mental hospitals, and convents. (p. 92)

Additional Readings

Danesi, Marcel. 2003. *Forever Young: The "Teen-Aging" of Modern Culture.* Toronto: University of Toronto Press. Danesi uses five years of interviews with adolescents and their parents to illustrate the "forever young" mentality and how the mass media exploit this mentality for economic purposes.

Goffman, Erving. 1959. *The Presentation of Self in Everyday Life.* New York: Doubleday. Goffman demonstrates his interactionist theory that the self is managed in everyday situations in much the same way that a theatrical performer carries out a stage role.

Graydon, Shari. 2001. "The Portrayal of Women in Media: The Good, the Bad and the Beautiful." In *Communications in Canadian Society,* 5th ed., edited by Craig McKie and Benjamin D. Singer. Scarborough, ON: Thomson

Educational Publishing, pp.179–195. Graydon outlines the mass media's role (with special attention to advertising) in constructing images and ideals of women in our society.

Hammett, Roberta F., and Kathy Sanford. 2007. *Boys, Girls, and the Myths of Literacies and Learning.* Toronto: CSPI/WP. Hammett and Sanford explore the ways in which gender influences learning; the authors also examine class, ethnicity, and sexuality as they relate to learning.

Maaka, Roger, and Chris Anderson. 2006. *The Indigenous Experience: Global Perspectives.* Toronto: CSPI/WP. Here, the authors present some of the richness and heterogeneity of indigenous colonial experiences around the globe.

 ## Online Learning Centre

Visit the *Sociology: A Brief Introduction* Online Learning Centre at www.mcgrawhill.ca/olc/schaefer to access quizzes, interactive exercises, video clips, and other research and study tools related to this chapter.

 ## Reel Society Video Clips

Reel Society video clips can be used to spark discussion about the following topic from this chapter:

- Agents of socialization

chapter 5

SOCIAL INTERACTION, GROUPS, AND SOCIAL STRUCTURE

KIDS DON'T PLAN TO LIVE ON THE STREET

Covenant House
covenanthouse.ca

BEDROOM

Social interaction is critical to society; without it, there is no shared sense of meaning or purpose. By supporting homeless youth, Covenant House of Canada helps them become part of the community, restoring meaning and purpose.

☐ **How do We Define and Reconstruct Reality?**

☐ **What are the Elements of Social Structure?**

☐ **What does a Global Perspective on Social Structure Look Like?**

☐ **How are Organizations Structured?**

☐ **How has the Workplace Changed?**

> **Boxes**

SOCIOLOGY IN THE GLOBAL COMMUNITY: Disability as a Master Status

RESEARCH IN ACTION: Immigrant Women's Social Networks

SOCIOLOGY IN THE GLOBAL COMMUNITY: McDonald's and the Worldwide Bureaucratization of Society

SOCIAL POLICY AND ORGANIZATIONS: The State of the Unions

The quiet of a summer Sunday morning in Palo Alto, California, was shattered by a screeching squad car siren as police swept through the city picking up college students in a surprise mass arrest. Each suspect was charged with a felony, warned of his constitutional rights, spread-eagled against the car, searched, handcuffed and carted off in the back seat of the squad car to the police station for booking.

After being fingerprinted and having identification forms prepared for his "jacket" (central information file), each prisoner was left isolated in a detention cell to wonder what he had done to get himself into this mess. After a while, he was blindfolded and transported to the "Stanford County Prison." Here, he began the induction process of becoming a prisoner—stripped naked, skin searched, deloused, and issued a uniform, bedding, soap and towel. By late afternoon, when nine such arrests had been completed, these youthful "first offenders" sat in dazed silence on the cots in their barren cells. These men were part of a very unusual kind of prison, an experimental or mock prison, created by social psychologists for the purpose of intensively studying the effects of imprisonment upon volunteer research subjects. When we planned our two-week-long simulation of prison life, we were primarily concerned about understanding the process by which people adapt to the novel and alien environment in which those called "prisoners" lose their liberty, civil rights, independence and privacy,

while those called "guards" gain social power by accepting the responsibility for controlling and managing the lives of their dependent charges. . . .

Our final sample of participants (10 prisoners and 11 guards) were selected from over 75 volunteers recruited through ads in the city and campus newspapers. . . . Half were randomly assigned to role-play being guards, the others to be prisoners. Thus, there were no measurable differences between the guards and the prisoners at the start of this experiment. . . .

At the end of only six days, we had to close down our mock prison because what we saw was frightening. It was no longer apparent to most of the subjects (or to us) where reality ended and their roles began. The majority had indeed become prisoners or guards, no longer able to clearly differentiate between role playing and self. There were dramatic changes in virtually every aspect of their behavior, thinking and feeling. In less than a week, the experience of imprisonment undid (temporarily) a lifetime of learning; human values were suspended, self-concepts were challenged and the ugliest, most base, pathological side of human nature surfaced. We were horrified because we saw some boys (guards) treat others as if they were despicable animals, taking pleasure in cruelty, while other boys (prisoners) became servile, dehumanized robots who thought only of escape, of their own individual survival, and of their mounting hatred for the guards.

☐ *(Zimbardo 1972:4; Zimbardo et al. 1974:61, 62, 63)*

In this study directed and described by social psychologist Philip Zimbardo, college students adopted the patterns of social interaction expected of guards and prisoners when they were placed in a mock prison. Sociologists use the term **social interaction** to refer to the ways in which people respond to one another, whether face to face, over the telephone, or on the computer. In the mock prison, social interactions between guards and prisoners were highly impersonal. The guards addressed the prisoners by number rather than name, and they wore reflective sunglasses that made eye contact impossible.

As in many real-life prisons, the simulated prison at Stanford University had a social structure in which guards held virtually total control over prisoners. The term **social structure** refers to the way in which a society is organized into predictable relationships. The social structure of Zimbardo's mock prison influenced how the guards and prisoners interacted. Zimbardo and his colleagues (2003:546) note that it was a real prison "in the minds of the jailers and their captives." His simulated prison experiment, first conducted more than 30 years ago, has subsequently been repeated (with similar findings) both in the United States and in other countries.

Zimbardo's experiment took on new relevance in 2004, in the wake of shocking revelations of prisoner abuse at the U.S.-run Abu Ghraib military facility in Iraq. Graphic photos showed U.S. soldiers humiliating naked Iraqi prisoners and threatening to attack them with police dogs. The structure of the wartime prison, coupled with intense pressure on military intelligence officers to secure information regarding terrorist plots, may have contributed to the breakdown in the guards' behaviour. But Zimbardo himself noted that the guards' depraved conduct could have been predicted simply on the basis of his research (Zarembo 2004; Zimbardo 2004, 2005).

The two concepts of social interaction and social structure are central to sociological study. They are closely related to socialization (see Chapter 4), the process through which people learn the attitudes, values, and behaviours appropriate to their culture. When the students in Zimbardo's experiment entered the mock prison, they began a process of resocialization. In that process, they adjusted to a new social structure and learned new rules for social interaction.

In this chapter, we will study social structure and its effect on our social interactions. What determines a person's status in society? How do our social roles affect our social interactions? What is the place of social institutions such as the family, religion, and government in our social structure? How can we better understand and manage large organizations such as multinational corporations? We'll begin by considering how social interactions shape the way we view the world around us. Next, we'll focus on the five basic elements of social structure: statuses, social roles, groups, social networks, and social institutions such as the family, religion, and government. We'll see that functionalists, conflict theorists, feminist theorists, and interactionists approach these institutions quite differently. We'll compare our modern social structure with simpler forms, using typologies developed by Émile Durkheim, Ferdinand Tönnies, and Gerhard Lenski.

Next, we'll examine how and why formal organizations, such as a corporation, college, or university, came into existence, touching on Max Weber's model of the modern bureaucracy in the process. Finally, we'll discuss recent changes in the workplace. The social policy section at the end of the chapter focuses on the status of organized labour today.

Use Your Sociological Imagination

If you had been selected to be a guard in the Stanford prison experiment, what meaning do you think the actions of the prisoners might have had for you? In what way do you think social reality was being constructed in the Stanford prison experiment?

☐ HOW DO WE DEFINE AND RECONSTRUCT REALITY?

When someone in a crowd shoves you, do you automatically push back? Or do you consider the circumstances of the incident and the attitude of the instigator before you react? Chances are you do the latter. According to sociologist Herbert Blumer (1969:79), the distinctive characteristic of social interaction among people is that "human beings interpret or 'define' each other's actions instead of merely reacting to each other's actions." In other words, our response to someone's behaviour is based on the *meaning* we attach to his or her actions. Reality is shaped by our perceptions, evaluations, and definitions.

These meanings typically reflect the norms and values of the dominant culture and our socialization experiences within that culture. As interactionists emphasize, the meanings that we attach to people's behaviour are shaped by our interactions with them and with the larger society. Social reality is literally constructed from our social interactions (Berger and Luckmann 1966).

How do we define our social reality? Consider something as simple as how we might regard tattoos. At one time, many Canadians might have considered tattoos weird or kooky. We associated them with fringe countercultural groups, such as punk rockers, biker gangs, and skinheads. Among many people, a tattoo elicited an automatic negative response. Now, however, so many people have tattoos—including society's trendsetters and major sports figures—and the ritual of getting a tattoo has become so legitimized, that mainstream culture now regards tattoos differently. At this point, as a result of increased social interaction with ink-adorned people, tattoos look perfectly natural to us in a number of settings.

The ability to define social reality reflects a group's power within a society. In fact, one of the most crucial aspects of the relationship between dominant and subordinate groups is the ability of the dominant or majority group to define a society's values. Sociologist William I. Thomas (1923), an early critic of theories of racial and gender differences, recognized that the "definition of the situation" could mould the thinking and personality of the individual. Writing from an interactionist perspective, Thomas observed that people respond not only to the objective features of a person or situation but also to the *meaning* that person or situation has for them.

For example, in Philip Zimbardo's mock prison experiment, student "guards" and "prisoners" accepted the definition of the situation (including the traditional roles and behaviour associated with being a guard or prisoner) and acted accordingly.

As we have seen throughout the last 40 years— through movements to bring about greater rights for members of such groups as women, racialized minorities, the elderly, gays and lesbians, and people with disabilities—an important aspect of the process of social change involves redefining or reconstructing social reality. Members of subordinate groups challenge traditional definitions and begin to perceive and experience reality in a new way. For example, in 1985, Rick Hansen began a two-year journey, circling the world in his wheelchair to raise awareness and money for people with spinal cord injuries. After being injured in an automobile accident that left him paralyzed at the age of 15, Hansen became a world-class athlete, winning international wheelchair marathons and world championships, and competing for Canada in the Paralympic Games. Continually breaking down stereotypes of people with disabilities, today, Hansen is the father of three daughters, the president and CEO of the Rick Hansen Foundation, an active environmentalist, and an athlete who enjoys fishing, pilates, tennis, kayaking, and sit-skiing.

Viewed from a sociological perspective, Rick Hansen was redefining social reality by challenging ways of thinking and terminology that restricted him and other people with disabilities.

Rick Hansen wheeled around the world to raise money for spinal cord research more than 20 years ago and founded the Man in Motion Foundation (now called the Rick Hansen Foundation). Rick represents a proactive attitude among Canadians who have disabilities and are breaking down societal stereotypes.

☐ WHAT ARE THE ELEMENTS OF SOCIAL STRUCTURE?

All social interaction takes place within a social structure, including those interactions that redefine social reality. For purposes of study, we can break down any social structure into five elements: *statuses*, *social roles*, *groups*, *social networks*, and *social institutions*. These elements make up social structure just as a foundation, walls, and ceilings make up a building's structure. The elements of social structure are developed through the lifelong process of socialization described in Chapter 4. In addition, human beings create the elements of social structure through a dynamic process involving meaningful interaction (Fleras 2003).

Statuses

We normally think of a person's status as having to do with influence, wealth, and fame. However, sociologists use the term **status** to refer to any of the full range of socially defined positions within a large group or society, from the lowest to the highest. Within our society, a person can occupy the status of CEO, fruit picker, son or daughter, violinist, teenager, resident of Alberta, dental technician, or neighbour. A person can hold a number of statuses at the same time.

Ascribed and Achieved Status

Sociologists view some statuses as ascribed and others as achieved (see Figure 5-1). An **ascribed status** is assigned to a person by society without regard for the person's unique talents or characteristics. Generally, the assignment takes place at birth; thus, a person's racial background, gender, and age are all considered ascribed statuses. While people may be born with certain ascribed statuses, these characteristics are significant mainly because of the social meanings they have in a given culture. Conflict theorists are especially interested in ascribed statuses, since they often confer privileges or reflect a person's membership in a subordinate group. The social meanings of race and ethnicity, gender, and age will be analyzed more fully in later chapters.

Think about It

The young woman in Figure 5.1 — "me" — occupies many positions in society, each of which involves distinct statuses. How would you define *your* statuses? Which have the most influence in your life?

> ▶ **FIGURE 5-1**

Social Statuses

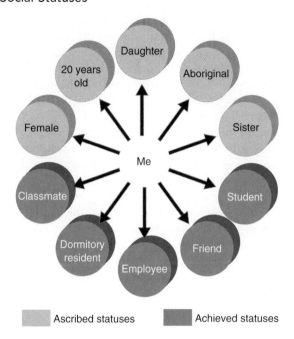

☐ Ascribed statuses   ☐ Achieved statuses

In most cases, we can do little to change an ascribed status. But we can attempt to change the traditional constraints associated with such statuses. For example, the Canadian Association of Retired Persons—an activist political group founded in 1984 to work for the rights of older people—have tried to modify society's negative and confining stereotypes of seniors. As a result of their work and that of other groups supporting older citizens, the ascribed status of "senior citizen" is no longer as difficult for millions of older people.

An ascribed status does not necessarily have the same social meaning in every society. In a cross-cultural study, sociologist Gary Huang (1988) confirmed the long-held view that respect for the elderly is an important cultural norm in China. In many cases, the adjective *old* is used respectfully: calling someone "old teacher" or "old person" is like calling a judge in North America "your honour." Huang points out that positive age-seniority language distinctions are uncommon in North America; consequently, we view the term *old man* as more of an insult than a celebration of seniority and wisdom. With the large baby boom population in Canada approaching what has been considered—until recently—retirement age, the meanings of *old age*, *senior citizen*, and *elderly* are being reconstructed; baby boomers are staying active for longer and many plan on working past age 65.

Unlike ascribed statuses, an **achieved status** comes to us largely through our own efforts. Both bank president

Whom do you see in this photo, a food service worker, an elderly food service worker, or an elderly woman? Our achieved and ascribed statuses determine how others see us.

and prison guard are achieved statuses, as are lawyer, pianist, sorority member, convict, and social worker. We must do something to acquire an achieved status—go to school, learn a skill, establish a friendship, invent a new product. But as we will see in the next section, our ascribed status heavily influences our achieved status. Being male, for example, decreases the likelihood that a person would consider a career in child care services.

Master Status

Each person holds many different and sometimes conflicting statuses; some may connote higher social position and some, lower position. How, then, do others view one's overall social position? According to sociologist Everett Hughes (1945), societies deal with inconsistencies by agreeing that certain statuses are more important than others. A **master status** is a status that dominates others and thereby determines a person's general position in society. For example, Arthur Ashe, who died of AIDS in 1993, had a remarkable career as a tennis star, but at the end of his life, his status as a well-known personality with AIDS may have outweighed his statuses as a retired athlete, author, and political activist. Throughout the world, many people with disabilities find that their status as "disabled" receives undue weight, overshadowing their actual ability to perform successfully in meaningful employment (see Box 5-1 on page 104).

Our society gives so much importance to race and gender that such labels often dominate our lives. These ascribed statuses frequently influence achieved status. Lee Williams, a long-serving porter for Canadian National Railway, was denied advancement into more senior positions because of racism (Manitoba Human Rights Commission 2004). Williams challenged the lack of opportunity for advancement of black railway workers under the Fair Employment Act and won his case; this allowed him and other black workers to move up the ranks to assume higher achieved status within the corporation. In Canada, ascribed statuses of race and gender can function as master statuses that have an important impact on a person's potential to achieve a desired professional and social status.

Social Roles

What Are Social Roles?

Throughout our lives, we acquire what sociologists call social roles. A **social role** is a set of expectations for people who occupy a given social position or status. Thus, in Canada, we expect that cab drivers will know how to get around a city, that receptionists will be reliable in handling phone messages, and that police officers will take action if they see a citizen being threatened. With each distinctive social status—whether ascribed or achieved—come particular role expectations. However, actual performance varies from individual to individual. One secretary may assume extensive administrative responsibilities, while another may focus on clerical duties. Similarly, in Philip Zimbardo's mock prison experiment, some students were brutal and sadistic guards; others were not.

Roles are a significant component of social structure. Viewed from a functionalist perspective, roles contribute to a society's stability by enabling members to anticipate the behaviour of others and to pattern their own actions accordingly. Yet, social roles can also be dysfunctional if they restrict people's interactions and relationships. If we view a person *only* as a "police officer" or "supervisor," it will be difficult to relate to him or her as a friend or neighbour.

Role Conflict

Imagine the delicate situation of a woman who has worked for a decade on an assembly line in an electrical plant, and has recently been named supervisor of her unit. How is this woman expected to relate to her long-time friends and co-workers? Should she still go out to lunch with them, as she has done almost daily for years? Is it her responsibility to recommend the firing of an old friend who cannot keep up with the demands of the assembly line?

Role conflict occurs when incompatible expectations arise from two or more social positions held by

Sociology in the Global Community

5-1

Disability as a Master Status

When the Canadian Transportation Agency ordered VIA Rail to make the passenger rail cars it had purchased several years ago accessible to people with disabilities, VIA responded by mounting a legal challenge. After a number of lower court decisions, in 2007, the Supreme Court of Canada—guided by the Canadian Charter of Rights and Freedoms—ruled that the rail service must be usable to people with and without disabilities.

Throughout history and around the world, people with disabilities have often been subjected to cruel and inhuman treatment. For example, in the early twentieth century, people with disabilities were frequently viewed as subhuman creatures who were a menace to society. In Alberta, between 1928 and 1972, over 2800 individuals were sterilized because they were deemed to be mentally "unfit." In Japan, more than 16 000 women with disabilities were involuntarily sterilized with government approval from 1945 to 1995. Sweden recently apologized for the same action taken against 62 000 of its citizens in the 1970s.

Such blatantly hostile treatment of people with disabilities generally gave way to a medical model that views people with disabilities as chronic patients. Increasingly, however, those concerned with the rights of people with disabilities have criticized this model as well. In their view, it is the unnecessary and discriminatory barriers present in the environment—both physical and attitudinal—that stand in the way of people with disabilities more than any biological limitations do. Applying a human-rights model, activists emphasize that those with disabilities face widespread prejudice, discrimination, and segregation. For example, some provinces and territories in Canada do not fund basic devices for people with disabilities, such as wheelchairs.

Drawing on the earlier work of Erving Goffman, contemporary sociologists have suggested that society has attached a stigma to many forms of disability and that this stigma leads to prejudicial treatment. People with disabilities frequently observe that other people often see them only as blind, wheelchair-ridden, and so forth, rather than as complex human beings with individual strengths and weaknesses, whose blindness or use of a wheelchair is merely one aspect of their lives. A review of studies of people with disabilities disclosed that most academic research on the subject does not differentiate gender, thereby perpetuating the view that a disability overrides other personal characteristics. Consequently, disability serves as a master status.

Without question, people with disabilities occupy a subordinate position in Canadian society. The first International Day of Persons with Disabilities was declared by the United Nations in 1992, and advocates from around the world continue to lobby for the adoption of an international convention on disability rights. Women and men involved in this movement are working to challenge negative views of disabled people and to modify the social structure by reshaping laws, institutions, and environments so that people with disabilities can be fully integrated into mainstream society.

The effort to overcome disability's master status is global in nature. Despite a regulation in China that universities may not reject students because of a physical disability, many universities do just that. In fact, in the last five years, the dozens of universities in Beijing alone have accepted only 236 students with any kind of disability, however minor. It appears that bias against those with disabilities runs deep in China, and many universities use a mandate to nurture physical development as an excuse to keep them out.

Kenya's constitution outlaws discrimination on the basis of many characteristics, including race, sex, tribe, place of origin, creed, and religion, but not on the basis of disability. The African nation of Botswana, however, has plans to assist those with disabilities, most of whom live in rural areas and need special services for mobility and economic development. In many countries, disability rights activists are targeting issues essential to overcoming master status and to being a full citizen; these issues include employment, housing, education, and access to public buildings.

Applying Theory

1. How would interactionist perspectives differ from conflict positions when it comes to the study of disabilities?
2. What emphases would feminist thinkers be most likely to bring to the study of disabilities?

Sources: Albrecht et al. 2001; Goffman 1963a; Murphy 1997; *Newsday* 1997; Ponczek 1998; Rosenthal 2001; Shapiro 1993; Willett and Deegan 2000.

the same person. Fulfillment of the roles associated with one status may directly violate the roles linked to a second status. In the example just given, the newly promoted supervisor will most likely experience a sharp conflict between her social and occupational roles.

Such role conflicts call for important ethical choices. The new supervisor will have to make a difficult decision about how much allegiance she owes her friend and how much she owes her employers, who have given her supervisory responsibilities.

Another type of role conflict occurs when individuals move into occupations that are not common among people with their ascribed status. Male preschool teachers and female police officers experience this type of role conflict. In the latter case, female officers must strive to reconcile their workplace role in law enforcement with the societal view of a woman's role, which does not embrace many skills needed in police work. And while female police officers encounter sexual harassment, as women do throughout the workforce, they must also contend with the "code of silence," an informal norm that precludes officers from implicating colleagues in wrongdoing (Fletcher 1995; S. Martin 1994).

Police officers may face role strain when they try to develop positive community relations while maintaining an authoritative position.

Use Your Sociological Imagination
If you were a male nurse, what aspects of role conflict might you experience? Now imagine you are a professional boxer and a woman. What conflicting role expectations might that involve? In both cases, how well do you think you would handle role conflict?

Role Strain

Role conflict describes the situation of a person dealing with the challenge of occupying two social positions simultaneously. However, even a single position can cause problems. Sociologists use the term **role strain** to describe the difficulty that arises when the same social position imposes conflicting demands and expectations.

Members of ethnic minority groups may experience role strain while working in the mainstream culture. Criminologist Larry Gould (2002) interviewed officers of the Navajo Nation Police Department in New Mexico about their relations with conventional law-enforcement officials, such as sheriffs and FBI agents. Besides enforc-

ing the law, Navajo Nation officers practise an alternative form of justice known as *peacemaking*, in which they seek reconciliation between the parties to a crime. The officers expressed great confidence in peacemaking, but worried that if they did not make arrests, other law-enforcement officials would think they were too soft, or "just taking care of their own." Regardless of the strength of their ties to traditional Navajo ways, all felt the strain of being considered "too Navajo" or "not Navajo enough."

Role Exit

Often, when we think of assuming a social role, we focus on the preparation and anticipatory socialization a person undergoes for that role. Such is true if a person is about to become an attorney, a chef, a spouse, or a parent. Yet, until recently, social scientists have given little attention to the adjustments involved in *leaving* social roles.

Sociologist Helen Rose Fuchs Ebaugh (1988) developed the term **role exit** to describe the process of disengagement from a role that is central to one's self-identity in order to establish a new role and identity. Drawing on interviews with 185 people—among them ex-convicts, divorced men and women, recovering alcoholics, ex-nuns, former doctors, retirees, and transsexuals—Ebaugh (herself a former nun) studied the process of voluntarily exiting from significant social roles.

Ebaugh has offered a four-stage model of role exit. The first stage begins with *doubt*. The person experiences frustration, burnout, or simply unhappiness with an accustomed status and the roles associated with the social position. The second stage involves a *search for alternatives*. A person who is unhappy with his or her career may

This college student in India has decorated his dorm room with photos of beautiful women and fast cars. They may signify his attempt to create a new identity, the final stage in his exit from the role of high school student living at home.

take a leave of absence; an unhappily married couple may begin what they see as a temporary separation.

The third stage of role exit is the *action stage* or *departure*. Ebaugh found that the vast majority of her respondents could identify a clear turning point that made them feel it was essential to take final action and leave their job, end their marriage, or engage in another type of role exit. Twenty percent of respondents saw their role exit as a gradual, evolutionary process that had no single turning point.

The last stage of role exit involves the *creation of a new identity*. Many of you reading this book participated in a role exit when you made the transition from high school to college or university. You left behind the role of offspring living at home and took on the role of a somewhat independent student living with peers in a dorm or apartment. Sociologist Ira Silver (1996) has studied the central role that material objects play in this transition. The objects students choose to leave at home (like stuffed animals and dolls) are associated with their prior identities. They may remain deeply attached to those objects, but do not want them to be seen as part of their new identities at college. The objects students bring with them symbolize how they now see themselves and how they wish to be perceived—iPods and wall posters, for example, are calculated to say, "This is me."

Groups

In sociological terms, a **group** is any number of people with similar norms, values, and expectations who interact with one another on a regular basis. The members of a women's basketball team, a hospital's business office, a synagogue, or a symphony orchestra constitute a group. However, the residents of a suburb would not be considered a group, since they rarely interact with one another at one time.

Groups play a vital part in a society's social structure. Much of our social interaction takes place within groups and is influenced by their norms and sanctions. Being a teenager or a retired person takes on special meanings when we interact within groups designed for people with that particular status. The expectations associated with many social roles, including those accompanying the statuses of brother, sister, and student, become more clearly defined in the context of a group.

Primary and Secondary Groups

Charles Horton Cooley (1902) coined the term **primary group** to refer to a small group characterized by intimate, face-to-face association and co-operation. The members of a street gang constitute a primary group; so do members of a family living in the same household, or a group of "sisters" in a college sorority.

Primary groups play a pivotal role both in the socialization process (see Chapter 4) and in the development of roles and statuses. Indeed, primary groups can be instrumental in a person's day-to-day existence. When we find ourselves identifying closely with a group, it is probably a primary group.

We also participate in many groups that are not characterized by close bonds of friendship, such as large college classes and business associations. The term **secondary group** refers to a formal, impersonal group in which there is little social intimacy or mutual understanding (see Table 5-1). Secondary groups often emerge in the workplace among those who share special understandings about their occupation. The distinction between primary and secondary groups is not always clear-cut, however. Some social clubs may become so large and impersonal that they no longer function as primary groups.

In-Groups and Out-Groups

A group can hold special meaning for members because of its relationship to other groups. For example, people in one group sometimes feel antagonistic toward or threatened by another group, especially if that group is perceived as being different either culturally or racially. To identify these "we" and "they" feelings, sociologists use two terms first employed by William Graham Sumner (1906): *in-group* and *out-group*.

Table 5-1 Comparison of Primary and Secondary Groups

Primary Group	Secondary Group
Generally small	Usually large
Relatively long period of interaction	Relatively short duration, often temporary
Intimate, face-to-face association	Little social intimacy or mutual understanding
Some emotional depth to relationships	Relationships generally superficial
Co-operative, friendly	More formal and impersonal

An **in-group** can be defined as any group or category to which people feel they belong. Simply put, it comprises everyone who is regarded as "we" or "us." The in-group may be as narrow as a teenage clique or as broad as an entire society. The very existence of an in-group implies that there is an out-group that is viewed as "they" or "them." An **out-group** is a group or category to which people feel they do *not* belong.

In-group members typically feel distinct and superior, seeing themselves as better than people in the out-group. Proper behaviour for the in-group is simultaneously viewed as unacceptable behaviour for the out-group. This double standard enhances the sense of superiority. Sociologist Robert Merton (1968) described this process as the conversion of "in-group virtues" into "out-group vices." We can see this differential standard operating in worldwide discussions of terrorism. When a group or a nation takes aggressive actions, it usually justifies them as necessary, even if civilians are hurt or killed. Opponents are quick to label such actions with the emotion-laden term of *terrorist* and appeal to the world community for condemnation. Yet this same group or nation may retaliate with actions that hurt civilians, which the first group will then condemn.

Conflict between in-groups and out-groups can turn violent on a personal as well as a political level. In 1999, two disaffected students at Columbine High School in Littleton, Colorado, launched a gunfire attack on the school that left 15 students and teachers dead, including the shooters. The gunmen, members of an out-group that other students referred to as the Trenchcoat Mafia, apparently resented taunting by an in-group referred to as the Jocks. Similar episodes have occurred in schools across North America, where rejected adolescents, overwhelmed by personal and family problems, peer group pressure, academic responsibilities, or media images of violence, have struck out against more popular classmates.

In-group members who actively provoke out-group members may have their own problems, including limited time and attention from working parents. Sociologists David Stevenson and Barbara Schneider (1999), who studied 7000 teenagers, found that despite many opportunities for group membership, young people spend an average of three and a half hours alone every day. While youths may claim they want privacy, they also crave attention, and striking out at members of an in-group or out-group, be they the wrong gender, ethnic group, or peer group, seems to be one way to get it.

Use Your Sociological Imagination

Try putting yourself in the shoes of an out-group member. What does your in-group look like from that perspective?

Reference Groups

Both in-groups and primary groups can dramatically influence the way an individual thinks and behaves. Sociologists call any group that individuals use as a standard for evaluating themselves and their own behaviour a **reference group**. For example, a high school student who aspires to join a social circle of hip-hop music devotees will pattern his or her behaviour after that of the group. The student will begin dressing like these peers, listening to the same music, and hanging out at the same stores and clubs.

Reference groups have two basic purposes: They serve a normative function by setting and enforcing standards of conduct and belief. The high school student who wants the approval of the hip-hop crowd will have to follow the group's dictates, at least to some extent. Reference groups also perform a comparison function by serving as a standard against which people can measure themselves and others. An actor will evaluate himself or herself against a reference group composed of others in the acting profession (Merton and Kitt 1950).

Reference groups may help the process of anticipatory socialization. For example, a college or university student majoring in finance may read *The Wall Street Journal*, study the annual reports of corporations, and listen to midday stock market news on the radio. Such a student is using financial experts as a reference group to which he or she aspires.

Often, two or more reference groups influence us at the same time. Our family members, neighbours, and co-workers all shape different aspects of our self-evaluation. In addition, reference group attachments change during the life cycle. A corporate executive who quits the rat race at age 45 to become a social worker will find new reference groups to use as standards for evaluation. We shift reference groups as we take on different statuses during our lives.

Coalitions

As groups grow larger, coalitions begin to develop. A **coalition** is a temporary or permanent alliance geared toward a common goal. Coalitions can be broad-based or narrow and can take on many different objectives. Sociologist William Julius Wilson (1999b) has described community-based organizations in Texas that include whites and Latinos, both working class and affluent, who have banded together to work for improved sidewalks, better drainage systems, and comprehensive street paving. Out of this type of coalition building, Wilson hopes, will emerge better interracial understanding.

Some coalitions are intentionally short-lived. Short-term coalition building is a key to success in popular "reality" TV programs like *Survivor*. In the first season of *Survivor*, the four members of the "Tagi alliance" banded together to vote fellow castaways off the island where they were sequestered. The political and business worlds can also foster many temporary coalitions. For example, in 1997, big tobacco companies joined with anti-smoking groups to draw up a settlement for reimbursing states for tobacco-related medical costs. Soon after the settlement was announced, the coalition members returned to their decades-long fight against each other (Pear 1997b).

Social Networks

Groups do not merely serve to define other elements of the social structure, such as roles and statuses; they also link the individual with the larger society. We all belong to a number of different groups, and through our acquaintances make connections with people in different social circles. These connections are known as a **social network**—that is, a series of social relationships that link a person directly to others, and through them indirectly to still more people. Social networks can centre on virtually any activity, from sharing job information to exchanging news and gossip or to sharing sex. Some networks may constrain people by limiting the range of their interactions, yet networks can also empower people by making vast resources available to them (Watts 2004; see Box 5-2 on page 109).

Involvement in social networks—commonly known as *networking*—is especially valuable in finding employment. Albert Einstein, who was a poor student, wasn't successful in finding a job until a classmate's father put him in touch with his future employer. These kinds of contacts—even those that are weak and distant—can be crucial in establishing social networks and facilitating the transmission of information.

In the workplace, networking pays off more for men than for women because of the traditional presence of men in leadership positions. One survey of executives found that 63 percent of the men used networking to find new jobs, compared to 41 percent

The Internet has added a massive new dimension to social interaction—even though you may not be totally sure whom you are "talking to."

Research in Action   5-2
Immigrant Women's Social Networks

Although sociologists have rightly given a good deal of attention to men's networks, there has been growing interest in the social networks created by women.

In her study of Hong Kong Chinese immigrant female entrepreneurs in Richmond, British Columbia, Frances Chiang (2001) used semi-structured interviews to document the experiences of 58 immigrant women. Chiang found that "co-ethnic informal networks," which she defined as personalized relationships established informally through friends, family, kin, and clients who share the same ethnic background, were used to attract, maintain, and increase clientele. According to Chiang, these networks were even more significant when gender was taken into account, in relation to female business owners and their female co-ethnic clientele, leading her to observe that "the unique femaleness of women-to-women relationships facilitated by co-ethnic gendered resources plays a key role in these women-run businesses" (2001:341). Among these immigrant female entrepreneurs, said Chiang, socializing with clients became a way of building trust and establishing good client relations.

Sociologist Pierrette Hondagneu-Sotelo (2001) conducted observation research and interviews among Hispanic women (primarily Mexican immigrants) who live in San Francisco and are employed as domestic workers in middle- and upper-class homes. These women engage in what sociologist Mary Romero has called "job work." That is, the domestic worker has several employers and cleans each home on a weekly or biweekly basis for a flat rate of pay for the work completed (in Spanish, *por el trabajo*) as opposed to being paid an hourly rate (*por la hora*). Job work typically involves low pay, no reimbursement for transportation costs, and no health-care benefits.

At first glance, we might expect that women engaged in such job work would be isolated from each other since they work alone. However, Hondagneu-Sotelo found that these Hispanic women have created strong social networks. Through interactions in various social settings—such as picnics, baby showers, church events, and informal gatherings at women's homes—they share such valuable information as cleaning tips, remedies for work-related physical ailments, tactics for negotiating better pay and gratuities, and advice on how to leave undesirable jobs.

Applying Theory

1. Have you ever participated in a job- or school-related network? If so, did you benefit from the opportunities it offered? In what way?

2. Suppose you want to land a professional job in the field of your choice. What people or organizations might help you to reach your goal? How would you get started?

Sources: Chiang 2001; Gabor 1995: Hondagneu-Sotelo 2001.

of the women. Thirty-one percent of the women used classified advertisements to find jobs, compared to only 13 percent of the men. Still, women at all levels of the paid labour force are beginning to make effective use of social networks. A study of women who were leaving the welfare rolls to enter the paid workforce found that networking was an effective tool in their search for employment. Informal networking also helped them to locate child care and better housing—keys to successful employment (Carey and McLean 1997; Henly 1999).

With advances in technology, we can now maintain social networks electronically; we don't need face-to-face contacts. Online network-building companies emerged in 2004, offering their services free of charge at first. People log in to these sites and create a profile. Rather than remaining anonymous, as they would with an online dating service, users are identified by name and encouraged to list friends—even trusted friends of friends—who can serve as job contacts, offer advice, or simply share interests. One site creates "tribes" of people who share the same characteristic—a religion, hobby, music preference, or post-secondary affiliation (Tedeschi 2004). Online social networking has a downside as well, as there are concerns that it may overexpose individuals, creating opportunities for misrepresentation or "inappropriate" network selves, as well as for creating a potential conflict between the virtual and non-virtual self.

Sociologist Manuel Castells (1997, 1998, 2000) views these emerging electronic social networks as fundamental to new organizations and the growth of existing businesses and associations. One such network, in particular, is changing the way people interact. *Texting* is the exchange of wireless emails over cell phones. It began first in Asia in 2000 and has since taken off in North America and Europe. Initially, texting was popular among young people, who sent each other shorthand messages such as "WRU" (Where are you?) and "CU2NYT" (See you tonight). Now, the world has seen the advantages of transmitting emails via cell phones or Blackberrys. Sociologists, however, caution that such devices create a workday that never ends, and that increasingly people are busy checking their digital devices rather than actually conversing with those around them.

The deployment of Canadian troops in Afghanistan as well as U.S. troops in the Middle East increased many people's reliance on email. Today, digital photos and sound files accompany email messages between soldiers and their families and friends. Well-established networks have developed to help those who are novices at electronic communication to connect to the Internet. Meanwhile, more seasoned users have begun to post their opinions of the Iraq war in online journals called Web logs, or *blogs*. Though critics may be skeptical of the identity, and thus the credibility, of some of the authors, the blogosphere has become yet another source of news about the war (Faith 2005; O'Connor 2004).

Use Your Sociological Imagination

If you were deaf, what impact might instant messaging, or texting, have on you?

Social Institutions

The mass media, the government, the economy, the family, and the health-care system are all examples of social institutions found in our society. **Social institutions** are organized patterns of beliefs and behaviour centred on basic social needs, such as replacing personnel (the family) and preserving order (the government).

A close look at social institutions gives sociologists insight into the structure of a society. Consider religion, for example. The institution of religion adapts to the segment of society that it serves. Religious work has very different meanings for religious leaders who serve a skid row area and those who serve a suburban middle-class community. Those assigned to a skid row mission will focus on tending to the ill and providing food and shelter. In contrast, religious leaders in affluent suburbs will be occupied with counselling those considering marriage and divorce, arranging youth activities, and overseeing cultural events.

Functionalist View

One way to understand social institutions is to see how they fulfil essential functions. Anthropologist David F. Aberle and his colleagues (1950) and sociologists Raymond Mack and Calvin Bradford (1979) have identified five major tasks, or functional prerequisites, that a society or relatively permanent group must accomplish if it is to survive:

1. *Replacing personnel.* Any group or society must replace personnel when they die, leave, or become incapacitated. This task is accomplished through such means as immigration, annexation of neighbouring groups, acquisition of slaves, or biological reproduction. The Shakers, a religious sect that came to North America in 1774, are a conspicuous example of a group that has *failed* to replace personnel. Their religious beliefs commit the Shakers to celibacy; to survive, the group must recruit new members. At first, the Shakers proved quite successful in attracting new members, reaching a peak of about 6000 people in the United States during the 1840s. As of 2004, however, the only Shaker community left in the States was a farm in Maine with five members—three men and two women (Sabbathday Lake 2004).

2. *Teaching new recruits.* No group or society can survive if many of its members reject the group's established behaviour and responsibilities. Thus, finding or producing new members is not sufficient; the group or society must also encourage recruits to learn and accept its values and customs. Such learning can take place formally, within schools (where learning is a manifest function), or informally, through interaction in peer groups (where instruction is a latent function).

3. *Producing and distributing goods and services.* Any relatively permanent group or society must provide and distribute desired goods and services to its members. Each society establishes a set of rules for the allocation of financial and other resources. The group must satisfy the needs of most members to some extent, or it will risk the possibility of discontent and ultimately disorder.

4. *Preserving order.* Throughout the world, indigenous and aboriginal peoples have struggled to protect themselves from outside invaders, with varying degrees of success. Failure to preserve order and defend against conquest leads to the death not only of a people, but also of a culture.

5. *Providing and maintaining a sense of purpose.* People must feel motivated to continue as members of a group or society in order to fulfil the first four requirements. After the September 11, 2001, airliner

Celebrating Canada Day helps to encourage patriotism and create a sense of purpose among Canadians.

of both perspectives agree that social institutions are organized to meet basic social needs, conflict theorists object to the idea that the outcome is necessarily efficient and desirable.

From a conflict perspective, the present organization of social institutions is no accident. Major institutions, such as education, help to maintain the privileges of the most powerful individuals and groups within a society, while contributing to the powerlessness of others. To give one example, public schools in Canada are financed largely through property taxes. This arrangement allows more affluent areas to provide their children with better-equipped schools and better-paid teachers than low income areas can afford. As a result, children from prosperous communities are better prepared to compete academically than children from impoverished communities. The structure of the nation's educational system permits and even promotes such unequal treatment of schoolchildren.

Conflict theorists argue that social institutions, such as education, have an inherently conservative nature. Without question, it has been difficult to implement educational reforms in Canada that promote equal opportunity—whether these reforms be increased access to English as a second language instruction or the inclusion of more students with disabilities in the classroom. From a functionalist perspective, social change can be dysfunctional, since it often leads to instability. However, from a conflict point of view, one might ask why we should preserve the existing social structure if it is unfair and discriminatory.

Feminist Perspectives

Feminist thinkers, such as Patricia Hill Collins (1998), argue that social institutions operate in gendered and racist environments. In schools, offices, and governmental institutions, assumptions about what people can do reflect the sexism and racism of the larger society. For instance, some people may assume that women cannot make tough decisions—even women in the top echelons of corporate management. Others might assume that all Aboriginal students at top universities in Canada represent equity policy admissions. Inequality based on gender, class, race, and ethnicity thrives in such an environment—to which

attacks in the United States, memorial services and community gatherings across the nation allowed people to affirm their allegiance to their country and bind up the psychic wounds inflicted by the terrorists. Patriotism, then, assists some people in developing and maintaining a sense of purpose. For others, tribal identities, religious values, or personal moral codes are especially meaningful. Whatever the motivator, in any society there remains one common and critical reality: if an individual does not have a sense of purpose, he or she has little reason to contribute to a society's survival.

This list of functional prerequisites does not specify *how* a society and its corresponding social institutions will perform each task. For example, one society may protect itself from external attack by amassing a frightening arsenal of weaponry, while another may make determined efforts to remain neutral in world politics and to promote co-operative relationships with its neighbours. No matter what its particular strategy, any society or relatively permanent group must attempt to satisfy all these functional prerequisites for survival. If it fails on even one condition, the society runs the risk of extinction.

Conflict View

Conflict theorists do not agree with the functionalist approach to social institutions. Although proponents we might add discrimination based on age, physical disability, and sexual orientation. The truth of this assertion can be seen in routine decisions by employers on how to advertise jobs as well as whether to provide fringe benefits, such as child care and parental leave.

Liberal feminists, or equality feminists, stress these types of benefits as a means of strengthening employment opportunities for women, thus promoting gender equality. Radical feminists, however, believe that a much more fundamental change must occur throughout the various social institutions in order to achieve gender equality: the elimination of patriarchy (the set of social relations that maintains male dominance).

Use Your Sociological Imagination

Would social networks be more important to a migrant worker in British Columbia than to someone with political and social clout? Why or why not?

Social institutions affect the way we behave. How might the worshippers at this mosque in Egypt interact differently in school or at work?

Interactionist View

Social institutions affect our everyday behaviour, whether we are driving down the street or waiting in a long shopping line. Sociologist Mitchell Duneier (1994a, 1994b) studied the social behaviour of the word processors, all women, who work in the service centre of a large Chicago law firm. Duneier was interested in the informal social norms that emerged in this work environment and the rich social network these female employees created.

The Network Center, as it is called, is a single, windowless room in a large office building where the law firm occupies seven floors. It is staffed by two shifts of word processors, who work either from 4:00 p.m. to midnight or from midnight to 8:00 a.m. Each word processor works in a cubicle with just enough room for her keyboard, terminal, printer, and telephone. Work assignments for the word processors are placed in a central basket and then completed according to precise procedures.

At first glance, we might think that these women labour with little social contact, apart from limited breaks and occasional conversations with their supervisor. However, drawing on the interactionist perspective, Duneier learned that despite working in a large office, these women find private moments to talk (often in the halls or outside the washroom) and share a critical view of the law firm's attorneys and day-shift secretaries. Indeed, the word processors routinely suggest that their assignments represent work that the "lazy" secretaries should have completed during the normal workday. Duneier (1994b) tells of one word processor who resented the lawyers' superior attitude and pointedly refused to recognize or speak with any attorney who would not address her by name.

Interactionist theorists emphasize that our social behaviour is conditioned by the roles and statuses we accept, the groups to which we belong, and the institutions within which we function. For example, the social roles associated with being a judge occur within the larger context of the criminal justice system. The status of "judge" stands in relation to other statuses, such as lawyer, plaintiff, defendant, and witness, as well as to the social institution of government. Although courts and jails have great symbolic importance, the judicial system derives its continued significance from the roles people carry out in social interactions (Berger and Luckmann 1966).

☐ WHAT DOES A GLOBAL PERSPECTIVE ON SOCIAL STRUCTURE LOOK LIKE?

Modern societies are complex, especially compared to earlier social arrangements. Sociologists Émile Durkheim, Ferdinand Tönnies, and Gerhard Lenski developed ways to contrast modern societies with simpler forms of social structure.

Durkheim's Mechanical and Organic Solidarity

In *Division of Labor* ([1893] 1933), Durkheim argued that social structure depends on the division of labour in a society—in other words, on the manner in which tasks are performed. Thus, a task such as providing food can be carried out almost totally by one individual, or it can be divided among many people. The latter pattern is typical of modern societies, in which the cultivation, processing, distribution, and retailing of a single food item are performed by literally hundreds of people.

In societies in which there is minimal division of labour, a collective consciousness develops that emphasizes group solidarity. Durkheim termed this collective frame of mind **mechanical solidarity**, implying that all individuals perform the same tasks. In this type of society, no one needs to ask, "What do your parents do?" since all are engaged in similar work. Each person prepares food, hunts, makes clothing, builds homes, and so forth. Because people have few options regarding what to do with their lives, there is little concern for individual needs. Instead, the group is the dominating force in society. Both social interaction and negotiation are based on close, intimate, face-to-face social contacts. Since there is little specialization, there are few social roles.

As societies become more technological, they rely on greater division of labour and no individual can go it alone. Dependence on others becomes essential for group survival. In Durkheim's terms, mechanical solidarity is replaced by **organic solidarity**, a collective consciousness resting on the need a society's members have for one another. Durkheim chose the term organic solidarity because in his view, individuals become interdependent in much the same way as organs of the human body.

Tönnies's *Gemeinschaft* and *Gesellschaft*

Ferdinand Tönnies (1855–1936) was appalled by the rise of an industrial city in his native Germany during the late 1800s. In his view, the city marked a dramatic change from the ideal of a close-knit community, which Tönnies termed a *Gemeinschaft*, to that of an impersonal mass society, known as a *Gesellschaft* (Tönnies [1887] 1988).

The **Gemeinschaft** (pronounced guh-MINE-shoft) is typical of rural life. It is a small community in which people have similar backgrounds and life experiences. Virtually everyone knows one another, and social interactions are intimate and familiar, almost as among kinfolk.

Social control in the *Gemeinschaft* is maintained through informal means such as moral persuasion, gossip, and even gestures. These techniques work effectively because people genuinely care how others feel about them. Social change is relatively limited in the *Gemeinschaft*; the lives of members of one generation may be quite similar to those of their grandparents.

In contrast, the **Gesellschaft** (pronounced guh-ZELL-shoft) is a community that is characteristic of modern urban life. In this community, most people are strangers who feel little in common with other residents. Social control rests on more formal techniques, such as laws and legally defined punishments. Social change is an important aspect of life in the *Gesellschaft*; it can be strikingly evident even within a single generation.

Table 5-2 summarizes the differences between the *Gemeinschaft* and the *Gesellschaft*. Sociologists have used these terms to compare social structures that stress close relationships with those that emphasize less personal ties. It is easy to view the *Gemeinschaft* with nostalgia, as a far better way of life than the rat race of contemporary existence. However, the more intimate relationships of the *Gemeinschaft* come at a price. The prejudice and discrimination found there can be quite confining; ascribed statuses such as family background often outweigh a person's unique talents and achievements. In addition, the *Gemeinschaft* tends to distrust individuals who seek to be creative or just to be different.

> ### Think about It
> How would you classify the communities with which you are familiar? Are they more *Gemeinschaft* or *Gesellschaft*?

Lenski's Socio-cultural Evolution Approach

Sociologist Gerhard Lenski (born 1924) takes a very different view of society and social structure. Rather than distinguishing between two opposite types of society, as Tönnies did, Lenski sees human societies as undergoing a process of change characterized by a dominant pattern known as **socio-cultural evolution**. This term refers to long-term trends in societies resulting from the interplay of continuity, innovation, and selection (Nolan and Lenski 2006:361).

In Lenski's view, a society's level of technology is critical to the way it is organized. Lenski defines **technology** as "cultural information about the ways in which the material resources of the environment may be used to satisfy human needs and desires" (Nolan and Lenski 2006:361).

Table 5-2 Comparison of the *Gemeinschaft* and *Gesellschaft*

Gemeinschaft	*Gesellschaft*
Rural life typifies this form.	Urban life typifies this form.
People share a feeling of community that results from their similar backgrounds and life experiences.	People have little sense of commonality. Their differences appear more striking than their similarities.
Social interactions are intimate and familiar.	Social interactions are likely to be impersonal and task-specific.
People maintain a spirit of co-operation and unity of will.	Self-interest dominates.
Tasks and personal relationships cannot be separated.	The task being performed is paramount; relationships are subordinate.
People place little emphasis on individual privacy.	Privacy is valued.
Informal social control predominates.	Formal social control is evident.
People are not very tolerant of deviance.	People are more tolerant of deviance.
Emphasis is on ascribed statuses.	Emphasis is on achieved statuses.
Social change is relatively limited.	Social change is very evident, even within a generation.

The available technology does not completely define the form that a particular society and its social structure take. Nevertheless, a low level of technology may limit the degree to which a society can depend on such things as irrigation or complex machinery. As technology advances, Lenski writes, a community changes from a pre-industrial to an industrial and finally a post-industrial society.

Pre-industrial Societies

How does a pre-industrial society organize its economy? If we know that, we can categorize the society. The first type of pre-industrial society to emerge in human history was the **hunting-and-gathering society**, in which people simply relied on whatever foods and fibres that were readily available. Technology in such societies is minimal. Organized into groups, people move constantly in search of food. There is little division of labour into specialized tasks.

Hunting-and-gathering societies are composed of small, widely dispersed groups. Each group consists almost entirely of people who are related to one another. As a result, kinship ties are the source of authority and influence, and the social institution of the family takes on a particularly important role. Tönnies would certainly view such societies as examples of the *Gemeinschaft*.

Social differentiation within the hunting-and-gathering society is based on ascribed statuses such as gender, age, and family background. Since resources are scarce, there is relatively little inequality in terms of material goods. By the close of the 20th century, hunting-and-gathering societies had virtually disappeared (Nolan and Lenski 2006).

Horticultural societies, in which people plant seeds and crops rather than merely subsist on available foods, emerged roughly 10 000 to 12 000 years ago. Members of horticultural societies are much less nomadic than hunters and gatherers. They place greater emphasis on the production of tools and household objects. Yet technology remains limited in these societies, whose members cultivate crops with the aid of digging sticks or hoes (Wilford 1997).

The last stage of pre-industrial development is the **agrarian society**, which emerged about 5000 years ago. As in horticultural societies, members of agrarian societies are engaged primarily in the production of food. However, new technological innovations such as the plow allow farmers to dramatically increase their crop yields. They can cultivate the same fields over generations, allowing the emergence of larger settlements.

The agrarian society continues to rely on the physical power of humans and animals (as opposed to mechanical power). Nevertheless, its social structure has more carefully defined roles than that of horticultural societies. Individuals focus on specialized tasks, such as the repair of fishing nets or blacksmithing.

Table 5-3 Stages of Socio-cultural Evolution

Societal Type	First Appearance	Characteristics
Hunting-and-gathering	Beginning of human life	Nomadic; reliance on readily available food and fibres
Horticultural	About 10 000 to 12 000 years ago	More settled; development of agriculture and limited technology
Agrarian	About 5000 years ago	Larger, more stable settlements; improved technology and increased crop yields
Industrial	1760–1850	Reliance on mechanical power and new sources of energy; centralized workplaces; economic interdependence; formal education
Post-industrial	1960s	Reliance on services, especially the processing and control of information; expanded middle class
Postmodern	Latter 1970s	High technology; mass consumption of consumer goods and media images; cross-cultural integration

Table 5-3 summarizes Lenski's three stages of socio-cultural evolution, as well as the stages that follow, which are described next.

Industrial Societies

Although the Industrial Revolution did not topple monarchs, it produced changes every bit as significant as those resulting from political revolutions. The Industrial Revolution, which took place largely in England from 1760 to 1830, was a scientific revolution focused on the application of non-animal (mechanical) sources of power to labour tasks. An **industrial society** is a society that depends on mechanization to produce its goods and services. Industrial societies rely on new inventions that facilitate agricultural and industrial production, and on new sources of energy, such as steam.

As the Industrial Revolution proceeded, a new form of social structure emerged. Many societies underwent an irrevocable shift from an agrarian-oriented economy to an industrial base. No longer did an individual or a family typically make an entire product. Instead, specialization of tasks and manufacturing of goods became increasingly common. Workers, generally men, but also women and even children, left their family homesteads to work in central locations such as factories.

The process of industrialization had distinctive social consequences. Families and communities could not continue to function as self-sufficient units. Individuals, villages, and regions began to exchange goods and services and to become interdependent. As people came to rely on the labour of members of other communities,

At first glance, this scene may seem a throwback to agrarian society, but look more closely. Today's farm is actually a highly mechanized, computer-dependent operation that is networked into the global economy.

the family lost its unique position as the source of power and authority. The need for specialized knowledge led to more formalized schooling, and education emerged as a social institution distinct from the family.

Post-industrial and Postmodern Societies

When Lenski first proposed the sociocultural evolutionary approach in the 1960s, he paid relatively little attention to how maturing industrialized societies may change with the emergence of even more advanced forms of technology. More recently, he and other sociologists have studied the significant changes in the occupational structure of industrial societies as they shift from manufacturing to service economies. In the 1970s, sociologist Daniel Bell wrote about the technologically advanced **post-industrial society**, whose economic system is engaged primarily in the processing and control of information. The main output of a post-industrial society is services rather than manufactured goods. Jobs in fields such as advertising, public relations, human resources, and computer information systems would be typical of a post-industrial society (D. Bell 1999).

Bell views the transition from industrial to post-industrial society as a positive development. He sees a general decline in organized working-class groups and a rise in interest groups concerned with national issues such as health, education, and the environment. Bell's outlook is functionalist, because he portrays the post-industrial society as basically consensual. As organizations and interest groups engage in an open and competitive process of decision making, Bell believes, the level of conflict among diverse groups will diminish, thus strengthening social stability.

Conflict theorists take issue with Bell's functionalist analysis of the post-industrial society. For example, Michael Harrington (1980), who alerted North America to the problems of the poor in his book, *The Other America*, questioned the significance that Bell attached to the growing class of white-collar workers. Harrington followed in the tradition of Marx by arguing that conflict between social classes will continue in the post-industrial society.

Sociologists have recently gone beyond discussion of the post-industrial society to the model of the postmodern society. As we discussed in Chapter 1, a **postmodern society** is a technologically sophisticated society that is preoccupied with consumer goods and media images and which consumes goods and information on a mass scale. Postmodern theorists take a global perspective, noting the ways in which particular aspects of culture cross national boundaries. For example, George Ritzer proposed a McDonaldization thesis where the principles of the fast-food company—"efficiency, calculability, predictability, control through the substitution of technology for people, and paradoxically, the irrationality of

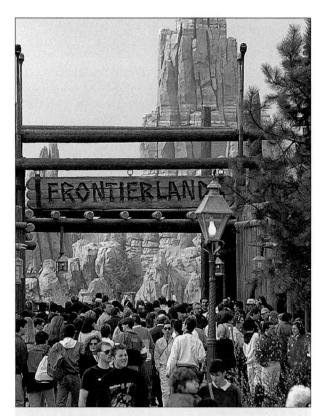

In a postmodern society, people consume goods, information, and media images en masse. Overseas, Disneyland Paris is popularizing U.S. media images, thus illustrating another characteristic of postmodern societies: globalization.

rationality" (e.g., people waiting in long lines, often in cars, for "fast food")—would spread to other sectors and around the world (2007:263).

Durkheim, Tönnies, and Lenski present three distinct visions of society's social structure. While they do differ, each is useful, and this book draws on all three. Lenski's sociocultural evolutionary approach emphasizes a historical perspective. It does not picture different types of social structures coexisting within the same society. Consequently, one would not expect a single society to include hunters and gatherers along with a postmodern culture. In contrast, Durkheim's and Tönnies's theories allow for the existence of different types of community—such as a *Gemeinschaft* and a *Gesellschaft*—in the same society. Thus, a rural Manitoba community located 150 kilometres from Winnipeg can be linked to the city by modern information technology. The main difference between these two theories is a matter of emphasis. While Tönnies emphasized the overriding concern in each type of community—one's own self-interest or the well-being of the larger society—Durkheim emphasized the division (or lack of division) of labour.

The work of these three thinkers reminds us that a major focus of sociology has been to identify changes in social structure and the consequences for human behaviour. At the macro level, we see society shifting to more advanced forms of technology. The social structure becomes increasingly complex, and new social institutions emerge to assume some functions that once were performed by the family. On the microlevel, these changes affect the nature of social interactions. Each individual takes on multiple social roles, and people come to rely more on social networks and less on kinship ties. As the social structure becomes more complex, people's relationships become more impersonal, transient, and fragmented.

☐ HOW ARE ORGANIZATIONS STRUCTURED?

Formal Organizations and Bureaucracies

As contemporary societies have shifted to more advanced forms of technology and their social structures have become more complex, our lives have become increasingly dominated by large secondary groups referred to as *formal organizations*. A **formal organization** is a group designed for a special purpose and structured for maximum efficiency. Canada Post, McDonald's, and the Vancouver Symphony are examples of formal organizations. Though organizations vary in their size, specificity of goals, and degree of efficiency, they are all structured to facilitate the management of large-scale operations. They also have a bureaucratic form of organization, which we describe in the next section.

In our society, formal organizations fulfil an enormous variety of personal and societal needs, shaping the lives of every one of us. In fact, formal organizations have become such a dominant force that we must create organizations to supervise other organizations, such as the Ontario Securities Commission (OSC) to regulate brokerage companies. While it sounds much more exciting to say that we live in the "computer age" than to admit that ours is the "age of formal organization," the latter is probably a more accurate description of our times (Azumi and Hage 1972; Etzioni 1964).

Ascribed statuses such as gender can influence how we see ourselves within formal organizations. For example, a study of women lawyers in some of the largest law firms found significant differences in the women's self-images, depending on the relative presence or absence of women in positions of power. In firms in which fewer than 15 percent of partners were women, the female lawyers were likely to believe that "feminine" traits were strongly devalued, and that masculinity was equated with

success. As one female attorney put it, "Let's face it, this is a man's environment, and it's sort of Jock City, especially at my firm." Women in firms where female lawyers were better represented in positions of power had a stronger desire for, and higher expectations of, promotion (Ely 1995:619).

Characteristics of a Bureaucracy

A **bureaucracy** is a component of formal organization that uses rules and hierarchical ranking to achieve efficiency. Rows of desks staffed by seemingly faceless people, endless lines and forms, impossibly complex language, and frustrating encounters with red tape—all these unpleasant images have combined to make *bureaucracy* a dirty word and an easy target in political campaigns. As a result, few people want to identify their occupation as "bureaucrat," despite the fact that all of us perform various bureaucratic tasks. In an industrial society, elements of bureaucracy enter into almost every occupation.

Max Weber ([1913–1922] 1947) first directed researchers to the significance of bureaucratic structure. He developed an *ideal type* of bureaucracy that would reflect the most characteristic aspects of all human organizations. By **ideal type**, Weber meant a construct or model for evaluating specific cases. In actuality, perfect bureaucracies do not exist; no real-world organization corresponds exactly to Weber's ideal type.

◀ P.8

Weber proposed that whether the purpose is to run a temple, a corporation, or an army, the ideal bureaucracy displays five basic characteristics. A discussion of those characteristics, as well as the dysfunctions of a bureaucracy, follows.

◀ P.13

1. **Division of labour.** Specialized experts perform specific tasks. In your college or university bureaucracy, the admissions officer does not do the job of registrar; the guidance counsellor doesn't see to the maintenance of buildings. By working at a specific task, people are more likely to become highly skilled and carry out a job with maximum efficiency. This emphasis on specialization is so basic a part of our lives that we may not realize it is a fairly recent development in Western culture.

   The downside of division of labour is that the fragmentation of work into smaller and smaller tasks can divide workers and remove any connection they might feel to the overall objective of the bureaucracy. In *The Communist Manifesto* (written in 1848), Karl Marx and Friedrich Engels charged that the capitalist system reduces workers to a mere "appendage of the machine" (L. Feuer 1989). Such a work arrangement, they wrote, produces extreme **alienation**—a condition of estrangement or dissociation from the surrounding society. According to both Marx and conflict theorists, restricting workers to very small tasks also weakens their job security, since new employees can be easily trained to replace them.

Although division of labour has certainly enhanced the performance of many complex bureaucracies, in some cases it can lead to **trained incapacity**; that is, workers become so specialized that they develop blind spots and fail to notice obvious problems.

Sometimes, the bureaucratic division of labour can have tragic results. In the wake of the coordinated attacks on the World Trade Center and the Pentagon on September 11, 2001, North Americans wondered aloud how the FBI and CIA could have failed to work together to detect the terrorists' elaborately planned operation. The problem, in part, turned out to be the division of labour between the FBI, which focuses on domestic matters, and the CIA, which operates overseas. Officials at these intelligence-gathering organizations, both of which are huge bureaucracies, are well-known for jealously guarding information from one another. Subsequent investigations revealed that they knew about Osama bin Laden and his al-Qaeda terrorist network in the early 1990s. Unfortunately, five federal U.S. agencies—the CIA, FBI, National Security Agency, Defense Intelligence Agency, and National Reconnaissance Office—failed to share their leads on the network. Although the hijacking of the four commercial airliners used in the massive attacks may not have been preventable, the bureaucratic division of labour definitely hindered efforts to defend against terrorism, undermining U.S. national security.

2. **Hierarchy of authority.** Bureaucracies follow the principle of hierarchy; that is, each position is under the supervision of a higher authority. A president heads a college or university bureaucracy; he or she selects members of the administration, who in turn hire their own staff. In the Roman Catholic Church, the pope is the supreme authority; under him are cardinals, bishops, and so forth.

3. **Written rules and regulations.** What if your sociology professor gave your classmate an "A" for having such a friendly smile? You might think that wasn't fair, that it was against the rules.

Rules and regulations, as we all know, are an important characteristic of bureaucracies. Ideally, through such procedures, a bureaucracy ensures uniform performance of every task. Thus, your classmate cannot receive an "A" for a nice smile,

"Frankly, at this point in the flow chart, we don't know what happens to these people..."

A hierarchy of authority may deprive individuals of a voice in decision making, but it does clarify who supervises whom.

because the rules guarantee that all students will receive essentially the same treatment.

Through written rules and regulations, bureaucracies generally offer employees clear standards for an adequate (or exceptional) performance. In addition, procedures provide a valuable sense of continuity in a bureaucracy. Individual workers will come and go, but the structure and past records of the organization give it a life of its own that outlives the services of any one bureaucrat.

Of course, rules and regulations can overshadow the larger goals of an organization to the point that they become dysfunctional. What if a hospital emergency room physician failed to treat a seriously injured person because he or she failed to present a health-care card. If blindly applied, rules no longer serve as a means to achieving an objective, but instead become important (and perhaps too important) in their own right. Robert Merton (1968) used the term **goal displacement** to refer to overzealous conformity to official regulations.

4. **Impersonality.** Max Weber wrote that in a bureaucracy, work is carried out *sine ira et studio*, "without hatred or passion." Bureaucratic

norms dictate that officials perform their duties without giving personal consideration to people as individuals. Although this norm is intended to guarantee equal treatment for each person, it also contributes to the often cold and uncaring feeling associated with modern organizations. Frequently, bureaucratic impersonality produces frustration and disaffection. Today, even small organizations screen callers with electronic menus.

5. **Employment based on technical qualifications.** Within the ideal bureaucracy, hiring is based on technical qualifications rather than on favouritism, and performance is measured against specific standards. Written personnel policies dictate who gets promoted, and people often have a right to appeal if they believe that particular rules have been violated. Such procedures protect bureaucrats against arbitrary dismissal, provide a measure of security, and encourage loyalty to the organization.

In this sense, the "impersonal" bureaucracy can be considered an improvement over non-bureaucratic organizations. College and university faculty members, for example, are, ideally, hired and promoted according to their professional qualifications, including degrees earned and research published, rather than because of whom they know. Once they are granted tenure, academics' jobs are protected against the whims of officialdom.

Although any bureaucracy will, ideally, value technical and professional competence, personnel

decisions do not always follow that ideal pattern. Dysfunctions within bureaucracy have become well publicized, particularly because of the work of Laurence J. Peter. According to the **Peter Principle**, every employee within a hierarchy tends to rise to his or her level of incompetence (Peter and Hull 1969). This hypothesis, which has not been directly or systematically tested, reflects a possible dysfunctional outcome of advancement on the basis of merit. Talented people receive promotion after promotion, until sadly, some of them finally achieve positions that they cannot handle with their usual competence (Blau and Meyer 1987).

Table 5-4 summarizes the five characteristics of bureaucracy. These characteristics, developed by Max Weber more than 80 years ago, describe an ideal type rather than an actual bureaucracy. Not every formal organization will possess all five of Weber's characteristics. In fact, wide variation exists among actual bureaucratic organizations.

Bureaucracy pervades modern life. Through McDonaldization, bureaucratization has grown unwieldy (see Chapter 3). As Box 5-3 on page 120 shows, the McDonald's organization provides an excellent illustration of Weber's concept of bureaucracy.

Bureaucratization as a Process

Have you ever had to speak to 10 or 12 individuals in a corporation or government agency just to find out which official has jurisdiction over a particular problem? While

Table 5-4   Characteristics of a Bureaucracy

Characteristic	Positive Consequence	Negative Consequence For the Individual	For the Organization
Division of labour	Produces efficiency in a large-scale corporation	Produces trained incapacity	Produces a narrow perspective
Hierarchy of authority	Clarifies who is in command	Deprives employees of a voice in decision making	Permits concealment of mistakes
Written rules and regulations	Let workers know what is expected of them	Stifle initiative and imagination	Lead to goal displacement
Impersonality	Reduces bias	Contributes to feelings of alienation	Discourages loyalty to company
Employment based on technical qualifications	Discourages favouritism and reduces petty rivalries	Discourages ambition to improve oneself elsewhere	Fosters Peter Principle to operate

Sociology in the Global Community

McDonald's and the Worldwide Bureaucratization of Society

5-3

In his book *The McDonaldization of Society*, sociologist George Ritzer notes the enormous influence of a well-known fast-food organization on modern-day culture and social life. Ritzer defines **McDonaldization** as "the process by which the principles of the fast-food restaurant are coming to dominate more and more sectors of U.S. society as well as of the rest of the world" (Ritzer 2004:1). Through this process, the business principles on which the fast-food industry is founded—efficiency, calculability, predictability, and control—have changed not only the way U.S. citizens do business and run their organizations, but also the way they live their lives. For example, busy families have come to rely on the takeout meals served up by fast-food establishments, and social groups from adolescents to senior citizens now meet at McDonald's.

Max Weber's five characteristics of bureaucracy are apparent in McDonald's restaurants, as well as in the global corporation behind them. Food preparation and order taking reflect a painstaking *division of labour*, implemented by a *hierarchy of authority* that stretches from the food workers up to the shift manager and store operator, and ultimately to the corporate board of directors. Store operators learn the company's *written rules and regulations*, which govern even the amount of ketchup or mustard placed on a hamburger, at Hamburger University (a mandatory training program run by McDonald's).

Little bonding occurs between servers and customers, creating a pervasive sense of *impersonality*. Together with McDonald's cookie-cutter architectural designs, this lack of personal character tends to disguise a restaurant's locale—not just the town or city it serves, but often the country or continent as well. Finally, employees are expected to have specific *technical qualifications*, although most of the skills they need to perform their routine tasks can be learned in a brief training period.

The real significance of McDonaldization is that it is not confined to the food-service industry. Worldwide, the giant fast-food establishment's brand of predictability, efficiency, and dependence on non-human technology have become customary in a number of services, ranging from medical care to wedding planning to education. Even sporting events reflect the influence of this kind of bureaucratization. Around the world, sports stadiums—which are now customarily given forgettable corporate names

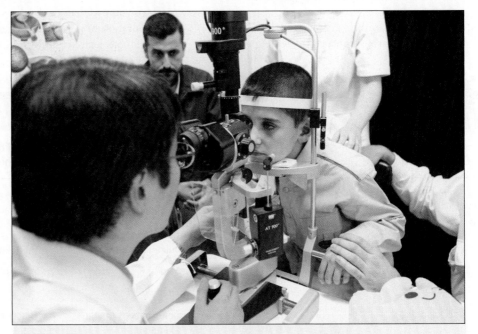

The worldwide success of highly efficient fast-food operations has led to the bureaucratization of many other services including eye care and other forms of medical treatment.

by sponsors who bid for "naming rights"—are becoming increasingly similar, both physically and in the way they present the sport to spectators. Swipe cards, "sports city" garages and parking lots, and automated ticket sales maximize efficiency. All seats offer spectators an unrestricted view, and a big screen guarantees them access to instant replays. Scores, player statistics, and attendance figures are updated automatically by computer and displayed on an automated scoreboard. Spectator enthusiasm is manufactured through digital displays urging applause or rhythmic chanting. At food counters, refreshments include well-known brands whose customer loyalty has been nourished by advertisers for decades. And, of course, the merchandising of teams' and even players' names and images is highly controlled.

Sources: Ormond 2005; Ritzer 2004.

McDonald's reliance on the five characteristics of bureaucracy is not revolutionary. What is new is the bureaucratization of services and life events that once were highly individualized, at times even spontaneous. More and more, societies around the globe are becoming McDonaldized.

Applying Theory

1. Do you patronize McDonald's and other fast-food establishments? If so, what features of these restaurants do you appreciate? Do you have any complaints about them?
2. Analyze life at your college or university using Weber's model of bureaucracy. What elements of McDonaldization do you see? Do you wish life were less McDonaldized?

on the telephone, have you ever been transferred from one department to another until you finally hung up in disgust? Sociologists have used the term **bureaucratization** to refer to the process by which a group, organization, or social movement becomes increasingly bureaucratic.

Normally, we think of bureaucratization in terms of large organizations. But bureaucratization can also take place within smaller businesses and groups. Sociologist Jennifer Bickman Mendez (1998) studied domestic houseworkers employed by a U.S. franchise. She found that housekeeping tasks were minutely defined, to the point that employees had to follow 22 written steps for cleaning a bathroom. Complaints and special requests went not to the workers, but to an office-based manager.

Oligarchy: Rule by a Few

Conflict theorists have examined the bureaucratization of social movements. The German sociologist Robert Michels (1915) studied socialist parties and labour unions in Europe before World War I and found that such organizations were becoming increasingly bureaucratic. The emerging leaders of the organizations—even some of the most radical—had a vested interest in clinging to power. If they lost their leadership posts, they would have to return to full-time work as manual labourers.

Through his research, Michels originated the idea of the **iron law of oligarchy**—it describes how even a democratic organization will eventually develop into a bureaucracy ruled by a few, which is called an oligarchy. Why do oligarchies emerge? People who achieve leadership roles usually have the skills, knowledge, or charismatic appeal

(as Weber noted) to direct, if not control, others. Michels argued that the rank and file of a movement or organization look to leaders for direction and thereby reinforce the process of rule by a few. In addition, members of an oligarchy are strongly motivated to maintain their leadership roles, privileges, and power.

Michels's insights continue to be relevant today. Contemporary labour unions in Canada, the U.S., and Western Europe bear little resemblance to those organized spontaneously by exploited workers. Conflict theorists have pointed to the longevity of union leaders, who are not always responsive to the needs and demands of the membership, and seem more concerned with maintaining their own positions and power. (The social policy section at the end of this chapter focuses on the status of labour unions today.)

Bureaucracy and Organizational Culture

How does bureaucratization affect the average individual who works in an organization? The early theorists of formal organizations tended to neglect this question. Max Weber, for example, focused on management personnel within bureaucracies, but had little to say about workers in industry or clerks in government agencies.

According to the **classical theory** of formal organizations, also known as the **scientific management approach**, workers are motivated almost entirely by economic rewards. This theory stresses that only the physical constraints on workers limit their productivity.

Therefore, workers may be treated as a resource, much like the machines that began to replace them in the twentieth century. Under the scientific management approach, managerial types attempt to achieve maximum work efficiency through scientific planning, established performance standards, and careful supervision of workers and production. Planning involves efficiency studies but not studies of workers' attitudes or job satisfaction.

Not until workers organized unions—and forced management to recognize that they were not objects—did theorists of formal organizations begin to revise the classical approach. Along with management and administrators, social scientists became aware that informal groups of workers have an important impact on organizations (Perrow 1986). An alternative way of considering bureaucratic dynamics, the **human relations approach**, emphasizes the role of people, communication, and participation in a bureaucracy. This type of analysis reflects the interest of interactionist theorists in small-group behaviour. Unlike planning under the scientific management approach, planning based on the human relations perspective focuses on workers' feelings, frustrations, and emotional need for job satisfaction.

The gradual move away from a sole focus on the physical aspects of getting the job done—and toward the concerns and needs of workers—led advocates of the human relations approach to stress the less formal aspects of bureaucratic structure. Informal groups and social networks within organizations develop partly as a result of people's ability to create more direct forms of communication than under the formal structure. Charles Page (1946) used the term *bureaucracy's other face* to refer to the unofficial activities and interactions that are such a basic part of daily organizational life.

A series of classic studies illustrates the value of the human relations approach. The Hawthorne studies alerted sociologists to the fact that research subjects may alter their behaviour to match the experimenter's expectations. The major focus of the Hawthorne studies, however, was the role of social factors in workers' productivity. One aspect of the research concerned the switchboard-bank wiring room, where 14 men were making parts of switches for telephone equipment. The researchers discovered that these men were producing far below their physical capabilities. The discovery was especially surprising because the men would have earned more money if they had produced more parts.

◀ P.36

What accounted for such an unexpected restriction of output? The men feared that if they produced switch parts at a faster rate, their pay rate might be reduced, or some of them might lose their jobs. As a result, this group of workers had established their own (unofficial) norm for a proper day's work and created informal rules and sanctions to enforce it. Yet, management was unaware of these practices and actually believed that the men were working as hard as they could (Roethlisberger and Dickson 1939).

Today, research on formal organizations is following new avenues. First, the proportion of women and visible minority group members in high-level management positions is still much lower than might be expected, given their numbers in the labour force. In 2006, roughly 47 percent of the Canadian workforce was made up of women while just over 4 percent of CEO positions in Canada were filled by women (Catalyst Canada 2007). A 2007 study showed that visible minority managers, professionals, and executives in Canada are more likely to perceive workplace barriers to their advancement than their white counterparts (Catalyst Canada 2007). Researchers are now beginning to look at the impact this gender and racial/ethnic imbalance—diversity issues—may have on managerial judgment, both formal and informal. Second, a company's power structure is only partly reflected in its formal organizational charts. In practice, core groups tend to emerge to dominate the decision-making process. Very large corporations—say, a General Electric or a Procter & Gamble—may have hundreds of interlocking core groups, each of which plays a key role in its division or region. Third, these organizations have traditionally been viewed as having fairly fixed boundaries. But today's production and service systems stretch across networks of independent or semi-independent companies—a fact that must be considered in studying corporate culture (Kleiner 2003; Scott 2004).

☐ HOW HAS THE WORKPLACE CHANGED?

Weber's work on bureaucracy and Michels's thinking on oligarchy are still applicable to the organizational structure and culture of the workplace. But today's factories and offices are undergoing rapid, profound changes unanticipated a century or more ago. Besides the far-reaching impact of technological advances such as computerization, workers must cope with organizational restructuring. In this section, we detail the dramatic changes evident in today's workplace.

Organizational Restructuring

To some extent, individual businesses, community organizations, and government agencies are always changing, if only because of personnel turnover. But since the late twentieth century, formal organizations have been experimenting with new ways of getting the job done, some of which have significantly altered the workplace.

Collective decision making, or the active involvement of employee problem-solving groups in corporate management, first became popular in North America in the 1980s. Management gurus had noted the dazzling success of Japanese automobile and consumer products manufacturers. In studying these companies, they found that problem-solving groups were one key to success. At first, such groups concentrated on small problems at specific points in the production line. But today, these groups often cross departmental and divisional boundaries to attack problems rooted in the bureaucratic division of labour. Thus, they require significant adjustment by employees long used to working in a bureaucracy (Ouchi 1981).

Another innovation in the workplace, called *minimal hierarchy*, replaces the traditional bureaucratic hierarchy of authority with a flatter organizational structure. Minimal hierarchy offers workers greater access to those in authority, giving them an opportunity to voice concerns that might not be heard in a traditional bureaucracy. This new organizational structure is thought to minimize the potential for costly and dangerous bureaucratic oversights.

Finally, organizational *work teams* have become increasingly common, even in smaller organizations. There are two types of work team. *Project teams* address ongoing issues, such as workplace health and safety. *Task forces* pursue non-recurring issues, such as a major building renovation. In both cases, team members are released to some degree from their regular duties in order to contribute to the organization-wide effort (Scott 2003).

The common purpose of work teams, minimal hierarchy, and collective decision making is to empower workers. For that reason, these new organizational structures can be exciting for the employees who participate in them. But these innovations rarely touch the vast numbers of workers who perform routine jobs in factories and office buildings. By 2008, it is estimated that roughly 33 percent of the total U.S. non-farm workforce will be part-time or temporary; in Canada, approximately 27 percent of current workers are in part-time or temporary jobs (Canadian Centre for Policy Alternatives [CCPA] 2007). Organizational innovations such as project teams and work teams, no doubt, will have little relevance for part-time and temporary workers who are increasingly being denied their share of the economic pie (CCPA 2007).

Telecommuting

Increasingly, in many industrial countries, workers are turning into telecommuters. **Telecommuters** are employees who work full-time or part-time at home rather than in an outside office, and who are linked to their supervisors and colleagues through computer terminals, phone lines, and fax machines. In countries such as Japan and the United States, telecommuting has become part of national policy. In 2007, Japan announced plans to double the number of telecommuters by 2010 (Song, 2007).

A Statistics Canada report revealed that the number of telecommuters in this country actually dipped slightly in 2005, after increasing steadily from 1991 to 2000. The report conjectured the use of laptops, BlackBerrys, and mobile phones and the growing proliferation of communication centres may have contributed to this dip, allowing people to work in a variety of locations, in addition to home (Statistics Canada 2007k). Despite the growing amount of time Canadians spend travelling to and from work and the environmental impact of this travel, the Canadian government has not made telecommuting a national priority.

What are the social implications of a shift toward the virtual office? From an interactionist perspective, the workplace is a major source of friendships; restricting face-to-face social opportunities could destroy the trust that is created by "handshake agreements." Thus, telecommuting may move society further along the continuum from *Gemeinschaft* to *Gesellschaft*. On a more positive

Telecommuters are linked to their supervisors and colleagues through computer terminals, phones, and fax machines.

note, telecommuting may be the first social change that pulls fathers and mothers back into the home, after years of being pushed out. Telecommuting could also increase autonomy and job satisfaction for many employees (Castells 2001; DiMaggio et al. 2001).

Use Your Sociological Imagination

If your first full-time job after college involved telecommuting, what do you think would be the advantages and disadvantages of working out of a home office? Do you think you would be satisfied as a telecommuter? Why or why not?

Electronic Communication

Electronic communication in the workplace has generated a lot of heat lately. On the one hand, emailing is a convenient way to push messages around, especially with the CC (carbon copy) button. It's democratic, too: lower-level employees are more likely to participate in email discussions than in face-to-face communications, giving organizations the benefit of their experience and views. But email doesn't convey body language, which in face-to-face communication can soften insensitive phrasing and make unpleasant messages (such as a reprimand) easier to take. It also leaves a permanent record, which can be a problem if messages are written thoughtlessly (DiMaggio et al. 2001). Email communication also runs the risk of being sent—unintentionally—to unanticipated recipients, such as in the case of a young Toronto man who, after applying for a government job in 2007, received an email from a lower-level government employee in which he was referred to in a racist manner. When the government worker emailed her colleague, she accidentally copied the message to the young job applicant as well. The premier of Ontario eventually called the young man to apologize on behalf of the provincial government (Diebel 2007).

Electronic communication has contributed significantly to the fragmentation of work. Today, productivity in the workplace is frequently hindered by email, pagers, cellphones, and pop-up windows, as well as face-to-face interruptions and cube drop-ins. In one observational study of office workers, researchers found that employees spent an average of only 11 minutes on any given project before being interrupted. Typically, 25 minutes passed before they returned to their original tasks. While multi-tasking may increase a person's efficiency in some situations, it has become an integral and not necessarily helpful feature of work for many employees (Mark et al. 2005; C. Thompson 2005).

Social Policy and Organizations
The State of the Unions

The Issue

How many people do you know who belong to a labour union? Chances are you can name fewer people than someone could 15 years ago. In 1991, unions represented 35.6 percent of workers in the Canadian economy; in 2006, they represented 30 percent (Statistics Canada 2007l). What has happened to diminish the representation for organized labour today? Have unions perhaps outlived their usefulness in a rapidly changing global economy dominated by the service industry? Are there differences between Canada and the United States in terms of legal impediments to union organization? Is Canada more labour friendly than the United States?

The Setting

Labour unions consist of organized workers sharing either the same skill (as in electronics) or the same employer (as in the case of postal employees). Unions began to emerge during the Industrial Revolution in England in the eighteenth century. Groups of workers banded together to extract concessions from employers, as well as to protect their positions. They frequently tried to protect their jobs by limiting entry to their occupation based on gender, race, ethnicity, citizenship, age, and sometimes rather arbitrary measures of skill levels. Today, we see less of this protection of special interests, but individual labour unions are still often the target of charges of discrimination (as are employers) (Form 1992).

The experience of labour unions varies widely in different countries. In some, such as Britain and Mexico, unions play a key role in the foundation of governments. In others, such as Japan and Korea, their role in politics is very limited and even their ability to influence the private sector is relatively weak. Stark differences exist between Canada and the United States in terms of union experiences. As Figure 5-2 illustrates, Canada's overall rate of unionization is more than double that of the United States. Although both countries have much lower rates of unionization in the private sector than in the public sector, Canada's percentages of union membership in both sectors far exceed those in the United States. The United States also exhibits greater disparities between rates of unionization for men and women and between rates for full-time and part-time employees (U.S. Bureau of Labor Statistics 2004). The increase in rates of unionization for women in Canada, which Statistics Canada (2004a) has referred to as a profound transformation in Canadian union membership, has not been duplicated in the United States. Unions in Canada sometimes can have a significant influence on employers and elected officials, but their effect may vary dramatically by type of industry and even region of the country.

Few people today would dispute the fact that the Canadian union movement is in transition. What accounts for this transition? Among the reasons offered are the following:

1. **The feminization of the movement.** In 1977, approximately 10 percent of female workers were unionized; by 2003, the number had risen to 30 percent. According to Statistics Canada (2004a), this growth can be attributed to such factors as the growing proportion of women in the paid labour force, their increased representation in the heavily unionized public sector, the rising unionization rate of part-time and temporary workers, and the expansion of unions into female-dominated and non-unionized or less-unionized workplaces, such as the service sector.

2. **The rising rate of unionization of the public sector and the falling rate of unionization of the private sector.** The rate of unionization of the public sector has remained stable for the last 30 years, while the rate for the private sector has fallen from 26 percent to 18 percent.

> ## Think about It
> What is the relationship between union membership and public or private sector employment in both Canada and the United States?

3. **The waning influence of international unions headquartered outside Canada.** In 1962, unions with headquarters outside the country accounted for two-thirds of union membership in Canada; in 2003, the proportion had fallen to just more than one-fourth.

4. **The changing scope of union membership.** The largest inroads in union membership have occurred among

▶ **FIGURE 5-2**

Comparison of Canadian and U.S. Unionization Rates

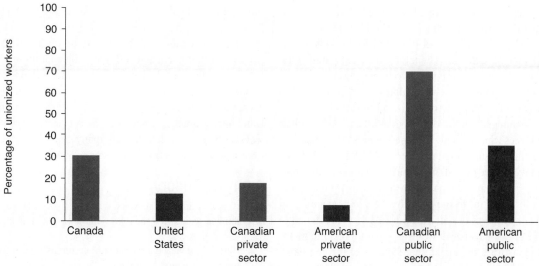

Sources: Statistics Canada 2004a; U.S. Bureau of Labor Statistics 2004.

women, youth, public administration workers, and child care and home support workers, while losses have been experienced among technical health workers (Statistics Canada 2004a). Labour market trends like globalization, the increase of self-employment, and the rise of non-standard work has altered people's relationship with work and weakened their ability to unionize.

Sociological Insights

Both Marxists and functionalists would view unions as a logical response to the emergence of impersonal, large-scale, formal, and often alienating organizations. This view certainly characterized the growth of unions in major manufacturing industries with a sharp division of labour. However, as manufacturing has declined, unions have had to look elsewhere for growth (Statistics Canada 2004a).

Today, labour unions in North America and Europe bear little resemblance to those early unions organized spontaneously by exploited workers. In line with the oligarchic model developed by Robert Michels (see page 121), unions have become increasingly bureaucratized under a self-serving leadership. Conflict theorists would point out that the longer union leaders are in office, the less responsive they are to the needs and demands of the rank and file and the more concerned they are with maintaining their own positions and power.

Yet, research shows that under certain circumstances union leadership can change significantly. Smaller unions are vulnerable to changes in leaders, as are unions whose memberships shift in composition, such as going from being predominantly male to female.

Many union employees encounter role conflict. For example, they agree to provide a needed service and then organize a "strike" to withhold it. This role conflict is especially apparent in the so-called helping occupations: teaching, social work, nursing, law enforcement, and paramedics. These workers may feel torn between carrying out their professional responsibilities and enduring working conditions they find unacceptable (Aronowitz and Di Fazio 1994).

Sociologists have observed another role conflict: employees who suddenly become "owners" of a business. Take the case of United Airlines (UAL). Since 1994, the employees have owned the majority of shares of the company. They may have changed the slogan from "fly the friendly skies" to "fly our friendly skies," but tensions still prevail. Union after union within UAL has threatened to strike or has enacted slowdowns, even though the members constitute the major shareholders of the company. Obviously, although everybody agreed to call the workers "owners," the pilots, mechanics, airline attendants, and others did not act like owners, and UAL management did not treat them like owners (L. Zuckerman 2001).

Policy Initiatives

United States law grants workers the right to organize via unions. But that country is unique among industrial democracies in allowing employers to actively oppose their employees' decision to organize (Comstock and Fox 1994). Wal-Mart, the largest employer in the United States—and the largest retailer in the world—is perhaps the most notable example of this (among its employees in the States, that is). In China, where, in 2004, Wal-Mart had over 40 store and 20 000 Chinese employees, the story is quite different. Here, Wal-Mart officials announced that if the employees decided to form a union, their wishes would be respected, as long as the union was affiliated with All-China Federation of Trade Unions (Meyerson 2004). This federation is dominated by the Communist Party in China and its unions are headed by members of the company management—hardly a genuine workers' movement (Meyerson 2004).

Within the United States, a major barrier to union growth exists in the 20 states that have so-called right-to-work laws. In these states, workers cannot be *required* to join or pay dues or fees to a union. The very term *right to work* reflects the anti-union view that a worker should not be forced to join a union, even if that union may negotiate on his or her behalf and achieve results that benefit the worker. In contrast to the United States, Canada has fewer legal impediments to union organization. Labour laws are under the control of the provinces and territories, and some jurisdictions are considered more labour friendly than others. For example, Quebec, Saskatchewan, and British Columbia will certify a bargaining unit without a vote as soon as the majority of workers in that particular unit have signed a union card (McKenna 2004). In the United States, where union activity is covered by federal law, employers can stall or block a vote on union organization for a significant period of time; once a much-delayed vote takes place, disgruntled workers may have left the company and the drive to unionize may have waned (McKenna 2004).

Applying Theory

1. If conflict thinker Karl Marx were alive today, how do you think he would view the role of unions in contemporary Canadian society?
2. How do you view the relevance of unions as a means of promoting gender equality?

CHAPTER RESOURCES

Summary

How do We Define and Reconstruct Reality?

- Through **social structure** (p. 100), a society is organized into predictable relationships based on **social interaction** (p. 100).
- People interact based on the meaning that situations or others' behaviour have for them. The ability to define reality reflects a group's power in society.

What are the Elements of Social Structure?

- An **ascribed status** (p. 102) is generally assigned to a person at birth, whereas an **achieved status** (p. 102) is attained largely through one's own effort. Some ascribed statuses, such as race and gender, can function as **master statuses** (p. 103) that affect one's potential to achieve a certain professional or social status.
- With each distinctive status—whether ascribed or achieved—come particular **social roles** (p. 103): the set of expectations for people who occupy that status.
- Much of our social behaviour takes place in **groups** (p. 106). When we find ourselves identifying closely with a group, it is probably a **primary group** (p. 106). A **secondary group** (p. 106) is more formal and impersonal.
- People tend to see the world in terms of **in-groups** (p. 107) and **out-groups** (p. 107), a perception often fostered by the very groups which they belong to or identify with.
- **Reference groups** (p. 107) set and enforce standards of conduct and serve as a source of comparison for people's evaluations of themselves and others.
- Groups serve as links to **social networks** (p. 108) and their vast resources.
- **Social institutions** (p. 110) are organized patterns of beliefs and behaviour centred on the provision of basic social needs as well as the production and reproduction of social relations. The mass media, the government, the economy, the family, and the health-care system are all examples of social institutions.
- Conflict theorists charge that social institutions help to maintain the privileges of the powerful while contributing to the powerlessness of others.

- Interactionist theorists stress that our social behaviour is conditioned by the roles and statuses we accept, the groups to which we belong, and the institutions within which we function.

What does a Global Perspective on Social Structure Look Like?

- Émile Durkheim thought that social structure depends on the division of labour in a society. According to Durkheim, societies with minimal division of labour have a collective consciousness called **mechanical solidarity** (p. 113); those with greater division of labour show an interdependence called **organic solidarity** (p. 113).
- Ferdinand Tönnies distinguished the close-knit community of *Gemeinschaft* (p. 113) from the impersonal mass society known as *Gesellschaft* (p. 113).
- Gerhard Lenski thinks that a society's social structure changes as its culture and technology become more sophisticated, a process he calls **socio-cultural evolution** (p. 113).

How are Organizations Structured?

- As societies have become more complex, large **formal organizations** (p. 117) have become more powerful and pervasive.
- Max Weber argued that in its ideal form, every **bureaucracy** (p. 117) has five basic characteristics: division of labour, hierarchical authority, written rules and regulations, impersonality, and employment based on technical qualifications. Carefully constructed bureaucratic policies can be undermined or redefined by an organization's informal structure, however.

How has the Workplace Changed?

- Organizational restructuring and new technologies have transformed the workplace through innovations such as *collective decision making*, *minimal hierarchy*, *work teams*, and *telecommuting*. At the same time, major shifts in the economy have reduced the power of **labour unions** (p. 125).

Critical Thinking Questions

1. People in certain professions seem particularly susceptible to role conflict. For example, journalists commonly experience role conflict when covering natural disasters, crimes, and other distressing situations. Should they offer assistance to the needy or cover breaking news? Select two other professions and discuss the role conflicts people in them might experience.
2. The functionalist, conflict, feminist, and interactionist perspectives can all be used in analyzing social institutions. What are the strengths and weaknesses in each perspective's analysis of those institutions?
3. Are primary groups, secondary groups, in-groups, out-groups, and reference groups likely to be found within a formal organization? What functions do these groups serve for a formal organization? What dysfunction might occur as a result of their presence?
4. Max Weber identified five basic characteristics of bureaucracy. Select an actual organization familiar to you (for example, your college or university, a workplace, a religious institution, or civic association you belong to) and apply Weber's analysis to that organization. To what degree does it correspond to Weber's ideal type of bureaucracy?

Key Terms

Achieved status   A social position that a person attains largely through his or her own efforts. (p. 102)

Agrarian society   The most technologically advanced form of pre-industrial society. Members are engaged primarily in the production of food, but increase their crop yields through technological innovations such as the plow. (p. 114)

Alienation   A condition of estrangement or dissociation from the surrounding society. (p. 117)

Ascribed status   A social position assigned to a person by society without regard for the person's unique talents or characteristics. (p. 102)

Bureaucracy   A component of formal organization that uses rules and hierarchical ranking to achieve efficiency. (p. 117)

Bureaucratization   The process by which a group, organization, or social movement becomes increasingly bureaucratic. (p. 121)

Classical theory   An approach to the study of formal organizations that views workers as being motivated almost entirely by economic rewards. (p. 121)

Coalition   A temporary or permanent alliance geared toward a common goal. (p. 108)

Formal organization   A group designed for a special purpose and structured for maximum efficiency. (p. 117)

Gemeinschaft   A close-knit community, often found in rural areas, in which strong personal bonds unite members. (p. 113)

Gesellschaft   A community, often urban, that is large and impersonal, with little commitment to the group or consensus on values. (p. 113)

Goal displacement   Overzealous conformity to official regulations of a bureaucracy. (p. 118)

Group   Any number of people with similar norms, values, and expectations who interact with one another on a regular basis. (p. 106)

Horticultural society   A pre-industrial society in which people plant seeds and crops rather than merely subsisting on available foods. (p. 114)

Human relations approach   An approach to the study of formal organizations that emphasizes the role of people, communication, and participation in a bureaucracy and tends to focus on the informal structure of the organization. (p. 122)

Hunting-and-gathering society   A pre-industrial society in which people rely on whatever foods and fibres are readily available in order to survive. (p. 114)

Ideal type   A construct or model for evaluating specific cases. (p. 117)

Industrial society   A society that depends on mechanization to produce its goods and services. (p. 115)

In-group   Any group or category to which people feel they belong. (p. 107)

Iron law of oligarchy   A principle of organizational life under which even a democratic organization will eventually develop into a bureaucracy ruled by a few individuals. (p. 121)

Labour union   Organized workers who share either the same skill or the same employer. (p. 125)

Master status   A status that dominates others and thereby determines a person's general position in society. (p. 103)

McDonaldization   The process by which the principles of the fast-food restaurant have come to dominate more and more sectors of U.S. society as well as of the rest of the world. (p. 120)

Mechanical solidarity   A collective consciousness that emphasizes group solidarity, characteristic of societies with minimal division of labour. (p. 113)

Organic solidarity   A collective consciousness that rests on mutual interdependence, characteristic of societies with a complex division of labour. (p. 113)

Out-group   A group or category to which people feel they do not belong. (p. 107)

Peter Principle   A principle of organizational life according to which every employee within a hierarchy tends to rise to his or her level of incompetence. (p. 119)

Post-industrial society   A society whose economic system is engaged primarily in the processing and control of information. (p. 116)

Postmodern society   A technologically sophisticated society that is preoccupied with consumer goods and media images. (p. 116)

Primary group   A small group characterized by intimate, face-to-face association and co-operation. (p. 106)

Reference group   Any group that individuals use as a standard for evaluating themselves and their own behaviour. (p. 107)

Role conflict   The situation that occurs when incompatible expectations arise from two or more social positions held by the same person. (p. 103)

Role exit   The process of disengagement from a role that is central to one's self-identity in order to establish a new role and identity. (p. 105)

Role strain   The difficulty that arises when the same social position imposes conflicting demands and expectations. (p. 105)

Scientific management approach   Another name for the classical theory of formal organizations. (p. 121)

Secondary group   A formal, impersonal group in which there is little social intimacy or mutual understanding. (p. 106)

Social institution   An organized pattern of beliefs and behaviour centred on basic social needs. (p. 110)

Social interaction   The ways in which people respond to one another. (p. 100)

Social network   A series of social relationships that link a person directly to others, and through them indirectly to still more people. (p. 108)

Social role   A set of expectations for people who occupy a given social position or status. (p. 103)

Social structure   The way in which a society is organized into predictable relationships. (p. 100)

Socio-cultural evolution   Long-term trends in societies resulting from the interplay of continuity, innovation, and selection. (p. 113)

Status   A term used by sociologists to refer to any of the full range of socially defined positions within a large group or society. (p. 102)

Technology   According to Gerhard Lenski, "cultural information about the ways in which the material resources of the environment may be used to satisfy human needs and desires." (p. 113)

Telecommuter   An employee who works full-time or part-time at home rather than in an outside office, and who is linked to a supervisor and colleagues through computer terminals, phone lines, and fax machines. (p. 123)

Trained incapacity   The tendency of workers in a bureaucracy to become so specialized that they develop blind spots and fail to notice obvious problems. (p. 118)

Additional Readings

Altman, Dennis. 2002. *Global Sex*. Chicago: University of Chicago Press. A look at how mass media, transportation, new technologies, and multinational corporations are reshaping our sexual practices and views in an increasingly globalized world.

Bakan, Joel. 2004. *The Corporation: The Pathological Pursuit of Profit and Power*. Toronto: Viking Canada. In this book, Bakan examines the modern business corporation—its history, its power, and its relationships to government, society, and the environment—likening it to a psychopathic personality.

Clement, Wallace, and Leah V. Vosko, eds. 2003. *Changing Canada: Political Economy as Transformation*. Montreal: McGill-Queen's University Press. The book examines how capitalism is producing new political transformations in Canada, including welfare state restructuring and new forms of resistance.

Jackson, Andrew. 2005. *Work and Labour in Canada: Critical Issues*. Toronto: Canadian Scholars' Press Inc/WP. A comprehensive examination of work and labour in the Canadian context.

Online Learning Centre

Visit the *Sociology: A Brief Introduction* Online Learning Centre at www.mcgrawhill.ca/olc/schaefer to access quizzes, interactive exercises, video clips, and other research and study tools related to this chapter.

 ## Reel Society Video Clips

Reel Society video clips, which appear on this book's Web site, can be used to spark discussion about the following topics from this chapter:

- Social Roles
- Groups

Chapter **6**

THE MASS MEDIA

Aboriginal Peoples Television Network

Aboriginal Peoples Television Network (APTN), launched in 1999 in Canada, is the first of its kind in the world with programming for, by, and about Aboriginal peoples.

☐ **What are the Theoretical Perspectives on the Mass Media?**

☐ **Who are the Media's Audiences?**

☐ **What does the Media Industry Look Like?**

  Boxes

HOW DOES TELEVISION PORTRAY THE FAMILY?

SOCIOLOGY IN THE GLOBAL COMMUNITY: Privacy and Censorship in the Digital Village

RESEARCH IN ACTION: Looking at Television from Four Perspectives

SOCIOLOGY IN THE GLOBAL COMMUNITY: The Digital Divide

SOCIAL POLICY AND THE MASS MEDIA: Media Violence

There *is* something happening here. The Net Generation has come of age. Growing up digital has had a profound impact on the way this generation thinks, even changing the way their brains are wired. And although this digital immersion presents significant challenges for young people—such as dealing with a vast amount of incoming information or ensuring balance between the digital and physical worlds—their immersion has not hurt them overall. It has been positive. The generation is more tolerant of racial diversity, and is smarter and quicker than their predecessors. These young people are remaking every institution of modern life, from the workplace to the marketplace, from politics to education, and down to the basic structure of the family. Here are some of the ways in which this is occurring.

- As employees and managers, the Net generation is approaching work collaboratively, collapsing the rigid hierarchy and forcing organizations to rethink how they recruit, compensate, develop, and supervise talent. I believe that the very idea of management is changing, with the exodus from corporations to start-ups just beginning.
- As consumers, they want to be "prosumers"— co-innovating products and services with producers. The concept of a brand is in the process of changing forever because of them.
- In education, they are forcing a change in the model of pedagogy, from a teacher-focused approach based on instruction to a student-focused model based on collaboration.
- Within the family, they have already changed the relationship between parents and children, since they are experts in something really important— the Internet.
- As citizens, the Net Generation is in the early days of transforming how government services are conceived and delivered and how we understand and decide what the basic imperatives of citizenship and democracy should be. For the growing numbers trying to achieve social change, there is a sea of change under way, ranging from civic activities to political engagement. The Net Gen is bringing political action to life more than in any previous generation.
- And in society as a whole, empowered by the global reach of the Internet, their civic activity is becoming a new, more powerful kind of social activism.

The bottom line is this: if you understand the Net Generation, you will understand the future. You will also understand how our institutions and society need to change today.

☐ *(Tapscott 2009:10–11)*

In his book *Grown Up Digital: How the Net Generation is Changing Your World*, Don Tapscott confronts the sweeping social change caused by the introduction of new means of communication. The chairman of nGenera Innovation Network, a management consulting company, Tapscott sees a huge generational divide between baby boomers and "N-Gen": those who were children, adolescents, or young adults at the turn of the twenty-first century. Like their parents—the boomers, who grew up with a new means of communication called television—the young people of N-Gen are defined by the new media that surround them. These "children of a digital age," he writes, are changing the way we live and work in ways that marketers, employers, and government planners have just begun to realize.

Both television and the Internet are **mass media**, a term that refers to the print and electronic means of communication that carry messages to widespread audiences. Print media include newspapers, magazines, and books; electronic media include radio, satellite radio, television, motion pictures, and the Internet. Advertising, which falls into both categories, is also a form of mass media.

The social impact of the mass media is obvious. Consider a few examples: In the 1950s, *TV dinners* were invented to accommodate the millions of "couch potatoes" who couldn't bear to miss their favourite television programs. Today, screen time encompasses not just television viewing but also playing video games and surfing the Internet. Candidates for political office rely on their media consultants to project a winning image both in print and in the electronic media. World leaders use all forms of media for political advantage, whether to gain territory or to bid on hosting an Olympic games. In parts of Africa and Asia, AIDS education projects owe much of their success to media campaigns. And during the 2003 invasion of Iraq, both the British and U.S. governments allowed journalists to be embedded with frontline troops as a means of "telling their story."

Few aspects of society are as central as the mass media. Through the media, we expand our understanding of people and events beyond what we experience in person. The media inform us about different cultures and lifestyles and about the latest forms of technology. For sociologists, the key questions are how the mass media affect our social institutions and how they influence our social behaviour.

Why are the media so influential? Who benefits from media influence and why? How do we maintain cultural and ethical standards in the face of negative media images? In this chapter, we consider the ways sociology helps us to answer these questions. First, we will look at how proponents of the various sociological perspectives view the media. Then, we will examine just who makes up the media's audience, as well as how the media operate, especially in their global reach. In the social policy section at the end of the chapter, we consider whether the violence shown in the media breeds violent behaviour in the audience.

Use Your Sociological Imagination

Can you think of any institutions of society which are not affected by the mass media?

☐ WHAT ARE THE THEORETICAL PERSPECTIVES ON THE MASS MEDIA?

Over the past decade, new technologies have made new forms of mass media available to households around the world. These new technologies have changed people's viewing and listening habits. Canadians spend a lot of time with the media, more and more of it on the Internet. Canadians have to a great extent moved away from broadcast TV and toward cable outlets (CRTC 2007). The Internet is increasingly popular among Canadians, while the popularity of traditional television and radio is declining (CRTC 2007). Adam Finkelstein of Instructional Multimedia Services at McGill University states, "It's not as if TV is disappearing; it's just that the Internet is really consuming it" (CTV 2007). A 2007 study by the Canadian Radio-television and Telecommunications Commission (CRTC) found that a growing number of Canadians are listening to radio and watching television online and are using cellphones, MP3 players, BlackBerrys, or other electronic devices to access the Internet. What do these changes in people's viewing and listening habits signify? In the following sections, we'll examine the impact of the mass media and changes in their usage patterns from the four major sociological perspectives (E. Nelson 2004).

Functionalist View

One obvious function of the mass media is to entertain. Except for clearly identified news or educational programming, we often think the explicit purpose of the mass media is to occupy our leisure time—from newspaper comics and crossword puzzles to the latest music releases on the Internet. While that is true, the media have other important functions. They also socialize us, enforce social norms, confer status, and promote consumption. An important dysfunction of the mass media is that they may act as a narcotic, desensitizing us to distressing events (Lazarsfeld and Merton 1948; C. Wright 1986).

Agent of Socialization

The media increase social cohesion by presenting a common, more or less standardized view of culture through mass communication. Sociologist Robert Park (1922) studied how newspapers helped immigrants adjust to their environment by changing their customary habits and teaching them the opinions of people in their new home country. Unquestionably, the mass media play a significant role in providing a collective experience ◀ P. 84 for members of society. Think about how the mass media bring together members of a community or even a nation by broadcasting important events (such as press conferences, parades, state funerals, and the Olympics) and by covering large disasters.

Which media outlets did North Americans turn to in the aftermath of the September 11, 2001 (9/11), tragedy? Although traditional television was used, the Internet also played a prominent role. About half of all U.S. Internet users—more than 53 million people—received some kind of news about the attacks online. Nearly three-fourths of Internet users communicated via email to show their patriotism, discuss events with their families, or reconnect with old friends. More than a third of Internet users read or posted material in online forums. In the first 30 days alone, the U.S. Library of Congress collected from one Internet site more than half a million pages having to do with the terrorist attacks. As a Library of Congress director noted, "The Internet has become for many the public commons, a place where they can come together and talk" (D.L. Miller and Darlington 2002; Mirapaul 2001:E2; Rainie 2001).

Of course, the socializing effects of the media can be used to promote the goals of dissident, even militant minorities. In the Palestinian-held Gaza Strip, Hamas—a group better known for its suicide-bombing campaigns (and the current ruling party of Palestine)—launched a television program meant to familiarize children with the Palestinian position on the disputed territories. In between lectures on revered historic landmarks such as

On Al Aksa TV in Gaza, two animal characters interact with Uncle Hazim, the popular host of a local children's show. Sponsored by the militant group Hamas, the show is meant to inculcate in the young the Palestinian people's claim to disputed territories in the Middle East.

Nablus and Al Aksa Mosque, the show's host, known as Uncle Hazim, takes on-air phone calls from viewers and talks with animal characters reminiscent of those on *Sesame Street*. The show omits all mention of violence and armed conflict in pursuit of Hamas's goals (Craig Smith 2006).

Other problems are inherent in the socialization function of the mass media. For instance, many people worry about the effect of using television as a babysitter and the impact of violent programming on viewer behaviour (see "Social Policy and the Mass Media: Media Violence" on page 152). Some people adopt a blame-the-media mentality, holding the mainstream media accountable for anything that goes wrong in society, especially with young people.

Enforcer of Social Norms

The media often reaffirm proper behaviour by showing what happens to people who act in a way that violates societal expectations. These messages are conveyed when villains get clobbered in cartoons or are thrown into jail on *Law and Order*. Yet, the media also often glorify deviant behaviour, whether it be physical violence, showing disrespect for a teacher, or illegal drug use.

The media play a critical role in shaping people's perceptions about the risks of narcotics use. Increases in substance use among youths in the United States during the 1990s were linked to a decline in warnings and anti-drug messages from the media, the proliferation of pro-use messages from the entertainment industry, and high levels of tobacco and alcohol product advertising and promotion. Media content analysis shows that in the 200 most popular movie rentals of 1996 and 1997, alcohol use appeared in 93 percent of the films, tobacco use in 89 percent, and illicit drug use in 22 percent, with marijuana and cocaine use shown most often. An analysis of the 1000 most popular songs during the same period showed that 27 percent referred to either alcohol or illicit drugs. In 1999, 44 percent of entertainment programs aired by the four major television networks portrayed tobacco use in at least one episode (Ericson 2001; D.F. Roberts et al. 1999).

In 1997, a U.S. federal law required television networks to provide one free minute for every minute the government bought for a public service announcement with an anti-drug message. The networks subsequently persuaded the government to drop the free minutes in exchange for aggressive anti-drug messages embedded in popular programs, such as *ER* and *The Practice*. Some people objected, saying that the networks were evading their legal responsibility in using the public airwaves, but criticism really mounted when word got out that a government agency was screening scripts in advance and even working on the storylines. Many critics felt that such public meddling could open the way for the government to plant messages in the media on other topics as well, such as abortion or gun control (Albiniak 2000).

Conferral of Status

The mass media confer status on people, organizations, and public issues. Whether it is an issue such as homelessness or a celebrity such as Paris Hilton, the mainstream media can, and do, single out one story from thousands of others and make that story become significant. *People* magazine has featured the late Princess Diana on its cover more than anyone else (Schaefer 2006). The magazine was not responsible for making Diana into a worldwide celebrity, but all the media outlets collectively created a notoriety that Princess Victoria of Sweden, for one, did not enjoy.

Another way the media confer celebrity status on individuals is by publishing information about what figures receive the most frequent Internet searches. Some newspapers and Web sites carry regularly updated lists of the most heavily researched individuals and topics of the week. The means may have changed since the first issue of *Time* magazine hit the stands in 1923, but the media still confer status—often electronically. Table 6-1 shows the fastest rising (and falling) searches on Google in 2007, illustrating the rise and fall of the status of various topics and people.

Table 6-1 Fastest Rising and Fastest Falling Global Searches on Google, 2007

Fastest Rising	Fastest Falling
1. iPod	1. World Cup*
2. Badoo	2. Mozart
3. Facebook	3. FIFA
4. dailymotion	4. Rebelde*
5. Webkinz	5. Kazaa
6. YouTube	6. Xanga
7. eBuddy	7. Webdetente
8. Second Life	8. Sudoku
9. Hi5	9. Shakira
10. Club Penguin	10. MP3

*Featured in the 2006 fastest-rising list.
Source: www.google.com/intl/en/press/zeitgeist2007.

Think about It

Do you think lists like the one in Table 6-1 capture of the spirit of the times? Why? Why not?

Promotion of Consumption

Twenty-thousand commercials a year—that is the number the average child in the United States watches on television, according to the American Academy of Pediatrics. Young people cannot escape commercial messages. They show up on high school scoreboards, at rock concerts, and as banners on Web pages. They are even embedded in motion pictures (remember Budweiser in *The Departed*?). Such *product placement* is nothing new. In the 1951 movie, *The African Queen*, an ad for Gordon's Gin was prominently displayed aboard the boat carrying Katharine Hepburn and Humphrey Bogart. But commercial promotion has become far more common today. Moreover, advertisers are attempting to develop brand or logo loyalty among younger and younger customers (Lasn 2003; Quart 2003).

Media advertising has several clear functions: it supports the economy, provides information about products, and underwrites the cost of media. In some cases, advertising becomes part of the entertainment industry.

How Does Television Portray the Family?   6-1

The media don't just present reality; they filter and interpret it. A good example of the media's interpretive portrayal of content is the way the family has been presented on television from the 1950s to the present.

Television networks in the United States continue to air their shows in Canada each day, as they have done for decades. Programs from south of the border, particularly dramas and comedies—in which families are commonly portrayed—are viewed substantially more often by Canadians than most domestic fare. In 2006, Statistics Canada reported that close to 82 percent of Canadians' viewing time of dramas and comedies was spent on foreign programs (mostly U.S. shows) (Statistics Canada 2006h). As a result, many U.S. television actors are household names in Canada (Meisel 2001). Canadians are constantly bombarded with U.S. images of family, since 80 percent of the characters on Canadian television, both in French and English shows, are from U.S. television (Graydon 2001).

One of the earliest and biggest hit shows on TV, *I Love Lucy* (1951–1957), starred a real-life married couple, Lucille Ball and Desi Arnaz. In a nod to audience sensibilities in the prim and proper 1950s, the two characters slept in separate beds and refrained from uttering the word *pregnant*, even when, in reality, Lucy was carrying the couple's first child. Viewers *did* glimpse signs of the cultural tension inherent in an Anglo–Latino relationship.

As the decades passed and Americans' concept of family life changed, portrayals of families on television changed with it. In *The Brady Bunch* (1969–1974), the show foreshadowed what would become a common phenomenon by the century's end—the blended family—as character Michael Brady merged his family of three sons with Carol Martin's family of three daughters. And though *The Cosby Show* (1984–1992) did not often embrace social commentary, it did present a picture of a two-income couple (physician and attorney) whose family was firmly rooted in the black upper middle class. Mainstream television programming, however, has traditionally portrayed white professional nuclear families.

More recent shows have continued to expand the boundaries of the televised portrayal of family life. *Family Guy* (1999–2002, 2005–present), an animated series about a dysfunctional Rhode Island family with a clueless dad, a talking dog, and a frighteningly precocious infant, offers an irreverent and relatively rare look at a working-class family. In *Two and a Half Men* (2003–present), two brothers, one of whom retains custody of his son after a divorce, show that today's households can come in all varieties.

The homegrown Canadian television show, *Little Mosque on the Prairie*, which has gained great popularity in both Canada and many countries around the world, portrays a bicultural family—one spouse is Muslim, the other is non-Muslim—in a small Saskatchewan town. The couple have a daughter who skilfully negotiates the meaning of her diverse ethnic background in her relationship with her parents and in interactions with community members.

Television has also shown childless, extended, single-father, single-mother, and gay households. What TV family looks most like yours? What kinds of families are rarely, if ever, shown on television?

Little Mosque on the Prairie

Corner Gas

A national survey showed that 14 percent of those who viewed the 2003 Super Bowl did so *only* for the commercials.

Yet, related to these functions are *dysfunctions*. Media advertising contributes to a consumer culture that creates "needs" and raises unrealistic expectations of what is required to be happy or satisfied. Moreover, because the media depend heavily on advertising revenue, advertisers can influence media content (FAIR 2001; Horovitz 2003).

Dysfunction: The Narcotizing Effect

As we have just noted, the mainstream media perform a *dysfunction*. Sociologists Paul Lazarsfeld and Robert Merton (1948) created the term **narcotizing dysfunction** to refer to the phenomenon in which the media provide such massive amounts of coverage that the audience becomes numb and fails to act on the information, regardless of how compelling the issue. Interested citizens may take in the information but make no decision or take no action, for example, to support victims of natural disasters such as wildfires on the West Coast or Hurricane Katrina.

Consider how often the media initiate a great outpouring of philanthropic support in response to natural disasters or family crises (think of the tsunami in Southeast Asia in December of 2004). But then what happens? Research shows that as time passes, viewer fatigue sets in. The mass media audience becomes numb, desensitized to the suffering, and may even conclude that a solution to the crisis has been found (Moeller 1999).

The media's narcotizing dysfunction was identified nearly 60 years ago, when just a few homes had television—well before the proliferation of electronic media. At that time, the dysfunction went largely unnoticed; but, today, commentators often point out the ill effects of addiction to television or the Internet, especially among young people. Issues such as street crime, global wars, and HIV/AIDS apparently are such overwhelming topics that some in the audience may feel they have acted—or at the very least learned all they need to know—simply by watching the news.

> ### Use Your Sociological Imagination
> You are a news junkie. Where do you gather your facts or information—from newspapers, radio, tabloids, magazines, TV newscasts, or the Internet? Explain your choice of medium.

Conflict View

Conflict theorists emphasize that the media reflect, and even exacerbate, many of the divisions in our society and world, including those based on gender, race, ethnicity, and social class. They point in particular to the media's ability to decide what is transmitted through a process called *gatekeeping*.

Gatekeeping

What story appears on page one of the morning newspaper? Which motion picture plays on three screens rather than just one at the local cineplex? What movie isn't released at all or can't get onto theatre screens? Behind these decisions are powerful figures—publishers, editors, film executives, and other media moguls.

The mass media constitute a form of big business in which profits are generally more important than the quality of the programming. Increasingly, television networks such as CNN and FOX have gained popularity, as the business of television is one in which viewer ratings are paramount. Within the mass media, a relatively small number of people control what eventually reaches the audience through a process known as **gatekeeping**. This term describes how material must travel through a series of checkpoints (or gates) before reaching the public. Thus, a select few decide what images to bring to a broad audience, particularly in countries such as Canada where media mergers have taken place. In many countries, the government plays a gatekeeping role. A study done for the World Bank found that in 97 countries, 60 percent of the top five TV stations and 72 percent of the largest radio stations are government-owned (World Bank 2001:183).

Gatekeeping prevails in all kinds of media. As sociologist C. Wright Mills ([1956] 2000b) observed, the real power of the media is that they can control what is being presented. In the recording industry, gatekeepers may reject a popular local band because it competes with a group already on their label. Even if a band lands a recording deal, radio programmers may reject the music because it does not fit the station's "sound." Television programmers may keep a pilot for a new TV series off the air because they believe it does not appeal to the target audience (which is sometimes determined by advertising sponsors). Similar decisions are made by gatekeepers in the publishing industry (Hanson 2005). Lost in all of this is the quality of the product itself.

Gatekeeping is not as dominant in at least one form of mass media: the Internet. You can send virtually any message to an electronic bulletin board, and create a Web page or a blog to advance any argument, including one that insists the earth is flat. The Internet is a means of quickly disseminating information (or misinformation) without going through any significant gatekeeping process.

Nevertheless, the Internet is not totally without restrictions. In many nations, laws regulate content on

Product placement (or "brand casting") is an increasingly important source of revenue for motion picture studios. This scene from *Austin Powers: The Spy Who Shagged Me* (1999), starring Canadian actor Mike Myers, doubles as a commercial for Starbucks.

topics such as gambling, pornography, and even politics. Popular Internet service providers will terminate accounts for offensive behaviour. In the fallout of 9/11, the Web auctioneer eBay did not allow people to sell parts of the World Trade Center via its online interface. A World Bank study found that 17 countries place significant controls on Internet content. For example, China routinely blocks search engines like Google and AltaVista from accessing the names of groups or individuals critical of the government (French 2004; World Bank 2001:187).

Critics of the content of mass media argue that the gatekeeping process reflects a desire to maximize profits. Why else, they argue, would movie star Julia Roberts, rather than Afghanistan's leader Hamid Karzai, make the cover of *Time* magazine? Later in this chapter, we consider the role that corporate structure plays in the makeup and delivery of mass media content. The gatekeeping process also receives criticism because much content that sees the light of day does not reflect the diversity of the audience.

Media Monitoring

In the past, the term **media monitoring** has been used to refer to interest groups' monitoring of media content. Recently, however, use of the term has expanded to include monitoring of individuals' media usage and choices without their knowledge. New technologies related to video on demand, downloading of audio/video clips, and satellite programming have created records of individual viewing and listening preferences. In 2006, Google opposed U.S. government efforts to obtain company records of users' Web-browsing activities. At the same time, members of the general public expressed concern both that companies such as Google were maintaining such records and that government agencies were interested in them. In Chapter 9, we will see that media and computer giants don't always oppose government efforts to monitor media usage. For example, Yahoo, Google, Microsoft, and Dell have co-operated with the Chinese government's efforts to restrict and monitor Internet use, raising human rights concerns in the process.

The U.S. government has also come under criticism recently for authorizing wiretaps of its citizens' telephone conversations without judicial approval. Government officials argue that the wiretaps were undertaken in the interest of national security, to monitor contacts between U.S. citizens and known terrorist groups following 9/11. But critics who take the conflict perspective, among others, are concerned by the blatant invasion of people's privacy (Gertner 2005).

What are the practical and ethical limits of media monitoring? In daily life, parents often oversee their children's online activities and scan the blogs they read—which are, of course, available for anyone to see. Many parents may see such monitoring of children's media use and communications as an appropriate part of adult supervision. Yet, their snooping sets an example for their children, who may use the technique for their own ends. Some media analysts have noted a growing trend among adolescents: the use of new media to learn not-so-public information about their parents (Delaney 2005). In Box 6-2 on page 139, we discuss the ways in which the predominance of digital technology has intensified concerns over privacy, safety, and censorship.

Dominant Ideology: Constructing Reality

Conflict theorists argue that the mass media maintain the privileges of certain groups. Moreover, while protecting their own interests, powerful groups may limit the media's representation of others. Karl Marx saw economic determinism as shaping the way in which media are viewed. The economic base of a capitalist society, founded on class distinction and exploitation, determines the nature of the other institutions, such as the family, the education

Sociology in the Global Community

6-2

Privacy and Censorship in the Digital Village

Imagine discovering that a complete stranger has been able to construct a profile of your identity; she or he has been able to find your social insurance number, the number of bedrooms in your home, the names of your former partners, the restaurants you frequent, and the number of vacations you take each year. Such invasions do occur, which has prompted the Canadian government to take action. To protect Canadian citizens from invasions of their privacy and unwanted use of their personal information, and to create trust and confidence in using the Internet to conduct business, the federal government has recently established new rules to protect Canadians' personal information.

In the past, Canadian privacy laws have had loopholes and were so patchy that it was often difficult to distinguish between data that were obtained legally and data that were gathered illicitly. The other side of the coin is the fear that government might restrict the flow of electronic information too much, stepping over the ethical boundary into censorship. Some observers, however, feel the government is fully justified in restricting pornographic information. The whole issue of privacy and censorship in this technological age is another case of culture lag, in which the material culture (the technology) is changing faster than the non-material culture (norms controlling the technology).

The typical consumer in Canada is included in dozens of marketing databases. These lists may seem innocent enough at first. Does it really matter if companies can buy lists for marketing with our names, addresses, and telephone numbers? Part of the problem is that computer technology has made it increasingly easy for any individual, business firm, or government agency to retrieve more and more information about any of us. For decades, information from motor vehicle offices, voter registration lists, and credit bureaus has been electronically stored, yet the incompatibility of different computer systems would prevent access from one system to another. Today, having some amount of information about a person has made it much easier to get further and perhaps more sensitive information.

The question of how much free expression should be permitted on the Internet relates to the issue of censorship. Some X-rated material is perfectly legal, if inappropriate for children who use the Net. Some of sites on the Web are clearly illegal, such as those that serve the needs of pedophiles who prey on young children. Some are morally and legally elusive, such as the "upskirt" sites (which post images taken by video cameras aimed under the skirts of unsuspecting women in public places) or the site that, in 2005, featured the exposed thong underwear of unsuspecting female students at the University of Victoria in British Columbia. This is another area in which we can see the results of culture lag. To protect the privacy and personal information of Canadians in the digital landscape, the federal government implemented the Personal Information Protection and Electronic Documents Act (PIPEDA) in 2004. PIPEDA sets out 10 key principles that organizations must follow when collecting, using, and disclosing Canadians' personal information. Central to the law are the following provisions:

- Organizations must seek the consent of individuals before collecting, using, or disclosing their personal information.
- Organizations must protect personal information with security safeguards according to the sensitivity of the information.
- Individuals may access personal information about themselves and have it corrected if necessary.
- The purposes for which the information is collected must be identified by the organization at the time of its collection.

PIPEDA provides a consistent set of provisions to protect Canadians' personal information and privacy, regardless of what province or territory they live in. It also allows Canadian companies to seamlessly do business with the European Union (EU), which has implemented legislation called the European Union Data Protection Directive.

Privacy and censorship are also global issues. In Myanmar, the government has ruled that fax machines and computer modems are illegal. In Saudi Arabia, access to the Internet was banned until 1999. Now, all Internet connections there are routed through a government hub where central computers block access to thousands of sites catalogued on a rapidly expanding censorship list—for example, all gambling sites, all freewheeling chat rooms, and all sites critical of the ruling Saudi family. By contrast, the openness of the Internet in other parts of the

Middle East allows scattered Palestinian refugees to communicate with one another and establish Web sites that provide a history of Palestinian settlements. Although China encourages expansion of the Internet, it has been wary of facilitating communication that it regards as disruptive. From time to time, the Chinese government shuts down Internet search engines, such as Google. Meanwhile, the British government is constructing an Internet spy centre that is geared to watch all online activity domestically. It will be able to track every Web site a person visits (Africa News Service 1998; Jehl 1999; MacLeod 2000; E. Rosenthal 1999, 2000; Wilkinson 1999).

Although some people chastise government efforts to curb the uses of some new technological tools, others decry their failure to limit certain aspects of these tools. Unlike Canada, the United States has developed an international reputation of being opposed to efforts to protect people's privacy. For example, the Center for Public Integrity, a non-partisan research organization, issued a report in 1998 that critiques the U.S. government for failing to approve legislation protecting the confidentiality of medical records. In another case, America Online revealed to a U.S. Navy investigator the identity of a sailor who had described his marital status online as gay. In 1998, both the Navy and America Online were forced to reach settlements for violating the privacy of the sailor. At the same time, the United States has been vocal in opposing the above-mentioned European Union Data Protection Directive. The U.S. technology industry does not want access to information blocked, since information is vital to global commerce. Such cases as these illustrate the fine line between safeguarding privacy and stifling the electronic flow of information (Fleras 2003).

The conflict over privacy and censorship is far from over. As technology continues to advance in the twenty-first century, there are sure to be new problems. One such concern arises from the use of social networking sites such as Facebook; if people are not paying attention to their privacy settings, their profiles, which can contain a lot of personal information, are open to anyone for viewing.

Applying Theory

1. How might interactionists study the ways that people can obtain information about other people?
2. Taking a conflict perspective, do you think corporations and employers have a right to monitor employees' Internet activities?
3. Are you more concerned about government censorship of electronic communication or about unauthorized invasion of your privacy?

Sources: Africa News Service 1998; Fleras 2003; Jehl 1999; Macleod 2000; Rosenthal 1999; Wilkinson 1999.

system, the legal system, and, more applicably, the media. The media are used to ensure that the economy—based on exploitative class relations—is maintained and that profits for the ruling class will grow. Marxist theorists see advertising as a key ingredient in the maintenance of advanced capitalism, as consumers are "created" in order to maximize the economic power of the ruling class. The Italian Marxist, Antonio Gramsci (1891–1937), took Marx's idea of economic determinism further to include the ways in which the ruling classes convince the oppressed groups to consent to their oppression. According to Gramsci, the term **hegemony** refers to a situation where the powerful groups are able to convince the less powerful to accept the way that the powerful group acts or sees the world as "normal" or "common sense." This helps to maintain the social, economic, and political interests of the dominant classes. For example, the mainstream media transmit messages that virtually define what we regard as the real world, even though those images frequently vary from what the larger society experiences.

Mass media decision makers are overwhelmingly white, male, and wealthy. It may come as no surprise, then, that many types of mainstream media tend to ignore the lives and ambitions of subordinate groups, among them working-class people of colour, gays and lesbians, people with disabilities, overweight people, and older people. Worse, media content may create false images or stereotypes of these groups that then become accepted as accurate portrayals of reality. **Stereotypes** are unreliable generalizations about all members of a group that do not recognize individual differences within the group. The television program *Beauty and the Geek*, for example, stereotypes men who don't fit the culturally defined image of a physically attractive male as "geeks" and also stereotypes women as being shallow and attracted only to men who conform to these culturally defined images.

Television content is a prime example of this tendency to ignore reality. How many overweight TV characters can you name? Even though in real life, 1 out of every 4 women is obese (30 or more pounds over a healthy body weight), only 3 out of 100 TV characters are portrayed as obese. Heavy-set television characters have fewer romances, talk less about sex, eat more often, and are more frequently the object of ridicule than their thinner counterparts (Hellmich 2001).

Racialized minorities groups are stereotyped in television shows. Almost all leading roles are cast to be white, as media racism persists in filtering images through a "Eurocentric prism of whiteness" (Fleras 2003:284). Blacks on prime-time TV tend to be featured mainly in crime-based dramas (Azam 2000). The misrepresentation, stereotyping, ignoring, caricaturing, trivializing, and ridiculing of racialized minorities leads one to ask the question, "Is the Canadian mainstream media racist or is there media racism in Canada?" (Fleras 2003). Canadian sociologist Augie Fleras asserts that, while it is difficult to prove Canada has racist media, one can look at evidence showing how racism has been institutionalized through organizational characteristics such as codified procedures that openly discriminate against minorities and argue convincingly that Canada does suffer from media racism. In Fleras's words, "Media racism exists in the foundational principles that govern media values, agendas, and priorities, [which] continue to be rooted in the primacy of whiteness as the standard by which others are judged" (2003:283).

Dominant Ideology: Whose Culture?

In the United States, on the popular television contest, *The Apprentice*, the dreaded dismissal line is, "You're fired." In Finland, on *Dilli* (The Deal), it's "*Olet vapautettu*" ("You're free to leave"); in Germany, on *Big Boss*, it's "*Sie haben frei*" ("You're off"). Although people ◄ P. 50–53 throughout the world decry American exports, from films to language to Bart Simpson, U.S. media models and popular culture are still widely imitated. Sociologist and cultural commentator Todd Gitlin describes U.S. pop culture as something that "people love, and love to hate" (2002:177; Wentz and Atkinson 2005).

This love–hate relationship is so enduring that the U.S. media have come to rely on overseas markets for major revenue streams. In fact, many motion pictures have brought in more monies abroad than at home. Through early 2006, for example, *Titanic* had earned a record breaking US$600 million in the United States and another US$1.2 billion from overseas box offices. Some Hollywood movies, however, are so insensitive to the global audience that they fail miserably overseas. The 2005 film, *Memoirs of a Geisha*, set in twentieth-century Japan, greatly offended moviegoers in that country because the three title roles went to Ziyi Zhang,

In Johannesburg, South Africa, musical artist Lebo Mathosa celebrates MTV's launch of the first local music channel on the African continent. African artists hope the channel will offer greater exposure to indigenous musicians. Like the mass media in most parts of the world, African television is dominated by Western constructions of reality, including musical styles.

Michelle Yeoh, and Gong Li—all non-Japanese performers. Ironically, Ziyi Zhang's casting also upset the Chinese government; it was outraged to see a leading Chinese star portray a Japanese geisha. In 2006, government officials banned the film's release in China (Banboza 2006).

We risk being ethnocentric if we overstress U.S. dominance in global popular culture. For example, *Survivor*, *Who Wants to Be a Millionaire*, and *Iron Chef*—immensely popular TV programs in the United States—came from Sweden, Britain, and Japan, respectively. Even *American Idol* originated in Britain, as *Pop Idol* featuring Simon Cowell. And the steamy telenovels of Mexico and other Spanish-speaking countries owe very little of their origin to Hollywood-produced soap operas. Unlike motion pictures, television is gradually moving away from U.S. domination and is more likely to be locally produced. By 2003, all the top 50 British TV shows were locally produced. *The West Wing* may appear on television in London, but it is shown late at night. Even U.S.-owned TV ventures, such as Disney, MTV, and CNN, have dramatically increased their locally produced programming overseas. The introduction of MTV Romania and MTV Indonesia in 2003 brought the number of local versions of the popular music channel to 38 (*The Economist* 2003a).

Nations that feel a loss of identity may try to defend against the cultural invasion from foreign countries, especially the economically dominant United States. Many developing nations have long argued for a greatly improved two-way flow of news and information between industrialized nations and developing nations. They complain that news from the developing world is scant, and what news there is reflects unfavourably on the developing nations. For example, what do you know about South America? Many people in North America will mention the topics that dominate the news from that continent: revolution and drugs. Most know little else about South America.

To remedy this imbalance, a resolution to monitor the news and content that cross the borders of developing nations was passed by the United Nations Educational,

Famed Chinese actress Ziyi Zhang played a Japanese geisha in the Hollywood-made film, *Memoirs* of a *Geisha* (2005). The decision to cast her in a Japanese role backfired in both Japan and China. Though U.S. films are usually well received abroad, cultural insensitivity can damage their box-office receipts.

Scientific, and Cultural Organization (UNESCO) in the 1980s. The United States disagreed with the proposal, which became one factor in the U.S. decision to withdraw from UNESCO in the mid-1980s. In 2005, the United States opposed another UNESCO plan, meant to reduce the diminishment of cultural differences. Hailed as an important step toward protecting threatened cultures, particularly the media markets in developing nations, the measure passed the UN's General Assembly by a vote of 148–2. The United States, one of the two dissenters, objected that the measure's wording was vague (Dominick 2005:455; Riding 2005).

Feminist Views

Many feminists share the view of conflict theorists that the mass media stereotype and misrepresent social reality. According to these views, the media powerfully influence how we look at women and men, communicating unrealistic, stereotypical, and limiting images of the sexes. Here are three problems feminists believe arise from media coverage (Wood 1994):

1. Women are under-represented, which suggests that men are the cultural standard and women are insignificant.
2. Men and women are portrayed in ways that reflect and perpetuate stereotypical views of gender. Women, for example, are often shown in peril, needing to be rescued by a male—rarely the reverse.
3. Depictions of male–female relationships emphasize traditional sex roles and normalize violence against women.

Educators and social scientists have long noted the stereotypical portrayal of women and men in the mass media. Women are often shown as being shallow and obsessed with beauty. They are more likely than men to be presented unclothed, in danger, or even physically victimized. Responding to the way advertising and the entertainment media objectify and even dehumanize women, Jean Kilbourne argues in her writings and film documentaries that "we [women] are the product." Feminist Vivian Gornick asserts that the portrayal of women in the media reflects "innumerable small murders of the mind and spirit [that] take place daily" (1979:ix; Cortese 1999; Goffman 1979; Kilbourne 2000a, 2000b).

A continuing, troubling issue for some feminists—particularly radical feminists—is pornography. Pornography frequently presents women as objects and attempts to normalize sexual violence by men toward women. Some feminists would argue that this type of objectification and imagery represents an implicit endorsement of violence against women and is a clear example of the unrelenting grip of patriarchal social structure and culture. According to radical feminist Leisbet van Zoonen, pornography is "a form of sexual violence against women, simultaneously a source and product of a deeply misogynistic society" (1994:19). The industry that creates sexually explicit adult images for videos, DVDs, and the Internet is largely unregulated, putting its own performers at risk. A 2002 health survey of triple-X, as the porn industry refers to itself, found that 40 percent of performers had at least one sexually transmitted disease, compared to 0.1 percent of the general population. The career span of these women and men is short, usually about 18 months, but the profits for the industry are continuous and enormous (Huffstutter 2003).

As in other areas of sociology, feminist researchers caution against assuming that what holds true for men's media use is true for everyone. Researchers, for example, have studied the different ways that women and men approach the Internet. Though men are only slightly more likely than women ever to have used the Internet, they are much more likely to use it daily. According to a 2005 study, about a third of men use the Internet every day, compared to a quarter of women. Not surprisingly, men account for 91 percent of the players in online sports fantasy leagues. But perhaps more socially significant is that women are more likely than men to maintain friendship networks through email (Boase et al. 2006; Fallows 2006; Rainie 2005).

Unlike feminist perspectives that point to necessary social action to change the media's portrayal of women, post-feminist views are those that individualize women's concerns, *discouraging* a radical change to social institutions, including the mass media. In her book, *Postfeminist News: Political Women in Media Culture*, Mary Douglas Vavrus argues that the ways in which women are portrayed in the mass media, and news programs in particular, promote a post-feminist view. Regrettably, these media accounts, according to Vavrus, encourage women's focus on private consumer lifestyles and middle-class aspirations while discouraging public life and political aspirations (2002).

Interactionist View

Interactionists are especially interested in shared understandings of everyday behaviour. These scholars examine the media on the microlevel to see how they shape day-to-day social behaviour. Increasingly, researchers point to the mass media as the source of major daily activity; some argue that television serves virtually as a primary group for many individuals who share TV viewing time together. Other mass media participation is not necessarily face to face. For example, we usually listen to the radio or read the newspaper as a solitary activity, although it is possible to share it with others (Cerulo et al. 1992; Waite 2000).

Interactionists note, too, that friendship networks can emerge from shared viewing habits or from recollection of a cherished television series from the past. Family members and friends often gather for parties centred on the broadcasting of popular events such as the Super Bowl or the Academy Awards. And, as we've seen, television often serves as a "babysitter" or "playmate" for children and even infants.

The power of the mass media encourages political leaders and entertainment figures to carefully manipulate their images through public appearances called photo opportunities (or photo ops). By embracing symbols (posing with celebrities or in front of prestigious landmarks), participants in these staged events attempt to convey self-serving definitions of social reality (M. Weinstein and D. Weinstein 2002).

The rise of the Internet has facilitated new forms of communication and social interaction, often referred to as "the new media." Grandparents can now keep up with their grandchildren via email. Gay and lesbian teens have online resources for support and information. People can even find their life partners through computer dating services. Social-networking sites, such as Facebook and MySpace, are popular among younger people, providing the opportunity to exchange information and to maintain and expand social contacts. As Figure 6-1 shows, throughout the world, the Internet is casting an increasingly wider net over social interactions.

Some troubling issues have been raised about day-to-day life on the Internet. What, if anything, should be done about extremist groups who use cyberspace to exchange messages of hatred? What, if anything, should be done about the issue of sexual "expression" on the Internet? How can children be protected from sexual predators? Should "hot chat" and X-rated film clips be censored? Or should expression be completely free?

Though the Internet has created a new platform for extremists and pornographers, it has also given people greater control over what they see and hear. That is, the Internet allows people to manage their media exposure so as to avoid sounds, images, and ideas they do not enjoy or endorse. The legal scholar, Cass Sunstein (2002), has referred to this personalized approach to news information gathering as *egocasting*. Other media commentators have observed the shift away from the dominance of *broadcasting* to what has become referred to as *narrowcasting*. One possible social consequence of this trend may be a less tolerant society. If we read, see, and hear

▶ **FIGURE 6-1**

The Internet Explosion

In little more than a decade, the World Wide Web has exploded, touching 600 million users in every single country on the earth. Still, a digital divide, measured in the form of relative bandwidth, separates rich countries from poor ones.

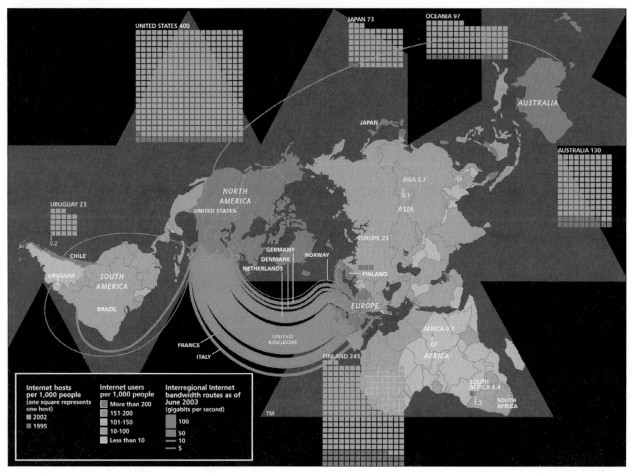

Source: National Geographic 2005:21 and the Buckminster Fuller Institute™.

only what we know and agree with, we may become much less prepared to meet with people from different backgrounds or converse with those who express new viewpoints.

Finally, while many people in Canada and elsewhere embrace the Internet, we should mention here that not everyone has equal access to it. The same people, by and large, who experience poor health, enjoy few job opportunities, and have been generally marginalized by society are left off the information highway. Figure 6-2 breaks down Internet usage by gender, age, income, and education. Note the large disparities in usage between those with high and low incomes, the younger and the older, and between those with more

or less education. Though educators and politicians have touted the potential benefits to the disadvantaged, Internet usage may be reinforcing existing inequality. Box 6-3 on page 146 places the topic of unequal Internet access in a global context.

The interactionist perspective helps us to understand one important aspect of the entire mass media system: the audience. How do we actively participate in media events? How do we construct with others the meaning of media messages? We will explore these questions in the section that follows. (Table 6-2 summarizes the various sociological perspectives on all media, and Box 6-4 on page 147 looks at television from those four perspectives.)

FIGURE 6-2

Who's on the Internet?

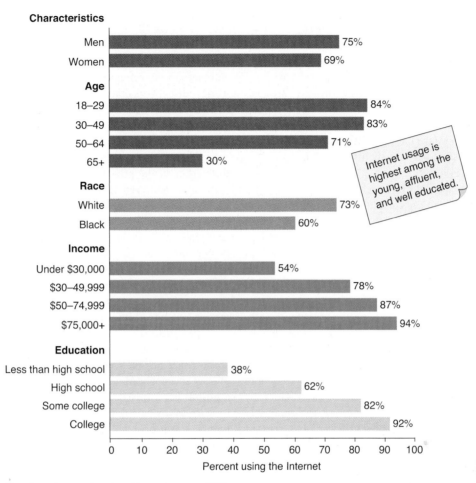

Note: Based on any location of Internet access, 2005.
Source: Statistics Canada 2006k, CANSIM Table 358-0125.

Table 6-2 Sociological Perspectives on the Mass Media

Theoretical Perspective	Emphasis	Theoretical Perspective	Emphasis
Functionalist	Socialization	Conflict	Gatekeeping
	Enforcement of social norms		Media monitoring
	Conferral of status		Construction of reality
	Promotion of consumption	Interactionist	Impact on social behaviour
	Narcotizing effect (dysfunction)		Source of friendship networks
		Feminist	Under-representation of women
			Misrepresentation of women

Sociology in the Global Community

The Digital Divide

6-3

Students in colleges and universities in North America expect to be able to use the Internet or leave messages through voice mail. They complain when the computer is "slow" or the electronic mailbox is "full." Despite their complaints, they take these services for granted and generally do not even pay directly for them. But in much of the world, it is very different.

The term **digital divide** refers to the "troubling gap between those who use computers and the Internet and those who do not" (Mehra et al. 2004:782). The digital divide takes into account the gap in use between developing and developed countries, as well as factors such as age, gender, income, and education.

The United Nations, which declared May 17 World Information Day in order to draw attention to the digital divide, has tried for years to assist Madagascar to upgrade its telephone system so that nation can handle a 300-band communication device—the slowest speed available. At such a glacial rate, it would take roughly two minutes to transmit this page of the book you're reading without the colour and without the graphics. By comparison, in Canada, most people are discarding systems 50 times faster and turning to devices that transmit information 180 times faster. The irony is that it costs more per minute to use a telephone in Madagascar and much of Africa than in Canada, so we have a continent paying more per minute to transmit information much more slowly.

This is but one example of the haves and have-nots in the information age. The Internet is virtually monopolized by North America and Europe and a few other industrial nations. As of 2005, a U.N. report notes that the digital divide between rich and poor countries persists and that one-third of developing countries have a broadband penetration rate that is less than 5 percent (UNCTAD 2006). High-income countries have the most

Internet hosts, computers directly connected to the worldwide network of interconnected computer systems. In contrast, in 2001, three countries had no Internet service provider at all: Guyana in South America, Guinea-Bissau in Africa, and North Korea.

This inequality is not new. We also find dramatic differences in the presence of newspapers, telephones, televisions, and even radios throughout the world. For example, in Madagascar, there are 3 telephone lines per 1000 people; and for all low-income nations, the average is 16. In Canada, there are more than 600 lines per 1000 people; for all high-income nations the average is 552. Often in developing nations, and especially their rural areas, radio and television transmission is sporadic, and the programming may be dominated by recycled information from the United States.

The consequences of the global digital divide for developing nations are far more serious than not being able to "surf the Net." Today, we have the true emergence of what sociologist Manuel Castells and others refer to as a **global economy** because the world has the capacity to work as a single unit in real time. However, if large numbers of people and, indeed, entire nations are disconnected from the information economy, their slow economic growth will continue, with all the negative consequences it has for people. The educated and skilled will immigrate to labour markets that are a part of this global economy, deepening the impoverishment of the nations on the periphery.

Applying Theory

1. What factors might contribute to the digital divide in developing nations?
2. What are some of the social and economic consequences for nations that are not "connected"? What groups are particularly vulnerable to not being connected?

Sources: Castells 1996, 2000; Fleras 2003; Matrix.Net 2000; Mehra et al. 2004; UNCTAD 2006; World Bank 2000a; Wresch 1996.

Research in Action   6-4
Looking at Television from Four Perspectives

Television to most of us is that box sitting on the shelf or hanging on the wall that diverts us, occasionally entertains us, and sometimes puts us to sleep. But sociologists look much more deeply at the medium. Here is what they find using the four sociological perspectives:

Functionalist View

In examining any aspect of society, including television, functionalists emphasize the contribution it makes to overall social stability. Functionalists regard television as a powerful force in communicating the common values of our society and in promoting an overall feeling of unity and social solidarity:

- Television vividly presents important national and international news. On a local level, television communicates vital information on everything from storm warnings and school closings to the locations of emergency shelters.
- Television programs transmit valuable learning skills (*Curious George*) and factual information (CBC's *The National*).
- Television "brings together" members of a community or even a nation by broadcasting important events and ceremonies (press conferences, parades, and state funerals) and through coverage of tragedies, such as the shocking murder of four RCMP officers in 2005.
- Television contributes to economic stability and prosperity by promoting and advertising services and (through shopping channels) serving as a direct marketplace for products.

Conflict View

Conflict theorists argue that the social order is based on coercion and exploitation. They emphasize that television reflects and even exacerbates many of the divisions of our society and world, including those based on gender, race, ethnicity, and social class:

- Television is a form of big business in which profits are more important than the quality of the product (programming).
- Television's network executives are overwhelmingly white, male, and prosperous; by contrast, television programs tend to ignore the lives and ambitions

of subordinate groups, among them working-class people, visible minorities, Aboriginal people, gays and lesbians, people with disabilities, and older people.
- Television distorts the electoral process in politics, as candidates with the most money (often backed by powerful lobbying groups) buy TV commercial time and saturate the air with negative attack ads.
- By exporting *Survivor*, *Desperate Housewives*, and other programs around the world, U.S. television undermines the distinctive traditions and art forms of other societies and encourages their cultural and economic dependence on the United States.

Interactionist View

In studying the social order, interactionists are especially interested in shared understandings of everyday behaviour. Consequently, interactionists examine television on the micro level by focusing on how day-to-day social behaviour is shaped by television:

- Neglectful parents use television as a "babysitter" or "playmate" for many children, often over long periods of time.
- Friendship networks can emerge from shared viewing habits or from recollections of an old, cherished TV series. Family members and friends often gather for parties centred on the broadcasting of popular events, such as a Stanley Cup playoff game, the Academy Awards, or even "reality" series like *Canadian Idol*.
- The frequent appearance of violence in the news and in entertainment programming creates feelings of fear and may actually make interpersonal relations more charged or aggressive.
- The power of television encourages political leaders and even entertainment figures to carefully manipulate symbols (by publicly posing with celebrities or in front of prestigious landmarks) and to attempt to convey self-serving definitions of social reality.

Feminist Views

Feminist theorists believe that gender is constructed by society; thus, television plays a major role not only in reflecting society's ideas about gender but also in constructing its own images:

- Television reinforces gender inequality through its portrayal of women as subordinate and powerless and men as dominant and powerful.
- Television objectifies women through its portrayal of women as objects to be admired for their physical appearance and sexual attractiveness.
- Television creates the false impression that most women are the same—young, white, middle-class, slim, and heterosexual.

Despite their differences, feminist theorists, functionalists, conflict theorists, and interactionists would agree that there is much more to television than simply "entertainment." They would also agree that television and other popular forms of culture are worthy subjects for serious study by sociologists.

Applying Theory

1. What functions does television serve? What might be some dysfunctions?
2. If you were a television network executive, which perspective would influence your choice of programs? Why?

☐ WHO ARE THE MEDIA'S AUDIENCES?

The mass media are distinguished from other social institutions by the necessary presence of an audience. It can be an identifiable, finite group, such as an audience at a jazz club or a Broadway musical, or a much larger and undefined group, such as MuchMusic viewers or readers of the same issue of *The Globe and Mail*. The audience may be a secondary group gathered in a large auditorium or a primary group, such as a family watching the latest Harry Potter video at home.

We can look at the audience from the level of both *microsociology* and *macrosociology*. At the micro level, we might consider how audience members, interacting among themselves, respond to the media, or in the case of live performances, actually influence the performers. At the macro level, we might examine broader societal consequences of the media's influence, such as the widespread early childhood education delivered through programming like *Sesame Street*.

Even if an audience is spread out over a wide geographic area and members don't know one another, it is still distinctive in terms of age, gender, income, political allegiance, education, and ethnicity. The audience for a ballet, for example, would differ substantially from the audience for country music.

Use Your Sociological Imagination

Think about the last time you were part of an audience. How similar or different from yourself were the other audience members? What might account for whatever similarities or differences you noticed?

The Segmented (or Niche) Audience

Increasingly, the media are marketing themselves to a *particular* audience (sometimes referred to as **narrowcasting**). Once a media outlet, such as a radio station or a magazine, has identified its audience, it targets that group—such a group can be called a **niche** or **segmented audience**. To some degree, this specialization is driven by advertising. Media specialists have sharpened their ability, through survey research, to identify particular target audiences. As a result, Nike would be much more likely to promote a new line of golf clubs on the Golf Channel, for example, than on an episode of *SpongeBob SquarePants*. The many more choices that the growing Internet and satellite/digital broadcast channels offer audiences also foster specialization. Members of these audiences are more likely to *expect* content geared to their own interests.

Marketing research has developed to the point that those who are interested can estimate the size of the audience for a particular performer. In fact, computer programs have been written to simulate not just specific audiences, but the connections among them. The specialized targeting of audiences has led some scholars to question the "mass" in mass media. For example, the British social psychologist, Sonia Livingstone, has written that the media have become so segmented, they have taken on the appearance almost of individualization (2004). Are viewing audiences so segmented that large collective viewerships are a thing of the past? The answer is not yet clear. Even though we seem to be living in an age of *personal* computers and *personal* digital assistants (PDAs), large formal organizations still do transmit public messages that reach a sizable, heterogeneous, and scattered audience.

Audience Behaviour

Sociologists have long researched how audiences interact with one another and how they share information after

In 2005, 50 Cent's "Candy Shop" became the top cellphone ring tone, with 1.9 million downloads. Because today's media provide multiple services, music fans can use the Internet to access recorded music and listen to it on their mobile phones (Gunderson 2006).

a media event. The role of audience members as opinion leaders particularly intrigues social researchers. An **opinion leader** is someone who influences the opinions and decisions of others through day-to-day personal contact and communication. For example, a movie or theatre critic functions as an opinion leader. Sociologist Paul Lazarsfeld and his colleagues (1948) pioneered the study of opinion leaders in their research on political voting behaviour in the 1940s. They found that opinion leaders encourage their relatives, friends, and co-workers to think positively about a particular candidate, perhaps pushing them to listen to the politician's speeches or read the campaign literature.

Today, film critics often attribute the success of low-budget independent films to word of mouth. This is another way of saying that the mass media influence opinion leaders, who in turn influence others. The audience, then, can be seen not as a group of passive people but as a dynamic collective of active consumers who are often inspired to interact with others after a media event (Croteau and Hoynes 2003; C.R.Wright 1986).

Despite the persuasive role of opinion leaders, not all members of an audience interpret media spectacles in the same way. Often, the response of listeners/viewers is influenced by their social characteristics, such as occupation, education, and income. Sociologist Darnell Hunt (1997) wondered how the social composition of audience members would affect the way they interpreted news coverage in the United States. Hunt gathered 15 groups from the Los Angeles area, whose members were equally divided among whites, blacks, and Hispanics. He showed each group a 17-minute clip from the televised coverage of the 1992 LA riots and asked members to discuss how they would describe what they had just seen to a 12-year-old. In analyzing the discussions, Hunt found that although gender and class did not cause respondents to vary their answers much, race did.

Hunt went beyond noting how racial identification was associated with perceptions; he analyzed how the differences were manifested. For example, black viewers were much more likely than Hispanics or whites to refer to the events in terms of "us" versus "them." Another difference was that black and Hispanic viewers were more animated and critical than white viewers as they watched the film clip. White viewers tended to sit quietly, still and unquestioning, suggesting that they were more comfortable with the news coverage than the blacks or Hispanics.

☐ WHAT DOES THE MEDIA INDUSTRY LOOK LIKE?

Who owns the media production and distribution process? The answer is an ever-shrinking group of very large corporations. As we will see in the following section, two social consequences of this trend are a reduction in the number of truly independent information outlets and an increase in corporate opportunities for cross-promotion.

Media Concentration

The United States is the major global exporter of media products and programs, and, as noted in Chapter 3, the influence of U.S. media on Canadian culture remains substantial. A few multinational corporations now dominate the publishing, broadcasting, and film industries, though they may be hard to identify, since global conglomerates manage many different subsidiary companies as brands. The Walt Disney Company alone owns 16 television channels that reach 140 countries. Disney (which includes ABC, ESPN, and Pixar, among many others) is a global media giant. Other conglomerates include AOL Time Warner (CNN, *Time* magazine, and HBO); Rupert Murdoch's News Corporation of Australia (Fox Network Television, book publisher HarperCollins, numerous newspapers and magazines, and 20th Century Fox); Sony of Japan (Columbia Pictures, IMAX, CBS Records, and Columbia Records); and Viacom (Paramount, MTV, CBS, UPN, Black Entertainment Television, Simon and Schuster, and Blockbuster). This concentration of media giants fosters considerable cross-promotion. For example, the release of the Warner Brothers film, *The Matrix Reloaded*, in 2003 was heavily promoted by both CNN and *Time* magazine. In fact, *Time* managed to devote its cover to the film's release in the midst of the war in Iraq.

Similar concerns have been raised about the situation in countries such as China, Cuba, Iraq, and North Korea, where various ruling parties own and control the media. The difference, which is considerable, is that in the United States the gatekeeping process is in the hands of private individuals, who desire to maximize profits. In the other countries, such as Canada, the same process is sometimes carried out by private business people but can also be done by political leaders and senior bureaucrats, who are mandated to strengthen Canada's cultural integrity.

As mentioned in Chapter 3, Canada has historically been concerned about cultural diffusion and U.S. cultural imperialism as they relate to Canadian cultural sovereignty. The establishment of the Canadian Broadcasting Corporation (CBC), which is publicly owned, could be viewed as an attempt to protect and preserve Canada's national cultural interests. Today, many still see the CBC as having an essential role in buffering Canadians from the forces—to some, the absorption—of globalization (i.e., Americanization). Canadians have been, and continue to be, particularly susceptible to U.S. cultural imperialism because of geographic, economic, social, and political ties with the United States. According to the independent organization Media Awareness Network, "Canada has long been the largest importer of American television programming. This is due to its geographic proximity to the U.S., as well as an inability to produce profitable programming for a small domestic market" (Media Awareness Network 2008:1). In 1968, the federal government set up the Canadian Radio-television and Telecommunications Commission (CRTC) to regulate media broadcasting in Canada. The job of the CRTC is to oversee the restrictions on foreign ownership of broadcast outlets, ensure adequate amounts of Canadian content, and provide a vision of broadcasting as a means of strengthening Canada's cultural, social, and economic structures (CBC 2006b). As a result of the CRTC mandate, for example, 35 percent of a radio station's programming in the daytime must be Canadian.

Media concentration on a global level is not the only concern of government regulators. Media concentration—on a national level—has long been a concern for regulators and many Canadians alike. The ownership of Canadian mass media outlets tends to be concentrated in the hands of a few companies that may own not only newspapers, but television and radio stations as well. For example, CTV-globemedia (CTVgm) is one of Canada's largest media conglomerates, owning multiple sectors of media (cross media ownership). The company owns the CTV television network, newspapers such as *The Globe and Mail*, and 27 conventional television stations across Canada; and it has interests in 35 specialty channels, including TSN (The Sports Network) and MuchMusic. CTVgm also owns CHUM Radio, which operates 35 radio stations across Canada. Another example of media concentration is that of Quebecor Media which owns 8 daily newspapers and 200 other local and community newspapers, as well as Videotron and its French-language TV network, and Canoe.com. Also, CanWest Global Communications owns 11 of Canada's biggest daily newspapers, including the *National Post*, *The Gazette* in Montreal, and the *Ottawa Citizen*. Many people who see media concentration as a threat to a diversity of views are concerned about media ownership in Vancouver, where both major daily newspapers—*The Vancouver Sun* and *The Province*—are owned by CanWest Global. In 2008, the CRTC announced policies to curb the concentration of media ownership, which included restrictions limiting one person or entity from 1) controlling two types of media (a local radio station, a local television station, or a local newspaper) in the same market; and 2) controlling more than 45 percent of the total television audience as a result of a merger or acquisition (CBC 2008a).

We should note one significant exception to the centralization and concentration of the media: the Internet. Research shows that more and more people, especially those under age 35, are receiving their media content—whether it be watching television, listening to radio, or reading online news reports—through the Internet. A 2007 CRTC report noted that in 2006, about 48 percent of Canadians with Internet access went online for up to 10 hours per week, while 52 percent of Canadians aged 18–24 went online for more than 10 hours per week (CRTC 2007). Currently, the World Wide Web is accessible through independent outlets to millions of producers of media content. Obviously, the producer must be technologically proficient and must have access to a computer, but compared to other media outlets, the Internet is readily available for aspiring content producers. Media conglomerates, well aware of the Internet's potential, have adapted to the new landscape and have been delivering their material via the Web for some time now. Still, for now, the Internet allows the individual to become a media entrepreneur with a potential audience of millions (Gamson and Latteier 2004; J. Schwartz 2004).

The Media's Global Reach

Has the rise of the electronic media created a "global village"? Canadian communications theorist Marshall McLuhan predicted it would more than 40 years ago. McLuhan envisioned the global village as an electronically interconnected world where people would experience mass culture as if they were all in the same hometown. This interconnectedness, however, would have a dark side, as it would exclude many people whose values were not those of the dominant ones being put forth by a particular medium. According to McLuhan, the mass media could potentially have the effect of creating a "Big Brother" society, where one voice prevailed (McLuhan 1962). Today, physical distance is no longer a barrier, and instant messaging is possible across the world. The mass media have indeed created a global village. Not all countries are equally connected, as Figure 6-3 shows; but the progress has been staggering, considering that voice transmission was just beginning a little over a century ago (McLuhan 1964; McLuhan and Fiore 1967).

> ### Think about It
> What is the economic and political significance of media penetration?

Cultural critic Todd Gitlin considers "global torrent" a more apt metaphor for the media's reach than "global village." The media permeate all aspects of everyday life. Take advertising, for example. Consumer goods are marketed vigorously worldwide, from advertisements on airport baggage carriers to imprints on sandy beaches. Little wonder that many people around the world may develop loyalty to a brand and may be as likely to sport a Nike, Coca-Cola, or Harley-Davidson logo as they are their favourite soccer or baseball insignia (Gitlin 2002; N. Klein 1999).

The key to creating a truly global network that reaches directly into workplaces, schools, and homes is the Internet. Although much of the online global transmission today is limited to print and pictures, the potential to send audio and video via the Internet will increasingly reach into every part of the world. Social interaction will then truly take place on a global scale.

▶ **FIGURE 6-3**

Media Penetration in Selected Countries

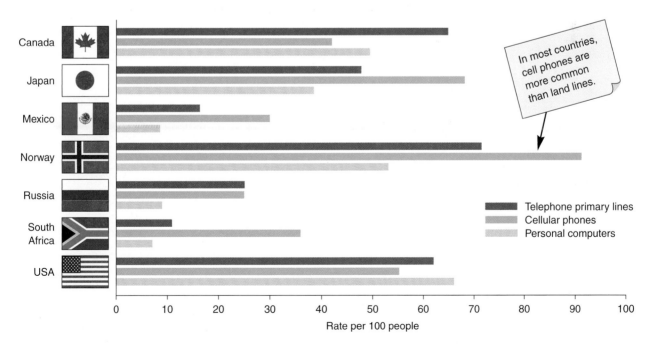

Note: Data for 2003 released in 2005.
Source: Bureau of the Census 2005:891.

These Bhutanese householders are watching the Oprah Winfrey Show on their brand-new television set. The Bhutanese were introduced to television in 1999. Since then, Canadian communications guru Marshall McLuhan's global village has become a reality in their remote Asian kingdom, where rulers have become concerned about the cultural impact of Western media.

the promotion of a world music that is not clearly identifiable with any single culture. Even the most future-oriented thinker would find the growth in the reach of the mass media in post-industrial and postmodern societies remarkable (Castells 2000, 2001; Croteau and Hoynes 2001, 2003).

The lack of one national home for the various forms of mass media raises a potential dilemma for media consumers. People worry that unhealthy influences and even crime pervade today's electronic global village, and that few if any controls prevent them. For example, the leaders of Bhutan worry about the impact of newly introduced tele-

The Internet has also facilitated other forms of communication. Reference materials and data banks can now be made accessible across national boundaries. Information related to international finance, marketing, trade, and manufacturing is literally just a keystroke away. We have seen the emergence of truly world news outlets and vision programming on their culture and their people. Similarly, in industrial countries, including Canada, officials are concerned about everything from online pornography to the menace posed by hackers. In the social policy section that follows, we'll discuss media violence and its influences.

Social Policy and the Mass Media
Media Violence

The Issue

Imagine a forensic expert in blood patterns working for a major city's police department, who is also a serial killer and who hides his double life from his sister, girlfriend, and co-workers. This is the premise of the popular television series, *Dexter*.

Scenes of violence are not limited to television; they are also common on the Internet, in motion pictures, and in video games. The video game, *Grand Theft Auto III: Vice City*, was a virtual urban war game. Companion Internet sites encouraged players to run over pedestrians, shoot the paramedics who show up, and loot the bodies for spare change. *Vice City* sold 1.4 million copies in the first three days of its release in 2002. Its 2004 sequel, *San Andreas*, featured crooked cops, rival gangs, and attackers kicking victims as they lay in pools of blood (*The Economist* 2005b; Houghton County 2005; Rainey 2004).

What effects do such violent scenes have on an audience? Will viewers engage in violent acts themselves? The idea for the electrical maze used in *Fear Factor* came from the Web site of a college student who had tested the painful experiment 80 times. The question of whether violence in the media leads people, especially youths, to become more violent has been raised since the early days of comic books, when *POW!* and *SPLAT!* were accompanied by vivid pictures of fights. Today, the mass media show far more violent and gruesome scenes, and every year, the amount of violence seems to increase. A recent study of U.S. network television showed an increase in violence at every hour of prime time. It's little wonder that in a 2005 national survey, 66 percent of viewers said there is too much violence on television—a higher level of concern than was expressed over cursing, explicit sexual content, or drug and alcohol abuse. Such views have led TV-watch groups to identify the best and worst shows.

The Setting

Canadians spend a great deal of time using media. According to a communications industry study, Canadians are turning in increasing numbers to online activities, with 70 percent of households having internet access. Television viewing in 2006, although down slightly from 2005, remained popular: the average per capita viewing time was 27.1 hours per week (CRTC 2007).

But, does watching hours of mass media with violent images cause one to behave differently? Today, the notion of exposure to media violence being linked to violent behaviour on the part of children and young people remains a hotly contested subject. This question is exceedingly complex, since many social factors influence behaviour. Some researchers use an experimental method in which participants are randomly assigned to view either violent or non-violent media and are later assessed for aggression. Other researchers survey subjects' media habits and aggressive behaviour or attitudes. The most comprehensive analysis of more than 200 studies of media violence and aggressive behaviour found that exposure to violence causes short-term increases in the aggressive behaviour of youths. Another more recent study found that less exposure to television and other media is related to less observed physical aggression (C. Anderson and Bushman 2001; J. Johnson et al. 2002; H. Paik and Comstock 1994; Robinson et al. 2001; U.S. Surgeon General 2001).

Other academics, however, assert that the scientific literature does not support the view that exposure to violence in television causes aggressive behaviour in children and adults (Faulkner 2001; Freedman 2002). There is a concern that the media may be used as a scapegoat, causing others to overlook social conditions such as poverty and parental neglect (Faulkner 2001). Canadian sociologist Augie Fleras contends that "there are many difficulties in uncovering a causal relationship between media [violence] and audience behaviour. Do people turn violent because of exposure to TV or are those who watch a lot of TV already prone to violence because of other factors in their life from lifestyle to neglect, rejection, and breakdowns" (2003:79).

Sociological Insights

The controversy surrounding violence and the media raises some basic questions about the functions of the media. If the media's functions are to entertain, socialize, and enforce social norms, how can violence be a part of its programming, especially when the offender rarely sees any consequences?

Even if a viewer does not necessarily become more violent from watching violent images, a kind of desensitization could be taking place. Using the premise of the *narcotizing dysfunction*, one might suggest that extended exposure to violent imagery leads to an increased tolerance and acceptance of violence in others. Sociologist George Gerbner theorized that attitudes about violent behaviour could be "cultivated" through exposure to television's violent images (Gerbner and Gross 1976). He claimed that people who are heavy watchers of TV are more inclined to see the world according to a "mean world" perspective. Gerbner's critics have argued that his views are over-simplified and do not take into account the relevance of such factors as age, gender, ethnicity, neighbourhood, and socio-economic conditions.

Both conflict and feminist theorists point out that the victims in violent scenes are often those who are marginalized in real life: women, children, the poor, ethnic minorities, gays, and the disabled. The media routinely portray sexual assault in a way that further devalues women, underscoring the view that they are powerless and should be fearful. Corresponding with this is the fact that many Hollywood television and movie productions in the mainstream media cast women as victims.

Interactionists are especially interested in whether violence in the media may become a script for real-life behaviour. Because aggression is a product of socialization, people may model themselves after the violent behaviour they see, especially if the situations approximate their own lives. Battling Doctor Octopus in *Spider-Man 2* is one thing, but what about violence that represents only a slight deviation from normal behaviour? In the 1993 film, *The Program*, high school football players proved their manhood by lying in the middle of a highway at night. After several young men died trying to prove their own manhood by imitating the scene, Touchstone Films ordered the removal of the scene from the film.

Policy Initiatives

According to the media organization, Media Awareness Network, violence in entertainment programming has been a policy issue in Canada since the 1970s, but the deregulation of children's programming in the United States and the emergence of the VCR in the 1980s brought concerns to the forefront (2007). In the early 1990s, Canadian broadcasting industry associations strengthened and revised their code's provisions on TV violence, which included the promise of the development of a classification system and the establishment of a time—9:00 p.m.—before which violence suitable for adults only could not be aired.

In the United States, the Surgeon General's 2001 report on youth violence recommended that parents use V-chip technology to screen the television programs their children watch. Yet, despite parental concerns, a 2001 national study showed that only 17 percent of parents used the V-chip to block programs with sexual or violent content. In general, most observers agree that parents should play a stronger role in monitoring their children's media consumption (Kaiser Family Foundation 2001; U.S. Surgeon General 2001).

Often, government studies are initiated by violent events that we desperately wish to explain. The U.S. Surgeon General's 2001 report on youth violence came in the fallout from the 1999 Columbine High School shootings in Littleton, Colorado. In the early 1990s, the Canadian government began to seriously examine media violence following "several tragic flashpoints, and a petition against media violence signed by 1.3 million Canadians" (Media Awareness Network 2007: 2). A senseless beating of a 5-year-old girl by three friends in Norway in 1994 led that country to look at violence in the media. In all these cases, initial calls for stiff government regulation eventually gave way to industry self-regulation and greater adult involvement in young people's viewing patterns (Bok 1998; Health Canada 1993).

Much of our knowledge of media violence comes from the study of children who watch traditional television programming. Some more recent studies have tried to assess the impact of video games. We should not lose sight of the fact that there are so many more types of media today; and we should especially be concerned with the role the Internet now plays in the delivery of media content. The Canadian Radio-television Telecommunications Commission (CRTC) in 1999 announced that it would regulate new media activities such as Web sites, video games, and online radio and TV, using their standards on violence in broadcasting. Much of this new media holds great promise for broadening educational horizons, but, unfortunately, new media can also offer a diet of violence.

Applying Theory

1. Do you know of anyone whose behaviour has become more aggressive from exposure to violence in the media? How was this aggression expressed? Have you noticed any changes in your own behaviour?

2. To what extent should the government act as a media regulator, especially in regard to violent content directed toward young people?

3. What role do you think parents should have in monitoring their children's viewing habits? Would you limit your children's access to new media? What alternative activities might children be offered?

CHAPTER RESOURCES

Summary

What are the Theoretical Perspectives on the Mass Media?

- The **mass media** (p. 133) are print and electronic instruments of communication that carry messages to often-widespread audiences. They pervade all social institutions, from entertainment to education to politics.
- From the functionalist perspective, the media entertain, socialize, enforce social norms, confer status, and promote consumption. They can be dysfunctional to the extent that they desensitize us to serious events and issues (the **narcotizing dysfunction**) (p. 137).
- Conflict theorists think the media reflect and even deepen the divisions in society through **gatekeeping** (p. 137), or control over which material reaches the public; **media monitoring** (p. 138), the covert observation of people's media usage and choices; imposed **hegemony** (p. 140), which is the process of creating acceptance of the views of the ruling class so that they are seen as "normal" by the exploited classes; and support of dominant ideology, which defines reality and overwhelms local cultures.
- Some feminist theorists point out that media images of the sexes communicate unrealistic, stereotypical, limiting, and sometimes violent perceptions of women.
- Interactionists examine the media on the micro level to see how they shape day-to-day social behaviour. Interactionists have studied shared TV viewing and staged public appearances intended to convey self-serving definitions of reality.

Who are the Media's Audiences?

- The mass media require the presence of an audience—whether it is small and well defined or large and amorphous. With the ever-increasing number of media outlets come more and more targeting of **segmented** (or **niche**) **audiences** (p. 148).
- Social researchers have studied the role of **opinion leaders** (p. 149) in influencing audiences.

What does the Media Industry Look Like?

- The media industry is becoming more and more concentrated, creating media conglomerates. This concentration raises concerns about how innovative and independent the media can be. In some countries, governments own and control the media.
- The Internet is the one significant exception to the trend toward centralization, allowing millions of people to produce their own media content.
- The media have a global reach thanks to new communications technologies, especially the Internet. Some people are concerned that the media's global reach will spread unhealthy influences to other cultures. Also of concern is the **digital divide** (p. 146) between developing and developed countries.

Critical Thinking Questions

1. What kind of audience is targeted by the producers of televised professional wrestling? By the creators of an animated film? By a rap group? What factors determine who makes up a particular audience?
2. Trace the production process for a new television situation comedy (sitcom). Who do you imagine are the gatekeepers in the process?
3. Use the functionalist, conflict, interactionist, and feminist perspectives to assess the effects of global TV programming on developing countries.

Key Terms

Digital divide The gap between developing and developed countries, in computer and Internet use as well as in factors such as age, gender, income, and education. (p. 146)

Gatekeeping The process by which a relatively small number of people in the media industry control what material eventually reaches the audience. (p. 137)

Global economy The economy of the world when people have the capacity to work as a single unit in real time. (p. 146)

Hegemony The process through which the views of the ruling class are accepted and seen as "normal" by the exploited classes. (p. 140)

Mass media Print and electronic means of communication that carry messages to widespread audiences. (p. 133)

Media monitoring The monitoring of media content by interest groups, as well as the monitoring of individuals' media usage and choices. (p. 138)

Narcotizing dysfunction The phenomenon in which the media provide such massive amounts of coverage that the audience becomes numb and fails to act on the information, regardless of how compelling the issue. (p. 137)

Narrowcasting Marketing of the media to a particular audience. (p. 148)

Opinion leader Someone who influences the opinions and decisions of others through day-to-day personal contact and communication (e.g., a film or theatre critic). (p. 149)

Segmented or **niche audience** A particular audience to which the media market themselves. (p. 148)

Stereotype An unreliable generalization about all members of a group that does not recognize individual differences within the group. (p. 140)

Additional Readings

Chomsky, Noam. 2002. *Media Control: The Spectacular Achievements of Propaganda,* Second Edition. New York: Seven Stories Press.

Gant, Scott. 2007. *We're All Journalists Now: The Transformation of the Press and Reshaping of the Law in the Internet Age.* Toronto: Simon and Schuster Canada.

Lorimer, Rowland. 2007. *Mass Communication in Canada*, Sixth Edition. Don Mills, ON: Oxford University Press.

 ## Online Learning Centre

Visit the *Sociology: A Brief Introduction* Online Learning Centre at www.mcgrawhill.ca/olc/schaefer to access quizzes, interactive exercises, video clips, and other research and study tools related to this chapter.

 ## Reel Society Video Clips

Reel Society video clips can be used to spark discussion about the following topics from this chapter:
- Sociological Perspectives on the Media
- The Media Industry

DEVIANCE AND SOCIAL CONTROL

Is marijuana use deviant behaviour? This woman is dressed as a marijuana leaf at the annual Amsterdam Cannabis Cup.

☐ **What is Social Control?**

☐ **What is Deviance?**

☐ **What is Crime?**

Boxes

RESEARCH IN ACTION: Street Kids

SOCIOLOGY IN THE GLOBAL COMMUNITY: Singapore: A Nation of Campaigns

RESEARCH IN ACTION: Labelling a Behaviour as a Crime: Road Rage

SOCIAL POLICY AND SOCIAL CONTROL: Illicit Drug Use in Canada

The smell of the Afghan poppy season is unmistakable, even from the open door of a Black Hawk helicopter. NATO soldiers in Helmand province see the expanse of purple and pink blossoms flashing by, but they do little to stop drug production; they worry instead about Taliban fighters mingling among the villagers, and are grateful to avoid being shot down.

Yet, the opium economy and the insurgency are mutually reinforcing; drugs finance the Taliban, while their violence encourages poppy cultivation. Not surprisingly, perhaps, both problems have grown more severe in recent years, nowhere more so than in Helmand.

According to the United Nations Office on Drugs and Crime (UNODC), the province is set to harvest another record crop this year, producing more opium (and from it heroin and other illegal drugs) than the rest of Afghanistan put together. Indeed, this surge has overshadowed the past decade's striking decline in the "Golden Triangle"—the border region of Thailand, Myanmar, and Laso—which UNODC says is "almost opium free."

Afghanistan has put a blot on what UNODC says is a hopeful global picture. Its latest *World Drug Report*, published on June 26, 2007, says that the market has largely stabilized for all classes of illicit drugs—including heroin, cocaine, amphetamines and cannabis. The global area under cultivation for both poppy and coca has declined over the past decade, although improving yields mean opium production has reached record levels while cocaine remains steady. Demand for opiates and cocaine is stable. Moreover, UNODC reckons that a startling 26 percent of global heroin production and 42 percent of cocaine output has been intercepted by government authorities. Meanwhile, cannabis cultivation in Morocco, the source of 70 percent of hashish in Europe, has dropped. World production of amphetamines and similar stimulants appears to be steady.

The drug business is by far the most profitable illicit global trade, says UNODC, earning some $320 billion annually, compared with estimates of $32 billion for human trafficking and $1 billion for illegal firearms. The runaway Afghan opium trade—worth around $60 billion at street prices in consuming countries—is arguably the hardest problem. Heroin is finding new routes to the consumer: for instance, through West Africa to North America, and via Pakistan and Central Asia to China.

. . . The impact is felt throughout Afghanistan. The opium trade is worth about $3.1 billion (less than a quarter of this is earned by farmers), the equivalent of about a third of Afghanistan's total economy. It has forced up the exchange rate, sucked in unproductive luxuries, and stoked a boom in construction, particularly around Kabul. In a country as poor as Afghanistan, opium rots any institution it touches. Some of the biggest drug barons are reputedly members of the national and provincial governments, even figures close to President Hamid Karzai. The whole chain of government that is supposed to impose the rule of law, from the ministry of interior to ordinary police, has been subverted. Poorly paid police are bribed to facilitate the trade. Some pay their superiors to get particularly "lucrative" jobs like border control.

☐ (*The Economist* 2007b)

In this excerpt from "A World Awash in Heroin" in the June 30, 2007, issue of *The Economist*, the mutually reinforcing relationship between the Taliban's influence in Afghanistan and poppy cultivation for the purpose of the global drug trade is exposed. Opium trade makes up about one-third of the Afghan economy. What behaviours should be considered deviant may not always be obvious. Take the issue of poppy production for the illicit global trade. On the one hand, we can view it as *deviant*, violating international standards of conduct; but on the other hand, it can be seen as *conforming* to local illicit drug culture because of poor socio-economic conditions. In Canada, people are socialized to have mixed feelings about both conforming and non-conforming behaviour. The term *conformity* can conjure up images of mindless imitation of a peer group—whether a group of teenagers with pierced tongues or a group of business executives dressed in similar grey suits. Yet, the same term can also suggest that an individual is co-operative or a "team player." What about those who do not conform? They may be respected as individualists, leaders, or creative thinkers who break new ground. Or they may be labelled as "troublemakers" and "weirdos" (Aronson 1999).

In this chapter, we examine the relationships among conformity, deviance, and social control. We begin by distinguishing between conformity and obedience and then look at two experiments regarding conforming behaviour and obedience to authority. The informal and formal mechanisms used by societies to encourage conformity and discourage deviance are analyzed. We give particular attention to the legal order and how it reflects underlying social values.

In the second part of the chapter, we focus on theoretical explanations for deviance, including the functionalist approach employed by Émile Durkheim and Robert Merton; the interactionist-based theories; labelling theory, which draws on both the interactionist and the conflict perspectives; conflict theory; and feminist theories.

In the third part of the chapter, we examine crime, a specific type of deviant behaviour. As a form of deviance subject to official, written norms, crime has been a special concern of policy makers and the public in general. We will look at various types of crime found in Canada, the ways crime is measured, and international crime rates. Finally, in the social policy section, we consider the use of illicit drugs in Canada.

Use Your Sociological Imagination

How do you think society views someone who deals in illegal drugs as opposed to, for example, someone who breaks and enters into a home? What kinds of questions would be raised by interactionist sociologists in their study of poppy growing in Afghanistan?

☐ WHAT IS SOCIAL CONTROL?

As we saw in Chapter 3, each culture, subculture, and group has distinctive norms governing what it deems appropriate behaviour. Laws, dress codes, bylaws of organizations, course requirements, and rules of sports and games all express social norms.

How does a society bring about acceptance of basic norms? The term **social control** refers to the techniques and strategies for preventing deviant human behaviour in any society. Social control occurs at all levels of society. In the family, we are socialized to obey our parents simply because they are our parents. Peer groups introduce us to informal norms, such as dress codes, that govern the behaviour of members. Universities establish standards they expect of their students. In bureaucratic organizations, workers encounter a formal system of rules and regulations. Finally, the government of every society legislates and enforces social norms.

Most of us respect and accept basic social norms and assume that others will do the same. Even without thinking, we obey the instructions of police officers, follow the day-to-day rules at our jobs, and move to the rear of elevators when people enter. Such behaviour reflects an effective process of socialization to the dominant standards of a culture. At the same time, we are well aware that individuals, groups, and institutions *expect* us to act "properly." If we fail to do so, we may face punishment through informal *sanctions*, such as fear and ridicule, or formal sanctions, such as jail sentences or fines. The impediment to effective social control is P. 57 that people often receive competing messages about how to behave. Although the state or government may clearly define acceptable behaviour, friends or fellow employees may encourage quite different behaviour patterns. Box 7-1 presents the latest research on a behaviour that is officially discouraged but nevertheless engaged in by some young people: living on the streets.

Research in Action
Street Kids

Fiona was a fairly typical 16-year-old, living in Prince George, British Columbia. She was struggling to complete high school and to learn how to get along with her mother's new common-law partner. Often, she and her mother's partner would argue over Fiona's contribution to the running of their household or whether she should be able to stay overnight at her boyfriend's apartment. Her mother's partner frequently would resort to verbal and physical abuse in attempting to make Fiona comply with his wishes. Although Fiona felt her mother loved her, she felt betrayed by her mother's silence when it came to protecting her from the abuse.

Fiona decided she couldn't endure the strain and sense of betrayal at home and convinced her boyfriend, Michael, to leave Prince George. They headed south, ending up on the West Coast—in Vancouver. Shortly after Fiona and Michael arrived in Vancouver, Michael's money supply ran out and he decided to return home. Fiona, also facing a shortage of cash, resorted to panhandling on Robson Street in downtown Vancouver and began living on the streets.

A major 2006 survey—of 762 youth across 9 communities in B.C.—by the McCreary Centre Society, entitled *Against the Odds*, noted that most street youth have experienced sexual or physical abuse, most having either run away or been kicked out of home. The study revealed that the majority of these young people "couch surf" or sleep in stairwells, parking lots, cars, and abandoned buildings or "squats."

Other major findings of the study revealed the following:

- One in three street-involved youth attended school.
- One in three were working in legal jobs.
- One in three females and one in ten males were gay, lesbian, or bisexual.
- Eighty-four percent surveyed said they grew up in B.C. (in 2000, 61 percent of street youth in Vancouver and 33 percent in Victoria were from outside the province; in 2006, only 20 percent of street youth in these cites were from outside the province).
- The percentage of Aboriginal youth has increased sharply since 2000; in Vancouver, it rose from 37 percent in 2000 to 65 percent in 2006.
- Four percent reported that they expected to be on the street in five years.
- Nine percent said they expected to be dead in five years.
- One-third said they expected to have a home in five years.

Applying Theory

1. Why do you think street kids might be likely to engage in activities such as panhandling? What sociological perspective(s) would be useful in studying this phenomenon?
2. Have you ever known someone who lived on the street? If so, what were his or her reasons for doing so?

Source: McCreary Centre Society 2006; Steffenhagen 2001, Ward 2007.

As of 2006, it was estimated that between 200 000 and 300 000 people in Canada were homeless (CBC 2007b), with roughly one-third of those people being between the ages of 16 and 24 (Youthworks 2006).

Functionalists contend that people must respect social norms if any group or society is to survive. In their view, societies literally could not function if massive numbers of people defied standards of appropriate conduct. By contrast, conflict theorists maintain that "successful functioning" of a society will consistently benefit the powerful and work to the disadvantage of other groups. They point out, for example, that widespread resistance to social norms was necessary to overturn the institution of slavery.

Conformity and Obedience

Techniques for social control operate on both the group level and the societal level. People whom we regard as our peers or as our equals influence us to act in particular ways; the same is true of people who hold authority over us or occupy awe-inspiring positions. Stanley Milgram made a useful distinction between these two important levels of social control (1975).

Milgram defined **conformity** as going along with peers—individuals of our own status, who have no special right to direct our behaviour. By contrast, **obedience** is defined as compliance with higher authorities in a hierarchical structure. Thus, a recruit entering military service will typically conform to the habits and language of other recruits and will obey the orders of superior officers. Students will conform to the drinking behaviour of their peers and will obey the requests of campus security officers.

Conformity to Prejudice

We often think of conformity in terms of rather harmless situations, such as members of an expensive health club who all work out in elaborate and costly sportswear. But researchers have found that people may conform to the attitudes and behaviour of their peers even when such conformity means expressing intolerance toward others.

Fletcher Blanchard, Teri Lilly, and Leigh Ann Vaughn (1991) conducted an experiment at a U.S. university and found that statements people overhear others make influence their own expressions of opinion on the issue of racism. A student employed by the researchers approached 72 white students as each was walking across the campus to get responses for an opinion poll she said she was conducting for a class. At the same time, a second white student—actually another working with the researchers—was stopped and asked to participate in the survey. Both students were then asked how their university should respond to anonymous racist notes that were sent to four black students. The student employed by the researchers always answered first. In some cases, she condemned the notes; in others, she justified them.

Blanchard and his colleagues (1991:102–103) conclude that "hearing at least one other person express strongly anti-racist opinions produced dramatically more strongly anti-racist public reactions to racism than hearing others express equivocal opinions or opinions more accepting of racism." A second experiment demonstrated that when the student working on behalf of the researchers expressed sentiments justifying racism, subjects were much *less* likely to express anti-racist opinions than were those who heard no one else offer opinions. In these experiments, social control (through the process of conformity) influenced people's attitudes, or at least the expression of those attitudes. In the next section, we will see that social control (through the process of obedience) can alter people's behaviour.

Obedience to Authority

If ordered to do so, would you comply with an experimenter's instruction to give people increasingly painful electric shocks? Most people would say no; yet, the research of social psychologist Stanley Milgram (1963, 1975) suggests that most of us *will* obey such orders. In Milgram's words, "Behaviour that is unthinkable in an individual. . . acting on his own may be executed without hesitation when carried out under orders" (1975:xi).

Milgram placed advertisements in New Haven, Connecticut, newspapers to recruit subjects for what was announced as a learning experiment at Yale University. Participants included postal clerks, engineers, high school teachers, and labourers. They were told that the purpose of the research was to investigate the effects of punishment on learning. The experimenter, dressed in a grey technician's coat, explained that in each testing, one subject would be randomly selected as the "learner" while another would function as the "teacher." However, this lottery was rigged so that the "real" subject would always be the teacher while an associate of Milgram's served as the learner.

At this point, the learner's hand was strapped to an electric apparatus. The teacher was taken to an electronic "shock generator" with 30 lever switches. Each switch was labelled with graduated voltage designations from 15 to 450 volts. Before beginning the experiment, subjects were given sample shocks of 45 volts to convince them of the authenticity of the experiment.

The experimenter instructed the teacher to apply shocks of increasing voltage each time the learner gave an incorrect answer on a memory test. Teachers were told that "although the shocks can be extremely painful, they cause no permanent tissue damage." In reality, the learner did not receive any shocks.

The learner deliberately gave incorrect answers and acted out a prearranged script. For example, at 150 volts, the learner would cry out, "Experimenter, get me out of here! I won't be in the experiment any more!" At 270 volts, the learner would scream in agony. When the shock reached 350 volts, the learner would fall silent. If the teacher wanted to stop the experiment, the experimenter would insist that the teacher continue, using such statements as, "The experiment requires that you continue" and "You have no other choice; you *must* go on" (Milgram 1975:19–23).

The results of this unusual experiment stunned and dismayed Milgram and other social scientists. A sample of psychiatrists had predicted that virtually all subjects would refuse to shock innocent victims. In their view, only a "pathological fringe" of less than 2 percent of the population would continue administering shocks up to the maximum level. Yet almost two-thirds of participants fell into the category of "obedient subjects."

Why did these subjects obey? Why were they willing to inflict seemingly painful shocks on innocent victims who had never done them any harm? There is no evidence that these subjects were unusually sadistic; few seemed to enjoy administering the shocks. Instead, in Milgram's view, the key to obedience was the experimenter's social role as a "scientist" and "seeker of knowledge."

In one of Stanley Milgram's experiments, a supposed victim received an electric shock when his hand rested on a shock plate. At the 150-volt level, the victim would demand to be released and would refuse to place his hand on the shock plate. The experimenter would then order the actual subject to force the victim's hand onto the plate, as shown in the photo. Though 40 percent of the true subjects stopped complying with Milgram at this point, 60 percent did force the victim's hand onto the shock plate, despite the victim's pretended agony.

Milgram pointed out that in the modern industrial world, we are accustomed to submitting to impersonal authority figures whose status is indicated by a title (professor, lieutenant, doctor) or by a uniform (the technician's coat). The authority is viewed as larger and more important than the individual; consequently, the obedient individual shifts responsibility for his or her behaviour to the authority figure. Milgram's subjects frequently stated, "If it were up to me, I would not have administered shocks." They saw themselves as merely doing their duty (Milgram 1975).

From an interactionist perspective, one important aspect of Milgram's findings is the fact that subjects in follow-up studies were less likely to inflict the supposed shocks as they were moved physically closer to their victims. Moreover, interactionists emphasize the effect of incrementally administering additional dosages of 15 volts. In effect, the experimenter negotiated with the teacher and convinced the teacher to continue inflicting higher levels of punishment. It is doubtful that anywhere near the two-thirds rate of obedience would have been reached had the experimenter told the teachers to administer 450 volts immediately to the learners (B. Allen 1978; Katovich 1987).

Milgram launched his experimental study of obedience to better understand the involvement of Germans in the annihilation of six million Jews and millions of other people during World War II. In an interview conducted long after the publication of his study, Milgram suggested that "if a system of death camps were set up in the United States of the sort we had seen in Nazi Germany, one would be able to find sufficient personnel for those camps in any medium-sized American town" (CBS News 1979:7–8).

Use Your Sociological Imagination

If you were a participant in Milgram's research on conformity, how far do you think you would go in carrying out orders? Do you see any ethical problem with the experimenter's manipulation of the control subjects?

Informal and Formal Social Control

The sanctions used to encourage conformity and obedience—and to discourage violation of social norms—are carried out through informal and formal social control. As the term implies, people use **informal social control** casually to enforce norms. Examples of informal social control include smiles, laughter, a raised eyebrow, and ridicule.

In Canada, the United States, and many other cultures, one common and yet controversial example of informal social control is parental use of corporal punishment. Adults often view spanking, slapping, or kicking children as a proper and necessary means of maintaining authority. Child development specialists counter that corporal punishment is inappropriate because it teaches children to solve problems through violence. They warn that slapping and spanking can escalate into more serious forms of abuse. Yet, despite the fact that pediatric experts now believe that physical forms of discipline are undesirable and encourage their patients to use non-physical means of discipline (Tidmarsh 2000), approximately 70 percent of Canadian parents have used physical punishment (Durrant and Rose-Krasnor 1995). In 1999, the Canadian Foundation for Youth and the Law challenged the constitutionality of section 43 of the Criminal Code of Canada, which allows parents to use reasonable force in disciplining their children. Section 43 was upheld.

Sometimes, informal methods of social control are not adequate to enforce conforming or obedient behaviour. In those cases, **formal social control** is carried out by authorized agents, such as police officers, physicians, school administrators, employers, military officers, and managers of movie theatres. It can serve as a last resort

Sociology in the Global Community
Singapore: A Nation of Campaigns
7-2

"Males with Long Hair Will Be Attended to Last!" "Throwing Litter from Apartments Can Kill!" "No Spitting!" These are some of the posters sponsored by the Singapore government in its effort to enforce social norms in this small nation of some four million people living in a totally urbanized area in Southeast Asia.

Although Singapore is governed by a democratically elected Parliament, one party has dominated the government since the country's independence in 1965. And it has not hesitated to use its authority to launch a number of campaigns to shape the social behaviour of its citizens. In most cases, these campaigns are directed against "disagreeable" behaviour: littering, spitting, chewing gum, failing to flush public toilets, teenage smoking, and the like. Courtesy is a major concern, with elaborate "Courtesy Month" celebrations scheduled to both entertain and educate the populace.

Some campaigns take on serious issues and are backed by legislation. For example, in the 1970s, Singapore's government asked its citizens to "Please Stop at Two" in family planning; tax and schooling benefits rewarded those who complied. However, this campaign was so successful that in the 1980s, the government began a "Have Three or More If You Can Afford To" campaign. In this case, it provided school benefits for larger families. In another attempt at social control, the government launched a "Speak Mandarin" campaign to encourage the multi-ethnic, multilingual population to accept Mandarin as the dialect of choice.

For the most part, Singaporeans cheerfully accept their government's admonitions and encouragement. They see the results of being clean and courteous: Singapore is a better place to live. Corporations also go along with the government and even help to sponsor some of the campaigns. As one corporate sponsor noted, "If [people] see Singapore as a clean country, they will view companies here as clean." Political scientist Michael Haas refers to this compliance as "the Singapore puzzle": citizens of Singapore accept strict social control dictates in exchange for continuing prosperity and technological leadership in the world.

Applying Theory

1. How would a functionalist thinker view an administration-sponsored campaign at your educational institution against drinking? What would be some latent functions of such a campaign?
2. According to conflict thinkers, why would these social-control campaigns work in Singapore?

Sources: Dorai 1998; Haas 1999; Haub and Cornelius 2000; Instituto del Tercer Mundo 1999.

when socialization and informal sanctions do not bring about desired behaviour. In Canada, for every 43 offences that occur, 1 person is sentenced to a penitentiary or prison. Of those who end up in a penitentiary or prison, a disproportionately high number are Aboriginal people, who account for between 8 and 10 percent of federal correctional institutions' populations, and an even greater percentage of the population in provincial and territorial institutions (A. Nelson and Fleras 1995).

Societies vary in deciding which behaviours will be subjected to formal social control and how severe the sanctions will be. In Singapore, chewing gum is prohibited, feeding birds can lead to fines of up to US$640, and there is even a US$95 fine for failing to flush the toilet (see Box 7-2). Singapore deals with serious crimes especially severely. The death penalty is mandatory for murder, drug trafficking, and crimes committed with firearms

(recently, a Canadian arrested for drug trafficking in Singapore came very close to being executed). Japan has created a special prison for reckless drivers. While some are imprisoned for vehicular homicide, others serve prison time for drunken driving and fleeing the scene of an accident (M. Elliott 1994).

Another controversial example of formal social control is the use of surveillance techniques. In 1992, police in Great Britain began to install closed-circuit television systems on "high streets" (the primary shopping and business areas of local communities) in an effort to reduce street crime. Within two years, three hundred British towns had installed or made plans to install such surveillance cameras, and the use of public surveillance had spread to North America. Supporters of surveillance believe that it makes the public feel more secure. Moreover, it can be cheaper to install and maintain cameras than to put more police officers on street patrol. For critics, however, the use of surveillance cameras brings to mind the grim, futuristic world presented by Britain's own George Orwell in his dystopian novel, *1984* (1949). In the world of *1984*, an all-seeing "Big Brother" represents an authoritarian government that watches people's every move and takes immediate action against anyone who questions the oppressive regime (Halbfinger 1998; Uttley 1993).

Law and Society

Some norms are so important to a society they are formalized into laws controlling people's behaviour. *Law* may be defined as governmental social control (D. Black 1995). Some laws, such as the prohibition against murder, are directed at all members of society. Others, such as fishing and hunting regulations, primarily affect particular categories of people. Still others govern the behaviour of social institutions (corporate law and laws regarding the taxing of non-profit enterprises).

Sociologists have become increasingly interested in the creation of laws as a social process. Laws are created in response to perceived needs for formal social control. Sociologists have sought to explain how and why such perceptions arise. In their view, law is not merely a static body of rules handed down from generation to generation. Rather, it reflects continually changing standards of what is right and wrong, of how violations are to be determined, and of what sanctions are to be applied (Schur 1968).

Sociologists representing varying theoretical perspectives agree that the legal order reflects underlying social values. Therefore, the creation of criminal law can be a most controversial matter. Should it be against the law to employ illegal immigrants in a factory (see Chapter 10), to have an abortion (see Chapter 11), or to smoke on a sidewalk? Such issues have been bitterly debated because they require a choice among competing values. Not surprisingly, laws that are unpopular—such as the Canadian law requiring the registration of firearms—

become difficult to enforce owing to lack of consensus supporting the norms.

Socialization is actually the primary source of conforming and obedient behaviour, including obedience to law. Generally, it is not external pressure from a peer group or authority figure that makes us go along with social norms. Rather, we have internalized such norms as valid and desirable and are committed to observing them. In a profound sense, we want to see ourselves (and to be seen) as loyal, co-operative, responsible, and respectful of others. In Canada and other societies around the world, people are socialized both to want to belong and to fear being viewed as different or deviant.

Control theory suggests that our connection to members of society leads us to systematically conform to society's norms. According to sociologist Travis Hirschi and other control theorists, we are bonded to our family members, friends, and peers in a way that leads us to follow the mores and folkways of our society while giving little conscious thought to whether we will be sanctioned if we fail to conform (1969). Socialization develops our self-control so well that we don't need further pressure to obey social norms. Although control theory does not effectively explain the rationale for every conforming act, it nevertheless reminds us that although the media may focus on crime and disorder, most members of nearly all

What's next in formal social control—iris checks? At Amsterdam's Schiphol Airport, a security official scans a passenger's irises. Like fingerprints, iris patterns are unique, but their greater complexity makes them a more accurate form of identification. This passenger may, or may not, choose to store her iris patterns on an identification card to expedite her boarding process.

societies conform to and obey basic norms (Gottfredson and Hirschi 1990; Hirschi 1969).

□ WHAT IS DEVIANCE?

Defining Deviance

For sociologists, the term deviance does not mean perversion or depravity. **Deviance** is behaviour that violates the standards of conduct or expectations of a group or society (Wickman 1991:85). In Canada, alcoholics, compulsive gamblers, and people with mental illnesses would all be classified as deviants. Being late for class is categorized as a deviant act; the same is true of dressing too casually for a formal wedding. On the basis of the sociological definition, deviance is universal, as we are all deviant from time to time. Each of us violates common social norms in certain situations.

Is being overweight an example of deviance? In North America and many other cultures, unrealistic standards of appearance and body image place a huge strain on people—especially on women and girls—based on how they look. Author Naomi Wolf has used the term *the beauty myth* to refer to an exaggerated ideal of beauty, beyond the reach of all but a few females, which has unfortunate consequences (1991). In order to shed their "deviant" image and conform to (unrealistic) societal norms, many women and girls become consumed with adjusting their appearances. For example, in a *People* magazine "health" feature, a young actress stated that she would always know it was time to eat when she passed out on the set. When females carry adherence to the beauty myth to an extreme, they may develop eating disorders or undertake costly and unnecessary cosmetic surgery procedures. Yet, what is deviant in our culture may be celebrated in another. In Nigeria, for example, being fat is a mark of beauty. Part of the coming-of-age ritual calls for young girls to spend months in a "fattening room." Among Nigerians, being thin at this point in the life course is deviant (Simmons 1998).

Deviance involves the violation of group norms, which may or may not be formalized into law. It is a comprehensive concept that includes not only criminal behaviour but also many actions not subject to prosecution. The public official who takes a bribe has defied social norms, but so has the high school student who refuses to sit in an assigned seat or cuts class. Of course, deviation from norms is not always negative, let alone criminal. A member of an exclusive social club who speaks out against its traditional policy of excluding women and Jews from admittance is deviating from the club's norms. So is a police officer who becomes a whistle-blower on corruption or brutality within the department.

Among the Kayan tribe in northern Thailand, females traditionally wear up to 5.5 kilograms of coils around the neck as a mark of beauty and tribal identity. Because deviance is socially constructed, it is subject to different social interpretations over time and across cultures.

Standards of deviance vary from one group (or subculture) to another. In Canada, it is generally considered acceptable to sing along at a folk or rock concert, but not at the opera. Just as deviance is defined by place, so, too, is it relative to time. For instance, drinking alcohol at 6:00 p.m. is a common practice in our society, but engaging in the same behaviour at breakfast is viewed as a deviant act and as symptomatic of a drinking problem.

From a sociological perspective, deviance is viewed according to normative standards. It is subject to social definitions within a particular society; in most instances, those individuals and groups with the greatest status and power define what is acceptable and what is deviant. For example, despite serious medical warnings about the dangers of tobacco as far back as 30 years ago, cigarette smoking continued to be accepted—in good part because of the power of tobacco farmers and cigarette manufacturers. It was only after a long campaign led by public health and anti-cancer activists that cigarette smoking became more of a deviant activity. Today, many local laws limit where people can smoke.

Although deviance can include relatively minor day-to-day decisions about our personal behaviour, in some cases, it can become part of a person's identity. This process is called *stigmatization*, as we will now see.

Deviance and Social Stigma

There are many ways a person can acquire a deviant identity. Because of physical or behavioural characteristics, some people are unwillingly cast in negative social roles. Once they have been assigned a deviant role, they have trouble presenting a positive image to others and may even experience lowered self-esteem. Whole groups of people—for instance, "short people" or "redheads"—may be labelled in this way (Heckert and Best 1997). The interactionist, Erving Goffman (see Chapters 1 and 4), introduced the term **stigma** to sociological theory to describe the labels society uses to devalue members of certain social groups (Goffman 1963a).

Prevailing expectations about beauty and body shape may prevent people who are regarded as ugly or obese from advancing as rapidly as their abilities permit. Both obese and anorexic people are assumed to be weak in character, slaves to their appetites or to media images. Because they do not conform to the beauty myth, they may be viewed as "disfigured" or "strange" in appearance, bearers of what Goffman calls a "spoiled identity." However, what constitutes disfigurement is a matter of interpretation. Of the more than one million cosmetic procedures done every year in Canada and the United States, many are performed on women who would be objectively defined as having a normal appearance. And although feminist sociologists have accurately noted that the beauty myth makes many women feel uncomfortable with themselves, many men, too, lack confidence in their appearance. The number of males who choose to undergo cosmetic procedures has risen sharply in recent years; in 2006, men accounted for 9 percent of such surgeries, up 8 percentage points from 2000 (American Society of Plastic Surgeons 2007b).

The American Board of Plastic Surgery, made up of doctors from both Canada and the United States, tracks the statistics on the number of cosmetic surgeries performed in both countries (see Table 7-1). Since 2000, the total number has increased by 20 percent.

Often, people are stigmatized for deviant behaviours they may no longer engage in. The labels, "compulsive gambler," "ex-convict," "recovering alcoholic," and "ex-mental patient" can stick with a person for life. Goffman draws a useful distinction between a prestige symbol that draws attention to a positive aspect of a person's identity, such as a wedding band or a badge, and a stigma symbol that discredits or debases a person's identity, such as a conviction for child molestation (1963a). Although stigma symbols may not always be obvious, they can become a matter of public knowledge. Some communities, for instance, publish the names and addresses, and in some instances even the pictures, of convicted sex offenders on the Web.

A person need not be guilty of a crime to be stigmatized. Homeless people often have trouble getting a job because employers are wary of applicants who cannot give a home address. Moreover, hiding homelessness is difficult, since agencies generally use the telephone to contact applicants about job openings. If a homeless person has access to a telephone at a shelter, the staff generally answer the phone by announcing the name of the institution—a sure way to discourage prospective employers. Even if a homeless person surmounts these obstacles and manages to get a job, she or he is often fired when the employer learns of the situation:

> Kim had been working as a receptionist in a doctor's office for several weeks when the doctor learned she was living in a shelter and fired her. "If I had known you lived in a shelter," Kim said the doctor told her, "I would never have hired you. Shelters are places of disease." "No," said Kim. "Doctors' offices are places of disease." (Liebow 1993:64–54)

Table 7-1 Selected Cosmetic Procedures in Canada and the United States			
	1998	**2004**	**2006**
Liposuction	172 079	324 891	302 789
Breast augmentation	132 378	264 041	329 396
Facelift	70 947	114 279	104 055
Nose reshaping	55 953	305 475	307 258
Tummy tuck	46 597	107 019	146 240
Breast lift	31 525	75 805	103 788
Male breast reduction	9023	13 963	19 881
Buttock lift	1246	3496	3710

Sources: Adapted from the American Society of Plastic Surgeons 2002, 2005, 2007a.

Regardless of a person's positive attributes, employers regard the spoiled identity of homelessness as sufficient reason to dismiss an employee.

Although some types of deviance will stigmatize a person, other types do not carry a significant penalty. Some good examples of socially tolerated forms of deviance can be found in the world of high technology.

Deviance and Technology

Technological innovations, such as pagers and voice mail, can redefine social interactions and the standards of behaviour related to them. When the Internet was first made available to the general public, no norms or regulations governed its use. Because online communication offers a high degree of anonymity, uncivil behaviour—speaking harshly of others or monopolizing chat rooms—quickly became common. Today, online bulletin boards designed to carry items of community interest must be policed to prevent users from posting commercial advertisements. Such deviant acts are beginning to provoke calls for the establishment of formal rules for online behaviour. For example, policy makers have debated the wisdom of regulating the content of Web sites featuring hate speech and pornography.

The sheer length of time people spend using the Internet may soon be an indication of deviance. Some psychiatrists and psychologists are now deciding whether or not Internet addiction may eventually be labelled a new disorder and, thus, a new form of deviant behaviour. Dr. Kimberly Young of the University of Pittsburgh has studied Internet addiction in the United States, placing it in the same category as pathological gambling and compulsive shopping. She found addicted users spent an average of 38 hours per week online, compared with 8 hours per week for non-addicts (Dalfen 2000). Canadians, according to a January 2000 *Media Matrix* study, use the Internet 27 percent more than their U.S. counterparts do (Dalfen 2000).

Some deviant uses of technology are criminal, though not all participants see it that way. The pirating of software, motion pictures, and CDs has become a big business. At conventions and swap meets, pirated copies of movies and CDs are sold openly. Some of the products are obviously counterfeit, but many come in sophisticated packaging, complete with warranty cards. When vendors are willing to talk, they say they merely want to be compensated for their time and the cost of materials, or that the software they have copied is in the public domain.

Though most of these black market activities are clearly illegal, many consumers and small-time pirates are proud of their behaviour. They may even think themselves smart for figuring out a way to avoid the "unfair" prices charged by "big corporations." Few people see the pirating

"I swear I wasn't looking at smut—I was just stealing music."

of a new software program or a first-run movie as a threat to the public good, as they would embezzlements from a bank. Similarly, most business people who "borrow" software from another department, even though they lack a site licence, do not think they are doing anything wrong. No social stigma attaches to their illegal behaviour.

Deviance, then, is a complex concept. Sometimes, it is trivial; sometimes, profoundly harmful. Sometimes, it is accepted by society and sometimes soundly rejected. What accounts for deviant behaviour and people's reaction to it? In the next section, we will examine four theoretical explanations for deviance.

Explaining Deviance

Why do people violate social norms? We have seen that deviant acts are subject to both informal and formal sanctions of social control. The non-conforming or disobedient person may face disapproval, loss of friends, fines, or even imprisonment. Why, then, does deviance occur?

Early explanations for deviance identified supernatural causes or genetic factors (such as "bad blood" or evolutionary throwbacks to primitive ancestors). By the 1800s, there were substantial research efforts to identify biological factors that lead to deviance and especially to criminal activity. Although such research was discredited in the twentieth century, contemporary studies, primarily by biochemists, have sought to isolate genetic factors leading to a likelihood of certain personality traits. Although criminality (much less deviance) is hardly a personality characteristic, researchers have focused on traits that might lead to crime, such as aggression. Of course, aggression can also lead to success in the corporate world, professional sports, or other areas of life.

The contemporary study of possible biological roots of criminality is but one aspect of the larger sociobiology debate. In general, sociologists reject any emphasis on genetic roots of crime and deviance. The limitations of current knowledge, the possibility of reinforcing racist and sexist assumptions, and the disturbing implications for rehabilitation of criminals have led sociologists to largely draw on other approaches to explain deviance (Sagarin and Sanchez 1988).

Functionalist Perspective

According to functionalists, deviance is a common part of human existence, with positive (as well as negative) consequences for social stability. Deviance helps to define the limits of proper behaviour. Children who see one parent scold the other for belching at the dinner table learn about approved conduct. The same is true of the driver who receives a speeding ticket, the department store cashier who is fired for yelling at a customer, and the university student who is penalized for handing in essays weeks overdue.

Durkheim's Legacy

Émile Durkheim investigated a range of social tacts that illuminated different forms of social solidarity within societies (1964, original edition 1895). In Durkheim's view, the punishments established within a culture (including both formal and informal mechanisms of social control) help to define acceptable behaviour and, thus, contribute to stability. If improper acts were not committed and then sanctioned, people might stretch their standards of what constitutes appropriate conduct.

Kai Erikson illustrated this boundary-maintenance function of deviance in his study of the Puritans of seventeenth-century New England (1966). By today's standards, the Puritans placed tremendous emphasis on conventional morals. Their persecution of Quakers and execution of women as witches represented continuing attempts to define and redefine the boundaries of their community. In effect, their changing social norms created "crime waves," as people whose behaviour was previously acceptable suddenly faced punishment for being deviant (Abrahamson 1978; N. Davis 1975).

Durkheim also introduced the term *anomie* into sociological literature (1951, original edition 1897). ◀ P.14 Anomie is a state of normlessness that typically occurs during a period of profound social change and disorder, such as during an economic collapse. People may become more aggressive or depressed, and this may result in higher rates of violent crime and suicide. Since there is much less agreement on what constitutes proper behaviour during times of revolution, sudden prosperity, or economic depression, conformity and obedience become less significant as social forces. It also becomes much more difficult to state exactly what constitutes deviance.

Merton's Theory of Deviance

What do a mugger and a teacher have in common? Each is "working" to obtain money that can then be exchanged for desired goods. As this example illustrates, behaviour that violates accepted norms (such as mugging) may be performed with the same basic objectives in mind as those of people who pursue more conventional lifestyles.

Using the above analysis, sociologist Robert Merton adapted Durkheim's notion of anomie to explain why people accept or reject the goals of a society, the socially approved means of fulfilling their aspirations, or both (1968). Merton maintained that one important cultural goal in capitalist societies is success, measured largely in terms of money. In addition to providing this goal for people, our society offers specific instructions on how to pursue success—go to school, work hard, do not quit, take advantage of opportunities, and so forth.

What happens to individuals in a society with a heavy emphasis on wealth as a basic symbol of success? Merton reasoned that people adapt in certain ways, either by conforming to or by deviating from such cultural expectations. Consequently, he developed the **anomie theory of deviance**, which posits five basic forms of adaptation (see Table 7-2).

Conformity to social norms, the most common adaptation in Merton's typology, is the opposite of deviance. It involves acceptance of both the overall societal goal ("become affluent") and the approved means ("work hard"). In Merton's view, there must be some consensus regarding accepted cultural goals and legitimate means for attaining them. Without such consensus, societies could exist only as collectives of people—rather than as unified cultures—and might function in continual chaos.

Table 7-2	Modes of Individual Adaptation	
Mode	**Institutionalized Means (Hard Work)**	**Societal Goal (Acquisition of Wealth)**
Non-deviant		
Conformity	+	+
Deviant		
Innovation	−	+
Ritualism	+	−
Retreatism	−	−
Rebellion	±	±

Note: + indicates acceptance; − indicates rejection; ± indicates replacement with new means and goals.
Source: Merton 1968:1940.

Of course, in a society such as ours, conformity is not universal. For example, the means for realizing objectives are not equally distributed. People in the lower social classes often identify with the same goals as those of more powerful and affluent citizens yet lack equal access to high-quality education and training for skilled work. Even within a society, institutionalized means for realizing objectives vary. For example, a Statistics Canada report found that in 1997, access to legalized gambling varied across provinces and territories. Lotteries were legal in all provinces and territories, government casinos were legal in approximately half of the provinces, and VLTs (video lottery terminals) were legal in most provinces (Marshall 1999).

The other four types of behaviour represented in Table 7-2 all involve some departure from conformity. The "innovator" accepts the goals of a society but pursues them through means regarded as improper. For example, Harry King, a professional thief who specialized in safecracking for 40 years, gave a lecture to a sociology class and was asked if he had minded spending time in prison. King responded:

> I didn't exactly like it. But it was one of the necessary things about the life I had chosen. Do you like to come here and teach this class? I bet if the students had their wishes they'd be somewhere else, maybe out stealing, instead of sitting in this dumpy room. But they do it because it gets them something they want. The same with me. If I had to go to prison from time to time, well, that was the price you pay. (Chambliss 1972:x)

Harry King saw his criminal lifestyle as an adaptation to the goal of material success or "getting something you want." Denied the chance to achieve success through socially approved means, some individuals (like King) turn to illegitimate paths of upward mobility.

In Merton's typology, the "ritualist" has abandoned the goal of material success and become compulsively committed to the institutional means. Work becomes simply a way of life rather than a means to the goal of success, as in the case of bureaucratic officials who blindly apply rules and regulations without remembering the larger goals of an organization. Certainly, this would be true of a welfare caseworker who refuses to assist a homeless family because their last apartment was in another district.

The "retreatist," as described by Merton, has basically withdrawn (or "retreated") from both the goals *and* the means of a society. In Canada, drug addicts and residents of skid row are typically portrayed as retreatists. There is also growing concern that adolescents addicted to alcohol will become retreatists at an early age.

The final adaptation identified by Merton reflects people's attempts to create a *new* social structure. The "rebel" feels alienated from dominant means and goals and may seek a dramatically different social order. Members of revolutionary political organizations, such as the Irish Republican Army (IRA) or right-wing militia groups, can be categorized as rebels according to Merton's model.

Merton has stressed that he was not attempting to describe five types of individuals. Rather, he offered a typology to explain the actions that people *usually* take. Thus, leaders of organized crime syndicates will be categorized as innovators, since they do not pursue success through socially approved means. Yet they may also attend church and send their children to medical school. Conversely, "respectable" people may occasionally cheat on their taxes or violate traffic laws. According to Merton, the same person will move back and forth from one mode of adaptation to another, depending on the demands of a particular situation.

Merton's theory, though popular, has had relatively few applications. Little effort has been made to determine to what extent all acts of deviance can be accounted for by his five modes. Moreover, although Merton's theory is useful in examining certain types of behaviour, such as illegal gambling by disadvantaged people functioning as innovators, his formulation fails to explain key differences in rates. Why, for example, do some disadvantaged groups have lower rates of reported crime than others? Why is criminal activity not viewed as a viable alternative by many people in adverse circumstances? Merton's theory of deviance does not answer such questions easily (Cloward 1959; Hartjen 1978).

Still, Merton has made a key contribution to the sociological understanding of deviance by pointing out that deviants (such as innovators and ritualists) share a great deal with conforming people. The convicted felon may hold many of the same aspirations as people with no criminal background. Therefore, we can understand deviance as socially created behaviour, rather than as the result of momentary pathological impulses.

Interactionist Perspective

The functionalist approach to deviance explains why rule violation continues to exist in societies despite pressures to conform and obey. However, functionalists do not indicate how a given person comes to commit a deviant act or why on some occasions crimes do or do not occur. The emphasis on everyday behaviour that is the focus of the interactionist perspective is reflected in two explanations of crime: cultural transmission and routine activities theory.

Cultural Transmission

White teenagers in the suburbs and cities attempt to achieve fame within a subculture of "taggers." These

The graffiti of teenagers can be seen on walls in most urban settings. According to interactionist Edwin Sutherland, teenagers are socialized into engaging in such deviant acts.

young people "tag" (spray graffiti on) poles, utility boxes, bridges, and freeway signs. Although law-enforcement officials prefer to view them as "visual terrorists," the taggers gain respect from their peers by being "up the most" on prominent walls and billboards and by displaying the flashiest styles. Even parents may tolerate or endorse such deviant behaviour by declaring, "At least my kid's not shooting people. He's still alive" (Wooden 1995:124).

These teenagers demonstrate that humans *learn* how to behave in social situations—whether properly or improperly. There is no natural, innate manner in which people interact with one another. These simple ideas are not disputed today, but this was not the case when sociologist Edwin Sutherland (1883–1950) first advanced the argument that an individual undergoes the same basic socialization process whether learning conforming or deviant acts.

Sutherland's ideas have been the dominating force in criminology. He drew on the **cultural transmission** school, which emphasizes that a person learns criminal behaviour through interactions with others. Such learning includes not only techniques of lawbreaking (for example, how to break into a car quickly and quietly) but also the motives, drives, and rationalizations of criminals. We can also use the cultural transmission approach to explain the behaviour of people who engage in habitual—and ultimately life-threatening—use of alcohol or drugs.

Sutherland maintained that through interactions with a primary group and significant others, people acquire definitions of proper and improper behaviour. He used the term **differential association** to describe the process through which exposure to attitudes *favourable* to criminal acts leads to violation of rules. Research suggests that this view of differential association also applies to such non-criminal deviant acts as sitting down during the singing of the national anthem or lying to a friend (E. Jackson, Tittle, and Burke 1986).

To what extent will a given person engage in activity regarded as proper or improper? For each individual, it will depend on the frequency, duration, and importance of two types of social interaction experiences—those that endorse deviant behaviour and those that promote acceptance of social norms. People are more likely to engage in norm-defying behaviour if they are part of a group or subculture that stresses deviant values, such as a street gang.

Sutherland offers the example of a boy who is sociable, outgoing, and athletic, and who lives in an area with a high rate of delinquency. The youth is very likely to come into contact with peers who commit acts of vandalism, fail to attend school, and so forth, and may come to adopt such behaviour. However, an introverted boy living in the same neighbourhood may stay away from his peers and avoid delinquency. In another community, an outgoing and athletic boy may join a baseball team or a scout troup because of his interactions with peers. Thus, Sutherland views learning improper behaviour as the result of the types of groups to which a person belongs and the kinds of friendships that person has with others (Sutherland and Cressey 1978).

According to its critics, however, the cultural transmission approach may explain the deviant behaviour of juvenile delinquents or graffiti artists, but it fails to explain the conduct of the first-time impulsive shoplifter or the impoverished person who steals out of necessity. Although not a precise statement of the process through which someone becomes a criminal, differential association theory does direct our attention to the paramount role of social interaction in increasing a person's motivation to engage in deviant behaviour (Cressey 1960; E. Jackson, Tittle, and Burke 1986; Sutherland and Cressey 1978).

Routine Activities Theory

Another more recent interactionist explanation considers the requisite conditions for a crime or deviant act to occur: there must be at the same time and in the same place a perpetrator, and a victim and/or an object of property. **Routine activities theory** contends that criminal victimization is increased when motivated offenders and suitable targets converge. It goes without saying that you cannot have car theft without automobiles, but the greater availability of more valuable automobiles to potential thieves *heightens* the likelihood that such a crime will occur. Campus and airport parking lots, where vehicles may be left in isolated locations for long periods, represent a new target for crime unknown just a generation ago. Routine activity of this nature can occur even in the home. For example, adults may save money by buying 24-packs of beer, but buying in bulk also allows juveniles to siphon off contents without attracting attention to their "crime." The theory derives its name of *routine* from the fact that the elements of a criminal or deviant act come together in normal, legal, and routine activities.

Advocates of this theory see it as a powerful explanation for the rise in crime during the past 50 years. Routine activity has changed to make crime more likely. Homes left vacant during the day or during long vacations are more accessible as targets of crime. The greater presence of consumer goods that are highly portable, such as video equipment and computers, also makes crime more likely (Cohen and Felson 1979; Felson 1998).

Some significant research supports the routine activities explanation. Studies of urban crime have documented the existence of "hot spots" where people are more likely to be victimized because of their routine comings and goings (Cromwell, Olson, and Avarey 1995; Sherman, Gartin, and Buerger 1989).

Perhaps what is most compelling about this theory is that it broadens our effort to understand crime and deviance. Rather than focus just on the criminal, routine activities theory also brings into the picture the behaviour of the victim. However, we need to resist the temptation to *expect* the higher victimization of some groups, such as racial and ethnic minorities, much less to consider it their own fault (Akers 1997).

Labelling Theory

The Saints and Roughnecks were two groups of high school males who were continually engaged in excessive drinking, reckless driving, truancy, petty theft, and vandalism. There the similarity ended. None of the Saints was ever arrested, but every Roughneck was frequently in trouble with police and townspeople. Why the disparity in their treatment? On the basis of his observational research in their high school, sociologist William Chambliss concluded that social class played an important role in the varying fortunes of the two groups (1973).

The Saints effectively produced a facade of respectability. They came from "good families," were active in

school organizations, expressed the intention of attending university, and received good grades. People generally viewed their delinquent acts as a few isolated cases of "sowing wild oats." By contrast, the Roughnecks had no such aura of respectability. They drove around town in beat-up cars, were generally unsuccessful in school, and were viewed with suspicion no matter what they did.

We can understand such discrepancies by using an approach to deviance known as **labelling theory**. Unlike Sutherland's work, labelling theory does not focus on why some individuals come to commit deviant acts. Instead, it attempts to explain why certain people (such as the Roughnecks) are *viewed* as deviants, delinquents, "bad kids," "losers," and criminals, while others whose behaviour is similar (such as the Saints) are not seen in such harsh terms. Reflecting the contribution of interactionist theorists, labelling theory emphasizes how a person comes to be labelled as deviant or to accept that label. Sociologist Howard Becker (1963:9; 1964), who popularized this approach, summed it up with this statement: "Deviant behavior is behavior that people so label." In Box 7-3 on page 172, we consider a behaviour that has only recently been identified and labelled a crime: road rage.

Labelling theory is also called the **societal-reaction approach**, reminding us that it is the *response* to an act and not the behaviour itself that determines deviance. For example, studies have shown that some school personnel and therapists expand educational programs designed for students who have learning disabilities to include those with behavioural problems. Consequently, a "troublemaker" can be improperly labelled as having a learning disability and vice versa.

A study by three British psychologists underscores the implications of using different labels to describe people with learning difficulties or disabilities. A total of 111 subjects completed a questionnaire designed to assess attitudes toward three labelled groups: "mentally subnormal adults," "mentally handicapped adults," and "people with learning difficulties." The researchers found that subjects reacted more positively to the label "people with learning difficulties" than to the other labels. Subjects view "people with learning difficulties" as more competent and as deserving of more rights than "mentally handicapped" or "mentally subnormal" individuals (Eayrs, Ellis, and Jones 1993).

Traditionally, research on deviance has focused on people who violate social norms. In contrast, labelling theory focuses on police, probation officers, psychiatrists, judges, teachers, employers, school officials, and other regulators of social control. These agents, it is argued, play a significant role in creating the deviant identity by designating certain people (and not others) as "deviant." An important aspect of labelling theory is the recognition that some individuals or groups have the power to *define* labels

Research in Action 7-3
Labelling a Behaviour as a Crime: Road Rage

You're cut off by a honking, cursing driver as you try to merge with traffic—road rage in action! Though this kind of anti-social behaviour isn't new, the concept of road rage is. Sociologists who have tried to trace its emergence want to know why it became socially significant only recently, even though bad driving dates back to the dawn of the automotive age.

It has been well documented that media portrayals of crime can influence the way we understand it, even if the social reality is quite different. Serial killers are extremely rare, but you wouldn't know it from watching television or the movies. And though news coverage of civil disorders emphasizes the lawlessness of the crowd, most people in the immediate vicinity of such disturbances behave in law-abiding fashion, even during the largest riots.

Thus, we should not be surprised to learn that the provocative term, *road rage*, emerged in the media in response to an extreme event: a series of deadly shootings committed by a driver on the Los Angeles Expressway more than 20 years ago. Once the term had become established in everyday usage, the idea that aggressive behaviour behind the wheel was on the increase became an accepted truism. In response to this perception, government officials launched campaigns to control aggressive driving, and legislators passed laws to distinguish road rage from other motor vehicle violations, such as tailgating or forcing another car off the road.

Like the attention the media give to serial killers, the focus on road rage may be overdone. One research study estimates that the odds of dying because of road rage are only 1 in 9.5 million, compared to the much more significant risk of being killed in an auto accident—a chance of about 1 in 16 000. Yet, the concept of road rage resonates with our notion of cars as super-powerful machines. As in Stephen King's novel, *Christine* (in which an "evil" car comes to "possess" its owner), cars have acquired almost a personality of their own in the popular imagination.

Once a form of deviance has been designated as unique, it may draw attention away from more pressing concerns.

Sources: Elliott 1999; Farrar 2005; Lupton 1999, 2001.

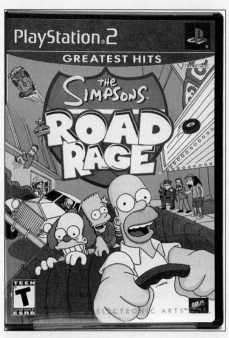

PlayStation2's interactive game *Road Rage* illustrates the wide usage of a label invented by the media just two decades ago.

Significantly, more common forms of aggression than road rage—such as "bar rage" or "party rage"—have not been singled out by special expressions. While road rage is far from a trivial or harmless behaviour, research suggests that its importance has been exaggerated by the power of labelling.

Applying Theory

1. What is the role of the audience in the creation of a new label such as *road rage*?
2. Can you think of another label for deviant behaviour that has come into currency recently? Do you know how it originated?

---

and apply them to others. This view recalls the conflict perspective's emphasis on the social significance of power.

In recent years, the practice of *racial* or *ethnic profiling*, in which people are identified as criminal suspects purely on the basis of their race or ethnicity, has come under public scrutiny. Studies conducted in the United States confirm the public's suspicions that in some jurisdictions, police officers are much more likely to stop black males than white males for routine traffic violations. In Canada, the United States, and many European countries, the events of September 11, 2001 (9/11), have caused civil rights activists to raise concerns about the use of racial profiling in safety and security policies and practices.

The labelling approach does not fully explain why certain people accept a label and others are able to reject it. In fact, this perspective may exaggerate the ease with which societal judgments can alter our self-image. Labelling theorists do suggest, however, that how much power a person has relative to others is important in determining that person's ability to resist an undesirable label. Competing approaches (including that of Sutherland) fail to explain why some deviants continue to be viewed as conformists rather than as violators of rules. According to Howard Becker, labelling theory was not conceived as the *sole* explanation for deviance (1973); its proponents merely hoped to focus more attention on the undeniably important actions of those people officially in charge of defining deviance (N. Davis 1975; compare with Cullen and Cullen 1978).

The popularity of labelling theory is reflected in the emergence of a related perspective, called social constructionism. According to the **social constructionist perspective**, deviance is the product of the culture we live in. Social constructionists focus specifically on the decision-making process that creates the deviant identity. They point out that "missing children," "deadbeat dads," "spree killers," and "date rapists" have always been with us but at times have become the major social concern of the moment because of intensive media coverage (Liska and Messner 1999; Wright, Gronfein, and Owens 2000).

Use Your Sociological Imagination

You are a teacher. What kinds of labels freely used in educational circles might be attached to your students?

Conflict Perspective

For many years, a husband who forced his wife to have sexual intercourse—without her consent and against her will—was not legally considered to have committed rape. The laws defined rape as pertaining only to sexual relations between people not married to each other. These laws reflected the overwhelmingly male composition of government and legal decision makers. Conflict theorists would not be surprised by this. They point out that people with power protect their own interests and define deviance to suit their own needs. It wasn't until 1983 in Canada that rape laws were broadened to sexual assault laws and it became a criminal act for a man to rape his wife.

Feminist legal scholar Catherine MacKinnon argues that male sexual behaviour represents "dominance eroticized," in that male sexuality is linked to dominance and power (1987). Edwin Schur expands on this view

of male sexuality, stating that "forced sex is the ultimate indicator and preserver of male dominance" (1983:148). Canadian laws have historically sanctioned the abuse of women within marriage, based on the assumption of male control and ownership of his family (H. Johnson 1996). According to Status of Women Canada (2000), female victims of spousal abuse are more likely to be subjected to sexual assault and more severe forms of violence, such as beating and choking, than are male victims.

Sociologist Richard Quinney is a leading exponent of the view that the criminal justice system serves the interests of the powerful (1974, 1979, 1980). Crime, according to Quinney, is a definition of conduct created by authorized agents of social control—such as legislators and law-enforcement officers—in a politically organized society (1970). He and other conflict theorists argued that law-making is often an attempt by the powerful to coerce others into their own morality (see also S. Spitzer 1975).

This helps to explain why our society has laws against gambling, drug usage, and prostitution, many of which are violated on a massive scale. (We examine these "victimless crimes" later in the chapter.) According to the conflict school, criminal law does not represent a consistent application of societal values but instead reflects competing values and interests.

Conflict theorists contend that the entire criminal justice system of Canada treats suspects differently on the basis of their racial, ethnic, or social class background. The case of Donald Marshall, an Aboriginal man from Nova Scotia who was wrongfully convicted of murder, and who served years in prison for a crime he did not commit, is one of the most illustrative examples of the bias against Aboriginal persons in Canadian legal history.

Today, Aboriginal men have the highest rate of over-representation in prisons of any group in Canada. Quinney argues that, through such differential applications of

Demonstrators in Vancouver show their support for safe-injection sites in that city.

social control, the criminal justice system helps to keep the poor and oppressed in their deprived position (1974). In his view, disadvantaged individuals and groups who represent a threat to those with power become the primary targets of criminal law. He maintains the real criminals in poor neighbourhoods are not the people arrested for vandalism and theft but rather absentee landlords and exploitative store owners. Even if we do not accept this challenging argument, we cannot ignore the role of the powerful in creating a social structure that perpetuates suffering.

The perspective advanced by labelling and conflict theorists forms quite a contrast to the functionalist approach to deviance. Functionalists view standards of deviant behaviour as merely reflecting cultural norms, whereas conflict and labelling theorists point out that the most powerful groups in a society can shape laws and standards and determine who is (or is not) prosecuted as a criminal. Thus, the label "deviant" is rarely applied to the corporate executive whose decisions lead to large-scale environmental pollution. In the opinion of conflict theorists, agents of social control and powerful groups can generally impose their own self-serving definitions of deviance on the general public.

Feminist Perspectives

Although feminist theories of deviance are diverse, most tend to challenge other mainstream theories on the grounds that women's experiences have not been included and that gender-based perspectives have not been employed. Feminist theories of deviance are generally eager to understand the gendered nature of institutions, such as the criminal justice system, and the inequities in the system that lead to differential treatment of men and women.

Many feminist perspectives contend that courts, prisons, law-enforcement agencies, welfare agencies, and families alike are organized on the basis of gender as well as power, class, race, and sexuality (Elliot and Mandell 1998). Of concern are ways in which such factors as gender, sexuality, class, and race intersect to produce patterns of and responses to deviant behaviour. As well, these perspectives in general hold the view that since gender relations are not "natural," but rather are produced by social, cultural, and historical conditions, gendered patterns of deviance will reflect these conditions. For example, the social acceptability of smoking for women (and the labelling of some women smokers as deviants) has been shaped by history, class, and sexuality. From the 1800s to the 1920s in North America, smoking by women was associated with prostitution and lesbianism. Women who smoked were labelled "sluts," "whores," and "sinners," and were considered "fallen women" (Greaves 1996:18).

As previously mentioned, feminist perspectives are varied. For example, liberal feminist perspectives tend to view women's rates of crime and deviance as a reflection of the degree to which they participate in all areas of social life—sports, politics, business, education, and so on. Because women are confronted with obstacles in their climb to the top corporate positions, they are limited in their opportunities to engage in particular deviant acts, such as corporate crime.

In contrast, radical feminist perspectives see patriarchy (the set of social relations that maintains male control) as the key to understanding female crime and deviance. Patriarchy, according to radical feminist analysis, puts men in control of women's bodies and minds and sets in place oppressive social institutions, such as the family and the law, in order to maintain control. Sexual offences for women, therefore, are more common, since men control the institutions that regulate activities such as prostitution. This imbalance of power results in a higher rate of arrest and conviction for the female prostitute than for the male customer.

We have seen that over the past century, sociologists have taken many different approaches in studying deviance, arousing some controversy in the process. Table 7-3 summarizes the various theoretical approaches to this topic.

☐ WHAT IS CRIME?

Crime is a violation of criminal law for which some governmental authority applies formal penalties. It represents a deviation from formal social norms administered by the state. Laws divide crimes into various categories, depending on the severity of the offence, the age of the offender, the potential punishment that can be levied, and the court that holds jurisdiction over the case.

Crimes tend to affect some groups more than others; for example, their impact can be gender-specific and age-specific. In Canada, of all the victims of crimes against the person, women and girls make up the vast majority of victims of sexual offences. In 2004, 70 percent of victims of sexual offences up to age 11 were female; in the same year, 89 percent of the victims between the ages of 12 and 17 and 93 percent of the victims over age 18 were female (Statistics Canada 2005g).

Types of Crime

Rather than relying solely on legal categories, sociologists classify crimes in terms of how they are committed and how society views the offences. In this section, we will examine four types of crime as differentiated by sociologists: professional crime, organized crime, white-collar crime, and so-called victimless crimes.

Table 7-3   Sociological Perspectives on Deviance

Approach	Perspective	Proponents	Emphasis
Anomie	Functionalist	Émile Durkheim Robert Merton	Adaptation to societal norms
Cultural transmission/ Differential association	Interactionist	Edwin Sutherland	Patterns learned through others
Routine activities	Interactionist	Marcus Felson	Impact of the social environment
Labelling/Social constructionist	Interactionist	Howard Becker	Societal response to acts
Conflict	Conflict	Richard Quinney	Dominance by authorized agents Discretionary justice
Feminist	Feminist/Conflict	Freda Adler Meda Chesney-Lind	Role of gender Women as victims and perpetrators

Professional Crime

Although the adage "crime doesn't pay" is familiar, many people do make a career of illegal activities. A **professional criminal** is a person who pursues crime as a day-to-day occupation, developing skilled techniques and enjoying a certain degree of status among other criminals. Some professional criminals specialize in burglary, safecracking, hijacking of cargo, pickpocketing, and shoplifting. Such people have acquired skills that reduce the likelihood of arrest, conviction, and imprisonment. As a result, they may have long careers in their chosen "professions."

Edwin Sutherland offered pioneering insights into the behaviour of professional criminals by publishing an annotated account written by a professional thief (1937). Unlike the person who engages in crime only once or twice, professional thieves make a business of stealing. They devote their entire working time to planning and executing crimes and sometimes travel across the nation to pursue their "professional duties." Like people in regular occupations, professional thieves consult with their colleagues concerning the demands of work, thus becoming part of a subculture of similarly occupied individuals. They exchange information on possible places to burglarize, on outlets for unloading stolen goods, and on ways of securing bail bonds if arrested.

Organized Crime

For our purposes, we will consider **organized crime** to be the work of a group that regulates relations among various criminal enterprises involved in the smuggling and sale of drugs, prostitution, gambling, and other illegal activities. In Canada, gangs are increasingly involved in organized crime, as "gang imperialism" (Taylor 1990) promotes linkages between gangs for the purpose of financial gain

(Astwood Strategy Corporation 2003). Organized crime dominates the world of illegal business just as large corporations dominate the conventional business world. It allocates territory, sets prices for goods and services, and acts as an arbitrator in internal disputes.

Organized crime is a secret, conspiratorial activity that generally evades law enforcement. Organized crime takes over legitimate businesses, gains influence over labour unions, corrupts public officials, intimidates witnesses in criminal trials, and even "taxes" merchants in exchange for "protection" (National Advisory Commission on Criminal Justice 1976). An example of the intimidation tactics used by organized crime is the gunning down of Montreal crime reporter Michel Auger in 2000. Auger specialized in stories on Quebec organized crime and biker gangs. Auger was shot five times, but recovered. Although it has not yet been proven that biker gangs were responsible for the execution-style attack, it came a day after his paper, *Le Journal*, printed one of his articles on biker-related murders.

There has always been a global element in organized crime. But law-enforcement officials and policymakers have acknowledged the emergence of a new form of organized crime that takes advantage of advances in electronic communications. *Transnational* organized crime includes drug and arms smuggling, money laundering, and trafficking in illegal immigrants and stolen goods such as automobiles (Office of Justice Programs 1999).

White-Collar and Technology-Based Crime

Income tax evasion, stock manipulation, consumer fraud, bribery and extraction of "kickbacks," embezzlement, and misrepresentation in advertising—these are all examples of **white-collar crime**: illegal acts committed in the course of business activities, often by affluent, "respectable" people. Perhaps one of the most notable examples of white-collar crime would be that of Canadian-born businessman Conrad Black—a member of the British House of Lords and a high-profile newspaper baron—who, in 2007, was found guilty on several criminal charges stemming from his many business ventures. Edwin Sutherland (1949, 1983) likened white-collar crime to organized crime because it is often perpetrated through occupational roles (Friedrichs 1998).

A new type of white-collar crime has emerged in recent decades: computer crime. The use of such high technology allows people to carry out embezzlement or electronic fraud without leaving a trace, or to gain access to a company's inventory without leaving home. An adept programmer can gain access to a firm's computer by telephone and then copy valuable files. It is virtually impossible to track such people unless they are foolish enough to call from the same phone each time. According to a study conducted in 2000 by the FBI and the Computer Security Institute, 70 percent of companies in the United States relying on computer systems reported theft of electronic information, for an estimated loss of US$265 million in 1999 alone (Zuckerman 2000).

Sutherland coined the phrase *white-collar crime* in 1939 to refer to acts by individuals (1940), but the term has been broadened more recently to include offences by organizations as well. *Organizational crime* is an offence committed

"BUT IF WE GO BACK TO SCHOOL AND GET A GOOD EDUCATION, THINK OF ALL THE DOORS IT'LL OPEN TO WHITE-COLLAR CRIME."

with the approval and encouragement of a company to advance its own interests (Coleman 1985). Corporations, for example, may engage in anti-competitive behaviour, acts that lead to environmental pollution, tax fraud, stock fraud and manipulation, the production of unsafe goods, bribery and corruption, and worker health-and-safety violations (Simpson 1993).

Given the economic and social costs of white-collar crime, you might expect the criminal justice system to take this problem quite seriously. Yet, research done in the United States shows that white-collar offenders are more likely to receive fines than prison sentences. In federal courts—where most white-collar cases end up—probation is granted to 40 percent of those who have violated antitrust laws, 61 percent of those convicted of fraud, and 70 percent of convicted embezzlers (Gest 1985). Amitai Etzioni's study (1985, 1990) found that in 43 percent of the incidents, either no penalty was imposed or the company was required merely to cease engaging in the illegal practice and to return any funds gained through illegal means (for a different view, see Manson 1986).

Moreover, conviction for such illegal acts does not generally harm a person's reputation and career aspirations nearly as much as conviction for street crime would. Apparently, being labelled a "white-collar criminal" does not carry the stigma of the label, "felon convicted of a violent crime." Conflict theorists are not surprised by such differential labelling and treatment. They argue that the criminal justice system largely disregards the white-collar crimes of the affluent, while focusing on crimes often committed by the poor. If an offender holds a position of status and influence, his or her crime is treated as less serious, and the sanction is much more lenient (Maguire 1988).

Use Your Sociological Imagination

As a newspaper editor, how might you treat stories on corporate crime differently from those on violent crimes?

Victimless Crimes

White-collar or street crimes endanger people's economic or personal well-being against their will (or without their direct knowledge). By contrast, sociologists use the term **victimless crimes** to describe the willing exchange among adults of widely desired, but illegal, goods and services (Schur 1965, 1985).

Although the term *victimless crime* is widely used, many people object to the notion that there is no victim when such offences take place. Excessive drinking, compulsive gambling, and illegal drug use contribute to an enormous amount of personal and property damage. And feminist sociologists contend that the so-called victimless crime of prostitution, as well as the more disturbing aspects of pornography, reinforce the misconception that women are "toys" who can be treated as objects rather than as people (Flavin 1998; Jolin 1994).

Nonetheless, some activists are working to decriminalize many of these illegal practices. Supporters of decriminalization are troubled by the attempt to legislate a moral code of behaviour for adults. In their view, it is impossible to prevent prostitution, gambling, and other victimless crimes. The already overburdened criminal justice system should instead devote its resources to "street crimes" and other offences with obvious victims. However, opponents of decriminalization insist that such offences do indeed have victims, in the sense that they can bring harm to innocent people. For example, a person with a drinking problem can become abusive to a spouse or children; a compulsive gambler or drug user may steal to pursue the obsession. According to critics of decriminalization, society must not give tacit approval to conduct that has such harmful consequences (National Advisory Commission on Criminal Justice 1976; Schur 1968, 1985).

The controversy over decriminalization reminds us of the important insights of labelling and conflict theories presented earlier. Underlying this debate are two interesting questions: Who has the power to define gambling, prostitution, and public drunkenness as "crimes"? And who has the power to label such behaviours as "victimless"? It is generally the government and, in some cases, the police and the courts.

Again, we can see that criminal law is not simply a universal standard of behaviour agreed on by all members of society. Rather, it reflects the struggle among competing individuals and groups to gain governmental support for their particular moral and social values. For example, such organizations as Mothers Against Drunk Driving (MADD) and Students Against Drunk Driving (SADD) have had success over the years in modifying public attitudes toward drunkenness. Rather than being viewed as a victimless crime, drunkenness is increasingly being associated with the potential dangers of driving while under the influence of alcohol. As a result, the mass media are giving greater (and more critical) attention to people who are guilty of drunk driving, and many provincial and territorial governments have instituted more severe fines and jail terms for a wide variety of alcohol-related offences.

Crime Statistics

Crime statistics are not as accurate as social scientists would like. However, since they deal with an issue of grave concern to people in many countries, they are frequently cited as if they were completely reliable. Such data do serve as an indicator of police activity, as well as an approximate indication of the level of certain types of crimes. Yet, it would be a mistake to interpret these data as an exact representation of the incidence of crime.

Public opinion polls reveal that Canadians believe the crime rate is increasing in this country, despite the release of statistics that indicate the national crime rate in 2006 hit its lowest point in 25 years (Statistics Canada 2007c). In 2006, the rate of violent crime in Canada did not increase from the previous year; the rate of attempted murder increased by 3 percent over the previous year, while homicides dropped by 10 percent—down 14 percentage points from 1996–2006. Youth crime rates increased in 2006, which was the first increase since 2003 (Statistics Canada 2007c).

In 2006, the overall crime rate fell in every province of Canada. Within Canada, however, vast regional differences exist in rates of crime. As Figure 7-1 illustrates, in 2006, Saskatchewan had the highest rate among the provinces (for the ninth year in a row), followed by Manitoba, British Columbia, and Alberta. Ontario had

▶ **FIGURE 7-1**

Crime Rates by Province and Territory, 2006

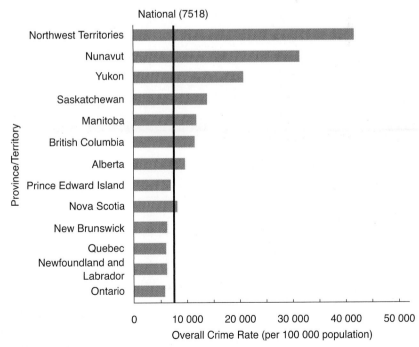

Source: Statistics Canada 2007b.

the lowest crime rate in the country. Youth crime rates, in 2005 and 2006, were up in all provinces except Quebec (Statistics Canada 2007c).

Canada's crime rates are significantly lower than those of our U.S. neighbours, particularly for violent crimes, such as homicide, for which the U.S. rate is more than three times greater than Canada's (Statistics Canada 2001b). Research has shown, however, that Canadian and U.S. rates converge in the area of spousal assault, showing that "Canadian men are just as, if not more, likely to beat their spouses as American men" (DeKeseredy and Schwartz 1998:vii).

International comparisons aside, results from *Women Abuse on Campus: Results from the Canadian National Survey* reveal that it is not only women in marital or cohabiting relationships who are in danger of abuse, but also those at post-secondary institutions who are in dating relationships (DeKeseredy and Schwartz 1998). Despite the fact that women attending post-secondary institutions in Canada are most likely to be sexually assaulted, not only by men they know but also by men who might actually like them, and that the assault is most likely to take place in a private location, they fear "stranger danger" (DeKeseredy and Schwartz 1998). Table 7-4 illustrates the perception of safety of 1835 Canadian female students on campuses across the country.

Sociologists have several ways of measuring crime. Historically, they have relied on official statistics, but under-reporting has always been a problem with such measures. Because members of racial and ethnic minority groups have not always trusted law-enforcement agencies, they have often refrained from contacting the police. Feminist sociologists and others have noted that many women do not report sexual assault or spousal abuse out of fear that officials will regard the crime as the women's fault. Partly because of the deficiencies of official statistics,

victimization surveys question ordinary people, not police officers, to learn how much crime occurs.

Unfortunately, like other crime data, victimization surveys have particular limitations. They require first that victims understand what has happened to them and then that victims disclose such information to interviewers. Fraud, income tax evasion, and blackmail are examples of crimes that are unlikely to be reported in victimization studies. Even though victimization surveys have their limitations, they can be helpful in augmenting police statistics. For example, both police statistics and victimization surveys report that, although the majority of violent-crime offenders tend to be males, victims are equally likely to be male or female (H. Johnson 1996).

International Crime Rates

If it is difficult to develop reliable crime data in Canada, it is even trickier to make useful cross-national comparisons. Nevertheless, with some care, we can offer preliminary conclusions about how crime rates differ around the world.

During the 1980s and 1990s, violent crimes were much more common in the United States than in Canada and Western Europe. Murders, rapes, and robberies were reported to the police at much higher rates in the United States. Yet, the incidence of certain other types of crime appears to be higher elsewhere. For example, England, Italy, Australia, and New Zealand all have higher rates of car theft than in the United States (Rotella 1999; Russell 1995).

Think about It

Do you think that women's feelings of safety on campus contribute to their overall assessment of the quality of their university?

Table 7-4   Reported Feelings of Safety on Campus and Surrounding Areas of 1835 Canadian Women Post-secondary Students

Activity	% Reporting Feeling Unsafe	% Reporting Feeling Very Unsafe
Walking alone after dark	36.1	25.9
Riding a bus or streetcar alone after dark	35.7	12.9
Riding a subway alone after dark	34.8	38.7
Walking alone to a car in a parking lot after dark	42.5	25.7
Waiting for public transportation alone after dark	41.0	31.2
Walking past men they don't know while alone after dark	36.3	38.9

Source: DeKeseredy and Schwartz 1998:3; Kelly and DeKeseredy 1993.

Why are rates of violent crime so much higher in the United States? Although there is no simple answer to this question, sociologist Elliot Currie has suggested a reason could be that U.S. society places greater emphasis on individual economic achievement than do other societies (1985, 1998). At the same time, many observers have noted that the culture of the United States has long tolerated, if not condoned, many forms of violence. When coupled with high rates of handgun ownership, sharp disparities between poor and affluent citizens, significant unemployment, and substantial alcohol and drug abuse, all these factors combine to produce a climate conducive to crime.

There are, however, disturbing increases in violent crime evident in other Western societies. For example, crime in Russia has skyrocketed since the overthrow of Communist Party rule (with its strict controls on guns and criminals) in 1991. Whereas there were fewer than 260 homicides in Moscow in 1978 and again in 1988, there are now more than 1000 homicides per year. Organized crime has filled a power vacuum in Russia (as well as a number of other former Eastern Bloc countries) since the end of communism; one result is that gangland shootouts and premeditated "contract hits" have become more common. Some prominent reformist politicians have been targeted as well. Russia is the only nation in the world that incarcerates a higher proportion of its citizens than the United States. Russia imprisons 580 per 100 000 of its adults on a typical day compared with 550 in the United States, 150 in Canada, fewer than 100 in Mexico or Britain, and only 16 in Greece (Currie 1998; Shinkai and Zvekic 1999).

Transnational Crime

More and more, scholars and police officials are turning their attention to **transnational crime**, or crime that occurs across multiple national borders. In the past, international crime was often limited to the clandestine shipment of goods across the border between two countries. But increasingly, crime is no more restricted by such borders than is legal commerce. Rather than concentrating on specific countries, international crime now spans the globe, leading us to the following question: How is crime exported as a function of globalization?

Historically, probably the most dreaded example of transnational crime has been the enslavement and trafficking of Africans. At first, governments did not regard slavery as a crime, but merely regulated it as they would the trade in goods, placing human life on the same level of importance as objects. In the twentieth century, transnational crime grew to embrace trafficking in endangered species, drugs, and stolen art and antiquities.

Transnational crime is not exclusive of some of the other types of crime we have discussed. For example, organized criminal networks are increasingly global. Technology definitely facilitates their illegal activities, such as trafficking in child pornography. Beginning in the 1990s, the United Nations began to categorize transnational crimes; Table 7-5 lists some of the more common types.

Bilateral co-operation in the pursuit of border criminals such as smugglers has been common for many years. The first global effort to control international crime began with the establishment of the International Criminal Police Organization (Interpol), a co-operative network of European police forces founded to stem the movement of political revolutionaries across borders. While such efforts to fight transnational crime may seem lofty—an activity with which any government should co-operate—they are complicated by sensitive legal and security issues. Most nations that have signed protocols issued by the United Nations, including the United States, have expressed concern over potential encroachments on their national judicial systems, as well as concern over their national security. Thus, they have been reluctant to share certain types of intelligence data. The 9/11 attacks increased both the interest in combatting transnational crime and sensitivity to the risks of sharing intelligence data (Deflem 2005; D. Felson and Kalaitzidis 2005).

Table 7-5 Types of Transnational Crime

Bankruptcy and insurance fraud

Computer crime (treating computers as both a tool and a target of crime)

Corruption and bribery of public officials

Environment crime

Hijacking of airplanes ("skyjacking")

Illegal drug trade

Illegal money transfers ("money laundering")

Illegal sales of firearms and ammunition

Infiltration of legal businesses

Networking of criminal organizations

Sea piracy

Terrorism

Theft of art and cultural objects

Trafficking in body parts (includes illegal organ transplants)

Trafficking in human beings (includes sex trade)

Source: Compiled by the author based on Mueller 2001 and United Nations Office on Drugs and Crime 2005.

Social Policy and Social Control
Illicit Drug Use in Canada

The Issue

Vancouver's municipal government spends more money per capita in dealing with illicit drugs than any other city in Canada (Bula 2000). In 2000, then mayor of Vancouver Philip Owen claimed that although Vancouver's drug problem is so well known and has been highlighted in many media reports, it does not mean that other big cities are not struggling with the same concerns. Owen stated, "Everyone has a drug problem, all the big-city mayors have talked about this. Every single one is looking for solutions. But nobody is prepared to stand up to the plate" (Bula 2000). In response to this problem, Vancouver authorities devised a drug strategy and harm-reduction plan. According to the former mayor, this is an "international crisis," and cities such as Yokohama, Japan, and Seattle, Washington, have asked for a copy of Vancouver's drug strategy (Bula 2000).

The Setting

National surveys have shown that in Canada, people living in British Columbia were most likely to report the personal use of illicit substances (A. Nelson and Fleras 1995). The drug "problem" is particularly apparent in Vancouver's Downtown Eastside, an area that is the poorest in all of Canada and that houses people who have some of the most severe social, economic, and health problems in the country. The death rate in the Downtown Eastside is high because of the growing incidence of hepatitis C and HIV, acquired through intravenous-injection drug use. Activities such as youth prostitution and panhandling become the means through which addicts can sustain their addiction.

Sociological Insights

Functionalists view alienation and anomie to be the cause of many forms of addiction, including alcohol and drug addiction (A. Nelson and Fleras 1995). The activities of addicts, according to functionalist theorists, have functional consequences for society. For example, they demonstrate the boundaries of so-called "rule-breaking behaviour," and they create social agreement and cohesion regarding unacceptable behaviours.

Conflict theorists, in contrast, ask the questions, "Who benefits?" and "Why is it that some drug users receive the label 'addict,' while other users do not?" Conflict thinkers argue that the state and its various agencies, such as prisons, police, and rehabilitation programs, serve to benefit from such labels because they create employment for correction officers, police officers, social workers, and counsellors. They also address the reasons why society does not label those addicted to prescription drugs and "legal" drugs, such as tobacco, in the same manner as it labels and scapegoats those addicted to such drugs as cocaine and heroin.

Feminist approaches to addiction are as diverse as feminist theories themselves. Some argue that for women, addiction grows out of their overall status of subordination in society; in other words, women's powerlessness leads to various forms of self-destructive escapes, such as drug use (Lundy 1991). Other feminist theories argue that the concept of gender and the various related roles and behaviours deny both men and women full expression of their own humanity; addiction becomes a metaphor for the gender stereotypes in our society (A. Nelson and Fleras 1995).

Interactionist approaches frame drug addiction in the context of continual action on the part of the drug addict and reaction on the part of those around her or him. They stress the process through which the person is identified as an "addict" and the impact that this label has on the person's sense of self. Goffman's dramaturgical approach is an example of this process of individual action and social reaction, in which the individual plays many roles, as would an actor. The drug addict, for example, may play one role in dealing with the police (for example, presenting himself or herself as someone trying to get "clean") while presenting a different image to peers.

Policy Initiatives

Vancouver's drug strategy and harm-reduction plan is the first of its kind in North America. It shifts the focus away from drug use as a criminal activity and toward drug use as a health-and-safety issue; under the plan, users would receive treatment rather than jail terms and special treatment beds would be allocated to young users.

The drug strategy and harm-reduction plan, similar to those implemented in many European cities, is based on a four-pillar approach:

1. **Enforcement.** This pillar includes a pilot drug-treatment court that would weigh various options of treatment, an increase in the police drug and

organized-crime squads to target larger dealers, and the creation of a "drug action team" that would respond to neighbourhood drug issues.

2. **Harm reduction.** This notion encompasses the creation of an overdose-death prevention campaign, the provision of short-term shelter and housing for drug users on the street, and the establishment of street-drug testing.

3. **Treatment.** The treatment element of the plan would provide treatment beds for young people outside the Downtown Eastside; special treatment for women who are pregnant and/or have children; needle exchanges in primary health-care clinics, hospitals, and pharmacies; pilot day centres for addicts; and different kinds of housing for users and those trying to go clean.

4. **Prevention.** This pillar of the plan would give communities and neighbourhoods more power to combat drug abuse and to develop a pilot citywide school curriculum on drugs and drug abuse.

As part of its harm-reduction strategy, in 2003, Vancouver opened its first safe-injection site (INSITE)—a facility where people with addictions can safely inject drugs in a clean, sterile environment rather than on the streets with needles that may be dirty. This site is the first of its kind in North America and, as a consequence, the whole world has been watching. In 2004, the International Narcotics Board (INB)—an independent United Nations

organization—criticized the Vancouver safe-injection site, claiming that it violated international drug treatises. Then mayor of Vancouver, Larry Campbell, dismissed the INB's criticisms, stating that, because of its overwhelming U.S. funding, the INB simply reflects the U.S. policy on the "war on drugs," which does not embrace the principle or practice of harm reduction. However, according to Colin Mangham, director of research for the Drug Prevention Network of Canada, the principle of harm reduction, as represented by INSITE, has overpowered the other three pillars of Vancouver's drug strategy to become the foundation of drug policy. Mangham states that drug policy has become so politicized, based upon an ideology of harm reduction, that the failures or deficiencies of INSITE are rarely discussed. For example, he notes that only a small percentage of intravenous drug users frequent INSITE for even a majority of their injections and, thus, a major problem of this harm-reduction approach is its inability to control a free-moving population of drug users (Mangham 2007).

Applying Theory

1. How might conflict sociologists explain why certain drugs, and the individuals who use them, have been treated so differently?
2. According to functionalist perspectives, what functions might drug or alcohol addiction have in society?

CHAPTER RESOURCES

Summary

What is Social Control?

- **Conformity** and **deviance** are two ways in which people respond to real or imagined pressures from others. In this chapter, we examined the relationship among conformity, deviance, and mechanisms of social control.
- **Social control** (p. 159) involves the mechanisms used by society to bring about conformity to social norms.

- Stanley Milgram defined **conformity** (p. 160) as going along with our peers; **obedience** (p. 160) is defined as compliance with higher authorities in a hierarchical structure.
- Some norms are so important to a society, that they are formalized into laws. Socialization is a primary source of conforming and obedient behaviour, including obedience to law.

What is Deviance?

- **Deviance** (p. 165) is behaviour that violates any social norm. Some forms of deviance carry a negative social **stigma** (p. 166), while other forms are more or less acceptable.
- From a functionalist point of view, deviance and its consequences help to define the limits of proper behaviour.
- Interactionists maintain that we learn criminal behaviour from interactions with others—an approach called **cultural transmission** (p. 170). They also stress that for crime to occur, there has to be a convergence of motivated offenders and suitable targets of crime; this approach is known as **routine activities theory** (p. 171).
- The theory of **differential association** (p. 170) holds that deviance results from exposure to attitudes favourable to criminal acts.

- **Labelling theory** (p. 171) is based upon the recognition that some people are viewed as deviant while others engaged in the same behaviour are not.
- The conflict perspective views laws and punishments as reflecting the interests of the powerful.
- Feminist perspectives on deviance are varied. Often, they emphasize that crimes involving women are defined and treated differently.

What is Crime?

- **Crime** (p. 174) represents a deviation from formal social norms administered by the state.
- Sociologists differentiate among **professional crime** (p. 175), **organized crime** (p. 175), **white-collar crime** (p. 175), **victimless crime** (p. 176), and **transnational crime** (p. 179).
- Crime statistics are among the least reliable social data, partly because so many crimes are not reported to law-enforcement agencies.

Critical Thinking Questions

1. What mechanisms of formal and informal social control are evident in your university or college classes and in day-to-day life and social interactions at your school?
2. What approach to deviance do you find most persuasive, that of functionalists, conflict theorists, interactionists, labelling theorists, or feminist theorists? Why is this approach more convincing than the others? What are the main weaknesses of each approach?

3. Rates of violent crime are lower in Canada, Western Europe, Australia, and New Zealand than in the United States. Draw on as many of the theories discussed in the chapter as possible to explain why Canada is a comparatively less violent society.
4. Why do you think a computer hacker might be viewed differently from a person who commits a break-and-enter or steals something from a department store?

Key Terms

Anomie theory of deviance   Robert Merton's theory that explains deviance as an adaptation either of socially prescribed goals or of the norms governing their attainment, or both. (p. 168)

Conformity   Going along with peers, individuals of a person's own status who have no special right to direct that person's behaviour. (p. 160)

Control theory   A view of conformity and deviance that suggests our connection to members of society leads us to systematically conform to society's norms. (p. 164)

Crime   A violation of criminal law for which some governmental authority applies formal penalties. (p. 174)

Cultural transmission   A school of criminology which argues that criminal behaviour is learned through social interactions. (p. 170)

Deviance   Behaviour that violates the standards of conduct or expectations of a group or society. (p. 165)

Differential association   A theory of deviance proposed by Edwin Sutherland which holds that violation of rules results from exposure to attitudes favourable to criminal acts. (p. 170)

Formal social control   Social control carried out by authorized agents, such as police officers, judges, school administrators, and employers. (p. 162)

Informal social control   Social control carried out casually by ordinary people through such means as laughter, smiles, and ridicule. (p. 162)

Labelling theory   An approach to deviance that attempts to explain why certain people are viewed as deviants while others engaging in the same behaviour are not. (p. 171)

Obedience Compliance with higher authorities in a hierarchical structure. (p. 160)

Organized crime The work of a group that regulates relations among various criminal enterprises involved in the smuggling and sale of drugs, prostitution, gambling, and other illegal activities. (p. 175)

Professional criminal A person who pursues crime as a day-to-day occupation, developing skilled techniques and enjoying a certain degree of status among other criminals. (p. 175)

Routine activities theory The notion that criminal victimization increases when there is a convergence of motivated offenders and suitable targets. (p. 171)

Social constructionist perspective An approach to deviance that emphasizes the role of culture in the creation of the deviant identity. (p. 173)

Social control The techniques and strategies for preventing deviant human behaviour in any society. (p. 159)

Societal-reaction approach Another name for **labelling theory**. (p. 171)

Stigma A label used to devalue members of deviant social groups. (p. 166)

Transnational crime Crime that occurs across multiple national borders. (p. 179)

Victimization surveys Questionnaires or interviews used to determine whether people have been victims of crime. (p. 178)

Victimless crime A term used by sociologists to describe the willing exchange among adults of widely desired, but illegal, goods and services. (p. 176)

White-collar crime Crimes committed by usually affluent individuals or corporations in the course of their daily business activities. (p. 175)

Additional Readings

Fong, Josephine Sui-Fun, ed. 2007. *Specific and Central Issues in Woman Abuse.* Toronto: CSPI/WP. A collection of articles on the abusive manifestations of male dominance in relationships and households in Canada.

Glasbeek, Amanda, ed. 2006. *Moral Regulation and Governance in Canada: History, Context, and Critical Issues.* Toronto: CSPI/WP. An array of readings on

issues of deviance, moral regulation, and governance from a Canadian perspective.

O'Grady, William. 2007. *Crime in the Canadian Context.* Don Mills, ON: Oxford University Press. In this book, O'Grady provides students with a thorough look at the issues and questions relevant to criminology in Canada.

 ## Online Learning Centre

Visit the *Sociology: A Brief Introduction* Online Learning Centre at www.mcgrawhill.ca/olc/schaefer to access quizzes,

interactive exercises, video clips, and other research and study tools related to this chapter.

 ## Reel Society Video Clips

Reel Society can be used to spark discussion about the following topics from this chapter:

- Conformity and obedience
- Informal and formal social control
- Deviance

chapter 8

STRATIFICATION IN CANADA

WE SEE WHAT MOST DON'T

We see the heartbreaking effects of poverty, homelessness, abuse and addiction every day. Last year in Canada, The Salvation Army served 2.5 million meals to the hungry, helped 10,000 people with addictions and provided one third of all shelter beds each night. This Christmas we ask you to open your eyes and your heart. And give.

Giving Hope Today

SalvationArmy.ca ~ 1.800.SAL.ARMY

Original Design: AGLC Inc. | Photography: Ostoa Photo

This Salvation Army advertisement shows that poverty is a reality in Canada, and the poor are often forgotten by, or invisible to, the rest of society.

☐ **What is Stratification?**

☐ **How are Stratification and Social Class Related?**

☐ **Does Social Mobility Exist?**

Boxes

SOCIOLOGY IN THE GLOBAL COMMUNITY: Slavery in the Twenty-First Century

SOCIOLOGY IN THE GLOBAL COMMUNITY: Poverty and Global Inequality

SOCIAL POLICY AND STRATIFICATION: Rethinking Social Assistance in North America and Europe

By the time most Canadians roll up their sleeves to begin a new year of work, Canada's best-paid 100 CEOs will already be having a good year: They'll pocket the national average wage of $38 998 by 10:33 a.m. on January 2nd.

And they will continue to earn the average Canadian wage every nine hours and 33 minutes for the rest of the year, according to a new report on CEO (chief executive officer) pay by the Canadian Centre for Policy Alternatives (CCPA).

"Most Canadians are heading back into work with a mound of Christmas bills and financial worries but for Canada's best-paid 100 CEOs it's like Santa Claus delivers every nine hours," says the report's author, Hugh Mackenzie, a CCPA research associate.

"That's what happens when you make an average of $8 528 304—which is the average of what Canada's 100 best-paid CEOs made in 2006."

On average, the best-paid 100 CEOs make more than 218 times as much as a Canadian working full-time for a full year at the average of weekly employment earnings.

"That represents a significant gap between the rich and the rest of us—especially the working poor who earn the minimum wage," Mackenzie says.

By 1:04 p.m. on New Year's Day, the top CEOs pocketed what will take a minimum wage worker all of 2008 to earn. Every four hours and four minutes, they will keep pocketing the annual income of a full-time, full-year minimum wage worker.

"We have to ask ourselves, are those at the top of the income heap really worth so much? And are those at the bottom really worth so little?"

☐ *(Mackenzie 2008)*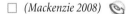

In his report, research associate Hugh Mackenzie of the Canadian Centre for Policy Alternatives draws attention to the gap between the average annual earnings of working Canadians and that of Canada's 100 highest-paid CEOs. In one day, these CEOs earned what most workers in Canada take an entire year to earn. Mackenzie asks the question, which is pertinent to the central theme of this chapter, "Are Canada's 100 highest-paid CEOs really worth more in a day than most Canadian workers are in a year?"

Ever since people first began to speculate about the nature of human society, their attention has been drawn to the differences between individuals and groups within any society. The term **social inequality** describes a condition in which members of a society have different amounts of wealth, prestige, or power. Some degree of social inequality characterizes every society.

When a system of social inequality is based on a hierarchy of groups, sociologists refer to it as **stratification**: a structured ranking of entire groups of people that perpetuates unequal economic rewards and power in a society. These unequal rewards are evident not only in the distribution of wealth and income but also in the distressing mortality rates of impoverished communities. Stratification involves the ways in which one generation passes on social inequalities to the next, thereby producing groups of people arranged in rank order from low to high.

Stratification is a crucial subject of sociological investigation because of its pervasive influence on human interactions and institutions. It inevitably results in social inequality because certain groups of people stand higher in social rankings, control scarce resources, wield power, and receive special treatment. As we will see in this chapter, the consequences of stratification are evident in the unequal distribution of wealth and income within industrial societies. The term **income** refers to salaries and wages. By contrast, **wealth** encompasses all of a person's material assets, including land, stocks, and other types of property.

Do you think that social inequality is an inevitable part of any society? How do you think government policy affects the life chances of the working poor? How are wealth and income distributed, and how much opportunity does the average worker have to move up the social ladder? What economic and political conditions explain the divide between rich nations and poor? In this chapter, we focus on the unequal distribution of socially valued rewards, and its consequences.

We will examine three general systems of stratification, paying particular attention to the theories of Karl Marx and Max Weber, as well as to functionalist, interactionist, conflict, and feminist theories. We see how sociologists define social class and examine the consequences of stratification for people's wealth and income, health, and educational opportunities. And we confront the question of social mobility, both upward and downward, focusing on stratification in Canada. Finally, in the social policy section, we address the issue of welfare reform in both North America and Europe.

Think about It

What determines how much or how little a person will receive for the work he or she contributes to society?

Use Your Sociological Imagination

What are the possible consequences of having a significant gap between the rich and the working poor who earn minimum wage?

☐ WHAT IS STRATIFICATION?

Systems of Stratification

Look at the three general systems of stratification examined here—slavery, castes, and social classes—as ideal types useful for purposes of analysis. Any stratification system may include elements of more than one type.

◀ P. 102 To understand these systems better, it may be helpful to review the distinction between achieved status and ascribed status, described in Chapter 5. Ascribed status is a social position "assigned" to a person without regard for that person's unique characteristics or talents. By contrast, achieved status is a social position attained by a person largely through his or her own effort. The two are closely linked. The nation's most affluent

Sociology in the Global Community   8-1
Slavery in the Twenty-First Century

Around the world, at least 27 million people were still enslaved at the beginning of the twenty-first century. And yet the 1948 Universal Declaration of Human Rights, which is supposedly binding on all members of the United Nations, holds that "no one shall be held in slavery or servitude; slavery and the slave trade shall be prohibited in all their forms" (Masland 1992:30, 32).

Canada considers any person a slave who is unable to withdraw his or her labour voluntarily from an employer. In many parts of the world, bonded labourers are imprisoned in virtual lifetime employment as they struggle to repay small debts. In other places, human beings are owned outright.

The Swiss-based human rights group Christian Solidarity International has focused worldwide attention on the plight of slaves in the African nation of Sudan. The organization solicits funds and uses them to buy slaves their freedom—at about $50 a slave.

In Ivory Coast, where 43 percent of the world's cocoa beans are produced, child slavery is used to produce and harvest crops. These children are beaten and forced to do hard labour—up to 100 hours per week (Sierra Club of Canada 2003).

Although contemporary slavery may be most obvious in developing countries, it also afflicts the industrialized nations of the West. Throughout Europe, guest workers and maids are employed by masters who hold their passports, subject them to degrading working conditions, and threaten them with deportation if they protest. Similar tactics are used to essentially imprison young women from Eastern Europe and Asia who have been brought (through deceptive promises) to work in the sex industries of Canada, the United States, Belgium, France, Germany, Greece, the Netherlands, and Switzerland.

Within Canada and other developed countries, illegal immigrants are forced to labour for years under terrible conditions, either to pay off debts or to avoid being turned over to immigration authorities. Estimates of the number of women brought into Canada as forced sex workers in 2000 vary from 8000 to 16 000.

Applying Theory

1. According to conflict theorists, why are many bonded labourers around the world in the position of slaves?
2. What explanations might some feminist sociologists have for the varying incidence rates of forced sex work from one country to another?

Sources: Fisher 1999; France 2000; Jacobs 2001; Masland 1992; Richard 2000.

---

families generally inherit wealth and status, while many members of racial and ethnic minorities inherit disadvantaged status. Age and gender, as well, are ascribed statuses that influence a person's wealth and social position.

Slavery

The most extreme form of legalized social inequality for individuals or groups is **slavery**. What distinguishes this oppressive system of stratification is that enslaved individuals are *owned* by other people. They treat these human beings as property, just as if they were household pets or appliances.

Slavery has varied in the way it has been practised. In ancient Greece, most slaves were captives of war and piracy. Although succeeding generations could inherit slave status, it was not necessarily permanent. A person's status might change depending on which city-state happened to triumph in a military conflict. In effect, all citizens had the potential of becoming slaves or of being granted freedom, depending on the circumstances of history. By contrast, in the United States, Canada, the Caribbean, and Latin America, where slavery was an ascribed status, racial and legal barriers prevented the freeing of slaves. As Box 8-1 shows, millions of people still live as slaves around the world.

Castes

Castes are hereditary systems of rank, usually religiously dictated, that tend to be fixed and immobile. The caste system is generally associated with Hinduism in India and other countries. In India, there are four major castes, called varnas. A fifth category, referred to as untouchables, is considered to be so lowly and unclean as to have no place within this system of stratification. There are also many minor castes. Caste membership is an ascribed status (at birth, children automatically assume the same position as their parents). Each caste is quite sharply defined, and members are expected to marry within that caste.

Caste membership generally determines a person's occupation or role as a religious functionary. An example of a lower caste in India is the Dons, whose main work is the undesirable job of cremating bodies. The caste system promotes a remarkable degree of differentiation. Thus, the single caste of chauffeurs has been split into two separate subcastes: drivers of luxury cars have a higher status than drivers of economy cars.

In recent decades, industrialization and urbanization have taken their toll on India's rigid caste system. Many villagers have moved to urban areas where their low-caste status is unknown. Schools, hospitals, factories, and public transportation facilitate contacts between different castes that were previously avoided at all costs. In addition, the government has tried to reform the caste system. India's constitution, adopted in 1950, includes a provision abolishing discrimination against untouchables, who had traditionally been excluded from temples, schools, and most forms of employment. Yet, the caste system prevails, and its impact is now evident in electoral politics, as various political parties compete for the support of frustrated untouchable voters who constitute one-third of India's electorate. For the first time, in the 1990s and early 2000s, India had someone from an untouchable background serving in the symbolic but high-status position of president. Meanwhile, however, dozens of low-caste people continue to be killed for overstepping their lowly status in life (Dugger 1999; Schmetzer 1999).

Social Classes

A **class system** is a social ranking based primarily on economic position in which achieved characteristics can influence social mobility. In contrast to slavery and caste systems, the boundaries between classes are imprecisely defined, and people can move from one stratum, or level, of society to another. Even so, class systems maintain stable stratification hierarchies and patterns of class divisions, and they, too, are marked by unequal distribution of wealth and power.

Income inequality is a basic characteristic of a class system. In 2005, the average after-tax family income in Canada was $62 700 (Statistics Canada 2007h). This figure does nothing to convey the income disparities in our society. In 2005, Canadian families in the top 20 percent of income accounted for 47 percent of total after-tax family income, while families in the bottom 20 percent earned 4 percent of total after-tax family income (Statistics Canada 2007h). Canada's rich are getting richer, with their collective net worth reaching an all-time high of $153.7 billion in 2006 (Mlynek et al. 2006/2007). The top 100 richest individuals include Vancouver entrepreneur Jimmy Pattison; Jeff Skoll of eBay; and Galen Weston, Sr., of George Weston Ltd., which controls the Loblaw supermarket chain. Table 8-1 shows the ranking of Canada's richest families—all of which are led by white males—and reveals the fortunes of each (in billions of dollars). In stark contrast to this increase in wealth among the rich, the rate of child poverty in Canada in 2006 increased 20 percent from 1989, bringing the number of children who live in poverty to more than one million or nearly one in six (Campaign 2000 2007).

Table 8-1 Canada's Richest Families, 2008

Family	Net worth, billions of CDN$
1. Thomson family (Thomson Reuters, Woodbridge Co. Ltd.)	18.45
2. Irving family (Irving Oil Ltd., J.D. Irving Ltd.)	7.11
3. Galen Weston (George Weston Ltd., Loblaws Cos. Ltd.)	6.58
4. Ted Rogers, Jr.* (Rogers Communications Inc.)	5.05
5. Jimmy Pattison (Jim Pattison Group)	4.93
6. Alex Schnaider (Midland Resources Holding Ltd.)	4.25
7. David Azrieli (Canpro Investments Ltd.)	4.15
8. Paul Desmarais (Power Corp.)	4.11
9. Barry Sherman (Apotex Group of Cos.)	3.77
10. Jeff Skoll (eBay Inc.)	3.14

*Ted Rogers, Jr. died December 2, 2008 at the age of 75.

Source: *Canadian Business* December 2008, http://www.canadianbusiness.com/rankings/rich/100/2008.

The people with the highest incomes, generally those heading private companies, earn well above even affluent wage earners. As the opening excerpt to this chapter illustrates, Canada's 100 highest-paid CEOs are paid more in one day than most Canadian workers make in one year (Canadian Centre for Policy Alternatives 2007). The compensation CEOs receive is not necessarily linked to conventional measures of success. For example, the U.S. economy worsened in 2002, and an analysis showed that the CEOs who received the highest compensation were generally those who authorized the largest layoffs (Klinger et al. 2002).

> ### Think about It
> Why are CEOs "worth" so much more than other workers?

A 2004 study conducted by Leger Marketing, on behalf of Amex Canada, revealed some characteristics of wealthy or affluent Canadians, defined as those with annual household incomes or investable assets of $200 000 or more (*The Globe and Mail* 2004a):

- Affluent Canadians take, on average, three vacations a year, expecting to pay $2000 per person.
- Affluent Canadians dine out, on average, seven times per month.
- Thirty-nine percent of affluent Canadians own two properties.
- Twenty-five percent of affluent Canadians send their children to private schools.
- Twenty-five percent of affluent Canadians belong to private clubs (e.g., golf, tennis).
- Forty percent of affluent Canadians have home theatres.

Statistics reflecting personal wealth or *net worth* (assets minus debts) demonstrate an enormous gap between the richest 20 percent and the poorest 20 percent of Canadian families. In 2005, for example, the poorest 20 percent of Canadian families had an average net worth of −$2400 (meaning that they owed more than they owned), while the richest 20 percent had an average net worth of $1 264 200 (Statistics Canada 2006i). What is most distressing about this disparity is that the poorest 20 percent control 0.1 percent of the total wealth of Canadian families, while the richest 20 percent control 69 percent of the total wealth.

Both of these groups, at opposite ends of the nation's economic hierarchy, reflect the importance of ascribed status and achieved status. Ascribed statuses, such as race, gender, and class, clearly influence a person's wealth and social position. And sociologist Richard Jenkins (1991) has researched how the ascribed status of having a disability marginalizes people in society. People with disabilities are particularly vulnerable to unemployment, are often poorly paid, and in many cases are on the lower rung of occupational ladders. Regardless of their actual performance on the job, people with disabilities are stigmatized as not "earning their keep." Such are the effects of ascribed status.

Social class is one of the independent or explanatory variables most frequently used by social scientists to shed light on social issues. In later chapters, we will analyze the relationships among social class and divorce patterns (Chapter 12), religious behaviour (Chapter 13), and formal schooling (Chapter 13), as well as other relationships in which social class is a variable.

Theoretical Perspectives on Social Stratification

Must some members of society receive greater rewards than others? Do people need to feel socially and economically superior to others? Can social life be organized without structured inequality? These questions have been debated for centuries, especially among political activists. Utopian socialists, religious minorities, and members of recent countercultures have all attempted to establish communities that, to some extent or other, would abolish inequality in social relationships.

Social science research has found that inequality exists in all societies—even the simplest. For example, when anthropologist Gunnar Landtman ([1938] 1968) studied the Kiwai Papuans of New Guinea, he initially noticed little differentiation among them. Every man in the village did the same work and lived in similar housing. However, on closer inspection, Landtman observed that certain Papuans—the men who were warriors, harpooners, and sorcerers—were described as "a little more high" than others. By contrast, villagers who were female, unemployed, or unmarried were considered "down a little bit" and were barred from owning land.

Stratification is universal in that all societies maintain some form of social inequality among members. Depending on its values, a society may assign people to distinctive ranks based on their religious knowledge, skill in hunting, beauty, trading expertise, or ability to provide health care. But why has such inequality developed in human societies? And how much differentiation among people, if any, is actually essential?

Functionalist and conflict sociologists offer contrasting explanations for the existence and necessity of social stratification. Functionalists maintain that a differential system of rewards and punishments is necessary for the efficient operation of society. Conflict theorists argue that competition for scarce resources results in significant political, economic, and social inequality. Some feminist sociologists argue that gender and its interconnections with race, age, class, and disability come together to produce various levels of inequality in society. Interactionist sociologists focus their attention on the interactions among individuals that serve to create and maintain social inequality.

Functionalist View

Would people go to school for many years to become physicians if they could make as much money and gain as much respect working as street cleaners? Functionalists say no, which is partly why they believe that a stratified society is universal.

In the view of Kingsley Davis and Wilbert Moore, society must distribute its members among a variety of social positions (1945). It must not only make sure that these positions are filled but also see that they are staffed by people with the appropriate talents and abilities. Rewards, including money and prestige, are based on the importance of a position and the relative scarcity of qualified personnel. Yet this assessment often devalues work performed by certain segments of society, such as women's work as homemakers or other occupations traditionally filled by women, or low-status work in fast-food outlets.

Davis and Moore argue that stratification is universal and that social inequality is necessary so that people will be motivated to fill functionally important positions (1945). But, critics say, unequal rewards are not the only means of encouraging people to fill critical positions and occupations. Personal pleasure, intrinsic satisfaction, and value orientations also motivate people to enter particular careers. Functionalists agree but note that society must use some type of reward to motivate people to enter unpleasant or dangerous jobs and jobs that require a long training period. This response does not justify stratification systems in which status is largely inherited, such as slave or caste societies. Similarly, it is difficult to explain the high salaries our society offers to professional athletes or entertainers on the basis of how critical these jobs are to the survival of society (R. Collins 1975; Kerbo 2000; Tumin 1953, 1985).

Even if stratification is inevitable, the functionalist explanation for differential rewards does not explain the wide disparity between the rich and the poor. Critics of the functionalist approach point out that the richest 10 percent of households account for 20 percent of the nation's income in Sweden, 25 percent in France, 28 percent in Canada, and 31 percent in the United States. In their view, the level of income inequality found in contemporary industrial societies cannot be defended—even though these societies have a legitimate need to fill certain key occupations (World Bank 2002:74–76).

Conflict View

Karl Marx's View of Stratification

Sociologist Leonard Beeghley aptly noted that "Karl Marx was both a revolutionary and a social scientist" (1978:1). Marx was concerned with stratification in all types of human societies, beginning with primitive agricultural tribes and continuing into feudalism. But his main focus was on the effects of economic inequality on all aspects of life in nineteenth-century Europe. The plight of the working class made him feel that it was imperative to strive for changes in the class structure of society.

In Marx's view, social relations during any period of history depend on who controls the primary mode of economic production, such as land or factories. Differential access to scarce resources shapes the relationships among groups. Thus, under the feudal estate system, most production was agricultural, and the land was owned by the nobility. Peasants had little choice but to work according to terms dictated by those who owned the land.

This family's expensive lifestyle and acquisitions underscore the unequal distribution of wealth and power in Canada.

Using this type of analysis, Marx examined social relations within **capitalism**—an economic system in which the means of production are largely in private hands and the main incentive for economic activity is the accumulation of profits (Rosenberg 1991). Marx focused on the two classes that began to emerge as the feudal estate system declined—the bourgeoisie and the proletariat. The **bourgeoisie**, or capitalist class, owns the means of production, such as factories and machinery, whereas the **proletariat** is the working class. In capitalist societies, the members of the bourgeoisie maximize profit in competition with other firms. In the process, they exploit workers, who must exchange their labour for subsistence wages. In Marx's view, members of each class share a distinctive culture. He was most interested in the culture of the proletariat, but he also examined the ideology of the bourgeoisie, through which it justifies its dominance over workers.

According to Marx, exploitation of the proletariat will inevitably lead to the destruction of the capitalist system because the workers will revolt. But, first, the working class must develop **class consciousness**—a subjective awareness of common vested interests and the need for collective political action to bring about

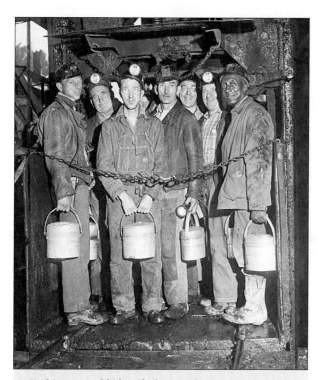

Karl Marx would identify these coal miners as members of the proletariat, or working class. For generations, miners were forced to spend their meagre wages at "company stores," whose high prices kept them perpetually in debt. The exploitation of the working class is a core principle of Marxist theory.

social change. Workers must often overcome what Marx termed **false consciousness**, or an attitude held by members of a class that does not accurately reflect its objective position. A worker with false consciousness may adopt an individualistic viewpoint toward capitalist exploitation ("I am being exploited by my boss"). By contrast, the class-conscious worker realizes that all workers are being exploited by the bourgeoisie and have a common stake in revolution (Vanneman and Cannon 1987).

For Karl Marx, class consciousness is part of a collective process whereby the proletariat comes to identify the bourgeoisie as the source of its oppression. Revolutionary leaders will guide the working class in its class struggle. Ultimately, the proletariat will overthrow the rule of the bourgeoisie and the government (which Marx saw as representing the interests of capitalists) and will eliminate private ownership of the means of production. In his utopian view, classes and oppression will cease to exist in the post-revolutionary workers' state.

How accurate were Marx's predictions? He failed to anticipate the emergence of labour unions, whose power in collective bargaining weakens the stranglehold that capitalists maintain over workers. Moreover, as contemporary conflict theorists note, he did not foresee the extent to which political liberties and relative prosperity could contribute to "false consciousness." Many people have come to view themselves as individuals striving for improvement within "free" societies with substantial mobility—rather than as downtrodden members of social classes facing a collective fate. Finally, Marx did not predict that communist party rule would be established and later overthrown in the Commonwealth of Independent States (the former Soviet Union) and throughout Eastern Europe. Still, the Marxist approach to the study of class is useful in stressing the importance of stratification as a determinant of social behaviour and the fundamental separation in many societies between two distinct groups, the rich and the poor.

The writings of Karl Marx are at the heart of conflict theory. Marx viewed history as a continuous struggle between the oppressors and the oppressed that would ultimately culminate in an egalitarian, classless society. In terms of stratification, he argued that the dominant class under capitalism manipulated the economic and political systems in order to maintain control over the exploited proletariat. Marx did not believe that stratification was inevitable, but he did see inequality and oppression as inherent in capitalism (Wright et al. 1982).

The Views of Ralf Dahrendorf

Like Marx, contemporary conflict theorists believe that human beings are prone to conflict over such scarce

As popular songs and movies suggest, long-haul truck drivers take pride in their low-prestige job. According to the conflict perspective, the cultural beliefs that form a society's dominant ideology, such as the popular image of the truck driver as hero, help the wealthy to maintain their power and control at the expense of the lower classes.

resources as wealth, status, and power. However, where Marx focused primarily on class conflict, more recent theorists have extended this analysis to include conflicts based on gender, race, age, and other dimensions. British sociologist Ralf Dahrendorf is one of the most influential contributors to the conflict approach.

Dahrendorf modified Marx's analysis of capitalist society to apply to *modern* capitalist societies (1959). For Dahrendorf, social classes are groups of people who share common interests resulting from their authority relationships. In identifying the most powerful groups in society, he includes not only the bourgeoisie—the owners of the means of production—but also the managers of industry, legislators, the judiciary, heads of the government bureaucracy, and others. In that respect, Dahrendorf has merged Marx's emphasis on class conflict with Weber's recognition that power is an important element of stratification (Cuff et al. 1990).

Conflict theorists, including Dahrendorf, contend that the powerful of today, like the bourgeoisie of Marx's time, want society to run smoothly so that they can enjoy their privileged positions. Because the status quo suits those with wealth, status, and power, they have a clear interest in preventing, minimizing, or controlling societal conflict.

Max Weber's View of Stratification

Unlike Karl Marx, Max Weber insisted that no single characteristic (such as class) totally defines a person's position within the stratification system. Instead, writing

in 1916, he identified three distinct components of stratification: class, status, and power (Gerth and Mills 1958).

Weber used the term **class** to refer to people who have a similar level of wealth and income. For example, certain workers in Canada try to support their families through minimum-wage jobs. According to Weber's definition, these wage earners constitute a class because they share the same economic position and fate. Although Weber agreed with Marx on the importance of this economic dimension of stratification, he argued that the actions of individuals and groups could not be understood solely in economic terms.

Weber used the term **status group** to refer to people who rank the same in prestige or lifestyle. An individual gains status through membership in a desirable group, such as the medical profession. But status is not the same as economic class standing. In our culture, a successful pickpocket may be in the same income class as a university professor. Yet, the thief is widely regarded as a member of a low-status group, whereas the professor holds high status.

For Weber, the third major component of stratification reflects a political dimension. **Power** is the ability to exercise our will over others. In Canada, power stems from membership in particularly influential groups, such as corporate boards of directors, government bodies, and interest groups. Conflict theorists generally agree that two major sources of power—big business and government—are closely interrelated (see Chapter 14).

In Weber's view, then, each of us has not one rank in society but three. Our position in a stratification system reflects some combination of class, status, and power. Each factor influences the other two, and in fact the rankings on these three dimensions often tend to coincide. Pierre Trudeau came from a wealthy family, attended exclusive schools, graduated from elite universities, such as Harvard and the Sorbonne, and went on to become prime minister of Canada. Like Trudeau, many people from affluent backgrounds achieve impressive status and power.

At the same time, these dimensions of stratification may operate somewhat independently in determining a person's position. Jean Chrétien had a small legal practice in Shawinigan, Quebec, but he used a political power base to work his way up into federal politics to eventually become prime minister. A widely published poet may achieve high status while earning a relatively modest income. Successful professional athletes have little power but enjoy a relatively high position in terms of class and status. To understand the workings of a culture more fully, sociologists must carefully evaluate the ways in which that culture distributes its most valued rewards, including wealth and income, status, and power (Duberman 1976; Gerth and Mills 1958).

One way for the powerful to maintain the status quo is to define and disseminate the society's dominant ideology. The term *dominant ideology* describes a set of cultural beliefs and practices that helps to maintain powerful social, economic, and political interests. For Karl Marx, the dominant ideology in a capitalist society serves the interests of the ruling class. From a conflict perspective, the social significance of the dominant ideology is that not only do a society's most powerful groups and institutions control wealth and property, but, even more important, they also control the means of producing beliefs about reality through religion, education, and the media (Abercrombie, Hill, and Turner 1980, 1990; Robertson 1988).

The powerful, such as leaders of government, also use limited social reforms to buy off the oppressed and reduce the danger of challenges to their dominance. For example, minimum wage laws and unemployment compensation unquestionably give some valuable assistance to needy men and women. Yet, these reforms also serve to pacify those who might otherwise rebel. Of course, in the view of conflict theorists, such manoeuvres can never entirely eliminate conflict, since workers will continue to demand equality, and the powerful will not give up their control of society.

Conflict theorists see stratification as a major source of societal tension and conflict. They do not agree with Davis and Moore (1945) that stratification is functional for a society or that it serves as a source of stability. Rather, conflict sociologists argue that stratification will inevitably lead to instability and social change (R. Collins 1975; Coser 1977).

Feminist Views

As we described earlier, feminist sociological perspectives comprise a diverse group of viewpoints. A central belief, however, unites the various feminist perspectives: gender inequality is pervasive and women are the subordinated and dominated sex. Feminist thinkers, however, differ greatly in their views on the root causes of gender inequality; on how gender inequality manifests itself in homes, workplaces, and political arenas; and on how to address this inequality. Radical feminists, for example, place great

emphasis on patriarchy—as a form of social organization and ideology. In 1971, radical feminist Kate Millet wrote:

> Our society . . . is a patriarchy. The fact is evident at once if one recalls that the military, industry, technology, universities, science, political offices, finances—in short, every avenue of power within our society, including the coercive force of the police, is entirely in male hands. (1971:25)

In effect, radical feminists maintain that gender stratification is systemic, permeating society and creating a culture in which male values and priorities prevail. Since women are excluded from this culture, they stand to be controlled and oppressed by it.

Liberal feminists, in contrast, recognize the inequality that women face but believe that it could be addressed by providing women with greater access to the public sphere and by making that sphere (i.e., workplaces) more "female friendly."

Liberal feminists, then, believe less in a systemic pattern of gender inequality and more in the necessity of approaches that would provide women with greater access to employment opportunities, upward mobility, and, eventually, economic equality.

Interactionist View

Although functionalist, conflict, and some feminist perspectives tend to use a macrosociological approach to examine social inequality, interactionist thinkers tend to be more micro in their orientation. They are interested in the "person-to-person" (Naiman 2004:19) ways in which social stratification is maintained, perhaps in the forms of interpersonal and non-verbal communication. Erving Goffman (1967) theorized on the activity of *deference*, a symbolic act that conveys appreciation from one person to another. The pattern of showing deference, in which one person is the giver and the other is the recipient, often is symbolic of the unequal power relations between the two and, thus, serves to maintain and perpetuate social inequality. For example, would an employee be more likely than an employer to open a door for the other? to call the other "Ms." or "Mr." rather than by a first name? to let the other lead in the conversation and not be prone to interrupt?

Judith Rollins's study (1985) of the person-to-person interactions between domestic workers and their employers, based on interviews and participant observation, showed the patterns of deference displayed between white female employers and primarily women who were members of a visible minority. Rollins found that touching (or the absence thereof), calling the domestic workers "girls" regardless of their age, and keeping certain spatial distances were all rituals of deference that served to maintain the social class inequality between the two women.

Anti-colonial Views

Anti-colonial views of stratification reject the notion that social inequality can be reduced to one element, such as class. Colonialism, as further discussed in Chapter 9, simply means rule by outsiders which includes political, social, economic, and cultural domination. Class reductionism—attributing all forms of oppression and inequality to class, while ignoring or minimizing factors such as race, colonialism, gender, and sexuality—is rejected by anti-colonial thinkers such as Albert Memmi in his work, *The Colonizer and the Colonized:*

> To observe the life of the colonizer and the colonized is to discover rapidly that the daily humiliations of the colonized, his objective subjugation, are not merely economic. Even the poorest colonizer thought himself to be—and actually was—superior to the colonized. This too was part of colonial privilege. The Marxist discovery of the importance of the economy in all oppressive relationships is not the point. This relationship has other characteristics which I believe I have discovered in the colonial relationship. (Memmi 1965:xii)

Aboriginal people of Canada, for example, continue to experience powerlessness and poverty as a result of a legacy of colonization (Green 2003). To reduce the unequal conditions experienced by Aboriginal people to simply a matter of "class" would be a totally inadequate explanation of their socio-economic position in Canada today. As Matthew Coon Come, former national chief of the Assembly of First Nations, stated:

> . . . Without adequate access to lands, resources, and without the jurisdictions required to benefit meaningfully and sustainably from them . . . no number of apologies, policies, token programs, or symbolic healing funds are going to remedy this fundamental socio-economic fact. (cited in Barnsley 1999:1)

Lenski's Viewpoint

Let's return to a question posed earlier—Is stratification universal?—and consider the sociological response. Some form of differentiation is found in every culture. Sociologist Gerhard Lenski, in his socio-cultural evolution approach, described how economic systems change as their level of technology becomes more complex, beginning with hunting and gathering and culminating eventually with industrial society. In subsistence-based, hunting-and-gathering societies, people focus on survival. Although some inequality and differentiation are evident, a stratification system based on social class does not emerge because there is no real wealth to be claimed.

As a society advances in technology, it becomes capable of producing a considerable surplus of goods. The emergence of surplus resources greatly expands the possibilities for inequality in status, influence, and power and allows a well-defined, rigid social class system to develop. To minimize strikes, slowdowns, and industrial sabotage, the elite may share a portion of the economic surplus with the lower classes, but not enough to reduce their own power and privilege.

As Lenski argued, the allocation of surplus goods and services controlled by those with wealth, status, and power reinforces the social inequality that accompanies stratification systems. Although this reward system may once have served the overall purposes of society, as functionalists contend, the same cannot be said for the large disparities separating the haves from the have-nots in current societies. In contemporary industrial society, the degree of social and economic inequality far exceeds what is needed to provide for goods and services (Lenski 1966; Nolan and Lenski 1999).

☐ HOW ARE STRATIFICATION AND SOCIAL CLASS RELATED?

Measuring Social Class

We continually assess how wealthy people are by looking at the cars they drive, the houses they live in, the clothes they wear, and so on. Yet, it is not so easy to locate an individual within our social hierarchies as it would be in slavery or caste systems of stratification. To determine someone's class position, sociologists generally rely on the objective method.

Objective Method

The **objective method** of measuring social class views class largely as a statistical category. Researchers assign individuals to social classes on the basis of criteria such as occupation, education, income, and residence. The key to the objective method is that the *researcher*, rather than the person being classified, identifies an individual's class position.

The first step in using this method is to decide what indicators or causal factors will be measured objectively, whether wealth, income, education, or occupation. The prestige ranking of occupations has proven to be a useful indicator of a person's class position. For one thing, it is much easier to determine accurately than income or wealth. The term **prestige** refers to the respect and admiration that an occupation holds in a society. "My daughter, the physicist" connotes something very different from "my daughter, the waitress." Prestige is independent of the particular individual who occupies a job, a characteristic that distinguishes it from esteem. **Esteem** refers to the reputation that a specific person has earned within an occupation. Therefore, one can say that the position of prime minister of Canada has high prestige, even though it has been occupied by people with varying degrees of esteem. A hairdresser may have the esteem of his clients, but he lacks the prestige of a corporation president.

Table 8-2 ranks the prestige of a number of well-known occupations. In a series of national surveys conducted in the United States, sociologists assigned prestige rankings to roughly 500 occupations, ranging from phy-

sician to newspaper vendor. The highest possible prestige score was 100, and the lowest was 0. Physician, lawyer, dentist, and professor were the most highly regarded occupations. Sociologists have used such data to assign prestige rankings to virtually all jobs. Similar studies in other countries have also developed useful prestige rankings of occupations (Hodge and Rossi 1964; Lin and Xie 1988; Treiman 1977).

Gender and Occupational Prestige

For many years, studies of social class tended to neglect the occupations and incomes of *women* as determinants

Table 8-2 Prestige Rankings of Occupations

Occupation	Score	Occupation	Score
Physician	86	Secretary	46
Lawyer	75	Insurance agent	45
Dentist	74	Bank teller	43
Professor	74	Nurse's aide	42
Architect	73	Farmer	40
Clergy	69	Correctional officer	40
Pharmacist	68	Receptionist	39
Registered nurse	66	Carpenter	39
High school teacher	66	Barber	36
Accountant	65	Child-care worker	35
Elementary school teacher	64	Hotel clerk	32
Airline pilot	60	Bus driver	32
Police officer or detective	60	Auto body repairer	31
Pre-kindergarten teacher	55	Truck driver	30
Librarian	54	Sales worker (shoes, clothes, etc.)	28
Firefighter	53	Garbage collector	28
Dental hygienist	52	Waiter and waitress	28
Social worker	52	Bartender	25
Electrician	51	Farm worker	23
Funeral director	49	Janitor	22
Mail carrier	47	Newspaper vendor	19

Note: 100 is the highest and *0* the lowest possible prestige score.

Source: J. Davis et al. 2005:2050–2051.

of social rank. In an exhaustive study of 589 occupations, sociologists Mary Powers and Joan Holmberg (1978) examined the impact of women's participation in the paid labour force on occupational status. Since women tend to dominate the relatively low-paying occupations, such as bookkeepers and child-care workers, their participation in the workforce leads to a general upgrading of the status of most male-dominated occupations. More recent research conducted in both the United States and Europe has assessed the occupations of husbands *and* wives in determining the class positions of families (Sørensen 1994). With more than half of all married women now working outside the home (see Chapter 11), this approach seems long overdue, but it also raises some questions. For example, how is class or status to be judged in dual-career families—by the occupation regarded as having greater prestige, the average, or some other combination of the two occupations?

Sociologists—and, in particular, feminist sociologists in Great Britain—are drawing on new approaches in assessing women's social class standing. One approach is to focus on the individual (rather than the family or household) as the basis of categorizing a woman's class position. Thus, a woman would be classified based on her own occupational status rather than that of her spouse (O'Donnell 1992).

Another feminist effort to measure the contribution of women to the economy reflects a more clearly political agenda. International Women Count Network, a global grassroots feminist organization, has sought to give a monetary value to women's unpaid work. Besides providing symbolic recognition of women's role in labour, this value would also be used to calculate pension programs and benefits that are based on wages received. In 1995, the United Nations placed an $11 trillion price tag on unpaid labour by women, largely in child care, housework, and agriculture. Whatever the figure today, the continued undercounting of many workers' contributions to a family and to an entire economy means virtually all measures of stratification are in need of reform (United Nations Development Programme 1995; Wages for Housework Campaign 1999).

Multiple Measures

Another complication in measuring social class is that advances in statistical methods and computer technology have multiplied the factors used to define class under the objective method. No longer are sociologists limited to annual income and education in evaluating a person's class position. Today, studies use as criteria the value of homes, sources of income, assets, years in present occupations, neighbourhoods, and considerations regarding dual careers. Adding these variables will not necessarily paint a different picture of class differentiation in Canada,

▶ **FIGURE 8-1**

Comparison of Family Income and Wealth in Canada, 2005

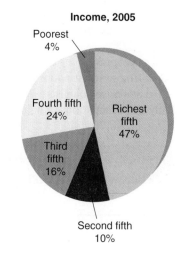

Income, 2005

- Poorest 4%
- Fourth fifth 24%
- Richest fifth 47%
- Third fifth 16%
- Second fifth 10%

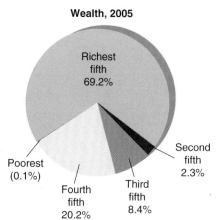

Wealth, 2005

- Richest fifth 69.2%
- Poorest (0.1%)
- Fourth fifth 20.2%
- Third fifth 8.4%
- Second fifth 2.3%

Note: Data do not add to 100 percent due to rounding.

Sources: Statistics Canada 2006i; Statistics Canada 2007h.

but it does allow sociologists to measure class in a more complex and multi-dimensional way. Whatever the technique used to measure class, the sociologist is interested in real and often dramatic differences in power, privilege, and opportunity in a society. The study of stratification is a study of inequality. Nowhere is this more evident than in the distribution of wealth and income. As Figure 8-1 illustrates, in Canada, there is greater inequality in wealth than in income.

Wealth and Income

Wealth in Canada is much more unevenly distributed than is income. As Figure 8-1 shows, in 2005, the richest

▶ **FIGURE 8-2**

Median Earnings by Decile, Families Raising Children, Canada, 1976–2004

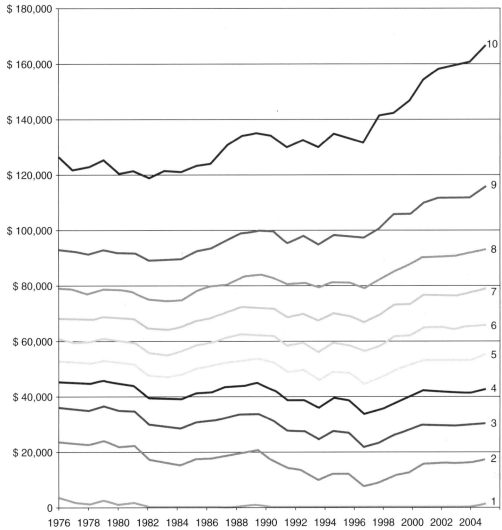

Source: Adapted from Yalnizyan 2007.

fifth of the population held 69 percent of the nation's wealth. Researchers have also found dramatic disparities in wealth between families headed by a single parent (particularly a mother) and those headed by two parents, between those headed by Aboriginal parents and by non-Aboriginal parents, and between those headed by parents who have a mental disability and by those who do not (Wolff 2002).

By all measures, income in Canada is distributed unevenly. Nobel Prize–winning economist Paul Samuelson has described the situation in the following words: "If we made an income pyramid out of building blocks, with each layer portraying $500 of income, the peak would be far higher than Mount Everest, but most people would be within a few feet of the ground" (Samuelson and Nordhaus 2001:386).

Recent data support Samuelson's analogy. As Figure 8-2 illustrates, in 2004, the average earnings of the richest tenth (or top 10 percent) of Canada's families raising children was 82 times that earned by of the poorest tenth (or bottom 10 percent). This ratio has tripled since 1976, when the average earnings of the top 10 percent was 31 times that of the bottom 10 percent (Yalnizyan 2007).

Survey data show that more than 50 percent of Canadians (as opposed to 38 percent of U.S. citizens) believe that government should take steps to reduce the income disparity between the rich and the poor. By contrast, 80 percent of people in Italy, 66 percent in Germany, and 65 percent in Great Britain support governmental efforts to reduce income inequality. It is not surprising, then, that many European countries, particularly in Scandinavia, provide more extensive "safety nets" to assist and protect the disadvantaged. By contrast, the strong cultural value placed on individualism in the United States leads to greater possibilities for both economic success and failure (Lipset 1996).

> ### Think about It
> In addition to generous raises and favourable government policies, what else might have accounted for the sharp rise in income for the richest 10 percent of Canadians?

Poverty

Approximately one out of every six children in Canada lives below the low-income cut-off established by the federal government. The 2006 *Report Card on Child and Family Poverty in Canada* (Campaign 2000 2007) reported that just over one million children are living in low-income households and that one-third of all Canadian children have experienced poverty for at least one year since 1996. The economic boom of the 1990s and early 2000s sidestepped these people. Despite the federal government's goal of eradicating child poverty by 2000, a UNICEF report showed that, in 2005, 15 percent of Canadian children lived below the low-income cut-off. The same report indicated that Canada's ranking among other countries, in respect to child poverty, had not changed from 2000 (UNICEF 2005). In this section, we'll consider just how we define *poverty* and who is included in that category (Bauman 1999; Proctor and Dalaker 2002).

Studying Poverty

The efforts of sociologists and other social scientists to better understand poverty are complicated by the difficulty of defining it. This problem is evident even in government programs that conceive of poverty in either absolute or relative terms. **Absolute poverty** refers to a minimum level of subsistence that no family should be expected to live below. Government policies concerning minimum wages, labour market barriers for excluded groups, housing standards, or school lunch programs for the poor imply a need to bring citizens up to some predetermined level of existence.

Although Canada's federal government does not have an official poverty line, it does have what is called a LICO (low-income cut-off), which is calculated for families of different sizes, and for individuals, living in different communities of varying size, from rural to urban. For example, a family of three living in a city of over 500 000 people, would have a LICO of $32 450 (see Table 8-3). If a family spends 20 percent more than the average family does on the essentials (e.g., clothing,

Table 8-3 Low Income Cut-Offs Before Tax, 2006

			Community Size		
Family Size	**500 000+** $	**100 000–499 999**	**30 000–99 999**	**Less than 30 000***	**Rural areas**
1	21 202	18 260	18 147	16 605	14 596
2	26 396	22 731	22 591	20 671	18 170
3	32 450	27 945	27 773	25 412	22 338
4	39 399	33 930	33 721	30 855	27 122
5	44 686	38 482	38 245	34 995	30 760
6	50 397	43,402	43 135	39 469	34 694
7	56 110	48 322	48 024	43 943	38 626

* Includes cities with a population between 15 000 and 30 000 and small urban areas (under 15 000).
Source: Statistics Canada 2006c.

▶ **FIGURE 8-3**

Poverty in Selected Industrial Countries (percentage of people living below the income poverty line)

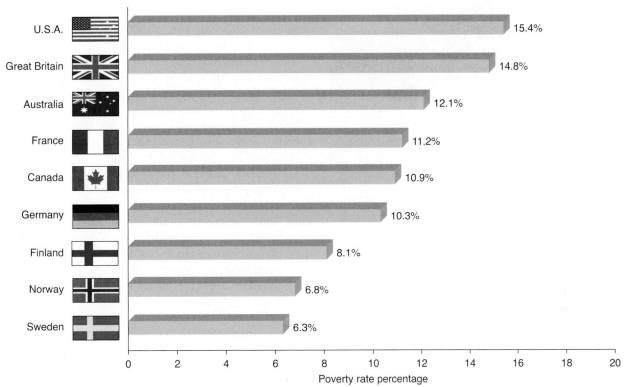

Source: United Nations Human Development Report 2006.

food, shelter), it falls below the LICO. As of 2006, a family spending more than 63 percent of its gross income on the necessities of clothing, food, and shelter would fall below the LICO. Figure 8-3 shows poverty rates in Canada and in other countries. Canada's poverty rate, although higher than those in Norway, Finland, and Sweden, is significantly lower than that of the United States.

If anything, this cross-national comparison understates the extent of poverty in the United States, since U.S. residents are likely to pay more for housing, health care, child care, and education than residents of other countries, where such expenses are often subsidized.

By contrast, **relative poverty** is a floating standard of deprivation by which people at the bottom of a society, whatever their lifestyles, are judged to be disadvantaged *in comparison with the nation as a whole.* Therefore, even if the poor of the 2000s are better off in absolute terms than the poor of the 1930s or 1960s, they are still seen as deserving special assistance.

Campaign 2000 is an organization made up of more than 90 national, provincial or territorial, and community groups focused on the goal of eliminating child and family poverty in Canada. In its 2004 report (Campaign 2000 2004), it stated that, despite continued economic growth and rising employment, child and family poverty remain a "social deficit" in Canada. The organization made the following recommendations to help alleviate poverty in Canada:

- Establish a multi-year social investment plan, which would include a maximum child benefit of $4900 a year.
- Establish a high-quality, universally accessible, publicly funded system of early learning and child care.
- Expand affordable housing programs.
- Create more good jobs that provide living wages.
- Renew the social safety net.

Who are the Poor?

Not only does the category of the poor defy any simple definition, but it also counters the common stereotypes about "poor people" that Barbara Ehrenreich addressed in her book *Nickel and Dimed* (2001). For example, many

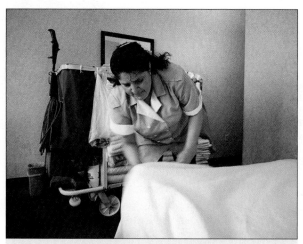

A hotel housekeeper hurries to make the bed and move on to the next room to be cleaned. At low wage rates, even full-time workers have difficulty staying out of poverty, especially if they have families.

people in Canada believe that the vast majority of the poor are able to work but will not. Yet, many poor adults do work outside the home. Sociological researchers call this group the **working poor**. A working poor individual is one who works a minimum number of hours a year and whose family income falls below the LICO. In 2004, in Canada, 551 900 individuals were in this category. Of this number, approximately one in five, or 19.5 percent, were immigrants (HRSDC 2007).

A sizable number of the poor live in urban areas. Poverty is no stranger in rural areas, however, ranging from Saskatchewan's hard-hit farming regions to fishing communities in Newfoundland and Labrador. Table 8-4 provides additional statistical information regarding these low-income people in Canada.

An increasing proportion of the low-income people in Canada are women, many of whom are single parents. Approximately 46 percent of Canadians with low incomes in 2000 were in lone-parent families that had at least one child under age 18; the vast majority of these families were headed by women. Canadian women's wages remain unequal to those of Canadian men, and many women in Canadian workplaces still hold jobs in female-dominated job ghettos. This alarming reality, known as the *feminization of poverty*, is evident not just in Canada but also around the world.

A major factor in the feminization of poverty has been the increase in the number of families with women as single heads of the household (see Chapter 12). In ◄ P.93 2005, 7.4 percent of all families of two persons or more in the Canada lived in poverty (below the LICO), compared to 29 percent of households headed by single mothers (Statistics Canada 2007m). Some feminist thinkers trace the higher rates of poverty among women to such factors as the difficulty in finding affordable child care, sexual harassment, and sex discrimination in the labour market, while others attribute it to more deep-rooted systemic factors (see Chapter 11).

Sociologist William Julius Wilson (1980, 1987, 1989, 1996) and other social scientists have used the term **underclass** to describe the long-term poor who lack training and skills. In Canada, this class is often associated with such factors as race, ethnicity, age, disability, geographic region, and age. For example, persistently and disproportionately represented in the so-called

Table 8-4 Low Income after Tax, by Selected Family Types, Canada, 2005

Individuals and Selected Family Types	Percentage in Low Income 2005
Unattached individuals	30.4
Couple families with no children	6.4
Couple families with children	6.7
Couple families with other relatives	2.2
Lone-parent families	25.9
Other non-elderly families	11.2
Elderly families	1.6

Source: Adapted by the author from Statistics Canada 2006c.

underclass of Canadian society are those of Aboriginal heritage. The social condition of Canada's Aboriginal people will be explored in greater detail in Chapter 10.

Conflict theorists, among others, have expressed alarm at the portion of Canada's population living on this lower rung of the stratification hierarchy and at society's reluctance to address the lack of economic opportunities for these people. Often, portraits of the underclass seem to "blame the victims" for their own plight while ignoring other factors that push people into poverty.

Analyses of the poor in general reveal that they are not a static social class. The overall composition of the poor changes continually, because some individuals and families near the top edge of poverty move above the poverty level after a year or two while others slip below it. Still, hundreds of thousands of people remain in poverty for many years at a time.

Explaining Poverty

Why is it that pervasive poverty continues within a nation of such vast wealth? Sociologist Herbert Gans has applied functionalist analysis to the existence of poverty and argues that various segments of society actually *benefit* from the existence of the poor (1995). Gans has identified a number of social, economic, and political functions that the poor perform for society:

- The presence of poor people means that society's dirty work—physically dirty or dangerous, dead-end and underpaid, undignified and menial jobs—will be performed at low cost.
- Poverty creates jobs for occupations and professions that service the poor. It creates both legal employment (public health experts, welfare caseworkers) and illegal jobs (drug dealers, numbers runners).
- The identification and punishment of the poor as deviants upholds the legitimacy of conventional social norms and mainstream values regarding hard work, thrift, and honesty.
- Within a relatively hierarchical society, the existence of poor people guarantees the higher status of the more affluent. As psychologist William Ryan has noted, affluent people may justify inequality (and gain a measure of satisfaction) by "blaming the victims" of poverty for their disadvantaged condition (1976).
- Because of their lack of political power, the poor often absorb the costs of social change. Under the policy of deinstitutionalization, people with mental illnesses released from long-term hospitals have been "dumped" primarily into low-income communities and neighbourhoods.

◀ P. 168

Similarly, halfway houses for rehabilitated drug abusers are often rejected by more affluent communities and end up in poorer neighbourhoods.

In Gans's view, then, poverty and the poor actually satisfy positive functions for many non-poor groups in society.

Life Chances

Max Weber saw class as closely related to people's **life chances**—that is, their opportunities to provide themselves with material goods, positive living conditions, and favourable life experiences (Gerth and Mills 1958). Life chances are reflected in such measures as housing, education, and health. Occupying a higher position in a society improves your life chances and brings greater access to social rewards. By contrast, people in the lower social classes are forced to devote a larger proportion of their limited resources to the necessities of life.

In times of danger, the affluent and powerful have a better chance of surviving than people of ordinary means. When the supposedly unsinkable British ocean-liner *Titanic* hit an iceberg in 1912, it was not carrying enough lifeboats to accommodate all its passengers. Plans had been made to evacuate only first- and second-class passengers. About 62 percent of the first-class passengers survived the disaster. Despite a rule that women and children would go first, about a third of those passengers were male. In contrast, only 25 percent of the passengers in third class survived. The first attempt to alert them to the need to abandon ship came at least 45 minutes after other passengers had been notified (D. Butler 1998; Crouse 1999; Riding 1998).

Class position also affects health in important ways. In fact, class is increasingly being viewed as an important predictor of health. The affluent avail themselves of improved health services while such advances bypass poor people. The chances of a child's dying during the first year of life are much higher in poor families than among the middle class. This higher infant mortality rate results in part from the inadequate nutrition received by low-income expectant mothers. Even when they survive infancy, the poor are more likely than the affluent to suffer from serious, chronic illnesses, such as arthritis, bronchitis, diabetes, and heart disease.

All these factors contribute to differences in the death rates of the poor and the affluent. Studies drawing on health data in Canada document the impact of class (as well as race) on mortality. Ill health among the poor only serves to increase the likelihood that the poor will remain impoverished (Link and Phelan 1995).

Like disease, crime can be particularly devastating when it attacks the poor. People in low-income families were more likely to be assaulted, raped, or robbed than were the most affluent people. Furthermore, if accused of a crime, a person with low income and status is likely to be represented by an overworked publicly funded lawyer. Whether innocent or guilty, the accused may sit in jail for months, unable to raise bail (Rennison 2002).

Some people have hoped that the Internet revolution would help level the playing field by making information and markets uniformly available. Unfortunately, however, not everyone is able to get onto the "information highway," and so yet another aspect of social inequality has emerged—the *digital divide* (see Chapter 6). People who are poor, who have less education, who are members of minority groups, or who live in rural communities are not getting connected at home or at work. For example, in 2003, 64 percent of all households had access to the Internet. However, about 88 percent of households whose head had a university degree had access to the Internet, while only 32 percent of those families whose head had less than a high school education did. As more-educated people continue to buy high-speed Internet connections, they will be able to take advantage of even more sophisticated interactive services, and the digital divide will grow larger (Statistics Canada 2004f).

Wealth, status, and power may not ensure happiness, but they certainly provide additional ways of coping with problems and disappointments. For this reason, the opportunity for advancement—for social mobility—is of special significance to those who are at the bottom of society looking up. These people want the rewards and privileges that are granted to high-ranking members of a society.

The social policy section that closes this chapter focuses on the Canadian welfare system, a government program that serves many women and men who are trapped in poverty. The aim of welfare reform has been to encourage these people to find jobs and become self-supporting. We'll also see how other governments have approached welfare reform, and what the results have been.

Use Your Sociological Imagination

Imagine a society in which there are no social classes— no differences in people's wealth, income, and life chances. What would such a society be like? Would it be stable, or would its social structure change over time?

□ DOES SOCIAL MOBILITY EXIST?

Jimmy Pattison, a self-made billionaire and international businessman, grew up in impoverished circumstances in Luseland, Saskatchewan. He began his business career by selling used cars. Today, he is one of the wealthiest individuals in Canada and sole owner of one of the largest companies in Canada. The rise of a child from a poor background to a position of great prestige, power, and financial reward is an example of social mobility. The term **social mobility** refers to movement of individuals or groups from one position of a society's stratification system to another. But how significant—how frequent, how dramatic—is mobility in such a class society as Canada?

Open versus Closed Stratification Systems

Sociologists use the terms open stratification system and closed stratification system to indicate the amount of social mobility in a society. An **open system** implies that the position of each individual is influenced by the person's achieved status. At the other extreme of social mobility is the **closed system**, which allows little or no possibility of moving up. The slavery and caste systems of stratification are examples of closed systems. In such societies, social placement is based on ascribed statuses, such as race or family background, which cannot be changed.

Types of Social Mobility

An airline pilot who becomes a police officer moves from one social position to another of the same rank. Each occupation has the same prestige ranking: 60 on a scale ranging from a low of 0 to a high of 100 (see Table 8-2 on page 195). Sociologists call this kind of movement **horizontal mobility**. However, if the pilot were to become a lawyer (prestige ranking of 75), he or she would experience **vertical mobility**, the movement from one social position to another of a different rank. Vertical mobility can also involve moving downward in a society's stratification system, as would be the case if the airline pilot became a bank teller (ranking of 43). Pitirim Sorokin was the first sociologist to distinguish between horizontal and vertical mobility ([1927] 1959). Most sociological analysis, however, focuses on vertical rather than horizontal mobility.

One way of examining vertical social mobility is to contrast intergenerational and intragenerational mobility. **Intergenerational mobility** involves changes in the social position of children relative to their parents. Thus, a plumber whose father was a physician provides an example of downward intergenerational mobility. A film star whose parents were both factory workers illustrates upward intergenerational mobility.

Intragenerational mobility involves changes in social position within a person's adult life. A woman who enters the paid labour force as a teacher's aide and eventually becomes superintendent of the school district experiences upward intragenerational mobility. A man who becomes a taxicab driver after his accounting firm goes bankrupt undergoes downward intragenerational mobility.

Social Mobility in Canada

The belief in upward mobility is an important value in our society. Does this mean that Canada is indeed the land of opportunity? This can only be the case if such ascriptive characteristics as race, gender, and family background have ceased to be significant in determining someone's future prospects. We can see the impact of these factors in the occupational structure.

Occupational Mobility

"You are three times more likely as a young man to move from rags to rags than rags to riches. And moving from riches to riches is the most likely of all." These are the words of the authors of a major Canadian study on the occupational mobility of 400 000 men between the ages of 16 and 19 (Corak and Heisz 1996). The authors concluded that although there is limited upward mobility in the middle ranges of the Canadian occupational hierarchy, the richest and poorest individuals tend to reproduce the income level of their fathers. This study is consistent with other studies of intragenerational mobility in Canada, which found that the majority of Canadians experienced no occupational mobility in their working lives (Creese, Guppy, and Meissner 1991). In Canada, achievement is not simply based on hard work and merit; ascribed characteristics, such as race, gender, and ethnicity, are significant in their influence on a person's chances for both intergenerational and intragenerational occupational mobility.

The Impact of Education

Education plays a critical role in social mobility. The impact of advanced education on adult status is clearly evident in Canada, as documented in statistics showing the relationship between the highest level of educational achievement and income and wealth in adulthood.

Generally, the higher a person's level of educational achievement, the higher his or her level of income and wealth (expressed as net worth). For example, according to the 2001 census, people with master's degrees in commerce made, on average, $88 396 per year, while those holding bachelor's degrees made, on average, $63 117 per year. The same pattern exists in the field of education: those with master's degrees had an average income of $50 379, while those with bachelor's degrees had an average income of $40 408. For other fields, such as history and agricultural science, the differences in earnings between those holding master's degrees and those holding bachelor's degrees were insignificant (*The Vancouver Sun* 2004a).

Although educational achievement is linked to social mobility, the stark reality is that the chance of achieving an education continues to be associated with family background. In 1999, 34 percent of students from the lowest socio-economic quartile did not complete high school, compared with 23 percent of students from the highest quartile; 20 percent of students from the quartile attended university, compared with 40 percent of those from the highest quartile (Canadian Education Statistics Council 2000). With the increased costs of tuition and other expenses associated with a post-secondary education, students who attend university are increasingly likely to have parents from the higher socio-economic groups.

The Impact of Race

The variables of race, class, and gender are intertwined in such a way as to produce diverse chances for both intergenerational mobility and intragenerational mobility. Canadian women who are racialized persons earn less than other Canadian women who are not. They also earn less than men, whether the men are racialized persons or not. For example, racialized women earned roughly $3000 a year less than non-racialized women, roughly $9000 less than racialized men, and roughly $18 000 less than non-racialized men (Statistics Canada 2006m). The glaring absence of racialized persons from corporate boardrooms, political office, and other positions of power and influence reflects a systemic pattern of inequality. As Joseph Mensah (2002:129) states in his book on blacks in Canada, "the unabashed racial discrimination in the job market impacts Blacks more than any other form of bigotry."

The Impact of Gender

Studies of mobility, even more than those of class, have traditionally ignored the significance of gender, but some research findings are now available that explore the relationship between gender and mobility.

Rita Tsang, president and CEO of Tour East Holidays (Canada) Inc., is one of the few women in Canada who have risen to the top of the corporate hierarchy. Despite the implementation of employment-equity policies, occupational barriers still limit women's social mobility.

Women's employment opportunities are much more limited than men's (as we will see in Chapter 11). Moreover, according to recent research, women whose skills far exceed the jobs offered them are more likely than men to withdraw entirely from the paid labour force. This withdrawal violates an assumption common to traditional mobility studies: that most people will aspire to upward mobility and seek to make the most of their opportunities.

In contrast to men, women's jobs are heavily concentrated in the sales and service areas. But the modest salary ranges and few prospects for advancement in many of these positions limit the possibility of upward mobility. Self-employment as shopkeepers, entrepreneurs, independent professionals, and the like—an important road to upward mobility for men—is difficult for women, who find it harder to secure the necessary financing. Although sons often follow in the footsteps of their fathers, women are less likely to move into their fathers' positions. Consequently, gender remains an important factor in shaping social mobility within Canada. Women in Canada (and in other parts of the world) are especially likely to be trapped in poverty and unable to rise out of their low-income status (Heilman 2001).

So far we have focused on stratification and social mobility within Canada. In the next chapter, we broaden our focus to consider stratification from a global perspective. In Box 8-2, we provide a look at global inequality.

Sociology in the Global Community
Poverty and Global Inequality

8-2

Rustica Banda is a midwife who delivers 10 to 13 babies a day at a community hospital near Lilongwe in Malawi, in sub-Saharan Africa. In 2004, sub-Saharan Africa had 25 million people living with human immunodeficiency virus/acquired immune deficiency syndrome (HIV/AIDS), more than half of whom were women. The percentage of women in the region living with HIV/AIDS is increasing, contributing to what has been called the "feminization of HIV/AIDS" (UNAIDS 2004). Because of a lack of state funding to local hospitals for wages and basic medical supplies, such as plastic gloves, Rustica Banda and others like her work for low wages in unsafe and dangerous conditions to care for patients, some of whom have HIV/AIDS. Banda attributes the poverty in her country to global economic interconnectedness; more specifically, to debts with other countries. Owing more than 1.5 times its annual income, Malawi is one of the most heavily indebted countries in the world. In 2003, the country spent more than twice its funding for health care in servicing its debt. In this context, Rustica Banda (*Guardian Unlimited* 2005) describes the conditions in her life:

> I have five children to support, as well as five orphaned grandchildren. There is a great staff shortage here in Mitunda. At any one time, there are only two nurses on duty.... The pregnant woman must buy her own things for labour; a plastic sheet to put on the bed to protect her from the blood of other patients.... I have to use my bare hands when collecting blood, even when I don't know the HIV status of the patient.... The government says it does not have money for salaries or to buy enough equipment to run the hospital. It has too many debts with other countries. I call on the state of Malawi to consider its nurses and our salaries; we should not be running away from the government hospitals. I also ask the G8 to cancel Malawi's debt.

Make Poverty History, an alliance of charities, religious organizations, trade unions, anti-poverty groups, rock stars, and celebrities, mobilized to promote global awareness (e.g., Live 8) and to apply pressure on the G8 leaders (that is, leaders of the richest countries: Canada, the United States, Great Britain, Italy, Germany, France, Russia, and Japan) when they met in Scotland in 2005 for the G8 Summit. Make Poverty History called for governments and international decision makers to change policies regarding three inextricably connected areas—trade, debt, and aid—as they relate to the dealings between the world's richest and poorest countries. Falling short of some anti-poverty and AIDS activist groups' expectations (Clark 2005), the G8 leaders did, however, agree to the following:

- to increase aid by US$25 billion annually to Africa by 2010
- to provide universal access to AIDS treatment by 2010
- to establish efforts to save 600 000 lives lost to malaria by 2015
- to train 20 000 additional peacekeepers for an African union peace force
- to call for trade talks to eliminate agricultural subsidies, which would help African products find markets

Applying Theory

1. Have you ever been involved in a fundraising or awareness-raising campaign in your community or university to fight poverty in Africa?
2. Do you think that Canada is doing enough in its efforts to close the gap between the rich and the poor countries of the world?

Social Policy and Stratification
Rethinking Social Assistance in North America and Europe

The Issue

- After five years of living on social assistance in Saskatchewan, a single mother of three is a success story. The 28-year-old has landed a job at a storage company and moved up to a $12-an-hour customer service position. However, another single mother employed in a nearby hotel for $8.00 per hour worries about being edged back into unemployment by the stiff competition for low-wage jobs.

- Hélène Desegrais, a single mother in Paris, France, waited for four months to obtain a place in government-subsidized daycare for her daughter. Now she can seek a full-time job, but she is concerned about government threats to curtail such services to keep taxes down (Simons 1997).

- Marcia Missouri of Worcester, Massachusetts, tacks up a handwritten advertisement in the public housing project in which she lives to say that she is available to clean yards and braid hair for a few extra dollars. The sign lists a friend's phone number; she doesn't have a phone of her own (Vobejda and Havenmann 1997).

These are the faces of people living on the edge—often women with children seeking to make a go of it amid changing social policies. Governments in all parts of the world are searching for the right approach to social assistance: How much subsidy should they provide? How much responsibility should fall on the shoulders of the poor?

The Setting

By the 1990s, there was intense debate in Canada over the issue of welfare. Welfare programs were costly, and there was widespread concern (however unfounded) that welfare payments discouraged recipients from seek-ing jobs. On the one hand, there were declarations to "end poverty as we know it" (Pear 1996:20); on the other, neo-conservative forces in Canada voiced concern about government spending.

A 2006 study released by the National Council of Welfare showed that the number of people receiving social assistance in Canada has decreased by more than one million between 1995 and 2005. A Statistics Canada study attributed the decline to new rules that make it tougher to qualify for social assistance and to improvements in the economies of various provinces. The greatest change in terms of family type of those collecting social assistance occurred among single mothers. In 1995, almost one-half of Canada's single mothers received social assistance; by 2000, that rate had declined to almost one-third. In 2005, according to the National Council of Welfare, nearly half a million of the roughly 1.7 million people receiving assistance were children (2006).

Countries vary widely in their commitment to social service programs. But some industrialized nations devote higher proportions of their expenditures to housing,

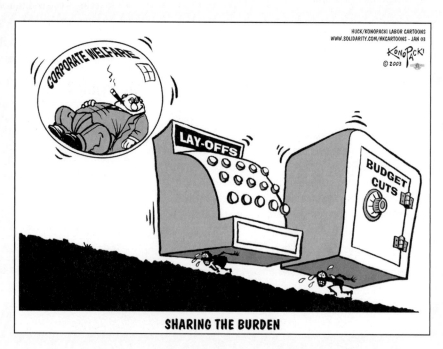

SHARING THE BURDEN

social security, welfare, health care, and unemployment compensation than Canada does. Data available in 2004 indicated that in Great Britain, 82 percent of health expenditures were paid for by the government; in Spain and Canada, 71 percent; but in the United States, only 44 percent (World Bank 2004:88–90).

Sociological Insights

Many sociologists tend to view the debate over welfare throughout industrialized nations from a conflict perspective: the "haves" in positions of policy making listen to the interests of other "haves," while the cries of the "have-nots" are drowned out. Critics of so-called welfare reform believe that Canada's economic problems are unfairly being blamed on welfare spending and the poor. From a conflict perspective, this backlash against welfare recipients reflects deep fears and hostility toward the country's poor and dispossessed. Sylvia Bashevkin, in her book, *Welfare Hot Buttons: Women, Work, and Social Policy Reform*, examines welfare reform in three countries—Canada, the United States, and the United Kingdom—over the last two decades (2002). She discovered similarities in the consequences of welfare reform in these three countries. In each, there was a decline in caseloads, an increase in the rates of employment of single mothers, and a backlash against poor women and welfare-reliant mothers. In Canada, single-parent households—overwhelmingly headed by women, disproportionately poor and, thus, more likely to require welfare assistance—make up an unprecedented one in four families (Statistics Canada 2007m). Bashevkin argues that we are moving toward a "duty state" where citizens are viewed as having a responsibilty and obligation to the state, based on a market exchange.

Those critical of the backlash note that "welfare scapegoating" conveniently ignores the lucrative government handouts that go to *affluent* individuals and families. British Columbia's government, for example, has reduced income taxes for all residents, including the wealthy, while at the same time reducing or eliminating government services and programs that most benefit the poor.

Those who take a conflict perspective also urge policy makers and the general public to look closely at *corporate welfare*—the tax breaks, direct payments, and grants that governments make to corporations—rather than to focus on the comparatively small allowances being given to mothers on social assistance and their children. Any suggestion to curtail such corporate welfare brings a strong response from special-interest groups that are much more powerful than any coalition on behalf of the poor. One example of corporate welfare is the airline bailout bill that was passed in the wake of 9/11. Within 11 days, the U.S. government had approved the bailout, whose positive impact was felt largely by airline executives and shareholders. Relatively low-paid airline employees were still laid off, and hundreds of thousands of low-wage workers in airports, hotels, and related industries received little or no assistance. Efforts to broaden unemployment assistance to help these marginally employed workers failed (Hartman and Miller 2001).

Policy Initiatives

The government likes to highlight success stories. It is true that many people who previously depended on tax dollars are now working and paying taxes themselves. But it is much too soon to say whether or not welfare reform will be successful. The new jobs that were generated by the booming economy of the late 1990s and early 2000s may be an unrealistic test of the system. Prospects for the chronically jobless—those people who are hard to train or who have drug or alcohol dependency, physical disabilities, or child-care needs—remain a challenge.

In the United States, fewer people are on welfare since the enactment of the welfare reform law in August 1996. By January 2002, nearly 7 million people had left the system, reducing the rolls to 5.4 million people. Yet, research showed that most adults who had gone off welfare had taken low-wage jobs that did not offer benefits. As they moved off welfare, their Medicaid coverage ended, leaving them without health insurance. Support has also been lacking for working parents who need high-quality child care. And assistance to immigrants, even those who are legal residents, continues to be limited (Department of Health and Human Services 2000, 2002; Ehrenreich and Piven 2002).

European governments have encountered some of the same citizen demands as those that occur in North America: Keep our taxes low, even if it means reducing services to the poor. However, nations in Eastern and

Central Europe have faced a special challenge since the fall of communism. The governments in those nations had traditionally provided an impressive array of social services, but they differed from capitalist systems in several important respects. First, the communist system was premised on full employment, so there was no need to provide employment insurance or social services focused on older people and those with disabilities. Second, subsidies, such as for housing and even utilities, played an important role. With new competition from the West and tight budgets, some of these countries are beginning to realize that universal coverage is no longer affordable and must be replaced with targeted programs. Even Sweden, despite its long history of social welfare programs, is feeling the pinch. Still, only modest cutbacks have been made in European social service programs, leaving them much more generous than those in Canada and the United States (Gornick 2001).

Both in North America and Europe, people are beginning to turn to private means to support themselves. For instance, they are investing money for their later years rather than depending on government social security programs. But that solution works only if you have a job and can save money. Increasing proportions of people are seeing the gap growing between themselves and the affluent with fewer government programs aimed at assisting them. Solutions are frequently left to the private sector, while government policy initiatives at the national level all but disappear.

Applying Theory

1. What might be the focus of some feminist sociologists as they study the changes in welfare reform in Canada and elsewhere?
2. How would you explain the trend of the decreasing number of Canadians receiving social assistance?
3. Have you or has anyone you know applied for social assistance? If so, what caused you or them to do so?

CHAPTER RESOURCES

Summary

What is Stratification?
- **Stratification** (p. 186) is the structured ranking of entire groups of people in a society, which leads to the perpetuation of **social inequality** (p. 186). Stratification is manifested in all cultures through systems of *stratification*, which include **slavery** (p. 187), **castes** (p. 187), and social **class** (p. 192).
- Karl Marx saw that differences in access to the means of production created social, economic, and political inequality and distinct classes of owners and labourers.
- Max Weber identified three analytically distinct components of stratification: **class** (p. 192), **status group** (p. 192), and **power** (p. 192).
- Functionalists argue that stratification is necessary to motivate people to fill society's important positions; conflict theorists see stratification as a major source of societal tension and conflict.

How are Stratification and Social Class Related?
- One measure of social class is occupational **prestige** (p. 194). A consequence of social class in Canada is that both **wealth** (p. 186) and **income** (p. 186) are distributed unevenly.
- The category of the "poor" defies any simple definition, and counters common stereotypes about "poor people." The long-term poor, who lack training and skills, form an **underclass** (p. 200).
- Functionalists find that the poor satisfy positive functions for many of the non-poor in capitalist societies.
- A person's **life chances** (p. 201)—opportunities for obtaining material goods, positive living conditions, and favourable life experiences—are related to social class. Occupying a high social position improves a person's life chances.

Does Social Mobility Exist?
- **Social mobility** (p. 202) is more likely to be found in an **open system** (p. 202) that emphasizes achieved status than in a **closed system** (p. 202) that focuses on ascribed chararacteristics.

- Race, gender, and class intersect to produce compounded chances for social mobility.

Critical Thinking Questions

1. How would functional thinkers explain the growing gap between the rich and the poor in Canada? What about among nations?
2. Sociological study of stratification generally is conducted at the macro level and draws most heavily on the functionalist and conflict perspectives. How might sociologists use the interactionist perspective to examine social class inequalities within a university?
3. Imagine you have the opportunity to do research on changing patterns of social mobility in a developing nation from a feminist perspective. What specific question would you want to investigate, and how would you go about it?
4. Why do you think companies like Nike and Wal-Mart do not produce products in their own country?

Key Terms

Absolute poverty   A standard of poverty based on a minimum level of subsistence below which families should not be expected to live. (p. 198)

Bourgeoisie   Karl Marx's term for the capitalist class, comprising the owners of the means of production. (p. 191)

Capitalism   An economic system in which the means of production are largely in private hands and the main incentive for economic activity is the accumulation of profits. (p. 191)

Castes   Hereditary systems of rank, usually religiously dictated, that tend to be fixed and immobile. (p. 187)

Class   A group of people who have a similar level of wealth and income. (p. 192)

Class consciousness   In Karl Marx's view, a subjective awareness held by members of a class regarding their common vested interests and need for collective political action to bring about social change. (p. 199)

Class system   A social ranking based primarily on economic position in which achieved characteristics can influence social mobility. (p. 188)

Closed system   A social system in which there is little or no possibility of individual mobility. (p. 202)

Esteem   The reputation that a particular individual has earned within an occupation. (p. 195)

False consciousness   A term used by Karl Marx to describe an attitude held by members of a class that does not accurately reflect their objective position. (p. 191)

Horizontal mobility   The movement of an individual from one social position to another of the same rank. (p. 202)

Income   Salaries and wages. (p. 186)

Intergenerational mobility   Changes in the social position of children relative to their parents. (p. 202)

Intragenerational mobility   Changes in a person's social position within his or her adult life. (p. 203)

Life chances   People's opportunities to provide themselves with material goods, positive living conditions, and favourable life experiences. (p. 201)

Objective method   A technique for measuring social class that assigns individuals to classes on the basis of such criteria as occupation, education, income, and place of residence. (p. 194)

Open system   A social system in which the position of each individual is influenced by his or her achieved status. (p. 202)

Power   The ability of people to exercise their will over others. (p. 192)

Prestige   The respect and admiration that an occupation holds in a society. (p. 194)

Proletariat   Karl Marx's term for the working class in a capitalist society. (p. 191)

Relative poverty   A floating standard of deprivation by which people at the bottom of a society, whatever their lifestyles, are judged to be disadvantaged in comparison with the nation as a whole. (p. 199)

Slavery   A system of enforced servitude in which people are legally owned by others and in which enslaved status is transferred from parents to children. (p. 187)

Social inequality   A condition in which members of a society have different amounts of wealth, prestige, or power. (p. 186)

Social mobility   Movement of individuals or groups from one position of a society's stratification system to another. (p. 202)

Status group   People who have the same prestige or lifestyle, independent of their class positions. (p. 192)

Stratification   A structured ranking of entire groups of people that perpetuates unequal economic rewards and power in a society. (p. 186)

Underclass   People who are poor for the long term and who lack training and skills. (p. 200)

Vertical mobility   The movement of a person from one social position to another of a different rank. (p. 202)

Wealth   An inclusive term encompassing all of a person's material assets, including land and other types of property. (p. 186)

Working poor   People who work a certain number of hours a year but whose family income still falls below the low-income cut-off (LICO). (p. 200)

Additional Readings

Curtis, James, Edward Grabb, and Neil Guppy, eds. 2004. *Social Inequality in Canada*, 4th ed. Don Mills, ON: Prentice Hall. A collection of 31 readings, focusing on Canada, that address all the major aspects or dimensions of social inequality.

Fleras, Augie, and Jean Leonard Elliott. 2006. *Unequal Relations: An Introduction to Race, Ethnic, and Aboriginal Dynamics in Canada*, 5th ed. Don Mills, ON: Prentice Hall. An examination of the paradoxes and contradictions of Canadian society as they relate to diversity and difference.

Galabuzi, Grace-Edward. 2005. *Canada's Economic Apartheid*. Toronto: CSPI/WP. This book draws attention to the growing racialization of the gap between rich and poor in Canada, and also challenges some of the myths about the economic performance of Canada's racialized minorities.

Grabb, Edward G. 2002. *Theories of Social Inequality*, 4th ed. Toronto: Harcourt. This book provides a comprehensive overview and analysis of both classical and contemporary theories of social inequality.

Online Learning Centre

Visit the *Sociology: A Brief Introduction* Online Learning Centre at www.mcgrawhill.ca/olc/schaefer to access quizzes, interactive exercises, video clips, and other research and study tools related to this chapter.

Reel Society Video Clips

Reel Society can be used to spark discussion about the following topics from this chapter:

- Understanding stratification
- Stratification by social class
- Social mobility

chapter 9

GLOBAL INEQUALITY

This UNICEF poster reminds affluent Western consumers that the brand-name jeans they wear may be produced by exploited workers in developing countries. In sweatshops throughout the developing world, non-union garment workers—some of them still children—labour long hours for extremely low wages.

☐ **What is the Global Divide?**

☐ **What Forms does Global Inequality Take?**

☐ **How does Stratification within Nations Compare?**

> **Boxes**

SOCIOLOGY IN THE GLOBAL COMMUNITY: The Global Disconnect

SOCIOLOGY IN THE GLOBAL COMMUNITY: Cutting Poverty Worldwide

SOCIOLOGY IN THE GLOBAL COMMUNITY: Stratification in Japan

SOCIAL POLICY AND GLOBAL INEQUALITY: Universal Human Rights

Amit is a member of India's rising middle class. The 22-year-old left his village to study at an urban university and considers himself a connoisseur of Western fashions. He enjoys watching Arnold Schwarzenegger films and National Basketball Association games beamed to India from the United States. The foreign media reaffirm his self-image as a citizen of the world. Yet at the same time Amit complains that the media threaten Indian family arrangements. "I want an arranged marriage," Amit says, "but I fear that Fashion Television, MTV, and [music] Channel V are distorting the desires of the younger generation."

India, with a population now in excess of 1 billion, is a massive experiment in "globalization"—the emergence of worldwide markets and communications that increasingly ignore national boundaries. People, jobs, goods, and media move to and from India at unprecedented speed and volume. Global consumer products entice Indians. And Indians,

Amit is a member of India's rising middle class. The 22-year-old left his village to study at an urban university and considers himself a connoisseur of Western fashions.

in turn, produce for the global market. Cable and satellite television broadcasts from around the world reach Indian homes and Hollywood has grabbed a significant share of the movie audience (India's huge Bollywood film industry notwithstanding). There is a fear that Western images and ideas will undermine traditional Indian culture....

Over the last two decades, more of what people around the world buy and watch is produced elsewhere; more of what they produce is made for a global market; and more local policies are shaped by outside decision

makers. In India, a foreign-exchange crisis in 1991 gave the International Monetary Fund leverage to demand the removal of restrictions on foreign investment and trade. With that economic liberalization, once scarce goods rapidly flowed into the Indian market. Taking advantage of cheap, well-trained labor, computer programming jobs appeared. International financiers arrived. Within five years, imports more than doubled, exports more than tripled and foreign capital investment more than quintupled.

Cultural globalization—international media—quickly followed as global advertisers tried to reach the new Indian market and government restrictions eased. In 1991, cable television in India reached 300,000 homes; in 1999, it reached 24 million. In 1991, only a few foreign films showed in the biggest cities, but by 2001, foreign films were dubbed into Hindi and screened throughout the country.

Given new opportunities for employment, consumption, and entertainment, affluent urban Indian men aspired to new goods and experimented with changes in family life. In contrast, studies show that the lives of middle-class Indian men have not been significantly transformed and while the research is less conclusive, the contrast seems to apply to women as well. (Unfortunately, the effects of globalization on poor urban and rural Indians have not been sufficiently studied—although we do know that rural and urban poverty have increased slightly since 1991.)

☐ *(Derné 2003:12–13)* ✎

In this excerpt from the journal *Contexts*, sociologist Steve Derné describes the effects of globalization on Indian society. Derné conducted observation research in India in 1991 and again in 2001. He found that through Western media, Indians like Amit were being exposed to more and more consumer products, most of which they could not afford to purchase. An Indian citizen is considered affluent if his or her income tops $2150 a year; only about 3 percent of the population fits that description. These high-income consumers can afford some foreign goods, as well as an occasional visit to Pizza Hut, where they spend about $6 per person. (In comparison, a full dinner at an Indian restaurant costs about $1.) In Canada and the United States, most people cannot afford the lifestyles

Students protesting sweatshop labour in developing countries mock Nike by repurposing the company's own slogan, "Just do it."

portrayed in the majority of Hollywood-produced movies and television programs. But the disconnect between desire and reality is much greater in India and most other countries around the globe (Derné 2003).

At the same time that Western media have been flooding India with images of material wealth, Canadian students have been questioning the labour conditions in the foreign factories that produce their university-logo-embroidered sweatshirts. Their concerns have given rise to a coalition called Students Against Sweatshops (SAS)—which can be found on college and university campuses across the continent. Because this issue combines women's rights, immigrant rights, environmental concerns, and human rights, it has linked diverse groups on campus. The student movement has been aimed at ridding campus stores of all products made in sweatshops, both at home and abroad. Pressed by their students, many colleges and universities have agreed to adopt anti-sweatshop codes governing the products they stock on campus. Nike and Reebok, partly in response to student protests, have raised the wages of some 100 000 workers in their Indonesian factories to about 20 cents an hour—still far below what is needed to raise a family (Appelbaum and Dreier 1999; Rivoli 2005).

Together, the apparel industry and the global consumer-goods culture focus our attention on worldwide social stratification—on the enormous gap between wealthy nations and poorer nations. In many respects, the wealth of rich nations depends on the poverty of poor nations. People in industrialized societies benefit when they buy consumer goods made by low-wage workers in developing countries. Yet, the low wages workers earn in multinationals' factories typically are comparatively high for those countries.

What economic and political conditions explain the divide between rich nations and poor? Within developing nations, how are wealth and income distributed, and how much opportunity does the average worker have to move up the social ladder? How do race and gender affect social mobility in these countries? In this chapter, we focus on global inequality, beginning with the global divide. We consider the impact of colonialism and neo-colonialism, globalization, the rise of multinational corporations, grinding poverty, and the trend toward modernization. Then, we focus on stratification within nations, in terms of the distribution of wealth and income and social mobility. The chapter closes with a social policy section on universal human rights.

Use Your Sociological Imagination

Have you ever considered some actions that might reduce the inequality between rich and poor nations?

People's needs and desires differ dramatically depending on where they live. On the left, eager customers line up outside a store in Edmonton at 6:00 a.m. for a Boxing Day sale. On the right, residents of Ethiopia line up to receive water.

□ WHAT IS THE GLOBAL DIVIDE?

In some parts of the world, the people who have dedicated their lives to fighting starvation refer to what they call "coping mechanisms"—ways in which the desperately poor attempt to control their hunger. Eritrean women will strap flat stones to their stomachs to lessen their hunger pangs. In Mozambique, people eat the grasshoppers that have destroyed their crops, calling them "flying shrimp." Though dirt eating is considered a pathological condition (called *geophapy*) among the well-fed, the world's poor eat dirt to add minerals and taste, and to provide immunological support to their diet. And in many countries, mothers have been known to boil stones in water, to convince their hungry children that supper is almost ready. As they hover over the pot, these women hope that their malnourished children will fall asleep (McNeil 2004).

Around the world, inequality is a significant determinant of human behaviour, opening doors of opportunity to some and closing them to others. Indeed, disparities in life chances are so extreme that in some places, the poorest of the poor may not be aware of them. Western media images may have circled the globe, but in extremely depressed rural areas, those at the bottom of society are not likely to see them. A few centuries ago, such vast divides in global wealth did not exist. Except for a very few rulers and landowners, everyone in the world was poor. In much of Europe, life was as difficult as it was in Asia or South America. This was true until the Industrial Revolution and rising agricultural productivity produced explosive economic growth. The resulting rise in living standards was not evenly distributed across the world.

Figure 9-1 compares the industrial nations of the world to the developing nations. Using total population as a yardstick, we see that the developing countries have more than their fair share of rural population, as well as of total births, disease, and childhood deaths. At the same time, the industrial nations of the world, with a much smaller share of total population, have significantly more income and exports than the developing nations. Industrial nations also spend more on health and the military than other nations, and they emit more carbon dioxide (CO_2) (Sachs 2005a; Sutcliffe 2002).

▶ **FIGURE 9-1**

Fundamental Global Inequality

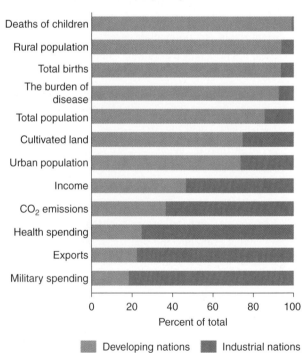

Note: In this comparison, industrial nations include Canada and the United States, Japan, and countries of Western Europe and Australasia. Developing nations include countries of Africa, Asia (except for Japan), Latin America, Eastern Europe, the Caribbean, and the Pacific.
Source: Adapted from Sutcliffe 2002:18.

WHAT FORMS DOES GLOBAL INEQUALITY TAKE?

The divide between industrial and developing nations is sharp, but sociologists recognize a continuum of nations, from the richest of the rich to the poorest of the poor. For example, in 2004, the average value of goods and services produced per citizen (or per capita gross national income) in the industrialized countries of the United States, Japan, Switzerland, Belgium, and Norway was more than $30 000. In at least 12 poorer countries, the value was just $900 or less. But most countries fell somewhere between those extremes, as Figure 9-2 shows.

Still, the contrasts are stark. Three forces discussed here are particularly responsible for the domination of the world marketplace by a few nations: the legacy of colonialism, the advent of multinational corporations, and modernization.

Think about It

What is the relationship among health spending, disease, and deaths of children? Among CO_2 emissions, income, and exports?

The Legacy of Colonialism

Colonialism occurs when a foreign power maintains political, social, economic, and cultural domination over a people for an extended period. Central to colonialism are values, beliefs, and ideas of inferiority/superiority regarding race and white superiority. In simple terms, colonialism is rule by outsiders. The long reign of the British Empire over much of North America, parts of Africa, and India is an example of colonial domination. The same can be said of French rule over Algeria, Tunisia, and other parts of North Africa. Relations between the colonial nation and colonized people are similar to those between the dominant capitalist class and the proletariat, as described by Karl Marx.

By the 1980s, colonialism had largely disappeared from the world. Most of the nations that were colonies before World War I had achieved political independence and established their own governments. However, for many of these countries, the transition to genuine self-rule was not yet complete. Colonial domination had established patterns of economic exploitation that continued even after nationhood was achieved—in part because former colonies were unable to develop their own industry and technology. Their dependence on more industrialized nations, including their former colonial masters, for managerial and technical expertise, investment capital, and manufactured goods kept former colonies in a subservient position. Such continuing dependence and foreign domination are referred to as **neo-colonialism**.

The economic and political consequences of colonialism and neo-colonialism are readily apparent. Drawing on the conflict perspective, sociologist Immanuel Wallerstein views the global economic system as being divided between nations that control wealth and nations from which resources are taken (1974, 1979a, 2000). Through his **world systems analysis**, Wallerstein has described the unequal economic and political relationships in which certain industrialized nations (among them the United States, Japan, and Germany) and their global corporations dominate the core of this system (see Figure 9-3). At the semi-periphery of the system are countries with marginal economic status, such as Israel, Ireland, and South Korea. Wallerstein suggests that the poor developing countries of Asia, Africa, and Latin America are on the periphery of the world economic system. The key to Wallerstein's analysis is the exploitative relationship of core nations toward non-core nations. Core nations and their corporations control and exploit non-core nations' economies. Unlike other nations, the core nations are relatively independent of outside control (Chase-Dunn and Grimes 1995).

The division between core and periphery nations is significant and remarkably stable. A study by the International Monetary Fund (IMF) found little change over the course of the *last 100 years* for the 42 economies that were studied (2000). The only changes were Japan's movement up into the group of core nations and China's movement down toward the margins of the semi-periphery nations. Yet, Immanuel Wallerstein (2000) speculates that the world system as we currently understand it may soon undergo unpredictable changes. The world is becoming increasingly urbanized, a trend that is gradually eliminating the large pools of low-cost workers in rural areas. In the future, core nations will have to find other ways to reduce their labour costs. The exhaustion of land and water resources through clear-cutting and pollution is also driving up the costs of production.

Wallerstein's world systems analysis is the most widely used version of **dependency theory**. According to this theory, even as developing countries make economic advances, they remain weak and subservient to core nations and corporations in an increasingly intertwined global economy. This interdependency allows industrialized nations to continue to exploit developing countries for their own gain. In a sense, dependency theory applies the conflict perspective on a global scale.

In the view of world systems analysis and dependency theory, a growing share of the human and natural resources of developing countries is being redistributed

▶ **FIGURE 9-2**

Gross National Income per Capita

This stylized map reflects the relative population sizes of the world's nations. The colour for each country shows the 2002 estimated gross national income (the total value of goods and services produced by the nation in a given year) per capita. As the map shows, some of the world's most populous countries—such as Nigeria, Bangladesh, and Pakistan—are among the nations with the lowest standard of living, as measured by per capita gross national income.

Key:
GNI per capita in 2004

- $3,000 and below
- $8,000–$19,100
- $3,100–$7,995
- Over $19,200
- No available data

Note: Size based on 2000 population estimates.

Sources: Haub 2005; Weeks 2002:22–23, 2005:32–33.

▶ **FIGURE 9-3**

World Systems Analysis at the Beginning of the Twenty-First Century

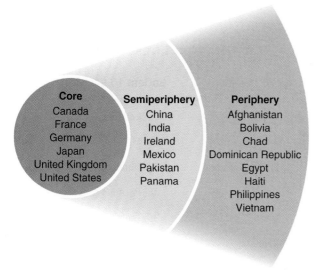

Core
Canada
France
Germany
Japan
United Kingdom
United States

Semiperiphery
China
India
Ireland
Mexico
Pakistan
Panama

Periphery
Afghanistan
Bolivia
Chad
Dominican Republic
Egypt
Haiti
Philippines
Vietnam

Note: Figure shows only a partial listing of countries.

to the core industrialized nations. This redistribution happens in part because developing countries owe huge sums of money to industrialized nations as a result of foreign aid, loans, and trade deficits. The global debt crisis has intensified the Third World dependency begun under colonialism, neo-colonialism, and multinational investment. International financial institutions are pressuring indebted countries to take severe measures to meet their interest payments. The result is that developing nations may be forced to devalue their currencies, freeze workers' wages, increase privatization of industry, and reduce government services and employment.

Closely related to these problems is **globalization**, the worldwide integration of government policies, cultures, social movements, and financial markets through trade and the exchange of ideas. Because world financial markets transcend governance by conventional nation states, international organizations such as the World Bank and the IMF have emerged as major players in the global economy. The function of these institutions, which are heavily funded and influenced by core nations, is to encourage economic trade and development and to ensure the smooth operation of international financial markets. As such, they are seen as promoters of globalization and defenders primarily of the interests of core nations. Critics call attention to a variety of issues, including violations of workers' rights, the destruction of the environment, the loss of cultural identity, and

discrimination against minority groups in periphery nations.

Some observers see globalization and its effects as the natural result of advances in communications technology, particularly the Internet and satellite transmission of the mass media. Others view it more critically, as a process that allows multinational corporations to expand unchecked, as we will see in the next section (Chase-Dunn et al. 2000; Feketekuty 2001; L. Feuer 1989; Pearlstein 2001).

Modernization

Around the world, millions of people are witnessing a revolutionary transformation of their day-to-day life. Contemporary social scientists use the term **modernization** to describe the far-reaching process by which periphery nations move from traditional or less developed institutions to those characteristic of more developed societies.

Wendell Bell, whose definition of modernization we are using, notes that modern societies tend to be urban, literate, and industrial (1981). These societies have sophisticated transportation and media systems. Their families tend to be organized within the nuclear family unit rather than the extended-family model (see Chapter 12). Thus, members of societies that undergo modernization must shift their allegiance from traditional sources of authority, such as parents, elders, and priests, to newer authorities, such as government officials.

Many sociologists are quick to note that terms such as *modernization* and even *development* contain an ethnocentric bias. The unstated assumption behind these terms is that "they" (people living in developing countries) are struggling to become more like "us" (in the core industrialized nations). Viewed from a conflict perspective, these terms perpetuate the dominant ideology of capitalist societies.

The term *modernization* also suggests positive change. Yet, change—if it comes at all—often comes slowly; and when it does, it tends to serve the affluent segments of industrial nations. This truism seems to apply to the spread of the latest electronic technologies to the developing world (see Box 9-1 on page 218).

A similar criticism has been made of **modernization theory**, a functionalist approach which proposes that modernization and development will gradually improve the lives of people in developing nations. According to this theory, even though countries develop at uneven rates, the development of peripheral countries will be assisted by innovations transferred from the industrialized world. Critics of modernization theory, including dependency theorists, counter that any such technology transfer only increases the dominance of core nations over developing countries and facilitates further exploitation. (Table 9-1, on page 219, summarizes the three major approaches to global inequality.)

Sociology in the Global Community
The Global Disconnect

9-1

Bogdan Ghirda, a Romanian, is paid 50 cents an hour to participate in multi-player Internet games like *City of Heroes* and *Star Wars*. He is sitting in for someone in an industrialized country who does not want to spend days ascending to the highest levels of competition in order to compete with players who are already "well armed." This arrangement is not unusual. Services based in the United States can earn hundreds of dollars for recruiting someone in a less developed country, like Ghirda, to represent a single player in an affluent industrial country.

Meanwhile, villagers in Arumugam, India, are beginning to benefit from their new Knowledge Centre. The facility, funded by a non-profit organization, contains five computers that offer Internet access—an amenity unknown until now to thousands of villagers.

These two situations illustrate the technological disconnect between the developing and industrial nations. Around the world, developing nations lag far behind industrial nations in their use of and access to new technologies. The World Economic Forum's Networked Readiness Index (NRI), a ranking of 104 nations, shows the relative preparedness of individuals, businesses, and governments to benefit from information technologies. As the accompanying table shows, the haves of the world—countries like Singapore, the United States, and Japan—are network ready; the have-nots—countries like Ethiopia, Bolivia, and Mozambique—are not.

For developing nations, the consequences of the global disconnect are far more serious than an inability to surf the Net. Thanks to the Internet, multinational organizations can now function as a single global unit, responding instantly in real time, 24 hours a day. This new capability has fostered the emergence of what sociologist Manuel Castells and others call a "global economy." But if large numbers of people—indeed, entire nations—are disconnected from the new global economy, their economic growth will remain slow and the well-being of their people will remain retarded. Those citizens who are educated and skilled will immigrate to other labour markets, deepening the impoverishment of these nations on the periphery.

Network Readiness Index

Top 10 Countries	Bottom 10 Countries
1. Singapore	95. Ecuador
2. Ireland	96. Mozambique
3. Finland	97. Honduras
4. Denmark	98. Paraguay
5. United States	99. Bolivia
6. Sweden	100. Bangladesh
7. Hong Kong	101. Angola
8. Japan	102. Ethiopia
9. Switzerland	103. Nicaragua
10. Canada	104. Chad

Remedying the global disconnect is not a simple matter. To gain access to new technologies, people in developing nations typically must serve the world's industrial giants, as Bogdan Ghirda does. Some may benefit from investment by non-governmental organizations (NGOs), as the villagers in India have. But progress to date has been slow. In 2005, in an effort to accelerate the diffusion of new technologies, the United Nations launched the Digital Solidarity Fund. The hope is that global information technology companies can be persuaded to set aside some of their profits to help developing nations connect to the Internet.

Applying Theory

1. For nations on the periphery, what are some of the social and economic consequences of the global disconnect?
2. According to conflict thinkers, what factors might complicate efforts to remedy the global disconnect in developing nations?

Sources: Castells 2000; *The Economist* 2005c; T. Thompson 2005; United Nations 2005b; World Economic Forum 2005.

Multinational Corporations

Worldwide, corporate giants play a key role in neocolonialism. The term **multinational corporation** refers to any commercial organization that is headquartered in one country but does business throughout the world. Such private trade and lending relationships are not new; merchants have conducted business abroad for hundreds of years, trading gems, spices, garments, and other goods. However, today's multinational giants are not merely buying and selling overseas; they are also *producing* goods all over the world (I. Wallerstein 1974).

Moreover, today's "global factories" (factories throughout the developing world that are run by multinational corporations) may now have the "global office" alongside them. Multinationals based in core countries are beginning to establish reservation services and centres for processing data and insurance claims in the periphery nations. As service industries become a more important part of the international marketplace, many companies are concluding that the low costs of overseas operations more than offset the expense of transmitting information around the world.

Do not underestimate the size of these global corporations. As Table 9-2 shows, the total revenues of multinational businesses are on a par with the total value of goods and services exchanged in *entire nations*. Foreign sales represent an important source of profit for multinational corporations—these sales encourage them to expand into

Protests occur at meetings of the World Trade Organization (WTO) around the world, like this one in Jakarta, Indonesia, in 2007. These protesters charge that multinational corporations dominate world trade policy at the expense of developing nations, and that industrial nations should be held accountable for the economic and financial problems they create.

other countries (in many cases, the developing nations). The economy of the United States is heavily dependent on foreign commerce, much of which is conducted by multinationals. Over one-fourth of all commerce in the United States has to do with either the export of goods to foreign countries or the import of goods from abroad (U.S. Trade Representative 2003).

Functionalist View

Functionalists believe that multinational corporations can actually help the developing nations of the world. They bring jobs and industry to areas where subsistence agriculture once served as the only means of survival.

Table 9-1   Three Approaches to Global Inequality: Sociological Approach, Perspective, and Explanation

Sociological Approach	Sociological Perspective	Sociological Explanation
World systems analysis	Functionalist and conflict	Unequal economic and political relationships maintain sharp divisions among nations.
Dependency theory	Conflict	Industrial nations exploit developing countries through colonialism and multinational corporations.
Modernization theory	Functionalist	Developing countries are moving away from traditional cultures and toward the cultures of industrialized nations.

Multinationals also promote rapid development through the diffusion of inventions and innovations from industrial nations. Viewed from a functionalist perspective, the combination of skilled technology and management provided by multinationals and the relatively cheap labour available in developing nations is ideal for a global enterprise. Multinationals can take maximum advantage of technology while reducing costs and boosting profits.

Through their international ties, multinational corporations also make the nations of the world more interdependent. These ties may prevent certain disputes from reaching the point of serious conflict. A country cannot afford to sever diplomatic relations or engage in warfare with a nation that is the headquarters for its main business suppliers or a key outlet for its exports.

Conflict View

Conflict theorists challenge this favourable evaluation of the impact of multinational corporations. They emphasize that multinationals exploit local workers to maximize profits. Starbucks—the international coffee retailer based in Seattle, Washington—gets much of its coffee from farms in Ethiopia. A recent documentary, entitled *Black Gold*, documented the dismal working conditions of the Ethiopian coffee workers (Kornell 2007).

The influence of multinational corporations abroad can be seen in this street scene from Manila, capital of the Philippines.

Table 9-2 Multinational Corporations Compared to Nations

Rank	Corporation	Revenues ($ millions)	Comparison Nation(s)	Gross Domestic Product ($ millions)
1.	Wal-Mart (USA)	$287 989	Sweden	$301 606
2.	BP-British Petroleum (Britain)	285 059	Saudi Arabia plus UAE	285 708
3.	Exxon Mobil (USA)	270 772	Norway plus Bangladesh	272 768
4.	Royal Dutch/Shell (Britain/Netherlands)	268 690	Poland plus Romania	266 514
5.	General Motors (USA)	193 517	Argentina plus Peru	190 173
6.	DaimlerChrysler (Germany)	176 688	South Africa plus Zimbabwe	177 636
7.	Toyota Motor (Japan)	172 616	Singapore plus Pakistan	174 166
8.	Ford Motor (USA)	172 233	Greece	172 203
9.	General Electric (USA)	152 866	Ireland	153 719
10.	Total (France)	152 609	Portugal	147 899

Notes: Total is an oil, petroleum, and chemical company. UAE refers to United Arab Emirates. Where two nations are listed, the country with the larger GDP is listed first. Revenues as tabulated by *Fortune* are for 2004. GDPs as collected by the World Bank are for 2003.

Sources: For corporate data, *Fortune* 2005:119; for GDP data, World Bank 2005:202D204.

The pool of cheap labour in the developing world prompts multinationals to move factories out of core countries. An added bonus for the multinationals is that the developing world discourages strong trade unions. In industrialized countries, organized labour insists on decent wages and humane working conditions, but governments seeking to attract or keep multinationals may develop a "climate for investment" that includes repressive anti-labour laws that restrict union activity and collective bargaining. If labour's demands become too threatening, the multinational firm will simply move its plant elsewhere, leaving a trail of unemployment behind. Nike, for example, moved its factories from the United States to Korea to Indonesia to Vietnam in search of the lowest labour costs. Conflict theorists conclude that on the whole, multinational corporations have a negative social impact on workers in *both* industrialized and developing nations.

Workers in Canada, the United States, and other core countries are beginning to recognize that their own interests are served by helping to organize workers in developing nations. As long as multinationals can exploit cheap labour abroad, they will be in a strong position to reduce wages and benefits in industrialized countries. With this in mind, in the 1990s, labour unions, religious organizations, campus groups, and other activists mounted public campaigns to pressure companies such as Nike, Starbucks, Reebok, The Gap, and Wal-Mart to improve wages and working conditions in their overseas operations (Global Alliance for Workers and Communities 2003; Gonzalez 2003).

Several sociologists who have surveyed the effects of foreign investment by multinationals conclude that although it may initially contribute to a host nation's wealth, it eventually increases economic inequality within developing nations. This conclusion holds true for both income and ownership of land. The upper and middle classes benefit most from economic expansion, whereas the lower classes are less likely to benefit. As conflict theorists point out, multinationals invest in limited economic sectors and restricted regions of a nation. Although certain sectors of the host nation's economy expand, such as hotels and expensive restaurants, their very expansion appears to retard growth in agriculture and other economic sectors. Moreover, multinational corporations often buy out or force out local entrepreneurs and companies, thereby increasing eco-

nomic and cultural dependence (Chase-Dunn and Grimes 1995; Kerbo 2003; I. Wallerstein 1979b).

Worldwide Poverty

What would a map of the world look like if we drew it to a scale that reflects the number of *poor* people in each country instead of the number of people, as in Figure 9-2 on page 216? As Figure 9-4 shows, when we focus on the poverty level rather than the population, the world looks quite different. Note the huge areas of poverty in Africa and Asia, and the comparatively small areas of affluence in industrialized North America and Europe. Poverty is a worldwide problem that blights the lives of billions of people.

In 2000, the United Nations launched the Millennium Project, whose objective is to eliminate extreme poverty worldwide by the year 2015 (see Box 9-2 on page 223). While 15 years may seem a long time, the challenge is great. Today, almost 3 billion people subsist on $2 a day or less. To accomplish the project's goal, planners estimate that industrial nations must set aside 0.7 percent of their **gross national product**—the value of a nation's goods and services—for aid to developing nations. At the time the Millennium Project was launched, only five countries were giving at that target rate: Denmark, Luxembourg, the Netherlands, Norway, and Sweden. To match their contribution proportionally, the United States would need to multiply its present aid level by 45 (Sachs 2005a).

Most garments carried in clothing stores in Canada are made in developing nations—in Immanuel Wallerstein's terms, nations at the semi-periphery or periphery of the core nations.

▶ **FIGURE 9-4**

Poverty Worldwide

The scale of this map is based on the number of people in each region who are chronically poor. The colours represent the income levels of those who are poorest.

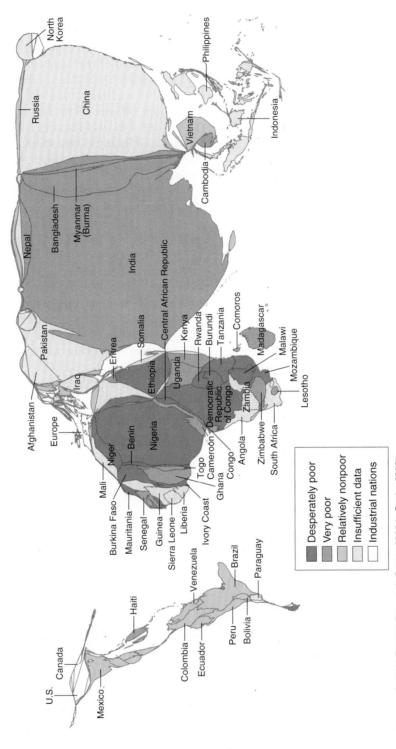

Legend:
- Desperately poor
- Very poor
- Relatively nonpoor
- Insufficient data
- Industrial nations

Source: Chronic Poverty Research Center 2005 in Sachs 2005b.

Sociology in the Global Community

Cutting Poverty Worldwide

9-2

The goal of the United Nations' Millennium Project is to cut the world's poverty level in half by 2015. The project has eight objectives:

1. *Eradicate extreme poverty and hunger.* Poverty rates are falling in many parts of the globe, particularly in Asia. But in sub-Saharan Africa, where the poor are hard-pressed, millions more have sunk deeper into poverty. In 2001, more than 1 billion people worldwide were living on less than $1 a day. These people suffer from chronic hunger. In 2006, an estimated 100 million of the world's children were malnourished—a statistic that has negative implications for their countries' economic progress.

2. *Achieve universal primary education.* While many parts of the developing world are approaching universal school enrollment, in sub-Saharan Africa, less than two-thirds of all children are enrolled in primary school.

3. *Promote gender equality and empower women.* The gender gap in primary school enrollment that has characterized the developing world for so long is slowly closing. However, women still lack equal representation at the highest levels of government. Worldwide, they hold only about 16 percent of all parliamentary seats. Numerous research studies have shown that advances in women's education and governance are critical to improved health and economic development.

4. *Reduce child mortality.* Death rates among children under age 5 are dropping, but not nearly fast enough. About 59 of every 1000 children die in the first year of life in developing nations, compared to just 3 of every 1000 in developed nations. Sadly, evidence indicates that progress toward reducing child mortality has slowed in recent decades.

5. *Improve maternal health.* Each year, more than half a million women die during pregnancy or childbirth. Progress has been made in reducing maternal death rates in some developing regions, but not in countries where the risk of giving birth is highest.

6. *Combat HIV/AIDS, malaria, and other diseases.* AIDS has become the leading cause of premature death in sub-Saharan Africa, where two-thirds of the world's AIDS patients reside. Worldwide, the disease is the fourth most frequent killer. Though new drug treatments can prolong life, there is still no

▶ **FIGURE 9-5**

Half Measures on Poverty

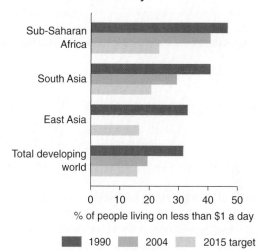

% of people living on less than $1 a day

■ 1990   ■ 2004   ■ 2015 target

Source: *The Economist*, July 7, 2007; based on data from The World Bank and the UN.

cure for this scourge. Moreover, each year, malaria and tuberculosis kill almost as many people as AIDS, severely draining the labour pool in many countries.

7. *Ensure environmental sustainability.* While most countries have publicly committed themselves to the principles of sustainable development (development that can be maintained across generations), sufficient progress has not been made toward reversing the loss of the world's environmental resources through rampant clear-cutting of forests and other forms of environmental destruction. Even so, many developing countries lack the infrastructure needed to support public health. Though access to safe drinking water has increased, half the developing world lacks toilets and other forms of basic sanitation.

8. *Develop a global partnership for development.* The United Nations Millennium Declaration seeks a global social compact in which developing countries pledge to do more to ensure their own development, while developed countries support them through aid, debt relief, and improved trade opportunities. However, despite the much publicized G8 summit (a meeting

of the heads of state of the eight major economies) in Gleneagles, Scotland, in 2005 and the accompanying Live 8 global concerts, the developed nations have fallen far short of the targets they set themselves.

Applying Theory

1. As a conflict thinker, do you think the Millennium Project's objectives are realistic, given the enormity of the obstacles that must be overcome? Why do you think the project's founders gave themselves only 15 years to accomplish their goal?

2. How are the project's eight objectives related to one another? Could some of the objectives be reached successfully without addressing the others? If you were a government planner with the resources to address just one objective, which would you pick, and why?

Sources: Haub 2005; Katel 2005; Sachs 2005a; United Nations 2005a; Weisbrot et al. 2005; World Bank 2006.

> **Think about It**
>
> What happens to society when corporations grow richer than countries and spill across international borders?

Privileged people in industrialized nations tend to assume that the world's poor lack significant assets. Yet, again and again, observers from these countries have been startled to discover how far even a small amount of capital can go. Numerous micro-finance programs, which involve relatively small grants or loans, have encouraged marginalized people to invest not in livestock, which may die, or jewellery, which may be stolen, but in technological improvements such as small cooking stoves. In Indonesia, for example, some 60 000 micro-loans have enabled families who once cooked their food in a pit to purchase stoves. Improvements such as this not only enable people to cook more food at a more consistent temperature; they can become the basis of small-scale home businesses (*The Economist* 2007c).

> **Think about It**
>
> To what degree does the map in Figure 9-4 minimize those countries you have studied or might want to visit? To what degree does it emphasize parts of the world about which you know very little?

When we see all the Coca-Cola and IBM signs going up in developing countries, it is easy to assume that globalization and economic change are effecting cultural change. But that is not always the case, researchers note. Distinctive cultural traditions, such as a particular religious orientation or a nationalistic identity, often persist, and can soften the impact of modernization on a developing nation. Some contemporary sociologists emphasize that both industrialized and developing countries are "modern." Researchers increasingly view modernization as movement along a series of social indicators—among them degree of urbanization, energy use, literacy, political democracy, and use of birth control. Clearly, some of these are subjective indicators; even in industrialized nations, not everyone would agree that wider use of birth control represents an example of progress (Armer and Katsillis 1992; Hedley 1992; Inglehart and Baker 2000).

Current modernization studies generally take a convergence perspective. Using the indicators we just noted, researchers focus on how societies are moving closer together, despite traditional differences. From a conflict perspective, the modernization of developing countries often perpetuates their dependence on and continued exploitation by more industrialized nations. Conflict theorists view such continuing dependence on foreign powers as an example of contemporary neo-colonialism.

☐ HOW DOES STRATIFICATION WITHIN NATIONS COMPARE?

At the same time that the gap between rich and poor nations is widening, so, too, is the gap between rich and poor citizens *within* nations. As we discussed earlier, stratification in developing nations is closely related to their relatively weak and dependent position in the global economy. Local elites work hand in hand with multinational corporations and prosper from such alliances. At the same time, the economic system creates and perpetuates the exploitation of industrial and agricultural workers. That's why foreign investment in developing countries tends to increase economic inequality. As Box 9-3 makes clear, inequality within a society is also evident in industrialized nations such as Japan (Bornschier et al. 1978; Kerbo 2003).

Distribution of Wealth and Income

In at least 26 nations around the world, the most affluent 10 percent of the population receives at least 40 percent of all income. The list includes the African nation of Namibia (the leader, at 65 percent of all income), as well as Colombia, Mexico, Nigeria, and South Africa. Figure 9-6 compares the distribution of income in selected industrialized and developing nations.

To varying degrees, based on the intersection of factors such as race, class, age, disability, sexuality and nationality, women in developing countries may find life especially difficult. Karuna Chanana Ahmed, an anthropologist from India who has studied women in develop-

ing nations, calls women the most exploited of oppressed people (2001). Beginning at birth, women may face sexual discrimination. They may be fed less than male children, denied educational opportunities, and hospitalized only when they are critically ill. As is the case in industrialized countries, inside or outside the home, women's work is frequently devalued. When economies fail, as they did in Asian countries in the late 1990s, women are the first to be laid off from work (J. Anderson and Moore 1993; Kristof 1998).

Only one-third of Pakistan's sexually segregated schools are for women, and one-third of those schools have no buildings. In Kenya and Tanzania, it is illegal for a woman to own a house. In Saudi Arabia, women were prohibited from driving until 2008, when the Saudi Shura Council recommended that they be allowed to drive a vehicle (with a number of stipulations such as obtaining the permission of a male relative) (Assyrian International News Agency 2008). We explore women's status throughout the world more fully in Chapter 11.

▶ **FIGURE 9-6**

Distribution of Income in Nine Nations

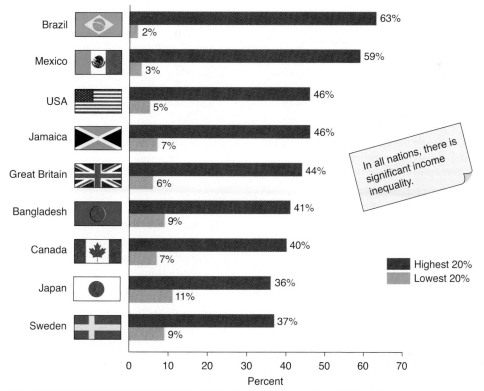

In all nations, there is significant income inequality.

Note: Data are considered comparable although based on statistics covering 1993 to 2001.

Source: World Bank 2005a:72–74.

Sociology in the Global Community

Stratification in Japan

9-3

A tourist visiting Japan may at first experience a bit of culture shock after noticing the degree to which everything in Japanese life is ranked: corporations, universities, even educational programs. These rankings are widely reported and accepted. Moreover, the ratings shape day-to-day social interactions: Japanese find it difficult to sit, talk, or eat together unless the relative rankings of those present have been established, often through the practice of meishi (the exchange of business cards).

The apparent preoccupation with ranking and formality suggests an exceptional degree of stratification. Yet, researchers have determined that Japan's level of income inequality is among the lowest of major industrial societies (see Figure 9-6 on page 225). The pay gap between Japan's top corporate executives and the nation's lowest-paid workers is about 8 to 1; the comparable figure for the United States would be 37 to 1.

One factor that works against inequality is that Japan is rather homogeneous—certainly when compared with the United States—in terms of race, ethnicity, nationality, and language. Japan's population is 98 percent Japanese. Still, there is discrimination against the nation's Chinese and Korean minorities; and the Burakumin, a low-status subculture, encounter extensive prejudice.

Perhaps the most pervasive form of inequality in Japan today is gender discrimination. Overall, women earn only about 65 percent of men's wages. A mere 9 percent of

Japanese managers are female—a ratio that is one of the lowest in the world. Even in developing countries, women are twice as likely to be managers as women in Japan.

In 1985, Japan's parliament—at the time, 97 percent male—passed an equal employment bill that encourages employers to end sex discrimination in hiring, assignment, and promotion policies. However, feminist organizations were dissatisfied because the law lacked strong sanctions. In a landmark ruling issued in late 1996, a Japanese court for the first time held an employer liable for denying promotions due to sex discrimination.

Progress has also been made in terms of public opinion. In 1987, 43 percent of Japanese adults agreed that married women should stay home; by 2000, the proportion had dropped to 25 percent. On the political front, Japanese women have made progress but remain under-represented. In a study of women in government around the world, Japan ranked near the bottom of the countries studied, with only 9 percent of its national legislators female.

Applying Theory

1. How might functionalist thinkers explain the relatively low level of income inequality in Japan?
2. Describe the types of gender discrimination found in Japan. How do you think feminist thinkers might explain why Japanese women occupy such a subordinate social position?

Sources: French 2003a, 2003b; Fujimoto 2004; Goodman and Kashiwagi 2002; Inter-Parliamentary Union 2006; Neary 2003.

Social Mobility

Mobility in Industrial Nations

Studies of intergenerational mobility in industrialized nations have found the following patterns:

1. Substantial similarities exist in the ways that parents' positions in stratification systems are transmitted to their children.
2. As in Canada, mobility opportunities in other nations have been influenced by structural factors, such as labour market changes that lead to the rise or decline of an occupational group within the social hierarchy.

3. Immigration continues to be a significant factor in shaping a society's level of intergenerational mobility (Ganzeboom et al. 1991; Haller et al. 1990; Hauser and Grusky 1988).

Cross-cultural studies suggest that intergenerational mobility has been increasing in recent decades, at least among men. Dutch sociologists Harry Ganzeboom and Ruud Luijkx, joined by sociologist Donald Treiman of the United States, examined surveys of mobility in 35 industrial and developing nations (1989). They found that almost all the countries studied had witnessed increased intergenerational mobility between the 1950s and the 1980s. In particular, they noted a common pattern of movement away from agriculture-based occupations.

Mobility in Developing Nations

Mobility patterns in industrialized countries are usually associated with intergenerational and intragenerational mobility. However, in developing nations, macro-level social and economic changes often overshadow microlevel movement from one occupation to another. For example, there is typically a substantial wage differential between rural and urban areas, which leads to high levels of migration to the cities. Yet, the urban industrial sectors of developing countries generally cannot provide sufficient employment for all those seeking work.

In large developing nations, the most socially significant mobility is the movement out of poverty. This type of mobility is difficult to measure and confirm, however, because economic trends can differ from one area of a country to another. For instance, China's rapid income growth has been accompanied by a growing disparity in income between urban and rural areas, and among different regions. Similarly, in India during the 1990s, poverty declined in urban areas but

In developing countries, people who hope to rise out of poverty often move from the country to the city, where employment prospects are better. The jobs available in industrialized urban areas offer perhaps the best means of upward mobility. This woman works in an electronics factory in Kuala Lumpur, Malaysia.

may have remained static at best in rural areas. Around the world, social mobility is also dramatically influenced by catastrophes such as crop failure and warfare (World Bank 2000).

Gender Differences and Mobility

Only relatively recently have researchers begun to investigate the impact of gender on the mobility patterns of developing nations. Many aspects of the development process—such as rural-to-urban migration just described—may result in the modification or abandonment of traditional cultural practices and even marital systems. The effects on women's social standing and mobility are not necessarily positive. As a country develops and becomes more urban, women's vital role in food production deteriorates, jeopardizing both their autonomy and their material well-being. Moreover, the movement of families to the cities weakens women's ties to relatives who can provide food, financial assistance, and social support.

In the Philippines, however, women have moved to the forefront of the indigenous peoples' struggle to protect their ancestral land from exploitation by outsiders. Having established their right to its rich minerals and forests, members of indigenous groups had begun to feud among themselves over the way in which the land's resources should be developed. Aided by the United Nations Partners in Development Programme, women volunteers established the Pan-Cordillera Women's Network for Peace and Development—a coalition of women's groups dedicated to resolving local disputes. The women mapped boundaries, prepared development plans, and negotiated more than 2000 peace pacts among community members. They have also run in elections, campaigned against social problems, and organized residents to work together for the common good (United Nations Development Programme 2000:87).

Studies of the distribution of wealth and income within various countries, together with cross-cultural research on mobility, consistently reveal stratification based on class, gender, and other factors within a wide range of societies. Clearly, a worldwide view of stratification must include not only the sharp contrast between wealthy and impoverished nations but also the layers of hierarchy *within* industrialized societies and developing countries.

Use Your Sociological Imagination

Imagine a day when the border between Canada and the United States is completely open? What would the two countries' economies be like? What would their societies be like?

Social Policy and Global Inequality
Universal Human Rights

The Issue

Poised at the brink of the third millennium, the world seemed capable of mighty feats, ranging from explorations of distant solar systems to the refinement of tiny genes within human cells. At the same time, though, came constant reminders of how quickly people and their fundamental human rights could be trampled.

Human rights are universal moral rights possessed by all people because they are human. The most important elaboration of human rights appears in the Universal Declaration of Human Rights, adopted by the United Nations in 1948. This declaration prohibits slavery, torture, and degrading punishment; grants everyone the right to a nationality and its culture; affirms freedom of religion and the right to vote; proclaims the right to seek asylum in other countries to escape persecution; and prohibits arbitrary interference with one's privacy and the arbitrary taking of a person's property. It also emphasizes that mothers and children are entitled to special care and assistance.

What steps, if any, can the world community take to ensure the protection of these rights? Is it even possible to agree on what those rights are?

The Setting

The 1990s brought the term *ethnic cleansing* into the world's vocabulary. In the former Yugoslavia, Serbian paramilitary groups attempted to "cleanse" Muslims from parts of Bosnia-Herzegovina, and ethnic Albanians from the province of Kosovo. In both of these regions, hundreds of thousands of people were killed in fighting, while many others were uprooted from their homes. Moreover, reports surfaced of substantial numbers of rapes of Muslim, Croatian, and Kosovar women by Serbian soldiers. In 1996, a United Nations tribunal indicted eight Bosnian Serb military and police officers for rape, thus marking the first time that sexual assault was treated as a war crime under international law (Power 2002). In 2007, the highest U.N. court ruled that Serbia failed to use its influence to prevent the genocide of Bosnian Muslims and punish those who carried out the killings; the court, however, ruled that Serbia—as a nation—did not commit genocide in the 1992–1995 war (*International Herald Tribune* 2007).

In the wake of the terrorist attacks in the United States on September 11, 2001, increased security and surveillance at U.S. airports and border crossings caused some observers to wonder whether human rights were not being jeopardized at home. At the same time, thousands of non-citizens of Arab and South Asian descent were questioned for no other reason than their ethnic and religious backgrounds. In the case of the Syrian-born Canadian Maher Arar, the consequences were much graver. While travelling home to Canada through the United States in 2002, Arar was detained and shipped to Syria where he was tortured and imprisoned for almost a year. The Canadian government co-operated with the U.S. authorities in supplying information—which it attempted to keep secret—leading to Arar's detainment. In 2006, an inquiry determined that Arar was an innocent citizen; shortly after, the Canadian government made an official apology and paid Arar $10.9 million in compensation plus legal fees. The United States government has made no such apology. Other North Americans have been placed in custody, sometimes without access to legal assistance. As the so-called war on terror moved overseas, human-rights concerns escalated. In 2005, the United Nations' secretary-general, Kofi Annan, criticized the United States and Britain for equating people who were speaking out against the presence of foreign troops in Afghanistan and Iraq with terrorists. For the foreseeable future, it seems, the United States and other Western countries will walk a delicate tightrope between human rights and the need to take national security measures (Parker 2004; Steele 2005).

Sociological Insights

By its very name, the Universal Declaration of Human Rights emphasizes that such rights should be universal. Even so, cultural relativism encourages understanding and respect for the distinctive norms, values, and customs of each culture. In some situations, conflicts arise between human rights standards and local social practices that rest on alternative views of human dignity. For example, is India's caste system an inherent violation of human rights? What about the many cultures of the world that view the subordinate status of women as an essential element in their traditions? Should human rights be interpreted differently in various world locations?

P. 64

In 2007, Canada's federal government reiterated its support of the United Nations convention on the elimination of all discrimination against women. Currently, the principle of gender equality is systematically integrated into Canada's development programs in countries around the world. The human-rights watchdog, Amnesty International, states, however, that Canada must also be mindful of domestic human-rights concerns, asserting that "there is no corner of the planet where women are safe from the threat or reality of violence. In the home, at work, on the street, in the midst of war, violence stalks women everywhere from Sudan to Colombia, India to Russia, Iran to Canada" (Amnesty International Canada 2005:2). In the late 1990s, certain Asian and African nations were reviving arguments about cultural relativism in an attempt to block sanctions by the United Nations Human Rights Commission. For example, female genital mutilation, a practice that is common in more than 30 countries around the world, has been condemned in Western nations as a human-rights abuse. This controversial practice often involves removal of the clitoris, in the belief that its excision will inhibit a young woman's sex drive, making her chaste and, thus, more desirable to her future husband. Though some countries have passed laws against the practice, these laws have largely gone unenforced. Immigrants from countries where genital mutilation is common often insist that their daughters undergo the procedure so they'll be protected from Western cultural norms that allow premarital sex. In this context, how does one define human rights (*Religious Tolerance* 2005)?

It is not often that a nation makes a bold statement related solely to human rights. Policy makers, including those in Canada and the United States, more frequently look at human-rights issues from an economic perspective. Function-alists would point out how much more quickly we become embroiled in "human-rights" concerns when oil is at stake, as in the Middle East, or when military alliances come into play, as in Europe. Governments ratify human-rights laws but resist independent efforts to enforce them within their own borders (Hafner-Burton and Tsutsui 2005).

Because international human rights can be highly contextual, they may also be difficult to enforce within the formal requirements of a country's legal process. Despite the apparent torture exposed in digital camera shots from Iraq and Afghanistan, for example, numerous investigations by the British and U.S. military have been inconclusive. Either because of the tenets of military necessity in wartime or because of an inability to locate the victims, many apparent violations have gone unpunished (Klug 2005).

Policy Initiatives

Human rights issues come wrapped up in international diplomacy. For that reason, many national policy makers hesitate to interfere in human-rights issues, especially if they conflict with what are regarded as more

A Chechen boy who witnessed his father's killing stands outside a refugee camp in Russia, where he and his brother are receiving mental health care from Médecins sans Frontières. Civilian assassinations are one of the many violations of human rights that typically occur during wartime.

pressing national concerns. Stepping up to fill the gap are international organizations such as the United Nations and non-governmental organizations (NGOs) like Médecins sans Frontières and Amnesty International. Most initiatives come from these international bodies.

Médecins sans Frontières (Doctors without Borders), the world's largest independent emergency medical-aid organization, won the 1999 Nobel Peace Prize for its work in countries worldwide. Founded in 1971 and based in Paris, the organization has 5000 doctors and nurses working in 80 countries. "Our intention is to highlight current upheavals, to bear witness to foreign tragedies and reflect on the principles of humanitarian aid," explains Dr. Rony Brauman, the organization's former president (Spielmann 1992:12; also see Daley 1999).

In recent years, awareness has been growing of lesbian and gay rights as an aspect of universal human rights. In 1994, Amnesty International published a pioneering report in which it acknowledged that "[lesbians and gay men] in many parts of the world live in constant fear of government persecution" (1994:2). The report examined abuses in Brazil, Greece, Mexico, Iran, the United States, and other countries, including cases of torture, imprisonment,

and extrajudicial execution. Later in 1994, the U.S. government issued an order that would allow lesbians and gay men to seek political asylum in the United States if they could prove they had suffered government persecution in their home countries solely because of their sexual orientation (Johnston 1994).

Ethnic cleansing in the former Yugoslavia, human-rights violations in Iraq and Afghanistan, increased surveillance in the name of counter-terrorism, violence against women inside and outside the family, governmental torture of lesbians and gay men—all these are vivid reminders that social inequality today can have life-and-death consequences. Universal human rights remain an ideal, not a reality.

Applying Theory

1. Why do definitions of *human rights* vary?
2. How might conflict and functionalist thinkers differ in their view of human-rights violations in time of war? in the aftermath of serious terrorist attacks such as those of September 11, 2001?
3. How might feminist thinkers assess Canada's respect for human rights, both at home and abroad?

CHAPTER RESOURCES

Summary

What is the Global Divide?
- Worldwide, stratification can be seen both in the gap between rich and poor nations and in the inequality within countries. In this chapter, we examined the global divide and stratification within the world economic system; the impact of **globalization** (p. 217), **modernization** (p. 217), and **multinational corporations** (p. 219) on developing countries; and the distribution of wealth and income in various nations.

- Developing nations account for most of the world's population and most of its births, but they also bear the burden of most of its poverty, disease, and childhood deaths.

What Forms does Global Inequality Take?
- Former colonized nations are kept in a subservient position, subject to foreign domination, through the process of **neo-colonialism** (p. 215).
- Drawing on the conflict perspective, sociologist Immanuel Wallerstein's **world systems analysis**

(p. 215) views the global economic system as one divided between nations that control wealth (core nations) and those from which capital is taken (periphery nations).

- According to **dependency theory** (p. 215), even as developing countries make economic advances, they remain weak and subservient to core nations and corporations in an increasingly integrated global economy.
- **Globalization** (p. 217) is a controversial trend that critics blame for contributing to the cultural domination of periphery nations by core nations.
- **Multinational corporations** (p. 219) bring jobs and industry to developing nations, but they also tend to exploit workers in order to maximize profits.

- Poverty is a worldwide problem that blights the lives of billions of people. In 2000, the United Nations launched the Millennium Project. Its goal is to eliminate extreme poverty worldwide by 2015.
- Many sociologists are quick to note that terms such as *modernization* and even *development* contain an ethnocentric bias.
- According to **modernization theory** (p. 217), development in periphery countries will be assisted by innovations transferred from the industrialized world.

How does Stratification within Nations Compare?
- The gap between rich and poor nations is widening, as is the gap between rich and poor citizens *within* nations.

Critical Thinking Questions

1. How have multinational corporations and the trend toward globalization affected you, your family, and your community? List both the pros and the cons. Have the benefits outweighed the drawbacks?
2. Imagine that you have the opportunity to spend a year in Mexico studying inequality in that nation. How would you draw on specific research designs (surveys, observation, experiments, existing sources) to better understand and document stratification in Mexico?
3. How active should the Canadian government be in addressing violations of human rights in other countries? At what point, if any, does concern for human rights turn into ethnocentrism through failure to respect the distinctive norms, values, and customs of another culture?

Key Terms

Colonialism   The maintenance of political, social, economic, and cultural dominance over a people by a foreign power for an extended period. (p. 215)

Dependency theory   An approach which contends that industrialized nations continue to exploit developing countries for their own gain. (p. 215)

Globalization   The worldwide integration of government policies, cultures, social movements, and financial markets through trade and the exchange of ideas. (p. 217)

Gross national product (GNP)   The value of a nation's goods and services. (p. 221)

Human rights   Universal moral rights possessed by all people because they are human. (p. 228)

Modernization   The far-reaching process by which periphery nations move from traditional or less-developed institutions to those characteristic of more developed societies. (p. 217)

Modernization theory   A functionalist approach that proposes that modernization and development will gradually improve the lives of people in developing nations. (p. 217)

Multinational corporation   A commercial organization that is headquartered in one country but does business throughout the world. (p. 219)

Neo-colonialism   Continuing dependence of former colonies on more industrialized foreign countries, including those that are former colonial masters. (p. 215)

World systems analysis   A view of the global economic system as one divided among certain industrialized nations that control wealth and developing countries that are controlled and exploited. (p. 215)

Additional Readings

Carroll, William. 2003. *Corporate Power in a Globalizing World.* Don Mills, ON: Oxford University Press. This book offers a systematic analysis of the Canadian corporate network in the global context, arguing that it constitutes the leading edge of the ruling class.

Seear, Michael. 2007. *An Introduction to International Health.* Toronto: CSPI/WS. In this book, Seear looks at the history of overseas aid and the determinants of health, poverty, and developing-world debt and malnutrition; he examines solutions as well.

Thobani, Sunera, and Tineke Hellwig, eds. 2006. *Asian Women: Interconnections.* Toronto: CSPI/WP. A collection of papers placing Asian women at the centre of the discussion, and examining the relationship of Asia to the West and northern countries.

Van der Gaag, Nikki. 2004. *The No-Nonsense Guide to Women's Rights.* Toronto: New Internationalist Publications. In this book, the author places poverty in a global context, focusing on those who suffer the most: women and children.

 Online Learning Centre

Visit the *Sociology: A Brief Introduction* Online Learning Centre at www.mcgrawhill.ca/olc/schaefer to access quizzes, interactive exercises, video clips, and other research and study tools related to this chapter.

RACIAL AND ETHNIC INEQUALITY

Racism is a reality for many people in our society. *Racism. Stop It!*, a national video contest, is part of the Canadian government's campaign against racial discrimination. It encourages Canada's youth to express in video their thoughts on eliminating racism.

☐ **What are Minority, Racial, and Ethnic Groups?**

☐ **What are Prejudice and Discrimination?**

☐ **How are Race and Ethnicity Studied?**

☐ **What are Some Patterns of Inter-group Relations?**

☐ **What are Some Groups that Make Up Canada's Multi-ethnic Character?**

Boxes

SOCIOLOGY IN THE GLOBAL COMMUNITY: Cultural Survival in Brazil

RESEARCH IN ACTION: Racism and the Mainstream Media

SOCIAL POLICY AND RACE AND ETHNICITY: Global Immigration et's be clear: There is also a New Canada out there. If Canadians can't see it themselves, they certainly pay attention when others see it on our behalf. Thus, *The Economist* magazine captured our attention in the fall of 2003 when it put on its cover a moose in sunglasses under the headline, "Canada's new spirit," and went on to laud our tolerance and cultural diversity and describe our major cities as vibrant, cosmopolitan places. . .

Our embrace of multiculturalism presents the most obvious manifestation of the New Canada. But it goes well beyond the mere fact of scores of different ethnic groups coexisting peacefully in our global cities, however notable an achievement that may represent in international terms.

Our schools ring out with the sound of different tongues, giving our children an early and everlasting lesson in the very Canadian balance of individual expression and social peace. The New Canada of which we speak flows from the long cherished frontier value of freedom. The New Canada is about the freedom to be who you are and still belong to the larger group. . . .

Immigration died down during the Depression and the Second World War. Then, starting in the postwar period, Canada attracted a wave of skilled and semi-skilled blue-collar workers from southern Europe. Many

of the children of this second wave sit proudly today in our legislatures and Parliament.

And then the third wave—the one that has so demonstrably changed the look of our cities over the past generation. Chinese, Sri Lankans, Filipinos, Sikhs, Ismailis, West Indians, North and sub-Saharan Africans—an influx that has changed our capacities but strengthened our fabric. Thanks to the education system and the media, integration occurs far faster than ever before—usually within the same generation for younger Canadians. As Queen's University professor Matthew Mendelsohn, a consultant on the New Canada series, points out, in France, Britain, Italy, the United States and elsewhere, anywhere from 30 to 50 percent of people say that relations between ethnic groups are a problem. In Canada, just 12 percent think so.

This process of ethnic diversification is inevitably changing our world outlook—making us less parochial in all our dealings. When you see a *pure laine* Québécois boy strolling down Rue St. Denis with his Haitian-Canadian girlfriend and their Moroccan-Canadian schoolmates, it is hard to imagine them being overly agitated about the hanging of Louis Riel. They are connected to a vibrant world, not stuck in an historical rant.

☐ *(Anderssen, Valpy, et al, 2004)*

This excerpt from the book by Erin Anderssen, Michael Valpy, and others depicts a "New Canada" characterized as tolerant, peaceful, and culturally diverse, with vibrant cosmopolitan cities. It is a Canada, according to the authors, where people, particularly those under the age of 30, do not consider similar ethnocultural background an important consideration in choosing a mate.

In Canada, 12 percent of Canadians say that relations among ethnic groups are a problem, in sharp contrast to such countries as France, Britain, Italy, and the United States, where 30 to 50 percent of the people say that relations among ethnic groups are a problem. Despite this seemingly glowing view of ethnic diversity in Canada, patterns of inequality exist and persist, whereby some groups are systematically subjugated by the dominant groups, restricting their access to opportunity and upward mobility.

Today, thousands of people who are members of racial and ethnic minorities continue to experience the often bitter contrast between the Canadian ideal of multiculturalism and the grim realities of poverty, prejudice, and discrimination. Class, gender, and the social definitions of race and ethnicity intersect to produce systems of inequality, not only in this country but throughout the world. High incomes, a good command of French or English, and hard-earned professional credentials do not always override racial and ethnic stereotypes or protect those who fit them from the sting of racism.

What is prejudice, and how is it institutionalized in the form of discrimination? In what ways have race and ethnicity affected the experience of immigrants from other countries? What are the fastest-growing minority groups in Canada today? In this chapter, we focus on the meaning of race and ethnicity. We begin by identifying the basic characteristics of a minority group and distinguishing between racial groups and ethnic groups. Then, we examine the dynamics of prejudice and discrimination. After considering the functionalist, conflict, feminist, and interactionist perspectives on race and ethnicity, we look at patterns of inter-group relations, particularly in Canada. Finally, in the social policy section, we explore issues related to immigration worldwide.

Use Your Sociological Imagination

Does Anderssen and Valpy's view of Canada match your own experience or situation? Do you think the statistic that only 12 percent of Canadians say that relations among ethnic groups are a problem masks the everyday experiences of many Canadians who face discrimination because of their skin colour or ethnocultural identity?

☐ WHAT ARE MINORITY, RACIAL, AND ETHNIC GROUPS?

Categories of people can often be thought of as "racial" and ethnic groups. The term **racial group** describes a category that is set apart and treated differently from others because of perceived physical differences. White, black, and Asian Canadians are all perceived to be racial groups in Canada. It is the culture of a particular society, however, that constructs and attaches social significance to these perceived differences, as we will see later. Unlike racialized groups, an **ethnic group** is set apart from others primarily because of its national origin or distinctive cultural patterns. In Canada, Italian Canadians, Jewish people, and Polish Canadians are all categorized as ethnic groups (even though Jewishness isn't, by definition, an ethnicity). Both types of groups are considered to be minority groups by sociologists, as the next section shows.

Minority Groups

A numerical minority is any group that makes up less than half of some larger population. The population of Canada includes thousands of numerical minorities, including television actors, green-eyed people, tax lawyers, and snowboarders. However, these numerical minorities are not considered to be minorities in the sociological sense; in fact, the number of people in a group does not necessarily determine its status as a social minority (or a dominant group). When sociologists define a minority group, they are primarily concerned with the economic and political power, or powerlessness, of that group. A **minority group** is a subordinate group whose members have significantly less control or power over their own lives than the members of a dominant or majority group have over their own.

In Canada, the term **visible minority** is used to refer to those Canadians who are non-white or are identified as being physically different from white Canadians of European descent, who compose the dominant group. Visible minorities, according to the official government definition, include such groups as South Asians, Japanese, Arabs, Latin Americans, and Chinese. Aboriginal people form a distinct and unique minority group in Canada; but for government and statistical purposes, they are not categorized as a minority group. Aboriginal people, however, have been and continue to be treated as a visible minority group, experiencing generations of systemic brutalization by whites of European descent—most notably via the residential school system. The cruel treatment that Aboriginal people have received from the dominant ethnic groups will be explained more fully later in this chapter.

Sociologists have identified five basic properties of a minority group: unequal treatment, physical or cultural traits, ascribed status, solidarity, and in-group marriage (Wagley and Harris 1958):

1. Members of a minority group experience unequal treatment as compared with members of a dominant group. For example, the management of an apartment complex may refuse to rent to blacks, Asians, or Jews. Social inequality may be created or maintained by prejudice, discrimination, segregation, or even extermination.

2. Members of a minority group share physical or cultural characteristics that distinguish them from the dominant group. Each society arbitrarily decides which characteristics are most important in defining the groups.

3. Membership in a minority group (or in a dominant group, for that matter) is not voluntary; people are born into the group. Thus, race and ethnicity are considered *ascribed* statuses. ◄ P. 102

4. Minority group members have a strong sense of group solidarity. William Graham Sumner, writing in 1906, noted that people make distinctions between members of their own group (the in-group) and everyone else (the out-group). When a group is the object of long-term prejudice and discrimination, the feeling of "us versus them" can and often does become extremely intense. ◄ P. 106

5. Members of a minority generally marry others from the same group. A member of a dominant group is often unwilling to marry into a supposedly inferior minority. In addition, the minority group's sense of solidarity encourages marriages within the group and discourages marriages to outsiders.

Race

As explained earlier, the term *racial group* refers to those minorities (and the corresponding dominant groups) set apart from others by what are perceived to be obvious physical differences. But what is an "obvious" physical difference? Each society determines which differences are important while ignoring other characteristics that could serve as a basis for social differentiation. In Canada, we see differences in both skin colour and hair colour. Yet, people learn informally that differences in skin colour have a dramatic social and political meaning, while differences in hair colour do not.

When observing skin colour, people in Canada tend to lump others rather casually into such categories as "black," "brown," "white," and "Asian." More subtle differences in skin colour often go unnoticed. However, this is not the case in some other societies. Many nations of Central America and South America have colour gradients distinguishing people on a continuum from light to dark skin colour. Brazil has approximately 40 colour groupings, while in other countries people may be described as "Mestizo Hondurans," "Mulatto Colombians," or "African Panamanians." What people see as obvious differences, then, are subject to each society's social definitions.

Three groups make up the largest visible minorities in Canada: those who identified themselves in the 2006 census as South Asian, Chinese, and black. Figure 10-1 provides information about where the vast majority of immigrants settle—Montreal, Vancouver, and Toronto. A high and growing number of immigrants to those cities are members of visible minority groups.

Biological Significance of Race

Viewed from a biological perspective, the term *race* would refer to a genetically isolated group with distinctive gene frequencies. But it is impossible to scientifically define or identify such a group. Contrary to popular belief, there are no "pure races." Nor are there physical traits—whether skin colour or baldness—that can be used to describe one group to the exclusion of all others. If scientists examine a smear of human blood under a microscope, they cannot tell whether it came from a Chinese, Aboriginal, or black Canadian. There is, in fact, more genetic variation *within* races than across them.

Migration, exploration, and invasion have led to the mixing of genetic material from people around the world. Research indicates that the percentage of North American blacks with white ancestry ranges from 20 percent to as much as 75 percent. Such statistics challenge the view that we can accurately categorize, for example, "black" and "white." Therefore, the belief that we are able to neatly categorize individuals according to race is a myth.

Some people would like to find biological explanations to help social scientists understand why certain peoples of the world have come to dominate others (see the discussion of sociobiology in Chapter 4). Given the absence of pure racial groups, there can be no satisfactory biological answers for such social and political questions. ◄ P. 75

▶ **FIGURE 10-1**

Share of Immigrants 10 Years or Less in Canada: Montreal, Toronto, and Vancouver, 1981, 1991, 2001, 2006

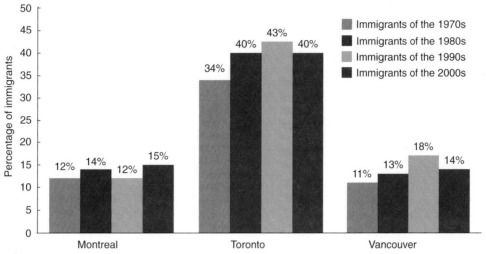

Legend:
■ Immigrants of the 1970s
■ Immigrants of the 1980s
■ Immigrants of the 1990s
■ Immigrants of the 2000s

Source: Statistics Canada 2003d, 2007g.

What Is the Social Construction of Race?

In the southern part of the United States, it was known as the "one-drop rule." If a person had even a single drop of "black blood," that person was defined and viewed as black, even if he or she *appeared* to be white. Clearly, race had social significance in that region, enough so that white legislators established official standards about who was "black" and "white."

The one-drop rule was a vivid example of **racialization**—the social processes by which people come to define a group as a "race" based in part on physical characteristics, but also on historical, cultural, and economic factors.

According to the 2006 census, approximately 13 million or 40 percent of Canadians reported having multiple ethnic origins. With rates of intermarriage increasing in Canada, so, too, is the multiplicity of backgrounds. In 2006, over 5 million Canadians—more than 16 percent—defined themselves as members of a visible minority group.

A dominant or majority group has the power not only to define itself legally but also to define a society's values. Sociologist William I. Thomas (1923), an early critic of theories of racial and gender differences, saw that the "definition of the situation" could mould the personality of the individual. To put it another way, Thomas, writing from the interactionist perspective, observed that people respond not only to the objective features of a situation or person but also to the *meaning* that situation or person has for them. Thus, we can create false images

Children who have one black parent are categorized as "black," even though they may appear to be "white." This is an example of how race is socially constructed.

or stereotypes that become real in their consequences. **Stereotypes** are unreliable generalizations about all members of a group that do not recognize individual differences within the group.

In the last 30 years, critics have pointed out the power of the mass media to perpetuate false racial and ethnic stereotypes. Television is a prime example: Almost all the leading dramatic roles are cast as whites, even in urban-based programs. Blacks tend to be featured mainly in crime-based dramas.

Use Your Sociological Imagination

Count the various ethnicities portrayed in Canadian television programming between the hours of 8 and 11 p.m. Using a TV remote control, how quickly do you think you could find a television show in which all the characters share your own background? What about a show in which all the characters share a different background from your own — how quickly could you find one of those?

Ethnicity

An ethnic group, unlike a racial group, is set apart from others because of its national origin or distinctive cultural patterns. Among the ethnic groups in Canada are people with a French-speaking background, which includes people from Tracadie, New Brunswick; Paris, France; Coderre, Saskatchewan; and Quebec City, Quebec. Other ethnic groups in Canada include Japanese, Irish, Italian, and Norwegian Canadians. Although these groupings are convenient, they serve to obscure differences *within* these ethnic categories as well as to overlook the mixed ancestry of so many ethnic people in Canada.

The Canadian census, however, does address this problem, to some extent, by providing Canadians with the option of giving single or multiple responses to the question of ethnic origin (see Table 10-1). For example, the 2006 census reported that 231 110 Canadians identified themselves as being of Jamaican origin, with 134 320 declaring this as their sole response and 96 785 declaring this as one of multiple responses.

The distinction between racial and ethnic minorities is not always clear-cut. Many members of racial minorities, such as Asian Canadians, may have significant cultural differences from other groups. At the same time, certain ethnic minorities, such as Indo-Canadians, may have physical differences that are perceived to set them apart from other residents of Canada.

Despite categorization problems, sociologists continue to feel that the distinction between racial groups and ethnic groups is socially significant. In most societies, including Canada, physical differences tend to be more visible than ethnic differences. Partly as a result of this fact, racialized stratification is more resistant to change than is stratification along ethnic lines. Members of an ethnic minority sometimes can become, over time, indistinguishable from the majority—although this process may take generations and may never include all members of the group. By contrast, members of a racialized minority find it much more difficult to blend in with the larger society and to gain acceptance from the majority. Michael Ornstein, of York University in Toronto, found, after studying the ethno-racial groups of Toronto from 1971 to 2001, that poverty is highly racialized. In his 2006 report, Ornstein found that the economic gap between European and non-European groups has been increasing over the past 30 years; he states that "as the population from non-European groups in Canada has increased from about four percent in 1971 to about 40 percent in 2001, the racialization of poverty has increased" (York University 2006).

□ WHAT ARE PREJUDICE AND DISCRIMINATION?

In recent years, university campuses across North America have been the scene of bias-related incidents. Student-run newspapers and radio stations have ridiculed racial and ethnic minorities; threatening literature has been stuffed under the doors of minority students; graffiti endorsing the views of white supremacist organizations, such as the Ku Klux Klan, have been scrawled on university walls. In some cases, there have even been violent clashes between groups of white and black students (Bunzel 1992; R. Schaefer 2004).

In April 2004, the United Talmud Torahs elementary school—a Jewish school in Montreal—was firebombed, destroying the school's library and adjoining offices and classrooms. The attack on the school was accompanied by a rash of anti-Semitic actions around the world. Since then, Jewish schools in Canada have spent millions of dollars implementing tighter security measures in an attempt to ensure the safety of their students and staff.

Prejudice

Prejudice is a negative attitude toward an entire category of people, often an ethnic or a racial minority. If you resent your roommate because he or she is sloppy, you are not necessarily guilty of prejudice. However, if you immediately stereotype your roommate on the basis of such characteristics as race, ethnicity, or religion, that is a form of prejudice. Prejudice tends to perpetuate false definitions of individuals and groups.

Table 10-1 Population by Selected Ethnic Origins, Canada, 2006 Census

Ethnic Origins	Total Responses	Single Responses	Multiple Responses
Total Population	31 241 030	18 319 580	12 921 445
Canadian	10 066 290	5 748 725	4 317 570
English	6 570 015	1 367 125	5 202 890
French	4 941 210	1 230 535	3 710 675
Scottish	4 719 850	568 515	4 151 340
Irish	4 354 155	491 030	3 863 125
German	3 179 425	670 640	2 508 785
Italian	1 445 335	741 045	704 285
Chinese	1 346 510	1 135 365	211 145
North American Indian	1 253 615	512 150	741 470
Ukrainian	1 209 085	300 590	908 495
Dutch (Netherlands)	1 035 965	303 400	732 560
Polish	984 565	269 375	715 190
East Indian	962 665	780 175	182 495
Russian	500 600	98 245	402 355
Welsh	440 965	27 115	413 855
Filipino	436 190	321 390	114 800
Norwegian	432 515	44 790	387 725
Portuguese	410 850	262 230	148 625
Métis	409 065	77 295	331 770
Swedish	334 765	28 445	306 325
Spanish	325 730	67 475	258 255
American	316 350	28 785	287 565
Hungarian (Magyar)	315 510	88 685	226 820
Jewish	315 120	134 045	181 070
Greek	242 685	145 250	97 435
Jamaican	231 110	134 320	96 785
Danish	200 035	33 770	166 265
Austrian	194 255	27 060	167 195
Romanian	192 170	79 650	112 515
Vietnamese	180 125	136 445	43 685
Belgian	168 910	33 670	135 240
Lebanese	165 150	103 855	61 295
Québécois	146 585	96 835	49 750
Korean	146 550	137 790	8 755
Swiss	137 775	25 180	112 800
Finnish	131 040	30 195	100 850
Pakistani	124 730	89 605	35 125

Source: Statistics Canada 2008a.

Sometimes, prejudice can result from ethnocentrism—the tendency to assume that your own culture and way of life represent the norm or are superior to all others.

Ethnocentric people judge other cultures by the standards of their own group, which leads quite easily ◄ P.64 to prejudice against cultures viewed as inferior.

One important and widespread form of prejudice is **racism**, the belief that one group is supreme and all others are innately inferior. When racism prevails in a society, members of minority groups generally experience prejudice, discrimination, and exploitation.

The activity level of organized hate groups appears to be increasing, both in reality and in virtual reality. Although only a few hundred such groups may exist, thousands of Web sites advocate racial hatred on the Internet. The technology of the Internet has allowed race-hate groups to expand far beyond their regional bases to reach millions (Marriott 2004).

Discriminatory Behaviour

Prejudice often leads to **discrimination**, the denial of opportunities and equal rights to individuals and groups based on some type of arbitrary bias. For example, perhaps a white corporate chief executive officer (CEO) with a prejudice against Indo-Canadians has to fill an executive position. The most qualified candidate for the job is of Indian descent. If the CEO refuses to hire this candidate and instead selects a less-qualified white person, he or she is engaging in an act of racial discrimination.

Prejudiced *attitudes* should not be equated with discriminatory *behaviour*. Although the two are generally related, they are not identical, and either condition can be present without the other. A prejudiced person does not always act on his or her biases. The white CEO, for example, might choose—despite his or her attitude—to hire the Indo-Canadian. This would be prejudice without discrimination. However, a white corporate CEO with a completely respectful view of Indo-Canadians might refuse to hire someone of Indian descent for executive posts out of fear that biased clients would take their business elsewhere. In this case, the CEO's action would constitute discrimination without prejudice.

Discrimination persists even for the most educated and qualified minority group members from the best family backgrounds. Despite their talents and experiences, they sometimes encounter attitudinal or organizational bias that prevents them from reaching their full potential. The term **glass ceiling** refers to an invisible barrier that blocks the promotion of a qualified individual in a work environment because of the individual's gender, race, or ethnicity (R. Schaefer 2006; Yamagata et al. 1997).

Glass ceilings continue to block women and minority-group men from top management positions in government, education, politics, and business. Even in *Fortune* magazine's 2002 listing of the most diversified corporations, white men held more than 80 percent of both the board of directors seats and of the top 50 paid positions in companies. The existence of this glass ceiling results principally from the fears and prejudices of many middle- and upper-level white male managers, who believe that the inclusion of women and minority group men in management circles will threaten their own prospects for advancement (Hickman 2002).

The Privileges of the Dominant

One aspect of discrimination that is often overlooked is the privilege dominant groups enjoy at the expense of others. For instance, there is often a tendency to focus more on the difficulty many women have in getting ahead at work, juggling paid and unpaid work at home, than on the ease with which many men avoid domestic work and manage to make their way in the world. Similarly, there may be more of a focus on discrimination against racial and ethnic minorities than on the advantages that the dominant groups enjoy. Indeed, most white people rarely think about their "whiteness," taking their status for granted. But sociologists and other social scientists are becoming increasingly interested in what it means to be "white," as white privilege is the other side of the proverbial coin of racial discrimination.

The feminist scholar Peggy McIntosh became interested in white privilege after noticing that most men would not acknowledge that there were privileges attached to being male—even if they would agree that being female had its disadvantages (1988). McIntosh wondered if white people suffer from a similar blind spot regarding their own racial privilege. Intrigued, McIntosh began to list all the ways in which she benefited from her whiteness. She soon realized that the list of unspoken advantages was long and significant.

McIntosh found that as a white person, she rarely needed to step out of her comfort zone, no matter where she went. If she wished to, she could spend most of her time with people of her own race. She could find a good place to live in a pleasant neighbourhood, buy the foods she liked to eat from almost any grocery store, and get her hair styled in almost any salon. She could attend a public meeting without feeling that she did not belong, that she was different from everyone else.

McIntosh discovered, too, that her skin colour opened doors for her. She could cash cheques and use credit cards without suspicion, browse through stores without being shadowed by security guards. She could be seated without difficulty in a restaurant. If McIntosh asked to see the manager of an establishment, she could assume he or she would be of her own race. If she needed help from a doctor or a lawyer, she could get it. It became evident that McIntosh's whiteness made her job of parenting easier. She did not need to worry about protecting her children from people who didn't like them. She could be sure that their textbooks would show pictures of people who looked like them, and that their history texts would describe white people's achievements. McIntosh knew that the television programs they watched would include white characters.

Finally, McIntosh had to admit that others did not constantly evaluate her in racial terms. When she appeared in public, she didn't need to worry that her clothing or behaviour might reflect poorly on white people. If she was recognized for an achievement, it was seen as her achievement, not that of an entire race. And no one ever assumed that the personal opinions she voiced should be those of all white people. Because Peggy McIntosh blended in with the people around her, she wasn't always onstage.

These are not all the privileges white people take for granted in North American life. White job seekers enjoy tremendous advantages over non-whites who face discrimination when it comes to employment opportunities (Pager and Quillian 2005; Ornstein 2006).

Whiteness confers privilege. White customers have different experiences from black customers. They are less likely than blacks to have their cheques or credit cards refused, and they are less likely to be viewed with suspicion by security guards.

Institutional Discrimination

Discrimination is practised not only by individuals in one-to-one encounters but also by institutions in their daily operations. Social scientists are particularly concerned with the ways in which structural factors, such as employment, housing, health care, and government operations, maintain the social significance of race and ethnicity. **Institutional discrimination** refers to the denial of opportunities and equal rights to individuals and groups that results from the normal operations of a society. This kind of discrimination consistently affects certain racial and ethnic groups more than others.

The following are examples of institutional discrimination:

- rules requiring that only English be spoken at a place of work, even when it is not a business necessity to restrict the use of other languages
- preferences shown by law schools and medical schools in the admission of children of wealthy and influential alumni, nearly all of whom are not members of minorities
- restrictive employment-leave policies, coupled with prohibitions on part-time work, that make it difficult for the heads of single-parent families (most of whom are women) to obtain and keep jobs

Racial or ethnic profiling, which is the use of the social construct of "race" as a consideration in suspect profiling in law enforcement and national security practices, is a form of institutional discrimination. A study released in 2005 and conducted by University of Toronto criminologist Scott Wortley using Kingston, Ontario, police statistics found that young black men and Aboriginal men had a greater chance of being stopped by the police than did members of other groups. More specifically, the study showed that a black man was 3.7 times more likely to be stopped by police than was a white man (CBC 2005).

Even the world of computers reflects a kind of discrimination—perhaps we could call this technological discrimination. As the Internet and computer technology spread globally, access to this technology is crucial in determining who moves ahead and who stays behind in our hard-wired society. In Canada, a disproportionate number of those with post-secondary education and higher

People from white ethnic groups tend to underestimate the value of racial privilege. Employers generally hire those with backgrounds similar to their own, as this all-white workplace gathering suggests.

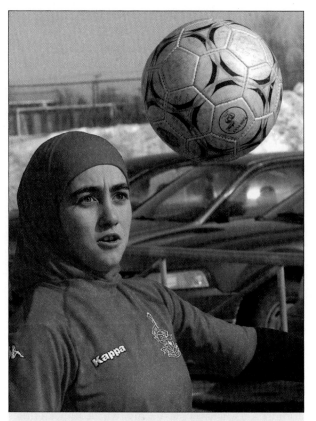

Asmahan Mansour, a member of Ottawa's under-12 girls soccer team, was ejected from a game by a referee in Laval, Quebec, after she refused to remove her hijab. The Quebec Soccer Federation defended the action of the referee, citing that wearing the hijab broke a safety rule of Fédération Internationale de Football Association (FIFA), soccer's international governing organization.

income are from white ethnic and non-Aboriginal groups. Similarly, a disproportionately high number of Aboriginal people are from lower income and lower education groups. As of 2003, Canadians with post-secondary education and higher income levels have been at the forefront of Internet use in the home (Statistics Canada 2004e). The significance of differential access to the Internet may only increase as better-paying jobs, and even information itself, become increasingly tied to computer access and literacy.

Use Your Sociological Imagination

Suddenly, you don't have access to a desktop computer — not at home, at school, or even at work. How will your life change?

For more than 20 years, employment-equity programs have been instituted in an attempt to make the workforce more diverse and to overcome discrimination. **Employment equity** comprises positive efforts to recruit historically disadvantaged groups for jobs, promotions, and educational opportunities. Some people, however, resent these programs, arguing that advancing one group's cause merely shifts the discrimination to another group. Critics argue that by giving priority to visible minorities in school admissions, for example, more qualified white ethnic group candidates may be overlooked.

Discriminatory practices continue to pervade nearly all areas of life in Canada today. In part, this is because various individuals and groups actually *benefit* from racial and ethnic discrimination in terms of money, status, and influence. Discrimination permits members of the majority to enhance their wealth, power, and prestige at the expense of others. Less-qualified people get jobs and promotions simply because they are members of the dominant group. Such individuals and groups will not surrender these advantages easily. We'll take a closer look at this functionalist analysis, as well as the conflict, feminist, and interactionist perspectives.

☐ HOW ARE RACE AND ETHNICITY STUDIED?

Relations among dominant and ethnic minority groups lend themselves to analysis from the four major perspectives of sociology. From the macro level, functionalists observe that racism toward ethnic minorities serves positive functions for dominant groups, whereas conflict theorists see the economic structure as a central factor in the exploitation of minorities. The feminist perspective looks at both micro-level and macro-level issues. The micro-level analysis of interactionist researchers stresses the manner in which everyday contact between people from different ethnic minorities contributes to tolerance or leads to hostility.

Functionalist Perspective

What possible use could racism have for society? Functionalist theorists, while agreeing that racism is hardly to be admired, point out that it indeed serves positive functions for those practising discrimination.

Anthropologist Manning Nash has identified three functions of racist beliefs for the dominant group (1962):

1. Racist views provide a moral justification for maintaining an unequal society that routinely deprives a minority of its rights and privileges. Slavery has been justified, for example, by those who believed that Africans were physically and spiritually subhuman and devoid of souls (Hoebel 1949).
2. Racist beliefs discourage the subordinate minority from attempting to question its lowly status, which would be to question the very foundations of society.
3. Racial myths suggest that any major societal change (such as an end to discrimination) would only bring greater poverty to the minority and lower the majority's standard of living. As a result, Nash suggests, racial prejudice grows when a society's value system (for example, one underlying a colonial empire or a regime perpetuating slavery) is being threatened.

Although racism may serve the interests of the powerful, such unequal treatment can also be dysfunctional to a society and even to its dominant group. Sociologist Arnold Rose has outlined four dysfunctions associated with racism (1951):

1. A society that practises discrimination fails to use the resources of all individuals. Discrimination limits the search for talent and leadership to the dominant group.
2. Discrimination aggravates social problems, such as poverty, delinquency, and crime, and places the financial burden to alleviate these problems on the dominant group.
3. Society must invest a good deal of time and money to defend its barriers to full participation of all members.

4. Racial prejudice and discrimination often undercut goodwill and friendly diplomatic relations between nations.

Conflict Perspective

Conflict theorists would certainly agree with Arnold Rose that racial prejudice and discrimination have many harmful consequences for society. Sociologists such as Oliver Cox (1948), Robert Blauner (1972), and Herbert M. Hunter (2000) have used **exploitation theory** (or Marxist class theory) to explain the basis of racial subordination. As P.190 we saw in Chapter 8, Karl Marx viewed the exploitation of the lower class as a basic part of the capitalist economic system. From a Marxist point of view, racism keeps minority group members in low-paying jobs, thereby supplying the capitalist ruling class with a pool of cheap labour. Moreover, by forcing racial minorities to accept low wages, capitalists can restrict the wages of *all* members of the proletariat. Workers from the dominant group who demand higher wages can always be replaced by minorities who have no choice but to accept low-paying jobs.

The conflict view of race relations seems persuasive in a number of instances. In the late nineteenth century, the Canadian government encouraged thousands of Chinese workers to come to Canada, without their families, to build the Canadian Pacific Railway. These men faced dangerous working and living conditions, and many died before the railway was completed in 1885. After the railway's completion, when their labour was no longer needed, the government attempted to force the workers to return to China. To discourage future immigration from China, the Canadian government imposed what was called a head tax on every Chinese immigrant.

However, the exploitation theory is too limited to explain prejudice in its many forms. Not all minority groups have been economically exploited to the same extent. In addition, some groups, such as the Jews, have been victimized by prejudice for other than economic reasons. Still, as Gordon Allport concludes, the exploitation theory correctly "points a sure finger at one of the factors involved in prejudice . . . rationalized self-interest of the upper classes" (1979:210).

Feminist Perspectives

Given the great diversity of feminist perspectives, it is, perhaps, not surprising to discover differences among these theories in their treatment of race. Some feminist perspectives have taken white, middle-class, heterosexual women's experiences to be the norm, while ignoring "the specificity of black, native, and other ethnic and cultural experiences" (Elliot and Mandell 1998:14). Although such perspectives as radical feminism treat women as a uniform, undifferentiated group whose major source of

Table 10-2   Sociological Perspectives on Race

Perspective	Emphasis
Functionalist	The dominant majority benefits from the subordination of racial minorities.
Conflict	Vested interests perpetuate racial inequality through economic exploitation.
Interactionist	Co-operative interracial contacts can reduce hostility.
Feminist	Race, class, and gender intersect to produce multiple levels of inequality.

oppression is sexism, other perspectives have strenuously challenged this point of view (Grant 1993; Brand 1993). Such perspectives as anti-racist and critical race feminism point out that gender is not the sole source of oppression; gender, race, and other sources of oppression intersect to produce multiple degrees of inequality. Anti-racist feminists argue that all people are racialized, gendered, and differently constructed—they do not participate on an equal footing in social interactions, and unequal power relations permeate all social institutions. According to Enakshi Dua, anti-racist feminism "attempts to integrate the way race and gender function together in structuring inequality" (1999:9). Like anti-racist feminism, critical race feminism examines the interconnection of race or racism and other forms of oppression, with gender, emphasizing the social difference and multiplicity within feminism (Hua 2003). Unlike white, middle-class women, immigrant women, visible minority women, and Aboriginal women, for example, experience the compounded effects of inequality associated with their race and class as well as their gender.

Patricia Hill Collins uses the term "outsiders-within" to describe the condition of black women situated in academic, legal, business, and other communities (1998). As outsiders-within, Hill Collins argues, these women are members of a given community but at the same time are dually marginalized in that community as women and as blacks; they find themselves unable to access the knowledge and possess the full power granted to others in the community.

Interactionist Perspective

An Aboriginal woman is transferred from a job on an assembly line to a similar position working next to a white man. At first, the white man is patronizing, assuming that she must be incompetent. She is cold and resentful; even when she needs assistance, she refuses to admit it. After a week, the growing tension between the two leads to a bitter quarrel. Yet, over time, each slowly comes to appreciate the other's strengths and talents. A year after they begin working together, these two workers become respectful friends.

This is an example of what interactionists call the *contact hypothesis* in action. The **contact hypothesis** states that interracial contact between people of equal status in co-operative circumstances will cause them to become less prejudiced and to abandon previous stereotypes. People begin to see one another as individuals and discard the broad generalizations characteristic of stereotyping. Note the factors of *equal status* and *co-operative circumstances*. In the example above, if the two workers had been competing for one vacancy as a supervisor, the racial hostility between them might have worsened (Allport 1979; R. Schaefer 2004; Sigelman et al. 1996).

As visible minorities slowly gain access to better-paying and more responsible jobs in Canada, the contact hypothesis may take on even greater significance. The trend in our society is toward increasing contact between individuals from dominant and subordinate groups. This may be one way of eliminating—or at least reducing—racial and ethnic stereotyping and prejudice. Another may be the establishment of interracial coalitions, an idea suggested by sociologist William Julius Wilson (1999b). To work, such coalitions would obviously need to be built on an equal role for all members.

Table 10-2 summarizes the four major sociological perspectives on race. No matter what explanation is given, the racialization of non-dominant groups has powerful consequences in the form of prejudice and discrimination.

□ WHAT ARE SOME PATTERNS OF INTERGROUP RELATIONS?

Racial and ethnic groups can relate to one another in a wide variety of ways, ranging from friendships and inter-marriages to the killing of those from particular minority groups, from behaviours that require mutual approval to behaviours imposed by the dominant group.

Conflict sociologists emphasize the ways in which dominant groups exercise their political, social, economic, and cultural domination over other groups. Historically, dominant groups—primarily white—have subjugated less powerful groups whom they perceived to be different; they constructed these groups as the "other." This subjugation, as we discussed in the previous chapter on global stratification, can take the form of colonialism, and, more recently, neo-colonialism. Thus, as conflict and some feminist sociologists have pointed out, "otherized" groups have historically been exploited, oppressed, and controlled by dominant groups through such systems as colonialism, globalized labour exploitation, slavery, and genocide (Hua 2003).

Genocide is the deliberate, systematic killing of an entire people or nation. For example, the killing of a million Armenians by Turkish authorities beginning in 1915 was genocide. *Genocide* is most commonly used as a descriptor for Nazi Germany's extermination of 6 million European Jews, as well as gays, lesbians, and the Romani people, during World War II. The term is also appropriate in describing the U.S. government's policies toward Native Americans in the nineteenth century. During the Seven Years' War (1756–1763), germ warfare decimated the North American Aboriginal population. Blankets contaminated with smallpox were distributed to Aboriginal groups that were allied with France (Harrison and Friesen 2004). In a recent example of genocide, in Rwanda in 1994, an estimated 800 000 Tutsis were slaughtered by Hutus in 100 days.

The *expulsion* of a people is another extreme means of acting out racial or ethnic prejudice. In 1979, Vietnam expelled nearly a million ethnic Chinese, partly as a result of centuries of hostility between Vietnam and neighbouring China. In a more recent example of expulsion, Sudan's government began a campaign of "ethnic cleansing" in its Darfur region. According to the global human rights watchdog, Human Rights Watch, the conflict has been mischaracterized and oversimplified as a clash between "Arab" and "non-Arab" African people; rather, "the ways in which both rebel groups and the Sudanese government have manipulated ethnic tensions have served to polarize much of the Darfur population along ethnic lines" (Human Rights Watch 2007:1). Many deaths have occurred and approximately 2.4 million people (including 200 000 refugees) have been displaced since 2003 (Human Rights Watch 2007). Genocide and expulsion are arguably the most extreme examples of hostile inter-group relations. Other patterns of inter-group relations that are explored by sociologists are assimilation, segregation, and multiculturalism. Each pattern defines the dominant group's actions and the responses of various minority groups. Inter-group relations are rarely restricted to just one of the three patterns,

although invariably one does tend to dominate. Therefore, think of these patterns primarily as ideal types.

Assimilation

Many Hindus in India complain about Indian citizens who copy the traditions and customs of the British. In Australia, Aborigines who have become part of the dominant society refuse to acknowledge their darker-skinned grandparents on the street. In Canada, some Poles, Ukrainians, and Jews, among others, have changed their ethnic-sounding family names to surnames that are typically found among British and Northern European families.

Assimilation is the process by which a person forsakes his or her own cultural tradition to become part of a different culture. Generally, it is practised by a minority group member who wants to conform to the standards of the dominant group. Assimilation can be described as an ideology in which $A + B + C \rightarrow A$. The majority A dominates in such a way that members of minorities B and C imitate A and attempt to become indistinguishable from the dominant group (Newman 1973).

Assimilation can strike at the very roots of a person's identity. Alphonso D'Abruzzo, for example, changed his name to Alan Alda (following the lead of his actor father, Robert Alda). Legendary Canadian rock singer Geddy Lee was born Gary Lee Weinrib; the British actor Joyce Frankenberg changed her name to Jane Seymour. Name changes, switches in religious affiliation, and dropping of native languages can obscure a person's roots and heritage. However, assimilation does not necessarily bring acceptance for the minority group individual. A Chinese Canadian may speak English fluently, achieve high educational standards, and become a well-respected professional or business person and *still* be seen as different. Some Canadians may reject him or her as a business associate, neighbour, or marriage partner, simply because she or he is seen as different.

> ### Use Your Sociological Imagination
> You have immigrated to another country with a very different culture. How are you treated?

Segregation

Separate schools, separate seating sections on buses and in restaurants, separate washrooms, even separate drinking fountains—these were all part of the lives of African Americans in the American South when segregation ruled in the first half of the twentieth century. **Segregation** is the physical separation of two groups of people in terms of residence, work-place, and social events. Generally, a dominant group imposes it on a minority group. Segregation is rarely complete, however. Inter-group contact inevitably occurs, even in the most segregated societies.

From 1948 (when it received its independence) to 1990, the Republic of South Africa severely restricted the movement of blacks and other non-whites by means of a wide-ranging system of segregation known as **apartheid**. Apartheid even included the creation of homelands where blacks were expected to live. However, decades of local resistance to apartheid, combined with international pressure, led to marked political changes in the 1990s. In 1994, a prominent black activist, Nelson Mandela, was elected as South Africa's president. This was the first election in which blacks (the majority of the nation's population) were allowed to vote. Mandela had spent almost 28 years in South African prisons for his anti-apartheid activities. His election was widely viewed as the final blow to South Africa's oppressive apartheid policy.

The most blatant form of segregation in Canada is that of the reserve system established by the federal government for Aboriginal peoples. Although Aboriginal people do have a choice as to where they live, they do not receive the same privileges off reserves as they would on them. Effectively, reserves segregate Aboriginal people by placing their schools, housing, recreational facilities, and medical services in remote areas, separate from the larger community. This segregation creates centres of "shiftlessness and inertia," where Aboriginal people are transformed into a "great family of wards, dependent on government for direction and assistance" (Harrison and Friesen 2004:187).

Some forms of segregation can be voluntary and, thus, may be referred to as **self-segregation**. An example of self-segregation is the residential segregation found in Canada's major cities, such as Toronto, Vancouver, and Montreal, where residents in Chinese-, Jewish-, and Indo-Canadian neighbourhoods remain residentially separated from other ethnic groups. The recent approval, in 2008, by the Toronto District School Board allowing the creation of Canada's first black-focused public school was considered to be segregation by opponents of the plan. Those in support of the move, which features a curriculum and

This public housing development in suburban Paris is home to African and Asian immigrants, most of them Muslim. Such racial and ethnic enclaves are characterized by limited job opportunities and underfinanced schools. In many other parts of the world as well, the segregation of racial and ethnic minorities accentuates the gap between the haves and have-nots.

teaching that focuses on black culture and history, believe that it will help to keep black students in school longer (CBC 2008b).

Box 10-1 discusses the cultural survival of indigenous peoples in Brazil, segregated on reserves.

Multiculturalism

In 1969, Canada's federal government adopted an official policy of bilingualism in response to the rise of nationalism in Quebec (Harrison and Friesen 2004). But in 1971, the government adopted a policy of multiculturalism in recognition of the growing number of Canadians who were from ethnic backgrounds other than British or French. The multiculturalism policy was, and still is, an attempt to establish a larger framework within which to respond to Canadian ethnic and racial diversity.

The meaning of multiculturalism in Canada goes beyond simply describing what is (or the obvious): that Canada is a country comprising people from many diverse ethnic and racial origins. **Multiculturalism**, officially, is a policy that attempts to promote ethnic and racial diversity in all aspects of Canadian life, and to establish diversity as a fundamental characteristic of the Canadian identity. The policy of multiculturalism, however, is not without its critics, who assert that it is simply window dressing that diverts attention from the economic

Sociology in the Global Community
Cultural Survival in Brazil

10-1

When the first Portuguese ships landed on the coast of what we now know as Brazil, more than 2 million people already inhabited the vast, mineral-rich land. They lived in small, isolated settlements, spoke a variety of languages, and embraced many different cultural traditions.

Today, over five centuries later, Brazil's population has grown to more than 180 million, only about 500 000 of whom are indigenous peoples descended from the original inhabitants. Over 200 different indigenous groups have survived, living a life closely tied to the land and the rivers, just as their ancestors did. But over the last two generations, their numbers have dwindled as booms in mining, logging, oil drilling, and agriculture have encroached on their land and their settlements.

Many indigenous groups were once nomads, moving around from one hunting or fishing ground to another. Now, they are hemmed in on the reservations the government confined them to, surrounded by huge farms or ranches whose owners deny their right to live off the land. State officials may insist that laws restrict the development of indigenous lands, but indigenous peoples tell a different story. In Mato Grosso, a heavily forested area near the Amazon River, loggers have been clear-cutting the land at a rate that alarms the Bororo, an indigenous group that has lived in the area for centuries. According to one elder, the Bororo are now confined to six small reservations of roughly 1300 square kilometres—

Sources: Chu 2005; Instituto del Tercer Mundo 2005.

much less than the area officially granted them in the nineteenth century.

Indigenous tribes are no match for powerful agri-business interests, one of whose leaders is also the governor of Mato Grosso. Blairo Maggi, head of the largest soybean producer in the world, has publicly trivialized the consequences of the massive deforestation occurring in Mato Grosso. Though Maggi recently said he would propose a three-year moratorium on development, opponents are skeptical that he will follow through on the promise.

Meanwhile, indigenous groups like the Bororo struggle to maintain their culture in the face of dwindling resources. Though the tribe still observes the traditional initiation rites for adolescent boys, members are finding it difficult to continue their hunting and fishing rituals, given the scarcity of fish and game in the area. Pesticides in the runoff from nearby farms have poisoned the water they fish and bathe in, threatening both their health and their culture's survival.

Applying Theory

1. How would conflict thinkers explain the relationship between indigenous groups and agri-business interests in Brazil?
2. How would functionalists explain the state of indigenous groups and their dwindling resources?

---

and political inequalities that persist among various ethnic groups (e.g., between members of visible minorities and members of other minorities).

Whether this policy of multiculturalism is reflected in today's mainstream media is discussed in Box 10-2.

☐ WHAT ARE SOME GROUPS THAT MAKE UP CANADA'S MULTI-ETHNIC CHARACTER?

Few societies have a more diverse population than Canada; the nation is truly a multiracial, multi-ethnic

society. Of course, this has not always been the case. The population of what is now Canada has changed dramatically since the arrival of French settlers in the 1600s. Immigration has largely been responsible for shaping the racial and ethnic makeup of our present-day society.

Canada's diversity is evident from the statistical profile presented in Table 10-1 on page 239. That diversity, particularly with regard to visible minority status, has been increasing dramatically in recent years. Between the early 1960s and the most recent census of 2006, there has been a marked shift away from Europe and toward Asia as the source of the majority of immigrants to Canada (Statistics Canada 2007n).

Research in Action   10-2
Racism and the Mainstream Media

Augie Fleras and Jean Lock Kunz, in their book *Media and Minorities* (2001), observe that Canada's mainstream media is frequently accused of being racist. Fleras and Lock Kunz provide some vignettes that illustrate the complexity of racism as it relates to media representations of male and female members of minority groups (pp. 30–31):

- After watching 114 hours of TV, the *Toronto Star* television critic concluded that members of minority groups are still under-represented on air, both in television shows and in advertisements, in relation to their populations and relative to whites. Advertisers justify this practice, stating that using members of minority groups could offend their customers.

- A one-month study of five major Canadian newspapers confirmed that Muslims are typically cast as barbaric fanatics by the media. Muslims are portrayed as violent people or terrorists whose fundamentalist religion condones their brutal acts.

- "When people of colour commit a crime . . . collective responsibility is imposed on an entire race . . . [while] white criminal violence is a matter of individual responsibility" (p. 31). For example, Paul Bernardo's killing of two teenage girls was seen as the fault of the individual, not of his entire race. "No one in the media asked, 'What's wrong with blue-eyed, blond-haired men of Italian descent?'" (p. 31).

In 2004, a report commissioned by the Canadian Radio-television and Telecommunications Commission (CRTC)—the body which regulates Canada's airways—reinforced the view that visible minorities were being misrepresented (CBC 2004a). The report emphasized the need for greater cultural diversity on Canadian television, and focus groups—consulted by the report's authors—complained about the persistent use of stereotypes and negatives images of visible minorities. The CRTC called on Canadian broadcasters to address these imbalances and misrepresentations and to revisit the issue in three or four years to see what progress—if any—had been made (CBC 2004a).

Similarly, before the 2002 fall season, executives of the major U.S. television networks once again renewed their commitment to diversify both who is on television and who is responsible for the content. It proved to be a tough commitment to keep. Only 2 of the 26 new fall series had even one minority person in a leading role. Furthermore, a Directors Guild of America report indicated that of all 826 episodes of the 40 most popular series in 2001, 80 percent were directed by white males and 11 percent by white females. That left only 9 percent directed by blacks, Latinos, or Asian Americans, who collectively account for more than 25 percent of U.S. television viewers.

In the 2003–2004 season, 74 percent of all characters in prime-time series were white. When minority groups

Ethnic Groups

The 2006 Canadian census revealed the 10 top ethnic origins to be, in descending order, Canadian, English, French, Scottish, Irish, German, Italian, Chinese, North American Indian, and Ukrainian. Below, we will explore some of the groups that make up Canada's multi-ethnic character.

Aboriginal People

The history of Aboriginal groups in Canada is one, first and foremost, of colonialism, the effects of which continue to be felt by Aboriginal people today. The historical legacy of oppression is one many Native people still cope with daily, as they continue to be marginalized

and struggle against various forms of racism. They have endured years of overt attempts on the part of the dominant culture to eradicate their Aboriginal identities.

The Indian Act of 1876 granted the federal government the power to control most aspects of Aboriginal life, denying First Nations people the right to vote or to buy land. This pivotal piece of legislation transformed Aboriginals from self-governing, autonomous peoples to externally regulated, controlled, and, thus, dependent ones. Ten years before the Indian Act, after breaking treaty after treaty to make way for European settlement, Canada's government decided that particular parcels of land would be used for reserves. Yet, as Lee Maracle argues in her 1996 book, *I Am Woman: A Native Perspective on Sociology and Feminism* (p. 92), Native people in do appear on U.S. television and in other forms of media, their roles tend to reinforce the stereotypes. In 2004, for example, nearly half of all Middle Eastern characters shown on television were criminals, compared to only 5 percent of white characters.

Beyond these excuses, real reasons can be found for the departure from the diversity exhibited in past shows and seasons. In recent years, the rise of more networks, cable TV, and the Internet has fragmented the broadcast entertainment market, siphoning viewers away from the general-audience sitcoms and dramas of the past.

Meanwhile, the mainstream network executives, producers, and writers remain overwhelmingly white and tend to write and produce stories about people like themselves. Marc Hirschfeld, an NBC executive, claims that some white producers have told him they don't know how to write for black characters. Stephen Bochco, producer of *NYPD Blue*, is a rare exception. His series, *City of Angels*, featured a mostly non-white cast, like the people Bochco grew up with in an inner-city neighbourhood. The series ran for 23 episodes before being cancelled in 2000.

In the long run, media observers believe, the major networks will need to integrate the ranks of gatekeepers before they achieve true diversity in programming. Adonis Hoffman, director of the Corporate Policy Institute, has urged network executives to throw open their studios and boardrooms to minorities. There are some signs of agreement from the networks. According to Doug Herzog, former president of Fox Entertainment, real progress means incorporating diversity from within.

Why does it matter that minority groups aren't visible on major network television, if they are well represented on other channels, such as Aboriginal Peoples Television Network (APTN)? The problem is that whites as well as visible minorities see a distorted picture of their society every time they turn on network TV. In the case of U.S. television, Hoffman states, "African Americans, Latinos, and Asians, while portrayed as such, are not merely walk-ons in our society—they are woven into the fabric of what has made this country great" (A. Hoffman 1997:M6).

Applying Theory

1. Do you watch network TV? If so, how well do you think it represents the diversity of Canadian society?
2. Have you seen a movie or TV show recently that portrayed members of a visible minority group in a sensitive and realistic way—as real people rather than as stereotypes or token walk-ons? If so, describe the show.

Sources: Bielby and Bielby 2002; Braxton and Calvo 2002; Children Now 2004; Directors Guild of America 2002; Fleras and Kunz 2001; A. Hoffman 1997; Navarro 2002; Poniewozik 2001; Soriano 2001; Wood 2000.

Canada, despite decades of colonization, have not had their culture "stolen":

> We have not "lost our culture" or had it "stolen." Much of the information that was available to us through our education process has been expropriated and consigned to deadwood leaves in libraries. The essence of Native culture still lives on in the hearts, minds, and spirits of our folk. Some of us have forsaken our culture in the interests of becoming integrated. This is not the same thing as losing something. The expropriation of the accumulated knowledge of Native peoples is one legacy of colonization. Decolonization will require the repatriation and rematriation of the knowledge by Native peoples themselves.

Almost 160 years ago, Egerton Ryerson, chief superintendent of education for Upper Canada, set out to "civilize" Aboriginal children through, as a federal government report published in 1847 described it, a "weaning from the habits and feelings of their ancestors and the acquirement of the language, arts and customs of civilized life." Residential schools established in the mid-nineteenth century, with mandatory attendance beginning in 1920, were run as a partnership between the federal government and the major churches. Thousands of Native children were excised from their families and communities to be "whitened" and "educated" in the ways of European culture.

Many of these children endured conditions of neglect, isolation, and emotional, physical, and sexual abuse. As many have argued, they were also the victims of a cultural genocide. The final report of the Royal

The ethnic mosaic of the Canadian community has marginalized First Nations peoples. In recent years, the Assembly of First Nations and local native groups have had great success in focusing attention on the ongoing discrimination to which they are subjected.

Commission on Aboriginal Peoples, issued in 1996, stated that "the schools were . . . part of the contagion of colonialization. In their direct attack of language, beliefs and spirituality, the schools had been a particularly virulent strain of that epidemic of empire, sapping children's bodies and beings" (D. Wilson 2000). The last residential schools closed in the mid-1980s; however, the now-adult survivors continue to struggle with the traumatic effects of their experiences as children in these schools.

British Columbia psychiatrist and professor Charles Brasfield, who runs a practice focusing on the needs of Aboriginal people, suggests that "residential school syndrome" might be a diagnostic term appropriately applied to survivors of the residential school system (2001:80). In his practice, Brasfield treats Aboriginal people who are trying to overcome nightmares, flashbacks, relationship problems, sleeping difficulties, and anger-management issues, all of which are rooted in their experiences in the residential schools. Not having good parenting role models while in the schools, many now lack parenting skills. Often, Brasfield sees his Aboriginal clients struggling to deal with alcohol or drug abuse.

In November 2005, the federal government announced plans to distribute a $2 billion compensation package to survivors of Aboriginal residential schools and, by 2008, more than $1.3 billion worth of claims had been paid. Approximately 86 000 former students are eligible to receive a $10 000 basic payment and $3000

for every year spent in a residential school. In addition, compensation will be offered for claims of sexual and physical abuse, and loss of language and culture. The Aboriginal Healing Foundation will receive five years of funding ($125 million), $60 million will be available for a truth and reconciliation process, and $10 million will be spent to commemorate what happened in the schools. In return, the recipients give up the right to sue the federal government and the churches that ran the schools, except in cases of sexual and serious physical abuse. An official apology on the part of the federal government for the abuses suffered by students of residential schools was issued by Prime Minister Stephen Harper in June 2008.

In addition to, and interrelated with, the effects of the residential schools' legacy, Aboriginal people have higher rates of poverty, suicide, tuberculosis, infant mortality, and incarceration than the non-Aboriginal population (Statistics Canada 2003h). Aboriginal people also have lower rates of education and employment than non-Aboriginals, as well as shorter life expectancies.

In 2006, the number of people who identified themselves as Aboriginal passed the 1 million mark (Statistics Canada 2008a). Between 1996 and 2006, the Aboriginal population increased 45 percent, while the non-Aboriginal population grew by 8 percent over the same period (Statistics Canada 2008a).

Despite more than a century of colonial oppression, Aboriginal people have made strides toward regaining self-determination and autonomy. For example, the 1999 ratification of a treaty with the Nisga'a of northern British Columbia established a precedent for Aboriginal land claims and political autonomy. Figure 10-2 shows an overview of the First Nations People of British Columbia.

Asian Canadians

Peter Li, author of *Chinese in Canada* (1988), argues that Asian, and Chinese in particular, is a racial distinctiveness and cultural inferiority articulated in the ideology and practice of Canada, while the normative order upholding Europeans as the desirable race is well entrenched (P. Li 2003). The social significance of race is also evident in public discourse, economic relations, and the arts and media (Fleras and Kunz 2001; P. Li 2003). Canadians are

▶ **FIGURE 10-2**

First Nations People of British Columbia

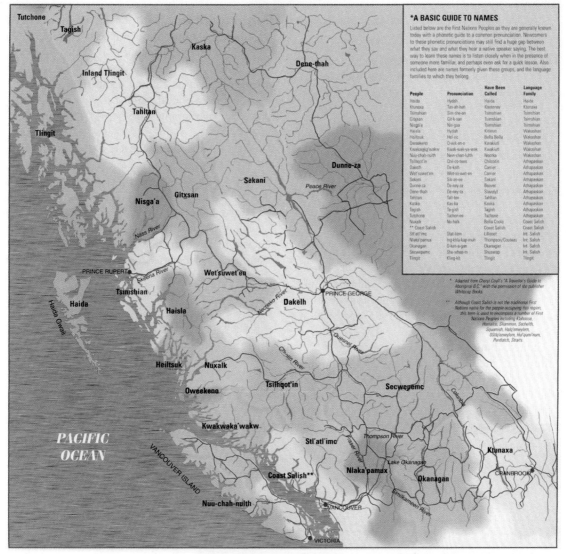

Source: Sovereign Indigenous Nations Territorial Boundaries in British Columbia.

fed a steady diet of mainstream media images in which Asians are portrayed as a homogeneous group, defined on the basis of a single racialized identity:

> We make up more than one half of the world's population, yet in spite of our numbers and contributions to the world, our images and perspectives are seldom seen. Our histories and our cultures are obscured, overlooked, buried or tokenized in a world dominated by Western classism. Our voices are seldom heard, our stories are left untold and our realities are seldom represented by those who control the means and resources to name and shape a picture of reality. (S. Park 1997)

These images are translated through the mainstream media into "us and them" scenarios (Fleras and Kunz 2001:131–132). For example, Asian Canadians are often portrayed in films as

- being foreigners who cannot be assimilated
- having no power or influence when playing leading roles
- having restricted features or mannerisms that are comical or sinister
- playing supporting roles even in the contexts that are unmistakably Asian

- having a negative or non-existent sexuality (for men)
- having regressive speech patterns that compound low intellectual capabilities
- having suicidal impulses in defence of honour, name, or country
- being overachievers but emotionally bankrupt

Given a normative social order in which Europeans were seen as desirable, the histories of Asian Canadians are ones in which institutional racism was entrenched in the social, political, and economic life of Canada. Chinese immigrants, who, for example, first came to Canada in the late 1850s to work in the mines, establish small businesses, and provide necessary labour for the building of the national railway, were viewed as a threatening and potentially dangerous "other" and treated accordingly. The Canadian government actively recruited Chinese labourers to complete the most dangerous phases of work on the Canadian Pacific Railway, paying them a fraction of the wages paid to white workers (Creese et al. 1991; Lampkin 1985). Institutional racism, as carried out by Canada's federal government, became more pronounced in 1885 with an act to restrict and regulate Chinese immigration to Canada. With this act began the imposition of a head tax of $50 in 1885, $100 in 1901, and $500 in 1904—a year's wages (A. Finkel et al. 1993)—to be paid by every Chinese immigrant entering Canada.

Institutional racism toward Chinese immigrants became even more wide-ranging in 1923, with the passing of the Chinese Exclusion Act, which, among other restrictions, barred the families of men working in Canada from joining them, resulting in years of separation of family members. Despite a history of institutional racism and current self-reported experiences of discrimination, Chinese Canadians are now among the best-educated groups in Canada, many having attained middle-class status, frequently as professionals (Derouin 2004; Nguyen 1982; Reitz 1980).

Other Asian groups have also endured various forms of racism, including institutional racism. In 1907, a Vancouver-bound ship carrying more than 1000 Japanese immigrants and some Sikh immigrants was met by a racist mob of workers protesting their arrival on the grounds that they were a threat to the job security of white workers. This anti-Asian riot, organized by the Asiatic Exclusion League, also targeted Asian-run businesses in downtown Vancouver. Vandals smashed windows and destroyed signs. Many years later, in 1941, Japanese Canadians faced a major attack of institutional racism by the Canadian government. The government rounded up Japanese Canadians who lived within one hundred miles (160 kilometres) of the Pacific Coast for reasons of "national security," regardless of whether or not they supported Japan's involvement in World War II. Japanese Canadians were placed in internment camps in the interior of British Columbia and on sugar beet farms in Alberta and Manitoba (David Suzuki, the Canadian environmentalist and television host/producer, spent part of his childhood with his family in an internment camp in British Columbia). Between 1943 and 1946, the federal government sold all the property and possessions of the internees, and new Japanese immigrants were barred from entering Canada until 1967, when of a new immigration policy was introduced based on a point system. In 1988, the federal government offered an apology and compensation to Japanese Canadians for the racist treatment they had received during the internment. In 2006, the federal government formally apologized to Chinese Canadians for both the head tax and other government measures to bar Chinese immigration between 1923 and 1947.

Institutional racism is also entrenched in the history of Indo-Canadians, with the case of the *Komagata Maru*—a ship carrying 376 passengers from India to Canada

A Chinese head tax receipt, issued by the Canadian Immigration Branch, Vancouver, August 2, 1918.

in 1914—being perhaps the most notable example. The ship remained anchored just off the Vancouver coast for two months, while debates based on racist ideologies on the part of the government and the public ensued. During this time, passengers and crew were left without adequate supplies of food and water and without proper medical care. Conditions on board deteriorated rapidly. Eventually, based on the view that the Indian passengers constituted the category of "other," and thus warranted racist treatment, the Canadian government did not allow the ship to dock, forcing it to return to India.

In 1939, the Supreme Court of Canada ruled that discrimination based on race was legally enforceable (F. Henry et al. 1995). This ruling remained in place until the multiculturalism policy of 1971 was

PP. 236, 237

enacted, which brought about the modification of rules of engagement and entitlement for the "containment" of ethnicity (Fleras and Kunz 2001). Today, Asian Canadians, who tend to settle in Toronto, Vancouver, and Montreal, are the fastest-growing segment of new immigrants to Canada. The diverse groups found within this category are often stereotyped as "model" or ideal minority groups, as many members tend to succeed, educationally and economically, even while enduring various forms of racism.

The success of many of the members of these visible minorities, particularly the Chinese, may be used to bolster the position of those who argue that all it takes to get ahead in Canada is hard work and effort (as discussed when we examined the functionalist view in Chapter 8). The implication of this view is that if some members of visible minorities do succeed, those who do not must suffer from personal inadequacies. However, in their review of the vertical mosaic thesis, Lian and Matthews concluded that "similar educational qualifications carried different economic values in the Canadian labour market for individuals of different 'racial' origins and that a 'coloured mosaic' now exists, in which educational achievement at any level fails to protect persons of visible minority background from being disadvantaged in terms of income they receive" (1998:475–476).

The disadvantage of having a visible minority background affects those born outside the country as well as

In 1914, passengers who arrived in Vancouver on the *Komagata Maru* were forced to turn back to India after a two-month standoff. Most of the passengers were Sikhs, and the remaining were Muslims and Hindus. Discriminatory laws at the time made it difficult for Asian immigrants to come to Canada.

others who are native Canadians (Pendakur and Pendakur 2002). A 2004 study showed that one-third of members of visible minorities in Canada—more than one million people—reported having been discriminated against or treated unfairly because of their ethnicity, culture, race, skin colour, language, accent, or religion (Derouin 2004). Asian Canadians reported lower levels of discrimination than members of the visible minority category did overall, with Chinese Canadians reporting marginally lower rates of discrimination than members of the Asian category did overall (see Figure 10-3).

It is imperative to keep in mind the ways in which categories, such as gender and age, intersect with a visible minority background, diversifying and compounding the degrees of discrimination experienced by many Canadians.

White Ethnic Groups

Unlike minority groups whose identities have been racialized, those of both dominant and minority white ethnic groups have not. As a result of their "invisibility," they experience a greater chance of social inclusion and, in the case of white minorities, a lesser chance of social exclusion through racism, discrimination, and exploitation after the initial adaptation period (Fleras and Elliott 1992). As Peter Li argues, "social inclusion of 'racial' groups that have been historically marginalized implies

▶ **FIGURE 10-3**

Percentage Reporting Discrimination or Unfair Treatment "Sometimes" or "Often" in the Previous Five Years, by Visible Minority Status, 2002

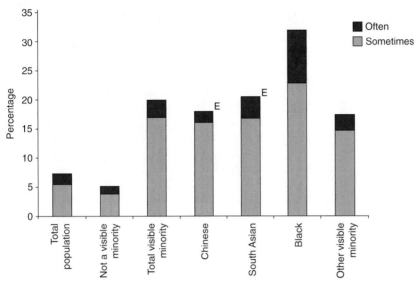

ᴱ Use with caution

Note: Refers to Canada's non-Aboriginal population aged 15 and older reporting discrimination or unfair treatment in Canada because of ethnocultural characteristics.

Source: Statistics Canada 2003c.

basis of perceived racial differences, required special permits for entry.

John Porter's landmark study *The Vertical Mosaic* (1965) used the concept of *charter groups* to represent the French and English, the so-called founding groups of Canadian society. Porter's work documented the imbalances in the distribution of power, wealth, and resources, showing that the British and French were more positively rewarded and evaluated than were newly arrived immigrants (Fleras and Elliott 1992; Kazemipur 2002). Porter's thesis study, as discussed in earlier chapters, in which various ethnic groups were hierarchically arranged such that European groups held higher socioeconomic positions than non-European groups, has been re-examined in more contemporary contexts. These studies show that whites are advantaged over non-whites in relation to occupational status and earnings (Geschwender 1994; Lautard and Loree 1984; Lautard and Guppy 1999; P. Li 1988). Even when such factors as demographic features are controlled for, substantial income disparities persist between Canadians of European origin and those of visible minority groups (Beach and Worswick 2003; Boyd 1984, 1992; P. Li 1992, 2000; Pendakur and Pendakur 1998). Studies conducted since the release of *The Vertical Mosaic*, which included the impact of the major influx of immigrants from non-European countries, have "resulted in an increase in the salience of race at the expense of ethnicity . . . as the 1960s' reforms in Canadian immigration policy have raised the number of visible minority immigrants, and along with it the potential to racial discrimination" (Kazemipur 2002).

Members of white ethnic groups, who continue to hold the bulk of economic and political power in Canada (federal and provincial or territorial), have co-opted Canada's ethnic and racial diversity for trade, investment, and commercial purposes. For example, in her article, "Multiculturalism, or the United Colours of Capitalism?", Katharyne Mitchell argues that Canada's multicultural character has been used by Canadian powerholders to attract transnational elites to Canada, by selling an ideology of racial harmony that may provide reassurance for nervous investors (Fleras and Kunz 2001).

◀ P.11

the use of 'race' as grounds to signify the value of people. In contrast, racial exclusion involves constructing social boundaries based on phenotypic features [physical appearance], by which individuals or groups are denied social opportunities, economic rewards and other privileges as a result of their 'racial designation'" (2003:1).

Given that *race* is a value-laden term, racial markers have provided the basis on which to distinguish the "desirable" from the "undesirable," "us" from "them" (Li 2003). The normative social order of Canada has favoured Europeans, positioning them as "us," institutionalizing their interests and cultural values and thus providing them greater power to set the norms of society. Initial immigrant policies were racist in orientation, intending to encourage assimilation, and had an exclusionary result (Fleras and Elliott 2003). "Preferred" groups were from Northern and Western Europe and, later, in response to the settlement needs of Western Canada, groups from Eastern and Southern Europe that, although lower in preferred ranking, were also deemed acceptable. These groups faced limited or no entry restrictions, while other groups, such as Jews and Mediterranean populations, "otherized" on the

Social Policy and Race and Ethnicity
Global Immigration

The Issue

Worldwide, there are an estimated 191 million immigrants, with the last 50 years seeing almost a doubling of immigration (UNFPA 2006). The increasing numbers raise questions for the recipient countries, the majority of which are developed. Who should be allowed in? Should immigration be expanded? At what point should it be curtailed?

The Setting

The migration of people is not uniform across time or space. At certain times, wars or famines may precipitate large movements of people either temporarily or permanently. Temporary dislocations occur when people wait until it is safe to return to their home areas. However, more and more migrants who cannot make adequate livings in their home nations are making permanent moves to developed nations. The major migration streams flow into North America, the oil-rich areas of the Middle East, and the industrial economies of Western Europe and Asia. Currently, seven of the world's wealthiest nations (including Canada, Germany, France, the United Kingdom, and the United States) shelter about one-third of the world's migrant population, but less than one-fifth of the total world population. As long as there are disparities in job opportunities among countries, there is little reason to expect this international migration trend to end.

Countries, such as Canada, that have long been a destination for immigrants have a history of policies to determine who has preference to enter. Often, clear racial and ethnic biases are built into these policies. Until the 1960s, Canadian immigration policy has favoured immigrants from Northern Europe and Britain. Immigrants who were members of visible minority groups were explicitly excluded and discriminated against, as Canadian politicians and policymakers believed that they were not a "good fit" for Canadian society. The first hundred years of post-Confederation immigration were essentially about European migration to Canada. Not all Europeans, however, were treated equally or looked on favourably by Canadian immigration policy. The British and Northern Europeans were preferred over Eastern and Southern Europeans, the latter being recruited only if there were not sufficient numbers of eligible British and Northern Europeans.

Since the late 1960s, policies in Canada have encouraged immigration of people from non-European nations.

This change has significantly altered the pattern of immigrants' country of birth. Previously, Europeans dominated; but for the last 20 years, immigrants have come primarily from Asia (see Figure 10-4).

People from Asia and the Middle East made up 58.3 percent of immigrants to Canada between 2001 and 2006 (Statistics Canada 2007d). The impact that immigration has on Canada, however, is not experienced equally by all Canadians; it has a much larger impact, for the most part, on those living in larger urban centres. More specifically, immigrants arriving in Canada between 2001 and 2006 tended to settle in Toronto, Montreal, and Vancouver and their suburbs (Statistics Canada 2007d). These three cities are also among the cities in the world with the largest foreign-born populations (see Figure 10-5).

Sociological Insights

Immigration can provide many valuable functions. For the destination society, it alleviates labour shortages, such as in the areas of health care, business, and technology in Canada. For the sending nation, migration can relieve economies unable to support large numbers of people. Often overlooked is the large amount of money that immigrants send back to their home nations. For example, worldwide, immigrants from Portugal alone send more than $4 billion annually back to their home country (World Bank 1995).

Immigration can be dysfunctional as well. Although studies generally show that immigration has a positive impact on the receiving nation's economy, areas experiencing high concentrations of immigrants may find it difficult to meet short-term social service needs. Critics of the way in which Canada's federal government is handling immigration say that although the country may be creating a few vibrantly multicultural urban centres, the government is also fostering cities that lack the services to deal with this growth and diversity. When migrants with skills or educational potential leave developing countries, it can be dysfunctional for those nations. No amount of payments sent back home can make up for the loss of valuable human resources from poor nations (Martin and Midgley 1999).

Conflict theorists note how much of the debate over immigration is phrased in economic terms. But this debate is intensified when the arrivals are of different racial and ethnic background from the host population.

▶ **FIGURE 10-4**

Place of Birth of Recent Immigrants to Canada, 2006

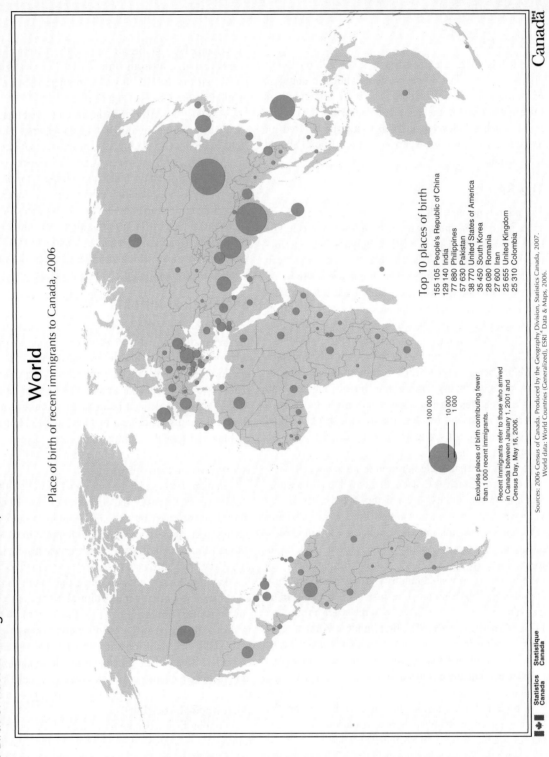

World

Place of birth of recent immigrants to Canada, 2006

Top 10 places of birth

155 105	People's Republic of China
129 140	India
77 880	Philippines
57 630	Pakistan
38 770	United States of America
35 450	South Korea
28 080	Romania
27 600	Iran
25 655	United Kingdom
25 310	Colombia

100 000

10 000

1 000

Excludes places of birth contributing fewer than 1 000 recent immigrants.

Recent immigrants refer to those who arrived in Canada between January 1, 2001 and Census Day, May 16, 2006.

Sources: 2006 Census of Canada. Produced by the Geography Division, Statistics Canada, 2007. World data: World Countries (Generalized), ESRI² Data & Maps, 2006.

Statistics Canada   Statistique Canada

Canada

Source: Statistics Canada 2006.

> **FIGURE 10-5**

Foreign Born as a Percentage of Metropolitan Population, 2006

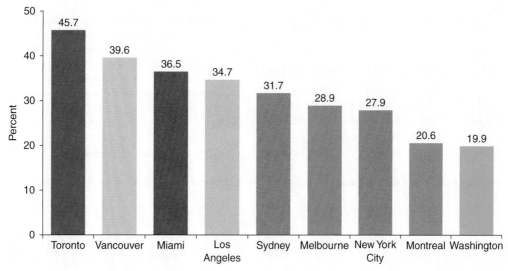

Note: The data from the United States is from 2005.
Sources: Statistics Canada, 2006j; Australian Bureau of Statistics, 2006 Census; United States Census Bureau, 2006 American Community Survey.

For example, Europeans often refer to "foreigners," but the term does not necessarily mean one of foreign birth. In Germany, "foreigners" refers to people of non-German ancestry, even if they were born in Germany; it does not refer to people of German ancestry born in another country who may choose to come to their "mother country." Fear and dislike of "new" ethnic groups may divide countries throughout the world (Martin and Widgren 1996). In Canada, fear or dislike of high levels of immigration is not as evident as that experienced in other countries.

Policy Initiatives

The long border with Mexico provides ample opportunity for illegal immigration into the United States. Throughout the 1980s, there was a perception among some observers that the United States had lost control of its borders. Feeling public pressure for immigration control, the U.S. Congress ended a decade of debate by approving the Immigration Reform and Control Act of 1986. The Act marked a historic change in immigration policy. For the first time, hiring of illegal aliens was outlawed, and employers caught violating the law became subject to fines and even prison sentences. Just as significant

a change was the extension of amnesty and legal status to many illegal immigrants already living in the United States. Almost two decades later, however, the 1986 immigration law appears to have had mixed results. Substantial numbers of illegal immigrants continue to enter the United States each year, with an estimated 11 million present in March 2005 (Passel 2006).

Of particular concern for Canadian policymakers is the distribution or dispersion of immigrants. The fact that the vast majority of newcomers to Canada have settled in large metropolitan regions has created a problem of "two solitudes—overtaxed megalopolises and waning small towns" (Jimenez and Lunman 2004: A5). In the large centres, pressure is placed on public housing, English-language courses, support services for immigrants, public transportation, and the cities' infrastructures in general. Policy-makers and politicians at all levels of government are currently devising strategies to deal with these challenges.

Throughout the world, globalization has had an overwhelming impact on immigration patterns. Overseas, the European Union (E.U.) agreement of 1997 gave the E.U.'s governing commission authority to propose a continent-wide policy on immigration. European Union policy allows residents of one E.U. country to live and work in another member state—an arrangement that is expected to become more complicated when nations such as Turkey become members of the E.U. In many E.U. countries, immigrants from Turkey's predominantly Muslim population are not welcome, no matter how pressing the local economy's need for labour (Denny 2004).

The intense debate over immigration reflects deep value conflicts in the cultures of many developed nations. One strand of the debate, for example, emphasizes egalitarian principles and a desire to be inclusive. At the same time, however, another strand is based on hostility to potential immigrants and refugees, reflecting not only racial, ethnic, and religious prejudice but also a desire to

maintain the dominant culture of the in-group by keeping out those viewed as outsiders.

Applying Theory

1. Did you or your parents or grandparents immigrate to Canada? If so, when? Where did your family come from, and why? Did you or they face discrimination?
2. Do you live, work, or study with recent immigrants to Canada? If so, are they well accepted in your community, or do they face prejudice and discrimination?
3. In your opinion, is there a backlash against immigrants in Canada?
4. In your view, does the functionalist perspective on race and ethnicity provide a realistic interpretation of unequal access to opportunity in Canada?

CHAPTER RESOURCES

Summary

What are Minority, Racial, and Ethnic Groups?

- **Racial groups** (p. 235) are socially constructed through a process of racialization, based on perceived physical differences, whereas an **ethnic group** (p. 235) is set apart primarily because of national origin or distinctive cultural patterns.
- When sociologists define a **minority group** (p. 235), they are primarily concerned with the economic and political power, or powerlessness, of the group.
- There is no biological basis for the concept of "race," and there are no physical traits that can be used to describe one racial group to the exclusion of all others.
- The meaning that people give to the physical differences between certain groups gives social significance to race and ethnicity, leading to **stereotypes** (p. 238).

What are Prejudice and Discrimination?

- **Prejudice** (p. 238) often leads to **discrimination** (p. 240), but the two are not identical; and each can be present without the other.
- **Institutional discrimination** (p. 241) results when the structural components of a society create or foster differential treatment of groups.

How are Race and Ethnicity Studied?

- Functionalists point out that discrimination is both functional and dysfunctional in society. Conflict theorists explain racial subordination by **exploitation theory** (p. 243).
- Some feminists point out that gender is not the sole source of oppression, and that gender, race, and class intersect to produce multiple degrees of inequality.
- Interactionists focus on the micro level of race relations, posing the **contact hypothesis** (p. 244) as a means of reducing prejudice and discrimination.

What are Some Patterns of Inter-group Relations?
- Three patterns describe typical inter-group relations in North America and elsewhere: **assimilation** (p. 245), **segregation** (p. 245), and **multiculturalism** (p. 246).
- In Canada, the ideal pattern of inter-group relations is multiculturalism. There is an ongoing debate over whether the ideal is, in fact, the reality of life for most minority Canadians.

What are Some Groups that Make Up Canada's Multi-ethnic Character?
- After a century and half of degradation, Canada's Aboriginal peoples are poised to reclaim their status as an independent, self-determining people.

- In Canadian society, the socially constructed category of "Asian" obscures the differences among various groups that are placed in this broad category.
- Non-white immigrants commonly find themselves stereotyped, portrayed as the "other," and marginalized by mainstream Canadian society.
- Porter's "vertical mosaic" is as accurate a portrayal of Canadian multiculturalism today as it was in 1965; however, *race* is now more salient than *ethnicity*.

Critical Thinking Questions

1. How is institutional discrimination even more powerful than individual discrimination? How would functionalists, conflict theorists, feminists, and interactionists examine institutional discrimination?
2. Do you think that multiculturalism in Canada is real or an ideal? Can you think of ways in which it might serve to mask the disparities between various ethnic and racial groups?

3. What place do you see Canada's Aboriginal peoples occupying in the twenty-first century? Do you think Aboriginal people will become more integrated into mainstream culture, or will they distance themselves from it by re-establishing their traditional communities?

Key Terms

Apartheid The former policy of the South African government designed to maintain the separation of blacks and other non-whites from the dominant whites. (p. 246)

Assimilation The process by which a person forsakes his or her own cultural tradition to become part of a different culture. (p. 245)

Contact hypothesis An interactionist perspective that states that interracial contact between people of equal status in co-operative circumstances will reduce prejudice. (p. 244)

Discrimination The process of denying opportunities and equal rights to individuals and groups because of prejudice or for other arbitrary reasons. (p. 240)

Employment equity A federal act that attempts to eliminate barriers faced in the area of employment. (p. 242)

Ethnic group A group that is set apart from others because of its national origin or distinctive cultural patterns. (p. 235)

Exploitation theory A Marxist theory that views racial subordination, such as that in Canada, as a manifestation of the class system inherent in capitalism. (p. 243)

Genocide The deliberate, systematic killing of an entire people or nation. (p. 245)

Glass ceiling An invisible barrier that blocks the promotion of a qualified individual in a work environment because of the individual's gender, race, or ethnicity. (p. 240)

Institutional discrimination The denial of opportunities and equal rights to individuals and groups that results from the normal operations of a society. (p. 241)

Minority group A subordinate group whose members have significantly less control or power over their own lives than the members of a dominant or majority group have over theirs. (p. 235)

Multiculturalism A policy that attempts to promote ethnic and racial diversity in all aspects of Canadian life, and to establish diversity as a fundamental characteristic of the Canadian identity. (p. 246)

Prejudice   A negative attitude toward an entire category of people, such as a racial or an ethnic minority. (p. 238)

Racial group   A group that is set apart and treated differently from others because of perceived physical attributes. (p. 235)

Racial or ethnic profiling   The use of a social construct of race as a consideration in suspect profiling in law enforcement and national security practices. (p. 241)

Racialization   The social processes by which people come to define a group as a "race," based in part on physical characteristics, but also on historical, cultural, and economic factors. (p. 237)

Racism   The belief that one race is supreme and all others are innately inferior. (p. 240)

Segregation   The act of physically separating two groups; often imposed on a minority group by a dominant group. (p. 245)

Self-segregation   The situation that arises when members of a minority deliberately develop residential, economic, or social network structures that are separate from those of the majority population. (p. 246)

Stereotypes   Unreliable generalizations about all members of a group that do not recognize individual differences within the group. (p. 238)

Visible minority   Canadians who are non-white or are identified as being physically different from white Canadians of European descent. (p. 235)

Additional Readings

Day, Richard J.F. 2000. *Multiculturalism and the History of Canadian Diversity*. Toronto: University of Toronto Press. The author contends that formal legislation cannot resolve culture-based issues. Day criticizes the federal government's policy as fantasy, arguing that equality is a myth in a society as diverse as Canada's.

Fleras, Augie, and Jean Lock Kunz. 2001. *Media and Minorities*. Scarborough, ON: Nelson Thompson. Fleras and Kunz examine how race, ethnicity, and aboriginality are interpreted by mainstream media and the public discourses produced and consumed as a result of these interpretations.

Satzewich, Vic, and Nick Liodakis. 2007. *'Race' and Ethnicity in Canada: A Critical Introduction*. Don Mills, ON: Oxford University Press. The authors aim to help students analyze and understand patterns of immigration, Aboriginal/non-Aboriginal relations, and race and ethnic relations in Canada, while taking the position of methodological and theoretical pluralism.

Schaefer, Richard T. 2002. *Racial and Ethnic Groups*, 9th ed. Upper Saddle River, NJ: Prentice Hall. Comprehensive in its coverage of race and ethnicity, Schaefer's text also discusses women as a subordinate minority and examines dominant–subordinate relations in Canada, Northern Ireland, Israel and the Palestinian territory, Mexico, and South Africa.

 ## Online Learning Centre

Visit the *Sociology: A Brief Introduction* Online Learning Centre at www.mcgrawhill.ca/olc/schaefer to access quizzes, interactive exercises, video clips, and other research and study tools related to this chapter.

 ## Reel Society Video Clips

 *Reel Society* video clips can be used to spark discussion about the following topics from this chapter:

- Minority groups
- Race
- Ethnicity
- Prejudice and discrimination

chapter 11

GENDER RELATIONS

This billboard in Hollywood, California, produced by the feminist advocacy group, Guerrilla Girls, points out the gender inequities in the motion picture industry. In all categories, including makeup, the overwhelming majority of Academy Awards have been awarded to men.

☐ **How is Gender Socially Constructed?**

☐ **How are Gender Relations Explained?**

☐ **How can Women be an "Oppressed Majority"?**

Boxes

SOCIOLOGY IN THE GLOBAL COMMUNITY: The Empowerment of Women through Education

RESEARCH IN ACTION: Differences in Male and Female Physicians' Communication with Patients

SOCIAL POLICY AND GENDER RELATIONS: Abortion and Sex Selection: The "New Eugenics"

Ottawa—By the time kids are 16 years old and starting to think about life after high school, girls are already showing they are stronger contenders than boys for going to university, says Statistics Canada.

In a study examining why women are outnumbering men on campus, the federal agency suggests that the academic stage is set years earlier, with 15-year-old boys trailing girls in marks, standardized test scores, and homework habits.

"The results suggest that understanding why girls outperform boys in the classroom may be a key to understanding the gender divide in university," says the study, entitled *Why Are Most University Students Women?*

Statistics Canada also points out potential roadblocks on the home front, where parents expect less of their teen boys than their girls. Sixty percent of boys are expected to graduate from university, compared with 70 percent of girls.

The study, written by Marc Frenette and Klarka Zeman, notes that a dramatic reversal has taken place on Canadian campuses in the last 30 years.

It's an international trend that experts widely described as the "feminization of education."

Among 19-year-olds in 2003, 39 percent of girls had attended university, compared with 26 percent of boys, said Statistics Canada.

That is a major change from the 1971 census, when 68 percent of university graduates aged 25–29 were men.

In 2004–2005, the last year in which statistics are available, women accounted for 58 percent of university students.

John Martin, who teaches criminology at University College of the Fraser Valley, in Abbotsford, British Columbia, bemoans the fact that "post-secondary education is definitely where the boys aren't."

He says that in his first-year classes this year, less than a quarter of his students are male. In his fourth-year classes, girls outnumber boys 10 to 1.

Martin blames the trend on the public schools, which he said switched gears through the 1970s to appeal to the learning style of girls because they weren't doing as well as boys.

"Boys are getting shafted," said Martin, starting in the early elementary school grades where there is "zero tolerance on horsing around" and boys are treated as learning disabled and put on medication if they misbehave.

Michael Hoy, an economist at University of Guelph, says that women may simply be more motivated than men to go university because the financial payback is bigger compared with the earnings of their high-school-educated counterparts.

Hoy co-authored a study last year that found university premiums for women between 1977 and 1992 was 16 percent higher than for men. Between 1993 and 2003, it was even higher for women, at 22 percent.

In other words, by 2003, the better-educated women earned $2.73 for every dollar earned by female high school graduates. For men, it was $2.13 to one dollar.

"There is a huge difference," said Hoy. "One reason girls are more likely to go to university is that they won't have as high job prospects if they don't."

The Statistics Canada data come from a massive international study of 15-year-olds as well as surveys of students and their parents.

In standardized reading tests, only 20 percent of boys scored in the top 25 percent, compared to 30 percent of girls. Boys were also more likely than girls to score in the bottom quarter.

In school markets, almost half of girls—46 percent—were honour role students with average marks of 80 percent or higher, compared to 32 percent of boys.

Girls also spent more time on homework, with 41 percent reporting they spent at least four hours a week on homework, compared to 30 percent of boys.

Also, 1 in 10 boys repeats a grade in school, compared with 6.5 percent of girls.

☐ *(Tibbetts 2007)*

In this *Vancouver Sun* article, Janice Tibbetts discusses a recently published study by Statistics Canada.

The study—entitled *Why are Most University Students Women?*—examines a trend in Canadian educational participation in which women are outnumbering men in Canadian universities. This trend—described as the "feminization of education"—is not solely a Canadian one, but rather is an international phenomenon. In Canada, it is a reversal of the previous pattern of men outnumbering women in university enrolment and graduation.

Expectations related to participation in post-secondary education are one example of how cultural norms may lead to differentiation based on gender. Such differentiation is evident in virtually every human society about which we have information. We saw in Chapters 9 and 10 that most societies establish hierarchies based on social class, race, and ethnicity. In this chapter, we examine the ways in which societies stratify their members on the basis of gender, in relation to social class, race, and ethnicity. We also see that increases in educational participation among women have not resulted in the elimination of the long-standing economic disparity between men and women in Canada.

We begin by looking at how various cultures, including our own, assign women and men to particular social roles. Then, we consider sociological explanations for gender stratification. Next, we focus on the diverse experiences of women as an oppressed majority, and analyze the social, economic, and political aspects of women's subordinate position in society. Here, we also examine the emergence of the feminist movement, its goals, and its contradictions. Finally, the social policy section provides a discussion about the links among abortion, new reproductive technology, and women's reproductive choices.

Use Your Sociological Imagination

Have you observed any differences, on the basis of gender, in the academic performance of your classmates?

☐ HOW IS GENDER SOCIALLY CONSTRUCTED?

How many air passengers do you think feel a start when the captain's voice from the cockpit belongs to a woman? Consciously or unconsciously, many assume that flying a commercial plane is a *man's* job. Gendered practices and organization are an integral part of our social world, so much so that we may take them for granted and only take notice when they deviate from conventional behaviour and expectations.

Although a few people begin life with an unclear sexual identity, the overwhelming majority begin with a definite sex and quickly receive societal messages about how to behave. Thus, the term **sex** is a biological category. Many societies have established distinctions between "female" and "male" that are not "natural" but are cultural and social. This is what is meant by *gender*. When we use the term **gender**, we are "using a shorthand term which encodes a crucial point: that our basic social identities as men and women are socially constructed rather than based on fixed biological characteristics" (Young 1988:98).

In studying gender, sociologists are interested in the gender-role socialization that leads women and men to behave differently. In Chapter 4, *gender roles* were defined as expectations regarding the proper behaviour, attitudes, and activities of men and women. The application of traditional gender roles leads to many

What type of body image do the media promote to young women in North America? The beauty ideal is one that encourages young women to be as thin and white as possible (Kilbourne 2000b).

◀ P. 80

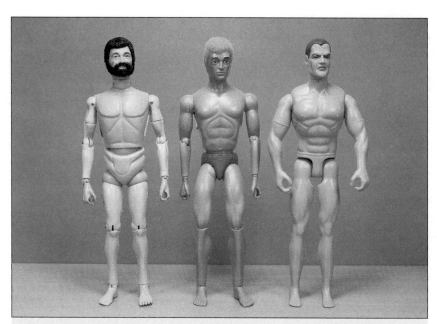

Society often exaggerates male–female differences in appearance and behaviour. In 1964, the GI Joe doll (left) had a realistic appearance, but by 1992 (middle), it had begun to acquire the exaggerated muscularity characteristic of professional wrestlers (right). The change intensified the contrast with ultra-thin female figures, like the Barbie doll (Angier 1998).

men. Yet our society still focuses on "masculine" and "feminine" qualities as if men and women must be evaluated in these terms. Clearly, we continue to "do gender," and this social construction of gender continues to define significantly different expectations for females and males in North America (Lorber 1994; L. Rosenbaum 1996; C. West and Zimmerman 1987).

Gender Roles in North America

Gender-Role Socialization

Male babies get blue blankets, while female babies get pink ones. Boys are expected to play with trucks, blocks, and toy soldiers; girls are given dolls and kitchen goods. Boys must be masculine—active, aggressive, tough, daring, and dominant—whereas girls must be feminine—soft, emotional, sweet, and submissive. These traditional gender-role patterns have been influential in the socialization of children in North America.

forms of differentiation between women and men. Both sexes are physically capable of learning to cook and sew, yet most Western societies determine that women should perform these tasks. Both men and women are capable of learning to weld and fly airplanes, but these functions are generally assigned to men.

Gender roles are evident not only in our work and behaviour but also in how we react to others. We are constantly "doing gender" without realizing it. If a father sits in the doctor's office with his son in the middle of a workday, he will probably receive approving glances from the receptionist and from other patients. "Isn't he a wonderful father?" runs through their minds. But if the boy's mother leaves *her* job and sits with the son in the doctor's office, she will not receive such silent applause.

We socially construct our behaviour so that male–female differences are either created or exaggerated. For example, men and women come in a variety of heights, sizes, and ages. Yet traditional norms regarding marriage and even casual dating tell us that in heterosexual couples, the man should be older, taller, and wiser than the woman. As we will see throughout this chapter, such social norms help to reinforce and legitimize patterns of male dominance.

In recent decades, women have increasingly entered occupations and professions previously dominated by

An important element in traditional views of proper "masculine" and "feminine" behaviour is fear of homosexuality. **Homophobia** is a fear of and prejudice against homosexuality. Homophobia contributes significantly to rigid gender-role socialization, since many people stereotypically associate male homosexuality with femininity and lesbianism with masculinity. Consequently, men and women who deviate from traditional expectations about gender roles are often presumed to be gay. Despite the advances made by the gay liberation movement, the continuing stigma attached to homosexuality in our culture places pressure on all males (whether gay or not) to exhibit only narrow masculine behaviour and on all females (whether lesbian or not) to exhibit only narrow feminine behaviour (Seidman 1994; see also Lehne 1995).

It is adults, of course, who play a critical role in guiding children into those gender roles deemed appropriate in a society. Parents are normally the first and most crucial agents of socialization. But other adults, older siblings, the mass media, and religious and educational institutions also exert an important influence on gender-role socialization in Canada and elsewhere.

It is not hard to test how rigid gender-role socialization can be. Just try transgressing some gender norms—say, by smoking a cigar in public if you are female or carrying a purse if you are male. That was exactly the assignment

Table 11-1   An Experiment of Gender Norm Violations by University Students

Norm Violations by Women	Norm Violations by Men
Send men flowers	Wear fingernail polish
Spit in public	Needlepoint in public
Use men's bathroom	Throw Tupperware party
Buy jock strap	Cry in public
Buy/chew tobacco	Have pedicure
Talk knowledgeably about cars	Apply to babysit
Open doors for men	Shave body hair

Sociology students were asked to behave in ways that might be regarded as violating gender norms. This is a sample of their actual choices over a seven-year period.
Source: Nielsen et al. 2000:287.

given to a group of sociology students. Professors asked the students to behave in ways that they thought violated norms of how a man or woman should act. The students had no trouble coming up with gender norm "transgressions" (see Table 11-1), and they kept careful notes on how others reacted to their behaviour, ranging from amusement to disgust (Nielsen, Walden, and Kunkel 2000).

> **Think about It**
> Do you agree that the actions taken by the students in Table 11-1 test the boundaries of conventional gender behaviour?

Gender-Role Socialization and Social Class

The 2000 movie *Billy Elliott* portrays the life of a young boy growing up in a British mining town and the gender socialization he undergoes. His father and older brother, both coal miners on strike, discover that Billy is secretly attending ballet classes rather than the boxing lessons he pretended to be taking. Billy's behaviour causes his father great concern and displeasure. He sees his son's dancing as a lack of conformity to gender-role expectations. Billy's father actively discourages him from pursuing his love of dance, until he comes to the realization that Billy possesses great talent. At that point, even though his son is defying cultural norms and community standards of appropriate male behaviour, the father begins to support and encourage Billy in his dream to become a professional dancer.

Research shows that patterns of gender socialization are not homogeneous, but rather vary according to the social class to which a person belongs. Working-class parents tend to be more concerned with their children's outward conformity to society's norms and roles (M. Kohn, Slomeznsky, and Schoenbach 1986). Middle-class parents, in contrast, tend to be more concerned with their children's motivation for certain behaviours and focus on developing such qualities as self-expression and self-control (Langman 1987). Upper-middle-class families are most likely to support more egalitarian gender relations and thus socialize their children accordingly (Langman 1987; Lips 1993). Children who are raised by middle-class, career-oriented mothers tend to hold more egalitarian attitudes relating to men's and women's roles (Tuck, Rolfe, and Adair 1994).

Women's Gender Roles

How does a girl come to develop a feminine self-image whereas a boy develops one that is masculine? In part, they do so by identifying with females and males in their families and neighbourhoods and in the media. If a young girl regularly sees female characters on television working as defence lawyers and judges, she may believe that she herself can become a lawyer and then a judge. And it will not hurt if women that she knows—her mother, sister, parents' friends, or neighbours—are lawyers. By contrast, if this young girl sees women portrayed in the media only as models, nurses, and secretaries, her identification and self-image will be quite different. Even if she does become a professional, she may secretly regret falling short of the media stereotype—a shapely, sexy young woman in a bathing suit (N. Wolf 1991).

Television is far from being alone in stereotyping women. Studies of children's books published in North

America in the 1940s, 1950s, and 1960s found that females were significantly under-represented in central roles and illustrations. Virtually all female characters were portrayed as helpless, passive, incompetent, and in need of a strong male caretaker. By the 1980s, there was somewhat less stereotyping in children's books, with some female characters shown to be active. An example of this change is seen in the 1980 children's book, *The Paper Bag Princess*, by Canadian writer Robert Munsch, where the female character is the active one who takes control of her life. Nevertheless, boys were still shown engaged in active play three times as often as girls (Kortenhaus and Demarest 1993). Females tended to be shown mostly in traditional roles, such as mother, grandmother, or volunteer, even though they also held non-traditional roles, such as working professional (Etaugh 2003).

Social research on gender roles reveals some persistent differences between men and women in North America and Europe. Women experience a mandate to both marry and be a mother. Often, marriage is viewed as the true entry into adulthood. And women are expected not only to become mothers but to *want* to be mothers. Obviously, men play a role in these events, but the events do not appear to be as critical in identifying the life course for a man. Society defines men's roles by economic success. Although women may achieve recognition in the labour force, it is not as important to their identity as it is for men (Doyle and Paludi 1998; Russo 1976).

Traditional gender roles have most severely restricted females. Throughout this chapter, we will see how women have been confined to subordinate roles within the political and economic institutions of Canada and elsewhere. Yet, it is also true that gender roles have restricted males.

Men's Gender Roles

> During the game I always played the outfield. Right field. Far right field. And there I would stand in the hot sun wishing I was anyplace else in the world. (Fager et al. 1971)

This is the childhood recollection of a man who, as a boy, disliked sports, dreaded gym classes, and had particular problems with baseball. Obviously, he did not conform to the socially constructed male gender role and no doubt paid the price for it.

Men's roles are socially constructed in much the same way as women's roles are. Family, peers, and the media all influence how a boy or a man comes to view his appropriate role in society. Robert Brannon (1976) and James Doyle (1995) have identified five aspects of the male gender role:

- anti-feminine element—show no "sissy stuff," including any expression of openness or vulnerability
- success element—prove their masculinity at work and sports

- aggressive element—use force in dealing with others
- sexual element—initiate and control all sexual relations
- self-reliant element—stay cool and unflappable

No systematic research has established all these elements as common aspects among boys and men, but specific studies have confirmed individual elements.

Being anti-feminine is basic to men's gender roles. Males who do not conform to the socially constructed gender role face constant criticism and even humiliation both from children when they are boys and from adults as men. It can be agonizing to be treated as a "chicken" or a "sissy"—particularly if such remarks come from a father or brothers. At the same time, boys who successfully adapt to cultural standards of masculinity may grow up to be inexpressive men who cannot share their feelings with others. They remain forceful and tough—but as a result they are also closed and isolated (Faludi 1999; McCreary 1994; Sheehy 1999). In his film *Tough Guise*, Jackson Katz presents the case of societal violence being a product of socialized maleness.

In the past 35 years, inspired in good part by the contemporary feminist movement (examined later in the chapter), increasing numbers of men in North America have criticized the restrictive aspects of the traditional male gender role. Some men have taken strong public positions in support of women's struggle for full equality and have even organized voluntary associations, such as the White Ribbon Campaign (WRC), founded in Canada in 1991 to end men's violence against women. Nevertheless, the traditional male gender role remains well entrenched as an influential element of our culture (Messner 1997).

Cross-Cultural Perspective

To what extent do actual biological differences between the sexes contribute to the cultural differences associated with gender? ◀ P. 72 This question brings us back to the debate over "nature versus nurture." In assessing the alleged and real differences between men and women, it is useful to examine cross-cultural data.

The research of anthropologist Margaret Mead points to the importance of cultural conditioning—as opposed to biology—in defining the social roles of males and females. In *Sex and Temperament* (1963, original edition 1935; 1973), Mead describes typical behaviours of each sex in three different cultures in New Guinea:

> In one [the Arapesh], both men and women act as we expect women to act—in a mild parental responsive way; in the second [the Mundugumor], both act as we expect men to act—in a fierce initiating fashion; and in the third [the Tchambuli], the men act according to our stereotypes for women—are catty, wear curls, and go shopping—while the women are energetic, managerial, unadorned partners. (Preface to 1950 ed.)

If biology determined all differences between the sexes, then cross-cultural differences, such as those described by Mead, would not exist. Her findings confirm the influential role of culture and socialization in gender-role differentiation. There appears to be no innate or biological reason to designate completely different gender roles for men and women.

In any society, gender stratification requires not only individual socialization into traditional gender roles within the family, but also the promotion and support of these traditional roles by other social institutions, such as religion and education. Moreover, even with all major institutions socializing the young into conventional gender roles, every society has women and men who resist and successfully oppose these stereotypes: strong women who become leaders or professionals, gentle men who care for children, and so forth. It seems clear that differences between the sexes are not dictated by biology. Indeed, the maintenance of traditional gender roles requires constant social controls—and these controls are not always effective.

Cultural conditioning is important in the development of gender role differences. Among the Bororo, a semi-nomadic people of West Africa, the male gender role includes ceremonial dancing (shown here), body painting, and other forms of personal adornment.

Use Your Sociological Imagination

How would your life and the lives of your family and friends be different if you lived in a society that was not gendered?

☐ HOW ARE GENDER RELATIONS EXPLAINED?

Cross-cultural studies indicate that societies dominated by men are much more common than those in which women play the decisive role. Sociologists have turned to all the major theoretical perspectives to understand how and why these social distinctions are established. Each approach focuses on culture, rather than biology, as the primary determinant of gender differences. Yet, in other respects, there are wide disagreements among advocates of these sociological perspectives. Box 11-1 discusses the role of education in the empowerment of women.

The Functionalist View

Functionalists maintain that gender differentiation has contributed to overall social stability. Sociologists Talcott Parsons and Robert Bales argued that to function most effectively, the family requires adults who will specialize in particular roles (1955). They viewed the traditional arrangement of gender roles as arising out of this need to establish a division of labour between marital partners.

Parsons and Bales contended that women take the expressive, emotionally supportive role and men the instrumental, practical role, with the two complementing each other. **Instrumentality** refers to emphasis on tasks, and a focus on more distant goals, as well as a concern for the external relationship between the family and other social institutions. **Expressiveness** denotes concern for the maintenance of harmony and the internal emotional affairs of the family. According to this theory, women's interest in expressive goals frees men for instrumental tasks, and vice versa. Women become "anchored" in the family as wives, mothers, and household managers; men are anchored in the occupational world outside the home. Of course, Parsons and Bales offered this framework in the 1950s, when many more women were full-time homemakers than

Sociology in the Global Community

The Empowerment of Women through Education

11-1

International declarations and targets to achieve certain rights for women include the education of girls and women as a key priority. For example, the U.N. Women's Conference in Cairo in 1990, the U.N. Social Summit in Copenhagen in 1995, the U.N. Conference in Beijing in 1995, and the U.N. Millennium Summit in 2000 all made declarations to close the gender gap in primary and secondary education by 2005. All four international conferences set a target date of 2015 for the provision of universal primary education in all countries. Many of these declarations may not be achieved by the stated target date; however, they are often used as benchmarks for the overall social and economic development of a country. As well, the declarations may be used by women's groups of various countries to lobby for the achievement of these goals locally (van der Gaag 2004).

Globally, great disparities exist among the young women of the world: in 2002, 95 percent or more of young women in the northern hemisphere were literate, while in the rest of the world, 11 countries had literacy rates of less than 10 percent for young women (van der Gaag 2004). Although sociocultural, gender-based barriers to education and literacy are factors that have been associated with the disempowerment of girls and women, educating girls and women has profound empowering benefits for them as individuals:

- It improves their health as well as that of their children.
- It decreases their fertility.
- It increases their productivity.
- It enhances their ability to make informed decisions.
- It increases their status and power within the family.
- It increases their opportunity to take on leadership roles in the community.

Sources: UNESCO 2002; van der Gaag 2004, UNICEF 2006.

- It decreases their chances, and their children's chances, of living in poverty.

These benefits are inextricably connected to those of the community as a whole. Many countries, recognizing the key role of education in their social and economic development, are addressing the issue of girls' and women's education through integrated socioeconomic, cultural, and institutional approaches, in order to improve the educational participation of girls and women (UNESCO 2002). In Benin, for example, school fees for girls are being eliminated in public primary schools in the rural areas, and a media campaign to sensitize parents on issues related to gender and education has been implemented (van der Gaag 2004). UNICEF's *State of the World's Children 2007* report states that even though women's education is linked to children's survival and development, almost one out of every five girls in developing countries won't complete primary education. The UNICEF report—subtitled *Women and Children: The Double Dividend of Gender Equality*—suggested seven initiatives to promote gender equality, one of which was to abolish school fees and to encourage investment in girls' education by parents and communities.

Applying Theory

1. Why is the education of girls and women such a powerful force in changing the social and economic conditions of a community as a whole?
2. In what way does the empowerment of women through education relate to class and race?
3. How might conflict sociologists explain the global disparities in girls' and women's access to education?

---

is true today. These theorists did not explicitly endorse traditional gender roles, but they implied that dividing tasks between spouses was functional for the family unit.

Given the typical socialization of women and men in North America, the functionalist view is initially persuasive. However, it would lead us to expect girls and women with no interest in children to become babysitters and mothers. Similarly, males who love spending time with children might be "programmed" into careers in the business world. Such differentiation might harm the individual who does not fit into prescribed roles

while also depriving society of the contributions of many talented people who are confined by gender stereotyping. Moreover, the functionalist approach does not convincingly explain why men should be categorically assigned to the instrumental role and women to the expressive role.

The Conflict Response

Viewed from a conflict perspective, this functionalist approach masks underlying power relations between men and women. Parsons and Bales never explicitly presented the expressive and instrumental tasks as unequally valued by society, yet this inequality is quite evident. Although social institutions may pay lip service to women's expressive skills, it is men's instrumental skills that are most highly rewarded—whether in terms of money or prestige. Consequently, according to feminists and conflict theorists, any division of labour by gender into instrumental and expressive tasks is far from neutral in its impact on women.

Conflict theorists contend that the relationship between females and males has traditionally been one of unequal power and ownership of resources, with men in a dominant position over women. Men may originally have become powerful in pre-industrial times because their size, physical strength, and freedom from child-bearing duties allowed them to dominate women physically. In contemporary societies, such considerations are not as important, yet cultural beliefs about the sexes are long established, as anthropologist Margaret Mead and feminist sociologist Helen Mayer Hacker (1951, 1974) both stressed. Such beliefs support a social structure that places males in controlling positions.

Thus, conflict theorists see gender inequality as the systematic subjugation of women. If we use an analogy to Marx's analysis of class conflict in capitalist societies, we can say that males are like the bourgeoisie, or capitalists; they control most of the society's wealth, prestige, and power. Females are like the proletarians, or ◀ P. 191 workers; they can acquire valuable resources only by following the dictates of their "bosses." Men's work is uniformly valued, while women's work (whether unpaid labour in the home or wage labour) is devalued.

Both functionalist and conflict theorists acknowledge that it is not possible to change gender roles drastically without dramatic revisions in a culture's social structure. Functionalists perceive potential for social disorder, or at least unknown social consequences, if all aspects of traditional gender stratification are disturbed. Yet, for conflict theorists, no social structure is ultimately desirable if it is maintained by oppressing a majority of its citizens. These theorists argue that gender stratification may be functional for men—who hold power and privilege—but it is hardly in the interests of women (R. Collins 1975; Schmid 1980).

Feminist Perspectives

As we have noted in earlier chapters, feminist perspectives encompass a wide-ranging and diverse group of theories focusing on gender inequality, its causes, and its remedies. Feminist perspectives, however, despite their diversity, share the belief that women have been subordinated, undervalued, under-represented, and excluded in male-dominated societies, which in practical terms means most of the world. As varied as political philosophies, feminist perspectives include postmodern feminism, global feminism, liberal feminism, Marxist feminism, socialist feminism, anti-racist feminism, cultural feminism, eco-feminism, and radical feminism, to name a few. We discussed some of these streams in the first chapter. To briefly recap these theories, liberal feminism advocates that women's equality can be attained through minor adjustments to key institutions, creating greater opportunities for women's advancement in the public sphere. Marxist feminism places capitalism, with its private ownership of resources and unequal class relations, at fault for the oppression of women. Socialist feminism, in contrast, is based on the belief that the inextricably connected systems of capitalism and patriarchy are responsible for women's subjugation. Radical feminists see the root of women's oppression as being embedded in the patriarchy that exists in all societies, whether they are capitalist, communist, or socialist.

Ongoing developments and debates in feminist theory are producing theories of global feminism, which acknowledge and pay attention to differences in power, material

Conflict theorists emphasize that men's work is uniformly valued, while women's work (whether unpaid labour in the home or wage labour) is devalued. These women are making tents in a factory.

resources, geographies, and histories (i.e., colonialism) and reject the use of the Western World as the normative standard (Weedon 1999).

Although it might appear that there has been an explosion in the growth of feminist perspectives since the mid-1960s, the critique of women's position in society and culture goes back to some of the earliest works that have influenced sociology. Among the most important are Mary Wollstonecraft's *A Vindication of the Rights of Women* (originally published in 1792), John Stuart Mill's *The Subjection of Women* (originally published in 1869), and Friedrich Engels's *The Origin of Private Property, the Family, and the State* (originally published in 1884).

Engels, a close associate of Karl Marx's, argued that women's subjugation coincided with the rise of private property during industrialization. Only when people moved beyond an agrarian economy could males "enjoy" the luxury of leisure and withhold rewards and privileges from women. Drawing on the work of Marx and Engels, some contemporary feminist theorists view women's subordination as part of the overall exploitation and injustice that they see as inherent in capitalist societies. Some radical feminist theorists, however, view the oppression of women as inevitable in *all* male-dominated societies, whether they be labelled "capitalist," "socialist," or "communist" (Feuer 1959; Tuchman 1992).

Feminist sociologists are more likely to embrace a political action agenda. Also, some feminist perspectives argue that the very discussion of women and society has been distorted by the exclusion of women from academic thought, including sociology. Perhaps one of the best examples of this exclusion of women from academic sociology is that of the U.S. sociologist Jane Addams (1860–1935). Although Addams made significant contributions to sociology through her work on women and the family, urban settlements, and working-class immigrants, she was viewed by mainstream sociology as an outsider and not as a legitimate member of academia. At the time, her efforts, while valued as humanitarian, were seen as unrelated to the research and conclusions being reached in academic circles, which, of course, were male academic circles (M. Andersen 1997; J. Howard 1999).

For most of the history of sociology, studies were conducted on male subjects or about male-led groups and organizations, and the findings were generalized to all people. For example, over many decades, studies of urban life focused on street corners, neighbourhood taverns, and bowling alleys—places where men typically congregated. Although the insights were valuable, they did not give a full impression of city life because they overlooked the areas where women were likely to gather (L. Lofland 1975).

Since men and women have had different life experiences, the issues they approach are different, and even when they have similar concerns, they approach them from different perspectives. For example, women who enter politics today typically do so for different reasons than men do. Men often embark on a political career to make business contacts or build on them, a natural extension of their livelihood; women generally become involved because they want to help. This difference in interests is relevant to the likelihood of their future success. The areas in which women achieve political recognition revolve around such social issues as day care, the environment, education, and child protection—areas that do not attract a lot of big donors. Men focus on tax policies, business regulation, and trade agreements—issues that excite big donors. Sometimes, women do become concerned with these issues but then they must constantly reassure voters that they are still concerned about "family issues." Male politicians who occasionally focus on family issues, however, are seen as enlightened and ready to govern (G. Collins 1998).

Feminist theorists emphasize that male dominance in Canada and the world goes far beyond the economic sphere. In fact, although on the surface economic inequality may appear to be separate from gender inequality, it is actually inextricably related to spousal abuse, sexual harassment, and sexual assault. Violence toward women by men is a major component of many interrelated experiences that contribute to women's inequality in Canada and elsewhere.

Gender inequality is embedded in the various institutions of Canadian society—the family, the workplace, the state, the mass media, the religious organizations—and thus produces a systemic pattern of discrimination. This systemic pattern of discrimination on the basis of gender does not work alone but rather is interconnected with race, class, sexual orientation, and disability to produce multiple layers of inequality and discrimination. Feminists who emphasize the intersection of many factors point to the diversity of women's lives and situations, maintaining that gender alone cannot fully explain how Canadian women experience inequality.

The Interactionist Approach

Although functionalists and conflict theorists studying gender stratification typically focus on macro-level social forces and institutions, interactionist researchers often examine gender stratification on the micro level of everyday behaviour. As an example, studies show that men initiate up to 96 percent of all interruptions in cross-sex (male–female) conversations. Men are more likely than women to change topics of conversation, to ignore topics chosen by members of the opposite sex, to minimize the contributions and ideas of members of the opposite sex, and to validate their own contributions. These patterns reflect the conversational (and, in a sense, political) dominance of males. Moreover, even when women

Table 11-2 Sociological Perspectives on Gender

Theoretical Perspective	Emphasis
Functionalist	Gender differentiation contributes to social stability
Conflict	Gender inequality is rooted in the female–male power relationship
Feminist	Women's subjugation is integral to society and social structure
Interactionist	Gender distinctions are reflected in people's everyday behaviour

occupy a prestigious position, such as that of physician, they are more likely to be interrupted than their male counterparts (A. Kohn 1988; Tannen 1990; C. West and Zimmerman 1983).

In certain studies, all participants are advised in advance of the overall finding that males are more likely than females to interrupt during a cross-sex conversation. After learning this information, men reduce the frequency of their interruptions, yet they continue to verbally dominate conversations with women. At the same time, women reduce their already low frequency of interruption and other conversationally dominant behaviours.

These findings regarding cross-sex conversations have been frequently replicated. They have striking implications when we consider the power dynamics underlying likely cross-sex interactions—employer and job seeker, professor and student, husband and wife, to name only a few. From an interactionist perspective, these simple, day-to-day exchanges are one more battleground in the struggle for sexual equality—as women try to "get a word in edgewise" in the midst of men's interruptions and verbal dominance (Tannen 1994a, 1994b).

Table 11-2 summarizes the major sociological perspectives on gender.

☐ HOW CAN WOMEN BE AN "OPPRESSED MAJORITY"?

Many people—both male and female—find it difficult to conceive of women as a subordinate and oppressed group. Yet, take a look at the political structure of Canada: Women remain noticeably under-represented. For example, in October 2007, none of the provincial or territorial premiers in Canada was female. Although the past decades have brought many firsts for women in Canadian public life—Beverly McLachlin as the first woman to serve as chief justice of the Supreme Court of Canada (2000), Catherine Callbeck of Prince Edward Island as the first female to be elected premier (1993), Kim Campbell as first woman to

serve as Canada's prime minister (1993)—women remain under-represented in both federal and provincial/territorial politics. In 2008, women made up approximately 22 percent of those elected to the federal House of Commons, while women, as a group, made up approximately 51 percent of the Canadian population.

This lack of women in the highest decision-making positions is evidence of their relative powerlessness in Canada. In Chapter 10, we identified five basic properties that define a minority or subordinate group. If we apply this model to the situation of women in Canada, we find that a numerical majority group fits our definition of a *subordinate minority* (Dworkin 1982; Hochschild 1973):

1. Women experience unequal treatment. In 2003 in Canada, women working on a full-time, full-year basis had average earnings that constituted 71 percent of what their male counterparts made (Statistics Canada 2006m).

    Visible minority women in Canada not only earned less than both visible and non-visible minority men but also earned less than other women. In 2000, female visible minority workers aged 15 years and over earned an average of approximately $3000 less than non-visible minority women. As Table 11-3 illustrates, these women, in turn, earned less than both visible minority men and non-visible minority men (Statistics Canada 2006m).

    The majority of women employed continue to work in occupations in which women have traditionally been concentrated—nursing and other health-related occupations; sales and service; clerical and administrative positions; and teaching (Statistics Canada 2006m).

    Moreover, women are increasingly dominating the ranks of the impoverished, leading to what has been called the *feminization of poverty*. In Canada, a large number of women will face poverty in their senior years due to low CPP (Canada Pension Plan) and OAP (Old Age Pension) benefits; newly arrived immigrant women are particularly

◀ P. 200

Table 11-3 Average Employment Earnings for Visible Minority Women Compared with Non-visible Minority Women, Visible Minority Men, and Non-visible Minority Men, 2000

Category	Earnings ($)
Women from Visible Minorities	20 043
Women from Non-visible Minorities	23 283
Men from Visible Minorities	28 929
Men from Non-visible Minorities	37 956

Note: Figures are for paid workers, 15 years and over, 2000.
Source: Statistics Canada 2006m.

vulnerable to poverty, as their contributions to CPP may be lower.

Globally, women and girls make up a disproportionate number of the world's poor. The United Nations Population Fund's *State of World Population Report 2000* stated that women and girls the world over are still being denied access to health care and education. In Canada, women make up a disproportionate number of those with low incomes; in 2003, 31 percent of unattached women 16 and over had low income (Statistics Canada 2006m).

2. Women, despite their diversity, share physical and cultural characteristics that distinguish them from the dominant group (men).
3. Membership in this subordinate group is involuntary.
4. Through the rise of contemporary feminism, women are developing a greater sense of group solidarity, as we will see later in the chapter.
5. Many women feel that their subordinate status is most irrevocably defined within the institution of marriage. Even when women are employed outside the home, they are still largely responsible for the care of their homes and families (TD Bank 2007).

A photo of Canada's provincial and territorial premiers taken in 2008 illustrates the obvious: that power and privilege in Canada are inextricably related to gender and race.

Sexism and Sex Discrimination

Just as visible minorities in Canada are victimized by racism, women suffer from the sexism of our society. **Sexism** is the ideology that one sex is superior to the other. The term is generally used to refer to male prejudice and discrimination against women. In Chapter 10, we noted that visible minorities can suffer from both individual acts of racism and institutional discrimination. *Institutional discrimination* ◄ P. 242 was defined as the denial of opportunities and equal rights to individuals or groups that results from the normal operations of a society. In the same sense, women suffer both from individual acts of sexism (such as sexist remarks and acts of violence) and from institutional sexism.

It is not simply that particular men in Canada and elsewhere are biased in their treatment of women. All the major institutions of our society—including the government, armed forces, large corporations, the media, universities, and the medical establishment—are controlled by men.

These institutions, in their "normal," day-to-day operations, often discriminate against women and perpetuate sexism. For example, if the central office of a nationwide bank sets a policy that single women are a bad risk for loans—regardless of their income and investments—the institution will discriminate against women as a group. It will do so even at bank branches in which loan officers hold no personal biases concerning women but are merely "following orders." We will examine institutional discrimination against women within the educational system in Chapter 13.

Our society is run by male-dominated institutions, yet with the power that flows to men comes responsibility and stress. Men have higher reported rates of certain types of mental illness, shorter life spans, and greater likelihood of death from heart attack or strokes (see Chapter 15). The pressure on some men to succeed—and then to remain on top in a competitive world of work—can be especially intense. This is not to suggest that gender stratification may be as damaging to men as it is to women. But it is clear that the relative power and privilege men (white men in particular) enjoy are no guarantee of well-being.

The Status of Women Worldwide

Inequality is a theme that figures large when we examine the status of the world's women.

It is estimated that women grow half the world's food, but they rarely own land. They constitute one-third of the world's paid labour force but are generally found in the lowest-paying jobs. Single-parent households headed by women—which appear to be on the increase in many nations—are typically found in the poorest sections of the population. The feminization of poverty has become a global phenomenon. As in Canada, women worldwide are under-represented politically; globally, in 2006, women made up fewer than 17 percent of parliamentarians (Inter-Parliamentary Union 2007).

A detailed overview of the status of the world's women, issued by the United Nations in 1995, noted that "too often, women and men live in different worlds—worlds that differ in access to education and work opportunities, and in health, personal security, and leisure time." Over a decade later—in 2006—a report by UNICEF echoed many of the same gender disparities, identifying a number of areas of continuing concern:

- Despite advances in education for girls and women in the developing world, for every 100 boys not attending primary school, 115 girls will be in the same situation.
- Women almost always work in occupations with lower status and pay than men do. In both developing and developed countries, many women work as unpaid family labourers.

- Globally, a disproportionately large number of women and girls are affected by HIV/AIDS.
- More than 130 million women and girls alive today have been subjected to genital mutilation, typically carried out by male practitioners who fail to use sterilized instruments. This can lead to immediate and serious complications from infection and to long-term health problems.
- In 2002, 150 million girls and 73 million boys under the age of 18 experienced forced sexual intercourse or other forms of physical and sexual violence (UNICEF 2006).

Not surprisingly, there is a link between the wealth of industrialized nations and the poverty of women in developing countries. Viewed from a conflict perspective or through the lens of Immanuel Wallerstein's world systems analysis, the economies of developing nations are controlled and exploited by industrialized countries and multinational corporations based in those countries. Much of the exploited labour in developing nations, especially in the non-industrial sector, is performed by women. Women workers typically toil long hours for low pay and contribute significantly to their families' incomes (Jacobson 1993).

◀ P. 225

In industrial countries, women's unequal status can be seen in the division of housework, as well as the jobs they hold and the pay they earn. Sociologist Makiko Fuwa (2004) analyzed gender inequality in 22 industrial countries using data from the International Social Survey Programme. Fuwa looked first at how couples divided up their housework. Then she compared that data to society-wide measures of women's presence in high-status occupations, as well as their wages relative to men's. Figure 11-1 shows that while gender differences in empowerment vary widely from one country to the next, equality between the sexes is rare.

Think about It

Ilow does Canada compare to a number of other industrialized countries in terms of gender inequality?

Women in the Paid Workforce in Canada

One of the most significant social changes witnessed in Canada over the past half-century has been the movement of women into the paid workforce. Even though the majority of Canadian women now work for pay outside the home, most continue to experience gendered patterns of inequality relating to pay, working conditions, and opportunities for advancement.

▶ **FIGURE 11-1**

Gender Inequality in Industrial Nations

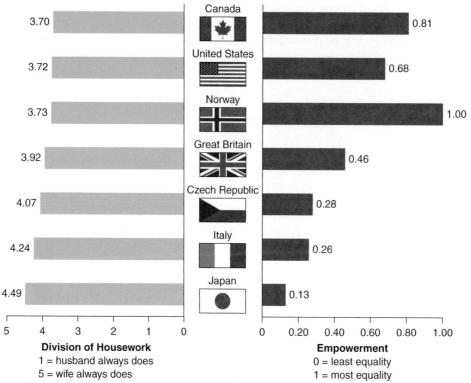

Division of Housework
1 = husband always does
5 = wife always does

Empowerment
0 = least equality
1 = most equality

Notes: Housework includes laundry, grocery shopping, dinner preparation, and care for sick family members. Empowerment includes the proportions of women in parliament, in management, and in professional/technical positions, as well as gender equality in income.
Source: Adapted from Fuwa 2004:757.

A Statistical Overview

No longer is the adult woman associated solely with the role of caregiver. Instead, millions of women—married and single, with and without children—are working in the labour force (see Figure 11-2). In 2006, 58.3 percent of all women in Canada aged 15 and over had jobs in the paid labour force, up from 42 percent in 1976. A majority of women are now members of the paid labour force, not full-time caregivers. The vast majority of employed women in Canada return to the paid labour force after giving birth. In 2006, 64.3 percent of all women with children under age 3 were employed, compared to 27.6 percent in 1976 (Statistics Canada 2007m).

Yet, women entering the job market find their options restricted in important ways. Particularly damaging is occupational segregation, or confinement to sex-typed "women's jobs." For example, in 2006, women accounted for 87.4 percent of all nursing, therapy, and other health-related jobs; 75 percent of all clerical, administrative jobs; and 56.8 percent of all sales and service jobs. Entering such sex-typed occupations places women in "service"

roles that parallel the traditional gender-role expectations of housewives "serving" their husbands and children.

Women are under-represented in occupations historically defined as "men's jobs," which often carry much greater financial rewards and prestige than women's jobs. For example, in 2006, women accounted for 47 percent of the paid labour force of Canada. Yet, they constituted only 26.3 percent of senior managers; 22 percent of those employed in natural science, engineering, and mathematics fields; and 6.5 percent in trades, transport, and construction. Canadian women have, however, made gains in the areas of business and finance, medicine, and dentistry, where they now account for over half of all professionals in these previously male-dominated fields (see Table 11-4).

Women from all groups, particularly those from visible minorities or those from older age groups, are at increased risk of encountering discrimination that prevents them ◀ P. 241 from reaching their full potential. As we saw in Chapter 10, the term *glass ceiling* refers to an invisible barrier that blocks the promotion of a qualified individual in a work environment because of the individual's gender,

▶ **FIGURE 11-2**

Employment of Women with Children under Age 16, by Family Status, 1976–2006

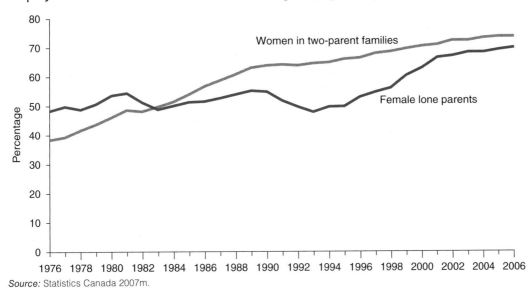

Source: Statistics Canada 2007m.

race, or ethnicity. A study of boards of directors in Canada found that only 12 percent of the seats on these boards were held by women (TD Bank 2007).

One response to the glass ceiling and other gender biases in the workplace is to start your own business

and work for yourself. This route to success, traditionally taken by men from immigrant and racial minority groups, has become more common among women as they have increasingly sought paid employment outside the home. Female entrepreneurs constitute a rapidly

Table 11-4 Canadian Women in Selected Occupations, 2006 Women as Percentage of Total Employed in Occupation	
Under-represented	
Trades, transport, and construction	6.5%
Natural sciences, engineering, mathematics	22.0%
Senior management	26.3%
Over-represented	
Nursing, therapy, other health-related	87.4%
Clerical and administrative	75.0%
Teaching	63.9%
Sales and service	56.8%
Roughly Equally Represented	
Business and finance	51.6%
Doctors, dentists, other health occupation	55.3%
Artistic, literary, recreational	54.1%

Source: Statistics Canada 2007m.

Research in Action 11-2
Differences in Male and Female Physicians' Communication with Patients

When Perri Klass told her 4-year-old son she would be taking him to the pediatrician, he replied, "Is she a nice doctor?" Klass, a professor of pediatrics, was struck by his innocent assumption that, like his mother, all pediatricians were female. "Boys can be doctors, too," she told him.

Not long ago, there would have been little potential for confusion on her son's part. Klass probably would not have been admitted to medical school, much less appointed a professor of medicine. But since the advent of the women's movement, the medical profession has been integrating women into its ranks. In Canada today, 53 percent of physicians under age 35 are female. Now, more than two dozen studies done over the past three and a half decades indicate that not only are women competent physicians, in some respects they are more effective than their male counterparts.

The female advantage is particularly noteworthy in physician–patient communication. Female primary-care physicians spend an extra two minutes talking with patients, or 10 percent more time than male primary-care physicians. They also engage in more patient-centred communication, more listening, asking questions about patients' personal well-being, and counselling patients about the concerns they bring to the doctor's office. Perhaps most important, female physicians tend to see their relationships with patients as active partnerships, in which they discuss several treatment options with patients rather than recommending a single course of treatment. From a sociological point of view, these differences between female and male physicians correspond to the gender differences in communication style that interactionist researchers have noted.

In some respects, female and male physicians do not differ. Researchers noted no differences in the quality or amount of time the two groups spend on purely medical matters, or on the length of time they spend conversing socially with patients.

Applying Theory

1. How might an interactionist approach be used to study gender differences in the way professors communicate with their students?

2. How might functionalist thinkers view differences in the communication styles of male and female doctors?

Sources: Canadian Medical Association 2007; Carroll 2003; Klass 2003:319; Kotulak 2005; Roter et al. 2002.

---

growing employment category in Canada. According to a report by TD Economics, the cumulative growth since 1987 of women's self-employment in the fields of finance, insurance, and real estate as well as professional, scientific and technical services is twice that of males (2007). In 2002, women represented 35 percent of the self-employed, up from 31 percent in 1985. (See Box 11-2 for a discussion of male and female physicians.)

The workplace patterns described here have one crucial result: Women earn much less money than men in Canada's paid labour force. In 2005, the average earnings of full-time female workers were about 71 percent of those for full-time male workers. Women in Canada are more likely to hold contract or temporary positions, giving them less pay and job security; 57 percent of contract workers are female (Statistics Canada 2005e). Given these data, it is hardly surprising to learn that many women are living in poverty, particularly when they must function as heads of households. In the discussion of poverty in Chapter 8, we noted that female heads of households and their children accounted for most of the nation's poor people living in families. Yet, not all women are in equal

danger of experiencing poverty. Aboriginal women as well as women who are members of visible minorities suffer from double jeopardy or multiple jeopardies. **Double jeopardy** refers to the discrimination that women experience as a result of the compounded effects of gender and race and ethnicity, while **multiple jeopardies** refers to the compounded effects of gender, race and ethnicity, class, age, or physical disability. Aboriginal women are more likely to live in poverty, to experience family violence, to be unemployed, to experience poor health, to be paid lower wages, to possess lower levels of education, and even to live shorter lives than non-Aboriginal women. Aboriginal women hold multiple memberships in disadvantaged categories and experience multiple forms of discrimination, all at the same time. Nelson and Robinson (1999:261) explain in this way:

> Women possessing multiple memberships in disadvantaged categories are in jeopardy of experiencing double, triple, or more forms of discrimination simultaneously. Since multiple jeopardies are difficult to disentangle, it is almost impossible to isolate which disadvantaged status has been accorded primary discrimination.

▶ **FIGURE 11-3**

Percentage of Workers Experiencing High Role Overload by Sex and Parental Status, 2001

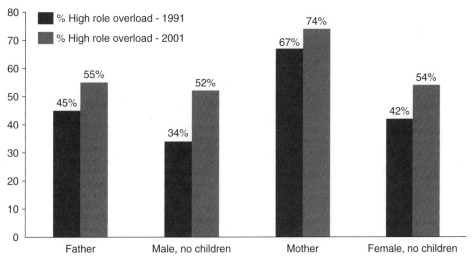

Legend:
- ■ % High role overload - 1991
- ■ % High role overload - 2001

Father: 45%, 55%
Male, no children: 34%, 52%
Mother: 67%, 74%
Female, no children: 42%, 54%

Source: Adapted from Duxbury and Higgins 2001, p. 22.

Social Consequences of Women's Employment

"What a circus we women perform every day of our lives. It puts a trapeze artist to shame." These words by the writer Anne Morrow Lindbergh (1955) attest to the lives of women today who try to juggle their work and family lives.

The consequence of this "role complexity" for women is to feel more time-stressed and to experience greater work-life conflict, which occurs when participation in one part of life (e.g., paid work) makes it difficult to fulfil responsibilities in another part (e.g., family) (Statistics Canada 2006m). Canadian research on "role overload"—having too much to do and too little time to do it—suggests that mothers in the paid labour force experience much greater high role overload than do fathers in the paid labour force (Duxbury and Higgins 2001) (see Figure 11-3).

> **Think about It**
>
> How might the percentages in Figure 11-3 be related to growing rates of depression and anxiety among working women?

This situation has many social consequences. For one thing, it puts pressure on child-care facilities and on public financing of daycare and even on the fast-food industry, which provides many of the meals that women used to prepare during the day. For another, it raises questions about what responsibility male wage earners have in the household.

Who does do the housework when women become wage earners? Studies indicate that there continues to be a clear gender gap in the performance of housework,

although the differences are narrowing (Statistics Canada 2006m). Joanna Hemm, a 34-year-old banquet server from Ottawa, expressed the reality of women's unpaid labour as follows:

> Men have their jobs. . . . When they come home they feel the need to unwind. They don't regard housework or cooking or cleaning as something that needs to be stuck to. (Freeze 2001)

Sociologist Arlie Hochschild has used the phrase "second shift" to describe the double burden—work outside the home followed by child care and housework—that many women face and few men share equitably (1989, 1990, 2005). On the basis of interviews with and observations

For some women, the workday never seems to end. Women who undertake most of the child care and housework in addition to working outside the home have a double burden, known as a "second shift."

of 52 couples over an 8-year period, Hochschild reports that the wives (and not their husbands) drive home from the office while planning domestic schedules and play dates for children—and then begin their second shift. Drawing on national studies, she concludes that women spend 15 fewer hours in leisure activities each week than their husbands do. In a year, these women work an extra month of 24-hour days because of the second shift; over a dozen years, they work an extra year of 24-hour days. Hochschild found that the married couples she studied were fraying at the edges, and so were their careers and their marriages. Juggling so many roles means that more things can go wrong for women, which contributes to stress. A recent poll of 381 Canadian government workers found that heavy family responsibilities had a profound impact on their paid jobs (Luciw 2007).

◀ P.93 With such reports in mind, many academics, policy analysts, and organizational experts have advocated greater governmental and corporate support for child care, more flexible family-leave policies, and other reforms designed to ease the burden on families (Moen and Roehling 2005).

Most studies of gender, child care, and housework focus on the time actually spent by women and men performing these duties. However, sociologist Susan Walzer was interested in whether there are gender differences in the amount of time that parents spend *thinking* about the care of their children (1996). Drawing on interviews

with 25 couples, Walzer found that mothers are much more involved than fathers in the invisible mental labour associated with taking care of a baby. For example, while involved in work outside the home, mothers are more likely to think about their babies and to feel guilty if they become so consumed with the demands of their jobs that they *fail* to think about their babies.

The very idea of what constitutes "work" in our society, whether it is done by men or women, at home or in the public sphere, is shaped by a "male-work role model" (Pleck and Corfman 1979). This model assumes that work will be full-time, continuous from graduation to retirement, that all other roles will be subordinate, and that a man's self-actualization will be based on this role. Implicit in this model is the assumption of paid work and stereotypical masculinity (A. Nelson and Robinson 2002). Since Canadian women, on average, engage in greater amounts of mental and physical labour in the care of their families and households, they run a greater risk of not having their labour considered as work.

The greater amounts of time women put into caring for their children, and to a lesser degree into housework, takes a special toll on women who are pursuing careers. In a 2005 survey published in the *Harvard Business Review*, about 40 percent of women indicated that they had voluntarily left work for months or years, compared to only 24 percent of men. As Figure 11-4 shows, Canadian women lawyers' major reason to choose another employer

▶ **FIGURE 11-4**

Reasons to Choose Work at Another [Law] Firm, by Gender

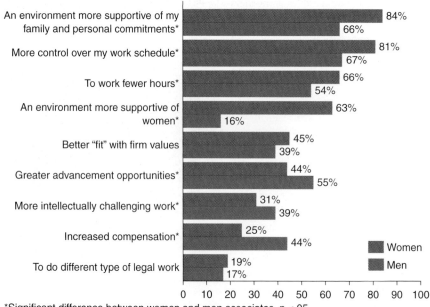

*Significant difference between women and men associates, p.<.05
Source: Catalyst 2005.

would be to find an environment more supportive of family and personal commitments, with 84 percent of the women respondents giving this reason as opposed to 66 percent of their male counterparts (Catalyst 2005).

Women: The Emergence of Feminism in Canada

Social movements involve the organized attempts of masses of people to bring about social change through their collective action. The women's movement, or feminist movement, is one such movement by which women and men have attempted to change their society—not only for the betterment of women but also for the betterment of society as a whole. Often, however, those in the movement have been white, middle-class women who fought for their own vision of social or moral reform—a vision that might improve the welfare of some women (depending on their race, ethnicity, and class) but not necessarily all. From the mid-nineteenth century to the mid-twentieth century, women's movements emerged in 32 countries worldwide (A. Nelson and Robinson 1999).

In Canada, the first wave of feminism beginning in the mid-nineteenth century had three faces—moral reform (or maternal feminism), liberalism, and socialism (Banks 1981). It concentrated largely on female suffrage and efforts to expand educational and employment opportunities for girls and women. Nellie McClung, perhaps Canada's foremost "maternal feminist," believed women were the "guardians of the race" and that it was therefore their responsibility to "lift high the standard of morality" (Adamson, Briskin, and McPhail 1998:31). During the 1920s, McClung and four fellow suffragettes—Irene Parlby, Henrietta Muir Edwards, Louise McKinney, and Emily Murphy—petitioned the Supreme Court of Canada to declare that women could become members of the Senate. The "Famous Five," as they were later known, appealed the negative decision of the Supreme Court of Canada to the British Privy Council. In 1929, the Privy Council declared that women were "persons" in the eyes of the law, making them eligible for appointment to the Senate. The "Persons case" marked a significant achievement for Canadian women.

The Famous Five were willing to fight for equality of some women; however, they were also willing to exclude others from their cause. Emily Murphy, Nellie McClung, and Louise McKinney were supporters of the eugenics movement, which espoused the desirability of certain races, ethnic groups, and classes. Emily Murphy, for example, spoke out against "aliens of colour," targeting the "black and yellow" races and advocating "whites-only" immigration and citizenship policies. The progress of the women's movement has affected Canadian women unevenly, depending on their race, ethnicity, and class.

Although women in Canada were granted the right to vote in federal elections in 1918 (Manitoba, Saskatchewan, Alberta, British Columbia, and Ontario had granted the provincial vote to women shortly before 1918), until 1960, Aboriginal women and men were entitled to vote only if they gave up their Indian status (Mossman 1994). It is worth noting that although Clare Brett Martin, in 1897, was the first woman to become a lawyer in the Commonwealth, "it was not until 1946 that the first Asian Canadian woman graduated from law school in Ontario" (A. Nelson and Robinson 1999: 493).

The second wave of feminism emerged in Canada in the 1960s, coinciding with the rise of feminist consciousness in the United States. The second wave of the movement in Canada focused on two areas of concern: (1) that women were treated differently and discriminated against (at home as well as in the paid workplace) and (2) that

Nellie McClung was one of a group of Canadian women's rights activists who later became known as the Famous Five. Although the Famous Five were concerned about the social injustice encountered by some Canadian women, their concerns excluded injustices because of ethnicity, race, and class.

women's unique qualities were undervalued (arguing for the recognition of these qualities) (Black 1993). This wave saw the huge growth of feminist perspectives in the social sciences, where feminist scholars challenged mainstream or "malestream" sociology's treatment of gender as it relates to studying crime, deviance, morality, aging, politics, and so on.

During this period, feminism began to become entrenched in institutions. Although essentially a grassroots movement, governments and international agencies around the world began to address some of the movement's concerns. In 1967, the Canadian government established the Royal Commission on the Status of Women, and the United Nations declared 1975–1985 the decade for women.

The third wave of feminism of the 1990s shifted focus away from common sources of oppression for women to multiple sources, acknowledging that what might be a source of oppression for some woman may not be for others. Today, there are movements on behalf of women in most countries of the world; however, the disparities of advantage and disadvantage remain great among the world's girls and women, not only between them and their male counterparts but also between females in developing and developed countries.

Social Policy and Gender Relations
Abortion and Sex Selection: The "New Eugenics"

The Issue

Today in Canada, a woman's decision to have an abortion is usually made in consultation with her doctor based on factors related to her overall health and well-being. However, as new reproductive and genetic technologies, referred to collectively as "reprogenetics" (McTeer 1999), emerge in our society and around the world, the twinning of abortion and reprogenetics presents new ethical and moral considerations. The most controversial of these is what some sociologists are calling "the new eugenics"—a new movement to promote the reproduction of those with particular characteristics, while attempting to limit or control the reproduction of those with other, less desirable traits. Thus, with new reproductive and genetic technologies, abortion has the potential to become no longer a choice a woman makes simply on the basis of her health and well-being, but an instrument of social control over what "type" (e.g., sex) of person is to be reproduced.

The Setting

Canada's first Criminal Code, established in 1892, made "procuring or performing an abortion a crime punishable by life imprisonment" (McTeer 1999:32). In 1968, amendments to the Criminal Code made abortion legal under certain conditions. The conditions included the approval of a special committee and that the abortion take place in an accredited hospital. However, hospitals and provincial or territorial governments were not required to establish the committee and many did not, thus making abortion inaccessible to many women in Canada, particularly those in non-urban areas. In 1988,

the law on abortion was changed again; today, it is a decision "left to the pregnant woman alone, and usually made in consultation with her doctor" (McTeer 1999:33).

In 1993, approximately 105 000 abortions were performed in Canada—27 abortions for every 100 live births. Race, class, and age differences are apparent as they relate to the incidence of abortion in Canada (Calliste 2001). For example, Aboriginal women in Canada were subjected to forced sterilization as a tactic of genocide, thus a policy of abortion on demand did not reflect their needs. In 1995, more than 42 percent of therapeutic abortions were performed on women between the ages of 18 and 24 (Statistics Canada 2000a).

In the late 1980s, the Canadian government called for the establishment of a royal commission investigating new reproductive technologies. These technologies and procedures included assisted reproduction, for example, artificial insemination (AI), in vitro fertilization (IVF), and direct ovum and sperm transfer (DOST); surrogacy (one woman carrying a pregnancy to term for another); and prenatal diagnosis (PND), which can include identification of the sex of the fetus. With the emergence of those technologies, the question becomes, "How can we as a society protect those who might be exploited or mistreated (e.g., surrogates, IVF-created human embryos, female fetuses) while still safeguarding women's reproductive rights relating to abortion and contraception?" (McTeer 1999).

In 1996, the Canadian government introduced Bill C-47, a legislative attempt to ban practices such as commercial surrogacy and sex selection for reasons other than those related to the health of the fetus (i.e., sex-linked hereditary diseases). Bill C-47, which set out to ban 13 different reproductive technological practices, died on the Order Paper when the 1997 federal election was called.

Sociological Insights

Sociologists see gender and social class as largely defining the issues surrounding abortion. The intense conflict over reproductive rights reflects broad differences over women's position in society. Sociologist Kristin Luker has offered a detailed study of activists in the pro-choice and pro-life movements (1984). Luker interviewed 212 activists, overwhelmingly women, who spent at least five hours a week working for one of these movements. According to Luker, each group has a consistent, coherent view of the world. Feminists involved in defending abortion rights typically believe that men and women are essentially similar: they support women's full participation in work outside the home and oppose all forms of sex discrimination. By contrast, most pro-life activists believe that men and women are fundamentally different. In their view, men are best suited for the public world of work, whereas women are best suited for the demanding and crucial task of rearing children. These activists are troubled by women's growing participation in work outside the home, which they view as destructive to the family and ultimately to society as a whole. The pro-life, or anti-abortion, activists see abortion as an act that denies nurturance and therefore diminishes the family, since the family is viewed as the major source of nurturance in society. Thus, these activists hold a view similar to that of functionalism, which connects the family to particular functions (Collier, Rosaldo, and Yanagisako 2001).

Feminist perspectives on abortion and reproductive technology have been led by the radical feminist vanguard, later to be joined by liberal and socialist perspectives (A. Nelson and Robinson 1999). The hope that technology would offer women escape from the "tyranny of their reproduction biology" (Firestone 1970) is now being tempered by the possible negative impact that technology could have on women's lives. Thus, radical feminist perspectives are now joined by many other forms of feminism in defining abortion, reproductive rights, and reproductive technologies as feminist issues (A. Nelson and Robinson 1999).

Policy Initiatives

The policies of the United States government and developing nations are intertwined. Throughout the 1980s, anti-abortion members of the U.S. Congress often successfully blocked foreign aid to countries that might use the funds to encourage abortion. And yet these developing nations generally have the most restrictive abortion

▶ **FIGURE 11-5**

The Global Divide on Abortion

Nations where abortion is permitted upon request

Note: Data current as of December 2004. Countries that prohibit abortion under any circumstances are Chile, El Salvador, Malta, and the Holy See (Vatican City).
Sources: Adapted from Gonnut 2001; United Nations Population Division 1998, 2004.

laws. As shown in Figure 11-5, it is primarily in Africa, Latin America, and parts of Asia that women are not able to terminate a pregnancy on request. As might be expected, illegal abortions are most common in these nations. In general, the more restrictive a nation's legislation on abortion, the higher its rate of unsafe abortions, for pregnancies may typically be terminated by unskilled health providers or by the pregnant women themselves.

Globally, countries' responses to new reproductive and genetic technologies vary in terms of the guidelines and legislation set in place to regulate their use. For example, Australia, Austria, Brazil, the Czech Republic, Denmark, Egypt, France, Germany, Hungary, Israel, Mexico, the Netherlands, Norway, Saudi Arabia, Singapore, South Africa, Spain, Sweden, Taiwan, Turkey, and the United Kingdom have some form of legislation to deal with how these technologies can be used. Other countries, such as Argentina, Egypt, Finland, Italy, Poland, Japan, South Korea, Switzerland, and the United States, have guidelines rather than legislation for the use of assisted reproductive technologies. Since the failure of Bill C-47 to become law, Canada's federal government has established a voluntary moratorium on certain reproductive and genetic practices. Greece, India, Jordan, and Portugal are among the countries that have neither legislation nor guidelines.

In India, and other countries where cultural preferences for male offspring remain strong, the coupling of prenatal diagnosis techniques, such as ultrasound and amniocentesis, which identify the sex of the fetus, and the use of abortion, can result in the birth of fewer female children. Although these Western-based prenatal diagnosis technologies can be used to identify and abort fetuses with genetic abnormalities, they also open the door to sex selection for cultural or social reasons. Saraswati Raju, a professor of gender and demography at Jawaharlal Nehru University in New Delhi, states that the fate of the female infant in India has been getting worse in recent decades (Lakshimi 2001). The most recent Indian census showed that the percentage of girls under age 6 has dropped since the previous census. Although the Indian government has banned the use of sex-selection tests and doctors' associations have discouraged their use, the tests persist and the government is unable to stop the practice. Despite widespread societal efforts to improve the status of girls and women in Indian society, a baby girl is viewed as a liability and a strong cultural preference for male children persists.

A recent report by UNICEF notes that "birth histories and census data reveal an unusually high proportion of male births and male children under [age] five in Asia, especially India and China, suggesting sex-selection through abortion and infanticide in the world's two most populous countries" (CBC 2006a).

Although it is rarer, sex selection can be used to produce female offspring as well. In 2000, a Scottish couple attempted to use a human rights bill in their country to force the British government to allow them to use sex-selection technology to produce a daughter. The couple already had four boys and recently had lost their 3-year-old daughter in a tragic accident.

According to Maureen McTeer, a former member of the Royal Commission on New Reproductive Technologies, sex selection violates our notions of equality as enshrined in the Canadian Charter of Rights and Freedoms and in our human-rights laws. In addition, she argues, allowing sex-selection practices at home would detract from Canada's international commitment to eliminate discrimination against women.

Applying Theory

1. According to conflict thinkers, who is most vulnerable to exploitation through the use of new reproductive and genetic technologies?
2. How might some feminist perspectives weigh the individual's right to reproduce against the society's need to regulate the use of these new technologies?
3. How might interactionist sociologists approach the study of reproductive or genetic technology for the purpose of selecting the sex of their offspring?

CHAPTER RESOURCES

Summary

How is Gender Socially Constructed?
- Like race, gender is an ascribed status that is socially constructed, providing a basis for social differentiation.
- The social construction of gender defines significantly different expectations for females and males.
- This social construction produces gender roles, which are revealed in our work and behaviour and in how we react to others.
- Females are restricted by gender roles, as are males.
- The research of anthropologist Margaret Mead points to the importance of cultural conditioning in defining the social roles of males and females.

How are Gender Relations Explained?
- Functionalists maintain that sex differentiation contributes to overall social stability, whereas conflict theorists contend that the relationship between females and males has been one of unequal power, with men in a dominant position over women. This dominance also shows up in everyday interactions.
- Feminist perspectives are diverse and vary in their explanation of the sources of women's inequality; they all agree, however, about the importance of social change, which would lead to greater equality.
- Interactionists study gender relations as reflections of everyday behaviour.

How can Women be an "Oppressed Majority"?
- Although numerically a majority, in many respects, women fit the definition of a subordinate minority group, within Canada and in most parts of the world.
- Women around the world experience **sexism** (p. 272) and institutional discrimination.
- Even though women have taken on more and more hours of paid employment outside the home, they continue to bear the primary responsibility for the care of their homes and families.

Critical Thinking Questions

1. Sociologist Barbara Bovee Polk suggests that women are oppressed because they constitute an alternative subculture that deviates from the prevailing masculine value system (1974). Does it seem valid to view women as an "alternative subculture"? In what ways do women support and deviate from the prevailing masculine value system evident in Canada?
2. In what ways is the social position of white women in Canada similar to that of Asian-Canadian women, black women, or Aboriginal women? In what ways is a woman's social position markedly different, given her racial and ethnic status?
3. In what ways do you think your behaviour, values, educational choices, or career plans have been influenced by gender socialization? Can you think of ways in which the social class of your family has influenced your gender socialization?
4. How might interactionist sociologists approach the emerging trend of more men engaging in cosmetic surgery?

Key Terms

Double jeopardy   Discrimination that women experience as a result of the compounded effects of gender and race and ethnicity. (p. 276)

Expressiveness   The concern for maintenance of harmony and the internal emotional affairs of the family. (p. 267)

Gender   Culturally and socially constructed identity as a man or a women. (p. 263)

Homophobia   Fear of and prejudice against homosexuality. (p. 264)

Instrumentality   The emphasis on tasks, along with a focus on more distant goals and a concern for the external relationship between the family and other social institutions. (p. 267)

Multiple jeopardies   Compounded effects of gender, race and ethnicity, class, age, or physical disability. (p. 276)

Sex   Biological category which distinguishes between female and male. (p. 263)

Sexism   The ideology that one sex is superior to the other. (p. 272)

Additional Readings

Crow, Barbara, and Lise Gotell, eds. 2009. *Open Boundaries: A Canadian Women's Studies Reader*, 3rd ed. Don Mills, ON: Prentice Hall. A very useful introductory reader for women's studies students and instructors.

Epstein, Cynthia Fuchs, Carroll Seron, Bonnie Oglensky, and Robert Saute. 1999. *The Part-Time Paradox: Time Norms, Professional Life, Family and Gender.* New York: Routledge. The authors explore the conflict and tension between the time demands of career and family life; they also examine the choice of part-time work as a solution.

Mandell, Nancy, ed. 2005. *Feminist Issues: Race, Class, and Sexuality*, 3rd ed. Don Mills, ON: Prentice Hall. In this book, a number of contributors cover a broad and diverse range of topics, including beauty, status and aging, violence, men in feminism, women and religion, and lesbianism.

Nelson, Adie. 2006. *Gender in Canada*, 3rd ed. Don Mills, ON: Prentice Hall. A comprehensive review of gender in Canada, covering such topics as intimate relations, gender and aging, marriage and parenting, work, and symbolic representations of gender.

 ## Online Learning Centre

Visit the *Sociology: A Brief Introduction* Online Learning Centre at www.mcgrawhill.ca/olc/schaefer to access quizzes, interactive exercises, video clips, and other research and study tools related to this chapter.

 ## Reel Society Video Clips

 *Reel Society* can be used to spark discussion about the following topics from this chapter:

- Gender roles in North America
- Cross-cultural perspective
- Sexism and sex discrimination
- The status of women worldwide

chapter 12

FAMILIES AND INTIMATE RELATIONSHIPS

Family Violence Hurts

Speak up!

But it's hard to know what to do. Now you can find out.

Visit **stopfamilyviolence.pe.ca**
Call 1-800-236-5196 or (902)368-5967
If you are in an emergency situation, call 911.

Premier's Action Committee on Family Violence Prevention

In contrast to the highly popularized view of families being safe and loving, many families are sources of danger and abuse. This poster, sponsored by Stop Family Violence, a government committee on family violence prevention in Prince Edward Island, calls attention to the needs of abused family members.

☐ **What is a Family?**

☐ **How do Sociologists Study Families?**

☐ **What are the Diverse Patterns of Marriage and Family?**

Boxes

SOCIOLOGY IN THE GLOBAL COMMUNITY: Domestic Violence
SOCIAL POLICY AND THE FAMILY: Reproductive Technology

He says that when his one-time girlfriend phoned him to let him know she was pregnant, she excitedly greeted him with the words, "Hello Papa."

The man had donated his sperm so that the ex-girlfriend and her lesbian partner could have a child.

Today, in a quarrel for the age in which we live, the man is in court to have himself recognized as the child's father so that, he says, he can develop "a loving and stable relationship" with the little child.

To the usual bitterness of any family-law dispute, this feud also features novel dimensions, from the ethical complexities of modern reproductive technologies to the new legal dynamics of same-sex marriages.

The litigation is "deciding the fate of this child in very arduous circumstances," Anne-France Goldwater, the lawyer for the biological mother, told a Quebec Superior Court hearing yesterday.

The case has raised concerns among lesbian couples who have had to turn to donors to become parents, said Laurie Arron, director of advocacy of the gay-rights group, Egale Canada. "Families come in all forms and the law should match the facts of a family," he said.

Details that can lead to the identification of the parties cannot be published. This story will refer to the biological mother as Jane.

The man says he and Jane used to date and remained friends even after they broke up and she soon began a relationship with a woman.

Jane eventually married her girlfriend.

Then, after they broke up, the man says in his court petition, he and Jane started talking about having a child.

"Much soul-searching went on by both parties and serious in-depth discussions took place," the man's motion says.

The man says that he has played an active role in the endeavour, that he was even at the hospital for the birth and that "it was always agreed between [himself] and [Jane] that they would both be actively involved in the child's life as mother and father of the child."

The two women say he wasn't the only man they approached and that the candidates were told the donor would not have legal status.

The women's lawyers cite an article of the Quebec Civil Code that states that there can be no bond of filiation if there hasn't been sexual intercourse. On the birth certificate, the two women are listed as the little child's parents.

The man says in his court filings that when he advised the couple that he would launch court proceedings, he was told all contact with the child would be ended and he "was advised not even to bother phoning."

"This attitude is totally destructive . . . depriving [the child's] rights to her father, preventing her from further developing a loving and stable relationship with [the father]," his motion says.

Last spring [2004], the man obtained a ruling granting him access to the child.

The women went to curtail that, fearing that any attachment between the toddler and the man could be cited eventually as a way for him to be the "psychological parent" of the child.

Mr. Justice Jean-Pierre Sénécal was to begin hearing the case yesterday. However, both sides wanted the case to unfold behind closed doors.

After a day-long debate, Judge Sénécal rejected the request, saying that as long as they did not identify the parties, the media should be present because the proceedings were in the public interest.

The case has been suspended while the issue of media access is taken to the Quebec Court of Appeal.

☐ *(Ha 2004)*

In the article from *The Globe and Mail* that opens the chapter, Tu Thanh Ha illustrates the diverse forms of families, underscored by social factors, such as the ethical complexities of modern reproductive technologies and new legal dynamics of same-sex marriage. New laws, new technologies, and new child-rearing patterns have all combined to create new forms of family life. Today, for example, more women are essential contributors to their families through their paid work, whether married or as a single parent. Blended families—the result of divorces and remarriages—are almost the norm. Many Canadians are seeking intimate relationships outside marriage, particularly in Quebec, whether it be in same-sex or opposite-sex cohabiting arrangements. And, of course, same-sex civil marriage became legal in Canada in 2005.

In this chapter, we address the subject of family and intimate relationships in Canada as well as in other parts of the world. As we will see, family patterns differ from one culture to another and within the same culture. A **family** can be defined as a set of people related by blood, marriage (or some other agreed-on relationship), or adoption who share the primary responsibility for reproduction and caring for members of society. A census family, as defined by Statistics Canada, is "a now-married couple, a common-law couple or a lone-parent with a child or youth who is under the age of 25 and who does not have his or her spouse living in the household. Now-married couples may or may not have such children and youth living with them" (Statistics Canada 2005c). Married couples and common-law couples are classified as husband-and-wife families and the partners in the couple are classified as spouses (Statistics Canada 2005c). With the 2005 passage of Bill C-38, the Civil Marriage Act, gays and lesbians can now be afforded spousal status, as their civil unions are legal in all Canadian jurisdictions.

In this chapter, we see that the family is universal—found in every culture—however varied in its organization. We will look at the family and intimate relationships from the functionalist, conflict, interactionist, and feminist points of view and at the variations in marital patterns and family life, including different family forms of child rearing. We pay particular attention to the increasing number of people in dual-income or single-parent families, the decline in the adult population that is married, and the legalization of same-sex marriage in Canada.

We examine divorce in Canada and consider diversity patterns, including cohabitation, remaining single, lesbian and gay relationships, and marriage without children. In the social policy section, we look at controversial issues surrounding the use of reproductive technology.

Use Your Sociological Imagination

What was your view of Bill C-38? What do you think the major reasons were for those who opposed the passage of the bill?

☐ WHAT IS A FAMILY?

Among Tibetans, a woman may be simultaneously married to more than one man, usually brothers. This system allows sons to share the limited amount of good land. A Hopi woman may divorce her husband by placing her belongings outside the door. A Trobriand Island couple signals marriage by sitting in public on a porch eating yams provided by the bride's mother. She may continue to provide cooked yams for a year while the groom's family offers in exchange such valuables as stone axes and clay pots (Haviland 1999).

As these examples illustrate, there are many variations in the family from culture to culture. Yet the family as a social institution is present in all cultures. Moreover, certain general principles concerning its composition, kinship patterns, and authority patterns are universal.

Composition of a Family

If we were to take our information on what a family is from what we see on television, we might come up with some very strange scenarios. The media don't always help us get a realistic view of the family. Moreover, many people still think of the family in very narrow terms—as a heterosexual married couple and their unmarried children living together, like the families in the old *Cosby Show*, *Family Ties*, or *Growing Pains*. However, this is but one type of family, what sociologists refer to as a **nuclear family**. The term nuclear family is well chosen, since this type of family serves as the nucleus, or core, upon which

German photographer Uwe Ommer took this and other photographs of families around the world. For 4 years, he travelled the world, visiting 130 countries on 5 continents in search of families in various societies. This photograph shows a Syrian family.

alized nations, including the United States, Great Britain, and Japan.

A family in which relatives—such as grandparents, aunts, or uncles—live in the same home as parents and their children is known as an **extended family**. Although not common, such living arrangements do exist in Canada. The structure of the extended family offers certain advantages over that of the nuclear family. Crises, such as death, divorce, and illness, put less strain on family members, since there are more people who can provide assistance and emotional support. In addition, the extended family constitutes a larger economic unit than the nuclear family. If the family is engaged in a common enterprise—a farm or a small business—the additional family members may represent the difference between prosperity and failure.

> **Think about It**
> What changes would you expect to see in Figure 12-1's percentages by 2011?

larger family groups are built. Some people in Canada may see the nuclear family as the preferred family arrangement. Yet, the 2006 Canadian census revealed that for the first time ever there were more couples without children than with children (Statistics Canada 2007d).

The proportion of households in Canada comprising married heterosexual couples with children at home has decreased steadily over the past 30 years, and this trend is expected to continue. At the same time, there have been increases in the number of single-parent households (see Figure 12-1). Similar trends are evident in other industri-

In considering these differing family types, we have limited ourselves to the form of marriage that is characteristic of Canada—monogamy. The term **monogamy** describes a form of marriage in which two people are married only to each other. Some observers, noting the rate of divorce in Canada, have suggested that "serial monogamy" is a more accurate description of marriage as it exists in this part of the world. Under **serial monogamy**, a person may have several spouses in his or her life but only one spouse at a time.

Some cultures allow an individual to have several spouses simultaneously. This form of marriage is known as **polygamy**. In fact, most societies throughout the

▶ **FIGURE 12-1**

Distribution of Census Families, 2001 and 2006

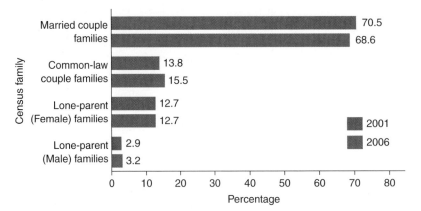

Source: Statistics Canada 2007d.

world, past and present, have preferred polygamy to monogamy. Anthropologist George Murdock sampled 565 societies and found that more than 80 percent had some type of polygamy as their preferred form (1949, 1957). Although polygamy steadily declined through most of the twentieth century, in at least five countries in Africa, 20 percent of men are still in polygamous marriages (Population Reference Bureau 1996).

There are two basic types of polygamy. According to Murdock, the most common—endorsed by the majority of cultures he sampled—was **polygyny**. Polygyny refers to the marriage of a man to more than one woman at the same time. The various wives are often sisters, who are expected to hold similar values and who have already had experience sharing a household. In polygynous societies, relatively few men actually have multiple spouses. Most individuals live in typical monogamous families; having multiple wives is viewed as a mark of status.

The other principal variation of polygamy is **polyandry**, under which a woman can have more than one husband at the same time. This is the case in the culture of the Todas of southern India. Polyandry, however, tends to be exceedingly rare in the world today. It has been accepted by some extremely poor societies that practise female infanticide (the killing of baby girls) and thus have a relatively small number of women. Like many other societies, polyandrous cultures devalue the social worth of women.

Kinship Patterns: To Whom are We Related?

Many of us can trace our roots by looking at a family tree or listening to elderly family members tell us about their lives—and about the lives of ancestors who died long before we were even born. Yet, a person's lineage is more than simply a personal history; it also reflects societal patterns that govern descent. In every culture, children encounter relatives to whom they are expected to show an emotional attachment. The state of being related to others is called **kinship**. Kinship is culturally learned and is not totally determined by biological or marital ties. For example, adoption creates a kinship tie that is legally acknowledged and socially accepted.

The family and the kin group are not necessarily the same. Although the family is a household unit, kin do not always live together or function as a collective body on a daily basis. Kin groups include aunts, uncles, cousins, in-laws, and so forth. In a society such as Canada, the kinship group may come together only rarely, as for a wedding or funeral. However, kinship ties frequently create obligations and responsibilities. We may feel compelled to assist our kin and feel free to call on relatives for many types of aid, including loans and babysitting.

Smile—it's family reunion time! The state of being related to others is called kinship. Kin groups include aunts, uncles, cousins, and so forth. This photo by Uwe Ommer shows a three-generation family from Armenia.

How do we identify kinship groups? The principle of descent assigns people to kinship groups according to their relationship to an individual's mother or father. There are three primary ways of determining descent. Generally in Canada, people follow the system of **bilateral descent**, which means that both sides of a person's family are regarded as equally important. For example, no higher value is given to the brothers of a father than to the brothers of a mother.

Most societies—according to George Murdock, 64 percent—give preference to one side of the family or the other in tracing descent. **Patrilineal** (from the Latin *pater*, "father") **descent** indicates that only the father's relatives are important in terms of property, inheritance, and emotional ties. Conversely, in societies that favour **matrilineal** (from the Latin *mater*, "mother") **descent**, only the mother's relatives are significant.

New forms of reproductive technology (discussed in the chapter-ending social policy section) will force a new way of looking at kinship. Today, a combination of biological and social processes can "create" a family member, requiring that more distinctions be made about who is related to whom (C. Cussins 1998).

Authority Patterns: Who Rules?

Imagine that you have recently married and must begin to make decisions about the future of your new family. You and your spouse face many questions. Where will you live? How will you furnish your home? Who will do the cooking, the shopping, and the cleaning? Whose friends will be invited to dinner? Each time a decision must be made, an issue is raised: Who has the power to make the

◀ P. 14 decision? In simple terms, who rules the family? The conflict perspective examines these questions in the context of gender stratification, in which men hold dominant positions over women in capitalist societies in general and in opposite-sex families in particular.

Societies vary in the way that power within the family is distributed. If a society expects males to dominate in all family decision making, it is termed a **patriarchy**. Frequently, in patriarchal societies, such as Iran, the eldest male wields the greatest power, although wives are expected to be treated with respect and kindness. A woman's status in Iran is typically defined by her relationship to a male relative, usually as a wife or daughter. In many patriarchal societies, a woman finds it more difficult to obtain a divorce than a man does (G. Farr 1999). By contrast, in a **matriarchy**, women have greater authority than men. Matriarchies, which are very uncommon, emerged among some of Canada's Aboriginal tribal societies and in nations in which men were absent for long periods of time for warfare or food gathering.

A third type of authority pattern, the **egalitarian family**, is one in which spouses are regarded as equals. This does not mean, however, that each decision is shared in such families. Wives may hold authority in some spheres, husbands in others. Many sociologists believe the egalitarian family has begun to replace the patriarchal family as the social norm in Canada.

☐ HOW DO SOCIOLOGISTS STUDY FAMILIES?

Do we really need the family? A century ago, Friedrich Engels, a colleague of Karl Marx's, described the family as the ultimate source of social inequality because of its role in the transfer of power, property, and privilege (1884). More recently, conflict theorists have argued that the family contributes to societal injustice, denies opportunities to women that are extended to men, and limits freedom in sexual expression and selection of a mate. By contrast, the functionalist perspective focuses on the ways in which the family gratifies the needs of its members and contributes to the stability of society. The interactionist view considers more intimate, face-to-face relationships.

Functionalist View

There are six paramount functions performed by the family, first outlined more than 65 years ago by sociologist William F. Ogburn (Ogburn and Tibbits 1934):

1. *Reproduction.* For a society to maintain itself, it must replace dying members. In this sense, the family contributes to human survival through its function of reproduction.

2. *Protection.* Unlike the young of other animal species, human infants need constant care and economic security. The extremely long period of dependency for children places special demands on older family members. In all cultures, it is the family that assumes ultimate responsibility for the protection and upbringing of children.

3. *Socialization.* Parents and other kin monitor a child's behaviour and transmit the norms, values, and language of a culture to the child (see Chapters 3 and 4). ◀ P. 80

4. *Regulation of sexual behaviour.* Sexual norms are subject to change over time (for instance, changes in customs for dating) and across cultures (Islamic Saudi Arabia compared with more permissive Denmark). However, whatever the time period or cultural values in a society, standards of sexual behaviour are most clearly defined within the family circle. The structure of society influences these standards. In male-dominated societies, for example, formal and informal norms generally permit men to express and enjoy their sexual desires more freely than women may.

5. *Affection and companionship.* Ideally, the family provides members with warm and intimate relationships and helps them feel satisfied and secure. Of course, a family member may find such rewards outside the family—from peers, in school, at work—and may perceive the home as an unpleasant place. Nevertheless, unlike other institutions, the family is obligated to serve the emotional needs of its members. We *expect* our relatives to understand us, to care for us, and to be there for us when we need them.

6. *Provision of social status.* We inherit a social position because of the "family background" and reputation of our parents and siblings. The family unit presents the newborn child with an ascribed status of race and ethnicity that helps to determine his or her place within a society's stratification system. Moreover, family resources affect children's ability to pursue certain opportunities, such as higher education and specialized lessons.

The family has traditionally fulfilled a number of other functions, such as providing religious training, education, and recreational outlets. Ogburn argued that other social institutions have gradually assumed many of these functions. Although the family once played a major role in religious life, this function has largely shifted to churches, synagogues, and other religious organizations. Similarly, education once took place at the family fireside; now it is the responsibility of professionals working in schools and universities. Even the family's traditional recreational function has been transferred to outside groups, such as soccer leagues, dance lessons, and Internet chat rooms.

Conflict View

Conflict theorists view the family not as a contributor to social stability, but as a reflection of the inequality in wealth and power found within the larger society. Feminist theorists and conflict theorists note that the family has traditionally legitimized and perpetuated male dominance. Throughout most of human history—and in a very wide range of societies—husbands have exercised overwhelming power and authority within the family. ◀ P.279 Not until the first wave of contemporary feminism in North America in the mid-nineteenth century was there a substantial challenge to the historic status of wives and children as the legal property of husbands.

Although the egalitarian family has become a more common pattern in North America in recent decades—owing in good part to the activism of feminists beginning in the late 1960s and early 1970s—male dominance within the family has hardly disappeared. Sociologists have found that women are significantly more likely to leave their jobs when their husbands find better employment opportunities, than men are when their wives receive desirable job offers (Bielby and Bielby 1992). And, unfortunately, many husbands reinforce their power and control over wives and children through acts of domestic violence. (Box 12-1 on page 301 considers cross-cultural findings about violence within the home.)

Conflict theorists also view the family as an economic unit that contributes to societal injustice. The family is the basis for transferring power, property, and privilege from ◀ P.14 one generation to the next. North America is widely viewed as a "land of opportunity," yet social mobility is restricted in important ways. Children "inherit" the privileged or less-than-privileged social and economic status of their parents (and, in some cases, of earlier generations as well). As conflict theorists point out, the social class of their parents significantly influences children's socialization experiences and the protection they receive. This means that the socio-economic status of a child's family will have a marked influence on his or her nutrition, health care, housing, educational opportunities, and, in many respects, life chances as an adult. For that reason, conflict theorists argue that the family helps to maintain inequality.

Interactionist View

Interactionists focus on the micro level of family and other intimate relationships. They are interested in how individuals interact with one another, whether they are gay, lesbian, or heterosexual couples, and so on. For example, interactionists have looked at the nature of family interactions

Interactionists are particularly interested in the ways in which mothers and fathers relate to each other and to their children. This mother and her two children are expressing a close and loving relationship, one of the foundations of a strong family.

and relationship quality (e.g., interparental conflict, parenting stress, love between parents and for their children), and have found that those factors, rather than the parents' sexual orientation, strongly predict children's behavioural adjustment (Chan, Rayboy, and Patterson 1998).

Another interactionist study might examine the role of the step-parent. The increased number of single parents who remarry has sparked an interest in those who are helping to raise other people's children. Although children likely do not dream about one day becoming a stepmom or stepdad, this is hardly an unusual occurrence today. Studies have found that stepmothers are more likely to accept the blame for bad relations with their stepchildren, whereas stepfathers are less likely to accept responsibility. Interactionists theorize that stepfathers (like most fathers) may simply be unaccustomed to interacting directly with children when the mother isn't there (Bray and Kelly 1999; Furstenberg and Cherlin 1991).

Feminist Views

No single theory fully represents how feminism conceptualizes the family. Feminist perspectives do, however, share certain assumptions in their study of family. Some of these assumptions include a rejection of the belief in the family's "naturalness" (Luxton 2001). Feminist

Table 12-1   Sociological Perspectives of the Family

Theoretical Perspective	Emphasis
Functionalist	The family as a contributor to social stability
	Roles of family members
Conflict	The family as a perpetuator of inequality
	Transmission of poverty or wealth across generations
Interactionist	Relationships among family members
Feminist	The family as a gendered institution
	Female-headed households

theorists argue that the family is a socially constructed institution and, thus, varies according to time and place. Families are not seen as "monolithic" or the same, but rather as diverse, flexible, and changeable. Although feminists' views on the family agree that women have a position of inequality and discrimination in the family, they argue that these, too, vary according to class, race, and ethnicity. The functional view of family is challenged by feminist theorists, who raise the question, "For whom and for whose interests is the family functional?"

Canadian feminist theorist Margrit Eichler argues that the ways in which sociologists study the family often contain biases (2001). These include a *monolithic bias*, which is a tendency to assume "the family" is uniform rather than diverse; a *conservative bias*, which treats recent changes in the family as fleeting and ignores or treats as rare some of the uglier aspects of family life (e.g., family violence); an *ageist bias*, which regards children and the aged only as passive members of families; a *sexist bias*, which is exhibited in such patterns as double standards and gender insensitivity; a *micro-structural bias*, which overemphasizes micro-level variables and neglects macro-level variables; a *racist bias*, which explicitly or implicitly assumes the superiority of the family form of the dominant group and ignores race and racism when relevant; and a *heterosexist bias*, which either ignores same-sex families or treats them as problematic and deviant.

Table 12-1 summarizes the four major theoretical perspectives on the family.

☐ WHAT ARE THE DIVERSE PATTERNS OF MARRIAGE AND FAMILY?

Historically, the most consistent aspect of family life in this country has been the high rate of heterosexual marriage. However, for the first time, according to the 2006 Canadian census, married people were the minority—51.5 percent of the adult population were not married in 2006. "Not married" in this context can mean never married, living in common-law relationships, divorced, separated, or widowed (Statistics Canada 2007i). Of those heterosexuals who separate or divorce, more men than women will go on to remarry or enter common-law relationships (Statistics Canada 2007i).

Here, we will examine various aspects of love, marriage, and parenthood in Canada, and we will contrast them with cross-cultural examples. In Western societies, romance and mate selection are often viewed as strictly a matter of individual preference. Yet, sociological analysis tells us that social institutions and distinctive cultural norms and values also play an important role.

Courtship and Mate Selection

"My rugby mates would roll over in their graves," says Tom Buckley of his online courtship and subsequent marriage to Terri Muir. But Tom and Terri are hardly alone these days in turning to the Internet for matchmaking services. By the end of 1999, more than 2500 Web sites were helping people find mates. You could choose from oneandonly.com, 2ofakind.com, or cupidnet.com, among others. One service alone claimed 2 million subscribers. Tom and Terri carried on their romance via email for a year before they met face to face. According to Tom, "email made it easier to communicate because neither one of us was the type to walk up to someone in the gym or a bar and say, 'You're the fuel to my fire'" (B. Morris 1999:D1).

Internet romance is only the latest of many courtship practices. In the central Asian nation of Uzbekistan and many other traditional cultures, courtship is defined largely through the interaction of two sets of parents. They arrange spouses for their children. Typically, a young Uzbekistani woman is socialized to eagerly anticipate her marriage to a man whom she will have met only once—when he is presented to her family at the time of the final inspection of her dowry. In Canada, by contrast, courtship is conducted primarily by individuals who may have a romantic interest in each other. In Western culture, courtship often requires these individuals to rely heavily on intricate games, gestures, and signals. Despite such differences, courtship—whether in Canada, Uzbekistan, or elsewhere—is influenced by the norms and values of the larger society (C.J. Williams 1995).

One unmistakable pattern in mate selection is that the process appears to be taking longer today than in the past. A variety of factors, including concerns about financial security and personal independence, has contributed to this delay in marriage. Most people are now well into their twenties before they marry, both in Canada and in other countries (see Figure 12-2).

Take our choice of a mate. Why are we drawn to a particular person in the first place? To what extent are these judgments shaped by the society around us?

▶ **FIGURE 12-2**

Percentage of People Aged 20 to 24 Ever Married, Selected Countries

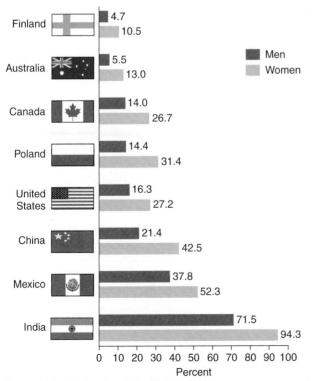

Source: United Nations Population Division 2004.

> ### Think about It
> Take a look at Figure 12-2. Why is the percentage of young women who are married particularly high in India, Mexico, and China, and particularly low in Finland and Australia?

Aspects of Mate Selection

Many societies have explicit or unstated rules that define potential mates as acceptable or unacceptable. These norms can be distinguished in terms of endogamy and exogamy. **Endogamy** (from the Greek *endon*, "within") specifies the groups within which a spouse must be found and prohibits marriage with others. For example, in Canada, many people are expected to marry within their own racial, ethnic, or religious group and are strongly discouraged or even prohibited from marrying outside the group. Endogamy is intended to reinforce the cohesiveness of the group by suggesting to the young that they should marry someone "of our own kind."

By contrast, **exogamy** (from the Greek *exo*, "outside") requires mate selection outside certain groups, usually outside the family or certain kinfolk. The **incest taboo**, a social norm common to virtually all societies, prohibits sexual relationships between certain culturally specified relatives. For people in Canada, this taboo means that Canadians must marry outside the nuclear family. We cannot marry our siblings; however, we are able to marry our first cousins.

Endogamous restrictions may be seen as preferences for one group over another. In the United States, such preferences are most obvious in racial barriers. Until the 1960s, some American states outlawed interracial marriages. This practice was challenged by Richard Loving (a white man) and Mildred Jeter Loving (a part-black, part-Aboriginal woman), who married in 1958. Eventually, in 1967, the U.S. Supreme Court ruled that it was unconstitutional to prohibit marriage solely on the basis of race. The decision struck down statutes in Virginia and 16 other American states.

In Canada, there is evidence to suggest that people are more likely to marry someone outside of their own ethnic group the longer they reside in Canada. Northern, Western, and Eastern European ethnic groups are the most likely to marry outside their own ethnic group, while Asians, Africans, and Latin Americans are the least likely. Despite the effort the federal government expends promoting the ideology and policies of multiculturalism, Canadian families are coming to resemble one another more and more through increased intermarriage among various ethnic groups. Although 11 percent of immigrants to this country report more than one ethnic background, approximately one-third of those born in Canada had a mixed ethnic background (Howell, Albanese, and Obusu-Mensah 2001).

Increasing numbers of exogamous unions force a society to reconsider its definitions of race and ethnicity. In Chapter 10, we noted that race is socially constructed in Canada and around the world. As increasing proportions of children in Canada come from backgrounds of more than one race or ethnicity, single ethnic and ◄ P.237 racial identifiers become less relevant. The Canadian census allows individuals to report two or more ethnicities as well as to respond to an "Other" category for race—this last category is aimed at those whose racial background does not fall neatly into one category (Howell et at. 2001).

The Love Relationship

Whatever the social construction of "love," most people would agree it is a complicated one. Nancy Netting, a professor of sociology at the University of British Columbia–Okanagan, has conducted three surveys, in 1980, 1990, and 2000. Netting's most recent data reveals some interesting trends: She found that students are having a great deal less casual sex. In 1980, 67 percent of men and 34 percent of women at her post-secondary institution described their sexual encounters as being a one-night stand or with a stranger. In 2000, the percentages had dropped to 14 and 8 respectively. "Back then, more people were saying, 'I don't love you but you seem like a nice person so why not get together,'" says Netting. "Now, people really weigh in their minds whether this is someone to take a chance on. They're trying to find the person they can love" (Intini 2007).

In North America, love is socially constructed as important in the courtship process. Living in their own home may make the affectional bond between two people especially important. The couple may be expected to develop its own emotional ties, free of the demands of other household members for affection. Sociologist William Goode observed that opposite-sex spouses in a nuclear family have to rely heavily on each other for the companionship and support that might be provided by other relatives in an extended-family situation (1959).

Given this social construction of love, parents in North America tend to value it highly as a rationale for marriage, and they encourage their children to develop intimate relationships based on heterosexual love and affection. In addition, songs, films, books, magazines, television shows, and even cartoons and comic books reinforce the theme of heterosexual love. At the same time, our society may expect parents and peers to help a person confine his or her search for a mate to "socially acceptable" members of the opposite sex.

The social construction of love-and-marriage, as witnessed in North America, is by no means a cultural

This interracial family from Botswana have what sociologists call an exogamous union. In many countries where politics are based on race, such families may feel they are outsiders. Still, their love for one another may hold the family together.

universal. In fact, in many cultures (both today and in the past), love and marriage are unconnected and are sometimes at odds with each other. For example, feelings of love are not a prerequisite for marriage among the Yaruros of inland Venezuela or in other cultures where there is little freedom for mate selection. The Yaruro male of marriageable age doesn't engage in the kind of dating behaviour so typical of young people in Canada. Rather, he knows that, under the traditions of his culture, he must marry one of his mother's brothers' daughters or one of his father's sisters' daughters. The young man's choice is further limited because one of his uncles selects the eligible cousin that he must marry (Freeman 1958; Lindholm 1999).

Many of the world's cultures give priority in mate selection to factors other than romantic feelings. In societies with **arranged marriages**, often engineered by parents or religious authorities, economic considerations play a significant role. The newly married couple is expected to develop a feeling of love *after* the legal union is formalized, if at all.

Within Canada, some subcultures carry on the arranged marriage practices of their native cultures (Nanda 1991). Young people among the Sikhs and Hindus who have immigrated from India, and among Islamic Muslims and Hasidic Jews, allow their parents or designated matchmakers to find spouses within their ethnic community. As one young Sikh declared, "I will definitely marry who my parents wish. They know me better than I know myself" (R. Segall 1998:48). This practice of arranged marriage may be gradually changing, however, because of the influence of the larger society's cultural practices. Young people who have emigrated without their families often turn to the Internet to find partners who share their background and goals. For example, matrimonial ads for the Indian community run on such Web sites as SuitableMatch.com and Indolink.com. One Hasidic Jewish woman noted that the system of arranged marriages "isn't perfect, and it doesn't work for everyone, but this is the system we know and trust, the way we couple, and the way we learn to love. So it works for most of us" (R. Segall 1998:53).

Use Your Sociological Imagination

Your parents or a matchmaker will arrange a marriage for you. What kind of mate will they select? Will your chances of having a successful marriage be better or worse than if you had selected your own mate?

Social Class Differences

Various studies have documented the differences in family organization among social classes in North America. The upper-class emphasis is on lineage and maintenance of family position. If you are in the upper class, you are not simply a member of a nuclear family; rather, you are a member of a larger family tradition. As a result, upper-class families are quite concerned about what they see as "proper training" for children.

Lower-class families do not often have the luxury of worrying about the "family name"; they must first struggle to pay their bills and survive the crises often associated with life in poverty. Such families are more likely to have only one parent in the home, creating special challenges in child care and financial needs. Children in lower-class families typically assume adult responsibilities—including marriage and parenthood—at an earlier age than children of affluent homes. In part, this is because they may lack the money needed to remain in school.

Social-class differences in family life are less striking than they once were. In the past, family specialists agreed that there were pronounced contrasts in child-rearing practices. Lower-class families were found to be more authoritarian in rearing children and more inclined to use physical punishment. Middle-class families were more permissive and restrained in punishing their children. However, these differences may have narrowed as more and more families from all social classes have turned to the same books, magazines, and even television talk shows for advice on rearing children (M. Kohn 1970; Luster, Rhoades, and Haas 1989).

Among the poor, women often play a significant role in the economic support of the family. According to the 2006 Canadian census, the median household income for single-parent families—80 percent being headed by women—was less than half that for two-parent families (Fenlon and Agrell 2007).

Many racial and ethnic groups appear to have distinctive family characteristics. However, racial and class factors are often closely related. In examining family life among racial and ethnic minorities, keep in mind that certain patterns may result from class as well as cultural factors.

Racial and Ethnic Differences

The ways in which race, ethnicity, gender, and class intersect contributes to the diversity of Canadian families. The subordinate status of racial and ethnic minorities and Canada's Aboriginal people has profound effects on the family life of these groups.

Aboriginal people are a heterogeneous group with different histories, geographies, languages, economies, and cultures. Their families, which often include those who are kin as well as those who come together in a common community purpose, have been fundamentally disrupted by hundreds of years of European domination. For example, the First Nations peoples of the Montagnais-Naskapi of the eastern Labrador peninsula underwent major changes in family structure and gender relations as they moved to trapping, introduced by Europeans, and away from traditional hunting and fishing. The division of labour between the sexes became more specialized and families began to get smaller, approaching the size of a nuclear family (Leacock 2001).

Aboriginal families have been devalued and undermined by the Canadian government and religious institutions. In the past, children were sent away from their homes to residential schools, where they were punished for speaking their own language and expressing their own culture. ◀ PP. 248– 250 There, they were often subjected to sexual and physical abuse at the hands of those who ran the schools— people who were assigned to be their guardians.

In the 1960s, many Aboriginal children were put up for adoption and taken in, most often, by white families in Canada and the United States, rather than by those from within their own band (Eichler 1997). Today, after years of cultural oppression under government control, problems of domestic abuse, youth suicide, and substance abuse plague Aboriginal families.

Research carried out in Nova Scotia and Ontario of opposite-sex couples demonstrates the links among race, class, and gender and their impact on black families (Calliste 2001). Significantly more black families were headed by women than non-black families; these women-headed black families earned approximately half of the income of their married counterparts, who in turn earned less than non-black families headed by married couples. The study concludes that the high rate of teenage pregnancy and the feminization of poverty need to be addressed by black community groups and government in the form of education, employment equity, sex education, and parenting sessions (Calliste 2001:417). Some similarities exist between Canadian and U.S. black families because race, class, and gender intersect to produce inequality for families in both countries.

Child-Rearing Patterns in Family Life

The Nayars of southern India acknowledge the biological role of the father, but the mother's eldest brother is responsible for her children (Gough 1974). By contrast, uncles play only a peripheral role in child care in North America. Caring for children is a universal function of the family, yet the ways in which different societies assign this function to family members can vary significantly. Within Canada, child-rearing patterns are varied. We'll look here at parenthood and grandparenthood, adoption, dual-income families, single-parent families, and stepfamilies. (See Figure 12-3 for proportions of children aged 14 and under living with married parents, common-law parents, and lone parents).

Parenthood and Grandparenthood

The socialization of children is essential to the maintenance of any culture. Consequently, parenthood is one of the most important (and most demanding) social ◀ P.82 roles in North America. Sociologist Alice Rossi (1968, 1984) has identified four factors that complicate the transition to parenthood and the role of socialization. First, there is little anticipatory socialization for the social role of caregiver. The normal school curriculum gives scant attention to the subjects most relevant to successful family life—such as child care and home maintenance. Second, only limited learning occurs during the period of pregnancy itself. Third, the transition to parenthood is quite abrupt. Unlike adolescence, it is not prolonged; unlike socialization for work,

▶ **FIGURE 12-3**

Distribution of Children Aged 14 and Under by Family Structure

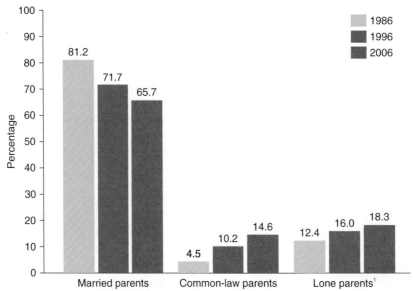

¹Historical comparisons for census families, particularly lone-parent families, must be interpreted with caution due to conceptual changes in 2001.
Source: Statistics Canada, 2007d.

The love expressed by this father to his child testifies to successful parenting. Even though parenthood is a crucial social role, society generally provides few clear guidelines.

you cannot gradually take on the duties of caregiving. Finally, in Rossi's view, our society lacks clear and helpful guidelines for successful parenthood. There is little consensus on how parents can produce happy and well-adjusted offspring—or even on what it means to be "well adjusted." For these reasons, socialization for parenthood involves difficult challenges for most men and women in North America.

One recent development in family life in Canada has been the extension of parenthood, as adult children continue to (or return to) live at home. The 2006 Canadian census revealed that 44 percent of adult children in their twenties lived in their parents' home, up 12 percent from 1986 (Statistics Canada 2007d). In some instances, financial constraints are at the heart of these living arrangements, particularly in the country's large urban centres. Although rents and real estate prices skyrocketed, salaries for younger workers did not keep pace, and many found themselves unable to afford their own homes. Moreover, with many marriages now ending in divorce—most commonly in the first seven years of marriage—divorced sons and daughters are returning to live with their parents, sometimes with their own children. Sociologist Monica Boyd at the University of Toronto states, "It has become normal" for parents to foster this living arrangement as a way of successfully launching their children (Andreatta 2007).

As life expectancy increases in North America, more and more parents are becoming grandparents and even great-grandparents. After interviewing many grandparents, sociologists Andrew Cherlin and Frank Furstenberg, Jr., identified three principal styles of grandparenting (1992):

1. More than half (55 percent) of grandparents surveyed functioned as "specialists in recreational caregiving." They enriched their grandchildren's lives through recreational outings and other special activities.
2. More than one-fourth (29 percent) carried on a "ritualistic" (primarily symbolic) relationship with their grandchildren. In some instances, this was because the grandparents lived far away from their grandchildren and could see them only occasionally.
3. About one-sixth (16 percent) of grandparents surveyed were actively involved in everyday routine care of their grandchildren and exercised substantial authority over them.

In Canada, more than 55 000 grandparents are raising their grandchildren on their own (Vallas 2005).

Adoption

In a legal sense, **adoption** is a "process that allows for the transfer of the legal rights, responsibilities, and privileges of parenthood" to a new legal parent or parents (E. Cole 1985:638). In many cases, these rights are transferred from a biological parent or parents (often called birth parents) to an adoptive parent or parents.

Viewed from a functionalist perspective, government has a strong interest in encouraging adoption. Policymakers, in fact, have both a humanitarian and a financial stake in the process. In theory, adoption offers a stable family environment for children who otherwise might not receive satisfactory care. Moreover, government data show that unwed mothers who keep their babies tend to be of lower socio-economic status and often require public assistance to support their children. Government can lower its social welfare expenses if children are transferred to economically self-sufficient families. From a conflict perspective, however, such financial considerations raise the ugly spectre of adoption as a means whereby affluent (often infertile) couples "buy" the children of the poor (C. Bachrach 1986). For decades during the last century, Native children were adopted into white families in Canada and the United States; this practice has since been identified as a form of cultural genocide (P. Johnson 1983).

With greater access to contraception and legal abortion, the rate of unplanned births to young women has declined since the 1950s, and the availability of Canadian infants has decreased. As well, more and more single mothers have been keeping their babies and supporting them through earnings or social assistance. In addition, the goals of family preservation in the Canadian child welfare system, and Canadians' current preference to adopt infants and younger children, will make the case for international adoption (most likely from developing countries) more compelling (M. Baker 2001). This supports the conflict view that the wealthier, more powerful countries have control over the poorer, less powerful countries. In this case, it involves the "purchase" of children.

Dual-Income Families

The idea of a family consisting of a wage-earning male spouse and a female spouse who stays at home has largely given way to the dual-income household. In Canada, dual-income families make up 63 percent of all households (TD Bank 2007). Why has there been such a rise in the number of dual-income families? A major factor is economic need. Manitoba Agriculture and Food, in 2004, estimated the costs of raising a child from birth to age 18 to be $166 762. Raising children in urban centres, where the bulk of the Canadian population resides, is expensive; housing costs over the past decade have increased dramatically in many cities across Canada. Other factors contributing to the rise of the dual-income model include the nation's declining birth rate (see Chapter 15), the increase in the proportion of women with post-secondary educations, the shift in the economy of North America from manufacturing to service industries, and the impact of the feminist movement in influencing societal attitudes.

Single-Parent Families

In recent decades, the stigma attached to "unwed mothers" and other single parents has significantly diminished. **Single-parent families**, in which there is only one parent to care for the children, can hardly be viewed as a rarity in Canada. In 2006, approximately 26 percent of families were run by a lone parent (up from 11 percent in 1981); the overwhelming majority of these families were female-headed. Variation and diversity exists among single-parent families. For example, according to Statistics Canada, almost half of black families were headed by a single parent, compared with 18 percent of other families (Canadian Press 2007). The interaction of race, class, and gender is evident in patterns of black family structure (Calliste 2001).

Although marital dissolution is the major cause of the increase in lone-parent families, never-married lone parents are growing in number. Never-married lone parents constituted 29.5 percent of all lone parents in Canada in 2006, while in 1951, they made up 1.5 percent of the total number of single parents (Statistics Canada 2007i).

The lives of single parents and their children are not necessarily more difficult than life in other types of families. It is as inaccurate to assume that a single-parent family is necessarily "deprived" as it is to assume that a two-parent family is always secure and happy. Nevertheless, life in a single-parent family can be extremely stressful, in both economic and emotional terms. Economic inequality and poverty are striking characteristics of lone-parent families. When compared with two-parent families, female-led (particularly those who are younger) lone-parent families are the most vulnerable to poverty, a fact that contributes to the phenomenon known as the "feminization of poverty."

A family headed by a single mother faces especially difficult problems if the mother is a teenager. Drawing on two decades of social science research, sociologist Kristin Luker observes:

> The short answer to why teenagers get pregnant and especially to why they continue those pregnancies is that a fairly substantial number of them just don't believe what adults tell them, be it about sex, contraception, marriage, or babies. They don't believe in adult conventional wisdom. (1996:11)

Why might low-income teenage women want to have children and face the obvious financial difficulties of motherhood? Viewed from an interactionist perspective, these women tend to have low self-esteem and limited options; a child may provide a sense of motivation and purpose for a teenager whose economic worth in our society is limited at best. Given the barriers that many young women face because of their gender, race, ethnicity, and class, many teenagers may believe that they have little to lose and much to gain by having a child.

Countries belonging to the Organisation for Economic Co-operation and Development (OECD; i.e., developed nations) have experienced an increase in lone-parent families since the early 1970s, with the greatest increase occurring in the United States (M. Baker 2001). However, poverty rates for these families vary among industrialized countries, depending on the availability of social welfare programs, the rates of male and female unemployment, government disincentives to work while receiving social assistance, and the availability of special employment training programs and child care.

Despite the current concern over the increase in the number of lone-parent families, this family type has existed for more than 100 years in Canada. In 1901, the ratio of lone-parent to two-parent families was only slightly lower than today's ratio. A major interdisciplinary study carried out at the University of Victoria, based on 1901 census data, concluded that the family has always been a variable and flexible institution. With unsanctioned or non-formalized divorce being more common in the past than is generally known, "there was much more volatility and shifting of marital status than anyone was prepared to admit at the state level" (Gram 2001).

The exact nature of these blended families has social significance for adults and children alike. Certainly, resocialization is required when an adult becomes a step-parent or a child becomes a stepchild and step-sibling. Moreover, an important distinction must be made between first-time stepfamilies and households where there have been repeated divorces, breakups, or changes in custodial arrangements.

In evaluating the rise of stepfamilies, some observers have assumed that children would benefit from remarriage because they'd be gaining a second custodial parent and, potentially, have greater economic security. However, after reviewing many studies on stepfamilies, sociologist Andrew Cherlin concluded that "the well-being of children in stepfamily households is no better, on average, than the well-being of children in divorced, single-parent households" (1999:421). Step-parents can play valuable and unique roles in their stepchildren's lives, but their involvement does not guarantee an improvement. In fact, standards may decline. Some studies conducted by an economist in the United States found that children raised in families with stepmothers are likely to have less health-care attention, education, and money spent on their nutrition than are children raised by biological mothers. The measures are also negative for children raised by a stepfather, but only half as negative as in the case of stepmothers. It may be that the stepmother recedes from the stepchild/stepchildren in an effort to avoid seeming too

Blended Families

For a couple or individual who separates or divorces and then goes on to form a second or third relationship, a **blended family** may be the result.

Blended families are an exceedingly complex form of family organization. Here is how one 13-year-old boy described his family:

Tim and Janet are my stepbrother and sister. Josh is my stepdad. Carin and Don are my real parents, who are divorced. And Don married Anna and together they had Ethan and Ellen, my half-sister and brother. And Carin married Josh and had little Alice, my half-sister. (A. Bernstein 1988)

When 9-year old Blake Brunson shows up for a basketball game, so do his eight grandparents—the result of his parents' remarriage.

intrusive, or relies mistakenly on the biological father to carry out these parental duties (Lewin 2000).

Family Violence in Canada

The family is often portrayed through the mass media and other institutions as a source of comfort, security, and safety, as a place to which its members retreat to escape the rough and tumble of the public world of work and school. This social construction of the family as a "haven in a heartless world" (Lasch 1977) often obscures the reality that many members of families face; that is, the family can be a source of conflict and, possibly, danger. Sociologists Gelles and Straus point out that "you are more likely to be physically assaulted, beaten, and killed in your own home at the hands of a loved one than anyplace else, or by anyone else in society" (1988:18). There are various types of family violence, including violence against women, violence against children, sibling violence, and violence against elders (DeKeseredy 2001).

In the five years leading up to and including 2004, Statistics Canada reported the estimated rate of spousal assault to be 7 percent for women and 6 percent for men in a current or previous spousal relationship (Statistics Canada 2006f). Statistics Canada's definition of spousal "violence" or "assault" includes being beaten, slapped, choked, or pushed; being threatened with a gun, knife, or other object; or being forced to engage in unwanted sexual activity. Women experience the more serious forms of spousal violence and are more likely to state that their spouse had been drinking before and during the time of the violent incident. Between 1993 and 1999, the overall decline in spousal assault against women in Canada may have been due to such factors as increased availability of shelters for abused women, increased reporting to police by victims of abuse, mandatory arrest policies for men who assault their wives, growth in the number of treatment programs for violent men, changes in the economic and social status of women that allow them to more easily leave violent relationships, and changes in society's attitudes recognizing assault of female spouses as a crime (Statistics Canada 2001d).

Contrary to a commonly held assumption that spousal violence ends after the breakdown of a marriage, violence continues and often occurs for the first time after the couple separates. In 2004 in Canada, "half of the women who reported experiencing spousal assault by a past partner indicated that the violence occurred after the couple separated, and in one-third of post-separation assaults, the violence became more severe or actually began after the separation" (Statistics Canada 2006e:38). Male "proprietariness" or sexual jealousy has often been used to explain patterns of male violence toward female ex-partners, particularly in acts of killing (Gartner, Dawson, and Crawford 2001).

Spousal homicide—the ultimate form of spousal violence—carries the greatest risk for women during marital separation. "Women killed by their spouses during marital separation also outnumber women in similar situations in the general population: 26 percent of female spousal homicide victims were separated compared with just 4 percent of women in the population" (Statistics Canada 2006e:38).

Although spousal violence against women occurs in all cultures, Aboriginal women run a greater risk of being harmed in episodes of family violence. From 1993 to 1999, 25 percent of Aboriginal women were assaulted by a current or former spouse, which was twice the rate of Aboriginal men and three times the rate of non-Aboriginal women (Statistics Canada 2001d).

Canadian children and youth who die from homicide are most likely to be killed by family members (Statistics Canada 2001d). Family members were responsible for 63 percent of solved homicides of children and youth recorded by police in Canada between 1974 and 1999. In 1998, the majority of cases of violence toward children where abuse had been substantiated involved inappropriate punishment, while the most common form of child sexual abuse was touching and fondling of genitals. Children's exposure to family violence (e.g., hearing or seeing one parent assault the other) was the most common form of emotional maltreatment (Statistics Canada 2001d).

(Box 12-1 presents a discussion of family violence in the global community.)

Divorce

"Do you promise to love, honour, and cherish . . . until death do you part?" Every year, people of all social classes, racial and ethnic groups, and, now, sexual orientations make this legally binding agreement. Yet, a number of these promises end in divorce. According to Statistics Canada, in 2003, the crude divorce rate was 223.7 for every 100 000 people in the population (2005i). Roughly 1 in 3 marriages ends in divorce within a 30-year period.

Statistical Trends in Divorce

Just how common is divorce? Surprisingly, this is not a simple question; divorce statistics are difficult to interpret.

The media frequently report that one out of every three opposite-sex marriages ends in divorce. And in 2004, the first same-sex legal divorce occurred in Canada. Figures can be misleading, since many marriages last for decades. They are based on a comparison of all divorces that occur in a single year (regardless of when the couples were married) against the number of new marriages in the same year.

Heterosexual divorce in Canada, and many other countries, began to increase in the late 1960s but then

Sociology in the Global Community

Domestic Violence

12-1

The phone rings two or three dozen times a day at the Friend of the Family Hotline in San Salvador, the capital city of El Salvador. Each time the staff receives a report of family violence, a crisis team is immediately dispatched to the caller's home. Caseworkers provide comfort to victims, as well as accumulate evidence for use in the attacker's prosecution. In the first three years of its existence, Friend of the Family handled more than 28 000 cases of domestic violence.

Wife battering and other forms of domestic violence are not confined to El Salvador. Drawing on studies conducted throughout the world, we can make the following generalizations:

- Women are most at risk of violence from the men they know.

- Violence against women occurs in all socioeconomic groups.

- Family violence is at least as dangerous as assaults committed by strangers.

- Though women sometimes exhibit violent behaviour toward men, the majority of violent acts that cause injury are perpetrated by men against women. Violence against men frequently goes unreported since male gender roles and domestic violence are incongruous in many cultures.

- Violence within intimate relationships tends to escalate over time.

- Emotional and psychological abuse can be at least as debilitating as physical abuse.

- Use of alcohol exacerbates family violence but does not cause it.

Using the conflict and feminist models, researchers have found that in relationships in which the inequality between men and women is great, the likelihood of assault on wives increases dramatically. This discovery suggests that much of the violence between intimates, even when sexual in nature, is about power rather than sex.

The family can be a dangerous place not only for women, children and the elderly. In 2003 and 2004, 95 000 women and children were admitted to 473 shelters across Canada (2003–2004 Transition Home Survey in Statistics Canada 2005f); between 1974 and 2003, women experienced spousal homicide rates four to five times greater than that of men (Statistics Canada 2005f).

Applying Theory

1. Do you know of a family that has experienced domestic violence? Did the victim(s) seek outside help, and, if so, was it effective?

2. Why might the degree of equality in a relationship correlate to the likelihood of domestic violence? How might conflict theorists explain this finding?

Sources: American Bar Association 1999; Gelles and Cornell 1990; Heise, Ellseberg, and Gottemuelle 1999; Rennison and Welchans 2000; Spindel, Levy, and Connor 2000; Statistics Canada 2005f; Valdez 1999; J. Wilson 2000.

---

started to level off and even decline since the late 1980s and remain relatively stable since 1999 (Statistics Canada 2005c). This is partly due to the aging of the baby boomer population and the corresponding decline in the proportion of people of marriageable age (see Figure 12-4).

Doug Norris, of the research firm Environics, notes, in his analysis of the 2006 Canadian census, that after separations and divorces Canadian women tend not to form unions again. Norris states, "When those relationships break up, women tend, for whatever reason, not to get into a second relationship. They live on their own, or perhaps as single parents, but they're not forming a couple. They are not remarrying, not going into a common law union to nearly the extent that males do, and that gap widens with age" (Fenlon and Agrell 2007).

Some people regard remarriage as an endorsement of the institution of marriage, but it does lead to the new challenges of a remarriage kin network comprising current and prior marital relationships. This network can be particularly complex if children are involved or if an ex-spouse remarries.

Factors Associated with Divorce

Perhaps the most important factor in the increase in heterosexual divorce throughout the twentieth century has been the greater social *acceptance* of divorce. It's no longer considered necessary to endure an unhappy marriage. Most importantly, various religious denominations have relaxed negative attitudes toward divorce, and most religious leaders no longer treat it as a sin. The growing

▶**FIGURE 12-4**

Marriage and Divorce Rates in Canada, 1967–2003

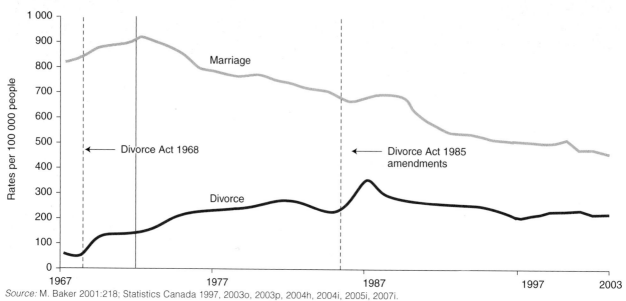

Source: M. Baker 2001:218; Statistics Canada 1997, 2003o, 2003p, 2004h, 2004i, 2005i, 2007i.

acceptance of divorce is a worldwide phenomenon. In 1998, a few months after a highly publicized divorce by pop superstar Seiko Matsuda, the prime minister of Japan released a survey showing that 54 percent of those polled supported uncontested divorce, compared with 20 percent in 1979 (Kyodo News International 1998a).

A few other factors deserve mention:

- No-fault divorce provisions, allowing a couple to end their marriage without fault on either side (such as specifying adultery), accounted for an initial surge in the divorce rate after they were introduced in 1985, although they appear to have had little effect beyond that.
- Divorce has become a more practical option in newly formed families, since they now tend to have fewer children than in the past.
- A general increase in family incomes, coupled with the availability of free legal aid for some poor people, has meant that more couples can afford the cost of divorce proceedings.
- As society provides greater opportunities for women, more and more wives are becoming less dependent on their husbands—both economically and emotionally. They may then feel more able to leave if the marriage seems hopeless.

Impact of Divorce on Children

According to Statistics Canada, nearly one in two divorces in Canada involve dependent children (2005d). For some of these children, divorce signals the welcome end to being witness to a very dysfunctional relationship. A study in the United States, conducted by sociologists Paul Amato and Alan Booth (1997), found that in roughly one-third of divorces, the children benefit from parental separation because it lessens their exposure to conflict. But in about 70 percent of all divorces, they found that the parents engaged in a low level of conflict; in these cases, the realities of divorce appear to be harder for the children to bear than living with the marital unhappiness. Other researchers, using differing definitions of conflict, have found greater unhappiness for children living in homes with marital differences. Still, it would be simplistic to assume that children are automatically better off following the breakup of their parents' marriage. The interests of the parents do not necessarily serve children well. A study based on a representative sample of heterosexual Canadians showed that although men experience moderate increases in their level of economic well-being after divorce, women experience a dramatic economic decline (Finnie 1993). Since women's wages are lower than men's, and since women are more likely to be awarded child custody, children of divorce often encounter serious economic consequences.

Divorce can obviously be a painful experience for children, but we should avoid labelling young people as "children of divorce," as if this *parental* experience is the singular event defining the life of a girl or boy. Large-scale studies in the United States and Britain have shown that some of the alleged negative effects of heterosexual divorce actually resulted from conditions (such as poverty) that existed *before* the parental separation. Moreover, if divorce does not lower children's access to resources and does not increase stress, its impact on children may be neutral or even positive. Divorce does not ruin the life of every child it touches, though its effect on a child is not always benign (Cherlin 1999; Wallerstein, Lewis, and Blakeslee 2000).

Use Your Sociological Imagination

In a society that maximizes the welfare of all family members, how easy should it be for couples to divorce? How easy should it be to get married? Remarried?

Cohabitation

One of the most dramatic trends of recent years in Canada has been the tremendous increase in the number of opposite-sex couples who choose to live together without marrying, engaging in what is commonly called **cohabitation**.

In 2006, 15.5 percent of all Canadian couples were cohabiting, up from 7.2 percent in 1986. Since 2001, common-law relationships have increased by 19 percent, five times faster than the growth in the number of married couples (Statistics Canada 2007d).

In much of Europe, cohabitation is so common that the general sentiment seems to be "love, yes; marriage, maybe." In Iceland, 62 percent of all children are born to single mothers; in France, Britain, and Norway, the proportion is roughly 40 percent. Government policies in these countries make few legal distinctions between married and unmarried couples or households (Lyall 2002).

In Canada, Quebec stands out from the rest of the country in its rates of marriage and cohabitation. The 2006 census found that 35 percent of couples in Quebec are in common-law relationships, making up 44.4 percent of the country's total number (Statistics Canada 2007d). Quebec residents are increasingly turning away from traditional institutions, such as church and state, in the establishment of their families. More people there than in any other jurisdiction live in common-law relationships; in 2006, the ratio was approximately one in every three couples.

Census figures have documented increases in cohabitation among older people in Canada with huge increases among those 40 and over; the number of Canadians between 60 and 64 living common-law rose 77 percent between 2001 and 2006 (Statistics Canada 2007d). Older couples may choose cohabitation rather than marriage for many reasons: because of religious dif-

ferences, to preserve the full pension benefits they receive as single people, out of fear of commitment, to avoid upsetting children from previous marriages, because one partner or both are not legally divorced, or because one or both have lived through a spouse's illness and death and do not want to experience that again. But some older couples simply see no need for marriage and report being happy living together as they are.

Zheng Wu, professor of sociology at the University of Victoria and expert in the area of cohabitation, states, "More people are substituting cohabitation for marriage and really treat it as marriage.... [Common] law has become a protected social institution" (Agrell 2007).

Remaining Single

Looking at TV programs today, you would be justified in thinking most households are composed of singles. Although this is not the case, it is true that more and more people in Canada are postponing entry into first marriages. In 1973, the average age of first marriage in Canada was approximately 25 years for men and 23 years for women; by 2003, the average age at first marriage was approximately 30 years and 28 years for men and women respectively, constituting an average increase for both sexes of five years (Statistics Canada 2007i). Partly because of the postponement of marriage and the increase in common-law relationships, married Canadians are now in the minority (Statistics Canada 2007i).

◀ P.273 The trend toward maintaining a single lifestyle for a longer period of time is related to the growing economic independence of young people. This is especially significant for women. Freed from financial needs, women don't necessarily have to marry to enjoy a satisfying life.

There are many reasons why a person may choose not to marry. Singleness is an attractive option for those who do not want to limit their sexual intimacy to one life partner. Also, some men and women do not want to become highly dependent on any one person—and do not want anyone depending heavily on them. In a society that values individuality and self-fulfilment, the single lifestyle can offer certain freedoms that married couples may not enjoy.

Remaining single represents a clear departure from societal expectations of the dominant culture; indeed, it has been likened to "being single on Noah's Ark." A single adult must confront the inaccurate view that he or she is always lonely, is a workaholic, and is immature. These stereotypes help support the traditional assumption in North America and most other societies that to be truly happy and fulfilled, a person must get married and raise a family. To help counter these societal expectations, singles have formed numerous support groups, such as the Alternatives to Marriage Project (www.unmarried.org).

Lesbian and Gay Relationships

> We were both raised in middle-class families, where the expectation was we would go to college, we would become educated, we'd get a nice white-collar job, we'd move up and own a nice house in the suburbs. And that's exactly what we've done. (*The New York Times* 1998:B2)

Sound like a heterosexual couple? The "we" described here is a gay couple.

The lives of lesbians and gay men vary greatly. Some live in long-term, monogamous relationships, legal or common-law. Some couples live with adopted children or children from former heterosexual marriages. The 2006 census in Canada counted 25 345 same-sex couples, up 32 percent from 2001. Same-sex couples make up 0.6 percent of all couples and live primarily in Canada's three largest cities—Vancouver, Toronto, and Montreal (Fenlon and Agrell 2007).

In the past, recognition of same-sex partnerships was not uncommon in Europe, including Denmark, Holland, Switzerland, France, Belgium, and parts of Germany, Italy, and Spain. In 2001, the Netherlands converted their "registered same-sex partnerships" into full-fledged marriages, with divorce provisions (S. Daley 2000).

Gay activist organizations emphasize that despite the passage of laws protecting the civil rights of lesbians and gay men, in some countries lesbian couples and gay male couples are prohibited from marrying—and, therefore, from gaining traditional partnership benefits. Some jurisdictions have passed legislation allowing for registration of domestic partnerships. A **domestic partnership** may be defined as two unrelated adults who reside together; agree to be jointly responsible for their dependants, basic living expenses, and other common necessities; and share a mutually caring relationship. Domestic-partnership benefits can apply to such areas as inheritance, parenting, pensions, taxation, housing, immigration, workplace fringe benefits, and health care. Although the most passionate support for domestic-partnership legislation has come from lesbian and gay male activists, the majority of those eligible for such benefits would be cohabiting heterosexual couples.

Domestic partnership legislation faces strong opposition from conservative religious and political groups. In the view of opponents, support for domestic partnership undermines the historic societal preference for the nuclear family. Advocates of domestic partnership counter that such relationships fulfil the same functions for the individuals involved and for society as the traditional family and should enjoy the same legal protections and benefits. The gay couple quoted at the beginning of this section consider themselves a family unit, just like the nuclear family that lives down the street in their suburb. They cannot understand why they have been denied a family membership at their municipal swimming pool and why they have to pay more than a married couple (*The New York Times* 1998).

In 2001, after a decade of court challenges and demonstrations over the rights of same-sex couples, Nova Scotia became the first jurisdiction in Canada to register same-sex and common-law relationships as legal domestic partnerships. This change allowed same-sex couples many of the same rights accorded married couples in that province—equal division of property and spousal support if the relationship dissolves, and full spousal benefits and pensions to partners. The registration of domestic partnerships, however, is not considered "marriage." In November 2004, Saskatchewan became the seventh Canadian jurisdiction (following Ontario, British

In 2005, Bill C-38 was passed by the Canada's federal government, making same-sex civil marriage legal in all jurisdictions. Here, a wedding witness signs the register following a same-sex marriage.

Columbia, Manitoba, Yukon, Quebec, and Nova Scotia) to allow same-sex marriage. The courts in the respective regions ruled that it was a violation of the Charter of Rights and Freedoms to discriminate against same-sex marriage. On December 21, 2004, same-sex marriage became legal in Newfoundland and Labrador. In September 2004, Canada's first same-sex divorce was granted in Ontario.

In 2005, Bill C-38 was passed by the federal government, making same-sex civil marriage legal in *all* jurisdictions in Canada. In 2006, for the first time, the Canadian census allowed individuals to indicate if they were in a same-sex marriage; 7465 couples indicated that they were (Fenlon and Agrell 2007). Canada was the third country in the world to legalize same-sex marriage, following Belgium and the Netherlands. Shortly after Canada's passage of Bill C-38, Spain's government announced the legalization of same-sex marriage.

Marriage is an emotionally charged issue among the gay and lesbian communities. Some believe that it represents a sign of legitimacy and normalization to their already established relationships. Others believe that marriage, given its history of patriarchy and oppression, is not an institution to be emulated by gay and lesbian couples. Nova Scotian Ross Boutilier, who, along with his partner, was among the first to register for domestic partnership, stated, "It does make a difference because it's a formalization of the understanding we have that we're in this together and this is an equal partnership" (K. Cox 2001).

The debate over the legalization of same-sex marriage played out over such concerns as rights (e.g., in the federal Department of Justice), human dignity and concern over the perpetuation of prejudicial attitudes (e.g., in the United Church of Canada), consequences for freedom of religion and conscience (e.g., in the Canadian Conference of Bishops), and the concern of being "over-inclusive" (e.g., by the attorney general of Alberta).

Marriage without Children

According to the 2006 census, for the first time in Canada, there were more families without children (42.7 percent) than with children (41.4 percent). Twenty years ago, more than half of Canadian couples had children, defined as offspring under 25 (Grewal 2007). Anne Milan, an analyst with Statistics Canada, attributes the trend to an aging population and to more women postponing or foregoing parenthood (Grewal 2007). Rates of childlessness began to increase for women born after 1941. These women entered young adulthood at a time when options were expanding for women in the form of advanced education and job opportunities. As well, this time in history witnessed the second wave of feminism, when ideas such as those expressed by Betty Friedan in

The Feminine Mystique (1963) challenged conventional views about full-time motherhood and caregiving. Despite changing attitudes and the expansion of educational and employment options for women born after this date, women today continue to "pay a price in the labour market for marriage and motherhood, and shoulder more responsibility for housework and child care at home than men" (Fox 2001:164). This reality contributes to the trend of women postponing marriage or never marrying, and postponing child-bearing or remaining child-free.

Childlessness within opposite-sex marriage has generally been viewed as a problem that can be solved through such means as adoption and artificial insemination. More and more couples today, however, choose not to have children and regard themselves as child-free, not childless. They do not believe that having children automatically follows from marriage, nor do they feel that reproduction is the duty of all married couples. Child-free opposite-sex couples have formed support groups (with names like "No Kidding") and set up Web sites (Terry 2000).

Economic considerations have contributed to this shift in attitudes; having children has become very expensive. Aware of the financial pressures, some couples are having fewer children and at a later age, and others are weighing the advantages of a child-free marriage. Alexis Victor who, with her partner, lives in an area of Toronto

"No, sorry, folks – you still can't afford to start a family."

with one of the highest rates of childlessness, states, "There aren't close-knit communities any more where you can raise well-adjusted, balanced children. The world's population is way too high, it needs to be balanced. We're both very busy" (Grewal 2007). Her partner, Gardiner Cranston, asks, " Why would you want to have kids in this city? . . . There's nothing for kids to enjoy. . . . You need at least $600 000 to buy a decent house" (Grewal 2007).

Meanwhile, some childless couples, both same sex and opposite sex, who desperately want children, may be

willing to try any means necessary to get pregnant. The social policy section that follows explores the controversy surrounding recent advances in reproductive technology.

> ## Use Your Sociological Imagination
> What would happen to our society if more married couples decided not to have children? How would society change if cohabitation or singlehood became the norm?

Social Policy and the Family
Reproductive Technology

The Issue

The 1997 feature film *Gattaca* tells the story of a future in which genetic engineering enhances people's genes. Those who are not "enhanced" in the womb—principally, those whose parents could not afford the treatments—suffer discrimination and social hurdles throughout their lives. To borrow a line from the movie, "Your genes are your resumé."

Far-fetched? Perhaps, but today we are commonly witnessing aspects of reproductive technology that were regarded as so much science fiction just a generation ago. In April 2007, it was revealed that a Quebec woman had frozen her eggs so that her 7-year-old daughter, who was infertile because of a genetic disorder, could use them in the future (CBC 2007c). "Test-tube" babies, frozen embryos, surrogate mothers, sperm and egg donation, and cloning of human cells are raising questions about the ethics of creating and shaping human life. How will these technologies change the nature of families and the definitions we have of motherhood and fatherhood? To what extent should social policy encourage or discourage innovative reproductive technology?

The Setting

In an effort to overcome infertility, many couples turn to a recent reproductive advance known as *in vitro fertilization* (IVF). In this technique, an egg and a sperm are combined in a laboratory dish. If the egg is fertilized, the resulting embryo (the so-called test-tube baby) is transferred into a woman's uterus. The fertilized egg could be transferred into the uterus of the woman from whom it was harvested or of a woman who has not donated the egg but who plays the role of surrogate (i.e., substitute). A surrogate mother carries the pregnancy to term and then transfers the child to the social mother. After this occurs, depending on the agreement between the social

mother and the surrogate mother, the child may or may not be a part of the surrogate mother's life.

These possibilities, and many more, make the definition and attending responsibilities of motherhood complicated and somewhat murky. How should motherhood be defined—as providing gestation, as providing care for the child, as providing the egg, or all or some combination of these?

Sociological Insights

Replacing personnel is a functional prerequisite that the family as a social institution performs. Obviously, advances in reproductive technology allow childless couples to fulfil their personal and societal goals. The new technology also presents opportunities not previously considered. A small but growing number of same-sex couples are using donated sperm or eggs to have genetically related children and fulfil their desire to have children and a family (Bruni 1998).

As we have mentioned, sometimes it is difficult to define relationships. For example, in 1995, a U.S. couple, John and Luanne Buzzanca, hired a married woman to carry a child to term for them—a child conceived of the sperm and egg of anonymous, unrelated donors. One month before the birth, John filed for divorce and claimed he had no parental responsibilities, including child support. Eventually, the court ruled that the baby girl had no legal parents; she is temporarily living with Luanne, who may seek to adopt the baby. Although this is an unusual case, it suggests the type of functional confusion that can arise in trying to establish kinship ties (Weiss 1998).

Feminist sociologist Margrit Eichler has developed a typology of motherhood in this age of new reproductive technology. She states that there can be up to 25 types of mothers, considering that mothers can now be "partial biological mothers—genetic but not gestational, or gestational but not genetic" (Eichler 1997:80). Her list of possible types of mothers include (1) genetic and gestational but not social mothers (mothers who have given up their child); (2) genetic, non-gestational, and non-social mothers (those who provide an egg); (3) non-genetic, but gestational, social, exclusive, full mothers (those who receive an egg); (4) a dead mother whose egg has been fertilized (mother number 1), implanted in a carrier (mother number 2), and transferred to a third woman (mother number 3).

Eichler adds that new reproductive technologies have had a far less dramatic impact on fatherhood, the most noticeable change coming in the form of what she calls "postmortem biological fathers" (Eichler 1997:72). This term refers to fatherhood that occurs after a man's death, when his sperm is harvested and used to impregnate a woman.

In the future depicted in *Gattaca*, the poor are at a disadvantage because they are not able to genetically control their lives. The conflict perspective would note that in the world today, the technologies available are often accessible only to the most affluent. In addition, a report by the 1993 Royal Commission on New Reproductive Technologies warned that these technologies could potentially be used for commercial purposes (e.g., surrogacy), making women of lower classes vulnerable to exploitation. Thus, today in Canada, there is a voluntary ban on the use of many technologies that could be used commercially and that would enable those with resources to "buy" a reproductive service and those with perhaps few resources to "sell" the services in demand.

Interactionists observe that the quest for information and social support connected with reproductive technology has created new social networks. Like other special-interest groups, couples with infertility problems band together to share information, offer support to one another, and demand better treatment. They develop social networks—sometimes through voluntary associations or Internet support groups—where they share information about new medical techniques, insurance plans, and the merits of particular physicians and hospitals. One Internet self-help group, Mothers of Supertwins, offers supportive services for mothers but also lobbies for improved counselling at infertility clinics to better prepare couples for the demands of many babies at one time (MOST 1999).

Policy Initiatives

In Japan, some infertile couples have caused a controversy by using eggs or sperm donated by siblings for in vitro fertilization. This violates an ethical (though not legal) ban on "extramarital fertilization," the use of genetic material from anyone other than a spouse for conception. Although opinion is divided on this issue, most Japanese agree that there should be government guidelines on reproductive technology. Many nations, such as Canada, Britain, and Australia, bar payments to egg donors—this results in there being very few donors in these countries. Even more countries limit how many times a man can donate sperm. Because the United States has no such restrictions, infertile foreigners with enough money to afford the costs involved view the States as a land of opportunity (Efron 1998; Kolata 1998).

In 2004, Canada enacted legislation (Bill C-13) to regulate assisted human reproduction and, in 2006, established the Assisted Human Reproduction Agency of Canada. This agency is responsible for overseeing and regulating assisted human reproduction in Canada, making sure that standards are followed and laws are enforced. Under Bill C-18, the following are some of practices which are not allowed:

- Cloning of people
- Selecting sex
- Making changes to human DNA
- Buying or selling embryos, sperm, eggs, or other human reproduction material

The following are some of the practices which *are* allowed:

- Using surrogate mothers
- Donating sperm, eggs, and other reproductive material
- Using human embryos and stem cells in research (CBC 2007)

In other countries where there are no strict guidelines and regulations regarding assisted human reproduction, hospitals are mixing donated sperm and eggs to create embryos that are frozen for future use. This raises the possibility of genetic screening as couples choose what they regard as the most "desirable" embryo—a "designer baby" in effect. Couples can select (some would say adopt) a frozen embryo that matches their requests in terms of race, sex, height, body type, eye colour, intelligence, ethnic and religious background, and even national origin (Begley 1999; Rifkin 1998).

Applying Theory

1. How might functional thinkers view the changing definitions of motherhood and fatherhood?
2. What concerns might some feminist thinkers raise over recent innovations in the area of reproductive technology?

CHAPTER RESOURCES

Summary

What is a Family?
- There are many variations in families from culture to culture and within the same culture.
- The structure of the **extended family** (p. 288) can offer certain advantages over that of the **nuclear family** (p. 287).
- All cultures determine kinship in one of these ways—by descent from both parents or **bilateral descent** (p. 289), from the father or **patrilineal descent** (p. 289), or from the mother or **matrilineal descent** (p. 289).
- Sociologists do not agree on whether the **egalitarian family** (p. 290) has replaced the **patriarchal family** (p. 290) as the social norm in Canada.

How do Sociologists Study Families?
- Functionalist sociologists have identified six basic functions of the family: reproduction, protection, socialization, regulation of sexual behaviour, companionship, and the provision of social status.
- Conflict theorists argue that the family contributes to societal injustice and denies opportunities to women that are extended to men.
- Interactionists focus on the micro level—on how individuals interact in the family.

- Feminist views on the family are diverse yet hold the common assumption that families are socially constructed.

What are the Diverse Patterns of Marriage and Family?
- In Canada, there is considerable variation in family life associated with sexual orientation, social class, race, and ethnic differences.
- Currently, the majority of all couples in Canada have both partners active in the paid labour force.
- Among the factors that contribute to the current divorce rate among couples in Canada are the greater social acceptance of divorce and the liberalization of divorce laws.
- More and more people are living together without marrying, thereby engaging in what is called **cohabitation** (p. 303). People are also staying single longer or deciding not to have children within marriage.
- In 2005, Canada passed Bill C-38, the Civil Marriage Act, which legalized same-sex civil marriages.
- Reproductive technology has advanced to such an extent that ethical questions have arisen about the creation and shaping of human life and, thus, the formation of families.

Critical Thinking Questions

1. Recent political discussions have focused on the definition of *family*. Should some governments promote the model of family that includes both same-sex and opposite-sex couples? Are there ways in which family might be defined other than on the basis of sexual orientation? If so, name them.
2. In an increasing proportion of couples in Canada, both partners work outside the home. What are the advantages and disadvantages of the dual-

income model for women, for men, for children, and for society as a whole?
3. Given the current rate of divorce in Canada, is it more appropriate to view divorce as dysfunctional or as a normal part of our marriage system? What are the implications of viewing divorce as normal rather than as dysfunctional?
4. What might be the focus of interactionist sociologists in their study of biological and non-biological parents' relationships with their children?

Key Terms

Adoption   A process that allows for the transfer of the legal rights, responsibilities, and privileges of parenthood to a new legal parent or parents. (p. 297)

Arranged marriages   marriages engineered by parents or religious authorities, in which economic considerations play a significant role. (p. 295)

Bilateral descent   A kinship system in which both sides of a person's family are regarded as equally important. (p. 289)

Blended family   The result when a couple or individual who separates or divorces and then goes on to form a new relationship, when children are involved (p. 299)

Cohabitation The practice of living together as a couple without marrying. (p. 303)

Domestic partnership Two unrelated adults who have chosen to share each other's lives in a relationship of mutual caring, who reside together, and who agree to be jointly responsible for their dependants, basic living expenses, and other common necessities. (p. 304)

Egalitarian family An authority pattern in which the adult members of the family are regarded as equals. (p. 290)

Endogamy The restriction of mate selection to people within the same group. (p. 293)

Exogamy The requirement that people select mates outside certain groups. (p. 293)

Extended family A family in which relatives—such as grandparents, aunts, or uncles—live in the same home as parents and their children. (p. 288)

Family A set of people related by blood, marriage (or some other agreed-on relationship), or adoption, who share the responsibility for reproducing and caring for members of society. (p. 287)

Incest taboo The prohibition of sexual relationships between certain culturally specified relatives. (p. 293)

Kinship The state of being related to others. (p. 289)

Matriarchy A society in which women dominate in family decision making. (p. 290)

Matrilineal descent A kinship system that favours the relatives of the mother. (p. 289)

Monogamy A form of marriage in which one woman and one man are married only to each other. (p. 288)

Nuclear family A married couple and their unmarried children living together. (p. 287)

Patriarchy A society in which men dominate in family decision making. (p. 290)

Patrilineal descent A kinship system that favours the relatives of the father. (p. 289)

Polyandry A form of polygamy in which a woman can have more than one husband at the same time. (p. 289)

Polygamy A form of marriage in which an individual can have several husbands or wives simultaneously. (p. 288)

Polygyny A form of polygamy in which a husband can have several wives at the same time. (p. 289)

Serial monogamy A life choice in which a person can have several spouses in his or her lifetime but only one spouse at a time. (p. 288)

Single-parent families Families in which there is only one parent to care for the children. Also known as lone-parent families. (p. 298)

Additional Readings

Baker, Maureen, ed. 2004. *Families: Changing Trends in Canada*, 5th ed. Whitby, ON: McGraw-Hill Ryerson. An edited collection by sociologists examining such areas as family violence, ethnic families, biases in family literature, and divorce and remarriage.

Milan, Anne. 2000. "One Hundred Years of Families." *Canadian Social Trends*. Statistics Canada, Catalogue No. 11-008 (Spring):2–13. This article provides a demographic overview of the changing Canadian family.

Weeks, Jeffrey, Brian Heaphy, and Catherine Donovan. 2001. *Same Sex Intimacies: Families of Choice and Other Life Experiments*. London, UK: Routledge. The authors examine the rich diversity of family types and intimate relationships.

Online Learning Centre

Visit the *Sociology: A Brief Introduction* Online Learning Centre at www.mcgrawhill.ca/olc/schaefer to access quizzes, interactive exercises, video clips, and other research and study tools related to this chapter.

Reel Society Video Clips

Reel Society can be used to spark discussion about the following topics from this chapter:

- Authority patterns
- Studying the family
- Marriage and family
- Diverse lifestyles

chapter 13

RELIGION AND EDUCATION

In this billboard distributed by Volkswagen of France, the figure of Jesus at the Last Supper says to his apostles, "Rejoice, my friends, for a new Golf is born." Although an image of Jesus is sacred for Christians, it is used here in a secular manner—to advertise cars.

☐ **What is Durkheim's Sociological Approach to Religion?**

☐ **What are the Major World Religions?**

☐ **What Role does Religion Play?**

☐ **What are the Components of Religion?**

☐ **What are the Forms of Religious Organization?**

☐ **What are some Sociological Perspectives on Education?**

☐ **What Makes Schools Formal Organizations?**

Boxes

I am the grandson of the late Joseph Michael Augustine.

My grandfather was a devout Catholic. He was baptized Catholic, raised with strong Christian beliefs and ascended into heaven shortly after our parish priest stood over his bedside to read him his last rites.

I record this religious aspect of his life in the home of one of his daughters—Aunt Madeline to me—where today I write from within a small, antiquated room in her basement. On each surrounding wall hang large, lifelike portraits of religious figures with names like Pontifex Pius X and Leo XIII and His Holiness Pope John XXIII. As was my grandfather, my aunt is a member of the Catholic Church.

With such strong ties to the Catholic religion, should I not feel ashamed of the fact that I do not even understand why each of these figures looming above me is holding the same pose, with right hand raised in the air and two fingers pointing upwards, obviously communicating to the observer something of righteous significance?

Or should I be ashamed that I choose not to understand the righteous significance of these men with all their symbolic gestures, and how they seemingly stare right though me, from every direction of this room, as if God might strike me down for recording such thoughts on religion.

I do not wish to be disrespectful, for my grandfather did not raise us in this way. I respect the Catholic religion, and my family for practising its teachings. However, I was raised in the generation where Aboriginal culture and spiritual traditions have since been reawakened, and despite being born into a strong Catholic family, I choose to honour our Great Spirit—God—through the practices and ceremonies originally given to the First Peoples of this land.

Rather than going to church, I attend a sweat lodge; rather than accepting bread and toast from the Holy Priest, I smoke a ceremonial pipe to come into Communion with the Great Spirit; and rather than kneeling with my hands placed together in prayer, I let sweetgrass be feathered over my entire being for spiritual cleansing and allow the smoke to carry my prayers into the heavens. I am a Mi'kmaq, and this is how we pray.

☐ *(Augustine 2000)*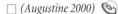

This excerpt from Noah Augustine's article "Grandfather was a Knowing Christian," which appeared in the *Toronto Star*, contrasts the religious beliefs of his grandfather to his own. Augustine, a Mi'kmaq, came to practise Aboriginal spiritual traditions—attending a sweat lodge and smoking a ceremonial pipe—even though he had been born into what he calls a "strong Catholic family." His grandfather, who was also a Mi'kmaq, practised Catholicism and was never "reawakened" by the spiritual traditions of his Aboriginal heritage. Noah Augustine's reawakening represents part of a growing trend among Aboriginal people in Canada in which Aboriginal spirituality is again being expressed after years of suppression by the dominant culture.

Religion plays a major role in people's lives, and religious practices of some sort are evident in every society. That makes religion a cultural universal, along with other general practices found in every culture, such as dancing, food preparation, the family, and personal names. At present, an estimated 4 billion people belong to the world's many religious faiths (see Figure 13-1 on the next page).

When religion's influence on other social institutions in a society diminishes, the process of **secularization** is said to be underway. During this process, religion will survive in the private sphere of individual and family life; it may even thrive on a personal level. But, at the same time, other social institutions—such as the economy, politics, and education—maintain their own sets of norms independent of religious guidance (Stark and Iannaccone 1992).

Education, like religion, is a cultural universal. As such, it is an important aspect of socialization—the lifelong process of learning the attitudes, values, and behaviour considered appropriate to members of a particular culture, as we saw in Chapter 4. When learning is explicit and formalized—when some people consciously teach, while others adopt the role of learner—the process of socialization is called **education**.

In this chapter, we first look at religion as it has emerged in modern industrial societies. We begin with a brief overview of the approaches that Émile Durkheim first introduced and those that later sociologists have used in studying religion. We explore religion's role in societal integration, social support, social change, and social control. We examine three important dimensions of religious behaviour—belief, ritual, and experience—as well as the basic forms of religious organization. We pay particular attention to the emergence of new religious movements.

In the second part of this chapter, we focus on the formal systems of education that characterize modern industrial societies, beginning with a discussion of four theoretical perspectives on education: functionalist, conflict, interactionist, and feminist. As we will see, education can both perpetuate the status quo and foster social change. An examination of schools as formal organizations—as bureaucracies and subcultures of teachers and students—follows. Two types of education that are becoming more common in North America today, adult education and home-schooling, merit special mention. We close the chapter with a social policy discussion of the controversy over religion in public schools.

Use Your Sociological Imagination

Why have Aboriginal people had their expressions of spirituality denied for generations? Have you ever attended a sweat lodge to observe or to receive spiritual cleansing? If so, what was the experience like for you?

☐ WHAT IS DURKHEIM'S SOCIOLOGICAL APPROACH TO RELIGION?

If a group believes that it is being directed by a "vision from God," sociologists will not attempt to prove or disprove this revelation. Instead, they will assess the effects of the religious experience on the group. What sociologists are

interested in is the social impact of religion on individuals and institutions (McGuire 1981:12).

Émile Durkheim was perhaps the first sociologist to recognize the critical importance of religion in human societies. He saw its appeal for the individual, but—more importantly—he stressed the social impact of religion. In Durkheim's view, religion is a collective act and includes many forms of behaviour in which people interact with others. As in his work on suicide,

▶ **FIGURE 13-1**

Religions of the World

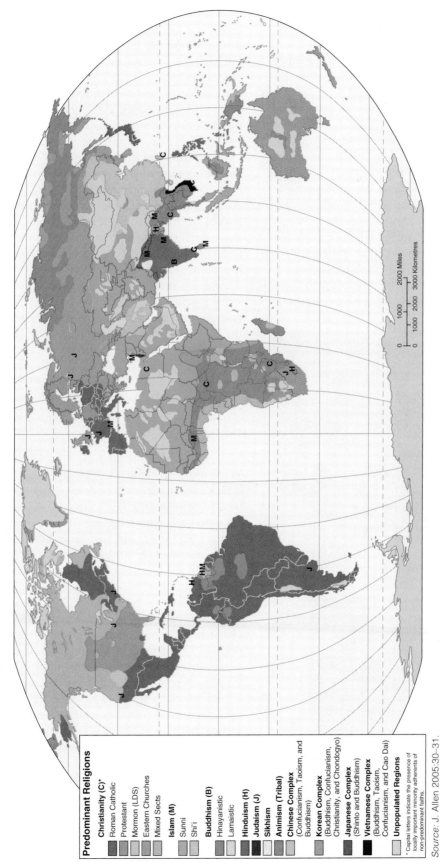

Predominant Religions

Christianity (C)*
Roman Catholic
Protestant
Mormon (LDS)
Eastern Churches
Mixed Sects

Islam (M)
Sunni
Shi'i

Buddhism (B)
Hinayanistic
Lamaistic

Hinduism (H)
Judaism (J)
Sikhism
Animism (Tribal)
Chinese Complex
(Confucianism, Taoism, and
Buddhism)
Korean Complex
(Buddhism, Confucianism,
Christianity, and Chondogyo)
Japanese Complex
(Shinto and Buddhism)
Vietnamese Complex
(Buddhism, Taoism,
Confucianism, and Cao Dai)
Unpopulated Regions

* Capital letters indicate the presence of
locally important minority adherents of
non-predominant faiths.

Source: J. Allen 2005:30–31.

Durkheim was not as interested in the personalities of religious believers as he was in understanding religious behaviour within a social context.

Durkheim defined **religion** as a "unified system of beliefs and practices relative to sacred things." In his view, religion involves a set of beliefs and practices that are uniquely the property of religion—as opposed to other social institutions and ways of thinking. Durkheim argued that religious faiths distinguish between certain events that transcend the ordinary and the everyday world (1947, original edition 1912). He referred to these realms as the *sacred* and the *profane*.

The **sacred** encompasses elements beyond everyday life that inspire awe, respect, and even fear. People become a part of the sacred realm only by completing some ritual, such as prayer or sacrifice. Believers have faith in the sacred; this faith allows them to accept what they cannot understand. By contrast, the **profane** includes the ordinary and commonplace. It can get confusing,

A Hindu holy man prays at the scared Ganges River in India. Hindus hold many aspects of life sacred, and emphasize the importance of being good in this life in order to advance in the next.

however, because the same object can be either sacred or profane depending on how it is viewed. A normal dining room table is profane, but it becomes sacred to Christians if it bears the elements of communion. A candelabra becomes sacred for Jews when it is a menorah. For Confucians and Taoists, incense sticks are not mere decorative items; they are highly valued offerings to the gods in religious ceremonies marking new and full moons.

Following the direction established by Durkheim almost a century ago, contemporary sociologists view religions in two different ways: First, they study the norms and values of religious faiths through examination of their substantive religious beliefs. For example, it is possible to compare the degree to which Christian faiths literally interpret the Bible, or Muslim groups follow the Qur'an (or Koran), the sacred book of Islam. Second, sociologists examine religions in terms of the social functions they fulfil, such as providing social support or reinforcing the social norms. By exploring both the beliefs and the functions of religion, we can better understand its impact on the individual, groups, and society as a whole.

□ WHAT ARE THE MAJOR WORLD RELIGIONS?

Worldwide, tremendous diversity exists in religious beliefs and practices. Overall, roughly 85 percent of the world's population adheres to some religion; only about 15 percent is non-religious. This level of adherence changes over time, and also varies by country and age group. In Canada in 2004, those who were non-religious accounted for 19 percent of the population, a 7 percent increase since 1985 (Clark and Schellenberg 2006l).

Christianity is the largest single religion in the world; the second largest is Islam (see Table 13-1). Although global news events often suggest an inherent conflict between Christians and Muslims, the two religions are similar in many ways. Both are monotheistic (based on a single deity); both include a belief in prophets, an afterlife, and a judgment day. In fact, Islam recognizes Jesus as a prophet, though not the son of God. Both faiths impose a moral code on believers, which varies from fairly rigid proscriptions for fundamentalists to relatively relaxed guidelines for liberals.

The followers of Islam, called Muslims, believe that Islam's holy scriptures were received from Allah (God) by the prophet Mohammad nearly 1400 years ago. They see Mohammad as the last in a long line of prophets, preceded by Adam, Abraham, Moses, and Jesus. Islam is more communal in its expression than Christianity,

Table 13-1 Major World Religions

Faith	Current Following, in Millions (and Percent of World Population)	Primary Location of Followers Today	Founder (and Approximate Date of Birth)	Important Texts (and Holy Sites)
Buddhism	379 (5.9%)	Southeast Asia, Mongolia, Tibet	Siddhartha Gautama (563 BC)	Triptaka (areas in Nepal)
Christianity	2133 (33.1%)	Europe, North America, South America	Jesus (6 BCE)	Bible (Jerusalem, Rome)
Hinduism	860 (13.3%)	India, Indian communities overseas	No specific founder (1500 BCE)	Sruti and Smrti texts (seven sacred cities, including Vavansi)
Islam	1309 (20.3%)	Middle East, Central Asia, North Africa, Indonesia	Mohammad (570 CE)	Qur'an, or Koran (Mecca, Medina, Jerusalem)
Judaism	15 (0.2%)	Israel, North America, France, Russia	Abraham (2000 BCE)	Torah, Talmud (Jerusalem)

Sources: Adapted from Barrett et al. 2005; Swatos 1998.

particularly than the latter's more individualistic Protestant denominations.

Consequently, in countries that are predominantly Muslim, the separation of religion and the state is not considered necessary or even desirable. In fact, Muslim governments often reinforce Islamic practices through their laws. Muslims do vary sharply in their interpretation of several traditions, some of which—such as the wearing of veils by women—are more cultural than religious in origin.

Like Christianity and Islam, Judaism is monotheistic. Jews believe that God's true nature is revealed in the Torah, which Christians know as the first five books of the Old Testament. According to these scriptures, God formed a covenant, or pact, with Abraham and Sarah, the ancestors of the tribes of Israel. Even today, Jews believe, this covenant holds them accountable to God's will. If they follow both the letter and spirit of the Torah, a long-awaited Messiah will one day bring paradise to earth. Although Judaism has a relatively small following compared to other major faiths, it forms the historical foundation for both Christianity and Islam. That is why Jews revere many of the same sacred Middle Eastern sites as Christians and Muslims.

Two other major religions developed in a different part of the world—India. The earlier one, Hinduism, originated circa 1500 BCE. Hinduism differs from Judaism, Christianity, and Islam in that it embraces a number of

gods and minor gods, although most worshippers are devoted primarily to a single deity, such as Shiva or Vishnu. Hinduism is also distinguished by a belief in reincarnation, or the perpetual rebirth of the soul after death. Unlike Judaism, Christianity, and Islam, which are based largely on sacred texts, Hindu beliefs have been preserved mostly through oral tradition.

A second religion, Buddhism, developed in the sixth century BCE as a reaction against Hinduism. This faith is founded on the teachings of Siddhartha Gautama (later called Buddha, or "the enlightened one"). Through meditation, followers of Buddhism strive to overcome selfish cravings for physical or material pleasures, with the goal of reaching a state of enlightenment, or nirvana. Buddhists created the first monastic orders, which are thought to be the models for monastic orders in other religions, including Christianity. Though Buddhism emerged in India, its followers were eventually driven out of that country by the Hindus. Buddhists are now found primarily in other parts of Asia. (Contemporary adherents of Buddhism in India are relatively recent converts.)

Although the differences among religions are striking, they are exceeded by variations within faiths. Consider the differences within Christianity, from relatively liberal denominations such as Presbyterians or the United Church of Canada to the more conservative Mormons and Greek Orthodox Catholics. Similar divisions exist within Hinduism, Islam, and the other world religions (Barrett et al. 2005; Swatos 1998).

☐ WHAT ROLE DOES RELIGION PLAY?

Since religion is a cultural universal, it is not surprising that it plays a basic role in human societies. In sociological terms, these include both manifest and latent functions. Among its *manifest* (open and stated) functions, religion defines the spiritual world and gives meaning to the divine. Religion provides an explanation for events that seem difficult to understand, such as what happens after death.

◄ P.13

The *latent* functions of religion are unintended, covert, or hidden. Even though the manifest function of church services is to offer a forum for religious worship, they might at the same time fulfil a latent function as a meeting ground for unmarried members.

Functionalists and conflict theorists both evaluate religion's impact as a social institution on human societies. We'll consider a functionalist view of religion's role in integrating society, in social support, and in promoting social change, and then look at religion as a means of social control from the conflict perspective. Note that, for the most part, religion's impact is best understood from a macro-level viewpoint, oriented toward the larger society. The social support function is an exception: it is best viewed on the micro level, directed toward the individual.

The Integrative Function of Religion

Émile Durkheim viewed religion as an integrative power in human society—a perspective reflected in functionalist thought today. Durkheim sought to answer a perplexing question: "How can human societies be held together when they are generally composed of individuals and social groups with diverse interests and aspirations?" In his view, religious bonds often transcend these personal and divisive forces. Durkheim acknowledged that religion is not the only integrative force—nationalism or patriotism may serve the same end.

How does religion provide this "societal glue"? Religion, whether it be Buddhism, Islam, Christianity, or Judaism, offers people meaning and purpose for their lives. It gives them certain ultimate values and ends to hold in common. Although subjective and not always fully accepted, these values and ends help a society to function as an integrated social system. For example, funerals, weddings, bar mitzvahs and bat mitzvahs, and confirmations serve to integrate people into larger communities by providing shared beliefs and values about the ultimate questions of life.

The integrative power of religion can be seen in the role that churches, synagogues, temples, and mosques have traditionally played and continue to play for immigrant groups in Canada. For example, Roman Catholic immigrants may settle near a parish church that offers services in their native language, such as Polish or Portuguese. Similarly, Korean immigrants may join a Presbyterian church with many Korean-Canadian members and with religious practices like those of churches in Korea. Like other religious organizations, these Roman Catholic and Presbyterian churches help to integrate immigrants into their new homeland.

Yet another example of the integrative impact of religion is provided by the Universal Fellowship of Metropolitan Community Churches. It was established in the United States in 1968 to offer a welcoming place of worship for lesbians and gays. This spiritual community is especially important today, given the many organized religions that are openly hostile to gay and lesbian people. The Metropolitan Community Church has 42 000 members in its local churches in 15 countries, including Canada, where there are 3 such churches in Toronto alone. As part of its effort to support lesbian and gay rights, the Metropolitan Community Church for years performed same-sex marriages, which it called "holy union ceremonies" (Stammer 1999). In 2005, Canada became the fourth country in the world to legally recognize same-sex marriage, a move that pleased many progressive activists and outraged other large factions. Many religious leaders argue that the government does not have the right to redefine marriage. The research of Canadian sociologist Reginald Bibby (2004) shows that religious affiliation and participation are closely linked to opposition to same-sex marriage. This relationship exists in both Canada and the United States; however, U.S. citizens are more likely to be against same-sex marriage.

In some instances, religious loyalties are *dysfunctional*; they contribute to tension and even to conflict between groups or nations. During the Second World War, the German Nazis attempted to exterminate the Jewish people; approximately 6 million European Jews were killed. In modern times, nations, such as Lebanon (Muslims versus Christians), Israel (Jews versus Muslims, as well as Orthodox versus secular Jews), Northern Ireland (Roman Catholics versus Protestants), and India (Hindus versus Muslims and, more recently, Sikhs), have been torn by clashes that are in large part based on religion.

Religious conflict (though on a less violent level) is evident in Canada as well. Christian fundamentalists in many communities battle against their liberal counterparts for control of the secular culture. The battlefield is an array of familiar social issues, among them multiculturalism, abortion, sex education in schools, and gay and lesbian rights.

Religion and Social Support

Most of us find it difficult to accept the stressful events of life—the death of a loved one, serious injury, bankruptcy, divorce, and so forth. This is especially true when something "senseless" happens. How, for example, can family and friends come to terms with the death of a talented university student, not even 20 years old, from a terminal disease?

Through its emphasis on the divine and the supernatural, religion allows us to "do something" about the calamities we face. In some faiths, adherents can offer sacrifices or pray to a deity in the belief that such acts will change their earthly condition. At a more basic level, religion encourages us to view our personal misfortunes as relatively unimportant in the broader perspective of human history—or even as part of an undisclosed divine purpose. Friends and relatives of the deceased university student may see this death as being "God's will" and as having some ultimate benefit that we cannot understand now. This perspective may be much more comforting than the terrifying feeling that any of us can die senselessly at any moment—and that there is no divine "answer" as to why one person lives a long and full life, while another dies tragically at a relatively early age.

Faith-based community organizations have taken on more and more responsibilities in the area of social assistance. In fact, as part of an effort to cut back on government-funded welfare programs, government leaders have advocated shifting the social "safety net" to private organizations in general and to churches and religious charities in particular. These organizations identify experienced leaders and assemble them into non-sectarian coalitions devoted to community development (K. Starr 1999).

Religion and Social Change

The Weberian Thesis

When someone seems driven to work and succeed, we often attribute the "Protestant work ethic" to that person. The term comes from the writings of Max Weber, who carefully examined the connection between reli-

Some churches, such as the Metropolitan Community Church in Toronto, perform marriage ceremonies joining same-sex couples.

gious allegiance and capitalist development. His findings appeared in his pioneering work *The Protestant Ethic and the Spirit of Capitalism* (1958a, original edition 1904).

Weber noted that in European nations with both Protestant and Catholic citizens, an overwhelming number of business leaders, owners of capital, and skilled workers were Protestant. In his view, this was no mere coincidence. Weber pointed out that the followers of John Calvin (1509–1564), a leader of the Protestant Reformation, emphasized the disciplined work ethic, worldly concerns, and rational orientation to life that have become known as the **Protestant ethic**. One by-product of the Protestant ethic was a drive to accumulate savings that could be used for future investment. This "spirit of capitalism," to use Weber's phrase, contrasted with the moderate work hours, leisurely work habits, and lack of ambition that he saw as typical of the times (Winter 1977; Yinger 1974).

Few books on the sociology of religion have aroused as much commentary and criticism as Weber's work. It has been hailed as one of the most important theoretical works in the field and as an excellent example of macrolevel analysis. Like Durkheim, Weber demonstrated that religion is not solely a matter of intimate personal beliefs. He stressed that the collective nature of religion has social consequences for society as a whole.

Weber provides a convincing description of the origins of European capitalism. But this economic system has subsequently been adopted by non-Calvinists in many parts of the world. Apparently, the "spirit of capitalism" has become a generalized cultural trait rather than a specific religious tenet (Greeley 1989).

Conflict theorists caution that Weber's theory—even if it is accepted—should not be regarded as an analysis of mature capitalism as reflected in the rise of multinational corporations that cross national boundaries. Marxists would disagree with Weber not on the origins of capitalism but on its future. Unlike Marx, Weber believed that capitalism could endure indefinitely as an economic system. He added, however, that the decline of religion as an overriding force in society opened the way for workers to express their discontent more vocally (R. Collins 1980).

◀ P.219

Liberation Theology

Sometimes, the clergy can be found in the forefront of social change. Many religious activists, especially in the Roman Catholic church in Latin America, support **liberation theology**—the use of a church in a political effort to eliminate poverty, discrimination, and other forms of injustice evident in a secular society. Advocates of this religious movement sometimes sympathize with Marxism. Many believe that radical change, rather than economic development in itself, is the only acceptable solution to the desperation of the masses in impoverished developing countries. Activists associated with liberation theology believe that organized religion has a moral responsibility to take a strong public stand against the oppression of the poor, members of racial and ethnic minorities, and women (C. Smith 1991).

Liberation theology may be seen by some as dysfunctional, however. Some Roman Catholics have come to believe that by focusing on political and governmental injustice, the clergy are no longer addressing their personal and spiritual needs. Partly as a result of such disenchantment, some Catholics in Latin America, for example, are converting to mainstream Protestant faiths or to Mormonism.

Use Your Sociological Imagination

The social support that religious groups provide is suddenly withdrawn from your community. How will your life or the lives of others change? What will happen if some religious groups stop pushing for social change?

Religion and Social Control: A Conflict View

Liberation theology is a relatively recent phenomenon and marks a break with the traditional role of churches. It was this traditional role that Karl Marx opposed. In his view, religion *impeded* social change by encouraging oppressed people to focus on other-worldly concerns rather than on their immediate poverty or exploitation. Marx described religion as "opium of the masses," particularly harmful to oppressed peoples. He felt that religion was widely used to "drug" less fortunate people into submission by offering a consolation for their harsh daily lives: the hope of salvation in an ideal afterlife. For example, Aboriginal children housed in residential schools in Canada were forbidden to practise their own forms of spirituality and were forced to adopt Christianity. These children were taught that obedience would lead to salvation and eternal happiness in the hereafter. Viewed from a conflict perspective, Christianity may have pacified certain oppressed groups and blunted the rage that often fuels rebellion (McGuire 1992; Yinger 1970).

Marx acknowledged that religion plays an important role in propping up the existing social structure. The values of religion, as already noted, reinforce other social institutions and the social order as a whole. From Marx's perspective, however, religion's promotion of stability within society only helps to perpetuate patterns of social inequality. According to Marx, the dominant religion reinforces the interests of those in power (Harap 1982).

Consider, for example, India's traditional caste system. It defined the social structure of that society, at least among the Hindu majority. The caste system was almost certainly the creation of the priesthood, but it also served the interests of India's political rulers by granting a certain religious legitimacy to social inequality.

◀ P.187

Contemporary Christianity, like the Hindu faith, reinforces traditional patterns of behaviour that call for the subordination of the less powerful. Like Marx, conflict theorists argue that to whatever extent religion actually influences social behaviour, it reinforces existing patterns of dominance and inequality.

From a Marxist perspective, religion functions as an "agent of depoliticization" (J. Wilson 1973). In simpler terms, religion keeps people from seeing their lives and societal conditions in political terms—for example, by obscuring the overriding significance of conflicting economic interests. Marxists suggest that by inducing a "false consciousness" among the disadvantaged, religion lessens the possibility of collective political action that can end capitalist oppression and transform society.

◀ P.14

Feminist Perspectives on Religion

Feminist thinkers draw attention to the reality that the positions of women in religious organizations tend to be ones of subjugation. Assumptions about gender often place women in subservient positions, both within many religious faiths and in the private sphere. In fact, as they do in the corporate world, women find it difficult to achieve leadership positions within many religious

Table 13-2 Sociological Perspectives on Religion

Theoretical Perspective	Emphasis
Functionalist	Religion as a source of social integration and unification Religion as a source of social support for individuals
Conflict	Religion as a potential obstacle to structural social change Religion as a potential source of structural social change (through liberation theology)
Interactionist	Individual religious expression through belief, ritual, and experience (see the next section of this chapter)
Feminist	Religious systems as gendered, reflecting dominant political and cultural assumptions

faiths. For example, only 20 percent of Anglican priests are female and approximately 40 percent of ordained ministers in the United Church of Canada are female (Harvey 2004). Among Canadian Aboriginals, however, women have traditionally been granted roles of spiritual leadership.

Female spiritual leaders are more likely to serve in subsidiary roles and to wait longer for desirable assignments. Although women may play a significant role as volunteers in religious communities, men are more likely to make the major theological and financial judgments for nationwide spiritual organizations.

Feminist perspectives on religion and female spirituality recognize the diversity of women's spiritual expression and reveal the ways in which religious systems are "gendered," reflecting dominant political and cultural assumptions (Stuckey 1998). These perspectives run the gamut from those suggesting that religions revise their messages and interpretations, to those unequivocally rejecting religious traditions as "irremediably sexist" (Stuckey 1998:269).

Table 13-2 summarizes the major sociological perspectives on religion.

☐ WHAT ARE THE COMPONENTS OF RELIGION?

All religions have certain elements in common, yet these elements are expressed in the distinctive manner of each faith. The patterns of religious behaviour, like other patterns of social behaviour, are of great interest to sociologists, since they underscore the relationship between religion and society.

Religious beliefs, rituals, and experience all help to define what is sacred and to differentiate the sacred from the profane. Let us now examine these three dimensions of religious behaviour.

Belief

Some people believe in life after death, in supreme beings with unlimited powers, and/or in supernatural forces. The strength of belief in God varies dramatically worldwide. **Religious beliefs** are statements to which members of a particular religion adhere. These views can vary dramatically from religion to religion.

The Christian and Jewish story of Adam and Eve—an account of creation—found in Genesis, the first book of the Old Testament and the Torah, is an example of a religious belief. Some people in Canada strongly adhere to this biblical explanation of creation. These people, known as *creationists*, are worried by the secularization of society and oppose teaching that directly or indirectly questions biblical scripture.

Use Your Sociological Imagination

Canada and the United States are similar in many ways. Why would religious participation in the U.S. be greater than that in Canada?

Ritual

Religious rituals are practices required or expected of members of a faith. Rituals usually honour the divine power (or powers) worshipped by believers; they also remind adherents of their religious duties and responsibilities. Rituals and beliefs can be interdependent; rituals generally involve the affirmation of beliefs, as in a public or private statement confessing a sin (Roberts 1995). Like any social institution, religion develops distinctive normative patterns to structure people's behaviour. Moreover, there are sanctions attached to religious rituals, whether rewards (bat mitzvah gifts) or penalties (expulsion from a religious institution for violation of norms).

▶ FIGURE 13-2

Religious Participation in Selected Countries, 1981 and 2001

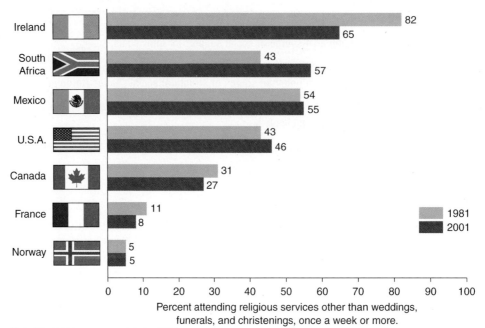

Note: World Values survey data for 2001.
Source: Noris and Inglehart 2004:74.

In North America, rituals may be very simple, such as saying grace at a meal or observing a moment of silence to commemorate someone's death. Yet, certain rituals, such as the process of canonizing a saint, are quite elaborate. Most religious rituals in our culture focus on services conducted at houses of worship. Attendance at a service, silent and spoken prayers, and singing of spiritual hymns and chants are common forms of ritual behaviour that generally take place in group settings. From an interactionist perspective, these rituals serve as important face-to-face encounters in which people reinforce their religious beliefs and their commitment to faith.

For Muslims, a very important ritual is the *hajj*, a pilgrimage to the Grand Mosque in Mecca, Saudi Arabia. Every Muslim who is physically and financially able is expected to make this trip at least once. Each year, 2 million pilgrims go to Mecca during the week-long period indicated by the Islamic lunar calendar. Muslims from all over the world make the *hajj*, including those in Canada, where many tours are arranged to facilitate this ritual.

Some rituals induce an almost trancelike state. The First Nations of the American Plains eat or drink peyote, a cactus containing the powerful hallucinogenic drug mescaline. Similarly, the ancient Greek followers of the god Pan chewed intoxicating leaves of ivy in order to become more ecstatic during their celebrations.

Of course, artificial stimulants are not necessary to achieve a religious "high." Devout believers, such as those who practise the pentecostal Christian ritual of "speaking in tongues," can reach a state of ecstasy simply through spiritual passion.

In recent decades, participation in religious ritual has tended to hold steady or decline in most countres. Figure 13-2 shows the change in religious participation in selected countries from 1981 to 2001.

Experience

In the sociological study of religion, the term **religious experience** refers to the feeling or perception of being in direct contact with the ultimate reality, such as a divine being, or of being overcome with religious emotion. A religious experience may be rather slight, such as the feeling of exaltation a person receives from hearing a choir sing Handel's "Hallelujah Chorus." But many religious experiences are more profound, such as a Muslim's experience on a *hajj*. In his autobiography, the late U.S. black activist Malcolm X wrote of his *hajj* and how deeply moved he was by the way that Muslims in Mecca came together across lines of race and colour. For Malcolm X, the colour blindness of the Muslim world "proved to me the power of the One God" (1964:338).

Pilgrims on hajj to the Grand Mosque in Mecca, Saudi Arabia. Islam requires all Muslims who are able to undertake a pilgrimage to the Holy Land.

Still another profound religious experience is being "born again"—that is, at a turning point in one's life, making a personal commitment to Jesus. According to a 2003 national survey, 42 percent of people in the United States claimed that they had a born-again Christian experience at some time in their lives. An earlier survey found that Baptists (75 percent) were the most likely to report such experiences; by contrast, only 21 percent of Catholics and 24 percent of Episcopalians stated that they had been born again. The collective nature of religion, as emphasized by Durkheim, is evident in these statistics. The beliefs and rituals of a particular faith can create an atmosphere either friendly or hostile to this type of religious experience. Thus, a Baptist would be encouraged to come forward and share such experiences with others,

whereas an Episcopalian who claimed to have been born again would receive much less interest (Newport 2004).

☐ WHAT ARE THE FORMS OF RELIGIOUS ORGANIZATION?

The collective nature of religion has led to many forms of religious association. In modern societies, religion has become increasingly formalized. Specific structures, such as churches and synagogues, are constructed for religious worship; individuals are trained for occupational roles within various fields. These developments make it possible to distinguish clearly between the sacred and secular parts of life—a distinction that could not be made in earlier societies in which religion was largely a family activity carried out in the home.

Sociologists find it useful to distinguish among four basic forms of organization: the ecclesia, the denomination, the sect, and the new religious movement or cult. We can see differences among these types of organizations in such factors as size, power, degree of

---

Use Your Sociological Imagination

Choose a religious tradition other than your own. How would your religious beliefs, rituals, and experience differ if you had been raised in that tradition?

commitment expected from members, and historical ties to other faiths.

Ecclesiae

An **ecclesia** (plural, *ecclesiae*) is a religious organization that claims to include most or all of the members of a society and is recognized as the national or official religion. Since virtually everyone belongs to the faith, membership is by birth rather than conscious decision. Examples of ecclesiae include the Lutheran church in Sweden, the Catholic church in Spain, Islam in Saudi Arabia, and Buddhism in Thailand. However, there can be significant differences even within the category of ecclesia. In Saudi Arabia's Islamic regime, leaders of the ecclesia hold vast power over actions of the state. By contrast, the Lutheran church in contemporary Sweden has no such power over the Riksdag (Parliament) or the prime minister.

Generally, ecclesiae are conservative in that they do not challenge the leaders of a secular government. In a society with an ecclesia, the political and religious institutions often act in harmony and mutually reinforce each other's power over their relative spheres of influence. Within the modern world, ecclesiae tend to be declining in power.

Denominations

A **denomination** is a large, organized religion not officially linked with the state or government. Like an ecclesia, it tends to have an explicit set of beliefs, a defined system of authority, and a generally respected position in society. Denominations claim as members large segments of a population. Generally, children accept the denomination of their parents and give little thought to membership in other faiths. Denominations also resemble ecclesiae in that generally few demands are made on members. However, there is a critical difference between these two forms of religious organization. Although the denomination is considered respectable and is not viewed as a challenge to the secular government, it lacks the official recognition and power held by an ecclesia (Doress and Porter 1977).

Although approximately 43 percent of all Canadians were Roman Catholic in 2001 (a question on religion is asked only once every 10 years and, therefore, was not asked in the 2006 Canada census), this country is marked by great religious diversity. With the exception of Aboriginal peoples, we are a country of immigrants, and Canadian religious diversity reflects patterns of immigration and population change.

Protestantism follows Catholicism in popularity and is practised by 29 percent of the population in Canada; 9.6 percent of people belonging to a Protestant denomi-nation are members of the United Church. From 1991 to 2001, the percentage of Muslims in Canada more than doubled, increasing to almost 600 000. The percentage of Jews increased by approximately 4 percent from one census period to the next, increasing to almost 330 000. The percentage of people declaring no religious affiliation rose from 12.3 percent in 1991 to 16.2 percent in 2001; at the same time, the percentage of those belonging to Protestant denominations dropped by approximately 8 percent. A significant increase in affiliation was reported in the category "Christian, not included elsewhere," which includes Christian fundamentalist denominations. That category rose 121 percent from 1991 to 2001. (See Table 13-3.)

These overall trends do not reveal the great diversity that exists regionally in relation to religious membership. In 2001, people in Yukon were the Canadians most likely to declare no religious affiliation (37 percent). By contrast, in Newfoundland and Labrador, less than 2 percent declared no religious affiliation (Statistics Canada 2003j).

Attendance at religious services tends to vary according to age, rural/urban setting, immigrant status, and family status. In 1998, married couples aged 25 to 44 with young children were more likely to worship regularly than those who were of the same age but child-free (Statistics Canada 2000b). Seniors aged 75 and over had the highest rates of attendance. Those born in Canada were less likely to be regular attendees of religious services than were immigrants. Approximately 50 percent of Asian immigrants who entered Canada between 1994 and 1998 attended worship services regularly, compared with approximately one in five European immigrants who entered the country during the same period. According to the 2001 General Social Survey by Statistics Canada, Canadians' attendance at religious services fell dramatically over the previous 15 years. In 2001, 20 percent of Canadians aged 15 and over attended religious services on a weekly basis, compared with 28 percent in 1986 (Statistics Canada 2003j).

In the past 20 years, some distinctions among denominations have started to blur. Certain faiths have even allowed members of other faiths to participate in some of their most sacred rituals, such as communion. Even more dramatic has been the appearance of **megachurches**—large congregations that often lack direct ties to a worldwide denomination.

Sects

A **sect** can be defined as a relatively small religious group that has broken away from some other religious organization to renew what it considers the original vision of the faith. Many sects, such as that led by Martin Luther during the Reformation, claim to be the "true church" because they seek to cleanse the established faith of what

Table 13-3   Major Religious Denominations, Canada, 1991 and 2001

	2001 number	%	1991[1] number	%	Percentage Change, 1991–2001
Roman Catholic	12 793 125	43.2	12 203 625	45.2	4.8
Protestant	8 654 854	29.2	9 427 675	34.9	−8.2
Christian Orthodox	479 620	1.6	387 395	1.4	23.8
Christian, not included elsewhere[2]	780 450	2.6	353 040	1.3	121.1
Muslim	579 640	2.0	253 265	0.9	128.9
Jewish	329 995	1.1	318 185	1.2	3.7
Buddhist	300 345	1.0	163 415	0.6	83.8
Hindu	297 200	1.0	157 015	0.6	89.3
Sikh	278 415	0.9	147 440	0.5	88.8
No religion	4 796 352	16.2	3 333 245	12.3	43.9

1. For comparability purposes, 1991 data are presented according to 2001 boundaries.
2. Includes persons who report "Christian," as well as those who report "Apostolic," "Born-again Christian," and "Evangelical."
Note: A question on religion is asked only once every 10 years and, therefore, was not asked in the 2006 Canada census.
Source: Statistics Canada 2003j.

they regard as extraneous beliefs and rituals (Stark and Bainbridge 1985). Max Weber termed the sect a "believer's church," because affiliation is based on conscious acceptance of a specific religious dogma (1958b:114, original edition 1916).

Sects are fundamentally at odds with society and do not seek to become established national religions. Unlike ecclesiae and denominations, sects require intensive commitments and demonstrations of belief by members. Partly owing to their "outsider" status in society, sects frequently exhibit a higher degree of religious fervour and loyalty than more established religious groups do. Recruitment focuses mainly on adults, and acceptance comes through conversion. One current-day sect is called the People of the Church, a movement within the Roman Catholic Church that began in Vienna, Austria. This sect has called for reforms of Catholicism, such as the ordination of women, local election of bishops, and optional celibacy for priests (*Religion Watch* 1995).

Sects also exist in the Islamic faith. See Box 13-1 for a discussion of Islamic sects in Canada.

New Religious Movements or Cults

In 1997, 38 members of the Heaven's Gate cult were found dead in Southern California after a mass suicide timed to occur with the appearance of the Hale-Bopp comet. They believed the comet hid a spaceship on which they could ride once they had broken free of their "bodily containers."

Partly as a result of the notoriety generated by such groups, the popular media have stigmatized the word *cult* by associating cults with the occult and the use of intense and forceful conversion techniques. The stereotyping of cults as uniformly bizarre and unethical has led sociologists to abandon the term and refer to a cult instead as a *new religious movement* (NRM). Although some NRMs, like the Branch Davidians, exhibit strange behaviour, many do not. They attract new members just like any other religion and often follow teachings similar to established Christian denominations but with less ritual.

It is difficult to distinguish sects from cults. A **new religious movement (NRM)** or **cult** is a generally small, secretive religious group that represents either a new religion or a major innovation of an existing faith. An example would be the Church of Scientology, to which a number of Hollywood actors belong. To its members, Scientology is an NRM; to its critics, it is a cult. NRMs are similar to sects in that they tend to be small and are often viewed as less respectable than more established religions.

However, unlike sects, NRMs normally do not result from schisms or breaks with established ecclesiae or denominations. Some cults, such as those focused on UFO sightings, may be totally unrelated to the existing faiths in a culture. Even when a cult does accept certain fundamental

Research in Action 13-1
Islam in Canada

The growing presence of Islam in Canada may, perhaps, lead to a better understanding of the significant diversity within Islam. Throughout the world, including in Canada, Muslims are divided into a variety of sects—the two major sects are Sunni and Shia (or Shiite). These divisions sometimes result in antagonism, just as rivalries between denominations of other faiths can cause friction. Yet, the Islamic faith is expressed in many different ways, even among Sunnis or Shia. To speak of Muslims as either Sunni or Shia would be like speaking of Christians as either Roman Catholic or Baptist.

Here, Muslim girls are playing basketball without compromising culturally appropriate norms.

The great majority of Muslims in Canada are Sunni Muslims—literally, those who follow the *Sunnah*, or way of the prophet. Compared to other Muslims, Sunnis tend to be moderate in their religious orthodoxy. The Shia, who come primarily from Iraq and Iran, are the second largest group. Shia Muslims are more attentive to guidance from accepted Islamic scholars than are Sunnis. In sufficient numbers, these two Muslim groups will choose to worship separately, even if they must cross ethnic or linguistic lines to do so. That certainly is the case in Canadian cities with large and varied Muslim communities.

Canada is home to roughly 700 000 Muslim Canadians, of which a minority—17 percent—feel that many or most Canadians are hostile toward their religion (Environics Research Group 2007b). A 2007 study by the Canadian research firm, Environics, surveyed 500 Muslim Canadians and 2045 members of the general population. The findings of the Environics study can be used alongside the results

Percentage of Muslims Who Feel that Either Some or Most of their Fellow Citizens are Hostile to their Group

Muslims in	Canada	Britain	Germany	France	Spain
Some	75	52	43	60	64
Most/many	17	42	51	39	31

Source: Environics Research Group 2007; Pew Global Attitudes 2006.

of a study of Muslims in Britain, Germany, France, and Spain conducted in 2005. Compared with their European counterparts, Canadian Muslims feel the least hostility from their fellow citizens. As we mentioned above, only 17 percent of Muslims in Canada feel hostility from most/many of their fellow citizens; in Germany, it was 51 percent; in Britain, 42 percent; in France, 39 percent; and in Spain, 31 percent.

The Environics poll revealed that a majority of Muslim Canadians—53 percent—responded that they would like to see Islamic sharia law adopted for divorce and family disputes while 86 percent do not believe governments should ban the wearing of headscarves by Muslim women in public places (including public schools). Haideh Moghissi, a sociologist at York University in Toronto, asserts that these concerns should probably be seen more as a "'political gesture than a religious one' by those

who have felt their community 'bearing the brunt of this suspicion and fear' since the September11, 2001, attacks" (CBC 2007).

On many college and university campuses in Canada, administrators have responded constructively to the growing numbers of Muslim students by hiring imams (prayer leaders) to minister to their needs, dedicating space for daily prayer, and providing for Muslim dietary restrictions.

Applying Theory

1. Is there a mosque in your community or a Muslim congregation on your campus? If so, are the members primarily Sunni or Shia?
2. Should communities be allowed to block the construction of mosques or dictate their appearance? What about a church or temple?

Sources: CBC 2007a; Decima Research Group 2007b; Pew Global Attitudes Project 2006; Ba-Yunus and Kone 2004; Belt 2002; Institute for Social Policy and Understanding 2004; P. King 2004; Leonard 2003; McCloud 1995; N. Paik 2001; T. Smith 2001.

tenets of a dominant faith—such as belief in Jesus as divine or Muhammad as a messenger of God—it will offer new revelations or new insights to justify its claim to be a more advanced religion (Stark and Bainbridge 1979, 1985).

Like sects, NRMs may undergo transformation over time into other types of religious organizations. An example is the Christian Science Church, which began as a new religious movement under the leadership of Mary Baker Eddy. Today, this church exhibits the characteristics of a denomination. New religious movements tend to be in the early stages of what may develop into a denomination, or they may just as easily fade away through loss of members or weak leadership (J. Richardson and van Driel 1997).

Comparing Forms of Religious Organization

How can we determine whether a particular religious group falls into the sociological category of ecclesia, denomination, sect, or NRM? As we have seen, these types of religious organizations have somewhat different relationships to society. Ecclesiae are recognized as national churches; denominations, although not officially approved by the state, are generally widely respected. By contrast, sects as well as NRMs are much more likely to be at odds with the larger culture.

Still, ecclesiae, denominations, and sects are best viewed as ideal types along a continuum rather than as

mutually exclusive categories. Table 13-4 summarizes some of the primary characteristics of these ideal types. Since Canada has no ecclesiae, sociologists studying this country's religions have naturally focused on denominations and sects. These religious forms have been pictured on either end of a continuum, with denominations being accommodating to the secular world and sects making a protest against established religions. New religious movements have also been included in Table 13-4 but are outside the continuum because they generally define themselves as a new view of life rather than in terms of existing religious faiths (Chalfant, Beckley, and Palmer 1994).

Advances in electronic communications have led to still another form of religious organization: the electronic church. Facilitated by cable television and satellite transmissions, *televangelists* direct their messages to more people—especially in the United States—than are served by all but the largest denominations. The Internet has given the electronic church another dimension: the religious blogosphere. According to a 2005 survey, roughly 1 million religious blogs (or Web logs) have been established in the United States alone, primarily to address people's views about religion or their personal spiritual experiences (D. Cohen 2005).

We turn now to another major social institution in every society: education. Education prepares citizens for the various roles demanded by other institutions,

Table 13-4 Characteristics of Ecclesiae, Denominations, Sects, and New Religious Movements

Characteristic	Ecclesia	Denomination	Sect	New Religious Movement (or Cult)
Size	Very large	Large	Small	Small
Wealth	Extensive	Extensive	Limited	Variable
Religious Services	Formal, little participation	Formal, little participation	Informal, emotional	Variable
Doctrines	Specific, but interpretation may be tolerated	Specific, but interpretation may be tolerated	Specific, purity of doctrine emphasized	Innovative, pathbreaking
Clergy	Well-trained, full-time	Well-trained, full-time	Trained to some degree	Unspecialized
Membership	By virtue of being a member of society	By acceptance of doctrine	By acceptance of doctrine	By an emotional commitment
Relationship to the State	Recognized, closely aligned	Tolerated	Not encouraged	Ignored or challenged

Source: Adapted from G. Vernon 1962; see also Chalfant et al. 1994.

including religion. Education and religion sometimes get intertwined, as we will see in this chapter's social policy section about the role of religion in the schools, and in Box 13-2, which examines the income and educational level of specific denominations in North America.

☐ WHAT ARE SOME SOCIOLOGICAL PERSPECTIVES ON EDUCATION?

Education is a massive industry in Canada as well as a major agent of socialization. In the last few decades, increasing numbers of people have obtained a high school diploma and at least some post-secondary education. (Figure 13-3 on page 328 shows where Canada ranks among other developed nations.) According to The Canadian Council of Learning, in 2004, only 10 percent of Canadians between the ages of 20 and 24 did not have a high school diploma or were not enrolled in school (2005).

Globally, enrolments in educational institutions have been increasing; however, vast regional and national differences exist in this overall trend. For example, in less developed regions, although progress has been made, only 79 percent of boys and 66 percent of girls finished primary education in 2002 (Unicef 2005). These numbers mask the fact that most girls in less developed countries receive less education than boys do, and in some of the world's poorest countries, fewer than half of young women receive the basic seven years of schooling (Unicef 2005). According to the United Nations Population Fund's *State of World Population Report 2000*, girls and women throughout the world are still routinely denied access to education. As a result, the United Nations Children's Fund reported in 2004, only 42 percent of women in the least-developed countries can read, compared with 62 percent of men (Unicef 2004).

The functionalist, conflict, interactionist, and feminist perspectives offer distinctive ways of examining education as a social institution.

Functionalist View

Like other social institutions, education has both manifest (open, stated) and latent (hidden) functions. The most basic *manifest* function of education is the transmission of knowledge. Schools teach students such things as how to read, how to speak foreign languages, and how to repair automobiles. Education has another important manifest function: it bestows status. Because many people believe this function is performed inequitably, we will consider this later, in the section on the conflict view of education.

Research in Action 13-2
Income and Education, Religiously Speaking

Sociologists have found that religions are distinguished not just by doctrinal issues, but by secular criteria as well. Research in the United States has consistently shown that denominations and faiths can be arranged in a hierarchy based on their members' social class. The associated differences in financial means have a noticeable impact on the religious bodies, affecting everything from the appearance of their houses of worship to their congregations' ability to undertake social outreach activities.

Analysis of the American General Social Survey shows that Jews, Presbyterians, and Episcopalians claim a higher proportion of affluent members than other faiths and denominations (see the top graph in the accompanying figure). Their relative affluence can often be seen in the architecture and furnishings of their houses of worship. Members of less affluent groups, such as Muslims and Baptists, may compensate for their lesser means by donating their time and talent to outreach programs. Or they may pledge a higher proportion of their income to their religious institutions.

As mentioned earlier in this text, income levels are positively associated with levels of education. Educational differences among faiths in the United States are even more striking, where Jews are three times more likely than Baptists to have a college education (see the bottom graph in the accompanying figure).

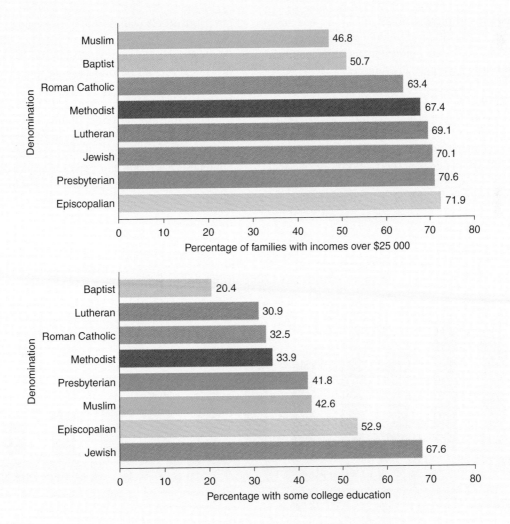

In Canada, according to Jean Lock Kunz, "the role of religion in labour market access deserves more attention" (2002:5). Lock Kunz comments:

> Does religious belief and affiliation facilitate or hinder labour market integration of racial minorities or immigrants? Compared to the Canadian-born, immigrants are more likely to participate in religious activities and, arguably, religious communities serve as a source of network. Yet, the public display of one's religious belief may hinder one's access to jobs. (2002:5).

A study in Canada among Muslim women in manufacturing and sales and service sectors found that those who wear hijab experience discrimination when applying for jobs (Persad and Lukas 2002). However, research by Minquin Wei suggests that Muslims rank the highest in returns (i.e., earnings) to education and job-market experience among Canadian women (2004).

Applying Theory

1. How would a conflict thinker explain the difference in income and education among the various religious groups?
2. Besides the obvious element of gender, what other elements might a feminist sociologist consider in an examination of the relationship among income, education, and religion?

Source: Adapted from data in the cumulative General Social Survey 1994–2004; see J. Davis et al. 2005; Lock Kunz 2002; Persad and Lukacs 2002; Wei 2004.

In addition to these manifest functions, education performs a number of *latent* functions: it transmits culture, promotes social and political integration, maintains social control, and serves as an agent of change.

Transmitting Culture

As a social institution, education performs a conservative function—transmitting the dominant culture. Schooling exposes each generation of young people to the existing beliefs, norms, and values of their culture. In our society, we learn respect for social control and reverence for established institutions, such as religion, the family, and government. Of course, this is also true in many other cultures.

In Britain, the transmission of the dominant culture in schools goes far beyond learning about monarchs and prime ministers. In 1996 in the U.K., the government's chief curriculum adviser—noting the need to fill a void left by the diminishing authority of the Church of England—proposed that British schools socialize students into a set of core values. These include honesty, respect for others, politeness, a sense of fair play, forgiveness, punctuality, non-violent behaviour, patience, faithfulness, and self-discipline (Charter and Sherman 1996).

▶ **FIGURE 13-3**

Percentage of Adults Ages 25 to 64 Who Have Completed Higher Education

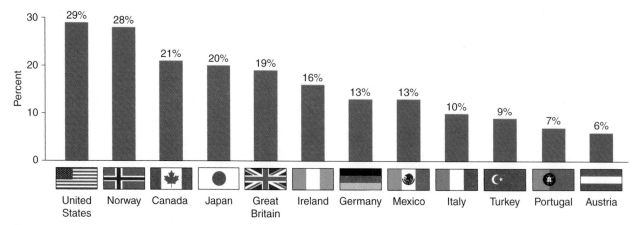

Source: Data for 2002 released in Bureau of the Census 2005:872.

Sometimes, nations need to reassess their ways of transmitting culture. When an economic crisis hit Asian countries in 1997 and 1998, many Asian students who had been studying abroad could no longer afford to do so. Their home countries had to figure out how to accommodate thousands more students pursuing higher education at home. In South Korea, people also began to question the content of the curriculum. Their schools traditionally teach Confucian values with a focus on rote memorization. This leads to an emphasis on accumulating facts as opposed to using reasoning. Entrance to university turns on a highly competitive exam that tests knowledge of facts. Once in university, a student has virtually no opportunity to change his or her program, and the classes continue to rely on memorization. The combination of an economic crisis and growing complaints about the educational process has caused government officials to re-evaluate the educational structure. Moreover, growth in juvenile crime, although low by North American standards, has led the government to introduce a new civic education program emphasizing honesty and discipline (Institute of International Education 1998; Woodard 1998).

At all levels of the education system in Canada, controversy surrounds the exclusion from the curriculum of authors and historical figures who do not represent the dominant culture. Critics charge that standard academic curricula have failed to represent the important contributions of immigrants, Aboriginal peoples, women, and visible minorities to history, literature, and other fields of study. Several underlying questions are raised by this debate and are still to be resolved: Which ideas and values are essential for instruction? Which cultures should be taught by the schools and post-secondary institutions of Canada?

Promoting Social and Political Integration

Many prestigious U.S. universities, such as Harvard, require their first-year students to live together on campus in order to foster a sense of community. Education serves the latent function of promoting social and political integration by transforming a population comprising diverse ethnic and religious groups into a society whose members share—to some extent—a common identity. Schools have historically played an important role in socializing the children of immigrants into the norms, values, and beliefs of the dominant culture. From a functionalist perspective, the common identity and social integration fostered by education contribute to societal stability and consensus (Touraine 1974).

In Canada, perhaps the most egregious example of an attempt to promote social integration through education is that of residential schools for First Nations children. Residential schools were established by the Canadian government and operated by the Roman Catholic, Anglican, United, and Presbyterian churches for the purpose of assimilating Aboriginal children into the dominant culture. Operating widely until the middle decades of the twentieth century, with the last ones closing in the 1980s, these schools had as their express purpose the goal of ◀ P. 248 cultural assimilation. Aboriginal children were taken from their homes and forced to speak languages other than their own. In residential schools, they learned the values and norms of the dominant European groups and at the same time learned that their own culture was inferior and thus needed to be replaced. In this process of promoting conformity to the dominant culture, many Aboriginal children were emotionally, physically, and sexually abused by those operating the residential schools. Today, many First Nations adults are enduring difficult lives because of their traumatizing experiences as children in these schools.

The attempt on the part of schools to promote social and political integration has resulted in Innu children today being taught with methods that are inappropriate to their culture (*The Globe and Mail* 2004b). A report by the federal government in 2004 stated that the education system was failing Innu children miserably by, among other things, not properly training teachers to deal with language and cultural differences.

Maintaining Social Control

In performing the manifest function of imparting knowledge, schools go far beyond teaching such skills as reading, writing, and mathematics. Like other social institutions, such as the family and religion, education prepares young people to lead productive and orderly lives as adults by introducing them to the norms, values, and sanctions of the larger society.

Through the exercise of social control, schools teach students various skills and values essential to their future positions within the labour force. They learn punctuality, discipline, scheduling, and responsible work habits, as well as how to negotiate their way through the complexities of a bureaucratic organization. As a social institution, education reflects the interests of the family and in turn prepares young people for their participation in yet another social institution: the economy. Students are being trained for what is ahead, whether it be the assembly line or a physician's office. In effect, then, schools serve as a transitional agent of social control—between parents and employers in the life cycle of most individuals (Bowles and Gintis 1976; M. Cole 1988).

Schools direct and even restrict students' aspirations in a manner that reflects societal values and prejudices. School administrators may allocate funds for athletic programs while giving much less support to music, art, and dance. ◀ P. 82 Teachers and guidance counsellors may encourage male students to pursue careers in the sciences but steer equally talented female students into careers as early child-hood educators. Such socialization into traditional gender roles can be viewed as a form of social control.

Serving as an Agent of Change

So far, we have focused on conservative functions of education—on its role in transmitting the existing culture, promoting social and political integration, and maintaining social control. Yet, education can also stimulate or bring about desired social change. Sex education classes were introduced in public schools in response to higher rates of sexual activity among teens. Special "girls only" science and mathematics classes were created in response to female graduates' low participation rates in such fields as science, technology, and engineering. Anti-racism programs in schools were created in response to the prevalence of racism in schools and society in general.

Education also promotes social change by serving as a meeting ground where distinctive beliefs and traditions can be shared. In 2004–2005, there were approximately 67 000 (full-time equivalent) international students in Canadian universities (CAUT 2007). Cross-cultural exchanges between these visitors and citizens of Canada ultimately broaden the perspective of both the hosts and their guests. The same is certainly true when students from Canada attend schools in Europe, Latin America, Africa, or Asia.

Numerous sociological studies have revealed that increased numbers of years of formal schooling are associated with openness to new ideas and more liberal social and political viewpoints. Sociologist Robin Williams points out that better educated people tend to

AngelaWilson, left, and Donna Harrow celebrate after Toronto public school trustees, on January 29, 2008, vote 11-9 to open an alternative Africentric school, in an effort to help curb the dropout rate of black students in the Greater Toronto Area.

have greater access to factual information, more diverse opinions, and the ability to make subtle distinctions in analysis. Formal education stresses both the importance of qualifying statements (in place of broad generalizations) and the need to be skeptical of (rather than simply accept) established truths and practices. As we saw in Chapter 2, the scientific method relies on *testing* hypotheses and reflects the questioning spirit that characterizes modern education (R. Williams et al. 1964).

Conflict View

Sociologist Christopher Hurn has compared the functionalist and conflict views of schooling (1985). According to Hurn, the functionalist perspective portrays contemporary education as basically benign. For example, it argues that schools rationally sort and select students for future high-status positions, thereby meeting society's need for talented and expert personnel. By contrast, the conflict perspective views education as an instrument of elite domination. Schools convince subordinate groups of their inferiority, reinforce existing social class inequality, and discourage alternative and more democratic visions of society.

Criticizing the functionalist view, conflict theorists argue that the educational system socializes students into values dictated by the powerful, that schools stifle individualism and creativity in the name of maintaining order, and that the level of change promoted by education is relatively insignificant. From a conflict perspective, the inhibiting effects of education are particularly apparent in the "hidden curriculum" as well as in the differential way in which status is bestowed.

The Hidden Curriculum

Schools are highly bureaucratic organizations. Many teachers rely on the rules and regulations of schools to maintain order. Unfortunately, the need for control and discipline can take precedence over the learning process. Teachers may focus on obedience to the rules as an end in itself. If this occurs, students and teachers alike become victims of what Philip Jackson has called the "hidden curriculum" (1968; see also P. Freire 1970).

The term **hidden curriculum** refers to standards of behaviour that are deemed proper by society and are taught subtly in schools. According to this curriculum, children must not speak until the teacher calls on them and must regulate their activities according to the clock or bells. In addition, they are expected to concentrate on their own work rather than assist other students who learn more slowly. A hidden curriculum is evident in schools around the world. For example, Japanese schools offer guidance sessions during lunch that seek to improve the classroom experience but also to develop healthy living skills. In effect, these sessions instil values and encourage behaviour useful for the Japanese business world, such as self-discipline and openness to group problem solving and decision making (Okano and Tsuchiya 1999).

In a classroom overly focused on obedience, value is placed on pleasing the teacher and remaining quiet rather than on creative thought and academic learn-◄ P.82 ing (Leacock 1969). Habitual obedience to authority may result in the type of distressing behaviour documented by Stanley Milgram in his classic obedience studies conducted in the 1960s.

Bestowal of Status

Both functionalist and conflict theorists agree that education performs the important function of bestowing status. As we noted earlier, an increasing proportion of people in Canada are obtaining high school diplomas; post-secondary certificates, diplomas, and degrees; and advanced professional degrees. From a functionalist perspective, this widening bestowal of status is beneficial not only to particular recipients but also to society as a ◄ P.190 whole. In the view of Kingsley Davis and Wilbert Moore, society must distribute its members among a variety of social positions (1945). Education can contribute to this process by sorting people into appropriate levels and courses of study that will prepare them for appropriate positions in the labour force.

Conflict sociologists are far more critical of the *differential* way education bestows status. They stress that schools sort pupils according to social class background. Although the educational system helps certain poor children to move into middle-class professional positions, it denies most disadvantaged children the same educational opportunities afforded children of the affluent. In this way, schools tend to preserve social class inequalities in each new generation (Giroux 1988; Pinkerton 2003).

Statistics Canada reported that in 2002, 53 percent of Canadian 18- to 24-year-olds whose family income was less than $30 000, had never taken post-secondary education; in contrast, 83 percent of those in the same age group whose family income was $80 000 or more had taken post-secondary education (CAUT 2007).

Even a single school can reinforce class differences by putting students in tracks. The term **tracking** refers to the practice of placing students in specific curriculum groups on the basis of test scores and other criteria. Tracking begins very early in the classroom, often in reading groups during grade 1. These tracks can reinforce the disadvantages that children from less affluent families may face if they haven't been exposed to reading materials, multimedia texts, and other forms of educational stimulation in their homes during their early childhood years.

Tracking and differential access to higher education are evident in many nations around the world. Japan's educational system mandates equality in school funding and insists that all schools use the same textbooks. Nevertheless, only the more affluent Japanese families can afford to send their children to *juku*, or cram schools. These afternoon schools prepare high school students for examinations that determine admission into prestigious colleges (Efron 1997).

According to a study of teachers' attitudes toward students in the outback in rural Australia—an area where sheep vastly outnumber people—students are being prepared to "stay in the bush." Only a small minority seek out electives geared toward preparation for university. However, beginning in the 1980s, parents in the outback questioned this agriculture-oriented curriculum in view of rural Australia's declining employment base (M. Henry 1989).

Conflict theorists hold that the educational inequalities resulting from tracking are designed to meet the needs of modern capitalist societies. Samuel Bowles and Herbert Gintis argue that capitalism requires a skilled, disciplined labour force and that the educational system of the United States is structured with this objective in mind (1976). Citing numerous studies, they offer support for what they call the **correspondence principle**.

According to this approach, schools with students from different social classes promote the values expected of individuals in each class and perpetuate social class divisions from one generation to the next. Thus, working-class children, assumed to be destined for subordinate positions, are more likely to be placed in high school vocational and general tracks, which emphasize close supervision and compliance with authority. By contrast, young people from more affluent families are largely directed to university preparatory tracks, which stress leadership and decision-making skills—corresponding to their likely futures. Although the correspondence principle continues to be persuasive, researchers have noted that the impact of race and gender on students' educational experiences may even overshadow that of class (M. Cole 1988).

Conflict views of the development of the Canadian school system have included the idea that urban-based priorities were imposed on rural schools because of the power of the industrial and mercantile elites located nearby, in local towns (H. Johnson 1960).

Interactionist View

In George Bernard Shaw's play, *Pygmalion*, later adapted into the hit Broadway musical, *My Fair Lady*, flower girl Eliza Doolittle is transformed into a "lady" by Professor Henry Higgins. He changes her manner of speech and teaches her the etiquette of "high society." When she is introduced into society as an aristocrat, she is readily accepted. People treat her as a "lady," and she responds as one.

The labelling approach suggests that if we treat people in particular ways, they may fulfil our expectations. Children labelled as "troublemakers" come to view ◀ P.171 themselves as delinquents. A dominant group's stereotyping of racial minorities may limit their opportunities to break away from expected roles.

Can this labelling process operate in the classroom? Because of their focus on micro-level classroom dynamics, interactionist researchers have been particularly interested in this question. Howard Becker studied public schools in low-income and more affluent areas of Chicago (1952). He noticed that administrators expected less of students from poor neighbourhoods, and he wondered if teachers were accepting this view. Subsequently, in *Pygmalion in the Classroom*, psychologist Robert Rosenthal, school principal Lenore Jacobson, and Elisha Babad documented what they referred to as a **teacher-expectancy effect**—the impact that a teacher's expectations about a student's performance may have on the student's actual achievements (1968). This appears to be especially true in lower grades, through grade 3 (Brint 1998).

In 1965 and 1966, children in a San Francisco elementary school were given a verbal and reasoning pretest. Rosenthal and Jacobson then *randomly* selected 20 percent of the sample and designated them as "spurters"—children of whom teachers could expect superior performance. The teachers then treated these children as superior students in the classroom. On a later verbal and reasoning test, the spurters were found to score significantly higher than before. Moreover, teachers evaluated them as more interesting, more curious, and better adjusted than their classmates. These results were striking. Apparently, teachers' perceptions that these students were exceptional led to noticeable improvements in performance.

Studies have revealed that teachers wait longer for an answer from a student believed to be a high achiever and are more likely to give such children a second chance. In one experiment, teachers' expectations were even shown to have an impact on students' athletic achievements. Teachers obtained better athletic performance—as measured in the number of sit-ups or push-ups performed—from those students of whom they *expected* higher numbers (R. Rosenthal, Babad, and Jacobson 1985).

Despite these findings, some researchers continue to question the accuracy of this self-fulfilling prophecy because of the difficulties in defining and measuring teacher expectancy. Further studies are needed to clarify the relationship between teacher expectations and actual student performance. Nevertheless, interactionists emphasize that ability alone may be less predictive of academic success than one might think (Brint 1998).

Feminist Views

In her 1928 book, *A Room of One's Own*, Virginia Woolf advocated the value of educational reform so that the female student could "live and write her poetry" (Woolf 1977:123). She contended that even if someone had to struggle in "poverty and obscurity" to bring about educational reform on behalf of girls and women, it was worthwhile. Although feminist perspectives on education are diverse, today, many share the view that educational institutions must attempt to prevent gendered patterns of inequality found in the larger society from being perpetuated in the classroom.

Feminist perspectives on education raise a wide range of concerns stemming from the historical exclusion of girls and women in education and the persistent "chilly climate" that many females experience in educational institutions that treat them as outsiders. Some perspectives have articulated the need to understand how the social construction of gender plays a role in the educational experiences of students from elementary school to university, and how these experiences are connected to such factors as race, class, and age (Mandell 1998). The

Although the Chinese government is attempting to address educational inequalities in China, girls continue to receive less education than boys—especially in rural areas.

Table 13-5 Sociological Perspectives on Education

Theoretical Perspective	Emphasis
Functionalist	Transmission of the dominant culture Integration of society Promotion of social norms, values, and sanctions Promotion of desirable social change
Conflict	Domination by the elite through unequal access to schooling Hidden curriculum Bestowal of status
Interactionist	Teacher-expectancy effect
Feminist	Educational systems exhibit and reproduce gendered patterns of inequality

hidden curriculum of the school system contributes to gender socialization through the use of language that is not gender-inclusive, curricula that are androcentric, and role models of male principals and female elementary school teachers that reinforce traditional patterns of male dominance and authority (Rees 1990).

Since the 1970s, Canadian universities and colleges have been developing women's studies programs that provide feminist frameworks for research, teaching, and educational reform.

Table 13-5 summarizes the four major theoretical perspectives on education.

☐ WHAT MAKES SCHOOLS FORMAL ORGANIZATIONS?

In many respects, today's schools, when viewed as an example of a formal organization, are similar to factories, hospitals, and business firms. Like these organizations, schools do not operate autonomously; they are influenced by the market of potential students. This is especially true of private schools. Currently, approximately 5 percent of students in Canada attend private schools (Mackie 2001). The parallels between schools and other types of formal organizations will become more apparent as we examine teaching as an occupational role and the student subculture (Dougherty and Hammack 1992).

Teachers: Employees and Instructors

Whether they serve as instructors of preschoolers or graduate students, teachers are employees of formal organizations with bureaucratic structures. There is an inherent conflict in serving as a professional within a bureaucracy. The organization follows the principles of hierarchy and expects adherence to its rules, but professionalism demands the individual responsibility of the practitioner. This conflict is very real for teachers, who experience all the positive and negative consequences of working in bureaucracies.

A teacher undergoes many perplexing stresses every day. Although teachers' academic assignments have become more specialized, the demands on their time remain diverse and contradictory. There are conflicts inherent in serving as an instructor, a disciplinarian, and an employee of a school district at the same time. For university professors, different types of role strain arise. Although formally employed as teachers, they are also expected to work on committees and are encouraged to conduct scholarly research. In many universities, security of position (tenure) is based primarily on the publication of original scholarship. As a result, instructors must fulfil goals that compete for time.

University professors rarely have to take on the role of disciplinarian, but this task has become a major focus of schoolteachers' work in such countries as Canada and the United States. Order is needed to establish an environment in which students can learn effectively. Some observers believe that schools have been the scene of increasingly violent misbehaviour in recent years, although these concerns may be overblown.

Canada is becoming an increasingly "schooled society" (Guppy and Davies 1998), which will contribute to the employment prospects of students wanting to become teachers. The Canadian Council on Learning (CCL) states that between 1971 and 2001 the percentage of "knowledge workers" almost doubled, with the highest level of knowledge intensity in the fields of health and education (2005).

As well, the demographic composition of teachers is changing, reflecting the aging population; a greater number of retiring teachers will need to be replaced in the near future. This trend is also occurring in the United States where, because of teacher shortages in some regions, school boards are advertising for and recruiting teachers from Canada.

The status of any job reflects several factors, including the level of education required, the financial compensation, and the respect given the occupation within society. The ◀ P. 194 teaching profession (see Table 8-2 on page 195) is feeling pressure in all three of these areas. First, the amount of formal schooling required for teaching remains high, and now the public has begun to call for new competency examinations for teachers. Second, statistics demonstrate that teachers' salaries are significantly lower than those of many professionals and skilled workers. Wages differ by field of study; graduates of education and social science, who are disproportionately female, earn less, for example, than graduates of computer science and engineering, who are disproportionately male (Statistics Canada 2006g). Finally, as we have seen, the overall prestige of the teaching profession has declined in the last fifteen years. Many teachers have become disappointed and frustrated and have left the educational world for careers in other professions. Many are simply "burned out" by the severe demands, limited rewards, and general sense of alienation that they experience on the job.

The Student Subculture

An important latent function of education relates directly to student life: Schools provide for students' social and recreational needs. Education helps toddlers and young children develop interpersonal skills that are essential during adolescence and adulthood. During high school and the years of post-secondary education, students may meet future partners and may establish lifelong friendships.

When people observe high schools and post-secondary institutions from the outside, students appear to constitute a cohesive, uniform group. However, the student subculture is actually much more complex and diverse. High school cliques and social groups may crop up based on ethnicity, social class, physical attractiveness, placement in courses, athletic ability, and leadership roles in the school and community. In his classic community study of "Elmtown," August Hollingshead found some 259 distinct cliques in a single high school (1975). These cliques, whose average size was five people, were centred on the school itself, on recreational activities, and on religious and community groups.

Adult Education

Picture a college or university student. Most likely, you will imagine a 19- or 20-year-old. This reflects the belief that education is something experienced and completed during the first two or three decades of life and rarely supplemented after that. However, many post-secondary institutions have witnessed a dramatic increase in the number of mature students pursuing higher education.

In 2001, students who were 22 years of age made up 31 percent of those continuing in post-secondary education who had no previous university/college credentials (Statistics Canada 2006n). As well, in 2000–2001, approximately 29 percent of undergraduates were 25 years of age or older (Statistics Canada 2003g). Obviously, sociological models of the post-secondary subculture will have to be revised significantly in light of the upward trends in adult education.

One explanation for the adult education boom is that society is changing rapidly in an age of technological innovation and a growing knowledge-based economy. Business firms have come to accept the view of education as lifelong and may encourage (or require) employees to learn job-related skills. Thus, administrative assistants are sent to special schools to be trained to use the latest computer software. Realtors attend classes to learn about alternative forms of financing for homebuyers. In occupation after occupation, long-time workers and professionals are going back to school to adapt to the new demands of their jobs. About 14 percent of Canadian workers participated in adult education between 1993 and 2001; on average, those who participated in adult education and who obtained a post-secondary certificate made significant gains in wages and earnings (Statistics Canada 2006g). Taking a conflict perspective, Canadian sociologist David Livingstone argues that, despite Canadians' growing technological proficiency and growing levels of training and education, employers are failing to fully utilize their skills, thus contributing to *underemployment* (1999).

Not all adult education happens at the formal level. According to Human Resources and Social Development Canada, "the extent and outcomes of informal learning in Canada are not currently well understood. While most available adult education and training data reflect formal training, there is growing recognition that informal learning is an important source of skill formation in modern economies" (2000:7). This type of learning involves self-directed activity done on the learner's own time and at a self-directed pace that aim to "enrich their ability to function within their communities and homes, to deal with family issues and enjoy their leisure time. Increasingly, people are also encouraged to view lifelong learning as a means of combating the mental deterioration associated with aging" (Silver, Williams, and McOrmond 2001:19). Although gender had little effect on whether or not a person was likely to study informally, gendered patterns of subject interest were found to exist. Women were more likely to study health and child care than were men, while men were more likely to study trade-related subjects (C. Silver et al. 2001).

Home-Schooling

When most people think of school, they think of bricks and mortar, and the teachers, administrators, and other employees who staff school buildings. But for an increasing number of students in Canada and the United States, home is the classroom and a parent is the teacher. Estimates of the number of children being home-schooled in Canada vary. The Home-School Legal Defense Association (HSLDA) estimates the number to be as high as 80 000, while Statistics Canada reported 19 114 registered home-schooled students in 1997 (Wake 2000). Statistics Canada warned, however, that those figures underestimate the total number, since many home-schools are not registered.

In the past, families that taught their children at home lived in isolated environments or held strict religious views at odds with the secular environment of public schools. But today, home-schooling is attracting a broader range of families not necessarily tied to organized religion. Poor academic quality, threat of school strikes, peer pressure, and school violence are

Today, many adults are returning to college and university to obtain further education, advance their careers, or change their line of work.

motivating many parents to teach their children at home. In addition, the growing presence of computers in the home and the availability of online educational resources have motivated some parents to educate their children themselves. Rates of home-schooling in Canada have increased every year since 1980. The greatest increases have been in Western Canada (particularly Alberta), where the number of registered home-schoolers grew by 10 percent between 1995–1996 and 1996–1997 (Wake 2000).

Although supporters of home-schooling feel that children can do just as well or better in home-schools as in public schools, critics counter that because home-schooled children are isolated from the larger community, they lose an important chance to improve their socialization skills. But proponents of home-schooling claim their children benefit from contact with others besides their own age group. They also see home-schools as a good alternative for children who suffer from attention deficit disorder (ADD) and learning disorders. Such children often do better in smaller classes, which present fewer distractions to disturb their concentration (National Homeschool Association 1999).

Quality control is an issue in home-schooling. Although home-schooling is legal in Canada, provincial and territorial governments require that parents register their children. In Alberta, where home-schooling is particularly popular, estimates point to a high number of unregistered children—children the government cannot monitor in terms of curricular and academic achievement. Many of these children are from families where the motivating factor to home-school is religion; these families believe that the secular school system does not reflect their values, particularly those concerning abortion, homosexuality, and evolution.

In 1988, the Supreme Court of Canada ruled that the Alberta government had a "compelling interest" in ensuring that the children of that province be properly educated (Mitchell 1999). This would mean making sure that home-schooled children followed a government-approved curriculum and that they were tested annually according to provincial standards. Despite the court ruling, many Christian parents continue to believe that the government should not be in the business of monitoring their children's education and that the values of secular education are not those to which they want their children exposed.

Home-schooling works, particularly for those who have made a commitment to it (D. Calhoun 2000; Matthews 1999; Paulson 2000). Home-schooling allows parents to integrate religion into their children's studies if they choose, but controversy brews when public schools do so, as you will see in the following social policy section.

Social Policy and Religion
Religion in Public Schools

The Issue

Should public schools be allowed to sponsor organized prayers in the classroom? Should the Lord's Prayer be part of the agenda at weekly school assemblies? How about reading Bible verses? Or just a collective moment of silence? Can public school athletes offer up a group prayer in a team huddle? Should students be able to initiate voluntary prayers at school events? Should a school be allowed to post the Ten Commandments in a hallway? Each of these situations has been an object of great dissension among those who see a role for prayer in public schools and those who want to maintain a strict separation of church and state.

Another area of controversy centres on the teaching of theories about the origin of humans and of the universe. Mainstream scientific thinking theorizes that humans evolved over billions of years from one-celled organisms and that the universe came into being 15 billion years ago as a result of a "big bang." But these theories are challenged by people who hold to the Biblical account of the creation of humans and the universe some 10 000 years ago—a viewpoint known as **creationism**. Creationists want their theory taught in the schools as the only one or, at the very least, as an alternative to the theory of evolution.

Who has the right to decide these issues? And what is considered the "right" decision? Religion in the public schools constitutes one of the thorniest issues in Canadian public policy today.

The Setting

In Canada, the Charter of Rights and Freedoms provides for freedom of religion. The Charter, along with the Canadian Constitution, protects the rights and privileges held by denominational schools at the time of Confederation in 1867. This has meant that in addition to the public school system, some provinces and territories fund Catholic school education, while Quebec, where the majority of schools are Catholic, funds Protestant education. In 1999, a government-mandated task force in Quebec recommended that the Catholic and Protestant status for public schools be abolished and replaced with "secular" public schools. In the case of non-denominational or so-called secular schools, where explicit religious affiliation is not established, the issue of religious content in the form of prayers and Bible readings has become a contentious one.

Quebec is not the only province to experience these tensions in the secular schools. In 1999, Saskatchewan became the fourth province in Canada to oppose prayer in public schools. In 1993, a complaint by nine Saskatoon parents launched a challenge against the 100-year-old tradition of encouraging public school teachers to say the Lord's Prayer in classrooms and at assemblies. The Saskatchewan Act, part of the provincial constitution, permitted prayer and Bible readings in the public schools. The group of nine Saskatoon parents, which included Muslims, Jews, Unitarians, and atheists, complained that this practice violated the Saskatchewan Human Rights Code. More specifically, they argued, it violated their children's (and other children's) right to freedom of conscience. They claimed that students were being denied the right to enjoy an education without discrimination because of creed or religion. As a result, in 1999, a board of inquiry ruled that it was discriminatory to require recitation of the Lord's Prayer in Saskatoon classrooms and assemblies.

Sociological Insights

Supporters of school prayer and of creationism feel that strict court rulings force too great a separation between what Émile Durkheim called the *sacred* and the *profane*. They insist that use of non-denominational prayer can in no way lead to the establishment of an ecclesia in Canada. Moreover, they believe that school prayer—and the teaching of creationism—can provide the spiritual guidance and socialization that many children today do not receive from parents or regular church attendance. Many communities also believe that schools should transmit the dominant culture of Canada by encouraging prayer.

A 1998 General Social Survey stated that 55 percent of adults in the United States disapproved of a Supreme Court ruling against the required reading of the Lord's Prayer or Bible verses in public schools. A national survey in 1999 showed that 68 percent of the public favoured teaching creationism along with evolution in public schools, and 40 percent favoured teaching *only* creationism. These numbers still hold up in 2009. No other Western society has such a large body of opinion supporting views that depart so much from contemporary scientific understanding. Perhaps this is a reflection of a deep-rooted and enduring strain of religious fundamentalism in the United States and the fact that religious belief in general is stronger there than in Canada and in other Western societies (Davis and Smith 1999; G. Johnson 1999; Lewis 1999).

Opponents of school prayer argue that a religious majority in a community might impose religious viewpoints specific to its faith, at the expense of religious minorities. Viewed from a conflict perspective, organized school prayer could reinforce the religious beliefs, rituals, and interests of the powerful; it could also violate the rights of the powerless, increase religious dissension, and threaten the multiculturalism of Canada. These critics question whether school prayer can remain truly voluntary. Drawing on the interactionist perspective and small-group research, they suggest that children will face enormous social pressure to conform to the beliefs and practices of a religious majority.

Policy Initiatives

A more recent case involving the Saskatoon Board of Education provides a good example of how in some communities policymakers are trying to find a compromise between those who want prayer in schools and those who do not. In 2001, two years after the Lord's Prayer was removed from the daily routine of public schools, the Saskatoon Public School Board considered a Christian education program for children of religious parents. Modelled after the Logos Christian Education program already in place in Edmonton public schools, Christian students would have received instruction in a separate classroom with a religious environment. Opposition to the proposal was raised by those who felt that the Logos program would have divided students along religious lines and undermined the basis of the public school system.

In 2006, the issue resurfaced in Manitoba, where the Public Schools Act allowed a petition from parents of at least 60 students (or 75 percent of that school's student population) to be voted on by the school board, for the approval of religious exercises during the school year. School trustee Gary Nelson, who voted against the motion, stated:

> What some, but not all, schools . . . had been doing when those petitions were received and approved by the board, was to broadcast the Lord's Prayer over the public address. Unfortunately, in so doing, the school was also providing the "religious exercise" to all of its students including those children whose parents did not request the Lord's Prayer. . . . The only real way for a school to comply with the Act, and the practice of most schools when they receive a petition, is also problematic. That is to segregate the children by either removing those children whose parents petitioned for prayer from the class; or to remove the children who were not named in the petition from the class. I am sure you can understand the problems that can occur when children are singled out: bullying, teasing, and ridicule often are the result. (G. Nelson 2006)

The activism of religious fundamentalists in the nation's public school system raises a more general question: Whose ideas and values deserve a hearing in classrooms? Critics see this campaign as one step toward sectarian religious control of public education. They worry that at some point in the future, teachers may not be able to use books or make statements that conflict with fundamentalist interpretations of the Bible. For advocates of a liberal education who are deeply committed to intellectual (and religious) diversity, this is a genuinely frightening prospect. University of Toronto education professor Ben Levin states, "I don't think issues on religion and language will ever be resolved in Canada; they're deeply contentious issues" (Wilson 2007).

Applying Theory

1. Do you think promoting religious observance is a legitimate function of the social institution of education?
2. Do you agree with a conflict view on the issue of organized school prayer?
3. Are there functions served by Christian fundamentalists and their allies attempting to reshape public education in Canada?

CHAPTER RESOURCES

Summary

What is Durkheim's Sociological Approach to Religion?
- Émile Durkheim stressed the social impact of religion and attempted to understand individual religious behaviour within the context of the larger society.

What are the Major World Religions?
- Eighty-five percent of the world's population adheres to some form of religion. Tremendous diversity exists in religious beliefs and practices, which may be heavily influenced by culture.

What Role does Religion Play?
- According to functionalists, religion serves the functions of integrating people in a diverse society and providing social support in time of need.
- Max Weber saw a connection between religious allegiance and capitalistic behaviour through a religious orientation known as the **Protestant ethic** (p. 317).
- **Liberation theology** (p. 318) uses the church in a political effort to alleviate poverty and social injustice.
- From a Marxist point of view, religion serves to reinforce the social control of those in power. It lessens the possibility of collective political action that can end capitalist oppression and transform society.

What are the Components of Religion?
- Religious components include **beliefs** (p. 319), **rituals** (p. 319), and **religious experience** (p. 320).

What are the Forms of Religious Organization?
- Sociologists have identified four basic types of religious organization: the **ecclesia** (p. 322), the **denomination** (p. 322), the **sect** (p. 322), and the **new religious movement (NRM)** or **cult** (p. 323). Advances in communication have led to a new type of church organization: the electronic church.

What are some Sociological Perspectives on Education?
- According to functionalist thinkers, transmission of knowledge and bestowal of status are manifest functions of **education** (p. 312). Among its latent functions are transmitting culture, promoting social and political integration, maintaining social control, and serving as an agent of social change.
- In the view of conflict theorists, education serves as an instrument of elite domination through the **hidden curriculum** (p. 330) and by bestowing status unequally.
- According to interactionist sociologists, the **teacher-expectancy effect** (p. 332) can sometimes have an impact on a student's actual achievements.

What Makes Schools Formal Organizations?
- Most schools in Canada today are organized on the basis of Weber's model of bureaucracy.

Critical Thinking Questions

1. From a conflict point of view, explain how religion could be used to bring about social change.
2. Why is it so difficult for women to become leaders of religious organizations?
3. What are the functions and dysfunctions of tracking in schools? Viewed from an interactionist perspective, how would the tracking of high school students influence the interactions between students and teachers? In what ways might tracking have positive and negative impacts on the self-concepts of various students?
4. Why are some religions granted greater social approval or higher status than others?

Key Terms

Correspondence principle   The tendency of schools to promote the values expected of individuals in each social class and to prepare students for the types of jobs typically held by members of their class. (p. 331)

Creationism   A literal interpretation of the Bible regarding the creation of humanity and the universe, used to argue that evolution should not be presented as established scientific fact. (p. 336)

Cult   See *new religious movement.*

Denomination   A large, organized religion not officially linked with the state or government. (p. 322)

Ecclesia   A religious organization that claims to include most or all of the members of a society and is recognized as the national or official religion. (p. 322)

Education   A formal process of learning in which some people consciously teach while others adopt the social role of learner. (p. 312)

Hidden curriculum   Standards of behaviour that are deemed proper by society and are taught subtly in schools. (p. 330)

Liberation theology   Use of a church, primarily Roman Catholicism, in a political effort to eliminate poverty, discrimination, and other forms of injustice evident in a secular society. (p. 318)

Megachurches   Large worship centres affiliated only loosely, if at all, with existing denominations. (p. 322)

New religious movement (NRM) or **cult**   A generally small, often secretive religious group that represents either a new religion or a major innovation of an existing faith. (p. 323)

Profane   The ordinary and commonplace elements of life, as distinguished from the sacred. (p. 314)

Protestant ethic   Max Weber's term for the disciplined work ethic, worldly concerns, and rational orientation to life emphasized by John Calvin and his followers. (p. 317)

Religion   A unified system of beliefs and practices relative to sacred things. (p. 314)

Religious beliefs   Statements to which members of a particular religion adhere. (p. 319)

Religious experience   The feeling or perception of being in direct contact with the ultimate reality, such as a divine being, or of being overcome with religious emotion. (p. 320)

Religious rituals   Practices required or expected of members of a faith. (p. 319)

Sacred   Elements beyond everyday life that inspire awe, respect, and even fear. (p. 314)

Sect   A relatively small religious group that has broken away from another religious organization to renew what it views as the original vision of the faith. (p. 322)

Secularization   The process through which religion's influence on other social institutions diminishes. (p. 312)

Teacher-expectancy effect   The impact that a teacher's expectations about a student's performance may have on the student's actual achievements. (p. 332)

Tracking   The practice of placing students in specific curriculum groups on the basis of test scores and other criteria. (p. 331)

Additional Readings

Adams, Michael. 2003. *Fire and Ice: The United States and Canada and the Myth of Converging Values*. Toronto: Penguin Books. A comparison of Canadian and U.S. values, including those related to religion. Adams's book reveals that Canadian and U.S. citizens have different beliefs about the role religion plays in their daily lives.

Davies, Scott, and Neil Guppy. 2006. *The Schooled Society: An Introduction to the Sociology of Education*. Don Mills, ON: Oxford University Press. Explores contemporary debates on schooling from a variety of perspectives within a Canadian context.

Wotherspoon, Terry. 2004. *The Sociology of Education in Canada: Critical Perspectives*, 2nd ed. Don Mills, ON: Oxford University Press. An introduction to the sociological understanding of education in Canada with an emphasis on the critical research and theories of education.

 ## Online Learning Centre

Visit the *Sociology: A Brief Introduction* Online Learning Centre at www.mcgrawhill.ca/olc/schaefer to access quizzes, interactive exercises, video clips, and other research and study tools related to this chapter.

 ## Reel Society Video Clips

Reel Society can be used to spark discussion about the following topics from this chapter:

- Durkheim and the sociological approach to religion
- Sociological explanations of religion
- World religions
- Components of religion
- Sociological perspectives on education
- Schools as formal organizations

chapter 14

POLITICS AND THE ECONOMY

Politically oriented messages are often meant for international as well as local consumption. In 2005, the Saudi Arabian government launched a public relations campaign featuring slogans like "Islam Is Moderation" and "Say No to Terrorism." On this poster, the English translation appears in much larger type than the Arabic message.

☐ **What Forms do Economic Systems Take?**

☐ **How do Forms of Power and Authority Differ?**

☐ **What are the Various Types of Government?**

☐ **How does Political Participation Manifest Itself in Canada?**

☐ **What are the Various Models of Power in Canada?**

☐ **How do Sociologists Conceptualize War and Peace?**

☐ **How is the Economy Changing?**

| Boxes |

SOCIOLOGY IN THE GLOBAL COMMUNITY: Capitalism in China
SOCIOLOGY IN THE GLOBAL COMMUNITY: Gender Quotas at the Ballot Box
SOCIAL POLICY AND THE ECONOMY: Global Offshoring

Just by reading this, chances are you're more politically engaged and plugged into current affairs than fellow Canadians who use television as their primary or only source of news, a new Statistics Canada report on media consumption says.

The study, based on data from a 2003 general social survey on social engagement, found the vast majority of Canadians—89 percent—follow news and current affairs daily or several times a week.

Of those frequent users, 91 per cent said they got some of their news from television, the "staple food" of the Canadian news diet, the report says. The majority, however, of frequent news consumers—72 percent—

get their information from two to four sources, with newspapers ranked second in 2003, followed by radio, internet and magazines.

The study found frequent news consumers tend to be more involved in non-voting political activities such as attending a public meeting, volunteering for a political party, signing a petition or participating in a march or demonstration.

Levels of civic engagement appear to be much higher among users who read news compared with those who watch television news only—67 percent of people who watched television news reported no involvement in political activities outside of voting, compared with 45 percent of people who used other media.

"This finding lends support to previous research that suggests that following the news and current affairs is related to being a more politically engaged citizen," the study's author, analyst Leslie-Anne Keown, noted.

"Moreover, these same studies argue that individuals who use media that require them to read and engage more actively with the material being presented have higher levels of civic engagement and more knowledge of current affairs than those who use television as their primary or only source of news."

The study found people who frequently follow news and current affairs more likely to be men, married, workers employed as professionals or managers, and those with incomes greater than $60 000.

The media results are taken from a sample of 18 000 Canadians surveyed as part of the larger General Social Survey in 2003.

☐ *(Fenlon 2007)*

How is the medium from which we gather our news related to our non-voting political activities such as volunteering for a political party, signing a petition, or attending a public meeting? The article by Brodie Fenlon in *The Globe and Mail* discusses a recent Statistics Canada report that suggests levels of civic engagement tend to be higher among those who read news, rather than those who watch television news only. Often, media outlets, whether they be print or electronic, operate—in varying degrees—within the frameworks of the existing political and economic systems. By **political system**, sociologists mean the social institution that is founded on a recognized set of procedures for implementing and achieving society's goals, such as the allocation of valued resources. Like religion and the family, the political system is a cultural universal: It is found in every society. In Canada, the political system holds the ultimate responsibility for addressing the social policy issues examined in this book: child care, the AIDS crisis, welfare reform, and so forth.

The term **economic system** refers to the social institution through which goods and services are produced, distributed, and consumed. As with social institutions such as the family, religion, and government, the economic system shapes other aspects of the social order and is in turn influenced by them. Throughout this book, you have been reminded of the economy's impact on social behaviour—for example, on individual and group behaviour in factories and offices. You have studied the work of Karl Marx and Friedrich Engels, who emphasized that a society's economic system can promote social inequality. And you have learned that foreign investment in developing countries can intensify inequality among residents.

It is hard to imagine two social institutions more intertwined than government and the economy. Besides serving as the largest employer in the nation, government at all levels regulates commerce and entry into many occupations. At the same time, the economy generates the revenue to support government services. In this chapter, we present a combined analysis of government and the economy. How does the power elite maintain its power? Is war necessary in settling international disputes? How have the trends toward deindustrialization and the outsourcing of service jobs affected our economy? We begin the chapter with a macro-level analysis of two ideal types of economic systems: capitalism and socialism. This theoretical discussion is followed by a case study of China's decision to allow capitalist entrepreneurial activity within its socialist economy. Next, we examine some general theories of power and authority, with the four major types of government in which that power and authority is exerted. We see how politics works, with particular attention to citizens' participation and the changing role of women. We look at two models of power in Canada, the elite and the pluralist models. Then, we touch briefly on war, peace, and terrorism, followed by a look at ways in which economies are changing in response to globalization. The chapter closes with a social policy section on global offshoring.

> **Use Your Sociological Imagination**
>
> Do you see any relationships within your age group in terms of the degree to which people are "plugged in" to news, the medium through which they receive the news, and their degree of political involvement (e.g., attending a demonstration, voting during elections, joining a political party)?

☐ WHAT FORMS DO ECONOMIC SYSTEMS TAKE?

The socio-cultural evolution approach developed by Gerhard Lenski categorizes pre-industrial society according to the way in which the economy is organized. The principal types of pre-industrial society, as you recall, are hunting-and-gathering societies, horticultural societies, and agrarian societies.

◄ P. 194

◄ P. 115 As we noted in Chapter 5, with the Industrial Revolution, a new form of social structure emerged: the **industrial society**, a society that depends on mechanization to produce its goods and services.

Two basic types of economic systems distinguish contemporary industrial societies: capitalism and socialism. As described in the following sections, capitalism and socialism serve as ideal types of economic system. No nation precisely fits either model. Instead, the economy of each individual state represents a mixture of capitalism and socialism, although one type or the other is generally more useful in describing a society's economic structure.

Capitalism

In pre-industrial societies, land functioned as the source of virtually all wealth. The Industrial Revolution changed all that. It required that certain individuals and institutions be willing to take substantial risks in order to finance new inventions, machinery, and business enterprises. Eventually, bankers, industrialists, and other holders of large sums of money replaced landowners as the most powerful economic force. These people invested their funds in the hope of realizing even greater profits, and thereby became owners of property and business firms.

The transition to private ownership of business was accompanied by the emergence of the capitalist economic system. **Capitalism** is an economic system in which the means of production are held largely in private hands and the main incentive for economic activity is the accumulation of profits. In practice, capitalist systems vary in the degree to which the government regulates private ownership and economic activity (D. Rosenberg 1991).

Immediately following the Industrial Revolution, the prevailing form of capitalism was what is termed **laissez-faire** ("let them do"). Under the principle of laissez-faire, as expounded and endorsed by British economist Adam Smith (1723–1790), people could compete freely, with minimal government intervention in the economy. Business retained the right to regulate itself and operated essentially without fear of government interference (Smelser 1963).

Two centuries later, capitalism has taken on a somewhat different form. Private ownership and maximization of profits still remain the most significant characteristics of capitalist economic systems. However, in contrast to the era of laissez-faire, capitalism today features government regulation of economic relations. Without restrictions, business firms can mislead consumers, endanger workers' safety, and even defraud the companies' investors—all in the pursuit of greater profits. That is why the government of a capitalist nation often monitors prices, sets safety and environmental standards for industries, protects the rights of consumers, and regulates collective bargaining between labour unions and management. Yet, under capitalism as an ideal type, government rarely takes over ownership of an entire industry.

Contemporary capitalism also differs from laissez-faire in another important respect: capitalism tolerates monopolistic practices. A **monopoly** exists when a single business firm controls the market. Domination of an industry allows the firm to effectively control a commodity by dictating pricing, quality standards, and availability. Buyers have little choice but to yield to the firm's decisions; there is no other place to purchase the product or service. Monopolistic practices violate the ideal of free competition cherished by Adam Smith and other supporters of laissez-faire capitalism.

Some capitalistic nations, such as Canada, restrict monopolies through federal legislation. Such laws prevent any business from taking over so much of the competition in an industry that it controls the market. The federal government allows monopolies to exist only in certain exceptional cases, such as the utility and transportation industries. Even then, regulatory agencies scrutinize these officially approved monopolies to protect the public. The protracted legal battle in the United States between the Justice Department and Microsoft, owner of the dominant operating system for personal computers, illustrates the uneasy relationship between governments and private monopolies in capitalistic countries.

Conflict theorists point out that although *pure* monopolies are not a basic element of the economy in countries such as Canada and the United States, competition is much more restricted than one might expect in a free enterprise system. In numerous industries, a few companies largely dominate the field and keep new enterprises from entering the marketplace.

As we have seen in earlier chapters, globalization and the rise of multinational corporations have spread the capitalistic pursuit of profits around the world. Especially in developing countries, governments are not always prepared to deal with the sudden influx of foreign capital and its effects on their economies. One particularly striking example of how unfettered capitalism can harm developing nations is found in the Democratic Republic of Congo (formerly Zaire). The Congo has significant deposits of the metal columbite-tantalite—*coltan*, for short—which is used in the production of electronic circuit boards. Until the market for cellphones, pagers, and laptop computers heated up, high-tech companies got much of their coltan from Australia. But at the height of consumer demand, they turned to miners in the Congo to increase their supply.

Predictably, the escalating price of the metal—as much as $400 a kilogram at one point, or more than three times the average Congolese worker's yearly wages—attracted undesirable attention. Soon, the neighbouring countries of Rwanda, Uganda, and Burundi, at war with one another and desperate for resources to finance the conflict, were raiding the Congo's national parks, slashing and burning to expose the coltan underneath the forest floor. Indirectly, the sudden increase in

A worker mines for coltan with sweat and a stick. The sudden increase in demand for the metal by U.S. computer manufacturers caused incursions into the Congo by neighbouring countries hungry for capital to finance a war. Too often, globalization can have unintended consequences for a nation's economy and social welfare.

the demand for coltan was financing war and the rape of the environment. Many manufacturers have since cut off their sources in the Congo in an effort to avoid abetting the destruction. But their action has only penalized legitimate miners in the impoverished country (Austin 2002; Delawala 2002).

Socialism

Socialist theory was refined in the writings of Karl Marx and Friedrich Engels. These European radicals were disturbed by the exploitation of the working class that ◀ P.9 emerged during the Industrial Revolution. In their view, capitalism forced large numbers of people to exchange their labour for low wages. The owners of an industry profit from the labour of workers primarily because they pay workers less than the value of the goods produced.

As an ideal type, a socialist economic system attempts to eliminate such economic exploitation. Under **socialism**, the means of production and distribution in a society are collectively rather than privately owned. The basic objective of the economic system is to meet people's needs rather than to maximize profits. Socialists reject the laissez-faire philosophy that free competition benefits the general public. Instead, they believe that the central government, acting as the representative of the people, should make basic economic decisions. Therefore, government ownership of all major industries—including steel production, automobile manufacturing, and agriculture—is a primary feature of socialism as an ideal type.

In practice, socialist economic systems vary in the extent to which they tolerate private ownership. For example, in Britain, a nation with some aspects of both a socialist and a capitalist economy, passenger airline service is concentrated in the government-owned corporation, British Airways. Yet, private airlines are allowed to compete with it.

Socialist countries typically offer government-financed medical care and other services to *all* citizens. In theory, the collective wealth of the people is used to provide health care, housing, education, and other key services to each individual and family.

Canada—also a mixture of socialist and capitalist elements—has a system of universal health care that is funded by taxpayer dollars and which, when it was established, was derogatorily declared as "socialist" by its opponents. (See the next chapter for a detailed account of the health-care system in Canada.)

Marx believed that socialist states would eventually "wither away" and evolve into *communist* societies. As an ideal type, **communism** refers to an economic system under which all property is communally owned and no social distinctions are made on the basis of people's ability to produce. In recent decades, the Soviet Union, the People's Republic of China, Vietnam, Cuba, and nations in Eastern Europe were popularly thought of as examples of communist economic systems. However, this usage represents an incorrect application of a term with sensitive political connotations. All nations known as communist in the twentieth century actually fell far short of the ideal type.

By the early 1990s, Communist parties were no longer ruling the nations of Eastern Europe. The first major challenge to Communist rule came in 1980, when Poland's Solidarity movement—led by Lech Walesa and backed by many workers—questioned the injustices of that society. Though martial law forced Solidarity underground, the movement eventually negotiated the end of Communist Party rule, in 1989. Over the next two years, Communist parties were overthrown by popular uprisings in the Soviet Union and throughout the Eastern Bloc. The former Soviet Union, Czechoslovakia, and Yugoslavia were subdivided to accommodate ethnic, linguistic, and religious differences.

As of 2009, China, Cuba, and Vietnam remained socialist societies ruled by Communist parties. Even in those countries, however, capitalism had begun to

Table 14-1   Characteristics of the Three Major Economic Systems

Economic System	Characteristics	Contemporary Examples
Capitalism	Private ownership of the means of production	Canada, Mexico,
	Accumulation of profits the main incentive	United States
Socialism	Collective ownership of the means of production	Germany, Russia,
	Meeting people's needs the basic objective	Sweden
Communism	Communal ownership of all property	Cuba, North Korea,
	No social distinctions made on basis of people's ability to produce	Vietnam

Note: Countries listed in column 3 are typical of one of the three economic systems, but not perfectly so. In practice, the economies of most countries include a mix of elements from the three major systems.

make inroads. In China, fully 25 percent of the country's production originated in the private business sector. (See Box 14-1, "Sociology in the Global Community: Capitalism in China," on page 346, for a fuller discussion.)

As we have seen, capitalism and socialism serve as ideal types of economic systems. In reality, the economy of each industrial society—including Canada, the United States, the European Union, and Japan—contains certain elements of both capitalism and socialism (see Table 14-1). Whatever the differences—whether a society more closely fits the ideal type of capitalism or socialism—all industrial societies rely chiefly on mechanization in the production of goods and services.

The Informal Economy

In many countries, one aspect of the economy defies description as either capitalist or socialist. In the **informal economy** (also known as the **underground economy**), transfers of money, goods, or services take place but are not reported to the government. Examples of the informal economy include trading services with someone— say, a haircut for a computer lesson; selling goods on the street; and engaging in illegal transactions, such as gambling or drug deals. Participants in this type of economy avoid taxes and government regulations.

Functionalists contend that bureaucratic regulations sometimes contribute to the rise of an informal economy. In the developing world, governments often set up burdensome business regulations that overworked bureaucrats must administer. When requests for licenses and permits pile up, delaying business projects, legitimate entrepreneurs find they need to "go underground"

to get anything done. Despite its apparent efficiency, this type of informal economy is dysfunctional for a country's overall political and economic well-being. Since informal firms typically operate in remote locations to avoid detection, they cannot easily expand when they become profitable. And given the limited protection for their property and contractual rights, participants in the informal economy are less likely than others to save and invest their income.

Whatever functions an informal economy may serve, it is in some respects dysfunctional for workers. Working conditions in these illegal businesses are often unsafe or dangerous, and the jobs rarely provide any benefits to those who become ill or cannot continue to work. Perhaps more significant, the longer a worker remains in the informal economy, the less likely that person is to make the transition to the regular economy. No matter how efficient or productive a worker, prospective employers expect to see experience in the formal economy on a job application. Experience as a successful street vendor or self-employed housecleaner does not carry much weight with interviewers (Light 2004).

Use Your Sociological Imagination

Some of your relatives are working full-time in the informal economy—for example, babysitting, lawn cutting, housecleaning—and are earning all their income that way. What will be the consequences for them in terms of job security and health care? Will you try to persuade them to seek formal employment, regardless of how much money they are making?

Sociology in the Global Community

Capitalism in China

14-1

Today's China is not the China of past generations; it stands on the brink of becoming the world's largest economy (see the accompanying Figure 14-1). In this country, where the Communist Party once dominated people's lives, few now bother to follow party proceedings. Instead, after a decade of rapid economic growth, most Chinese are more interested in acquiring the latest consumer goods. Ironically, it was party officials' decision to transform China's economy by opening it up to capitalism that reduced the once omnipotent institution's influence.

The Road to Capitalism

When the communists assumed the leadership of China in 1949, they cast themselves as the champions of workers and peasants and the enemies of those who exploited workers—namely landlords and capitalists. Profit making was outlawed, and those who engaged in it were arrested. By the 1960s, China's economy was dominated by huge state-controlled enterprises, such as factories. Even private farms were transformed into community-owned organiza-

tions. Peasants essentially worked for the government, receiving payment in goods based on their contribution to the collective good. In addition, they could receive a small plot of land on which to produce food for their families or for exchange with others. But, while the centralization of production for the benefit of all seemed to make sense ideologically, it did not work well economically.

In the 1980s, the government eased restrictions on private enterprise somewhat, permitting small businesses with no more than seven employees. But business owners could not hold policymaking positions in the Communist Party, at any level. Late in the decade, party leaders began to make market-oriented reforms, revising the nation's legal structure to promote private business. For the first time, private entrepreneurs were allowed to compete with some state-controlled businesses. By the mid-1990s, impressed with the results of the experiment, party officials had begun to hand some ailing state-controlled businesses over to private entrepreneurs, in hopes they could be turned around.

▶ **FIGURE 14-1**

World's Largest Economies, 2020 (Forecast)

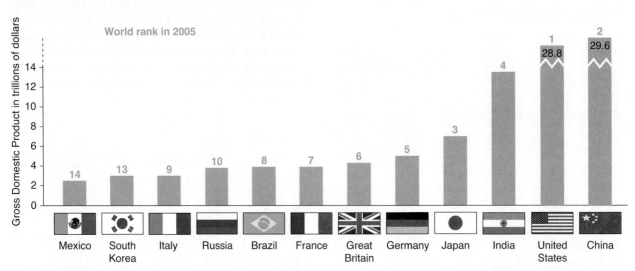

Note: Data standardized in terms of estimated purchasing power parity to eliminate differences in buying power. Countries ranked in 2005, when Spain was ranked 11 and Canada was 12.
Source: The Economist 2006.

The Chinese Economy Today

Today, entrepreneurs, who would have weathered government harassment during the Communist Party's early years, are among the nation's wealthiest capitalists. Some even hold positions on government advisory boards. The growing free-market economy they spawned has brought significant inequality to Chinese workers, however, especially between urban and rural workers. Though the move toward market-driven development has been slowing, questions are still being raised about the accumulation of wealth by a few (Kahn 2006).

This burgeoning metropolis isn't located in North America or Europe, but in China. Spurred by an influx of investment by multinational corporations, Shanghai has experienced rapid economic growth. In 1985, the city had one skyscraper; now, it has over 300.

Chinese capitalists have had to compete with multinational corporations, which can operate more easily in China now, thanks to government economic reforms. General Motors (GM) first became interested in China in 1992, hoping to use the nation's low-cost labour to manufacture cars for overseas markets. But more and more, foreign-owned enterprises like GM are selling to the Chinese market. By 2003, GM's Chinese operation was producing 110 000 automobiles a year for Chinese consumers, at a profit twice as high as that in the United States (Kahn 2003a).

Chinese Workers in the New Economy

For the Chinese workforce, the loosening of state control over the economy has meant a rise in occupational mobility, which was severely limited in the early days of Communist Party rule. The new markets created by private entrepreneurs are allowing ambitious workers to advance their careers by changing jobs or even cities. On the other hand, many middle-aged urban workers have lost their jobs to rural migrants seeking higher wages. Moreover, the privately owned factories that churn out lawn chairs and power tools for multinational corporations offer limited opportunities and very long hours. Hourly wages average less than 5 percent of the hourly wage

for manufacturing workers in Canada and approximately 25 percent of those in Mexico (Banister 2005).

In many of these small businesses, worker safety is not a priority. Just south of Shanghai, in the over 7000 small, privately owned hardware factories that operate in the region, there are unofficially 2500 serious injuries a year. Nationally, China recorded 140 000 workplace deaths in 2002—up 30 percent from the year before (Bradsher 2004; Iritani and Dickerson 2002; Kahn 2003b).

For the average worker, party membership is less important now than in the past. Instead, managerial skill and experience are much in demand. Hong Kong sociologist Xiaowei Zang (2002) surveyed 900 workers in a key industrial city and found that party members still had an advantage in government and state-owned companies, where they earned higher salaries than other workers. But in private businesses, seniority and either managerial or entrepreneurial experience were what counted. As might be expected, being male and well educated also helped.

Women have been slower to advance in the workplace than men. Traditionally, Chinese women have been relegated to subservient roles in the patriarchal family structure. Communist Party rule has allowed them to make significant gains in employment, income, and education, although not as quickly as promised. For rural women in China, the growth of a market economy has meant a choice between working in a factory or on a farm. Given recent economic changes, which have been massive, scholars are waiting to see whether Chinese women will maintain the progress they began under communism (Bian 2002; Lu et al. 2002; Shu and Bian 2003).

With the growth of a middle class and more people gaining access to education, many Chinese are seeking the same opportunities as their Western counterparts. The struggle has been particularly notable in the Chinese people's desire for open, unrestricted access to the World Wide Web. China requires even U.S.-based companies like Google, Yahoo, Microsoft, and Cisco Systems to alter their search engines and blogging tools so as to block access to unapproved Web sites. In most countries of the world, for example, a Web search for images of Tiananmen Square will call up photos of the 1989 crackdown on student protesters, in which soldiers in tanks attacked unarmed students. But on the other side of what has been dubbed the Great Firewall of China, the same search yields only photos of visiting diplomats posing in the square (Grossman and Beech 2006).

Applying theory

1. What research topics might be relevant to feminist sociologists studying the Chinese economy today?
2. What might conflict thinkers stress in studying the economic changes currently occurring in China?

☐ HOW DO FORMS OF POWER AND AUTHORITY DIFFER?

In any society, someone or some group—whether it be a tribal chief, a dictator, or a parliament—makes important decisions about how to use resources and how to allocate goods. Another cultural universal, then, is the exercise of power and authority. Inevitably, the struggle for power and authority involves **politics**, which political scientist Harold Lasswell tersely defined as "who gets what, when, and how" (1936). In their study of politics and government, sociologists are concerned with social interactions among individuals and groups and their impact on the larger political and economic order.

Power

Power lies at the heart of a political system. According to Max Weber, **power** is the ability to exercise one's will over others. To put it another way, whoever can control the behaviour of others is exercising power.

Power relations can involve large organizations, small groups, or even people in an intimate association.

Because Weber developed his conceptualization of power in the early 1900s, he focused primarily on the nation–state and its sphere of influence. Today, scholars recognize that the trend toward globalization has brought new opportunities, and with them new concentrations of power. Power is now exercised on a global as well as a national stage, as countries and multinational corporations compete to control access to resources and manage the distribution of capital (Sernau 2001).

There are three basic sources of power within any political system: force, influence, and authority. **Force** is the actual or threatened use of coercion to impose one's will on others. When leaders imprison or even execute political dissidents, they are applying force; so, too, are terrorists when they seize or bomb an embassy or assassinate a political leader. **Influence**, on the other hand, refers to the exercise of power through a process of persuasion. A citizen may change his or her view of

"Which country is the least mad at us?"

This cartoon, published in 1957, is still relevant in the U.S. today. The extent of the tension between the United States and other countries should not be exaggerated, however. Though other countries may dislike U.S. foreign policy, they do not necessarily dislike U.S. citizens.

a political leadership candidate because of a newspaper editorial, the character assessment given by the candidate's ex-colleague, or a stirring speech by a political activist at a convention rally. In each case, sociologists would view such efforts to persuade people as examples of influence. Now, let's take a look at the third source of power, *authority*.

Types of Authority

The term **authority** refers to institutionalized power that is recognized by the people over whom it is exercised. Sociologists commonly use the term in connection with those who hold legitimate power through elected or publicly acknowledged positions. A person's authority is often limited. Thus, a referee has the authority to decide whether a penalty should be called during a hockey game, but has no authority over the price of tickets to the game.

The emotional appeal that former prime minister Pierre Trudeau had to many Canadians was an example of charismatic authority.

Max Weber ([1913] 1947) developed a classification system for authority that has become one of the most useful and frequently cited contributions of early sociology ([1913] 1947). He identified three ideal types of authority: traditional, rational-legal, and charismatic. Weber did not insist that only one type applies to a given society or organization. All can be present, but their relative importance will vary. Sociologists have found Weber's typology valuable in understanding different manifestations of legitimate power within a society.

Traditional Authority

Until the middle of the last century, Japan was ruled by a revered emperor whose absolute power was passed down from generation to generation. In a political system based on **traditional authority**, legitimate power is conferred by custom and accepted practice. A king or queen is accepted as ruler of a nation simply by virtue of inheriting the crown; a tribal chief rules because that is the accepted practice. The ruler may be loved or hated, competent or destructive; in terms of legitimacy, that does not matter. For the traditional leader, authority rests in custom, not in personal characteristics, technical competence, or even written law. People accept the ruler's authority because that is how things have always been done. Traditional authority is

absolute when the ruler has the ability to determine laws and policies.

Rational-Legal Authority

The Constitution Acts of 1867 and 1982, give our government the authority to make and enforce laws and policies. Power made legitimate by law is known as **rational-legal authority**. Leaders derive their rational-legal authority from the written rules and regulations of political systems, such as a constitution. Generally, in societies based on rational-legal authority, leaders are thought to have specific areas of competence and authority but are not thought to be endowed with divine inspiration, as in certain societies with traditional forms of authority.

Charismatic Authority

Joan of Arc was a simple peasant girl in medieval France, yet she was able to rally the French people and lead them into major battles against English invaders. How was this possible? As Weber observed, power can be legitimized by the charisma of an individual. The term **charismatic authority** refers to power made legitimate by a leader's exceptional personal or emotional appeal to his or her followers.

Charisma lets a person lead or inspire without relying on set rules or traditions. In fact, charismatic authority is derived more from the beliefs of followers than from the actual qualities of leaders. So long as people *perceive* a leader as having qualities that set him or her apart from ordinary citizens, that leader's authority will remain secure and often unquestioned.

Unlike traditional rulers, charismatic leaders often become well known by breaking with established institutions and advocating dramatic changes in the social structure and the economic system. Their strong hold over their followers makes it easier to build protest movements that challenge the dominant norms and values of a society. Thus, charismatic leaders such as Joan of Arc, Gandhi, and Martin Luther King, Jr., all used their power to press for changes in accepted social behaviour. But so did Adolf Hitler, whose charismatic appeal turned people toward violent and destructive ends in Nazi Germany.

Observing from an interactionist perspective, sociologist Carl Couch points out that the growth of the electronic media has facilitated the development of charismatic authority (1996). During the 1930s and 1940s, the heads of state of the United States, Britain, and Germany all used radio to issue direct appeals to citizens. Now, television and the Internet allow leaders to "visit" people's homes and communicate with them. In both Taiwan and South Korea in 1996, troubled political leaders facing re-election campaigns spoke frequently to national audiences and exaggerated military threats from neighbouring China and North Korea, respectively.

As we noted earlier, Weber used traditional, rational-legal, and charismatic authority as ideal types. In reality, particular leaders and political systems combine elements of two or more of these forms. Pierre Trudeau, arguably one of the most remarkable prime ministers in Canadian history, wielded power through the rational-legal and charismatic forms of authority.

> **Use Your Sociological Imagination**
>
> What would our government be like if it were founded on traditional rather than rational-legal authority? What difference would it make to the average citizen?

☐ WHAT ARE THE VARIOUS TYPES OF GOVERNMENT?

Each society establishes a political system through which it is governed. In modern industrial nations, these formal systems of government make a significant number of critical political decisions. We will survey five basic types of government here: monarchy, oligarchy, dictatorship, totalitarianism, and democracy.

Monarchy

A **monarchy** is a form of government headed by a single member of a royal family, usually a king, queen, or some other hereditary ruler. In earlier times, many monarchs claimed that God had granted them a divine right to rule. Typically, they governed on the basis of traditional forms of authority, sometimes accompanied by the use of force. By the beginning of the twenty-first century, however, monarchs held genuine governmental power in only a few nations, such as Monaco. Most monarchs now have little practical power; they serve primarily ceremonial purposes.

Oligarchy

An **oligarchy** is a form of government in which a few individuals rule. An old method of governing that flourished in ancient Greece and Egypt, oligarchy now often takes the form of military rule. In developing nations in Africa, Asia, and Latin America, small factions of military officers will forcibly seize power, either from legally elected regimes or from other military cliques.

Strictly speaking, the term *oligarchy* is reserved for governments that are run by a few selected individuals. However, the People's Republic of China can be classified as an oligarchy if we stretch the meaning of the term. In China, power rests in the hands of a large but exclusive ruling *group*, the Communist Party. In a similar vein, drawing on conflict theory, one might argue that many industrialized nations of the West should be considered oligarchies (rather than democracies), since only a powerful few—leaders of big business, government, and the military—actually rule. Later in this chapter, we examine the "elite model" of political systems in greater detail.

Dictatorship and Totalitarianism

A **dictatorship** is a government in which one person has nearly total power to make and enforce laws. Dictators rule primarily through the use of coercion, which often includes torture and executions. Typically, they *seize* power rather than being freely elected (as in a democracy) or inheriting power (as in a monarchy). Some dictators are quite charismatic and manage to achieve a degree of popularity, though their supporters' enthusiasm is almost certainly tinged with fear. Other dictators are bitterly hated by the people over whom they rule.

Frequently, dictators develop such overwhelming control over people's lives that their governments are called *totalitarian*. (Monarchies and oligarchies may also achieve this type of dominance.) **Totalitarianism** involves virtually complete government control and surveillance over all aspects of a society's social and political life. Germany

North Korea has a totalitarian government whose leadership attempts to control all aspects of people's lives. This billboard, a blatant example of government propaganda, portrays the country's ruthless leader as a benevolent father figure.

during Hitler's reign, the former Soviet Union, and North Korea today are classified as totalitarian states.

Political scientists Carl Friedrich and Zbigniew Brzezinski have identified the traits that are typical of totalitarian states (1965:22). They include the widespread use of ideological propaganda and state control of the media and the economy.

Democracy

In a literal sense, **democracy** means government by the people. The word *democracy* originated in two Greek roots—*demos*, meaning "the populace" or "the common people," and *kratia*, meaning "rule." Of course, in large nations such as Canada, government by the people is impractical at the national level. Canadians cannot vote on every important issue that comes before their elected representatives. Consequently, popular rule is generally maintained through **representative democracy**, a form of government in which certain individuals are selected to speak for the people.

Canada is commonly classified as a *representative democracy*, since the elected members to the federal parliament and provincial legislatures make our laws. However, critics have questioned how *representative* our democracy really is. Do parliament and the provincial legislatures genuinely represent the masses? Are the people of Canada legitimately self-governing, or has our government become a forum for powerful elites? We explore these issues in the remainder of the chapter.

☐ HOW DOES POLITICAL PARTICIPATION MANIFEST ITSELF IN CANADA?

Citizens of Canada take for granted many aspects of their political system. They are accustomed to living in a nation with a Charter of Rights and Freedoms, an elected prime minister, provincial or territorial and local governments distinct from the federal government, and so forth. Yet each society has its own ways of governing itself and making decisions. Just as Canadian residents expect candidates from numerous political parties to compete for public office, residents of Cuba and the People's Republic of China are accustomed to one-party rule. In this section, we examine several aspects of political participation within Canada.

Participation and Apathy

In theory, a representative democracy will function most effectively and fairly if an informed and active electorate communicates its views to government leaders. Unfortunately, that is hardly the case in Canada. Many citizens are familiar with the basics of the political process, however, decreasing numbers of Canadians identify with a political party (Mendelsohn 2002) and only a small minority (often members of the higher social classes) actually participate in political organizations. Very few Canadians belong to a political party.

In the 1980s, it became clear that many people in Canada were beginning to be turned off by political parties, politicians, and big government. The most dramatic indication of this growing alienation came from voting statistics. Today, voters appear to be less enthusiastic than ever about elections. In 2008, voter turnout for the federal election—at 59 percent—was the lowest since Confederation in 1867 (CBC 2008c).

While a few nations still command high voter turnout, it is increasingly common to hear national leaders in

▶ **FIGURE 14-2**

Voter Turnout Worldwide

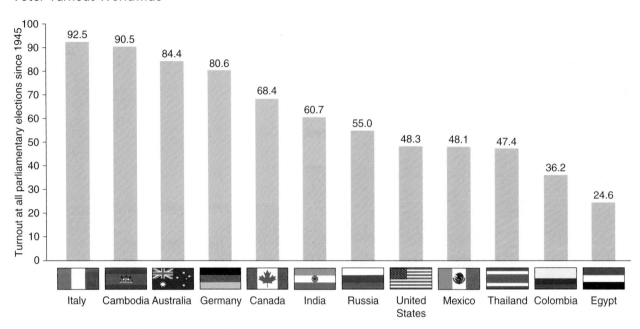

Source: International Institute for Democracy and Electoral Assistance 2005.

other countries complain of voter apathy. Despite lower rates of voter turnout in the recent past, Canada, from 1945 to 2005, has had a higher rate of turnout than the United States (see Figure 14-2). In 2008, however, voter turnout in the U.S. for the Presidential election, in which Barack Obama was elected, was 64 percent. This was the highest turnout since 1908, and greater than the voter turnout in the 2008 federal election in Canada.

In the end, political participation on the part of citizens makes government accountable to the voters. If participation declines, government operates with less of a sense of accountability to society. This issue is most serious for the least powerful individuals and groups in society. In Canada, voter turnout has been particularly low among members of younger age groups. In 2000, approximately 25 percent of eligible voters in the 18–24 age group voted in that year's federal election. A 2007 study by Elections Canada surveyed non-voters in the 2000 federal election and found that younger Canadians were much more likely not to vote because they were "just not interested"; 59 percent of 18- to 20-year-olds as opposed to 34 percent of 58- to 67-year-olds gave this response (Elections Canada 2007).

Women in Politics

Women continue to be dramatically under-represented in the halls of government. As we mentioned in Chapter 11,

most women in Canada (with the notable exception of Aboriginal women) were granted the right to vote in federal elections in 1918. It wasn't until 1929, however, that women in Canada were considered "persons" under the law, making them eligible for appointment to the Canadian Senate.

Canadians are socialized to see freedom of expression as an essential part of the democratic process. These people have gathered on Parliament Hill to protest the war in Iraq at a meeting of the leaders of Canada, the United States, and Mexico in 2007.

▶ **FIGURE 14-3**

Women in National Legislatures, Selected Countries, 2006

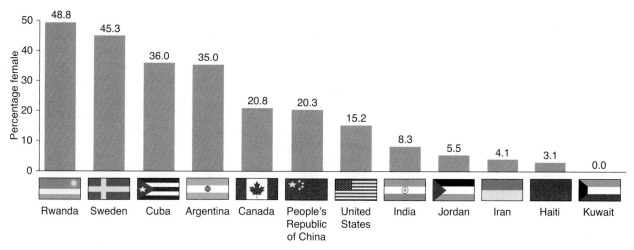

Notes: Data are for lower legislative houses only, as of March 31, 2006; data on upper houses, such as the U.S. Senate or the U.K. House of Lords, are not included. In 2005, the all-male Kuwaiti Parliament granted women the right to vote and serve in elected offices, which cleared the way for women to run for office in 2006. In 2006 and 2008, 27 women ran for office, but none were elected.
Source: Inter-Parliamentary Union 2006.

Sexism has been the most serious barrier to women interested in holding office. Female candidates continue to attempt to overcome the prejudices of both men and other women regarding women's fitness for leadership. Although Canada has had one female prime minister, Kim Campbell in 1993, her tenure was short-lived and she did not obtain her position through a federal ◀ P. 272 election. Campbell earned the top job by winning her party's leadership race to succeed the retiring prime minister, Brian Mulroney. In 2006, approximately 21 percent of members of the House of Commons were female—this despite the fact that women make up 51 percent of the Canadian population. The proportion of women in the federal parliament has remained relatively unchanged over the last decade. There are no female provincial or territorial premiers in Canada today. Moreover, women may encounter prejudice, discrimination, and abuse *after* they are elected.

Female politicians may be enjoying more electoral success now than in the past, but there is evidence that the media cover women in politics differently from their male counterparts. A content analysis of newspaper coverage showed that reporters wrote more often about a female candidate's personal life, appearance, or personality than a male candidate's, and less often about her political positions and voting record. Furthermore, when political issues were raised in newspaper articles, reporters were more likely to illustrate them with statements made by male candidates than by female candidates (Devitt 1999).

Although the proportion of women in legislatures has increased in Canada and many other nations, women still do not account for half the members of the national legislature in any country. The African Republic of Rwanda ranks the highest, with 48.8 percent of its legislative seats held by women. Overall, Canada in 2006 ranked 44th among 188 nations in the proportion of women serving as national legislators (Inter-Parliamentary Union 2005). To remedy this imbalance, many countries—including the world's largest democracy, India—have reserved a minimum number of legislative seats for women. (Figure 14-3 shows the representation of women in selected national legislatures; Box 14-2 on page 354 discusses the issue of gender quotas in politics.)

A gender gap becomes apparent when we examine the relationship between gender and politics. In the 2008 Canadian federal election, for example, the largest number of female candidates running for elected office—in parties with over 65 candidates—represented the Liberal Party, followed by (in descending order), the New Democratic Party (NDP), the Green Party, the Bloc Québécois, and the Conservative Party. Of the four major political parties (Liberal, Conservative, NDP, and Bloc Québécois), the NDP had the largest percentage of women elected as members of Parliament in 2008.

A gender gap has also emerged in relation to voting patterns in Canada. Between 1993 and 2000, Canadian men tended to support more conservative, right-wing political parties, while Canadian women did not. Research suggests that gender differences in values and

Sociology in the Global Community   14-2
Gender Quotas at the Ballot Box

Worldwide, women are under-represented in government. In national legislatures, they make up only 16 percent of the total membership—far below their share of the world's population in 2005.

To remedy this situation, many countries have adopted quotas for female representatives. In some, the government sets aside a certain proportion of seats for women, usually from 10 to 30 percent. In others, political parties have decided that 20 to 40 percent of their candidates should be women. Thirty-two countries now have some kind of female quota system.

In sheer numbers, India has seen the biggest gains in female representation. After a third of all village council seats were set aside for women, almost a million Indian women won election to local office. In South Africa, another country with quotas, women now hold 33 percent or more of the seats in both houses of Parliament. As previously mentioned, in Canada, where there are no quotas, 21 percent of the seats in the federal parliament are held by women. In Norway, where all parties must have 50 percent women on their party lists, 38 percent of all seats are filled by women.

In Africa, quotas have been particularly popular in countries where women contributed to independence movements. South African women fought hard against apartheid and received constitutional guarantees against discrimination in return. Ugandan women fought in the National Resistance Army in the 1980s, earning new respect—and new political power—from men. Women now comprise almost 24 percent of Uganda's parliament and form a minimum required percentage of all elected bodies in that country.

With support from President Yoweri Museveni (under whom a woman, Wandira Kazibwe, was elected vice president in 1994), Ugandan women have used their new-found power to enact new privileges for themselves. Married women can now share property ownership with their husbands, and widows can retain property after their husbands' death. Women legislators have also increased educational opportunities for girls in an effort to reduce the harsh poverty in their country. In President Museveni's opinion, the presence of women in government has helped to stabilize politics in Uganda. And in a country where women produce much of the wealth, he notes, they deserve to be empowered.

Applying Theory

1. How might a conflict thinker explain why Canada has so few women in government compared to some other nations?
2. What interpretation might a functionalist sociologist give to the low rates of female representation in elected politics?

Sources: Center for American Women and Politics 2006; Hanes 2005; Inter-Parliamentary Union 2006; A. Simmons and Wright 2000; Vasagar 2005; Wax 2005.

---

beliefs have contributed to corresponding gender differences in terms of party support (Gidengil et al. 2003). Canadian women were less likely to support cutting taxes, doing less for minorities, and reducing expenditures on government-sponsored welfare programs, policies, and proposals—policies which tend to be on the platforms of conservative political parties (Gidengil et al. 2003).

Use Your Sociological Imagination

Imagine a world in which women, not men, held the majority of elective offices. What kind of world would it be?

☐ WHAT ARE THE VARIOUS MODELS OF POWER IN CANADA?

Who really holds power in Canada? Do "the people" genuinely run the country through our elected representatives? Or is it true that behind the scenes a small elite controls both the government and, to a lesser extent, the economic system? In exploring these critical questions, social scientists have developed views on nations' power structures: the power elite and the pluralist models.

Power Elite Models

Karl Marx believed that nineteenth-century representative democracy was essentially a sham. He argued that industrial societies were dominated by relatively small numbers of people who owned factories and controlled natural resources. In Marx's view, government officials and military leaders were essentially servants of this capitalist class and followed their wishes. Therefore, any key decisions made by politicians inevitably reflected the interests of the dominant bourgeoisie. Like others who see the world as holding an **elite model** of power relations, Marx believed that society is ruled by a small group of individuals who share a common set of political and economic interests.

Mills's Model

Sociologist C. Wright Mills took this model a step further in his pioneering work, *The Power Elite* ([1956] 2000b). Mills described a small group of military, industrial, and government leaders who controlled the fate of a country— the **power elite**. Power rested in the hands of a few, both inside and outside government.

A pyramid illustrates the power structure of Mills's model (see the left-hand visual in Figure 14-4). At the top are the corporate rich, leaders of the executive branch of government, and heads of the military (whom Mills called the "warlords"). Directly below are local opinion leaders, members of the legislative branch of government, and leaders of special-interest groups. Mills contended that these individuals and groups would usually follow the wishes of the dominant power elite. At the bottom of the pyramid are the unorganized, exploited masses.

The power elite model is, in many respects, similar to the work of Karl Marx. The most striking difference is that Mills believed that the economically powerful coordinate their manoeuvres with the military and political establishments to serve their common interests. Yet, reminiscent of Marx, Mills argued that the corporate rich were perhaps the most powerful element of the power elite (first among "equals"). And the powerless masses at the bottom of Mills's model certainly bring to mind Marx's portrait of the oppressed workers of the world, who have "nothing to lose but their chains."

A fundamental element in Mills's thesis is that the power elite not only includes relatively few members but also operates as a self-conscious, cohesive unit. Although not necessarily diabolical or ruthless, the elite comprises similar types of people who interact regularly with one another and have essentially the same political and economic interests. Mills's power elite is not a conspiracy, but rather a community of interest and sentiment among a small number of influential people (A. Hacker 1964).

Admittedly, Mills failed to clarify when the elite opposes protests and when it tolerates them; he also did not provide detailed case studies that would substantiate the interrelationships among members of the power elite. Nevertheless, his challenging theories forced scholars

▶ **FIGURE 14-4**

Power Elite Models

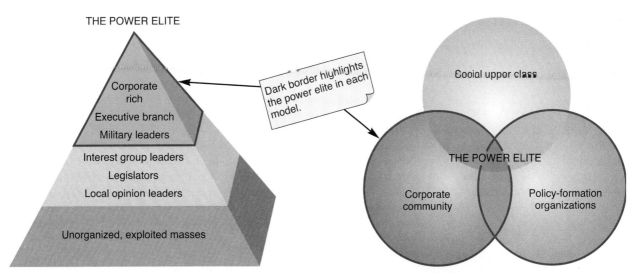

a. C. Wright Mills's model, 1956

b. G. William Domhoff's model, 2006

Source: Left, author based on C.W. Mills [1956] 2000b; right, G.W. Domhoff 2006:105.

to look more critically at the democratic political systems of Canada and the United States. In Canada, Fox and Ornstein revealed the existence of expensive networks linking corporations with the federal cabinet, Senate, and bureaucracy; they also showed the growth of these links over the last three decades of the period they examined (1986).

In commenting on the scandals that have rocked major financial outfits and corporations such as Freddie Mac, Fannie Mae, Enron, and Arthur Andersen over the last several years, observers in the United States have noted that members of the business elite are closely linked to these events as well. In a study of the members of the boards of directors of Fortune 1000 corporations, researchers found that each director can reach *every* other board of directors in just 3.7 steps. That is, by consulting acquaintances of acquaintances, each director can quickly reach someone who sits on each of the other 999 boards. Furthermore, the face-to-face contact directors regularly have in their board meetings makes them a highly cohesive elite. Finally, the corporate elite is not only wealthy, powerful, and cohesive, but also overwhelmingly white and male (G. Davis 2003, 2004; Kentor and Jang 2004; Mizruchi 1996; Strauss 2002).

Domhoff's Model

Over the last three decades, sociologist G. William Domhoff, co-author with Richard L. Zweigenhaft of *Diversity in the Power Elite*, has agreed with Mills that a powerful elite runs the developed world (2006). He finds that it is still largely white, male, and upper class. But Domhoff stresses the role played both by elites of the corporate community and by the leaders of policy-formation organizations, such as chambers of commerce and labour unions. Many of the people in both groups are also members of the social upper class.

While these groups overlap, as shown by the right-hand visual in Figure 14-4, they do not necessarily agree on specific policies. Domhoff notes that in the electoral arena, in the United States, two different coalitions have exercised influence. A corporate–conservative coalition has played a large role in both of the major political parties in the U.S., generating support for particular candidates through direct-mail appeals. A liberal–labour coalition in the U.S. is based in unions, local environmental organizations, a segment of the minority group community, liberal churches, and the university and arts communities (Zweigenhaft and Domhoff 2006).

Pluralist Model

Several social scientists insist that power in capitalist countries, such as Canada, is shared more widely than the elite models indicate. In their view, a pluralist model more accurately describes the nation's political system.

According to the **pluralist model**, many competing groups within the community have access to government, so that no single group is dominant.

The pluralist model suggests that a variety of groups play a significant role in decision making. Typically, pluralists make use of intensive case studies or community studies based on observation research. One of the most famous—an investigation of decision making in New Haven, Connecticut—was reported by Robert Dahl (1961). Dahl found that although the number of people involved in any important decision was rather small, community power was nonetheless diffuse. Few political actors exercised decision-making power on all issues. One individual or group might be influential in a battle over urban renewal, but have little impact on educational policy.

The pluralist model, however, has not escaped serious questioning. Domhoff re-examined Dahl's study of decision making and argued that Dahl and other pluralists had failed to trace how local elites who were prominent in decision making belonged to a larger national ruling class (1978, 2006). In addition, studies of community power, such as can be found in Dahl's work, examine decision making only on issues that become part of the political agenda. They fail to address the potential power of elites to keep certain matters entirely out of the realm of government debate.

Many sociologists and political scientists have criticized the pluralist model for failing to account for the exclusion of disadvantaged groups (the poor, women, Aboriginal peoples) from the political process. The pluralist claim that diverse and conflicting groups have access to government, with no single group being dominant, is seriously flawed. For example, members of Parliament in Canada do not reflect the characteristics of the Canadian population in terms of race, ethnicity, gender, education, or class (Dyck 2006).

In the United States, drawing on her studies of Chicago politics, Dianne Pinderhughes points out that the residential and occupational segregation of blacks and their long political disenfranchisement violates the logic of pluralism—which would hold that such a substantial minority should always have been influential in community decision making (1987). This critique applies to many cities across the United States, where other large racial and ethnic minorities, among them Asian Americans, Puerto Ricans, and Mexican Americans, are relatively powerless.

Historically, pluralists have stressed ways in which large numbers of people can participate in or influence governmental decision making. New communications technologies like the Internet and other digitized messaging devices are increasing the opportunity to be heard, not just in countries such as Canada and the United States but also in developing countries the world over. One common point of the elite and pluralist perspectives stands out, however: In Canada's political system, power is unequally distributed. All citizens may be equal in theory, yet those who are high in the nation's power structure are "more equal." New communications technology may or may not change that distribution of power, but any change, if it happens, will take time.

☐ HOW DO SOCIOLOGISTS CONCEPTUALIZE WAR AND PEACE?

Perhaps the ultimate test of power, no matter what a nation's power structures, involves broaching the decision to go to war. Because the rank and file of the military is generally drawn from the lower classes—the least powerful groups in society—such a decision has life-and-death consequences for people far removed from the centre of power. In the long run, if the general population is not convinced that war is necessary, military action is unlikely to succeed. Thus, war is a risky way in which to address conflict between countries. In this section we contrast war and peace as ways of addressing societal conflict, and more recently, the threat of terrorism.

Conflict is a central aspect of social relations. Too often, it becomes ongoing and violent, engulfing innocent bystanders as well as intentional participants. Sociologists Theodore Caplow and Louis Hicks have defined **war** as conflict between organizations that possess trained combat forces equipped with deadly weapons (2002:3). This meaning is broader than the legal definition, which typically requires a formal declaration of hostilities.

War

Sociologists approach war in three different ways: There are those who take a global view to study how and why two or more nations become engaged in military conflict; those

who take a nation-state view to stress the interaction of internal political, socio-economic, and cultural forces; and those who take a micro-level view to focus on the social impact of war on individuals and the groups they belong to (Kiser 1992).

From a micro-level point of view, war can bring out the worst as well as the best in people. In 2004, graphic images of the abuse of Iraqi prisoners of war by U.S. soldiers at Iraq's Abu Ghraib prison shocked the world. For social scientists, the deterioration of the guards' behaviour brought to mind Philip Zimbardo's mock prison experiment, conducted in 1971. Though the results of the experiment, which we highlighted in Chapter 5, have been applied primarily to civilian correctional facilities, Zimbardo's study was actually funded by the Office of Naval Research. In July 2004, the U.S. military began using a documentary film about the experiment to train military interrogators to avoid mistreatment of prisoners (Zarembo 2004; Zimbardo 2004).

Peace

Sociologists have considered **peace** both as the absence of war and as a proactive effort to develop cooperative relations among nations. While we focus here on international relations, it is worth noting that in the 1990s, 90 percent of the world's armed conflicts occurred *within*

A representative of the International Red Crescent Society delivers an aid parcel in the southern Iraqi town of Safwan. Red Crescent provides emergency aid to victims of war and disaster in Muslim communities. Such non-governmental organizations (NGOs) help to bind countries together, promoting peaceful relations.

Table 14-2   Likelihood of Terrorist Attack in Canada

Do you think it is very, somewhat, not very, or not at all likely that Canada will be the victim of a terrorist attack within the next two years? (Answers are given as percentages of those polled.)

	September/October 2001	December 2001*	January 2002	March 2002
Very likely	16%	13%	11%	11%
Somewhat likely	39%	37%	31%	26%
Not very likely	33%	33%	41%	46%
Not at all likely	10%	14%	15%	15%
Don't know/not applicable	2%	4%	3%	3%

* Social Cohesion Study, Government of Canada
Source: Adapted from Baker 2002. *Canada after September 11th: A public opinion perspective*, Environics Research Group, FOCUS CANADA study, 2002. Reprinted with permission.

rather than between states. Often, outside powers became involved in these internal conflicts, either as supporters of particular factions or in an attempt to broker a peace accord. In 28 countries where such conflicts occurred—none of which would be considered core nations in world systems analysis—at least 10 000 people died (Kriesberg 1992; Dan Smith 1999).

Sociologists and other social scientists who draw on sociological theory and research have tried to identify conditions that deter war. One of their findings is that international trade may act as a deterrent to armed conflict. As countries exchange goods, people, and then cultures, they become more integrated and less likely to threaten each other's security. Viewed from this perspective, not just trade but immigration and foreign exchange programs have a beneficial effect on international relations.

Another means of fostering peace is the activity of international charities and activist groups called non-governmental organizations (NGOs). The Red Cross, Doctors Without Borders, and Amnesty International donate their services wherever they are needed, without regard to nationality. In the last decade or so, these global organizations have been expanding in number, size, and scope. By sharing news of local conditions and clarifying local issues, they often prevent conflicts from escalating into violence and war. Some NGOs have initiated ceasefires, reached settlements, and even ended warfare between former adversaries.

Finally, many analysts stress that nations cannot maintain their security by threatening violence. Peace, they contend, can best be maintained by developing strong mutual security agreements between potential adversaries (Etzioni 1965; Shostak 2002).

Terrorism

In recent years, Canada, the United States, and many countries in Europe and elsewhere have begun to recognize that their security can be threatened not just by nation-states, but by political groups that operate outside the bounds of legitimate authority.

Immediately after the September 11, 2001, attacks in the United States, the majority of Canadians (55 percent) thought a terrorist attack was likely to take place in Canada within a two-year period; however, by March 2002, only 37 percent of Canadians thought such an attack was likely (Baker 2002). See Table 14-2 for more details.

Acts of terror, whether perpetrated by nation-states, a few, or many people, can be a powerful political force. Formally defined, **terrorism** is the use or threat of violence against random or symbolic targets in pursuit of political aims. For terrorists, the end justifies the means. They believe the status quo is oppressive, and desperate measures are essential to end the suffering of the deprived. Convinced that working through formal political processes will not effect the desired political change, terrorists insist that illegal actions—often directed against innocent people—are needed. Ultimately, they hope to intimidate others and thereby secure their position or bring about a new political order.

An essential aspect of contemporary terrorism involves use of the media. Terrorists may wish to keep secret their individual identities, but they want their political messages and goals to receive as much publicity as possible. Drawing on Erving Goffman's dramaturgical approach, sociologist Alfred McClung Lee has likened terrorism to the theatre, where certain scenes are played out in predictable fashion. Whether through calls to the media, anonymous manifestos, or other means, terrorists typically admit responsibility for and defend their violent acts.

☐ HOW IS THE ECONOMY CHANGING?

◄ P.219 As advocates of the power elite model point out, the trend in capitalist societies has been toward concentration of ownership by giant corporations, especially transnational ones. For example, in 1998, there were 3882 mergers in the United States alone, involving $1.4 trillion in business. The nature of national economies is changing in important ways, in part because each nation's economy is increasingly intertwined with and dependent on the global economy.

In the following sections, we examine the economy and the nature of work from four theoretical perspectives: conflict, functionalist, feminist, and interactionist. We also examine developments in the global economy that have interested sociologists: the changing face of the workforce, deindustrialization, the emergence of e-commerce, and the rise of a contingency or non-standard workforce. As these trends show, any change in the economy inevitably has social and political implications and soon becomes a concern of policymakers.

Conflict View

Conflict theorists view the economy as the central institution of a society and as the institution that defines the character of the entire society and, correspondingly, the quality of people's lives. In 1887, Karl Marx laid the foundation for the conflict perspective in his critique of capitalism. According to Marx's framework of economic determinism, the economy was the base of society, determining the character of all other institutions: the family, religion, the education system, the legal system, and the mass media. In capitalist societies, according to Marx, the economy is based on a division of classes: those who own the means of production (i.e., the factories and the workplaces), called the bourgeoisie, and those who work for the owners of the means of production, the proletariat. These classes are in conflict with each other, as the owning class exploits the workers to maximize profits. The nature of work, therefore, in capitalist societies is one in which workers experience great inequality, exploitation, and alienation. Work, for Marx, was central to human happiness and fulfilment; however, the conditions inherent in the capitalist economy denied workers the actualization of this basic human desire. In Marx's view, the alienation of the proletariat from the product that was being produced, from the way in which it was produced, from themselves, and from their fellow workers was rooted in the nature of the capitalist economy.

Today, conflict thinkers still maintain the view that the interests of the dominant economic class and the working class are opposed and, for the most part, incompatible. Conflict theorist Richard Edwards has called the workplace in capitalist economies "contested terrain" in which struggle and competition between these two groups is inevitable (1979).

Functionalist View

Although conflict thinkers see the capitalist economy as the basis for inequality, and, thus, as an institution requiring radical change, functionalist thinkers view the economy in an uncritical fashion. The economy, for functionalists, is an integral part of the whole society in which the various institutions (family, religion, education, and so on) contribute to the functioning of that society through their interdependence and interrelationships. Functionalists believe that the economy, with workplaces containing diverse jobs and occupations, serves to provide order and regulation.

Functional sociologists Kingsley Davis and Wilbur Moore, in their classic argument on the function of social stratification, maintain that an economy based on inequality, such as the capitalist economy, ensures that the best people reach the top positions of the workplace (1945). Critics of this view, such as Melvin Tumin, maintain that those who are disadvantaged because of ascribed characteristics, such as class, race, and gender, may, in fact, be the "best," but because of the barriers they face in hiring and employment practices (e.g., the glass ceiling), they rarely make it to the top positions in the economy (1953). Today, when we examine who makes it to the highest positions of the Canadian economy, clearly, the economy is more "functionally" beneficial to some Canadians than to others.

Feminist Views

Although feminist perspectives are diverse, many point to the economy as a source of gender inequality. As with conflict thinkers, Marxist feminists, for example, maintain that the principle of private ownership, central to capitalist economies, creates massive inequalities between those who own and those who work. Marxist feminists believe that at the heart of gender inequality is the fact that it is men who own the means of production and women who are used as a reserve of surplus labour—labour to be included or excluded at the whim of the owning class. Marxist feminists believe, therefore, that the root of women's opposition lies in the nature of the capitalist economy, where women's work in the paid workforce constitutes exploited labour and work done in the home goes unpaid.

▶ **FIGURE 14-5**

Employment of Canadian Women Aged 15 and over, 1976–2006

Source: Adapted by the author from Statistics Canada 2007m.

In contrast to the Marxist feminists' view, socialist feminists maintain that because the capitalist economy and patriarchy are inextricably connected, both must be eliminated to bring about gender equality. For example, socialist feminists state that the economy could change from being privately owned to being publicly owned; however, this would not ensure the elimination of patriarchal values, beliefs, and norms, which perpetuate sexism.

Liberal feminism, which tends to be moderate in its recommendations for change, suggests how the economy could be tweaked, rather than overhauled, to provide women with greater access to jobs and economic power.

Interactionist View

Interactionist sociologists examine the meaning that people give to work and the economy. Using this theoretical perspective allows us to see not only what work means to people but also why they work, why they choose to retire, how they view being unemployed, and how they view work relative to other aspects of their lives. Do people work only because they need money to feed and house themselves and their families? Or do they also work for intrinsic reasons, such as self-fulfilment and a sense of identity? Sociologist Robert Wuthnow found that although people said that the most important reason for working was for the money, when asked what they preferred about their jobs, 48 percent said "a feeling of accomplishment" (1996). Work also may provide people with a social network, a feeling of engagement in the larger society, or a sense of attachment to a community.

The Changing Face of the Canadian Workforce

The workforce in Canada is constantly changing. During World War II, when men were mobilized to fight abroad, women entered the workforce in large numbers. During the postwar years, however, many women retreated to the household, where domesticity and family life took primacy over paid employment. During the 1970s, a trend began that proved to be one of the most significant forces of social change in the latter half of the twentieth century—the changing role of women in Canadian society. Of particular significance—as we've outlined in previous chapters—is the growing number of women in the paid workforce with children under 6 years of age. These women thus have an accompanying need for quality child care. In 2006, 58 percent of all women 15 years of age and over were part of the paid workforce; this percentage is up from 42 percent in 1976 (Statistics Canada 2007m). Figure 14-5 shows the increases in the percentage of women aged 15 and over in the workforce. In addition, the federal government's Employment Equity Act of 1986 established the existence of four target groups: women, people of Aboriginal descent, people with disabilities, and members of visible minorities. It was the government's plan to increase the representation of these groups in the Canadian workforce.

Although predictions are not always reliable, sociologists and labour specialists foresee a workforce increasingly comprising women and members of racial and ethnic minorities. In 1960, there were twice as many men in the paid labour force as women. Today, women constitute slightly less than half of all Canadians 15 years of age and older in the paid labour force. It's likely that by 2015, the total numbers of male and female workers will be the equal.

The Canadian employment landscape increasingly reflects the diversity of the population as ethnic and visible minority immigrants enter the labour force. All immigrants, however, do not face the same treatment when entering the Canadian workforce. Visible minority immigrants experience greater inequality in income and employment than do those immigrants whose identities are not racialized. The "double jeopardy" of being a member of a visible minority and female compounds the effects of inequality in the workforce, resulting in lower incomes and fewer employment opportunities. The impact of this changing labour force is not merely statistical. A more diverse workforce means that relationships among workers are more likely to cross gender, racial, and ethnic lines. Interactionists note that people will find themselves supervising and being supervised by people very different from them. In response to these changes, 75 percent of businesses had instituted some type of cultural diversity training programs by 2000 (Melia 2000).

◀ PP. 240, 241, 242

Deindustrialization

What happens when a company decides it is more profitable to move its operations out of an established community to another part of the country or out of the country altogether? People lose jobs; stores lose customers; the local government's tax base declines and it cuts services. This devastating process has occurred again and again in the past decade or so.

The term **deindustrialization** refers to the systematic, widespread withdrawal of investment in basic aspects of productivity, such as factories and plants. Giant corporations that deindustrialize are not necessarily refusing to invest in new economic opportunities. Rather, the targets and locations of investment change, and the need for permanent or standard labour decreases as technology continues to automate production. First, there may be a relocation of plants from central cities to the suburbs. The next step may be relocation from suburban areas to jurisdictions where labour laws place more restrictions on unions. Finally, a corporation may simply relocate *outside* Canada to a country, such as Mexico,

with a lower rate of prevailing wages. General Motors, for example, decided to build a multi-billion-dollar plant in Spain rather than in Kansas City (Bluestone and Harrison 1982; Rifkin 1995).

Although deindustrialization may involve relocation, in some instances, it takes the form of corporate restructuring as companies seek to reduce costs in the face of growing worldwide competition. When such restructuring occurs, the impact on the bureaucratic hierarchy of formal organizations can be significant. A large corporation may choose to sell off or entirely abandon less productive divisions and eliminate layers of management viewed as unnecessary. Wages and salaries may be frozen and fringe benefits cut—all in the name of "restructuring." Increasing reliance on automation also spells the end of work as we have known it.

The term **downsizing** was introduced in 1987 to refer to reductions in a company's workforce. Downsizing contributed to the elimination of 60 percent of the workforce in British Columbia's sawmills between 1979 and 1998. According to the Economic Council of Canada, between 1988 and 1995, the manufacturing sector lost

In Seoul in 2001, protesting employees of the dot-com industry took to the streets to demand job security and better working conditions. The year before, South Korean workers had logged longer hours than those in 199 other countries (Webb 2001).

400 000 jobs—17 percent of its workforce. The deindustrialization of Canada contributed to lower levels of job creation—the rate of job creation fell from 2 percent per year in the 1980s to 1 percent per year in the 1990s. Overall, though, from 1975 to 1995, there was a net increase of 2.8 million jobs in Canada. These jobs, however, were in the service sector, where wages are typically lower, benefits are fewer, and part-time work is more common. Two-thirds of these new jobs went to women, which serves to perpetuate the "pink ghetto" phenomenon, in which women are over-represented in areas of employment that provide fewer rewards, opportunities, and benefits.

Viewed from a conflict perspective, the unprecedented attention given to downsizing in the mid-1990s reflected the continuing importance of social class in Canada. Conflict theorists note that job loss, affecting factory workers in particular, has long been a feature of deindustrialization. But when large numbers of middle-class managers and other white-collar employees with substantial incomes began to be laid off, suddenly there was great concern in the media over downsizing. By mid-2000, downsizing was being applied to dot-com companies, the sector of the economy that had flourished in the 1990s (Richtel 2000; Safire 1996; R. Samuelson 1996a, 1996b).

The social costs of deindustrialization and downsizing cannot be minimized. Layoffs in auto plants in Ontario have led to substantial unemployment in various communities; this can have a devastating impact on both the micro and macro levels. On the micro level, the unemployed person and his or her family must adjust to a loss of spending power. Both marital happiness and family cohesion may suffer as a result. Although many dismissed workers eventually re-enter the paid labour force, they often must accept less desirable positions with lower salaries and fewer benefits. Unemployment and underemployment are tied into many of the social problems discussed throughout this book, among them the need for child care, the controversy over welfare, and immigration issues.

On the societal, or macro, level, the impact on a community of a plant closing can be as difficult as it is for an individual worker and his or her family. As we noted earlier, the community will experience a significant loss of tax revenues. It then becomes more difficult to support police and fire protection, schools, parks, and other public services. Moreover, rising unemployment in a community leads to a reduced demand for goods and services. Sales by retail firms and other businesses fall off, and this can lead to further layoffs.

E-commerce

Another development following close on the heels of deindustrialization was the emergence of e-commerce, as online businesses compete with bricks-and-mortar establishments. **E-commerce** refers to the numerous ways that people with access to the Internet can do business from their computers. Amazon.com, for example, began in 1995 as a supplier of books but soon became the prototype for online businesses, branching into selling a variety of merchandise, including toys and hardware equipment. By 2002, Amazon.com boasted customers in 220 countries. The growth of e-commerce means jobs in a new line of industry as well as growth for related industries, such as warehousing, packing, and shipping.

Although e-commerce will not immediately overwhelm traditional businesses, it has brought new social dynamics to the retail trade. Consider the impact on traditional retail outlets and on face-to-face interaction with local store owners. Even established companies, such as Chapters, Indigo, A&B Sound, and Mattel, have their own online "stores," bypassing the retail outlets that they courted for years in order to directly reach customers with their merchandise. Mega-malls once replaced personal ties to stores for many shoppers; the growth of e-commerce with its "cybermalls" is just the latest change in the economy.

Some observers note that e-commerce offers more opportunities to consumers in rural areas (assuming they have the necessary high-tech infrastructure) and those with disabilities. To its critics, however, e-commerce signals more social isolation, more alienation, and greater disconnect for the poor and disadvantaged who are not a part of the new information technology (Amazon.com 2001; Drucker 1999; Stoughton and Walker 1999).

The Contingency Workforce

In the past, the term *temp* typically conjured up images of a replacement receptionist or a worker covering for someone on vacation. However, along with the deindustrialization and downsizing described above, contingency work—work that is considered atypical or non-standard—has emerged.

The downsizing of both the public and the private sectors in the 1980s was accompanied by the growth of non-standard work in Canada. Non-standard work is contingent on the employer's needs; it can include part-time and temporary work, work that is contracted or outsourced, and self-employment. In 1990, the Economic Council of Canada released a report making the distinction between "good jobs" (i.e., work that is done on an ongoing basis and provides some degree of continuity and security) and "bad jobs" (i.e., work that is non-standard). Grant Schellenberg and Christopher Clark wrote a report for the Canadian Council for Social Development in which they argue that new forms of employment are one of the strategies used by corporations to achieve flexibility in a changing economic environment—an environment greatly transformed by free trade, global

Non-standard jobs are often filled by women and younger people. These jobs are part-time or temporary, contracted or outsourced, and often in self-employed areas.

well. In 2000, this type of work made up 34 percent of the total employment sector; ten years before, it made up roughly 25 percent of the total employment sector. In 1997, it was 19 percent (Status of Women Canada 2003).

Both unemployed workers and entrants to the paid labour force accept positions as temporary or part-time workers. Some do so for flexibility and control over their work time, but others accept these jobs because they are the only ones available. Young people and women are especially likely to fill non-standard positions (Johanis and Meguerditchian 1996). A 2006 study by Brian Cooke and Isik Urla Zeytinglu found that women in non-standard jobs were more vulnerable than their male counterparts. The authors found that males in non-standard jobs tended to be treated much like their "standard" counterparts while "some employers apparently perceive that females in non-standard contracts either do not need, or should not get, training" (2006:31).

During the 1970s and 1980s, temporary workers typically held low-skill positions at fast-food restaurants, telemarketing firms, and other service industries. Today, the contingent workforce is evident at virtually *all* skill levels and in *all* industries. Clerical "temps" handle word processing and filing duties, managers are hired on a short-term basis to reorganize departments, freelance writers prepare speeches for corporate executives, and blue-collar workers fill in for a few months when a factory receives an unusually high number of orders.

markets, new technologies, and shifting customer demands (1996). Incidentally, this so-called flexibility also allows for employees to hire workers without having to provide benefits, such as pensions, health care, dental plans, and disability insurance. The private sector is not alone in its shift toward non-standard work; the public sector has increased its rates of non-standard work as

Use Your Sociological Imagination

What will the Canadian workforce look like in 2020? Consider workers' ages, genders, and ethnicities. How much education will workers need? Will they work full-time or part-time? What will be the most common occupations?

Social Policy and the Economy
Global Offshoring

The Issue

Anney Unnikrishnan's situation is not unusual. In fact, she is one of 245 000 Indians who work in global call centres, answering phone calls from all over the world or dialing out to solicit business. Anney received her MBA in India before taking the entrance exams to Purdue University. But after concluding that she couldn't afford Purdue, she realized that

because North American corporations were setting up shop in India, she didn't need to emigrate to the United States. Anney sums up what she considers her enviable position in this way: "So I still get my rice and sambar (a traditional Indian dish). . . . I don't need to . . . learn to eat coleslaw and cold beef . . . and I still work for a multinational. Why should I go to America?" (Friedman 2005:28).

Offshoring is global. It occurs not just between North America and India, but between North America and Europe and between other industrial and developing countries. Online services in the United States enlist Romanians to represent well-to-do video-game players (see Box 9-1 on page 218). Japan enlists Chinese speakers of Japanese—a legacy of Japan's bitter occupation of China—to create databases or develop floor plans for Japanese construction firms. In Africa, over 54 000 people work in call centres, some specializing in French and others serving the English-speaking market. People all over the world are affected by this issue (Friedman 2005; Lacey 2005).

The Setting

North American firms have been outsourcing certain types of work for generations. For example, moderate-sized businesses such as furniture stores and commercial laundries have long relied on outside trucking firms to make deliveries to their customers. The new trend toward **offshoring** carries this practice one step further, by transferring other types of work to foreign contractors. Now, even large companies are turning to overseas firms, many of them located in developing countries. Offshoring has become the latest tactic in the time-worn business strategy of raising profits by reducing costs.

Offshoring began when companies in North America and Europe started transferring manufacturing jobs to foreign factories, where wage rates were much lower. But the transfer of work from one country to another is no longer limited to manufacturing. Office and professional jobs are being exported, too, thanks to advanced telecommunications and the growth of skilled, English-speaking labour forces in developing nations with relatively low wage scales. The trend includes even those jobs that require considerable training, such as accounting and financial analysis, computer programming, claims adjustment, telemarketing, and hotel and airline reservations. Today, when you call a toll-free number to reach a customer service representative, chances are that the person who answers the phone will not be speaking from Canada.

In 2004, the import of computer, information, and other business services to Canada totalled $18 billion; types of firms in Canada utilizing offshoring include architecture, engineering, informatics, publishing, data entry, and payroll administration (Statistics Canada 2007k).

Sociological Insights

Because offshoring, like outsourcing in general, tends to improve the efficiency of business operations, it can be viewed as functional to society. Offshoring also increases economic interdependence in the production of goods and services, both among enterprises located just across town from one another and among those across the globe from each other.

Conflict theorists question whether this aspect of globalization furthers social inequality. While moving high-tech work to India does help to lower a company's costs, the impact on those technical and service workers who are displaced may be devastating. Certainly some middle-class workers in industrial countries may be alarmed

The number of jobs that can be offshored is growing. Some U.S.-based online tutoring services have begun to employ people such as Somit Basak. Based in New Delhi, India, Basak earns about US$200 a month, or $1.40 an hour—very little compared to roughly CDN$15–$30 an hour that online tutors in Canada earn.

by the trend. Though economists favour some assistance for workers who have been displaced by offshoring, they oppose broad-based efforts to block the practice.

There is a downside to offshoring for foreigners, as well. Although outsourcing is a significant source of employment for India's upper middle class, hundreds of millions of other Indians have seen little to no positive impact from the trend. Most households in India do not possess any form of high technology—only about 1 out of 10 have a telephone, and just 3 out of 1000 own a computer. Instead of improving these people's lives, the new business centres have siphoned water and electricity away from those who are most in need. On the other hand, the new call centres have brought significant improvements in India's infrastructure, particularly in telecommunications and power generation. The long-term impact of offshoring on India and other developing nations is difficult to predict (Waldman 2004a, 2004b, 2004c).

Policy Initiatives

Offshoring became a political flashpoint in the United States during the 2004 presidential election. The Democratic candidate, Senator John Kerry, proposed repealing the tax deduction U.S. companies receive for the wages and benefits they pay to offshore workers. Despite such political rhetoric, however, little legislative action has been taken. Most policymakers, while they bemoan the loss of jobs, see offshoring as part of the "natural" process of globalization, one more manifestation of the gains that come from international trade. In their view, the resulting dislocation of workers at home is just another job change—one that more and more workers will have to adjust to at some point during their lifetimes (Friedman 2005; Migration News 2005b). Furthermore, a Statistics Canada report found "no clear evidence that occupations potentially subject to service offshoring displayed smaller employment growth than other occupations in recent years" (Statistics Canada 2007k:1).

Applying Theory

1. What do you think should be done, if anything, about the growing trend toward offshoring? Do you see it as a serious political issue?
2. How might the number of international students who are educated in Canada contribute to the trend toward offshoring?

CHAPTER RESOURCES

Summary

What Forms do Economic Systems Take?
- Although systems of **capitalism** (p. 343) vary in the degree to which the government regulates private ownership and economic activity, they all emphasize the profit motive and private ownership.
- **Socialist** (p. 344) economic systems, in contrast, aim to eliminate economic exploitation and meet people's needs.

How do Forms of Power and Authority Differ?
- There are three basic sources of **power** (p. 348) within any political system: **force** (p. 348), **influence** (p. 348), and **authority** (p. 349).

- Max Weber identified three ideal types of authority: **traditional** (p. 349), **rational-legal** (p. 349), and **charismatic** (p. 349).

What are the Various Types of Government?
- There are five basic types of government: **monarchy** (p. 350), **oligarchy** (p. 350), **dictatorship** (p. 350), **totalitarianism** (p. 350), and **democracy** (p. 351).

How does Political Participation Manifest Itself in Canada?
- Political participation may make government accountable to its citizens, but voters display varying degrees of apathy, both in Canada and in other countries.

- Women are still under-represented in politics, but are becoming more successful at winning election to public office.

What are the Various Models of Power in Canada?
- Advocates of the **elite model** (p. 355) of the Canadian power structure see the nation as being ruled by a small group of individuals—a **power elite** (p. 355)—who share common political and economic interests, whereas advocates of a **pluralist model** (p. 356) believe that power ought to be shared more widely among conflicting groups.

How do Sociologists Conceptualize War and Peace?
- Sociologists approach **war** (p. 357) in three different ways: There are those who take a global view, those who take a nation-state view, and those who take a micro-level focus. Sociologists

have considered **peace** (p. 357) both as the absence of war and the proactive effort to develop cooperative relations among nations.

How is the Economy Changing?
- The nature of the Canadian economy and those around the world is changing. Sociologists are especially interested in the changing face of the workforce and the effects of **deindustrialization** (p. 361).
- **Offshoring** (p. 364), or the transfer of work to overseas contractors, has become a global phenomenon involving both developed and developing nations. Today, even professional services can be outsourced to nations, like India, that possess a large, well-educated English-speaking population willing to work for comparatively low wages.

Critical Thinking Questions

1. How are the decision makers of Canada different from those whose lives are being affected by their decisions?
2. Who really holds power at the college or university you attend? Describe the distribution of power at your school, drawing on the elite and pluralist models where relevant.
3. Do you vote during provincial/territorial or federal elections? If not, why not? What do you

think the implications of growing political apathy might be?
4. If you had the power to change the way in which electoral politics work, how would you increase the diversity of those elected to represent Canadians?
5. Why do you think there are age-related patterns in voter turnout?
6. How are changes in the global economy affecting the economic well-being of Canada?

Key Terms

Authority Institutionalized power that is recognized by the people over whom it is exercised. (p. 349)

Capitalism An economic system in which the means of production are held largely in private hands and the main incentive for economic activity is the accumulation of profits. (p. 343)

Charismatic authority Power made legitimate by a leader's exceptional personal or emotional appeal to his or her followers. (p. 349)

Communism As an ideal type, an economic system under which all property is communally owned and no social distinctions are made on the basis of people's ability to produce. (p. 344)

Deindustrialization The systematic, widespread withdrawal of investment in basic aspects of productivity, such as factories and plants. (p. 361)

Democracy In a literal sense, government by the people. (p. 351)

Dictatorship A government in which one person has nearly total power to make and enforce laws. (p. 350)

Downsizing Reductions taken in a company's workforce as part of deindustrialization. (p. 361)

E-commerce Business involving the numerous ways that people with access to the Internet and other new media can do business. (p. 362)

Economic system The social institution through which goods and services are produced, distributed, and consumed. (p. 342)

Elite model A view of society as being ruled by a small group of individuals who share a common set of political and economic interests. (p. 355)

Force The actual or threatened use of coercion to impose one's will on others. (p. 348)

Industrial society A society that depends on mechanization to produce its goods and services. (p. 342)

Influence The exercise of power through a process of persuasion. (p. 348)

Informal economy Transfers of money, goods, or services that are not reported to the government. (p. 345)

Laissez-faire A form of capitalism under which people compete freely, with minimal government intervention in the economy. (p. 343)

Monarchy   A form of government headed by a single member of a royal family, usually a king, queen, or count some other hereditary ruler. (p. 350)

Monopoly   Control of a market by a single business firm. (p. 343)

Offshoring   The transfer of work to foreign contractors. (p. 364)

Oligarchy   A form of government in which a few individuals rule. (p. 350)

Peace   The absence of war; or a proactive effort to develop cooperative relations among nations. (p. 357)

Pluralist model   A view of society in which many competing groups within the community have access to government, so that no single group is dominant. (p. 356)

Political system   The social institution that is founded on a recognized set of procedures for implementing and achieving society's goals. (p. 342)

Politics   In Harold Lasswell's words, "who gets what, when, and how." (p. 348)

Power   The ability to exercise one's will over others. (p. 348)

Power elite   A small group of individuals who share a common set of political and economic interests. (p. 355)

Rational-legal authority   Power made legitimate by law. (p. 349)

Representative democracy   A form of government in which certain individuals are selected to speak for the people. (p. 351)

Socialism   An economic system under which the means of production and distribution are collectively owned. (p. 344)

Terrorism   The use or threat of violence against random or symbolic targets in pursuit of political aims. (p. 358)

Totalitarianism   Virtually complete government control and surveillance over all aspects of a society's social and political life. (p. 350)

Traditional authority   Legitimate power conferred by custom and accepted practice. (p. 349)

Underground economy   See **informal economy**.

War   Conflict between organizations that possess trained combat forces equipped with deadly weapons. (p. 357)

Additional Readings

Dyck, Rand. 2006. *Canadian Politics*, concise 3rd ed. Scarborough, ON: Nelson Publishing. A comprehensive overview of Canadian politics that includes coverage of political culture, socialization, and participation, as well as the mass media and public opinion polls.

Kloby, Jerry. 2003. *Inequality, Power, and Development: Issues in Political Sociology.* Amherst, NY: Prometheus Books. An examination of the relationship between transnational corporate exploitation, Western political institutions, free trade, and international financial institutions.

Knuttila, Murray, and Wendee Kubik. 2000. *State Theories: Classical, Global, and Feminist Perspectives*, 3rd ed. Halifax, NS: Fernwood Publishers. A review of various perspectives on the state.

Shalla, Vivian (ed.). 2006. *Working in a Global Era: Canadian Perspectives.* Toronto: CSPI/WP. A collection of readings on the role of Canadian labour in the global working world, written from a critical perspective.

 ## Online Learning Centre

Visit the *Sociology: A Brief Introduction* Online Learning Centre at www.mcgrawhill.ca/olc/schaefer to access quizzes, interactive exercises, video clips, and other research and study tools related to this chapter.

 ## Reel Society Video Clips

Reel Society can be used to spark discussion about the following topics from this chapter:

- Power and authority
- Economic systems
- The changing economy

chapter 15

POPULATION, HEALTH, AND COMMUNITIES

This Chinese billboard promotes the government's policy of allowing only one child per family. For several decades, the People's Republic of China has been struggling with a population explosion that threatens to outstrip the nation's ability to provide for all its citizens.

- ☐ **What is Demography?**
- ☐ **What are the Patterns of World Population?**
- ☐ **What are the Fertility Patterns in Canada?**
- ☐ **What is Social Epidemiology?**
- ☐ **What are the Sociological Perspectives on Health and Illness?**
- ☐ **What is the Health-Care Situation in Canada?**
- ☐ **How have Communities Changed?**
- ☐ **What is Urbanization, and What are its Consequences?**
- ☐ **What are some Types of Communities?**

Boxes

SOCIOLOGY IN THE GLOBAL COMMUNITY: Population Policy in China
RESEARCH IN ACTION: The Store Wars
SOCIAL POLICY AND HEALTH: The AIDS Crisis

Tent City is not a city and we don't live in tents. We live in shacks and shanties on the edge of Canada's largest metropolis where the river meets the lake. There's a fence dividing these 27 acres from the rest of Toronto, and on this side we've built what dwellings we can with the rubble of the scrap yard, a no-man's landfill caught in confusion between the city and private business. Sometimes it seems like a community and sometimes like chaos. Junk Town would be a better name.

Picture a dump, littered with cast-outs of the last millennium. Refrigerators, stuffed animals, shoes, original paintings on torn canvasses, photo albums, three hundred broken bicycles and toboggans and hockey sticks. Televisions and microwaves, lamps and cash registers, headless Cabbage Patch Kids and enough books to start a library or a bookstore or your own education.

Now picture dozens of the country's thieves and drug addicts, vagabonds, and ex-cons. They're drunk, hungry and tired of running. It's getting old and getting cold, and one night they find themselves in this place, with the rest of the discards, on the edge of the world but smack in the middle of it all.

They look around and realize that everything they've been hustling for is right here: stereos and VCRs, room to move, a perfect hideout and waterfront property. They aren't way out in the lonesome countryside or the goddamn suburbs or trapped in the same old city. In fact, the city looks perfect from here—the lake, the downtown high-rises, the sun setting beneath the tallest free-standing structure in the world—it's like a picture postcard. And best of all, there are no laws and no cops—as long as they stay on this side of the fence. It's all private property. No one can tell them what to do, no one but Home Depot, the company that owns the land.

So they dig into a corner of the rubble for something they can use to build. There's so much, they could make anything. But for now they just throw together a few shelters using tarps and old office furniture. They buy some beer, light a fire, call it Tent City and decide to stay. The smoke rises for everyone to see, like a warning or an invitation. They drink and wait.

For almost four years people have been squatting here, and now some days the population reaches sixty or so. The singularity of this place has drawn media attention from all over the world, as well as a flood of well-meaning, but mostly redundant, donations—if only salvation could be bought with wool hats and toothbrushes. This remains, as much as such a thing is possible, a society of anarchy.

The rules are made up nightly. Repercussions are rarely considered in advance, or recorded for future reference. It is a useful, using and sometimes useless place. The castoffs of the megacity are snatched up, played with, eaten, worn, painted over and tossed into the mud. China plates are disposable, pillowcases never washed. If this place has a credo, it is: Grab what you can, stay drunk and mind your own damn business.

The protocol for moving into Tent City is one of invitation or recommendation. I unknowingly broke protocol. I came without a clue and nothing to lose, to learn about this place, write a book and lie [down] rent free. During the month I've spent so far, I've realized there is no way to live here and a hundred possible stories to be written. Some people beg, some squeegee windows, some steal, some work jobs, some sell themselves, sell others, sell drugs. Most do drugs, some do nothing at all. I don't yet know what I'm going to do.

□ *(Bishop-Stall 2004)*

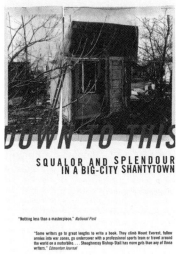

SHAUGHNESSY BISHOP-STALL

DOWN TO THIS

SQUALOR AND SPLENDOUR IN A BIG-CITY SHANTYTOWN

"Nothing less than a masterpiece." *National Post*

"Some writers go to great lengths to write a book. They climb Mount Everest, follow armies into war zones, go undercover with a professional sports team or travel around the world on a motorbike. . . . Shaughnessy Bishop-Stall has more guts than any of those writers." *Edmonton Journal*

This selection from Shaughnessy Bishop-Stall's *Down to This: Squalor and Splendour in a Big-City Shantytown* highlights the coexistence of wealth and poverty within a confined urban area—in this particular case, Toronto. The former "Tent City," as it was known, was littered with the excesses and throwaways of our consumer culture—children's toys, bikes, and electronics—and was inhabited by people drawn there for a variety of reasons. All the residents, however, shared the condition of being marginalized by the larger society. Some were dealing drugs, begging, or squeegeeing windows, and others were working in low-paying jobs. The residents formed their own community on land owned by Home Depot and filled it with shacks and shanties on the edge of what social commentators have often called "Toronto the Good."

In this chapter, we explore communities of all sorts, from rural towns to inner-city neighbourhoods and the suburbs that surround them. In sociological terms, a **community** may be defined as a spatial or political unit of social organization that gives people a sense of belonging. The sense of belonging can be based either on shared residence in a particular city or neighbourhood, such as Tent City, or on a common identity, such as that of homeless people, street vendors, or gays and lesbians. Whatever the members have in common, communities give people the feeling that they are part of something larger than themselves (Dotson 1991; see also Hillery 1955).

Communities are deeply affected by the two other topics covered in this chapter: health and population patterns. Population patterns determine which communities will grow and prosper and which will wither and die. Population patterns can also promote or undermine the health of those who live in communities. How is the world's population changing, and what effect will it have on our communities? Throughout the world, why have large communities grown at the expense of small villages? How do a population's health and well-being vary from one community to another and from one part of the world to another?

In this chapter, we try to answer these questions by taking a sociological overview of the world's population and its effects on our communities and health. We begin with Thomas Robert Malthus's analysis of population trends and Karl Marx's critical response. Brief overviews of population and fertility patterns follow, with particular emphasis on the current problem of overpopulation. Next, we trace the development of communities from pre-industrial cities to the birth of the modern megalopolis. We consider two different views of urbanization, one stressing its functions and the other its dysfunctions. And we compare three very different types of communities: the city, the suburb, and the rural area. Finally, we see how functionalists, conflict theorists, interactionists, and feminist theorists study health issues. We discover that the distribution of disease in a population varies with social class, race and ethnicity, gender, and age. In the social policy section that closes the chapter, we explore the most pressing health problem in the world today: the AIDS crisis.

> **Use Your Sociological Imagination**
>
> Do you think that communities such as Tent City are an inevitable part of big-city neighbourhoods?

☐ WHAT IS DEMOGRAPHY?

The study of population issues engages the attention of both natural and social scientists. The biologist explores the nature of reproduction and casts light on factors that affect **fertility**, the level of reproduction among women of child-bearing age. The medical pathologist examines and analyzes trends in the causes of death. Geographers, historians, and psychologists also have distinctive contributions to make to our understanding of population. Sociologists, more than these other researchers, focus on the *social* factors that influence population rates and trends.

In their study of population issues, sociologists are keenly aware that various elements of population—such as fertility and **mortality** (the amount of death)—are profoundly affected by the norms, values, and social patterns of a society. Fertility is influenced by people's age of entry into sexual unions and by their use of contraception—both of which, in turn, reflect the social and religious values that guide a particular culture. Mortality is shaped by a nation's level of nutrition, acceptance of immunization, and provisions for sanitation, as well as its general commitment to health care and health education. Migration from one country to another can depend on marital and kinship ties, the relative degree of tolerance of diversity in various societies, and people's evaluations of employment opportunities.

Demography is the scientific study of population. It draws on several components of population, including size, composition, and territorial distribution, to understand the social consequences of population. Demographers study geographical variations and historical trends in their effort to develop population forecasts. They also analyze the structure of a population—the age, gender, race, and ethnicity of its members. A key figure in this type of analysis was Thomas Robert Malthus.

Malthus's Thesis and Marx's Response

The Reverend Thomas Robert Malthus (1766–1834) was educated at Cambridge University in Britain and spent his life teaching history and political economy. He strongly criticized two major institutions of his time— the church and slavery—yet his most significant legacy for contemporary scholars is his still-controversial *Essays on the Principle of Population*, published in 1798.

Essentially, Malthus held that the world's population was growing more rapidly than the available food supply. Malthus argued that the food supply increases in an arithmetic progression (1, 2, 3, 4, and so on), whereas the population expands by a geometric progression (1, 2, 4, 8, and so on). According to his analysis, the gap between the food supply and the population will continue to grow over time. Even though the food supply will increase, it will not increase nearly enough to meet the needs of an expanding world population.

Malthus advocated population control to close the gap between the rising population and the food supply, yet he explicitly denounced artificial means of birth control because they were not sanctioned by religion. For Malthus, the appropriate way to control population was to postpone marriage. He argued that couples must take responsibility for the number of children they choose to bear; without such restraint, the world would face widespread hunger, poverty, and misery (Malthus, Huxley, and Osborn 1960, original edition 1824; Petersen 1979). Today, Malthus's ideas have spawned a legacy of population policies that facilitate racial inequality, class exploitation, and gender subordination (Kuumba 1999).

Karl Marx strongly criticized Malthus's views on population. Marx pointed to the nature of economic relations in Europe's industrial societies as the central problem. He could not accept the Malthusian notion that a rising world population, rather than capitalism, was the cause of social ills. In Marx's opinion, there was no special relationship between world population figures and the supply of resources (including food). If society were well ordered, increases in population should lead to greater wealth, not to hunger and misery.

Of course, Marx did not believe that capitalism operated under these ideal conditions. He maintained that capitalism devoted its resources to the financing of buildings and tools rather than to more equitable distribution of food, housing, and other necessities of life. Marx's work is important to the study of population because he linked overpopulation to the unequal distribution of resources—a topic that will be taken up again later in this chapter. His concern with the writings of Malthus also testifies to the importance of population in political and economic affairs.

The insights of Malthus and Marx regarding population issues have come together in what is termed the *neo-Malthusian view*. Best exemplified by the work of Paul Ehrlich (1968; Ehrlich and Ehrlich 1990), author of *The Population Bomb*, neo-Malthusians agree with Malthus that world population growth is outstretching natural resources. However, in contrast to the British theorist, they insist that birth-control measures are needed to regulate population increases. Neo-Malthusians have a Marxist flavour in their condemnation of developed nations that, despite their low birth rates, consume a disproportionately large share of world resources. Although rather pessimistic about the future, these theorists do see a way forward and stress that birth control and sensible use of resources are essential responses to rising world population (Tierney 1990; Weeks 2002; for a critique, see Commoner 1971).

Studying Population Today

The relative balance of births and deaths is no less important today than it was during the lifetime of Malthus and Marx. The suffering that Malthus spoke of is certainly a reality for many people of the world who are hungry and poor. Malnutrition remains the largest contributing factor to illness and death among children in the developing countries. Almost 18 percent of these children will die before age 5—a rate more than 11 times higher than in developed nations. Warfare and large-scale migration intensify problems of population and food supply. For example, strife in Bosnia, Iraq, and Sudan caused very uneven distribution of food supplies, leading to regional concerns about malnutrition and even starvation. Combatting world hunger may require reducing human births, dramatically increasing the world's food supply, or perhaps both at the same time. The study of population-related issues, then, seems to be essential.

In Canada and most other countries, the census is the primary mechanism for collecting population information.

A **census** is an enumeration or counting of a population. The Constitution Act of Canada requires that a full census be held every 10 years to determine the breakdown of ridings by province/territory represented in the House of Commons. The five-year census, which is mandated by Statistics Canada, provides the basis for government policies and decision making for social programs, such as housing, health care, daycare, and federal–provincial/territorial transfer payments. The questions asked on the census reflect changing social and political patterns and reveal the dynamic nature of Canadian society. Table 15-1 shows some of the milestones of the Canadian census that demonstrate changing values and attitudes on such matters as unpaid work, common-law and same-sex partnerships, and fertility of those who have mental illnesses. As well, the study of our population is supplemented by vital statistics; these records of births, deaths, marriages, and divorces are gathered through a registration system maintained by governments. In addition, Statistics Canada provides up-to-date information based on surveys of such topics as educational trends, the status of women, children, racial and ethnic minorities, agricultural crops, medical care, and time spent on leisure and recreational activities, to name only a few.

In administering a nationwide census and conducting other types of research, demographers employ many of the skills and techniques described in Chapter 2, including questionnaires, interviews, and sampling. The precision of population projections depends on the accuracy of a series of estimates that demographers must make. First, they must determine past population trends and establish a base population as of the date at which the forecast began. Next, birth rates and death rates must be established, along with estimates of future fluctuations. In making projections for a nation's population trends, demographers must consider migration as well, since a significant number of individuals may enter and leave a country.

Elements of Demography

Demographers communicate population facts with a language derived from the basic elements of human life—birth and death. The **birth rate** (or, more specifically, the *crude birth rate*) is the number of live births per 1000 population in a given year. In 2005, for example, there were an estimated 10.84 live births per 1000 people in Canada. The birth rate provides information on the actual reproductive patterns of a society.

One way demography can project future growth in a society is to make use of the **total fertility rate (TFR)**. The TFR is the average number of children born alive to any woman, assuming that she conforms to current fertility rates. The TFR estimated for Canada in 2005 was 1.53 live births per woman, as compared with nearly 6 births per woman in a developing country, such as Niger.

Table 15-1　Selected Milestones in the History of the Census in Canada

1921:	The population questions no longer include those on "insanity and idiocy" and fertility.
1931:	Questions are added to gauge the extent and severity of unemployment, and to analyze its causes.
1956:	The first five-year national census is conducted. It is introduced to monitor the rapid economic growth and urbanization that took place during the postwar years.
1971:	The majority of respondents now complete the census questionnaire themselves, a process called *self-enumeration*. Under the new Statistics Act, it becomes a statutory requirement to hold censuses of population and of agriculture every five years.
1986:	The Census of Population contains a question on disability, which is also used to establish a sample of respondents for the first post-censal survey on activity limitation. Also for the first time, the Census of Agriculture asks a question on computer use for farm management.
1991:	For the first time, the census asks a question on common-law relationships.
1996:	A question on unpaid work is included in the census.
2001:	The definition of *common-law* is expanded to include both opposite-sex and same-sex partners. Also, the Census of Agriculture asks about production of certified organic products.
2006:	A question on where individuals received their highest level of education is included.

Source: Adapted from Flanders 2001:4; Statistics Canada 2006j.

Mortality, like fertility, is measured in several different ways. The **death rate** (also known as the crude death rate) is the number of deaths per 1000 population in a given year. In 2005, Canada had an estimated death rate of 7.73 per 1000 population. The **infant mortality rate** is the number of deaths of infants under one year of age per 1000 live births in a given year. This particular measure serves as an important indicator of a society's level of health care; it reflects prenatal nutrition, delivery procedures, and infant screening measures. The infant mortality rate also functions as a useful indicator of future population growth, since those infants who survive to adulthood will contribute to further population increases.

Nations vary widely in the rate of death of newborn children. In 2005, the estimated infant mortality rate for Canada was 4.75 deaths per 1000 live births, whereas for the world as a whole it was an estimated 50.11 deaths per 1000 live births. At the same time, some nations have lower rates of infant mortality than Canada, including Switzerland, Japan, and Sweden.

A general measure of health used by demographers is **life expectancy**, the median number of years a person can be expected to live under current mortality conditions. Usually the figure is reported as life expectancy at birth. At present, Japan reports a life expectancy at birth of 82 years, slightly higher than Canada's figure of 80 years. By contrast, life expectancy at birth is less than 45 years in several developing nations, including Zambia (see Figure 15-1).

The **growth rate** of a society is the difference between births and deaths, plus the difference between immigrants (those who enter a country to establish permanent residence) and emigrants (those who leave a country permanently) per 1000 population. For the world as a whole, the growth rate is simply the difference between

▶ **FIGURE 15-1**

Life Expectancy in Selected Countries

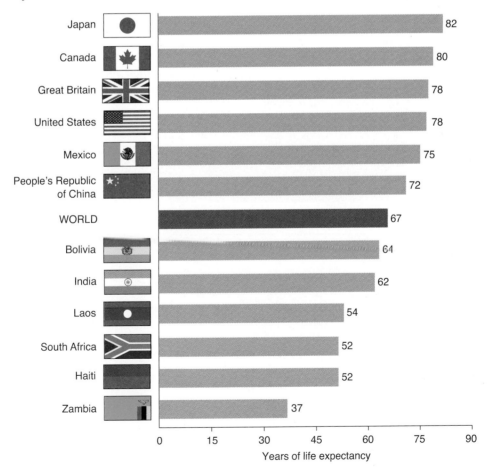

Source: Haub 2005.

births and deaths per 1000 population, since worldwide immigration and emigration must of necessity be equal. In 2007, Canada had an estimated growth rate of 1 percent, compared with an estimated 1.14 percent for the entire world (Haub 2005).

□ WHAT ARE THE PATTERNS OF WORLD POPULATION?

One important aspect of demographic work involves study of the history of population. But how is this possible? After all, official national censuses were relatively rare before 1850. Researchers interested in early population must turn to archaeological remains of settlements, burial sites, baptismal and tax records, and oral history sources.

On October 13, 1999, in a maternity clinic in Sarajevo, Bosnia-Herzegovina, Helac Fatina gave birth to a son, who has been designated as the 6 billionth person on this planet. Yet, until modern times, there were relatively few humans living in the world. One estimate placed the world population of a million years ago at only 125 000 people. As Table 15-2 indicates, the population has exploded in the past 200 years and continues to accelerate rapidly (World Health Organization 2000:3).

Demographic Transition

The phenomenal growth of the world population in recent times can be accounted for by changing patterns of births and deaths. Beginning in the late eighteenth century—and continuing until the middle of the twentieth century—there was a gradual reduction in death rates in Northern and Western Europe. People were able to live longer because of advances in food production, sanitation, nutrition, and public health care. Although death rates fell, birth rates remained high; as a result, there was unprecedented population growth during this period of European history. However, by the late nineteenth century, the birth rates of many European countries began to decline, and the rate of population growth also decreased (Bender and Smith 1997).

The changes in birth rates and death rates in nineteenth-century Europe serve as an example of *demographic transition*. Demographers use this term to describe an observed pattern in changing vital statistics. Specifically, **demographic transition** is the change from high birth rates and death rates to relatively low birth rates and death rates. This concept, which was introduced in the 1920s, is now widely used in the study of population trends.

As illustrated in Figure 15-2, demographic transition is typically viewed as a three-stage process:

1. *Pre-transition stage:* high birth rates and death rates with little population growth
2. *Transition stage:* declining death rates, primarily the result of reductions in infant deaths, along with high to medium fertility—resulting in significant population growth
3. *Post-transition stage:* low birth rates and death rates with little population growth

---

Table 15-2 Estimated Time for Each Successive Increase of One Billion People in World Population

Population Level	Time Taken to Reach New Population Level	Year of Attainment
First billion	Human history before 1800	1804
Second billion	123 years	1927
Third billion	32 years	1959
Fourth billion	15 years	1974
Fifth billion	13 years	1987
Sixth billion	12 years	1999
Seventh billion	13 years	2012
Eighth billion	15 years	2027
Ninth billion	18 years	2045

Source: Bureau of the Census 2005f.

▶ **FIGURE 15-2**

Demographic Transition

Demographers use the concept of *demographic transition* to describe changes in birth rates and death rates during stages of a nation's development. This graph shows the pattern that took place in developed nations. In the first stage, both birth rates and death rates were high, so that there was little population growth. In the second stage, the birth rate remained high while the death rate declined sharply, which led to rapid population growth. By the last stage, which many developing countries have yet to enter, the birth rate also declined and there was again little population growth.

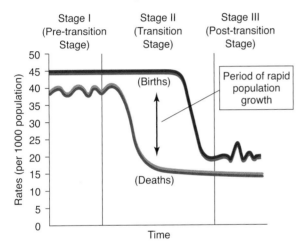

Demographic transition should be regarded not as a "law of population growth" but rather as a generalization of the population history of industrial nations. This concept helps us understand the growth problems faced by the world in the 1990s. About two-thirds of the world's nations have yet to pass fully through the second stage of demographic transition. Even if such nations make dramatic advances in fertility control, their populations will nevertheless increase greatly because of the large base of people already at prime child-bearing age.

The pattern of demographic transition varies from nation to nation. One particularly useful distinction is the contrast between the transition now occurring in developing nations—which include roughly two-thirds of the world's population—and that which occurred over almost a century in more industrialized countries. Demographic transition in developing nations has involved a rapid decline in death rates without adjustments in birth rates.

Specifically, in the post–World War II period, the death rates of developing nations began a sharp decline. This revolution in "death control" was triggered by antibiotics, immunization, insecticides (such as DDT, used

to strike at malaria-bearing mosquitoes), and largely successful campaigns against such fatal diseases as smallpox. Substantial medical and public health technology was imported almost overnight from more developed nations. As a result, the drop in death rates that had taken a century to happen in Europe was telescoped into two decades in many developing countries.

Birth rates had time to adjust. Cultural beliefs about the proper size of families could not possibly change as quickly as the falling death rates. For centuries, couples had given birth to as many as eight or more children, knowing that perhaps only two or three would survive to adulthood. Families were more willing to accept technological advances that prolonged life than to abandon fertility patterns that reflected centuries of tradition and religious training. The result over time was a huge increase in the global population.

Throughout the world, population patterns vary widely. As this scene in Warsaw, Poland, suggests, Eastern Europe has been losing population as the birth rate falls and young people emigrate to other countries. In Africa, by contrast, the population is growing. Over the next four decades, Somalia is expected to double in population.

Sociology in the Global Community
Population Policy in China

Recently, in a residential district in Shanghai, a member of the local family-planning committee knocks on the door of a childless couple. Why, she inquires, have they not started a family?

Such a question would have been unthinkable in 1979, when family-planning officials, in an attempt to avoid a looming population explosion, began resorting to sterilization to enforce the government rule of one child per family. Since then, the government has quietly begun to grant exceptions to the one-child policy to adults who are offspring of only-child families. In 2002, Chinese authorities extended the privilege to all families, but at a price. A new family-planning law imposes "social compensation fees" to cover the cost to society of an additional child. The fee, which is substantial, is equivalent to 20 years' worth of a rural farm family's income.

Chinese families are beset, too, by the unforeseen results of their attempts to circumvent the one-child policy. In the past, in an effort to ensure that their one child would be a male capable of perpetuating the family line, many couples chose to abort female fetuses, or quietly allowed female infants to die of neglect. As a result, among children 1 to 4 years old, China's sex ratio (the ratio of males to females) is now about 119 to 100—well above the normal rate at birth of 105 to 100. The difference in birth rates translates into 1.7 million fewer

Sources: Glenn 2004; N. Riley 2004; Yardley 2005.

female births per year than normal—and, down the line, into many fewer child-bearers than normal.

As a result of the rising sex ratio, Chinese officials have begun to worry about a future with too few women. The government now pays the parents of daughters to speak with other parents in an attempt to persuade them to raise girls. Officials have also increased the criminal penalties doctors face for performing prenatal scans and aborting pregnancies for the purpose of sex selection.

Another legacy of the one-child policy is a shortage of caregivers for the elderly. Coupled with improvements in longevity, the generation-long decline in births has greatly increased the ratio of dependent elders to able-bodied children. The migration of young adults to other parts of China has further compromised the care of the elderly. To compound the crisis, barely one in four of China's elders receives any pension at all. No other country in the world faces the prospect of caring for such a large population of seniors with so little social support.

Applying Theory

1. How would a conflict perspective contribute to your understanding of the one-child policy in China?
2. What issues or topics might you raise as a sociologist examining this policy?

The Population Explosion

Apart from war, rapid population growth has been perhaps the dominant international social problem of the past 40 years. Often, this issue is referred to in emotional terms as the "population bomb" or the "population explosion." Such striking language is not surprising, given the staggering increases in world population during the twentieth century (refer to Table 15-2). The population of our planet rose from 1 billion around the year 1800 to 6.4 billion by 2005.

By the middle 1970s, demographers had observed a slight decline in the growth rate of many developing nations (Kent and Haub 2005). These countries were still experiencing population increases, yet their *rates* of increase had declined as death rates could not go much

lower and birth rates began to fall. It appears that family-planning efforts have been instrumental in this demographic change. Beginning in the 1960s, governments in certain developing nations sponsored or supported campaigns to encourage family planning. For example, in good part as the result of government-sponsored birth-control campaigns, Thailand's total fertility rate fell from 6.1 births per woman in 1970 to only 1.7 in 2005. And China's strict one-child policy resulted in a *negative* growth rate in some urban areas; see the accompanying Box 15-1.

Through the efforts of many governments (among them Canada's) and private agencies (such as Planned Parenthood), the fertility rates of many developing countries have declined. However, some critics, reflecting a

▶ **FIGURE 15-3**

Population Structure of Canada and Kenya, 2007 (estimated)

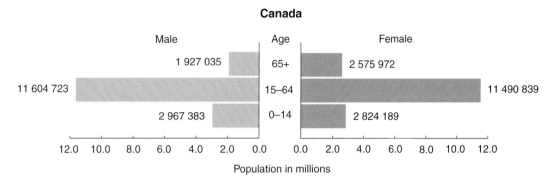

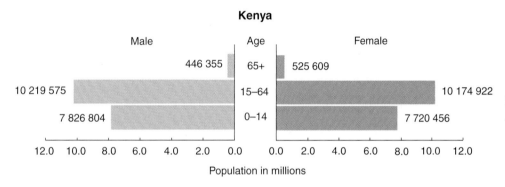

Source: Central Intelligence Agency 2007.

conflict perspective, have questioned why Canada and other industrialized nations are so enthusiastic about population control in the developing world. In line with Marx's response to Malthus, they argue that large families and even population growth are not the causes of hunger and misery. Rather, the unjust economic domination by the developed countries of the world results in an unequal distribution of world resources and in widespread poverty in exploited developing nations (Fornos 1997).

Even if family-planning efforts are successful in reducing fertility rates, the momentum toward a growing world population is well established. The developing nations face the prospect of continued population growth, since a substantial proportion of their population is approaching child-bearing years. This is evident in Figure 15-3, comparing the population structures of Canada and Kenya.

A **population pyramid** or population structure is a special type of bar chart that distributes the population by gender and age; it is generally used to illustrate the population structure of a society. As Figure 15-3 shows, a substantial portion of the population of Kenya consists of children under the age of 15, whose child-

bearing years are still to come. Thus, the built-in momentum for population growth is much greater in Kenya (and in many developing countries in other parts of the world) than in Western Europe or Canada.

Consider also India, which, in 2000, surpassed 1 billion in population. At some point between the years 2040 and 2050, India's population will surpass China's. The substantial momentum for growth built into India's age structure means that the nation will face a staggering increase in population in the coming decades—even if its birth rate declines sharply (Population Reference Bureau 2004).

Population growth is not a problem in all nations. Its effects, however, as feminist thinkers have pointed out, are undoubtedly gendered. A handful of countries are even adopting policies that *encourage* growth. Some of these countries include Russia, France, and Japan, where total fertility rates have fallen sharply. Nevertheless, a global perspective underscores the serious consequences that could result from overall continued population growth.

A tragic new factor has emerged in the last two decades that will restrict worldwide population growth: the spread of HIV/AIDS. Currently, about 39 million people around the world are infected with the HIV virus. According to the United Nations, 4.9 million people were newly infected with the virus in 2004. Of that number, 47 percent were women. In sub-Saharan Africa, the hardest-hit region with 25.4 million people infected, 57 percent are women between the ages of 15 and 49. Women are disproportionately affected because of such factors as sexual violence, less access to education, and lack of power to refuse sexual contact or insist on condom use (United Nations 2004). As a result of the increasing number of the disease's implications for women, the reality of the "feminization of AIDS" has been acknowledged by academics, politicians, and journalists alike. The social policy section at the end of this chapter considers the AIDS crisis and the devastating effects on African communities.

☐ WHAT ARE THE FERTILITY PATTERNS IN CANADA?

During the past four decades, Canada and other industrial nations have passed through two different patterns of population growth—the first marked by high fertility and rapid growth (stage II in the theory of demographic transition), the second marked by declining fertility and little growth (stage III). Sociologists are keenly aware of the social impact of these fertility patterns.

The Baby Boom

The most recent period of high fertility in Canada has often been referred to as the *baby boom*. The return of soldiers after World War II, high wages, and general prosperity during the postwar period encouraged many married couples to have children and purchase homes. In addition, several sociologists—as well as feminist author Betty Friedan (1963)—have noted that there were pervasive pressures on women during the 1950s to marry and become mothers and homemakers (Bouvier 1980).

The dramatic increase in births between 1946 and 1966 produced an age cohort in Canada that made up approximately one-third of the population. By the end of the boom in 1966, the age structure reflected a young, dependent population with a high percentage of Canadians under 15 years of age. As the baby boomers have aged, society has responded to their needs in education, recreation, consumer preferences, housing, and so on. Now, a significant challenge to society is to meet the needs of aging baby boomers as they begin to require greater medical attention at a time when health-care resources are severely strained.

Use Your Sociological Imagination

The country you are living in is so heavily populated that basic resources, such as food, water, and living space, are running short. What will you do? How will you respond to the crisis if you are a government social planner? a politician?

Stable Population Growth

Although the total fertility rate of Canada has remained low in the past two decades, the nation continues to grow in size because of two factors: the momentum built into our age structure by the postwar population boom and immigration. In 2005, Canada's fertility rate was 1.54 children per woman, below the 2.1 children needed to sustain the population (Statistics Canada 2007a). Despite low levels of fertility, Canada's population grew 5.4 percent between 2001 and 2006. This growth of population represented, in part, a demographic "echo" of the baby boom generation, many of whom are now parents (with some even inching closer to the traditional retirement age of 65). Because of the upsurge of births beginning in the late 1940s—in 1956, the fertility rate in Canada was 4 children per woman—there were, between 2001 and 2006, more people in their child-bearing years than in older age groups (where most deaths occur). Most of the growth, however, was due to international migration to Canada (Weeks 2007).

In the 1980s and early 1990s, some analysts projected that there would be relatively low fertility levels and moderate net migration over the coming decades. As a result, it seemed possible that Canada might reach **zero population growth (ZPG)** in the near future. Zero population growth is the state of a population in which the number of births plus immigrants equals the number of deaths plus emigrants. In the recent past, although some nations have achieved ZPG, it has been relatively short-lived. Yet, today, 78 countries—including all 42 in Europe—are showing a *decline* in population (Haub 2004; Longman 2004).

What would a Canadian society with stable population growth be like? In demographic terms, it would be quite different from the Canada we live in today. There would be relatively equal numbers of people in each age group, and the median age of the population would be higher.

By 2026, the percentage of Canadians age 65 and older would increase to 21.2 percent from 13.2 percent in 2006 (Canadian Press 2007). Based on this projection, the population pyramid of Canada would look more like a rectangle. There would also be a much larger proportion of older people, especially age 75 and over. They would place a greater demand on the nation's social-service programs and health-care institutions. As the population ages, many predict that labour shortages will occur. Occupations that are likely to be in demand include skilled and technical trade workers, teachers, health-care workers, information technology experts, and academics (Armstrong 2002).

The economy would be less volatile under ZPG, since the number of entrants into the paid labour force would remain stable. Zero population growth would also lead to changes in family life. With fertility rates declining, women would devote fewer years to child-rearing and to the social roles of motherhood; the proportion of married women entering the labour force would continue to rise (Spengler 1978; Weeks 2002).

According to the latest United States Census Bureau projections, the United States is *not* moving toward ZPG. Instead, the U.S. population is growing faster than was expected. Previous projections indicated that the U.S. population would stabilize between 290 million and 300 million by the middle of this century, but demographers now believe that by 2050, the population of the United States will reach 391 million. In contrast to Canada where most of the population increase was due to international migration, the United States owes its population rise to natural increase, where the number of births exceeded the number of deaths (Weeks 2007).

Canada's actual rate of population growth between 2001 and 2006 was the highest of all the G-8 industrialized countries. As you can see, population growth owes much to the age structure of a given region or country.

An Aging Canadian Population

As an index of aging, the United Nations uses the proportion of individuals 65 years of age and older to classify a population as "young," "mature," or "aged" (McVey and Kalbach 1995). A population is "young" if its proportion of older adults is under 4 percent; it is considered "mature" if its proportion of those 65 years of age and older is between 4 and 8 percent; and it is considered "aged" if this age group makes up 8 percent or more (McVey and Kalbach 1995). Canada became an "aged" population according to census data by 1971, when 8.1 percent of Canadians were 65 years of age and older. By 2006, 13.7 percent of the population were 65 years of age and older, following a steady increase of the proportion of this group in the total population (Statistics Canada 2007j). According to population projections, the numbers of seniors in Canada could double in the next 25 years (Statistics Canada 2007j).

National averages of aging, however, mask great diversity within Canada as it relates to such factors as region, gender, race, and ethnicity. There is a vast variation among regions in the percentage of the older age group, resulting in some regions being classified as "aged" populations while others are considered "young." According to the 2006 census, Saskatchewan, for example, has the oldest population, with 15.4 percent of its population 65 years of age or older, while Nunavut has the youngest population, with only 2.7 percent of their residents 65 years of age or older. Although Canada's overall population is aging, regional responses in the form of specialized housing, health care, caregiving services, and other social services may vary.

Gender differences sharply punctuate overall rates of aging in Canadian society. The proportion of older women in Canada has been increasing steadily since 1961. Given women's greater life expectancy, they constitute a disproportionate number of the aged. Because of women's lower average incomes and overall financial security, they are more likely to experience poverty than their male counterparts. The feminization of poverty, then, is accentuated by an aging population of which women make up a disproportionately high number. Although some may view their greater life expectancy as a positive gain, for many women, particularly immigrants, women of colour, Aboriginal women, and those of lower social class, living longer means an even greater chance of living in poverty. Aboriginal men and women are more likely to suffer from poor health and have lower life expectancies because of the prevailing conditions of poverty in their lives. This situation will be discussed in more detail in the upcoming sections on health.

☐ WHAT IS SOCIAL EPIDEMIOLOGY?

Social epidemiology is the study of the distribution of disease, impairment, and general health status across a population. In the preamble to its 1946 constitution, the World Health Organization (WHO) defined **health** as a "state of complete physical, mental, and social well-being, and not merely the absence of disease and infirmity" (Leavell and Clark 1965:14). Epidemiology initially concentrated on the scientific study of epidemics (and, more largely, pandemics), focusing on how they started and spread. Contemporary social epidemiology is much broader in scope, concerned not only with epidemics but also with non-epidemic diseases, injuries, drug addiction and alcoholism, suicide, and mental illness. Epidemiology draws on the work of a wide variety of scientists and researchers, among them physicians, sociologists, public health officials, biologists, veterinarians, demographers, anthropologists, psychologists, and meteorologists.

Researchers in social epidemiology commonly use two concepts: incidence and prevalence. **Incidence** refers to the number of *new* cases of a specific disorder occurring within a given population during a stated period of time, usually a year. For example, the incidence of HIV in Canada in 2005 was 2518 cases. By contrast, **prevalence** refers to the total number of cases of a specific disorder that exist at a given time. The prevalence of HIV in Canada in 2006 was about 61 000 cases (Public Health Agency of Canada 2006).

When incidence figures are presented as rates, or as the number of reports per 100 000 people, they are called **morbidity rates**. (The term **mortality rate**, you will recall, refers to the incidence of *death* in a given population.) Sociologists find morbidity rates useful because they reveal that a specific disease occurs more frequently among one segment of a population than another. As we will see, social class, race, ethnicity, gender, and age can all affect a population's morbidity rates.

Social Class

Social class is clearly associated with differences in morbidity and mortality rates. Studies in Canada and other countries have consistently shown that people in the lower classes have higher rates of mortality and disability. Health Canada has identified 12 determinants of health, which include income and social status, employment, education, gender, and culture (see Table 15-3).

Table 15-3 Twelve Determinants of Health Identified by Health Canada

- Income and social status
- Employment and working conditions
- Education
- Social environments
- Physical environments
- Healthy child development
- Personal health practices and coping skills
- Health services
- Social support networks
- Biology and genetic endowment
- Gender
- Culture

Source: Health Canada 2002.

Although available data do suggest the relationship between health and social class, they mask the vast diversity within Canada. For example, because social class, race, and gender intersect, Aboriginal women are affected by poor health to a much greater degree than non-Aboriginal women. Aboriginal women, who, on average, have lower incomes, were almost three times as likely to report a heart problem in 1997 as were all other Canadian women. As well, Aboriginal women have rates of suicide three times as high as those of non-Aboriginal women (Aboriginal Women's Health and Healing Research Group 2007).

Numerous studies document the impact of social class on health. An examination of data from 11 countries in North America and Europe found strong associations between household income and health, and between household income and life expectancy, when comparing families of similar size. Researchers from the Harvard School of Public Health found that higher overall mortality rates—as well as higher incidence of infant mortality and deaths from coronary heart disease, cancer, and homicide—were associated with lower incomes.

Why is class linked to health? Crowded living conditions, substandard housing, poor diet, and stress all contribute to the ill health of many low-income people in Canada. In certain instances, limited education and literacy may lead to a lack of awareness of measures necessary to maintain good health.

Another factor in the link between class and health is evident at the workplace: the occupations of people in the working and lower classes of Canada tend to be more dangerous than those of more affluent citizens. Miners, for example, must face the possibility of injury or death from explosions and cave-ins; they are also likely to develop respiratory diseases, such as black lung. Workers in textile mills may contract a variety of illnesses caused by exposure to toxic substances, including one disease commonly known as brown lung disease (R. Hall 1982). In recent years, the nation has learned of the perils of asbestos poisoning, a particular worry for construction workers.

In the view of Karl Marx and other contemporary conflict theorists, capitalist societies, such as Canada, would be seen as caring more about maximizing profits than about the health and safety of industrial workers. As a result, government agencies do not take forceful action to regulate conditions in the workplace, and workers suffer many preventable, job-related injuries and illnesses.

Research also shows that the lower classes are more vulnerable to environmental pollution than the affluent; this is the case not only where the lower classes work but also where they live (Moffatt 1995).

Sociologists Link and Phelan maintain that socioeconomic status is "a fundamental cause of disease" since it is linked to access to resources "that can be used to avoid risks or minimize the consequences of disease once it occurs… resources that include money, knowledge, power, prestige and kinds of interpersonal resources embodied in the concepts of social support and social network" (Link and Phelan 1995:87).

Race and Ethnicity

Health profiles of many racial and ethnic minorities reflect the social inequality evident in Canada. The most glaring examples of the relationship between race and ethnicity and health can be found within Canada's Aboriginal communities. The health of Aboriginal people reflects patterns of exclusion, past and present, that have limited and continue to limit their access to many of the social determinants of health—such determinants as income, employment, education, and literacy. Aboriginal people not only experience a lack of material resources but also face limited opportunities, isolation, discrimination, and racism.

A 1996 study prepared at the request of the Canadian Task Force on the Periodic Health Examination concluded that Aboriginal people "sustain a disproportionate share of the burden of physical disease and mental illness" (MacMillan, Offord, and Dingle 1996:1569). Many Aboriginal populations have an increased risk of death from alcoholism, homicide, suicide, and pneumonia; overall death rates for both men and women are higher among the Aboriginal population than their counterparts in the wider Canadian population (Health Canada 2006). Rates of tuberculosis (TB) in on-reserve First Nations communities are 8 to 10 times higher than the Canadian average (Health Canada 2006). Aboriginal communities have identified such problems as substance abuse, unemployment, suicide, and family violence as concerns affecting their members' health. The health of Aboriginal people as well as that of other disadvantaged ethnic and racial minorities is interwoven with the conditions of poverty and marginalization.

Gender

A large body of research indicates that, in comparison with men, women experience a higher prevalence of many illnesses, though they tend to live longer. Females born in 2004 have a life expectancy of 82.6 years; males born at the same time are expected to live for about 78 years. The difference in life expectancy between Canadian men and women has been attributed to such factors as risk-taking behaviour, such as drinking and dangerous driving on the part of males; levels of danger associated with male-dominated occupations, such as mining and construction; and women's tendency to use health-care services more often and at earlier stages of

their illness. The difference in life expectancy between men and women decreased to a gap of 4.8 years in 2004 from a gap of 7.4 years in 1979 (Statistics Canada 2006m). The narrowing of the gap has been attributed to a reduction of deaths because of cardiovascular disease in men, partly from a decrease in smoking. Smoking rates for women, however, have been increasing steadily for roughly three decades, contributing to higher rates of lung cancer and heart disease (Lem 2000). Many predict that the narrowing of the gender gap in life expectancy will continue in the twenty-first century because of women's changing roles and their exposure to stress, as well as the general aging of the population.

Studies suggest that the genuine differences in morbidity between women and men may be less pronounced than previously assumed (Macintyre, Hunt, and Sweeting 1996). Using the 1994 National Population Health Survey (NPHS) data, Canadian sociologists found no "clear excess of ill-health among women" (McDonough and Walters 2000:3). The researchers concluded that there is a need to further examine gender differences rather than to operate on the widely held assumption that women experience greater ill-health even though they live longer. The authors also concluded that although existing gender differences should not be minimized, for many age groups, the health of women and men is more similar than previously assumed. Other researchers argue that women are much more likely than men to seek treatment, to be diagnosed as having diseases, and thus to have their illnesses reflected in data examined by epidemiologists.

From a conflict perspective, women have been particularly vulnerable to the medicalization of society, with everything from birth to beauty treated in an increasingly medical context. Such medicalization may contribute to women's higher morbidity rates as compared with those of men. Ironically, although women have been especially affected by medicalization, medical researchers have women from clinical studies. Female physicians and researchers charge that sexism is at the heart of such research practices and insist that there is a desperate need for studies with female subjects.

Moreover, many feminist researchers state the need for greater investigation into the health effects of discrimination as a function of gender, race, sexual orientation, or disability, as well as how these variables interact to produce varying levels of health and disease. They argue that since gender is not a uniform category, research approaches are needed that will lead to a better understanding of the "dynamics of diversity" among and within the various groups of Canadian women (Vissandjee 2001:3).

Research on the relationship between culture and gender as they relate to health reveals that immigrant women's experiences differ from those that are depicted to be the Canadian "norm" (Repper et al. 1996). Certain immigrant women, for example, are less likely to participate in cancer-screening programs (e.g., mammograms and pap smears), while others with concerns arising from female genital mutilation are reluctant to consult health-care providers (Vissandjee 2001).

Despite renewed attention to women's health, recent studies confirm that women still are sometimes neglected by the medical establishment. A study published in the *Canadian Medical Association Journal* in 2007 found that seriously ill women—particularly those who are older—are about one-third less likely to be treated in an intensive care unit (ICU) than male patients with comparable conditions; women, as a result, are more likely to die of a critical illness (Picard 2007). As well, in the United States, even federally funded clinical research ignores the requirement since 1993 that their data be analyzed to see if women and men respond differently. Similarly, a content analysis of medical journals in the 1990s found that even the most recently published research focuses primarily on men—no studies excluded men, 20 percent excluded women, and another 30 percent failed to report the findings from female participants (General Accounting Office 2000; Vidaver et al. 2000).

Age

Health is the overriding concern of the elderly. Most older people in Canada report having at least one chronic illness, but only some of these conditions are potentially life threatening or require medical care. At the same time, health problems can affect the quality of life of older people in important ways. Arthritis and visual or hearing impairments can interfere with the performance of everyday tasks.

As the Canadian population ages, led by the baby boom generation, to which roughly one-third of all Canadians belong, our society will experience a greater prevalence of particular types of diseases. The Vancouver Brain Research Centre predicts that in 20 years, brain diseases, such as Alzheimer's and Parkinson's diseases, to which older people are more prone, will be the leading cause of death and disability among Canadians (Fong 2001). In Canada today, approximately 300 000 people have Alzheimer's disease, while another 100 000 have Parkinson's disease. Since the likelihood of contracting these diseases increases with age, some predict that 750 000 Canadians will be afflicted with Alzheimer's and 300 000 will have Parkinson's by 2020 (Fong 2001). The incidence of diseases related to vision (e.g., glaucoma and macular degeneration) is currently on the increase and will continue to rise as the baby boomers make their way into the senior years; the same is true of stroke. Overall,

these afflictions will surpass heart disease and cancer, which currently are the leading causes of death and disability. Gender is of particular importance in the study of health and aging, since women on average live longer lives. Living longer means older women are at increased risk of disease, and thus greater life expectancy can actually be viewed as a threat to women's health (Rodin and Ickovics 1990). Despite the fact that women make up a greater proportion of the elderly and therefore have greater health-care needs, they receive little research attention (M.L. Weber 1998).

Social support is a key factor related to the health of both older men and women. In older women, research reveals that depression is more strongly related to social support than to physical health (Albarracin, Fishbein, and Goldstein de Muchinik 1997). Older people tend to visit doctors more frequently and require hospitalization more often than do their younger counterparts (Canadian Institute for Health Information 2000). Given the demographic shift toward an older population accentuated by baby boomers, it is obvious that the disproportionate use of the health-care system in Canada by older people is a critical factor in all discussions about the cost of health care and possible reforms of the health-care system.

Sexual Orientation

Since heterosexuality is assumed to be the norm in Canadian society, there is a lack of attention paid to gays and lesbians in health research (M.L. Weber 1998). There does, however, tend to be more research carried out on gays than on lesbians (Lynch and Ferri 1997). Lesbians, then, face the combined effects of sexism and sexual orientation as they relate to health research and provision of health care. Research on health is conducted using mainly white, middle-class women, which results in a lack of knowledge about the health of bisexual women, older lesbians, lesbians of colour, and lesbians from rural areas (Hart 1995).

The assumption of diversity is, however, being integrated into some health-care systems, such as the Vancouver–Richmond Health Board, which represents the needs of lesbian, gay, bisexual, and transgender patients as well as other groups who traditionally have not been adequately served by the health-care system. As well, there have been concerns expressed over the curricula of Canadian medical schools regarding gay, lesbian, and bisexual issues. Medical schools are being prompted to ensure that the doctors they graduate are competently trained to care for *all* Canadians (Robinson and Cohen 1996).

In sum, to achieve the goal of 100 percent access and zero health disparities, public health officials must overcome inequities that are rooted not just in age but in social class, race and ethnicity, gender, and sexual orientation. If that were not enough, they must also deal with a geographical disparity in health-care resources. Dramatic differences in the availability of physicians, hospitals, and nursing homes also exist between urban and rural areas within the same province or territory. In the next section, we will look at the sociological perspectives on health and illness, some of which address these inequities in health care.

□ WHAT ARE THE SOCIOLOGICAL PERSPECTIVES ON HEALTH AND ILLNESS?

From a sociological point of view, social factors contribute to the evaluation of a person as "healthy" or "sick." People define themselves as healthy or sick on the basis of criteria established by each individual, relatives, friends, co-workers, and medical practitioners. Because health is relative, we can view it in a social context and consider how it varies in different situations or cultures (Twaddle 1974; Wolinsky 1980).

Why is it that you may consider yourself sick or well when others do not agree? Who controls definitions of health and illness in our society, and for what ends? What are the consequences of viewing yourself (or being viewed) as ill or disabled? Drawing on four sociological perspectives—functionalism, conflict theory, interactionism, and feminist theories—we can gain greater insight into the social context shaping definitions of health and treatment of illness.

An Overview

As you know, the sociological approaches should not be regarded as mutually exclusive. In the study of health-related issues, they share certain common themes. First, any person's health or illness is more than an organic condition, since it is subject to the interpretation of others. Owing to the impact of culture, family and friends, and the medical profession, health and illness are not purely biological occurrences but are sociological occurrences as well. Second, since members of a society (especially industrial societies) share the same health delivery system, health is a group and societal concern. Although health may be defined as the complete well-being of an individual, it is also the result of his or her social environment. As we will see, such factors as a person's social class, race and ethnicity, gender, and age can influence the likelihood of contracting a particular disease (Cockerham 1998).

Functionalist Approach

Illness entails at least a temporary disruption in a person's social interactions both at work and at home. Consequently, from a functionalist perspective, "being sick" must be controlled so that not too many people are released from their societal responsibilities at any one time. Functionalists contend that an overly broad definition of illness would disrupt the workings of a society.

"Sickness" requires a person to take on a social role, even if temporarily. The **sick role** refers to societal expectations about the attitudes and behaviour of a person viewed as being ill. Sociologist Talcott Parsons, well known for his contributions to functionalist theory (see Chapter 1), has outlined the behaviour required of people considered "sick" (1951, 1972, 1975). They are exempted from their normal, day-to-day responsibilities and generally are not blamed for their condition. Yet, they are obligated to try to get well, and this may include seeking competent professional care. Attempting to get well is particularly important in the world's developing countries. In modern automated industrial societies, we can absorb a greater degree of illness or disability, but in horticultural or agrarian societies, the availability of workers is far more critical (Conrad 2000).

◀ P.13

According to Parsons's theory, physicians function as "gatekeepers" for the sick role, either verifying a patient's condition as "illness" or designating the patient as "recovered." The ill person becomes dependent on the doctor because the latter can control valued rewards (not only treatment of illness but also excused absences from work and school). Parsons suggests that the doctor–patient relationship is somewhat like that between parent and child. Like a parent, the physician helps the patient to return to society as a full and functioning adult (A. Segall 1976).

The concept of sick role is not without criticism. First, patients' judgments regarding their own state of health may be related to their gender, age, social class, and ethnic group. For example, younger people may fail to detect warning signs of a dangerous illness while the elderly may focus too much on the slightest physical malady. Second, the sick role may be more applicable to people experiencing short-term illnesses than to those with recurring, long-term illnesses. Finally, even simple factors, such as whether a person is employed or not, seem to affect willingness to assume the sick role—as does the impact of socialization into a particular occupation or activity. For example, beginning in childhood, athletes learn to define certain ailments as "sports injuries" and therefore do not regard themselves as sick. Nonetheless, sociologists continue to rely on Parsons's model for functionalist analysis of the relationship between illness and societal expectations for the sick (Curry 1993).

Conflict Approach

Functionalists seek to explain how health-care systems meet the needs of society as well as those of individual patients and medical practitioners, but conflict theorists take issue with this view. They express concern that the profession of medicine has assumed a pre-eminence that extends well beyond whether to excuse a student from school or an employee from work. Sociologist Eliot Freidson has likened the position of medicine today to that of state religions yesterday—it has an officially approved monopoly on the right to define health and illness and to treat illness (1970:5). Conflict theorists use the term **medicalization of society** to refer to the growing role of medicine as a major institution of social control (Conrad and Schneider 1992; McKinlay and McKinlay 1977; Zola 1972, 1983).

Social control involves techniques and strategies for regulating behaviour in order to enforce the distinctive norms and values of a culture. Typically, we think of informal social control as occurring within families and peer groups, and formal social control as carried out by authorized agents, such as police officers, judges, school administrators, and employers. However, viewed from a conflict perspective, medicine is not simply a "healing profession"; it is a regulating mechanism as well.

◀ P. 159

How does medicine manifest its social control? First, it has greatly expanded its domain of expertise in recent decades. Physicians have become much more involved in examining a wide range of issues, among them sexuality (including homosexuality), old age, anxiety, obesity, child development, alcoholism, and drug addiction. Society tolerates such expansion of the boundaries of medicine because we hope that these experts can bring new "miracle cures" to complex human problems, as they have to the control of certain infectious diseases. The social significance of medicalization is that once a problem is viewed using a *medical model*—once medical experts become influential in proposing and assessing relevant public policies—it becomes more difficult for "common people" to join the discussion and exert influence on decision making. It also becomes more difficult to view these issues as being shaped by social, cultural, or psychological factors, rather than simply by physical or medical factors (Caplan 1989; Conrad and Schneider 1992; P. Starr 1982).

Second, medicine serves as an agent of social control by retaining absolute jurisdiction over many health-care procedures. Public health officials have even attempted to guard their jurisdiction by placing such health-care professionals as chiropractors and nurse-midwives outside the realm of acceptable medicine. Despite the

Midwives demonstrate in an effort to be included in the "legitimate" field of obstetrics in Canada. Physicians continue to exert control in marginalizing the role of midwives.

fact that midwives first brought professionalism to child delivery, they have been portrayed as having invaded the "legitimate" field of obstetrics in North America. Nurse-midwives have sought licensing as a way to achieve professional respectability, but physicians continue to exert power to ensure that midwifery remains a subordinate occupation (Friedland 2000).

The medicalization of society is but one concern of conflict theorists as they assess the workings of health-care institutions. As we have seen throughout this book, when analyzing any issue, conflict theorists seek to determine who benefits, who suffers, and who dominates at the expense of others. Viewed from a conflict perspective, there are glaring inequities in health-care delivery within Canada. For example, northern and rural areas tend to be underserved because medical services concentrate where people are numerous or wealthy.

Similarly, from a global perspective, there are obvious inequities in health-care delivery. In 2003, Canada had 2.1 physicians per 1000 people, while African nations had fewer than 1 per 1000. This situation is only worsened by the "brain drain"—the immigration to industrialized nations of skilled workers, professionals, and technicians who are desperately needed by their home countries. As part of this brain drain, physicians and other health-care professionals have come to developed countries from developing countries such as India, Pakistan, and various African states. Conflict theorists view such emigration out of the developing world as yet another way in which the world's core industrialized nations enhance their quality of life at the expense of developing countries (World Bank 2000a:190–91).

In another example of global inequities in health care, multinational corporations based in industrialized countries have reaped significant profits by "dumping" unapproved drugs on unsuspecting consumers in the developing world. In some cases, fraudulent capsules and tablets are manufactured and marketed as established products in developing countries. These "medications" contain useless ingredients or perhaps one-tenth of the needed dosage of a genuine medication. Even when the drugs dumped on developing countries are legitimate, the information available to physicians and patients is less likely to include warnings of side effects or health hazards and more likely to include undocumented testimonials than in industrialized nations (Silverman, Lydecker, and Lee 1990).

Conflict theorists emphasize that inequities in health-care resources have clear life-and-death consequences. For example, in 2005, the infant mortality rate in Sierra Leone was estimated to be 165 infant deaths per 1000 live births. By contrast, Japan's infant mortality rate was only 2.8 deaths per 1000 live births and Sweden's was 3.1. From a conflict perspective, the dramatic differences in infant mortality rates around the world (see Figure 15-4) reflect, at least in part, unequal distribution of health-care resources based on the wealth or poverty of various communities and nations.

In 2005, the United States had a rate of 6.6 infant deaths per 1000 live births (although it is estimated that the rate in some poor, inner-city neighbourhoods in that country exceeds 30 deaths per 1000 live births). Despite the wealth of the United States, at least 22 nations have lower infant mortality rates, among them Canada, Britain, and Japan. Conflict theorists point out that, unlike the United States, Canada and these other countries offer some form of government-supported health care for all citizens, which typically leads to greater availability and better use of prenatal care than is the case in the United States.

► **FIGURE 15-4**

Infant Mortality Rates in Selected Countries

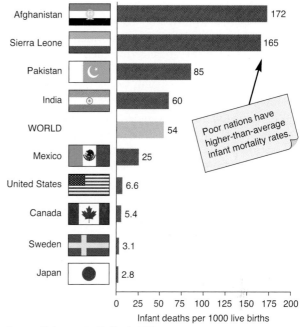

Source: Data reported in Haub 2005.

Interactionist Approach

In examining health, illness, and medicine as a social institution, interactionists generally focus on micro-level study of the roles played by health-care professionals and patients. They emphasize that the patient should not always be viewed as passive, but instead as an actor who often shows a powerful intent to see the physician (Alonzo 1989; Zola 1983).

Sometimes, patients play an active role in health care by *failing* to follow a physician's advice. For example, some patients stop taking medications long before they should, some take an incorrect dosage on purpose, and others never even fill their prescriptions. Such noncompliance results in part from the prevalence of self-medication in our society; many people are accustomed to self-diagnosis and self-treatment. Conversely, patients' active involvement in their own health care can sometimes have very *positive* consequences. Some patients read books about preventive health-care techniques, attempt to maintain healthful and nutritious diets, carefully monitor any side effects of medication, and adjust dosage based on such perceived side effects.

Labelling theorists suggest that the designation "healthy" or "ill" generally involves social definition by others. Just as police officers, judges, and other regulators of social control have the power to define certain people as criminals, health-care professionals (especially physicians) have the power to define certain people as "sick."

An example from history illustrates the labelling of women by the medical profession as fragile and possessing a limited source of energy. During the early years of the last century, women who expended energy pursuing intellectual activities (such as advanced education) were perceived to be endangering their womanhood. The medical establishment viewed the female body as a closed system of energy in which use of the brain would leave less energy to be used in other parts, such as the reproductive system. Women's brains and ovaries, according to doctors of the time, competed for the same supply of energy. Women who spent too much energy in intellectual pursuits were labelled "unhealthy" and unwomanly:

> A young woman… who consumed her vital force in intellectual activities was necessarily diverting these energies from the achievement of true womanhood. She would become weak and nervous, perhaps sterile… capable of bearing only sickly and neurotic children…. The brain and ovary could not develop at the same time. (Smith-Rosenberg and Rosenberg 1974:340)

Patriarchical views of women's health during this period even went so far as to suggest that male semen had a therapeutic and soothing effect on the female reproductive organs (Smith-Rosenberg 1986).

By the late 1980s, the power of a label—"person with AIDS"—had become quite evident. This label often P. 103 functions as a master status that overshadows all other aspects of a person's life. Once someone is told that he or she has tested positive for HIV, the virus associated with AIDS, that person is forced to confront immediate and difficult questions: "Should I tell my family members, my sexual partner(s), my friends, my co-workers, my employer? How will these people respond?" People's intense fear of this disease has led to prejudice and discrimination—even social ostracism— against those who have (or are suspected of having) AIDS. Consequently, a person who has AIDS must deal with not only the serious medical consequences of the disease but also with the distressing social consequences associated with the label.

According to labelling theorists, we can view a variety of life experiences as illnesses or not. Recently, premenstrual syndrome, post-traumatic disorders, and hyperactivity have been labelled as medically recognized disorders. Following the 1991 Gulf War against Iraq, more than 21 000 U.S. soldiers and other personnel reported a variety of symptoms ranging from fatigue and rashes to respiratory disorders. These symptoms have come to be called the Gulf War Syndrome (or illness); in 2008, the U.S. government officially recognized a clear link between the combat situation and subsequent symptoms. (Rutten 2008).

Probably the most noteworthy recent medical example of labelling is the case of homosexuality. For years, psychiatrists classified being gay or lesbian as a mental disorder subject to treatment. This official sanction by the psychiatry profession became an early target of the growing gay and lesbian rights movement in North America. In 1974, members of the American Psychiatric Association voted to drop homosexuality from the standard manual on mental disorders (Adam 1995; Charmaz and Paterniti 1999; Monteiro 1998).

Interactionist perspectives attempt to illuminate the social meaning of illness, as well as how these meanings affect a person's self-concept and relationships with others. For example, in the case of someone suffering from a mental illness, such as depression, interactionist approaches might shed light on the social stigma of the illness. In addition, these approaches might focus on how the stigma of the illness affects the individual's interpersonal relationships with family, friends, and co-workers. The interactionist perspective has been especially helpful in unravelling cultural differences that affect health care in a multicultural society, such as that of Canada. For example, regular exercise is not part of the culture of some ethnic groups; attitudes on diet, smoking, drinking, and body image, as well as fatalistic views of illness, may be culturally specific (Levy and Hawks 1996). Cultural sensitivity is necessary at all levels of health-care delivery in order to effectively treat a diverse patient population where many face language barriers, racism, social isolation, and inequality. Determining the different cultural meanings that individuals might attach to a doctor's report, a referral to a medical specialist, or a health survey are examples of how interactionists might approach the study of health and illness.

Feminist Approaches

Many feminist approaches to health and illness have pointed to a historical pattern of concentrating on women's reproductive potential, overshadowing a diversity of concerns related to health and illness. Early research on women focused on their roles as mothers and wives as they related to women's mental health, while comparable studies on men focused more on their physical health and job conditions. This bias still can be found in the research literature, even though most women now work in the paid labour force.

Other feminist perspectives point out the need to recognize that patterns of women's health and illness are as diverse as Canadian women themselves and that this diversity (e.g., poor women, immigrants, refugees, women of colour, lesbians, disabled women) must not

Table 15-4 Sociological Perspectives on Health and Illness

	Functionalist	Conflict	Interactionist	Feminist
Major emphasis	Control of the number of people who are considered sick	Overmedicalization Gross inequities in health care	Doctor–patient relationship Interaction of medical staff	Need to recognize patterns women's health and illness as diverse and not uniform
Controlling factors	Physician as gatekeeper	Medical profession Social inequalities	Medical profession	Medical profession
Proponents	Talcott Parsons	Paul Starr Thomas Szasz Irving Zola	Doug Maynard	Dorothy Smith

be masked by talking about "women" as a universal category. One feminist sociologist argues:

> Women are often discussed as a single group defined chiefly by their biological sex, members of an abstract universal (and implicitly white) category. In reality, we are a mixed lot, our gender roles and options shaped by history, culture and deep divisions across class and colour lines…. Traditionally, women as a group are defined by this reproductive potential. Usually ignored are the many ways that gender as a social reality gets into the body and transforms our biology. (Krieger and Fee 1994:18)

Sociological investigations of women's health must, many feminist theorists argue, shift the focus from reproduction potential and roles as mothers and wives to women's health and illness, to reflect the diversity of Canadian women.

The four sociological perspectives on health and illness are summarized, and their key proponents listed, in Table 15-4.

☐ WHAT IS THE HEALTH-CARE SITUATION IN CANADA?

In 1947, Swift Current, Saskatchewan, became the first region in North America to embrace a public hospital insurance program, in which all of its citizens were provided access to hospital services without direct payment. The following year, Premier Tommy Douglas introduced a program for all of Saskatchewan, based largely on the Swift Current model. Ten years later, the federal government followed suit by introducing the first national hospital insurance plan in North America. In 1962, Saskatchewan was again at the forefront of public health care when it introduced North Americas' first medicare

program, which would cover doctors' fees incurred outside hospitals. The program sparked the highly profiled Saskatchewan doctors' strike, which saw many physicians threatening to leave the province if this perceived threat to "free enterprise" in medical care went through. Critics of the medicare plan accused the government of "communist" and "socialist" tendencies, and of attempting to destroy the private relationship between physicians and patients.

The doctors' strike, which lasted three weeks, became the focus of media attention not only in Canada but also in the United States. The American Medical Association supported the dissenting Saskatchewan doctors in their attempt to resist the public administration of medical care and to preserve "free enterprise."

In 1968, the public administration of medical care became national policy, after the provinces and territories moved to implement their own insurance plans for in-hospital care. Justice Emmett Hall, after carrying out a review of the Canadian health-care system in 1979, reported it to be among the best in the world. He did, however, warn that the system was being weakened by extra billing by doctors and that user fees were creating a "two-tiered" system. These unresolved issues still pose a threat to the principles of accessibility, universality, and public administration, which, as discussed in a later section, are cornerstones of Canadian medicare.

The Role of Government in Health Care in Canada

In 1984, the federal government's Canada Health Act became the basis for the administration of our health-care system, known as *medicare*. The Health Act set out to ensure (in theory) that all Canadians receive access to hospital and doctors' services on the basis of need, not on the ability to pay. It also sets the conditions and criteria under which the provinces and territories receive transfer payments—payments that are then used to finance health-care services in their respective jurisdictions. The principles of the Canada Health Act are as follows (Health Canada 2001):

1. *Public administration*: Health care in a province or territory must be carried out by public institutions on a non-profit basis.
2. *Comprehensiveness*: All services carried out by hospitals and doctors and deemed to be medically necessary must be insured.
3. *Universality*: All residents of a province or territory are entitled to uniform health coverage.
4. *Portability*: Health coverage must be maintained when a person moves or travels across provinces and territories or outside Canada.
5. *Accessibility*: Reasonable access to necessary medical services should be available to all Canadians.

In many respects the principles of public administration, comprehensiveness, universality, portability, and accessibility represent Max Weber's ideal types; that is, they act as abstract measuring rods against which we are able to compare our perceptions of reality. For example, most Canadians would be able to give an example of how our health-care system today may not measure up to at least one of these principles. Whether the concern is waiting lists for surgery, access to specialists in remote locations, the growth of private, fee-for-service clinics, long waits in hospital emergency wards, waiting lists for specialized tests, such as MRIs, the closing of rural hospitals the reduction of beds in urban hospitals, or the shortage of nurses nationwide, Canadians consider the delivery of health-care services a concern of top priority (Canadian Institute for Health Information 2001). Canadians living in northern or rural areas or outside major metropolitan areas, immigrants, those with low incomes, Aboriginal persons, and people with disabilities represent some of the groups vulnerable to the so-called crisis in the Canadian health-care system.

☐ HOW HAVE COMMUNITIES CHANGED?

As we noted at the outset of this chapter, a community is a spatial or political unit of social organization that gives people a sense of belonging. The nature of community has changed greatly over the course of history—from early hunting-and-gathering societies to highly modernized post-industrial cities, as we will now see.

For most of human history, people used very basic tools and knowledge to survive. They satisfied their need for an adequate food supply through hunting, foraging for fruits or vegetables, fishing, and herding. In comparison with later industrial societies, early civilizations were much more dependent on the reproductive cycle of ◀ P.114 the physical environment and much less able to alter that environment to their advantage. The emergence of horticultural societies, in which people actually cultivated food rather than merely gathering fruits and vegetables, led to many dramatic changes in human social organization.

It was no longer necessary to move from place to place in search of food. Because people had to remain in specific locations to cultivate crops, more stable and enduring communities began to develop. As agricultural techniques became more and more sophisticated, a co-operative division of labour involving both family members and others developed. It gradually became possible for people to produce more food than they actually needed for themselves. They could then provide food, perhaps as part of an exchange, to others who might be involved in non-agricultural labour. This transition from subsistence to surplus represented a critical step in the emergence of cities.

Eventually, people produced enough goods to cover both their own needs and those of people not engaged in agricultural tasks. Initially, the surplus was limited to agricultural products, but it gradually evolved to include all types of goods and services. Residents of a city came to rely on community members who provided craft products and means of transportation, gathered information, and so forth (Nolan and Lenski 1999).

With these social changes came an even more elaborate division of labour, as well as a greater opportunity for differential rewards and privileges. As long as everyone was engaged in the same tasks, stratification was limited to such factors as gender, age, and perhaps the ability to perform the task (a skilful hunter could win unusual respect from the community). However, the surplus allowed for expansion of goods and services, leading to greater differentiation, a hierarchy of occupations, and social inequality. Therefore, surplus was a precondition not only for the establishment of cities but also for the division of members of a community into social classes (see Chapter 8). The ability to produce goods for other communities marked a fundamental shift in human social organization.

Pre-industrial Cities

It is estimated that, beginning about 10 000 BCE, permanent settlements free from dependence on crop cultivation emerged. Yet, by today's standards of population, these early communities would barely qualify as cities. The **pre-industrial city**, as it is termed, generally had only a few thousand people living within its borders and was characterized by a relatively closed class system and limited mobility. Status in these early cities was usually based on ascribed characteristics, such as family background; and education was limited to members of the elite. All the residents relied on perhaps 100 000 farmers and their own part-time farming to provide them with the needed agricultural surplus. The Mesopotamian city of Ur had a population of about 10 000 and was limited to roughly 90 hectares (220 acres) of land, including the canals, the temple, and the harbour.

Why were these early cities so small and relatively few in number? Several key factors restricted urbanization:

- *Reliance on animal power (from both humans and beasts of burden) as a source of energy for economic production.* This limited people's ability to make use of and alter the physical environment.
- *Modest levels of surplus produced by the agricultural sector.* Between 50 and 90 farmers may have been required to support one city resident (Davis [1949] 1995).
- *Problems in transportation and storage of food and other goods.* Even an excellent crop could easily be lost as a result of such difficulties.
- *Hardships of migration to the city.* For many peasants, migration was both physically and economically impossible. A few weeks of travel was out of the question without more sophisticated techniques of food storage.
- *Dangers of city life.* Concentrating a society's population in a small area left it open to attack from outsiders, as well as more susceptible to extreme damage from plagues and fires.

A sophisticated social organization is also an essential precondition for urban existence. Specialized social roles bring people together in new ways through the exchange of goods and services. A well-developed social organization ensures that these relationships are clearly defined and generally acceptable to all parties.

Table 15-5 summarizes the contrasts between pre-industrial and industrial cities as outlined by Sjoberg. Admittedly, Sjoberg's view of city life is an ideal type, since inequality did not vanish with the emergence of urban communities.

Industrial and Post-industrial Cities

Imagine how life could change by harnessing the energy of air, water, and other natural resources to power

society's tasks. Advances in agricultural technology led to dramatic changes in community life, but so did the process of industrialization. The Industrial Revolution, which began in the middle of the eighteenth century, ◀ P. 115 focused on the application of non-animal sources of power to labour tasks. Industrialization had a wide range of effects on people's lifestyles as well as on the structure of communities. Emerging urban settlements became centres not only of industry but also of banking, finance, and industrial management.

The factory system that developed during the Industrial Revolution led to a much more refined division of labour than was evident in pre-industrial cities. The many new occupations that were created produced a complex set of relationships among workers. Thus, the **industrial city** was not merely more populous than its pre-industrial predecessors; it was also based on very different principles of social organization.

In comparison with pre-industrial cities, industrial cities have a more open class system and more mobility. After initiatives in industrial cities by women's-rights groups, labour unions, and other political activists, formal education gradually became available to many children from poor and working-class families. Although ascribed characteristics, such as gender, race, and ethnicity, remained important, a talented or skilled individual had a greater opportunity to better his or her social position. In these and other respects, the industrial city is genuinely a "different world" from the pre-industrial urban community.

In the latter part of the twentieth century, a new type of urban community emerged. The **post-industrial city** is a city in which global finance and the electronic flow of information dominate the economy. Production ◀ P. 116 is decentralized and often takes place outside urban centres, but control is centralized in multinational corporations whose influence transcends urban and even national boundaries. Social change is a constant feature of the post-industrial city. Economic restructuring and spatial change seem to occur each decade, if not more frequently. In the post-industrial world, cities are forced into increasing competition for economic opportunities, which deepens the plight of the urban poor (Phillips 1996; Smith and Timberlake 1993).

Use Your Sociological Imagination

What would the ideal city of the future look like? Describe its architecture, public transportation, neighbourhoods, schools, and workplaces. What kinds of people would live and work there?

Table 15-5   Comparing Types of Cities

Pre-industrial Cities (through eighteenth century)	Industrial Cities (eighteenth through mid-twentieth century)	Post-industrial Cities (beginning late twentieth century)
Closed class system—pervasive influence of social class at birth	Open class system—mobility based on achieved characteristics	Wealth based on ability to obtain and use information
Economic realm controlled by guilds and a few families	Relatively open competition	Corporate power dominates
Beginnings of division of labour in creation of goods	Elaborate specialization in manufacturing of goods	Sense of place fades, transitional networks emerge
Pervasive influence of religion on social norms	Influence of religion limited to certain areas as society becomes more secularized	Religion becomes more fragmented; greater openness to new religious faiths
Little standardization of prices, weights, and measures	Standardization enforced by custom and law	Conflicting views of prevailing standards
Population largely illiterate; communication by word of mouth	Emergence of communication through posters, bulletins, and newspapers	Emergence of extended electronic networks
Schools limited to elites and designed to perpetuate their privileged status	Formal schooling open to the masses and viewed as a means of advancing the social order	Professional, scientific, and technical personnel are increasingly important

Sources: Based on Phillips 1996:132–135; Sjoberg 1960:323–328.

☐ WHAT IS URBANIZATION, AND WHAT ARE ITS CONSEQUENCES?

The 2006 census showed that 80 percent of Canadians live in urban centres, compared with 78.5 percent in 1996. The 2006 census also revealed that 54 percent of Canada's population is concentrated in four broad urban areas: Southern Ontario, Montreal and environs, the lower mainland of British Columbia and southern Vancouver Island, and the Calgary–Edmonton corridor.

Urbanization can be seen throughout the rest of the world, too. In 1900, only 10 percent of the world's people lived in urban areas; by 2000, that proportion had risen to around 50 percent. By the year 2025, the number of city dwellers could reach 5 billion (Koolhaas et al. 2001:3). During the nineteenth and twentieth centuries, rapid urbanization occurred primarily in Europe and North America. But since World War II, the population of cities in developing countries has exploded: see Figure 15-5 (Koolhaas et al. 2001:3).

Some metropolitan areas have spread so far that they have connected with other urban centres. Such a densely populated area, containing two or more cities and their suburbs, has become known as a **megalopolis**. An example is the so-called Golden Horseshoe region of Southern Ontario, which encompasses such communities as Hamilton, Burlington, and the Greater Toronto Area. Even when it is divided into autonomous political jurisdictions, the megalopolis can be viewed as a single economic entity. The megalopolis is also evident in Great Britain, Germany, Italy, Egypt, India, Japan, and China.

Functionalist View: Urban Ecology

Human ecology is concerned with the relationships between people and their environment. Human ecologists have long been interested in how the physical environment shapes people's lives (for example, rivers can serve as a barrier to residential expansion) and also how people influence the surrounding environment (air-conditioning has accelerated the growth of major metropolitan areas in the American Southwest). **Urban ecology** focuses on such relationships as they emerge in urban areas. Although the urban ecological approach examines social change in cities, it is nevertheless functionalist in

▶ **FIGURE 15-5**

Global Urbanization, 2015 (projected)

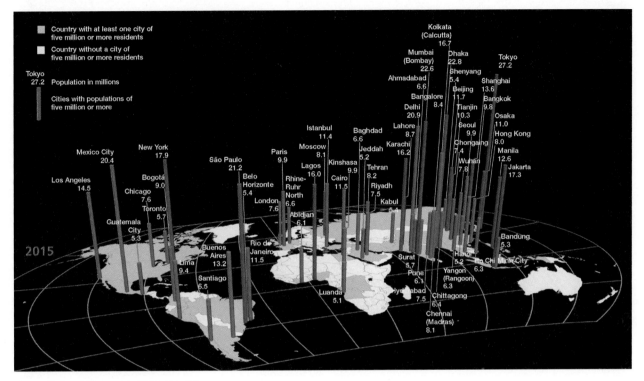

Source: National Geographic 2005: 104–105.

its orientation because it emphasizes that different elements in urban areas contribute to stability.

Early urban ecologists, such as Robert Park (1916, 1936) and Ernest Burgess (1925), concentrated on city life but drew on the approaches used by ecologists who studied plant and animal communities. With few exceptions, urban ecologists trace their work back to the **concentric-zone theory** devised in the 1920s by Burgess (see the left-hand visual in Figure 15-6). Using Chicago as an example, Burgess proposed a theory for describing land use in industrial cities. At the centre, or nucleus, of such a city is the central business district. Large department stores, hotels, theatres, and financial institutions occupy this highly valued land. Surrounding this urban centre are succeeding zones that contain other types of land use and that illustrate the growth of the urban area over time.

Note that the creation of zones is a *social* process, not the result of nature alone. Families and business firms compete for the most valuable land; those possessing the most wealth and power are generally the winners. The concentric-zone theory proposed by Burgess also represented a dynamic model of urban growth. As urban growth proceeded, each zone would move even farther from the central business district.

Because of its functionalist orientation and its emphasis on stability, the concentric-zone theory tended to understate or ignore certain tensions apparent in metropolitan areas. For example, the growing use by the affluent of land in a city's peripheral areas was uncritically approved, while the arrival of visible minorities in white neighbourhoods has been described by some sociologists in such terms as "invasion" and "succession." Moreover, the urban ecological perspective gave little thought to gender inequities, such as the establishment of men's private golf clubs and softball leagues in city parks without any programs for women's sports. Consequently, the urban ecological approach has been criticized for its failure to address issues of gender, race, and class.

By the middle of the twentieth century, urban populations had spilled beyond the traditional city limits. No longer could urban ecologists focus exclusively on growth in the central city, for large numbers of urban residents were abandoning the cities to live in suburban areas. As a response to the emergence of more than one focal point in some metropolitan areas, Chauncy D. Harris and Edward Ullman (1945) presented the **multiple-nuclei theory** (see the right-hand visual in Figure 15-6). In their view, not all urban growth radiates outward from a central business

▶ **FIGURE 15-6**

Comparison of Ecological Theories of Urban Growth

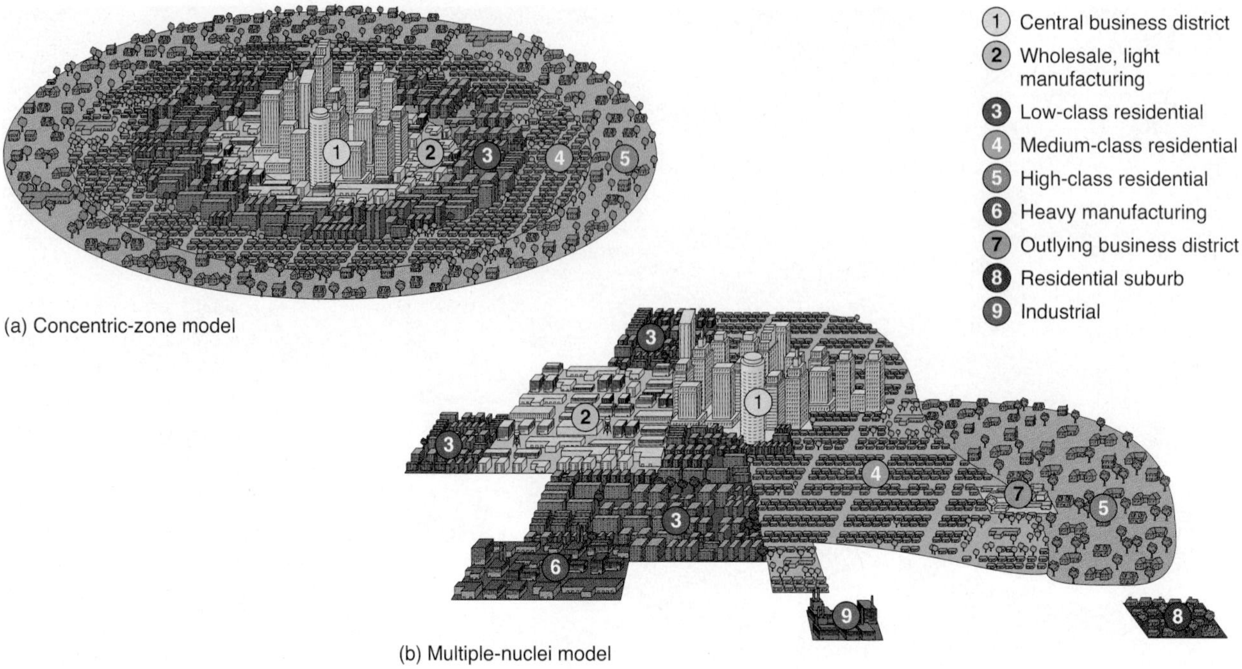

(a) Concentric-zone model

1 Central business district
2 Wholesale, light manufacturing
3 Low-class residential
4 Medium-class residential
5 High-class residential
6 Heavy manufacturing
7 Outlying business district
8 Residential suburb
9 Industrial

(b) Multiple-nuclei model

Source: C. Harris and Ullmann 1945:13.

district. Instead, a metropolitan area may have many centres of development, each of which reflects a particular urban need or activity. Thus, a city may have a financial district, a manufacturing zone, a waterfront area, an entertainment centre, and so forth. Certain types of business firms and certain types of housing will naturally cluster around each distinctive nucleus (Squires 2002).

The rise of suburban shopping malls is a vivid example of the phenomenon of multiple nuclei within metropolitan areas. Initially, all major retailing in cities was located in the central business district. Each residential neighbourhood had its own grocers, bakers, and butchers, but people travelled to the centre of the city to make major purchases at department stores. However, as major metropolitan areas expanded and the suburbs became more populous, an increasing number of people began to shop nearer their homes. Today, the suburban mall is a significant retailing and social centre for communities across Canada.

In a refinement of multiple-nuclei theory, contemporary urban ecologists have begun to study what journalist Joel Garreau (1991) has called "edge cities." These communities, which have grown up on the outskirts of major metropolitan areas, are economic and social centres with identities of their own. By any standard of measurement—height of buildings, amount of office space, presence of medical facilities, presence of leisure-time facilities, or, of course, population—edge cities qualify as independent cities rather than as large suburbs.

Whether they include edge cities or multiple nuclei, more and more metropolitan areas are characterized by spread-out development and unchecked growth. A David Suzuki Foundation report, entitled *Understanding Sprawl*, argues that, in some parts of Canada, urban sprawl is the largest creator of greenhouse gas emissions, as it segregates houses from stores and workplaces, forcing residents to rely on cars to get around (Gurin 2003). Large corporations are capitalizing on this so-called sprawl by building stores and services that depend on the use of the automobile. The former CEO of Starbucks, Orin Smith, recently stated that the suburbs and small towns in the United States would be the focus of growth for the coffee juggernaut; allowing people to stay in their cars by increasingly using drive-throughs—another huge source of pollution—is one of the company's goals. Smith states:

> We know from our studies that the reason our most frequent users—and as well our most infrequent users—don't use us more is because there are not enough of us and we're not convenient enough. . . . [North] Americans don't want to walk, so if you have to go more than two blocks, they don't go. (*The Vancouver Sun* 2004b)

Conflict View: New Urban Sociology

Contemporary sociologists point out that metropolitan growth is not governed by waterways and rail lines, as a purely ecological interpretation might suggest. From a conflict perspective, communities are human creations that reflect people's needs, choices, and decisions—but some people have more influence over these decisions than others do. Drawing on conflict theory, an approach that has come to be called the **new urban sociology** considers the interplay of local, national, and worldwide forces and their effect on local space, with special emphasis on the impact of global economic activity (Gottdiener and Hutchison 2006).

New urban sociologists note that ecological approaches typically have avoided examining the social forces, largely economic in nature, that have guided urban growth. For example, central business districts may be upgraded or abandoned, depending on whether urban policymakers grant substantial tax exemptions to developers. The suburban boom in the post–World War II era was fuelled by highway construction and federal housing policies that channelled investment capital into the construction of single-family homes rather than affordable rental housing in cities. Similarly, although some observers suggest that the growth of Sunbelt cities in the United States is due to a "good business climate," new urban sociologists counter that this term is actually a euphemism for hefty state and local government subsidies and anti-labour policies intended to attract manufacturers (Gottdiener and Feagin 1988; M. Smith 1988).

The new urban sociology draws generally on the conflict perspective and more specifically on sociologist Immanuel Wallerstein's world systems analysis. ◀ P.215 Wallerstein argues that certain industrialized nations (among them, the United States, Japan, and Germany) hold a dominant position at the *core* of the global economic system. At the same time, the poor developing countries of Asia, Africa, and Latin America are on the *periphery* of the global economy, where they are controlled and exploited by core industrialized nations. Through the use of world systems analysis, new urban sociologists consider urbanization from a global perspective. They view cities not as independent and autonomous entities but rather as the outcome of decision-making processes directed or influenced by a society's dominant classes and by core industrialized nations. New urban sociologists note that the rapidly growing cities of the world's developing countries were shaped first by colonialism and then by a global economy controlled by core nations and multinational corporations (Gottdiener and Feagin 1988; Smith 1995).

The urban ecologists of the 1920s and 1930s were aware of the role that the larger economy played in urbanization, but their theories emphasized the ◀ P.220 impact of local rather than national or global forces.

By contrast, through a broad, global emphasis on social inequality and conflict, new urban sociologists are interested in such topics as the existence of an underclass, the power of multinational corporations, deindustrialization, homelessness, and residential segregation.

Developers, builders, and investment bankers are not especially interested in urban growth when it means providing housing for middle- or low-income people. This lack of interest contributes to the problem of homelessness. These urban elites counter that the nation's

Though the African country of Kenya is mostly rural, Nairobi, a city with almost a million residents, is a modern urban area with international business connections. According to world systems analysis, the cities of developing nations exist on the periphery of the global economy, controlled and exploited by the more powerful industrialized nations.

Table 15-6 Comparing Approaches to Urbanization

	Urban Ecology	New Urban Sociology
Theoretical Perspective	Functionalist	Conflict
Primary Focus	Relationship of urban areas to their spatial setting and physical environment	Relationship of urban areas to global, national, and local forces
Key Source of Change	Technological innovations, such as new methods of transportation	Economic competition and monopolization of power
Initiator of Actions	Individuals, neighbourhoods, communities	Real estate developers, banks and other financial institutions, multinational corporations
Allied Disciplines	Geography, architecture	Political science, economics

housing shortage and the plight of the homeless are not the fault of the elites—and insist that they do not have the capital needed to construct and support such housing. But affluent people *are* interested in growth and *can* somehow find capital to build new shopping centres, office towers, and professional sports facilities.

Why, then, can't they provide the capital for affordable housing? ask new urban sociologists. Part of the answer is that developers, bankers, and other powerful real estate interests view housing in quite a different manner from tenants and most homeowners. For a tenant, an apartment is shelter, housing, a home. But for developers and investors—many of them large (and sometimes multinational) corporations—an apartment is simply a housing investment. These financiers and owners are primarily concerned with maximizing profit, not with solving social problems (Feagin 1983; Gottdiener and Hutchison 2000).

As we have seen throughout this textbook, in studying such varied issues as deviance and race and ethnicity, no single theoretical approach necessarily offers sociologists the only valuable perspective. As is shown in Table 15-6, urban ecology and new urban sociology offer significantly different ways of viewing urbanization that enrich our understanding of this complex phenomenon.

Interactionist View

Sociologist Louis Wirth argued that a relatively large and permanent settlement leads to distinctive patterns of behaviour, which he called **urbanism** (1928, 1938). He identified three critical factors contributing to urbanism: the size of the population, the population density, and the heterogeneity (variety) of the population. A frequent result of urbanism, according to Wirth, is that we

become insensitive to events around us and restrict our attention to the primary groups to which we are emotionally attached.

Wirth suggested that urbanization brings with it a way of life resulting from such factors as the spatial segregation of people according to class, race and ethnicity, and occupation. In this way of life, human interaction changes from being based on primary relationships (i.e., face to face, personal, and ongoing) to secondary relationships (i.e., detached, impersonal, and fragmented). Although people in urban areas, according to Wirth, gain greater autonomy, independence, and freedom from community norms and sanctions, they also lose the sense of intimacy, connection, and support that accompany primary forms of interaction.

Urban life is noteworthy for its diversity, so it would be a serious mistake to see all city residents as being alike. Sociologist Herbert J. Gans has distinguished among five types of people found in cities (1991):

1. *Cosmopolites.* These residents remain in cities to take advantage of unique cultural and intellectual benefits. Writers, artists, and scholars fall into this category.
2. *Unmarried and child-free people.* Such people choose to live in cities because of the active nightlife and varied recreational opportunities.
3. *Ethnic villagers.* These urban residents prefer to live in their own tight-knit communities. Typically, immigrant groups isolate themselves in such neighbourhoods to avoid resentment from well-established urban dwellers.
4. *The deprived.* Very poor people and families have little choice but to live in low-rent, and often run-down, urban neighbourhoods.

5. *The trapped.* Some city residents want to leave urban centres but cannot because of their limited economic resources and prospects. Gans includes the "downward mobiles" in this category—people who once held higher social positions but who are forced to live in less prestigious neighbourhoods owing to the loss of a job, death of a wage earner, or old age. Both elderly individuals living alone and families may feel "trapped" in part because they resent changes in their communities. Their desire to live elsewhere may reflect their uneasiness with unfamiliar immigrant groups who have become their neighbours.

These categories remind us that the city represents a choice (even a dream) for certain people and a nightmare for others. Gans's work underscores the importance of neighbourhoods in contemporary urban life. Ernest Burgess, in his study of life in Chicago in the 1920s, paid special attention to the ethnic neighbourhoods of that city. Many decades after Burgess conducted his study, residents in such districts as Chinatown or Greektown in many large urban centres continue to feel attached to their own ethnic communities rather than to the larger unit of a city. Even outside ethnic enclaves, a special sense of belonging can take hold in a neighbourhood.

The term *defended neighbourhood* is one which is used to refer to people's definitions of their community boundaries. Neighbourhoods acquire unique identities because residents view them as geographically separate—and socially different—from adjacent areas. The **defended neighbourhood**, in effect, becomes a sentimental union of similar people. Neighbourhood phone directories, community newspapers, school and parish boundaries, and business advertisements all serve to define an area and distinguish it from nearby communities.

Feminist Views

Feminist perspectives outlining the ways in which gender intersects with the conditions of city life have long been absent from the sociological literature. Studies on urban life have generally neglected the impact of industrialization and urbanization on the lives of women—women in the private sphere caring for their children, and those, as has increasingly been the case, also employed in workplaces in urban areas. Recently, urban studies have highlighted the ways in which patriarchy underpins how social life is organized, both in private and in public spheres or urban centres (Garber and Turner 1995).

As is consistent with the research in Chapter 11 on female students' feelings of safety on Canadian university campuses, safety is a major concern for women living in urban centres. In 2004, Statistics Canada revealed that 58 percent of women worried about their safety waiting for or using public transportation alone after dark (twice the proportion of male nighttime users). Women, in contrast to men, were almost three times as likely to be afraid to walk in their neighbourhoods after dark (Statistics Canada 2005j).

☐ WHAT ARE SOME TYPES OF COMMUNITIES?

Communities vary substantially in the degree to which their members feel connected and share a common identity. Ferdinand Tönnies used the term *Gemeinschaft* ◀ P.113 to describe a close-knit community in which social interaction among people is intimate and familiar ([1887]1988). It is the kind of place where people in a coffee shop will stop talking when anyone enters, because they are sure to know whoever walks through the door. A shopper at the small grocery store in this town would expect to know every employee and probably every other customer as well. By contrast, the ideal type of *Gesellschaft* describes modern urban life, in which people feel little in common with others. Their social relationships often are a result of interactions focused on immediate tasks, such as purchasing a product. Contemporary city life in Canada generally resembles a *Gesellschaft*.

The following sections will examine different types of communities found in Canada, focusing on the distinctive characteristics and problems of central cities, suburbs, and rural communities.

Central Cities

In terms of land mass, Canada is the second-largest nation in the world. Yet, more than two-thirds of the population is located near the U.S. border on land that comprises a mere fraction of the nation's total geographical area. As we have mentioned, more than half of Canada's population is heavily concentrated in four urban regions or **central cities**. Even those who live outside central cities, such as residents of suburban and rural communities, find that urban centres heavily influence their lifestyles.

Urban Dwellers

Many urban residents are the descendants of European immigrants—Irish, Italians, Jews, Poles, and others—who came to Canada in the nineteenth and early twentieth centuries. With a "vertical mosaic" firmly entrenched in Canada, the cities socialized newcomers to the norms, values, and language of their new homeland and gave them unequal opportunity to work their way up the economic

Large cities in Canada, such as Toronto (shown here), are becoming increasingly diverse due to international migration.

to the cities. City governments argue that the provincial and federal governments ought to carry more of the burden for the cost of upgrading roads and bridges, repairing crumbling sewers, and refurbishing and expanding public transportation systems.

A critical problem for the cities is mass transportation. In 1951, there were five people for every registered vehicle in Canada; by the mid-1980s, there were two people for every registered vehicle and that number has remained steady (Statistics Canada 2006o). Next to the United States, Canada has the highest rate of car ownership in the world. Growing traffic congestion in metropolitan areas has led many cities to recognize a need

ladder. In addition, a substantial number of Canadians of European descent came to the cities from rural farming areas in the period following World War II.

Cities in Canada are the destinations of immigrants from around the world, particularly those from China, India, the Philippines, and Hong Kong. Yet, unlike those who came to this country 100 years ago, current immigrants are arriving at a time of rapidly increasing housing costs in the larger cities. This makes it more difficult for them to find decent housing.

Some urban planners argue that Canada's federal government has failed to disperse recent immigrants to areas outside the cities in which these ethnic neighbourhoods are located. Larry Bourne, a University of Toronto geographer, states that "we're turning a half-dozen cities into intensely multicultural and multilingual places and creating these fantastically vibrant but underserviced cities while the rest of the country remains homogeneous with a declining and aging population" (Jimenez and Lunman 2004).

Issues Facing Cities

People and neighbourhoods vary greatly within any city in Canada. Yet, all residents of a central city—regardless of social class, racial, and ethnic differences—face certain common problems. Crime, air pollution, noise, crumbling infrastructures, congested roads and freeways, inadequate public transportation—these unpleasant realities and many more are an increasing feature of contemporary urban life. Municipal governments of large metropolitan cities, such as Toronto, have long been lobbying the federal and provincial governments to increase the amount of revenue that is transferred

C stands for "congestion." In 2003, to alleviate gridlock, officials in London, England, began to charge vehicles about $15 a day to enter designated congestion zones. At least initially, significant traffic reductions resulted, leading city planners around the world to consider adopting the idea.

for safe, efficient, and inexpensive mass transit systems. However, the federal government has traditionally given much more assistance to highway programs than to public transit. Conflict theorists note that such a bias favours the relatively affluent (automobile owners) as well as corporations such as auto manufacturers, tire makers, and oil companies. Meanwhile, low-income residents of metropolitan areas, who are much less likely to own cars than are members of the middle and upper classes, face higher fares on public transit along with deteriorating service (Mason 1998).

Suburbs

The term *suburb* was derived from the Latin *sub urbe*, meaning "under the city." Until recent times, most suburbs were just that—tiny communities totally dependent on urban centres for jobs, recreation, and even water.

Today, the term **suburb** defies any simple definition. The term generally refers to any community near a large city or any territory within a metropolitan area that is not included in the central city. Large cities and the suburbs that surround them make up a metropolitan area in which people live in one part of the area and work or go to school in another (e.g., living in Delta, British Columbia, and working in Vancouver). In the 2006 census, Statistics Canada considered Census Metropolitan Areas (CMAs) to be urban, suburban, and rural areas of more than 100 000 people that are socially and economically integrated.

Three social factors differentiate suburbs from cities. First, suburbs are generally less dense than cities; in the newest suburbs, there are often no more than four dwellings on a hectare of land. Second, the suburbs consist almost exclusively of private space. Private ornamental lawns replace common park areas for the most part. Third, suburbs have more exacting building design codes than cities, and these codes have become increasingly precise in the last decade. Although the suburbs may be diverse in population, such design standards give the impression of uniformity.

It can also be difficult to distinguish between suburbs and rural areas. Certain criteria generally define suburbs: Most people work at urban (as opposed to rural) jobs, and local governments provide services, such as water supply, sewage disposal, and fire protection. In rural areas, these services are less common, and a greater proportion of residents are employed in farming and related activities.

Suburban Expansion

Whatever the precise definition of a suburb, it is clear that suburbs have expanded. In fact, suburbanization was the most dramatic demographic trend in Canada throughout the twentieth century. Suburban areas grew at first along railroad lines, then at the terminal points of streetcar tracks, and, by the 1950s, along the nation's growing systems of freeways and expressways. The suburban boom has been especially evident since World War II.

According to University of Toronto demographer David Foot, increased urbanization was arguably the most controversial finding of the 2001 census. However, he believes that the real trend was suburbanization, not urbanization (Foot 2002). For example, the City of Toronto has grown by 4 percent since 1996, while the Greater Toronto Area's growth was twice that number.

Suburbanization was the most dramatic demographic trend in Canada throughout the twentieth century. The exacting building design codes often give the impression of uniformity.

Foot notes that similar patterns occurred in Edmonton, Montreal, Calgary, and Vancouver. Foot contends that during the 1980s and 1990s, the baby boom generation moved to the suburbs to raise their children (what he refers to as the "echo boom"). When considering whether such a trend will continue, Foot looks at the issue this way: "Migration to these urban clusters from the rest of the country will, undoubtedly, continue to contribute to this suburban growth. And most aging boomers will not immediately sell their suburban homes because they are hoping that their future grandchildren will come and visit" (Foot 2002: A17). Numbers from the 2006 census show that the trend of suburbanization has continued. Between 2001 and 2006, the percentage growth of suburban residents was greater than that of the core city itself (Weeks 2007).

Diversity in the Suburbs

In Canada, race and ethnicity remain the most important factors distinguishing cities from suburbs. Nevertheless, the common assumption that suburbia includes only prosperous whites is far from correct. In the last 20 years, we have witnessed the diversification of suburbs in terms of race and ethnicity. For example, by 2001, more than 40 percent of the people living in the Vancouver suburb of Richmond were Chinese; Richmond also has a significant South Asian population. Like the rest of the nation, members of racial and ethnic minorities are becoming suburban dwellers (El Nasser 2001; Frey 2001).

The term *ethnoburbia* was coined in the 1990s by geographer Wei Li. Ethnoburbia refers to the growing trend toward **ethnoburbs**—suburbs that are ethnically diverse and contain a wide variety of income groups whose members are white-collar and well educated. The ethnoburb serves not only as an ethnic residential suburb but also as a community centre and place of business (Li 1999). In the United States, a study of suburban residential patterns in 11 metropolitan areas found that Asian Americans and Hispanics tend to reside in equivalent socio-economic areas with whites—that is, affluent Hispanics live alongside affluent whites, poor Asians near poor whites, and so on. However, the case for African Americans is quite distinct. Suburban blacks live in poorer suburbs than whites do, even after taking into account differences in individuals' income, education, and home ownership.

Again, in contrast to prevailing stereotypes, the suburbs include a significant number of low-income people from diverse backgrounds, including both visible-minority and non-visible-minority groups. Poverty is not conventionally associated with the suburbs, partly because the suburban poor tend to be scattered among more affluent people. In some instances, suburban communities intentionally hide social problems, such as homelessness, so they can maintain a "respectable image." Soaring housing costs have contributed to suburban poverty, which surpassed city poverty in the U.S. in 2005 (Berube and Kneebone 2006).

Some urban and suburban residents are moving to communities even more remote from the central city or to fully rural areas. Initial evidence suggests that this move to rural areas is only intensifying the racial disparities in some metropolitan areas (Bureau of the Census 1997b; Holmes 1997).

Rural Communities

As we have seen, the people of Canada live mainly in large urban centres. Yet, in 2001, 20 percent of the population lived in rural areas and small towns, outside commuting distance to larger cities (Statistics Canada 2002e). As is true of the suburbs, it would be a mistake to view rural communities as fitting into one set image. Grain farms, coal mining towns, cattle ranches, and gas stations along the Trans-Canada Highway are all part of the rural landscape of Canada.

The historic stereotype of the farmer is a white male. Yet, women have long played a significant role in agriculture, both in Canada and throughout the world. Women participate actively in agriculture—on large and small farms, and in profitable and failing family businesses. Farming women are almost always married and generally have families. In Canada, the percentage of farms operated exclusively by women remains low (Statistics Canada 2006m). Segregation by gender is typical of farm labour: men are more likely to be engaged in fieldwork, while women are more likely to serve their farms as accountants, personnel and equipment managers, and purchasing agents. Many studies have documented the high degree of stress that farming women experience as they attempt to fulfil many demanding social roles (Keating and Munro 1988).

A study by Statistics Canada released in 2004, using data from the 2001 census, showed that a disproportionately high number of self-employed Canadians live in rural areas and small towns, outside the commuting distances to larger cities. In 2001, some 620 000 self-employed Canadians lived in rural areas, accounting for 1 in every 4 self-employed workers in the country (Statistics Canada 2004j). Between 1981 and 2001, rates of self-employment through farming declined substantially, while rates of non-farm self-employment were steady from 1981 to 1986 and increased throughout the 1990s. Provinces and territories heavily dependent on farming have seen their farming workforce rates decline, with many farm families leaving the rural areas for the larger cities. In 1976 in Saskatchewan, for example, 25 percent of the province's workforce was in farming, as opposed to only 11 percent in 2001.

In 2004, the federal government appointed a Canada research chair in the new rural economy. The appointee studies the linkages between technological change and economic growth in rural areas. The focus of this research on rural life includes an examination of how information and knowledge-intensive technologies play a role in the sustainability of rural areas in Canada.

In smaller communities, the construction of oversized malls (known as *power centres*) that usually contain large businesses, such as Wal-Mart, Home Depot, or Costco, can create its own problems. Although many residents welcome the new employment opportunities and the convenience of one-stop shopping, local merchants see their long-time family businesses endangered by formidable 200 000-square-foot competitors with national reputations. Even when such big-box discount stores provide a short-term boost to a local economy (and they do not always do so), they can undermine a town's sense of community and identity. Box 15-2 chronicles

Research in Action   15-2
Store Wars

No organization exists in a vacuum, especially not a corporate giant. Executives of Wal-Mart know that. The epitome of the superstore (or big-box store), Wal-Mart has become the centre of controversy in towns and cities across North America, despite the familiar smiley-face logo and its red, white, and blue corporate image. The reason: a new Wal-Mart can have powerfully negative effects on the surrounding community.

Wal-Mart was founded in 1962 by Sam Walton, whose strategy was to locate new stores in rural communities, where competition from other retailers was weak and unions were not organized. Over the years, as the enormously successful discount chain expanded, Wal-Mart began to move into the fringes of metropolitan areas as well. But the residents of the communities Wal-Mart moved into did not always welcome their new neighbour.

Residents of smaller communities worried that Wal-Mart would destroy the small-town atmosphere they treasured. Would their cozy grocery store, known for its personal service, survive the discount giant's competition? Would their quaint and charming Main Street fall into decline? Would full-time jobs with accompanying benefits give way to part-time employment? (Studies have shown that superstores ultimately *reduce* employment.) One community's grassroots opposition to Wal-Mart, chronicled in the television documentary, *Store Wars*, ultimately lost its battle because of Wal-Mart's promised low prices and increased tax revenues. But citizens in many other communities have won injunctions against the big-box giant, at least temporarily.

On the urban fringes, too, residents have mobilized to stop new superstores; for example, in one case, environmentalists sounded the alarm over a proposed Wal-Mart superstore to be located next to a marsh that sheltered endangered wildlife.

But the issue is more complicated in these areas, because communities on the urban fringe are hardly untouched by economic development—they are affected by what many have called *urban sprawl*. New houses that dot the suburbs surrounding new stores, built on lots carved out of farmland or forest, have had an environmental impact themselves. In fact, the trend toward the superstore seems to parallel the emergence of the megalopolis, whose boundaries push farther and farther outward, eating up open space in the process. Recognizing the drawbacks of urban sprawl, some planners are beginning to advocate "smart growth"—restoring the central city and its older suburbs rather than abandoning them for the outer rings.

In his book, *Wal-Mart: Template for Twenty-First Century Capitalism* (2005), labour historian Nelson Lichtenstein states that Wal-Mart rules suburbia and smaller centres across both Canada and the United States; the company's next move, however, will be to infiltrate the urban market, where it is significantly less dominant. In British Columbia, for example, Wal-Mart has 30 stores, but none in the City of Vancouver.

Wal-Mart executives are unapologetic about the chain's rapid expansion which, as of 2004, even included 20 000 Chinese sales associates working in 40 stores in China. They argue that their aggressive competition has lowered prices and raised working people's standard of living. And they say they have given back to the communities where their stores are located by donating money to educational institutions and local agencies.

Applying Theory

1. Is there a Wal-Mart, Home Depot, or some other superstore near you? If so, was its opening a matter of controversy in your community?

2. What do you think of the "smart growth" movement? Should communities attempt to redirect business and residential development, or should big-box developers be free to build wherever and whatever they choose? What insights might some feminist sociologists provide to this discussion?

Sources: Ibata 2001; Kaufman 2000; Lichtenstein 2005; *Maine Times* 2001; Meyerson 2004; PBS 2001; Simon 2001; Smart Growth 2001; Wal-Mart 2001; Wal-Mart Watch 2000.

---

the "store wars" that often ensue when a power centre announces plans to come to a community.

Rural communities that do survive may feel threatened by provincial and territorial governments that, in the name of fiscal responsibility, have cut such services as health care, education, legal and court services, and various other social programs in rural areas. Many rural residents must now travel to larger urban areas to seek medical treatment or counselling or to attend court hearings.

On a more positive note, advances in electronic communication have allowed some people in Canada to work wherever they want. For those who are concerned about quality-of-life issues (e.g., clean environment, affordable housing, community cohesion, lack of congestion), working at home in a rural area that has access to the latest high-tech services is the perfect arrangement. No matter where people make their homes—whether in the city, the suburbs, or a rural village—economic and technological change will have an impact on their quality of life.

Social Policy and Health
The AIDS Crisis

The Issue

In his novel, *The Plague*, Albert Camus (1948:34) wrote, "There have been as many plagues as wars in history, yet always plagues and wars take people equally by surprise." Regarded by many as the distinctive plague of the modern era, AIDS certainly caught major social institutions—particularly the government, the health-care system, and the economy—by surprise when it was first noticed by medical practitioners in the early 1980s. It has since spread around the world. While encouraging new therapies have been developed to treat AIDS, there is currently no way to eradicate the disease by medical means. Therefore, it is essential to protect people by reducing the transmission of the fatal virus. But how is that to be done, and whose responsibility is it? What is the role of social institutions in preventing the spread of AIDS?

The Setting

AIDS is the acronym for *acquired immune deficiency syndrome*. Rather than being a distinct disease, AIDS is actually a predisposition to disease that is caused by a virus, the human immunodeficiency virus (HIV). The virus gradually destroys the body's immune system, leaving the carrier vulnerable to infections such as pneumonia that those with healthy immune systems can generally resist. Transmission of the virus from one person to another appears to require either intimate sexual contact or exchange of blood or bodily fluids (whether from contaminated hypodermic needles or syringes, transfusions of infected blood, or transmission from an infected mother to her child before or during birth).

The first cases of AIDS in Canada were reported in 1982. While the numbers of new cases and deaths have recently shown some evidence of decline, an estimated 58 000 people in Canada were living with AIDS or HIV by the end of 2005 (Public Health Agency of Canada 2006). Women account for a growing proportion of new cases; Aboriginal people make up 13 percent of that

figure. Worldwide, AIDS is stabilizing, with an estimated 38.6 million people infected (see Figure 15-7). The disease is not evenly distributed; those areas least equipped to deal with it—the developing nations of sub-Saharan Africa—face the greatest challenge (Maugh 2004; UNAIDS 2006; World Health Organization 2005).

Sociological Insights

Dramatic crises like the AIDS pandemic are likely to bring about certain transformations in a society's social structure. From a functionalist perspective, if established social institutions cannot meet a crucial need, new social networks are likely to emerge to perform that function. In the case of AIDS, self-help groups—especially in the gay communities of major cities—have organized to care for the sick, educate the healthy, and lobby for more responsive public policies.

The label, "person with AIDS" or "HIV-positive," often functions as a master status. People who have AIDS or are infected with the HIV virus face a powerful dual stigma. Not only are they associated with a lethal and contagious disease, but they also have to contend with a disease that disproportionately afflicts already stigmatized groups, such as gay males and intravenous drug users. This link to stigmatized groups delayed recognition of the severity of the AIDS pandemic. The media took little interest in the disease until it seemed to be spreading beyond the gay community.

Viewed from a conflict perspective, policymakers were slow to respond to the AIDS crisis because those in high-risk groups—gay men and IV drug users—were comparatively powerless. Furthermore, a study done in 2002 documented the fact that females and minority groups are less likely than others to receive experimental treatments for the HIV infection (Gifford et al. 2002).

On the micro level of social interaction, observers once forecast that AIDS would lead to a more conservative sexual climate—among both homosexuals and heterosexuals—in which people would be much more

▶ **FIGURE 15-7**

Adults and Children Living with HIV/AIDS

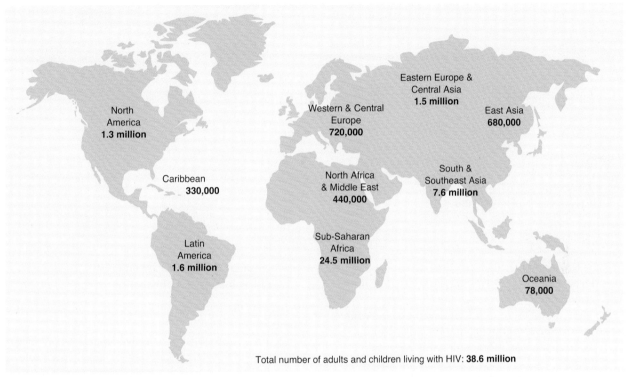

Total number of adults and children living with HIV: **38.6 million**

Note: Midpoint estimates for 2005 released in May 2006; world range is 33.4 to 46.0 million.
Source: UNAIDS 2006:505–540.

cautious about becoming involved with new partners. Yet, it appears that many sexually active people have not heeded precautions about so-called safe sex. Data from studies conducted in the early 1990s indicated a growing complacency about AIDS, even among those who were most vulnerable (Bernstein 2004).

Policy Initiatives

AIDS has struck all societies, but not all nations can respond in the same manner. Studies done in North America show that, today, people with HIV or AIDS who receive appropriate medical treatment are living longer than they did in the past. This advance may put additional pressure on policymakers to address the issues raised by the spread of AIDS.

In some nations, cultural practices may prevent people from dealing realistically with the AIDS pandemic. They may not be likely to take the necessary preventive measures, including open discussion of sexuality, homosexuality, and drug use. Prevention has shown signs of

working among target groups, such as drug users, pregnant women, and gay men and lesbians, but preventive initiatives are few and far between in developing nations.

The prescribed treatment to reduce mother-to-baby transmission of AIDS costs about US$300. That amount is roughly equivalent to the average annual income in much of the world where the risk of AIDS is greatest (such as Africa, which accounted for 71 percent of the world's deaths from AIDS in 2005). The medication for adult patients with HIV is even more costly (McNeil 2004; UNAIDS 2006:508; World Health Organization 2005:3).

The high cost of drug-treatment programs has generated intensive worldwide pressure on the major pharmaceutical companies to lower the prices to patients in developing nations, especially in sub-Saharan Africa. In 2001, bowing to this pressure, several of the companies agreed to make the combination therapies available at cost. Even at these much lower prices, however, in the poorest nations, relatively few of those who were sick enough to need treatment were receiving it. In many nations, social institutions simply are not equipped to distribute medicine to those who need it (McNeil 2004).

Applying Theory

1. What perspective might feminist sociologists bring to the discussion on the global crisis of HIV/AIDS?

2. From a conflict perspective, what groups would be less likely to receive experimental treatments for HIV/AIDS? Why?

3. If you were an interactionist sociologist who wanted to understand why some people knowingly ignore the dangers of AIDS, how would you go about studying the problem?

CHAPTER RESOURCES

Summary

What is Demography?

- **Demography** (p. 371) is the scientific study of population.
- Thomas Robert Malthus suggested that the world's population was growing more rapidly than the available food supply and that this gap would increase over time. However, Karl Marx saw capitalism, rather than a rising world population, as the cause of social ills.
- The primary mechanism for obtaining population information in Canada and most other countries is the **census** (p. 372).

What are the Patterns of World Population?

- Developing nations face the prospect of continued population growth because a substantial portion of their population is approaching child-bearing age. Many developed nations have begun to stabilize their population growth.

What are the Fertility Patterns in Canada?

- Canada's fertility rate in 2006 was 1.54 children, below the 2.1 children needed to sustain the population.

What is Social Epidemiology?

- **Social epidemiology** (p. 379) is the study of disease, health, and disability, across a population.
- Studies have consistently shown that people in the lower classes have higher rates of **mortality** (p. 380) and disability than those in upper classes.
- Ethnic minorities have higher rates of **morbidity** (p. 380) and **mortality** than do the dominant groups. Older people are vulnerable to particular diseases, such as Alzheimer's.

What are the Sociological Perspectives on Health and Illness?

- The functionalist perspective on health and illness sees physicians as "gatekeepers" for the **sick role** (p. 383), either verifying a person's condition as "ill" or designating the person as "recovered."
- Conflict theorists use the term **medicalization of society** (p. 384) to refer to medicine's growing role as a major institution of social control. Feminist theorists look at the ways in which the institution of medicine is gendered.

What is the Health-Care Situation in Canada?

- Canada's health-care system, as set out in the Canada Health Act, is based on the principles of public administration, comprehensiveness, universality, portability, and accessibility (p. 388).

How have Communities Changed?

- Stable **communities** (p. 388) emerged when humans became farmers and their surplus production allowed others to inhabit **pre-industrial cities** (p. 389).
- Mechanization of production brought about the **industrial city** (p. 389), characterized by a large population and domination of factories. Globalization and technology have led to the emergence of the **post-industrial city** (p. 389), where corporate offices are dominant rather than factories.

What is Urbanization, and What are its Consequences?

- **Urban ecology** (p. 390) is a functionalist view of urbanization which focuses on how the different elements of the urban area are interrelated and contribute to stability.
- **New urban sociology** (p. 393) is a conflict view of urbanization, which considers the interplay of a community's political and economic interests as well as the impact of the global economy on communities. This view draws on Immanuel Wallerstein's *world-systems analysis* (see Chapter 9 for a discussion of this term).

What are some Types of Communities?

- Types of communities include **central cities** (p. 395), **suburbs** (p. 397), and **rural communities** (p. 398).

Critical Thinking Questions

1. Some European nations are now experiencing population declines. Their death rates are low and their birth rates are even lower than in stage III of the demographic transition model. Does this pattern suggest that there is now a fourth stage in the demographic transition? Even more important, what are the implications of negative population growth for an industrialized nation in the twenty-first century?

2. How would you characterize the relationship between you and your doctor? How does the dimension of power play into that relationship?

3. How has your home community changed over the years you have lived there? Have there been significant changes in the community's economic base? Have the community's social problems intensified or lessened over time? What are the community's future prospects?

Key Terms

Birth rate The number of live births per 1000 population in a given year. Also known as the *crude birth rate*. (p. 372)

Census An enumeration, or counting, of a population. (p. 372)

Central cities Large urban areas where population is concentrated. (p. 395)

Community A spatial or political unit of social organization that gives people a sense of belonging. (p. 370)

Concentric-zone theory A theory for describing land use in industrial cities, where the centre (or nucleus) of a city is the central business district. (p. 391)

Death rate The number of deaths per 1000 population in a given year. Also known as the *crude death rate*. (p. 373)

Defended neighbourhood A sentimental union of similar people, where inhabitants apply their own definitions of community boundaries. (p. 395)

Demographic transition A term used to describe the change from high birth rates and death rates to relatively low birth rates and death rates. (p. 374)

Demography The scientific study of population. (p. 371)

Ethnoburb A suburb that is ethnically diverse. (p. 398)

Fertility The amount of reproduction among women of child-bearing age. (p. 370)

Growth rate The difference between births and deaths, plus the differences between immigrants and emigrants, per 1000 population. (p. 373)

Health As defined by the World Health Organization, a "state of complete physical, mental, and social well-being, and not merely the absence of disease and infirmity." (p. 379)

Human ecology A field of study concerned with the relationships between people and their environment. (p. 390)

Incidence The number of *new* cases of a specific disorder occurring within a given population during a stated period. (p. 379)

Industrial city The city that emerged following the Industrial Revolution; a centre of banking, finance, and industrialization, with a more open class system. (p. 389)

Infant mortality rate The number of deaths of infants under one year of age per 1000 live births in a given year. (p. 373)

Life expectancy The median number of years a person can be expected to live under current mortality conditions. (p. 373)

Medicalization of society The growing role of medicine as a major institution of social control. (p. 384)

Megalopolis A densely populated area, containing two or more cities and their suburbs. (p. 390)

Morbidity rate The incidence of diseases in a given population. (p. 380)

Mortality Number of deaths. (p. 370)

Mortality rate The incidence of death in a given population. (p. 380)

Multiple-nuclei theory A response to the emergence of more than one focal point in some metropolitan areas. In this view, a metropolitan area may have many centres of development, each of which reflects a particular urban need or activity. (p. 391)

New urban sociology Sociologists in this field consider the interplay of local, national, and worldwide forces and their effect on local space, with special emphasis on the impact of global economic activity. (p. 393)

Population pyramid A special type of bar chart that shows the distribution of population by gender and age. (p. 377)

Post-industrial city A city in which global finance and the electronic flow of information dominate the economy. (p. 389)

Pre-industrial city An old city that had a few thousand people living within its borders and was also characterized by a relatively closed class system and limited mobility. (p. 389)

Prevalence The total number of cases of a specific disorder that exist at a given time. (p. 380)

Sick role Societal expectations about the attitudes and behaviour of a person viewed as being ill. (p. 383)

Social epidemiology The study of the distribution of disease, impairment, and general health status across a population. (p. 379)

Suburb A term that generally refers to any community near a large city or any territory within a metropolitan area that is not included in the central city. (p. 397)

Total fertility rate (TFR) The average number of children born alive to a woman, assuming that she conforms to current fertility rates. (p. 372)

Urban ecology A field of study that focuses on various relationships as they emerge in urban areas; it emphasizes that different elements in urban areas contribute to stability. (p. 390)

Urbanism Louis Wirth's term for a distinctive pattern of behaviour emanating from a relatively large and permanently settled community. (p. 394)

Zero population growth (ZPG) The state of a population with a growth rate of zero, achieved when the number of births plus immigrants is equal to the number of deaths plus emigrants. (p. 378)

Additional Readings

Beaujot, Roderic, and Don Kerr, eds. 2007. *The Changing Face of Canada: Essential Readings in Population*. Toronto: CSPI/WP. Two demographers and other contributors trace how Canada's population has changed dramatically over time.

Decter, Michael. 2004. *Healing Medicare: Managing Health Care System Change the Canadian Way*. Toronto: McGilligan Books. This book provides a plan for the reform of the Canadian health-care system, offering suggestions on how to ensure the system remains affordable and high quality.

Kalipeni, Ezekiel, Susan Craddock, Joseph Oppong, and Jayati Ghosh, eds. 2004. *HIV and AIDS in Africa: Beyond Epidemiology*. Oxford, UK: Blackwell Publishing. An edited work covering a vast scope of HIV/AIDS–related topics and their impact on African nations.

Online Learning Centre

Visit the *Sociology: A Brief Introduction* Online Learning Centre at www.mcgrawhill.ca/olc/schaefer to access quizzes, interactive exercises, video clips, and other research and study tools related to this chapter.

Reel Society Video Clips

Reel Society can be used to spark discussion about the following topics from this chapter:

- Demography: The study of population
- Social epidemiology and health

chapter 16

GLOBALIZATION, THE ENVIRONMENT, AND SOCIAL CHANGE

In 2002, amid charges that wealthy nations were "dumping" large quantities of surplus wheat and other commodities on the world market, jeopardizing the value of crops produced in poor countries, the global charity Oxfam launched a campaign to ensure fair trade with nations that depend on a single crop, such as wheat, coffee, or rice. These photos of well-known personalities were taken to advertise the effort, beginning in 2005. From left to right: singer/actor Alanis Morissette, actor Colin Firth, and singer Chris Martin of Coldplay.

- ☐ **What are Social Movements?**
- ☐ **How can Social Change be Explained?**
- ☐ **What Forms does Resistance to Social Change Take?**
- ☐ **How does Globalization Affect Global Social Change?**
- ☐ **What Impact does Social Change have on the Environment?**

Boxes

SOCIOLOGY IN THE GLOBAL COMMUNITY: A New Social Movement in Rural India
RESEARCH IN ACTION: The Human Genome Project
SOCIAL POLICY AND GLOBALIZATION: Transnationals

Chuck D is an unlikely hero of the digital age. With hit albums such as *Yo! Bum Rush the Show* and *Fear of a Black Planet*, the founder of the rap group Public Enemy would seem to inhabit a world far removed from the more conspicuous pioneers of cyberspace, from the Netscapes and Yahoos! and AOLs. In 1998, however, Chuck D stormed into cyberspace. Rather than giving his latest songs to Def Jam, the label that had produced his music for over a decade, the rap artist instead released his music directly onto the Internet, at www.public-enemy.com. It shouldn't have been such a big deal, really: one artist, a handful of songs, and a funky distribution method that probably reached several thousand fans. But in the music business this was very big news. For Chuck D had taken one of the industry's most sacred practices and thrown it, quite literally, into space. With just a couple of songs, he challenged how music was sold and, even more fundamentally, how it was owned. "This is the beginning," proclaimed the rapper, "of the end of domination."

As far as Chuck D was concerned, putting music online was a matter of power, of using new technologies to right old wrongs and give recording artists the influence and money that was rightfully theirs. To the recording industry, however, it was heresy. . . .

Had Chuck D been an isolated case, the studios most likely could have looked the other way. They could have dismissed Chuck D as a simple renegade, a rapper gone bad, and forgotten him and his website. But the problem was that Chuck D, potentially, was everywhere. In cyberspace, any recording artist could distribute his or her music online; any musician could become a mini-studio, circumventing the record labels and their complex, clunky rules. . . .

Matters reached a head in 1999, when a 19-year-old college dropout named Shawn Fanning joined Chuck D in storming the frontier. Backed by his uncle in Boston, Fanning created Napster, a revolutionary system that allowed thousands—even millions—of users to trade their music online. Within months of its release, Napster had become a social phenomenon and a massive commercial threat. Universities complained that Napster was suddenly consuming huge chunks of their Internet bandwidth, and the music industry condemned it as piracy of the most blatant sort: "STEALING," as one music lawyer described it, "in big letters." Ironic foes such as Prince and the rock band Metallica joined the labels in pursuit of these new pirates, while prophets predicted the death of the recorded music industry. "A revolution has occurred in the way music is distributed," wrote one observer, "and the big record companies are in a state of panic."

☐ *(Spar 2001:327–329)*

RULING THE WAVES

Cycles of
Discovery, Chaos, and Wealth
from the Compass to the Internet

DEBORA L. SPAR

In this selection from *Ruling the Waves: Cycles of Discovery, Chaos, and Wealth from the Compass to the Internet*, political scientist Debora L. Spar (2001) describes the economic repercussions of a recent change in the way popular music is distributed. To young people, the advent of Napster meant that, suddenly, free music was available to them over the Internet. But to musicians and smaller record labels, Napster was a revolutionary new technology with the potential to shift the balance of power from the corporate giants that produced popular music to the artists who created and performed it. The global distribution of digitized music via the Internet, then, changed both the way people behaved—how they selected, obtained, and listened to music—and the cultural institution that is the music business.

The invention of the personal computer and its worldwide integration into people's day-to-day lives is another example of the social change that often follows the introduction of a new technology. **Social change** has been defined as significant alteration over time in behaviour patterns and culture (W. Moore 1967). But what constitutes a "significant" alteration? Certainly, the dramatic rise in formal education documented in Chapter 13 represents a change that has had profound social consequences. Other social changes that have had long-term and important consequences include the emergence of slavery as a system of stratification (see Chapter 8), the Industrial Revolution (Chapters 5 and 15), the increased participation of women in the paid labour force in Canada and other industrialized countries (Chapter 11), and the worldwide population explosion (Chapter 15). In many instances, the social movements that we cover in this chapter have played an important role in promoting social change.

How does social change happen? Is the process unpredictable, or can we make certain generalizations about it? Has globalization contributed to social change? And how has our environment been affected by social change? In this chapter, we examine the process of social change, with special emphasis on the impact of globalization and the effects on our environment. We begin with social movements—collective efforts to bring about deliberate social change. Then, we turn to the unanticipated social change that occurs when innovations such as new technologies sweep through society. Efforts to explain long-term social change have led to the development of theories of change; we consider the evolutionary, functionalist, conflict, feminist, and interactionist approaches to change. We see how vested interests attempt to block changes that they see as threatening. We see, too, that the process of globalization means that these social changes often happen on a global scale. And we look at what social change has done to our environment. Finally, in the social policy section, we discuss a controversial effect of global social change, the creation of **transnationals**—immigrants with an allegiance to more than one nation.

Use Your Sociological Imagination

Do you see the widespread availability of music online as reinforcing a generation gap between a younger crowd that thinks music should be common property and an older faction that views music as private intellectual property?

☐ WHAT ARE SOCIAL MOVEMENTS?

Although such factors as physical environment, population, technology, and social inequality serve as sources of change, it is the collective effort of individuals organized in social movements that ultimately leads to change. Sociologists use the term **social movement** to refer to an organized collective activity to bring about or resist fundamental change in an existing group or society (Benford 1992). Herbert Blumer recognized the special importance of social movements when he defined them as "collective enterprises to establish a new order of life" (1955:19).

In many nations, including Canada, social movements have had a dramatic impact on the course of history and the evolution of the social structure. Consider the actions of environmentalists, feminists, anti-globalization protesters, and anti-poverty activists. Members of each social movement stepped outside traditional channels for bringing about social change, yet had a noticeable influence on public policy. In Eastern Europe, equally dramatic collective efforts helped to topple Communist party regimes in a largely peaceful manner, in nations that many observers had thought were "immune" to such social change (Ramet 1991).

Though social movements imply the existence of conflict, we can also analyze their activities from a functionalist perspective. Even when they are unsuccessful, social movements contribute to the formation of public opinion. Initially, people thought the ideas of Margaret Sanger and other early advocates of birth control were radical, yet contraceptives are now widely available in North America. Moreover, functionalists view social movements as training grounds for leaders of the political establishment. Former heads of state such as Cuba's Fidel Castro and South Africa's Nelson Mandela came to power after serving as leaders of revolutionary movements. Poland's Lech Walesa, Russia's Boris Yeltsin, and the Czech playwright Vaclav Havel all led protest movements against Communist party rule and later became leaders of their countries' governments.

Because social movements know no borders, even nationalistic movements like those led by Castro and Walesa are deeply influenced by global events. Increasingly, social movements are taking on an international dimension from the start. Global enterprises, in particular, lend themselves to targeting through international mobilization, whether they are corporations like McDonald's, events such as the Olympics, or governmental bodies like the World Trade Organization (WTO). Global activism is not new, however; it is generally held that it began with the writing of Karl Marx, who sought to mobilize oppressed peoples in other industrialized countries. Today, activist networking is facilitated by the Internet and by relatively cheap travel costs. Participation in transnational activism is much wider now than in the past, and passions are quicker to ignite (Della Porta and Tarrow 2005; Tarrow 2005).

How and why do social movements emerge? Obviously, people are often discontented with the way things are. But what causes them to organize at a particular moment in a collective effort to effect change? Sociologists rely on two explanations for why people mobilize: the relative deprivation and resource mobilization approaches.

Relative Deprivation Approach

Those members of a society who feel most frustrated and disgruntled by social and economic conditions are not necessarily the worst off in an objective sense. Social scientists have long recognized that what is most significant is the way in which people *perceive* their situation. As Karl Marx pointed out, although the misery of the workers was important to their perception of their oppressed state, so was their position *in relation to* the capitalist ruling class (Marx and Engels [1847] 1955).

The term **relative deprivation** is defined as the conscious feeling of a negative discrepancy between legitimate expectations and present actualities (J. Wilson 1973).

◀ P. 199 In other words, things aren't as good as you hoped they would be. Such a state may be characterized by scarcity rather than a complete lack of necessities (as we saw in the distinction between absolute and relative poverty in Chapter 8). A relatively deprived person is dissatisfied because he or she feels downtrodden relative to some appropriate reference group. Thus, blue-collar workers who live in apartments, though hardly at the bottom of the economic ladder, may nevertheless feel deprived in comparison to corporate managers and professionals who live in lavish homes in exclusive suburbs.

In addition to the feeling of relative deprivation, two other elements must be present before discontent will be channelled into a social movement. People

Social movements are not limited to local issues; globalization and the rise of the Internet have facilitated international protests. In December 2005, these South Koreans travelled to Hong Kong to protest against free trade at a meeting of the World Trade Organization.

must feel that they have a *right* to their goals, that they deserve better than what they have. For example, the ◀ P.215 struggle against European colonialism in Africa intensified when growing numbers of Africans decided that it was legitimate for them to have political and economic independence. At the same time, the disadvantaged group must perceive that its goals cannot be attained through conventional means. This belief may or may not be correct. Whichever is the case, the group will not mobilize into a social movement unless there is a shared perception that members can end their relative deprivation only through collective action (Morrison 1971).

Critics of this approach have noted that people don't need to feel deprived to be moved to act. In addition, this approach fails to explain why certain feelings of deprivation are transformed into social movements, whereas in other similar situations, no collective effort is made to reshape society. Consequently, in recent years, sociologists have paid increasing attention to the forces needed to bring about the emergence of social movements (Alain 1985; Finkel and Rule 1987; Orum 1989).

Resource Mobilization Approach

It takes more than desire to start a social movement. It helps to have money, political influence, access to the media, and personnel. The term **resource mobilization** refers to the ways in which a social movement utilizes such resources. The success of a movement for change will depend in good part on what resources it has and how effectively it mobilizes them (see also Gamson 1989; Staggenborg 1989a, 1989b). Sociologist Anthony Oberschall has argued that to sustain social protest or resistance, there must be an "organizational base and continuity of leadership" (1973:199). As people become part of a social movement, norms develop to guide their behaviour. Members of the movement may be expected to attend regular meetings of organizations, pay dues, recruit new adherents, and boycott "enemy" products or speakers. An emerging social movement may give rise to special language or new words for familiar terms. In recent years, social movements have been responsible for such new terms of self-reference as *blacks, African Canadians, African Americans* (used to replace *Negroes*), *senior citizens* (used to replace *old folks*), *gays* (used to replace *homosexuals*), and *people with disabilities* (used to replace *the handicapped*).

Leadership is a central factor in the mobilization of the discontented into social movements. Often, a movement will be led by a charismatic figure, such ◀ P.349 as Nelson Mandela or Dr. Martin Luther King Jr. As Max Weber described it in 1904, *charisma* is that quality of an individual that sets him or her apart from

ordinary people. Of course, charisma can fade abruptly, which helps to account for the fragility of certain social movements (A. Morris 2000).

Yet many social movements do persist over long periods because their leadership is well organized and ongoing. Ironically, as Robert Michels noted, politi- ◀ P.121 cal movements that are fighting for social change eventually take on some of the aspects of the bureaucracy that they were organized to protest (1915). Leaders tend to dominate the decision-making process without directly consulting followers. The bureaucratization of social movements is not inevitable, however. More radical movements that advocate major structural change in society and embrace mass actions tend not to be hierarchical or bureaucratic (Fitzgerald and Rodgers 2000).

Why do certain individuals join a social movement while others who are in similar situations do not? Some of them are recruited to join. Karl Marx recog- ◀ P.190 nized the importance of recruitment when he called on workers to become aware of their oppressed status and to develop a class consciousness. Like theorists of the resource-mobilization approach, Marx held that a social movement (specifically, the revolt of the proletariat) would require leaders to sharpen the awareness of the oppressed. They would need to help workers to overcome feelings of **false consciousness**, or attitudes that do not reflect workers' objective position, in order to organize a revolutionary movement. Similarly, one of the challenges faced by feminists of the late 1960s and early 1970s in North America was to convince women that they were being deprived of their rights and of socially valued resources. As we mentioned in an earlier discussion on the feminist movement in Canada (see Chapter 11), white, middle-class women have often fought for their vision of social or moral reform, which did not necessarily serve the interests of all women.

Gender and Social Movements

Sociologists point out that gender is an important element in understanding social movements. In male-dominated societies, such as Canada, many women—particularly those who are older, disabled, and/or members of a visible minority—may find it more difficult than men to assume leadership positions in social movement organizations. While women often serve disproportionately as volunteers in these movements, their work is not always recognized, nor are their voices as easily heard as men's. Morseover, gender bias causes the real extent of women's influence to be overlooked. Traditional examination of the socio-political system tends to focus on such male-dominated corridors of power as legislatures and corporate boardrooms, to the neglect of the socially constructed female-dominated domains such as households, community-based groups, and faith-based networks. But efforts to influence family conditions, child-rearing, relationships between parents and schools, and spiritual values are clearly significant to a culture and society (Ferree and Merrill 2000; Noonan 1995).

Scholars of social movements now realize that gender can affect even the way we view organized efforts to bring about or resist change. For example, an emphasis on using rationality and cold logic to achieve goals helps to obscure the importance of passion and emotion in successful social movements. It would be difficult to find any movement—from labour battles to voting rights to animal rights—in which passion was not part of its activities. Yet, calls for a more serious study of the role of emotion are frequently seen as applying only to the women's movement, because emotion continues to be characterized as stereotypically feminine (Ferree and Merrill 2000; V. Taylor 1995).

New Social Movements

Beginning in the late 1960s, European social scientists observed a change in both the composition and the targets of emerging social movements. Previously, traditional social movements had focused on economic issues, often led by labour unions or by people who shared the same occupation. However, many social movements that have become active in recent decades—including the contemporary women's movement, the peace movement, and the environmental movement—do not have the social class roots typical of the labour protests in Canada, the United States, and Europe over the past century (Tilly 1993, 2004).

The term **new social movement** refers to organized collective activities that address values and social identities, as well as improvements in the quality of life. These movements may be involved in developing collective identities. Many have complex agendas that go beyond a single issue; some cross national boundaries. Educated, middle-class people are significantly represented in some of these new social movements, such as the anti-globalization movement. Box 16-1 describes a new social movement among exploited textile workers in rural India.

New social movements generally do not view government as their ally in the struggle for a better society. While they typically do not seek to overthrow the government, they may criticize, protest, or harass public officials. Researchers have found that members of new social movements show little inclination to accept established authority, even scientific or technical authority. This characteristic is especially evident in the environmental and anti–nuclear power movements, whose activists present their own experts to counter those of government or big business (Garner 1996; Polletta and Jasper 2001;

A. Scott 1990). In Canada, for example, Earth Day was one of the original green movements in the country. Activists protested against large companies that caused environmental damage and encouraged other Canadians to be more mindful of how they dispose of household garbage. In 2008, millions of Canadians turned off their lights during Earth Hour. Eighteen years after its initial launch, Earth Day Canada now has garnered numerous corporate sponsors, a move which has offended many unions and social justice organizations (Welsh 2008).

The environmental movement is one of many new movements with a worldwide focus. In their efforts to reduce air and water pollution, curtail global warming, and protect endangered animal species, environmental activists have realized that strong regulatory measures within a single country are not sufficient. Similarly, labour union leaders and human-rights advocates cannot adequately address exploitative sweatshop conditions in a developing country if a multinational corporation can simply move the factory to another country, where workers earn even less. Whereas traditional views of social movements tended to emphasize resource mobilization on a local level, new social movement theory offers a broader, global perspective on social and political activism. Table 16-1 summarizes the sociological approaches that have contributed to social movement theory. Each has added to our understanding of the development of social movements.

Use Your Sociological Imagination

Try to imagine a society without any social movements. Under what conditions could such a society exist? Would you want to live in it?

☐ HOW CAN SOCIAL CHANGE BE EXPLAINED?

We have defined social change as significant alteration over time in behaviour patterns and culture. Social change can occur so slowly as to be almost undetectable to those it affects, but it can also happen with breathtaking rapidity.

Explanations of social change are clearly a challenge in the diverse and complex world we inhabit today. Nevertheless, theorists from several disciplines have sought to analyze social change. In some instances, they have examined historical events to arrive at a better understanding of contemporary changes. We will review five theoretical approaches to change—evolutionary, functionalist, conflict, feminist, and interactionist theoriesy—and then we will take a look at resistance to change.

Sociology in the Global Community 16-1
A New Social Movement in Rural India

In the mid-1980s, 5000 striking textile workers came home from Bombay to mobilize support in their rural villages and gather food for strikers in the city. As the strike wore on, some remained in their villages and sought employment on government drought-relief projects. However, there weren't enough jobs for rural residents, much less for these new migrants from Bombay.

This experience was the origin of a new social movement in rural India. With unemployment threatening an expanded population in rural areas, activists formed what came to be called the Shoshit, Shetkari, Kashtakari, Kamgar, Mukti Sangharsh (SSKKMS), which means "exploited peasants, toilers, workers liberation struggle." The initial goal of the movement was to provide drought relief for villagers, but the deeper goal was to bring more power to rural areas.

The SSKKMS was unusual compared to other social movements in India: about half its participants and many of its leaders were women. This was no accident, for the movement also sought to address gender inequities. At a meeting in 1986, Indutai Patankar—a pioneer in the rural women's movement—declared:

> We have gathered here to discuss our problems as women and a rural poor. . . . Not only do we work twice as hard as men but we also do not get equal wages, no child care. . . . We have to organize as women with the other oppressed toilers in urban and rural areas. (Desai 1996:214)

Sociologist Manisha Desai views the SSKKMS as an **example of a** new social movement because it incorporates concrete, material targets as well as broad ideological goals—goals that in this case included greater access to water for the poor and gender equality.

Women and men from the movement were equally involved in many forms of political activism, including such direct-action tactics as roadblocks.

In addition to addressing issues of gender stratification, the SSKKMS openly confronted the pervasive inequities associated with the *dalit*, or oppressed people from lower castes (previously called untouchables). Movement activists insisted that both women and landless peasants (most of whom were *dalits*) should have equal access to water once dams were completed. This is a critical issue in the lives of rural Indian women, who typically spend many hours a day in search of safe drinking water.

In her analysis of the SSKKMS, Desai emphasizes that the movement does not have a single focus, but is committed to multiple struggles for social and economic justice (1996). As with any social movement, there are contradictions in the SSKKMS. A middle-class leadership core generally articulates goals for the many exploited villagers in this mass movement. While in one rural area, all local assemblies must be at least 30 percent female, rural women sometimes serve simply as fronts for the hidden agendas of their male relatives. Nevertheless, Desai's study of the SSKKMS underscores the fact that social movements in general—and new social movements in particular—are found *throughout* the world, not solely in industrialized nations.

Applying Theory

1. If you were a conflict thinker, why would you think so many women participated in the SSKKMS?
2. What would happen if "powerless" people in Canada formed a similar movement? According to conflict thinkers, would it succeed? Why or why not?

Evolutionary Theory

The pioneering work of Charles Darwin (1809–1882) in biological evolution contributed to nineteenth-century theories of social change. Darwin's approach stresses a continuing progression of successive life forms. For example, human beings came at a later stage of evolution than reptiles and represent a more complex form of life. Social theorists seeking an analogy to this biological model originated

evolutionary theory, in which society is viewed as moving in a definite direction. Early evolutionary theorists generally agreed that society was progressing inevitably to a higher state. As might be expected, they concluded—in ethnocentric fashion—that their own behaviour and culture were more advanced than those of earlier civilizations.

◄ P.7 August Comte (1798–1857), a founder of sociology, was an evolutionary theorist of change. He saw human societies as moving forward in their thinking,

Table 16-1 Contributions to Social Movement Theory	
Approach	**Emphasis**
Relative deprivation approach	Social movements are especially likely to arise when rising expectations are frustrated.
Resource mobilization approach	The success of social movements depends on which resources are available and how effectively they are used.
New social movement theory	Social movements arise when people are motivated by value issues and social identity questions.

from mythology to the scientific method. Similarly, Émile Durkheim ([1893]1933) maintained that society progressed from simple to more complex forms of social organization.

Today, evolutionary theory influences sociologists in a variety of ways. For example, it has encouraged sociobiologists to investigate the behavioural links between humans and other animals (Maryanski 2004). Many sociologists, as we previously mentioned in Chapter 1, are critical of evolutionary theory on the grounds that it attempts to provide justification for class differentiation and domination of the powerful over the powerless.

Functionalist Theory

Because functionalist sociologists focus on what *maintains* a system, not on what changes it, they might seem to offer little to the study of social change. Yet, as the work of sociologist Talcott Parsons demonstrates, functionalists have made a distinctive contribution to this area of sociological investigation.

Parsons (1902–1979), a leading proponent of functionalist theory, viewed society as being in a natural state of equilibrium. By "equilibrium," he meant that society tends toward a state of stability or balance. Parsons ◀ P.13 would view even prolonged labour strikes or civilian riots as temporary disruptions in the status quo rather than as significant alterations in social structure. Therefore, according to his **equilibrium model**, as changes occur in one part of society, adjustments must be made in other parts. If not, society's equilibrium will be threatened and strains will occur.

Reflecting the evolutionary approach, Parsons maintained that four processes of social change are inevitable (1966). The first, *differentiation*, refers to the increasing complexity of social organization. The transition from "medicine man" to physician, nurse, and pharmacist is an illustration of differentiation in the field of health. This process is accompanied by *adaptive upgrading*, by

which social institutions become more specialized in their purposes. The division of physicians into obstetricians, internists, surgeons, and so forth is an example of adaptive upgrading.

The third process Parsons identified is the *inclusion* of groups that were previously excluded because of their gender, race, ethnicity, or social class. Medical schools have practised inclusion by admitting increasing numbers of women and visible minorities. Lastly, Parsons contends that societies experience *value generalization*, the development of new values that tolerate and legitimate a greater range of activities. The acceptance of preventive and alternative medicine is an example of value generalization: society has broadened its view of health care. All four processes identified by Parsons stress consensus—societal agreement on the nature of social organization and values (B. Johnson 1975; Wallace and Wolf 1980).

Though Parsons's approach explicitly incorporates the evolutionary notion of continuing progress, the dominant theme in his model is stability. Society may change, but it remains stable through new forms of integration. For example, in place of the kinship ties that provided social cohesion in the past, people develop laws, judicial processes, and new values and belief systems.

Functionalists assume that social institutions would not persist unless they continued to contribute to society. This assumption leads them to conclude that drastically altering institutions will threaten societal equilibrium. Critics note that the functionalist approach virtually disregards the use of coercion by the powerful to maintain the illusion of a stable, well-integrated society (Gouldner 1960).

Conflict Theory

The functionalist perspective minimizes the importance of change. It emphasizes the persistence of social life, and sees change as reform, allowing for the maintenance of society's equilibrium. In contrast, conflict theorists contend that social institutions and practices persist because powerful groups have the ability to maintain the status quo. Change—possibly in the form of revolution—has crucial significance, since it is needed to correct social injustices and inequalities.

Karl Marx accepted the evolutionary argument that societies develop along a particular path. However, unlike Auguste Comte and Herbert Spencer, Marx did not view each successive stage as an inevitable improvement over the previous one. History, according to Marx, proceeds through a series of stages, each of which exploits a class of people. Ancient society exploited slaves; the estate system of feudalism exploited serfs; modern capitalist society exploits the working class. Ultimately, through a socialist revolution led by the proletariat, human society will move toward the final stage of development: a classless communist society, or "community of free individuals," as Marx described it in 1867 in *Das Kapital* (see Bottomore and Rubel 1956:250).

As we have seen, Marx had an important influence on the development of sociology. His thinking offered insights into such institutions as the economy, the family, religion, and government. The Marxist view of social change is appealing because it does not restrict people to a passive role in responding to inevitable cycles or changes in material culture. Instead, Marxist theory offers a tool for those who wish to seize control of the historical process and gain their freedom from injustice. In contrast to functionalists' emphasis on stability, Marx argues that conflict is a normal and desirable aspect

◀ P.9

of social change. In fact, change must be encouraged as a means of eliminating social inequality (Lauer 1982).

One conflict theorist, Ralf Dahrendorf, has noted that the contrast between the functionalist perspective's emphasis on stability and the conflict perspective's focus on change reflects the contradictory nature of society (1958). Human societies are stable and long-lasting, yet they also experience serious conflict. Dahrendorf found that the functionalist and the conflict approaches were ultimately compatible, despite their many points of disagreement. Indeed, Parsons spoke of new functions that result from social change, and Marx recognized the need for change so that societies could function more equitably.

Feminist Theories

Unlike other sociological perspectives, social change is the hallmark of feminist perspectives. Feminist sociologists, diverse as they are, share a desire to deepen their understanding of society in order to change the world; it is their desire to make it more just and humane (Lengermann and Niebrugge-Brantley 1998). Confronting social injustice in order to promote change for those groups in society who are disadvantaged by their "social location"—their class, race, ethnicity, sexual preference, age, or global location—is a key feature of feminist perspectives. As feminist sociologist Patricia Hill Collins explains, change is sought for "people differently placed in specific political, social, and historic contexts characterized by injustice" (1998:xiv).

On the outskirts of Buenos Aires, Argentina, a shantytown forms a stark contrast to the gleaming skyscrapers in the wealthy downtown area. Marxists and conflict theorists see social change as a way of overcoming the kind of social inequality evident in this photograph.

Table 16-2 Sociological Perspectives on Social Change

Evolutionary	Social change moves society in a definite direction, frequently from simple to more complex.
Functionalist	Social change must contribute to society's stability.
	Modest adjustments or reforms must be made to accommodate social change.
Conflict	Fundamental social change is necessary to correct social injustices and inequalities.
Feminist	Social change is necessary to bring about equality for women.
Interactionist	Constant adjustment and change occur through social interaction.

Increasingly, feminist perspectives advance the view that acknowledging women's differences must be paramount in guiding the direction of social change. The interests of white, middle-class women, for example, must not be assumed to represent the interests of all women. Social change must be inclusive of the interests of women of diverse backgrounds. As feminist theorists Rosemary Hennessy and Chrys Ingraham ask, "What are the consequences of this way of thinking for transforming the inequities in women's lives?" and "How is this way of explaining the world going to improve life for all women?" (Lengermann and Niebrugge-Brantley 1998: 445):

Interactionist Theory

The symbolic interactionist perspective sees people as active agents or actors and the social world as being active, so constant adjustment and change occur through social interaction. People give meaning to events as they interpret their own "social reality." Movements for social change, therefore, are not the results of external or objective factors, but rather a social construction based on the meaning or interpretation the participants give to their actions. As Herbert Blumer notes, and as mentioned in Chapter 15:

> Human beings interpret or "define" each other's actions instead of merely reacting to each other's actions. Their response is not made directly to the actions of one another but instead is based on the meaning which they attach to such actions. Thus, human interaction is mediated by the use of symbols, by interpretation, or by ascertaining the meaning of one another's actions. (1969:180)

More recent theories, founded on the principles of symbolic interactionism, are based on the assumption that social movements involve participants, opponents, and bystanders engaged in a process that is interactive, symbolically defined, and negotiated (Buechler 2000). Using the work of Erving Goffman—who suggested that our interpretation of events depends on the way we "frame" them—theories, such as that of Steven M. Buechler,

articulate the relationship between this framing and social movement theory:

> In the context of social movements, framing refers to the interactive, collective ways that movement actors assign meaning to their activities in the conduct of social movement activism. The concept of framing is designed for discussing the social construction of grievances as a fluid and variable process of social interaction. (2000:41)

Social movements may modify or recreate their frames to advance their goals. An example would be an environmental group whose frame was global deforestation but who reframes it to air quality and the health effects on children (e.g., increasing rates of childhood asthma).

Table 16-2 summarizes the differences among the five major theories of social change.

☐ WHAT FORMS DOES RESISTANCE TO SOCIAL CHANGE TAKE?

Efforts to promote social change are likely to meet with resistance. In the midst of rapid scientific and technological innovations, many people are frightened by the demands of an ever-changing society. Moreover, certain individuals and groups have a stake in maintaining the existing state of affairs. Social economist Thorstein Veblen (1857–1929) coined the term **vested interests** to refer to those people or groups who will suffer in the event of social change. For example, in the United States, the American Medical Association (AMA) has taken strong ◄ P.384 stands against national health insurance and the professionalization of midwifery. National health insurance could lead to limits on physicians' income, and a rise in the status of midwives could threaten the pre-eminent position of doctors as deliverers of babies. In general, those with a disproportionate share of society's wealth, status, and power, such as members of the American Medical Association, have a vested interest in preserving the status quo (Starr 1982; Veblen 1919).

Economic and Cultural Factors

Economic factors play an important role in resistance to social change. For example, it can be expensive for manufacturers to meet high standards for the safety of products and workers, and for the protection of the environment. Conflict theorists argue that in a capitalist economic system, many firms are not willing to pay the price of meeting strict safety and environmental standards. They may resist social change by cutting corners or by pressuring the government to ease regulations. Communities, too, protect their vested interests, often in the name of "protecting property values." The abbreviation *NIMBY* stands for "not in my backyard," a cry often heard when homeowners protest the arrival of nearby landfills, prisons, nuclear power facilities, big-box malls, and even bike trails and group homes for people with developmental disabilities. The targeted community may not challenge the need for the facility, but may simply insist that it be located elsewhere. The NIMBY attitude has become so common that it is almost impossible for policymakers to find acceptable locations for facilities such as hazardous waste dumps (Jasper 1997).

Like economic factors, cultural factors frequently shape resistance to change. William F. Ogburn distinguished between material and non-material aspects of culture (1922). *Material culture* includes inventions, artifacts, and technology; *non-material culture* encompasses ideas, norms, communications, and social organization. Ogburn pointed out that one cannot devise methods for controlling and using new technology before the introduction of a technique. Thus, non-material culture typically must respond to changes in material culture. Ogburn introduced the term **culture lag** to refer to the period of maladjustment when the non-material culture is still struggling to adapt to new material conditions. One example is the Internet—its rapid uncontrolled growth raises questions about whether to regulate it, and if so, how much.

◀ P. 52

In certain cases, changes in material culture can strain the relationships between social institutions. For example, new means of birth control have been developed in recent decades. Large families are no longer economically necessary, nor are they commonly endorsed by social norms. But certain religious faiths, among them Roman Catholicism, continue to oppose "unnatural" methods of limiting family size, such as contraception and abortion. This issue represents a lag between aspects of material culture (technology) and non-material culture (religious beliefs). Conflicts may also emerge between religion and other social institutions, such as government and the educational system, over the dissemination of birth control and family-planning information (M. Riley et al. 1994a, 1994b).

Resistance to Technology

Technological innovations are examples of changes in material culture that often provoke resistance. The Industrial Revolution, which took place largely in England during the period 1760 to 1830, was a scientific revolution focused on the application of non-animal sources of power to labour tasks. As this enormous change proceeded, societies came to rely on new inventions that facilitated agricultural and industrial production, and on new sources of energy such as steam. In some industries, the introduction of power-driven machinery reduced the need for factory workers and made it easier for factory owners to cut wages.

◀ P. 389

Strong resistance to the Industrial Revolution emerged in some countries. In England, beginning in 1811, masked craft workers took extreme measures: They mounted nighttime raids on factories and destroyed some of the new machinery. The government hunted these rebels, known as **Luddites**, and ultimately banished or hanged them. In a similar effort in France, angry workers threw their wooden shoes (*sabots*) into factory machinery to destroy it, giving rise to the term *sabotage*. While the resistance efforts of the Luddites and the French workers were short-lived and unsuccessful, they have come to symbolize resistance to technology.

Are we now in the midst of a second industrial revolution, with a contemporary group of Luddites engaged in resisting? Many sociologists believe that we are living in a *post-industrial society*. It is difficult to pinpoint exactly when this era began. Generally, it is viewed as having begun in the 1950s, when for the first time the majority of workers in industrial societies became involved in services rather than in the actual manufacture of goods (D. Bell 1999, Fiala 1992).

◀ P. 389

Just as the Luddites resisted the Industrial Revolution, people in many countries have resisted post-industrial technological changes. The term *neo-Luddites* refers to those who are wary of technological innovations, and who question the incessant expansion of industrialization, the increasing destruction of the natural and agrarian world, and the "throw-it-away" mentality of contemporary capitalism, with its resulting pollution of the environment. Neo-Luddites insist that whatever the presumed benefits of industrial and post-industrial technology, such technology has distinctive social costs, and may represent a danger to the future of both the human species and our planet (Bauerlein 1996; Rifkin 1995; Sale 1996; Snyder 1996).

☐ HOW DOES GLOBALIZATION AFFECT GLOBAL SOCIAL CHANGE?

We are at a truly dramatic time in history to consider global social change. Maureen Hallinan, in her 1997 presidential address to the American Sociological Association, asked those present to consider just a few of the recent political events: the collapse of communism; terrorism in various parts of the world, including the United States; major regime changes and severe economic disruptions in Africa, the Middle East, and Eastern Europe; the spread of AIDS; and the computer revolution. Just a few months after her remarks came the first verification of the cloning of a complex animal, Dolly the sheep.

In this era of massive social, political, and economic change on a global scale, is it possible to predict change? Some technological changes seem obvious, but the collapse of communist governments in the former Soviet Union and Eastern Europe in the early 1990s took people by surprise. Yet, prior to the Soviet collapse, sociologist Randall Collins, a conflict theorist, had observed a crucial sequence of events that most observers had missed (1986, 1995).

In seminars as far back as 1980, and in a book published in 1986, Collins had argued that Soviet expansionism had resulted in an overextension of resources, including disproportionate spending on military forces. Such an overextension will strain a regime's stability. Moreover, geopolitical theory suggests that nations in the middle of a geographic region, such as the Soviet Union, tend to fragment into smaller units over time. Collins predicted that the coincidence of social crises on several frontiers would precipitate the collapse of the Soviet Union.

And that is just what happened. In 1979, the success of the Iranian Revolution had led to an upsurge of Islamic fundamentalism in nearby Afghanistan, as well as in Soviet republics with substantial Muslim populations. At the same time, resistance to Communist party rule was growing both throughout Eastern Europe and within the Soviet Union itself. Collins had predicted that the rise of a dissident form of communism within the Soviet Union would likely facilitate the breakdown of the regime. Beginning in the late 1980s, Soviet leader Mikhail Gorbachev chose not to use military power and other types of repression to crush dissidents in Eastern Europe. Instead, he offered plans for democratization and social reform of Soviet society, and seemed willing to reshape the Soviet Union into a loose federation of somewhat autonomous states. But in 1991, six republics on the western periphery declared their independence, and within months, the entire Soviet Union had formally disintegrated into Russia and a number of other independent nations.

In her 1997 address, Hallinan cautioned that we need to move beyond the restrictive models of social change—the linear view of evolutionary theory and the assumptions about equilibrium in functionalist theory. She and other sociologists have looked to the "chaos theory" advanced by mathematicians to understand erratic events as a part of change. Hallinan noted that upheavals and major chaotic shifts do occur, and that sociologists must learn to predict their occurrence, as Collins did with the Soviet Union. For example, imagine the dramatic non-linear

Would protests by people within and outside of Myanmar (Burma) change its military junta? These monks, holding photos of the country's opposition leader, Aung San Suu Kyi (right) and her late father General Aung San, protest outside Myanmar's embassy in Colombo, Sri Lanka, in May 2008. They are demanding that the military government accept international aid for its cyclone-affected citizens and release all political prisoners.

social change that will result from major innovations in communications and biotechnology—topics we will discuss next.

Privacy and Censorship in a Global Village

As we saw in the chapter-opening excerpt, new technologies like the personal computer and the Internet have brought about sweeping social change. While much of that change has been beneficial, there have been some negative effects. Recent advances in computer technology have made it increasingly easy for business firms, government agencies, and even criminals to retrieve and store information about everything from our buying habits to our Web-surfing patterns. In public places, at work, and on the Internet, surveillance devices now track our every move, be it a keystroke or an ATM withdrawal. At the same time that these innovations have increased others' power to monitor our behaviour, they have raised fears that they might be misused for criminal or undemocratic purposes. In short, new technologies threaten not just our privacy, but our freedom from crime and censorship (Rheingold 2003).

In recent years, concern about the criminal misuse of personal information has been underscored by the thief of customer information from some huge databases. In 2007, for example, hackers stole customer information from the computer systems of the parent company of Winners and Home Sense, affecting 2 million Canadian credit card accounts. Unfortunately, technologies that facilitate the sharing of information have also created new types of crime.

From a sociological point of view, the complex issues of privacy and censorship can be considered illustrations of culture lag. As usual, the material culture (technology) is changing faster than the non-material culture (norms for controlling the use of technology). Too often, the result is an anything-goes approach to the use of new technologies.

Legislation regarding the surveillance of electronic communications has not always upheld citizens' right to privacy. In 1986 in the United States, for example, the federal government passed the Electronic Communications Privacy Act, which outlawed the surveillance of telephone calls except with the permission of both the U.S. attorney general and a federal judge. Telegrams, faxes, and email did not receive the same degree of protection, however (Eckenwiler 1995). In 2001, one month after the terrorist attacks of September 11, Congress passed the Patriot Act, which relaxed existing legal checks on surveillance by law-enforcement officers. Federal agencies are now freer to gather data electronically, including credit card receipts and banking records.

Sociologists' views on the use and abuse of new technologies differ depending on their theoretical perspective. Functionalists take a generally positive view of the Internet, pointing to its manifest function of facilitating communication. From their perspective, the Internet performs the latent function of empowering those with few resources—from hate groups to special interest organizations—to communicate with the masses. Conflict theorists, in contrast, stress the danger that the most powerful groups in a society will use technology to violate the privacy of the less powerful. Indeed, officials in the People's Republic of China have attempted to censor online discussion groups and Web postings that are critical of the government (see Chapter 14).

Biotechnology and the Gene Pool

Another field in which technological advances have spurred global social change is biotechnology. Sex selection of fetuses, genetically engineered organisms, cloning of sheep and cows—these have been among the significant yet controversial scientific advances in the field ◀P.53 of biotechnology in recent years. George Ritzer's concept of McDonaldization applies to the entire area of biotechnology. Just as the fast-food concept has permeated society, no phase of life now seems exempt from therapeutic or medical intervention. In fact, sociologists view many aspects of biotechnology as an extension of the recent trend toward the medicalization of society, which we discussed in Chapter 15. Through genetic manipulation, the medical profession is expanding its turf still further (Clarke et al. 2003).

Today's biotechnology holds itself out as totally beneficial to human beings, but it is in constant need of monitoring. As we will see, biotechnological advances have raised many difficult ethical and political questions, among them the desirability of tinkering with the gene pool, which could alter our environment in unexpected and unwanted ways (D. Weinstein and M. Weinstein 1999).

One startling biotechnological advance is the possibility of altering human behaviour through genetic engineering. Fish and plant genes have already been mixed to create frost-resistant potato and tomato crops. More recently, human genes have been implanted in pigs to provide human-like kidneys for organ transplants (Schmitz 1999).

One of the latest developments in genetic engineering is gene therapy. Geneticists working with mouse fetuses have managed to disable genes that carry an undesirable trait and replace them with genes carrying a desirable trait. Such advances raise staggering possibilities for altering animal and human life forms. Still, gene therapy remains highly experimental, and must be considered a long shot (Kolata 1999).

In Spain, Greenpeace members protest the European Union's proposed approval of a strain of genetically modified corn. The insect-resistant sweet corn produces a substance that is toxic to corn borers and earworms but not to humans. Nevertheless, transnational activists have raised questions about its potential health effects. Their vocal opposition has disrupted international trade and caused friction among countries.

burgeoning populations of Africa and Asia (Golden 1999; Schurman 2004).

Another form of biotechnology with a potentially wide-ranging impact is the Human Genome Project. This effort involves teams of scientists around the world in sequencing and mapping all 30 000 to 40 000 human genes in existence, collectively known as the **human genome.** Supporters say that the resulting knowledge could revolutionize doctors' ability to treat and even prevent disease. But sociologists worry about the ethical implications of such research. Box 16-2 provides an overview of the many issues the project has raised.

The debate on genetic engineering escalated in 1997 when scientists in Scotland announced that they had cloned a sheep (the aforementioned Dolly). After many unsuccessful attempts, they had finally been able to replace the genetic material of a sheep's egg with DNA from an adult sheep, creating a lamb that was a clone of the adult. The very next year, Japanese researchers successfully cloned cows. These developments raised the possibility that in the near future, scientists would be able to clone human beings.

William F. Ogburn probably could not have anticipated such scientific developments when he wrote of culture lag 75 years earlier. However, the successful cloning of sheep and cows illustrates again how quickly material culture can change, and how non-material culture moves more slowly in absorbing such changes.

While cloning grabs the headlines, controversy has been growing concerning genetically modified (GM) food. The idea behind the technology is to increase food production and make agriculture more economical. But critics use the term *Frankenfood* (as in "Frankenstein") to refer to everything from breakfast cereals made from genetically engineered grains to "fresh" GM tomatoes. Members of the anti-biotech movement object to tampering with nature; they are concerned about the possible health effects of GM food. Supporters of genetically modified food include not just biotech companies, but those who see the technology as a way to help feed the

☐ WHAT IMPACT DOES SOCIAL CHANGE HAVE ON THE ENVIRONMENT?

Sociologists and others may debate the potential impact of biotechnology, but technological change has already had serious environmental consequences. We can see signs of despoliation almost everywhere: Our air, our water, and our land are being polluted, whether we live in Kitchener, Ontario, or Lagos, Nigeria. In some parts of the United States, each summer brings power failures or brownouts to sweltering cities as the voracious consumption of electricity exceeds the supply. In some parts of Canada, summer has become a time of frequent smog alerts, warning the elderly and those who suffer from respiratory conditions to remain indoors.

In recent years, public attention has turned to global warming, manifested in the shrinking of the polar ice caps and the increasing ferociousness of tropical storms as they cross warmer-than-normal ocean waters. Human activities have contributed to the documented warming of the planet over the last half century, through the altered chemical composition of the atmosphere and the buildup of greenhouse gases such as carbon dioxide, methane, and nitrous oxide. While environmental problems may be easy to identify scientifically, however, devising socially and politically acceptable solutions is much more

Research in Action   16-2
The Human Genome Project

Together with geneticists, pathologists, and microbiologists, sociologist Troy Duster of New York University has been grappling with the ethical, legal, and social issues raised by the Human Genome Project since 1989. An original member of the oversight committee appointed to deal with such matters, he does not expect that his work will be done any time soon.

Duster, who is also past president of the American Sociological Association, has been asked to explain why his committee is taking so long to conclude its work. In reply, he lists the many issues raised by the massive project. First, he is concerned that the medical breakthroughs made possible by the project will not benefit all people equally. He notes, for example, that biotechnology firms have used the project's data to develop a test for cystic fibrosis in white North Americans, but not for the same syndrome in Zuni Indians. Biotechnology companies are profit-making ventures, not humanitarian organizations. So while the scientists involved in the Human Genome Project hope to map the genes of all the world's peoples, not everyone may benefit from the project in practical ways.

Duster's committee has also struggled with the question of informed consent—making sure that everyone who donates genes to the project will do so voluntarily, after being informed of the risks and benefits. In Western societies, scientists commonly obtain such consent from the individuals who participate in their research. But according to Duster, many non-Western societies do not acknowledge the individual's right to make such decisions. Instead, a leader makes the decision for the group as a whole. "When Western-trained researchers descend upon a village," Duster asks, "who should they turn to for consent?" (Duster 2002:69). And what if the answer is no?

Race, too, is a knotty problem for Duster's committee. DNA analysis shows conclusively that there are no genetic differences among the races. Given that analysis, many geneticists do not want to invest more time and effort in research on racial differences. As a sociologist, Duster knows that race is socially constructed. Yet he also knows that for millions of people around the world, race has a significant effect on their health and well-being. More to the point, Duster knows that a group's economic and political power helps to determine which diseases scientists study.

On the other hand, Duster worries that some researchers may be putting too much emphasis on biological differences between the so-called races. He notes that those racial

Troy Duster, a sociologist at New York University, also teaches and directs the American Cultures Center at the University of California, Berkeley.

groups who are socially disadvantaged suffer much higher rates of disease than advantaged groups. In the United States, for example, African American men suffer from prostate cancer at twice the rate of white men. Yet, in the Caribbean and sub-Saharan Africa, black men have a much lower rate of prostate cancer than American men, white or black. How can genes explain this disparity? Duster suspects that the explanation for African Americans' higher disease rates lies not in their genes, but in their stressful environment, where they are routinely subjected to racial profiling and other forms of institutional discrimination. "We may be 99.9 percent alike at the level of DNA," Duster writes, "but if that were the end of the story, we could all pack up and go home" (Duster 2002:70).

Applying Theory

1. What other criteria besides the power of a racial or ethnic group could be used to determine how much research is done on diseases that affect the group?

2. As an interactionist sociologist, how might you study members of the tribe who want to participate in a research project?

Sources: Dreifus 2006: Duster 2002.

THE FOUR TRUCK DRIVERS OF THE APOCALYPSE

Pollution, overdevelopment, warfare, and consumerism all pose a challenge to our environment.

difficult. In the following sections, we will survey some identifiable environmental problems and see what sociologists have to say about them (Easterbrook 2006; Gore 2006).

Environmental Problems: An Overview

In recent decades, the world has witnessed serious environmental disasters. In 1986, for example, a series of explosions set off a catastrophic nuclear reactor accident at Chernobyl, a part of Ukraine (in what was then the Soviet Union). Thousands of people died, and some 400 000 residents had to be evacuated. For nearly 31 kilometres in any direction, the area became uninhabitable. High levels of radiation were found as far as 48 kilometres from the reactor site, and radioactivity levels climbed well above normal even in Sweden and Japan. According to one estimate, the Chernobyl accident and the resulting nuclear fallout may ultimately result in 100 000 cases of cancer worldwide (Chernobyl Forum 2005).

Much more common than nuclear power plant disasters are oil spills in the ocean or coastal waters, typically from supertankers. The heavier types of crude or fuel oil, such as that carried by the *Exxon Valdez* in 1989, can contaminate the shoreline for years following a spill, even after a massive cleanup. Globally, oil spills occur regularly. In 2002, the oil tanker *Prestige* spilled twice as much fuel as the *Valdez*, greatly damaging coastal areas off Spain and France.

While reactor accidents, oil spills, and other environmental disasters understandably grab the headlines, it is the silent, day-to-day deterioration of the environment that ultimately poses a devastating threat to humanity. Examining all our environmental problems in detail would be impossible, but three broad areas of concern stand out: air pollution, water pollution, and the impact of globalization.

Air Pollution

Worldwide, more than 1 billion people are exposed to potentially health-damaging levels of air pollution. Unfortunately, in cities around the world, residents have come to accept smog and polluted air as normal. Urban air pollution is caused primarily by emissions from automobiles and secondarily by emissions from electric power plants and heavy industries. Smog not only limits visibility; it can also lead to health problems as uncomfortable as eye irritation and as deadly as lung cancer. Such problems are especially severe in developing countries. The World Health Organization has estimated that up to 700 000 premature deaths *per year* could be prevented if pollutants were brought down to safer levels (Carty 1999; World Resources Institute 1998).

People are capable of changing their behaviour, but they are also unwilling to make such changes permanent. During the 1984 Olympics in Los Angeles, residents were asked to carpool and stagger their work hours to relieve traffic congestion and improve the quality of the air athletes would breathe. These changes resulted in a remarkable 12 percent drop in ozone levels. But when the Olympians left, people reverted to their normal behaviour and the ozone levels climbed back up. Similarly, at the 2008 Olympics, China took drastic action to ensure that Beijing's high levels of air pollution did not mar the games. For a two-month period, all construction work in the city ceased, polluting factories and power plants closed down, and roads were swept and sprayed with water several times a day. But this temporary solution was hardly a solution to China's ongoing pollution problems (McCright and Dunlap 2003; Nussbaum 1998; ABC Radio Australia 2006).

Water Pollution

Around the world, water pollution is a growing concern. Oceans, lakes, rivers, and streams are becoming increasingly polluted as a result of waste dumping, fuel leaks from shipping, and occasional oil spills. In North America, dumping of waste materials by industries and local governments has polluted streams, rivers, and lakes. Accidents contribute to the contamination of soil and water. For example, in July 2007, in the Vancouver suburb of Burnaby, a construction crew accidentally ruptured a major crude oil pipeline, causing the spewing of oil over homes and gardens and the environmental contamination of soil and water. Consequently, many bodies of water have become unsafe for drinking, fishing, and swimming.

Less dramatic than large-scale accidents or disasters, but more common in many parts of the world, are problems with the basic water supply. Worldwide, over 1 billion people lack safe and adequate drinking water, and 2.4 billion have no acceptable means of sanitation—a problem that further threatens the quality of water supplies. The health costs of unsafe water are enormous (United Nations 2003).

The Impact of Globalization

Globalization can be both good and bad for the environment. On the negative side, it can create a race to the bottom, as polluting companies relocate to countries with less stringent environmental standards. Similarly, globalization allows multinationals to reap the resources of developing countries for short-term profit. From Mexico to China, the industrialization that often accompanies globalization has increased pollution of all types.

Yet globalization can have a positive impact, as well. As barriers to the international movement of goods, services, and people fall, multinational corporations have an incentive to carefully consider the cost of natural resources. Overusing or wasting resources makes little sense, especially when they are in danger of depletion (Kwong 2005).

Globalization has also encouraged efforts at multilateral environmental agreements. The Kyoto Protocol is intended to reduce global emissions of heat-trapped gases, which can contribute to global warming and climate change. To date, 141 countries have signed the accord. But the United States, which produces 24 percent of the world's carbon dioxide, has refused to sign, arguing that doing so would place the nation at a disadvantage in the global marketplace. Thirty-five other developed nations have agreed to a 5 percent reduction in the greenhouse gases they produce—a goal they must reach by 2012 (Landler 2005). Although Canada signed the Kyoto Protocol, necessary action has not been taken by the federal government to ensure that Canada meets its emissions targets.

What are the basic causes of our growing environmental problems? Some observers, such as Paul Ehrlich and Anne Ehrlich, see the pressure of world population

In a makeshift recycling centre, a woman in China uses a hammer to open an old cathode ray tube. She wants the copper that is inside, but in the process she will release several pounds of lead into the soil and groundwater. Scientists have found alarmingly high levels of toxic heavy metals in the rivers that flow by such rural recycling operations.

growth as the central factor in environmental deterioration. They argue that population control is essential in preventing widespread starvation and environmental decay. Barry Commoner, a biologist, counters that the primary cause of environmental ills is the increasing use of technological innovations that are destructive to the world's environment—among them plastics, detergents, synthetic fibres, pesticides, herbicides, and chemical fertilizers. Conflict theorists see the despoliation of the environment through the lens of world systems analysis (Commoner 1971, 1990; Ehrlich 1968; Ehrlich and Ehrlich 1990; Ehrlich and Ellison 2002).

Conflict View of Environmental Issues

In Chapter 9, we drew on world systems analysis to show how a growing share of the human and natural resources of developing countries is being redistributed to the core industrialized nations. This process only intensifies the

Vacation in an unspoiled paradise! Increasingly, people from developed countries are turning to ecotourism as an environmentally friendly way to see the world. The new trend bridges the interests of environmentalists and business people, especially in developing countries. These birdwatchers are vacationing in Belize.

gram). The money their residents spend on ocean cruises each year could provide clean drinking water for everyone on the planet. Ice cream expenditures in Europe alone could be used to immunize every child in the world. Thus, conflict theorists charge, the most serious threat to the environment comes from the global consumer class (G. Gardner et al. 2004).

Allan Schnaiberg further refines this analysis by criticizing the focus on affluent consumers as the cause of environmental troubles (1994). In his view, a capitalist system creates a "treadmill of production" because of its inherent need to build ever-expanding profits. This treadmill necessitates creating an increasing demand for products, obtaining natural resources at minimal cost, and manufacturing products as quickly and cheaply as possible—no matter what the long-term environmental consequences.

destruction of natural resources in poorer regions of the world. From a conflict perspective, less affluent nations are being forced to exploit their mineral deposits, forests, and fisheries in order to meet their debt obligations. The poor turn to the only means of survival available to them: They plow mountain slopes, burn plots in tropical forests, and overgraze grasslands (Livernash and Rodenburg 1998).

Brazil exemplifies this interplay between economic troubles and environmental destruction. Each year, more than 5.7 million acres of forest are cleared for crops and livestock. The elimination of the rain forest affects worldwide weather patterns, heightening the gradual warming of the earth. These socio-economic patterns, with their harmful environmental consequences, are evident not only in Latin America but in many regions of Africa and Asia (*National Geographic* 2002). Conflict theorists are well aware of the environmental implications of land use policies in the developing world, but they contend that focusing on developing countries is ethnocentric. Who, they ask, is more to blame for environmental deterioration: the poverty-stricken and "food-hungry" populations of the world or the "energy-hungry" industrialized nations? These theorists point out that the industrialized nations of North America and Europe account for only 12 percent of the world's population but are responsible for 60 percent of worldwide consumption and, thus, a disproportionately large ecological footprint (see Figure 16-1 for the 2006 World Consumption Carto-

Environmental Justice

Deline, Northwest Territories, is an Aboriginal community of about 800 people. A uranium mine near the town used many local people to work as labourers without providing necessary safety measures. As a result, the town—now dubbed "A Village of Widows"—has one of the highest cancer rates in Canada. The workers (mostly men) were not the only ones exposed to the hazards of uranium mining; their families were also unknowingly exposed to hazardous waste landfills and dumps, which contaminated their food sources and water.

Observations like this one have given rise to **environmental justice**, a legal strategy based on claims that ethnic minorities are subjected disproportionately to environmental hazards. The approach has had some success. In 1998, a U.S. chemical company called Shintech dropped plans to build a plastics plant in a poor black community in Mississippi after opponents filed a civil rights complaint with the Environmental Protection Agency (EPA) in the United States. EPA administrator Carol Browner praised the company's decision: "The principles applied to achieve this solution should be incorporated into any blueprint for dealing with environmental justice issues in communities across the nation" (Associated Press 1998:18).

Following reports from the EPA and other organizations documenting the discriminatory location of hazardous waste sites, then U.S. president Bill Clinton issued an executive order in 1994 that requires all federal agencies to

▶ **FIGURE 16-1**

World Consumption Cartogram, 2006

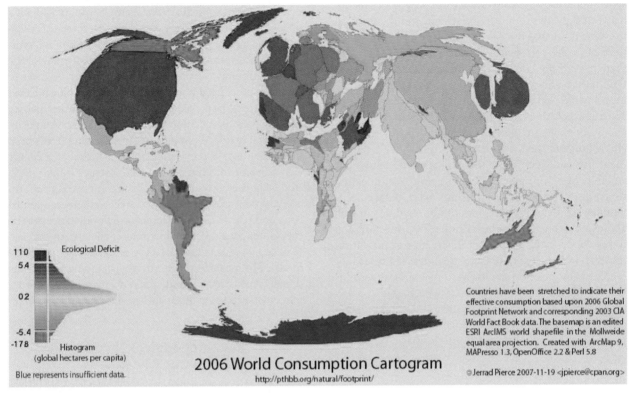

Source: Pierce 2006.

ensure that low-income and minority communities have access to better information about their environment, and an opportunity to participate in shaping government policies that affect their health. Initial efforts to implement the policy have aroused widespread opposition because of the delays it imposes in establishing new industrial sites. Some observers question the wisdom of an order that slows economic development in areas that are in dire need of employment opportunities. Others point out that such businesses employ few unskilled or less skilled workers, and only make the environment less livable (Pellow 2002).

Meanwhile, the poor and oppressed continue to bear the brunt of environmental pollution. In the 1990s, the U.S. government, unable to find a disposal site for spent nuclear fuel, turned to tribal reservations. Agents eventually persuaded a tiny band of Goshute Indians in Skull Valley, Utah, to accept more than 44 000 barrels of the hot, highly radioactive substance, which will remain dangerous for an estimated 10 000 years. The government is currently attempting to implement the plan despite opposition from surrounding towns and cities, whose residents object to the movement of the material through their communities. This is not the first time the U.S.

government has prevailed upon the impoverished tribe to accept environmentally objectionable installations. The military's nerve gas storage facility resides on or near the reservation, along with the Intermountain Power Project, which generates coal-fired electrical power for consumers in California (Eureka County 2006; Skull Valley Band Goshute 2006).

As is evident from this discussion, much of the literature on environmental justice (EJ) is based on U.S. studies and cases (Bryant and Mohai 1992; Bullard 1990; Hofrichter 1993). In 2001, however, Alice Nabalamba published a Canadian study using 1996 census data in which she investigated the links among socio-economic status, visible minority group status, and the location of pollution sources in Toronto, Hamilton, and the Niagara region. Nabalamba's findings suggest that poorer people are more likely than the general population to live in neighbourhoods near sources of pollution and industrial land use. Nabalamba predicts that future use of land for industrial discharges, waste treatment, disposal, storage, and so on, will continue to affect those Canadians of lower socio-economic status—those who have, obviously, less political clout to fight back (2001).

Feminist View: Eco-feminism

None of the various feminist perspectives addresses the links between gender and the environment as directly as eco-feminism does. Eco-feminism forges an alliance between the environmental movement and the feminist movement, between ecology and feminist principles. Central to the core tenets of eco-feminism is the belief that, historically, men have dominated and exploited both nature and women. Androcentric thinking, rooted in principles of dualism and hierarchy, has justified activities that have led to men's domination over nature and women. Eco-feminists reject this way of thinking and acting and the harm that it has caused the environment. Instead, they argue that women inherently have a closer, more intimate, and less exploitive connection to nature. Women's relationships with nature, eco-feminists contend, are not ones of domination, control, and exploitive self-interest but rather of protection and nurturance. Critics of eco-feminism suggest that arguing that women have inherent qualities of nurturance reduces their position to a form of biological determinism. Biological determinism has long been used as a justification for the separation, exclusion, and oppression of women, because their differences, in an androcentric world, have been interpreted as inferiorities.

Interactionist View

The symbolic interactionist perspective focuses on the meaning or symbolic significance that people attribute to one another's actions. Through social interaction, "human beings interpret or 'define' each other's actions instead of merely reacting to each other's actions" (Blumer 1969:79). Symbolic interactionism, therefore, may concentrate on the meaning we give to one another's actions as they relate to environmental practices. For example, your neighbour's use of a blue box for recycling might be interpreted as a sign that he or she is a good citizen, with the blue box as a symbol of concern for the environmental sustainability of the local community, or simply as an opportunity to meet or chat with other neighbours as they place their blue boxes at the roadside to be picked up. The interactionist perspective encompasses the phenomenon of social constructionism, in which individuals continually construct and reconstruct their meaning of environmental practices. Sociologists Clay Schoenfeld, Robert Meir, and Robert Griffin (1979) studied how environmental issues become the concerns of everyday citizens and how concern for an environmental issue one year (e.g., child labour or deforestation) may be supplanted by a different environmental concern the next year (e.g., public transportation or genetically modified foods). The meaning we give to human interaction is continually reconstructed; thus, different environmental issues may emerge as being of a higher profile than others are.

Use Your Sociological Imagination

Your community is designated as a site for the burial of toxic waste. How would you react? Would you organize a protest? Or would you make sure the authorities carry the project out safely? How can such sites be chosen fairly?

Social Policy and Globalization
Transnationals

The Issue

Imagine that as you leave your university convocation ceremony, diploma in hand, a stranger approaches and offers you a job. If you are willing to relocate to a foreign, non-English-speaking country, he says, you can earn $300 000 a year for the kind of work you have always thought of as menial labour. You can do the job for one year or several years. The only catch is that you must enter the country illegally, and remain there until you are ready to give up your job. The opportunity he is describing isn't new to you. In fact, you have many friends and relatives who have done exactly that.

The lure of fast, easy money that is described in this story may seem incredible to you, but it is real for many people in developing nations. Incomes in developing nations are so low that the wages an immigrant can earn in Canada, even at the most menial job, seem like a fortune. Back in the home country, their purchasing power is the equivalent of approximately $300 000 income in North America—a huge economic incentive to immigrate. But while the opportunity to become rich may encourage even highly skilled foreigners to immigrate, these migrant workers—even those with legal status—enjoy far fewer rights than native-born workers.

▶ **FIGURE 16-2**

Labour Migration

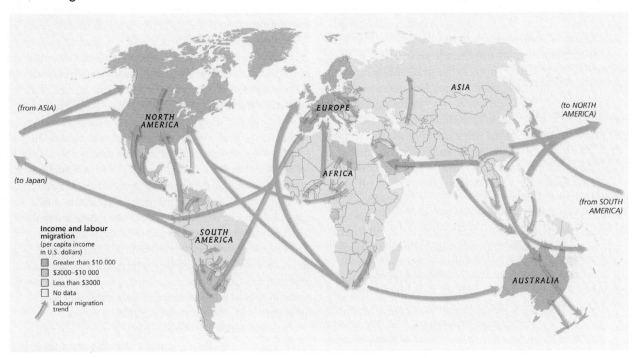

Source: National Geographic 2005:16.

The Setting

The accompanying Figure 16-2 shows the worldwide movement of workers with and without legal authorization to immigrate. Several areas, such as the European Union, have instituted international agreements that provide for the free movement of labourers. But in most other parts of the world, immigration restrictions give foreign workers only temporary status. Despite such legal restrictions, the labour market has become an increasingly global one. Just as globalization has integrated government policies, cultures, social movements, and financial markets, it has unified what once were discrete national labour markets.

Globalization has changed the immigrant experience as well as the labour market. In generations past, immigrants read foreign language newspapers to keep in touch with events in their home countries. Today, the Internet gives them immediate access to their countries and kinfolk. In this global framework, immigrants are less likely than they were in the past to think of themselves as residents of just one country. **Transnationals** are immigrants who

have an allegiance to more than one country and who sustain multiple social relationships that link their societies of origin with their societies of settlement.

Immigrants from Haiti and Jamaica, for example, identify with Canada; but at the same time they maintain close ties to their Caribbean homeland, frequently sending *remittances*, most often for the stated purpose of providing food for their parents back home (Simmons et al. 2005). In poor countries, the volume of transnational remittances—perhaps $80 billion worldwide—is easily the most reliable source of foreign income, far outstripping the value of foreign-aid programs (Fox 2005; Kapur and McHale 2003).

Sociological Insights

Sociologists did not begin to investigate transnationalism until the early 1990s. They are finding that new technologies which facilitate international travel and communications are accelerating the transnational movement of workers. Two other forces tend to promote transnationalism: Nationalism encourages émigrés to express continued allegiance to their homelands, and multiculturalism has legitimized the expression of those loyalties in receiving nations. Finally, international human rights organizations have joined faith-based groups in stressing universal human rights, regardless of a person's citizenship status. Whether these diverse influences will further the emergence of a global workforce composed of global citizens or simply fuel nationalistic fervour remains to be seen (Waldinger and Fitzgerald 2004).

As with other issues, sociologists differ in their opinion of transnationals, depending on their theoretical perspective. Functionalists see the free flow of immigrants, even when it is legally restricted, as one way for economies to maximize their use of human labour. Given the law of supply and demand, they note, countries with too few workers will inevitably attract labourers, while those with too many will become unattractive to residents.

Conflict theorists charge that globalization and international migration have increased the economic gulf between developed and developing nations. Today, residents of North America, Europe, and Japan consume 32 times more resources than the billions of people who live in developing countries. Through tourism and the global reach of the mass media, people in the poorer countries have become aware of the affluent lifestyle common in developed nations—and, of course, many of them now aspire to it (Diamond 2003).

Sociologists who follow world systems analysis (see Chapter 9) suggest that the global flow of people, not just goods and resources, should be factored into the relationship between core and periphery societies. The global economic system, with its sharp contrast between have and have-not nations, is responsible for the creation of the informal social networks that link those seeking a better life with those who already enjoy prosperity.

Interactionists are interested in the day-to-day relationships transnationals have with the people around them, from those of their country of origin to those of the host country and fellow workers from other countries. They are particularly concerned with how transnationals see their own identities and those of their children. In effect, transnationals negotiate their identities, depending on which social network they belong to at the moment. Some sociologists note that while being a transnational can be exhilarating, it can also isolate a person, even in a city of millions. Others worry that transnationals may become so cosmopolitan that they will lose touch with their national identities (Calhoun 2003; Plüss 2005; Rajan and Sharma 2006).

Policy Initiatives

The International Labor Organization has complained that the intense economic competition created by globalization is unravelling the social welfare systems of many countries. The Canadian Council on Social Development (CCSD) produced a personal security index which is used to assess Canadians' perception of their personal financial security. In 2003, the CCSD reported that although Canadians, over the previous five years, had more disposable income and were more confident in their job security, they were less satisfied with the adequacy of their incomes and had little confidence in government income-support programs. In general, Western European nations are among the most secure with Sweden topping the list; Eastern European countries that once were part of the Soviet Union are among the least secure. To alleviate the pressure created by a failing social service system, workers will often move to countries that offer both good jobs and good social services—a trend that strains receiving nations' safety nets. In 2005, voters in both France and the Netherlands rejected the proposed European Union constitution, in part because of concerns about a potential influx of workers from developing countries like Turkey (Standing 2004).

Another unresolved transnational issue is voter eligibility. Not all nations allow dual citizenship; even those countries that do may not allow absent nationals to vote. Canada permits dual citizenship and allows émigrés to continue to vote, as do the United States and Great Britain. Mexico, in contrast, has been reluctant to allow citizens who have emigrated to vote. Mexican politicians worry that the large number of Mexicans who live abroad (especially those in the United States) might vote differently from local voters, causing different outcomes (Sellers 2004).

Finally, the controversial issue of illegal immigration has yet to be settled, perhaps because of culture lag. That is, both public attitudes and government policies (non-material culture) have not kept pace, much less adjusted to, the increasing ease of migration around the globe (material culture). Though globalization has created a global labour market—one that many countries depend on, legal or illegal—the general public's attitude toward illegal immigrants remains hostile, especially in the United States.

Applying Theory

1. According to conflict thinkers, what role does globalization play in relation to the gulf between developing and developed countries?
2. Suppose you are an interactionist thinker. What topic of research might you construct relating to transnationals?

CHAPTER RESOURCES

Summary

What are Social Movements?

- **Social movements** (p. 407) are more structured than other forms of collective behaviour and persist over longer periods.
- A group will not mobilize into a social movement without a shared perception that its **relative deprivation** (p. 408) can be ended only through collective action.
- The success of a social movement depends in good part on effective resource mobilization.
- **New social movements** (p. 410) tend to focus on more than just economic issues, and often cross national boundaries.

How can Social Change be Explained?

- Early advocates of the **evolutionary theory** (p. 412) of social change believed that society was progressing inevitably toward a higher state.
- Talcott Parsons, a leading advocate of functionalist theory, viewed society as being in a natural state of equilibrium or balance.
- Conflict theorists as well as feminist theorists see change as having crucial significance, since it is needed to correct social injustices and inequalities.

What Forms does Resistance to Social Change Take?

- In general, those with a disproportionate share of society's wealth, status, and power have a **vested interest** (p. 414) in preserving the status quo, and will resist change.
- The period of maladjustment when a non-material culture is still struggling to adapt to new material conditions is known as **culture lag** (p. 415).

How does Globalization Affect Global Social Change?

- We are living in a time of sweeping social, political, and economic change—change that occurs not just on a local or national basis, but on a global scale.

What Impact does Social Change have on the Environment?

- Advances in biotechnology have raised difficult ethical questions about genetic engineering and the sex selection of fetuses.
- Air pollution, water pollution, and the impact of globalization are three major areas of environmental concern. Though globalization can contribute to environmental woes, it can also have beneficial effects.
- Conflict theorists charge that the most serious threat to the environment comes from Western industrialized nations.

Critical Thinking Questions

1. Select one social movement that is currently working for change in Canada. Analyze that movement, drawing on the concepts of relative deprivation, resource mobilization, and false consciousness.
2. In the last few years, we have witnessed phenomenal growth in the use of cellular phones around the world. Analyze this form of material culture in terms of culture lag. Consider usage, government regulation, and privacy issues.
3. Imagine that you have been asked to study the issue of air pollution in the largest city in your province or territory. How might you draw on surveys, observation research, experiments, and existing sources to study the issue?

Key Terms

Culture lag   A period of maladjustment when the non-material culture is still struggling to adapt to new material conditions. (page p. 415)

Environmental justice   A legal strategy based on claims that racial minorities are subjected disproportionately to environmental hazards. (p. 422)

Equilibrium model The functionalist view that society tends toward a state of stability or balance. (p. 412)

Evolutionary theory A theory of social change that holds that society is moving in a definite direction. (p. 411)

False consciousness A term used by Karl Marx to describe an attitude held by members of a class that does not accurately reflect their objective position. (p. 409)

Human genome The 30 000 to 40 000 human genes in existence. (p. 418)

Luddites Rebellious craft workers in nineteenth-century England who destroyed new factory machinery as part of their resistance to the Industrial Revolution. (p. 415)

New social movement An organized collective activity that addresses values and social identities, as well as improvements in the quality of life. (p. 410)

Relative deprivation The conscious feeling of a negative discrepancy between legitimate expectations and present actualities. (p. 408)

Resource mobilization The ways in which a social movement utilizes such resources as money, political influence, access to the media, and personnel. (p. 409)

Social change Significant alteration over time in behaviour patterns and culture, including norms and values. (p. 407)

Social movement An organized collective activity to bring about or resist fundamental change in an existing group or society. (p. 407)

Transnational An immigrant with an allegiance to more than one nation. (p. 425)

Vested interests Those people or groups who will suffer in the event of social change, and who have a stake in maintaining the status quo. (p. 414)

Additional Readings

Bantjes, Rod. 2007. *Social Movement in a Global Context*. Toronto: CSPI/WP. In this book, Bantjes focuses on interpreting the resurgence in popular protest, emphasizing the global context.

Burdon, Roy. 2003. *The Suffering Gene: Environmental Threats to Our Health*. Montreal: McGill-Queen's University Press. An examination of the effects of a toxic environment on human genes.

Hessing, Melody, Rebecca Ragion, and Catriona Sandilands. 2004. *This Elusive Land: Women and the Canadian Environment*. Vancouver: UBC Press. An interdisciplinary anthology that introduces readers to women's experiences and perceptions of the natural environment.

 ## Online Learning Centre

Visit the *Sociology: A Brief Introduction* Online Learning Centre at www.mcgrawhill.ca/olc/schaefer to access quizzes, interactive exercises, video clips, and other research and study tools related to this chapter.

 ## Reel Society Video Clips

Reel Society can be used to spark discussion about the following topics from this chapter:

- Social Movements
- The Environment

GLOSSARY

Numbers following the definitions indicate pages where the terms were identified. Consult the index for further page references.

A

Absolute poverty A standard of poverty based on a minimum level of subsistence below which families should not be expected to live. (198)

Achieved status A social position that a person attains largely through his or her own efforts. (102)

Activity theory An interactionist theory of aging that argues that elderly people who remain active and socially involved will be best adjusted. (88)

Adoption A process that allows for the transfer of the legal rights, responsibilities, and privileges of parenthood to a new legal parent or parents. (297)

Ageism Prejudice and discrimination against the elderly. (91)

Agrarian society The most technologically advanced form of pre-industrial society. Members are engaged primarily in the production of food, but increase their crop yields through technological innovations such as the plow. (114)

Alienation A condition of estrangement or disassociation from the surrounding society. (117)

Anomie The loss of direction felt in a society when social control of individual behaviour has become ineffective. (8)

Anomie theory of deviance Robert Merton's theory that explains deviance as an adaptation either of socially prescribed goals or of the norms governing their attainment, or both. (168)

Anticipatory socialization Processes of socialization in which a person "rehearses" for future positions, occupations, and social relationships. (91)

B

Apartheid The former policy of the South African government designed to maintain the separation of blacks and other non-whites from the dominant whites. (246)

Argot Specialized language used by members of a group or subculture. (60)

Arranged marriages Marriages engineered by parents or religious authorities, in which economic considerations play a significant role. (295)

Ascribed status A social position assigned to a person by society without regard for the person's unique talents or characteristics. (102)

Assimilation The process by which a person forsakes his or her own cultural tradition to become part of a different culture. (245)

Authority Institutionalized power that is recognized by the people over whom it is exercised. (349)

B

Bilateral descent A kinship system in which both sides of a person's family are regarded as equally important. (289)

Birth rate The number of live births per 1000 population in a given year. Also known as the *crude birth rate*. (372)

Blended family The result when a couple or individual who separates or divorces then goes on to form a new relationship, when children are involved. (299)

Bourgeoisie Karl Marx's term for the capitalist class, comprising the owners of the means of production. (191)

Bureaucracy A component of formal organization that uses rules and hierarchical ranking to achieve efficiency. (117)

Bureaucratization The process by which a group, organization, or social movement becomes increasingly bureaucratic. (121)

C

Capitalism An economic system in which the means of production are largely in private hands and the main incentive for economic activity is the accumulation of profits. (191, 343)

Career choice The first phase of occupational socialization. (86)

Castes Hereditary systems of rank, usually religiously dictated, that tend to be fixed and immobile. (187)

Causal logic The relationship between a condition or variable and a particular consequence, with one event leading to the other. (30)

Census An enumeration, or counting, of a population. (372)

Central cities Large urban areas where population is concentrated. (395)

Charismatic authority Power made legitimate by a leader's exceptional personal or emotional appeal to his or her followers. (349)

Class A group of people who have a similar level of wealth and income. (192)

Class consciousness In Karl Marx's view, a subjective awareness held by members of a class regarding their common vested interests and need for collective political action to bring about social change. (199)

Class system A social ranking based primarily on economic position in which achieved characteristics can influence mobility. (188)

Classical theory An approach to the study of formal organizations that views workers as being motivated almost entirely by economic rewards. (121)

Closed system A social system in which there is little or no possibility of individual mobility. (202)

Coalition A temporary or permanent alliance geared toward a common goal. (108)

Code of ethics The standards of acceptable behaviour developed by and for members of a profession. (26)

Cognitive theory of development Jean Piaget's theory explaining how children's thought progresses through four stages. (79)

Cohabitation The practice of living together as a couple without marrying. (303)

Colonialism The maintenance of political, social, economic, and cultural dominance over a people by a foreign power for an extended period. (215)

Commitment Part of the third phase of occupational socialization, it involves a worker enthusiastically accepting the pleasurable duties; this acceptance comes with the recognition by the person of the positive tasks of an occupation. (86)

Communism As an ideal type, an economic system under which all property is communally owned and no social distinctions are made on the basis of people's ability to produce. (344)

Community A spatial or political unit of social organization that gives people a sense of belonging. (370)

Concentric-zone theory A theory for describing land use in industrial cities, where the centre (or nucleus) of a city is the central business district. (391)

Concrete operational The third stage in Piaget's theory of cognitive development. (79)

Conditioning Part of the third phase of occupational socialization, it involves a worker reluctantly adjusting to the more unpleasant aspects of a job. (86)

Conflict perspective A sociological approach that assumes that social behaviour is best understood in terms of conflict or tension between competing groups. (14)

Conformity Going along with our peers, individuals of a person's own status, who have no special right to direct that person's behaviour. (160)

Contact hypothesis An interactionist perspective that states that interracial contact between people of equal status in co-operative circumstances will reduce prejudice. (244)

Content analysis The systematic coding and objective recording of data, guided by some rationale. (38)

Control group Subjects in an experiment who are not introduced to the independent variable by the researcher. (36)

Control theory A view of conformity and deviance that suggests our connection to members of society leads us to systematically conform to society's norms. (164)

Control variable A factor held constant to test the relative impact of an independent variable. (33)

Correlation A relationship between two variables whereby a change in one coincides with a change in the other. (30)

Correspondence principle The tendency of schools to promote the values expected of individuals in each social class and to prepare students for the types of jobs typically held by members of their class. (331)

Counterculture A subculture that deliberately opposes certain aspects of the larger culture. (61)

Creationism A literal interpretation of the Bible regarding the creation of humanity and the universe, used to argue that evolution should not be presented as established scientific fact. (336)

Crime A violation of criminal law for which some governmental authority applies formal penalties. (174)

Cult See **new religious movement.** (323)

Cultural imperialism The influence or imposition of the material or nonmaterial elements of a culture on another culture or cultures. (63)

Cultural relativism The viewing of people's behaviour from the perspective of their own culture. (64)

Cultural transmission A school of criminology that argues which argues that criminal behaviour is learned through social interactions. (170)

Cultural universals General practices found in every culture. (50)

Culture The totality of learned, socially transmitted customs, knowledge, material objects, and behaviour. (49)

Culture lag A period of maladjustment when the nonmaterial culture is still struggling to adapt to new material conditions. (52, 415)

Culture shock The feeling of surprise and disorientation that is experienced when people witness cultural practices different from their own. (62)

D

Death rate The number of deaths per 1000 population in a given year. Also known as the *crude death rate.* (373)

Defended neighbourhood A sentimental union of similar people, where inhabitants apply their own definitions of community boundaries. (395)

Degradation ceremony An aspect of the socialization process within total institutions, in which people are subjected to humiliating rituals. (92)

Deindustrialization The systematic, widespread withdrawal of investment in basic aspects of productivity, such as factories and plants. (361)

Democracy In a literal sense, government by the people. (351)

Demographic transition A term used to describe the change from high birth rates and death rates to relatively low birth rates and death rates. (374)

Demography The scientific study of population. (371)

Denomination A large, organized religion not officially linked with the state or government. (322)

Dependency theory An approach that contends that industrialized nations continue to exploit developing countries for their own gain. (215)

Dependent variable The variable in a causal relationship that is subject to the influence of another variable. (30)

Deviance Behaviour that violates the standards of conduct or expectations of a group or society. (165)

Dictatorship A government in which one person has nearly total power to make and enforce laws. (350)

Differential association A theory of deviance proposed by Edwin Sutherland which holds that violation of rules results from exposure to attitudes favourable to criminal acts. (170)

Diffusion The process by which a cultural item is spread from group to group or society to society. (51)

Digital divide The gap between developing and developed countries, in computer and Internet use, as well as in factors such as age, gender, income, and education. (146)

Discovery   The process of making known or sharing the existence of an aspect of reality. (50)

Discrimination   The process of denying opportunities and equal rights to individuals and groups because of prejudice or other arbitrary reasons. (240)

Disengagement theory   A functionalist theory of aging that contends that society and the aging individual mutually sever many of their relationships. (88)

Domestic partnership   Two unrelated adults who have chosen to share each other's lives in a relationship of mutual caring, who reside together, and who agree to be jointly responsible for their dependents, basic living expenses, and other common necessities. (304)

Dominant ideology   A set of cultural beliefs and practices that helps to maintain powerful social, economic, and political interests. (59)

Double jeopardy   Discrimination that women experience as a result of the compounded effects of gender and race and ethnicity. (276)

Downsizing   Reductions taken in a company's workforce as part of deindustrialization. (361)

Dramaturgical approach   A view of social interaction, popularized by Erving Goffman, that examines people as if they were theatrical performers. (16)

Dysfunction   An element or a process of society that may disrupt a social system or lead to a decrease in stability. (13)

E

Ecclesia   A religious organization that claims to include most or all of the members of a society and is recognized as the national or official religion. (322)

E-commerce   Business involving the numerous ways that people with access to the Internet and other new media can do business. (362)

Economic system   The social institution through which goods and services are produced, distributed, and consumed. (342)

Education   A formal process of learning in which some people consciously teach while others adopt the social role of learner. (312)

Egalitarian family   An authority pattern in which the adult members of the family are regarded as equals. (290)

Elite model   A view of society as being ruled by a small group of individuals who share a common set of political and economic interests. (355)

Employment equity   A federal act that attempts to eliminate barriers faced in the area of employment. (242)

Endogamy   The restriction of mate selection to people within the same group. (293)

Environmental justice   A legal strategy based on claims that racial minorities are subjected disproportionately to environmental hazards. (422)

Equality feminists   Another term for *liberal feminists*, who endorse individual freedom and equality of opportunity in the public and economic spheres. (78)

Equilibrium model   The functionalist view that society tends toward a state of stability or balance. (13, 412)

Esteem   The reputation that a particular individual has earned within an occupation. (195)

Ethnic group   A group that is set apart from others because of its national origin or distinctive cultural patterns. (235)

Ethnoburb   A suburb that is ethnically diverse. (398)

Ethnocentrism   The tendency to assume that our own culture and way of life represent the norm or are superior to all others. (64)

Ethnography   The study of an entire social setting through extended, systematic observation. (34)

Eurocentrism   The dominance of European cultural patterns which contribute to the view of non-European people and cultural patterns as being "other." (63)

Evolutionary theory   A theory of social change that holds that society is moving in a definite direction. (412)

Exogamy   The requirement that people select mates outside certain groups. (293)

Experiment   An artificially created situation that allows the researcher to manipulate variables. (36)

Experimental group   Subjects in an experiment who are exposed to an independent variable introduced by a researcher. (36)

Exploitation theory   A Marxist theory that views racial subordination, such as that in Canada, as a manifestation of the class system inherent in capitalism. (243)

Expressiveness   The concern for maintenance of harmony and the internal emotional affairs of the family. (267)

Extended family   A family in which relatives—such as grandparents, aunts, or uncles—live in the same home as parents and their children. (288)

F

Face-work   The efforts of people to maintain the proper image and avoid embarrassment in public. (76)

False consciousness   A term used by Karl Marx to describe an attitude held by members of a class that does not accurately reflect its objective position. (191, 409)

Family   A set of people related by blood, marriage (or some other agreed-on relationship), or adoption, who share the responsibility for reproducing and caring for members of society. (287)

Feminist perspectives   Sociological approaches that attempt to explain, understand, and change the ways in which gender socially organizes our public and private lives in such a way as to produce inequality between men and women. (14)

Fertility   The amount of reproduction among women of child-bearing age. (370)

Folkways   Norms governing everyday social behaviour whose violation raises comparatively little concern. (56)

Force   The actual or threatened use of coercion to impose one's will on others. (348)

Formal norms   Norms that generally have been written down and that specify strict rules for punishment of violators. (56)

Formal operational   The fourth stage in Piaget's theory of cognitive development. (79)

Formal organization   A group designed for a special purpose and structured for maximum efficiency. (117)

Formal social control   Social control carried out by authorized agents, such as police officers, judges, school administrators, and employers. (162)

Functionalist perspective   A sociological approach that emphasizes the way that parts of a society are structured to maintain its stability. (12)

G

Game stage In interactionist theory, the third stage of Mead's three-stage model for the emergence of self. (76)

Gatekeeping The process by which a relatively small number of people in the media industry control what material eventually reaches the audience. (137)

Gemeinschaft A close-knit community, often found in rural areas, in which strong personal bonds unite members. (113)

Gender Culturally and socially constructed identity as a man or a woman. (263)

Gender roles Expectations regarding the proper behaviour, attitudes, and activities of males and females. (80)

Gender socialization An aspect of socialization through which we learn the attitudes, behaviours, and practices associated with being male and female according to our society and social groups within it. (80)

Generalized others A term used by George Herbert Mead to refer to the attitudes, viewpoints, and expectations of society as a whole that a child takes into account in his or her behaviour. (16)

Genocide The deliberate, systematic killing of an entire people or nation. (245)

Gerontology The scientific study of the sociological and psychological aspects of aging and the problems of the aged. (87)

Gesellschaft A community, often urban, that is large and impersonal, with little commitment to the group or consensus on values. (113)

Glass ceiling An invisible barrier that blocks the promotion of a qualified individual in a work environment because of the individual's gender, race, or ethnicity. (240)

Global economy The economy of the world when people have the capacity to work as a single unit in real time. (146)

Globalization The worldwide integration of government policies, cultures, social movements, and financial markets through trade and the exchange of ideas. (51, 217)

Goal displacement Overzealous conformity to official regulations of a bureaucracy. (118)

Gross national product (GNP) The value of a nation's goods and services. (221)

Group Any number of people with similar norms, values, and expectations who interact with one another on a regular basis. (106)

Growth rate The difference between births and deaths, plus the differences between immigrants and emigrants, per 1000 population. (373)

H

Habit training A relatively formal period of infant socialization, during which caregivers impose routines on the infant. (80)

Hawthorne effect The unintended influence that observers or experimenters can have on their subjects. (37)

Health As defined by the World Health Organization, a "state of complete physical, mental, and social well-being, and not merely the absence of disease and infirmity." (379)

Hegemony The process through which the views of the ruling class are accepted and seen as "normal" by the exploited classes. (140)

Hidden curriculum Standards of behaviour that are deemed proper by society and are taught subtly in schools. (330)

Homophobia Fear of and prejudice against homosexuality. (264)

Horizontal mobility The movement of an individual from one social position to another of the same rank. (202)

Horticultural society A pre-industrial society in which people plant seeds and crops rather than merely subsisting on available foods. (114)

Human ecology A field of study concerned with the relationships between people and their environment. (390)

Human genome The 30 000 to 40 000 human genes in existence. (418)

Human relations approach An approach to the study of formal organizations that emphasizes the role of people, communication, and participation in a bureaucracy and tends to focus on the informal structure of the organization. (122)

Human rights Universal moral rights possessed by all people because they are human. (228)

Hunting-and-gathering society A pre-industrial society in which people rely on whatever foods and fibres are readily available in order to survive. (114)

Hypothesis A speculative statement about the relationship between two or more variables. (30)

I

Ideal type A construct or model for evaluating specific cases. (8, 117)

Impression management The altering of the presentation of the self to create distinctive appearances and satisfy particular audiences. (76)

Incest taboo The prohibition of sexual relationships between certain culturally specified relatives. (293)

Incidence The number of new cases of a specific disorder occurring within a given population during a stated period. (379)

Income Salaries and wages. (186)

Independent variable The variable in a causal relationship that causes or influences a change in a second variable. (30)

Industrial city The city that emerged following the Industrial Revolution; a centre of banking, finance, and industrialization, with a more open class system. (389)

Industrial society A society that depends on mechanization to produce its goods and services. (115, 342)

Infant mortality rate The number of deaths of infants under one year of age per 1000 live births in a given year. (373)

Influence The exercise of power through a process of persuasion. (348)

Informal economy Transfers of money, goods, or services that are not reported to the government. (345)

Informal norms Norms that generally are understood but are not precisely recorded. (56)

Informal social control Social control carried out by people casually by ordinary people through such means as laughter, smiles, and ridicule. (162)

In-group Any group or category to which people feel they belong. (107)

Innovation The process of introducing new elements into a culture through either discovery or invention. (50)

Institutional discrimination The denial of opportunities and equal rights to individuals and groups that results from the normal operations of a society. (241)

Instrumentality The emphasis on tasks, along with a focus on more distant goals and a concern for the external relationship between the family and other social institutions. (267)

Interactionist perspective A sociological approach that generalizes about fundamental or everyday forms of social interaction. (15)

Intergenerational mobility Changes in the social position of children relative to their parents. (202)

Interview A face-to-face or telephone questioning of a respondent to obtain desired information. (34)

Intragenerational mobility Changes in a person's social position within his or her adult life. (203)

Invention The combination of existing cultural items into a form that did not previously exist. (50)

Iron law of oligarchy A principle of organizational life under which even democratic organizations will eventually develop into a bureaucracy ruled by a few individuals. (121)

K

Kinship The state of being related to others. (289)

L

Labelling theory An approach to deviance that attempts to explain why certain people are viewed as deviants while others engaging in the same behaviour are not. (171)

Labour union Organized workers who share either the same skill or the same employer. (125)

Laissez-faire A form of capitalism under which people compete freely, with minimal government intervention in the economy. (343)

Language An abstract system of word meanings and symbols for all aspects of culture. It also includes gestures and other nonverbal communication. (53)

Latent functions Unconscious or unintended functions; hidden purposes. (13)

Law Governmental social control. (56)

Liberal feminism The stream of feminism that asserts that women's equality can be obtained through the extension of the principles of equality of opportunity and freedom. (14)

Liberation theology Use of a church, primarily Roman Catholicism, in a political effort to eliminate poverty, discrimination, and other forms of injustice evident in a secular society. (318)

Life chances People's opportunities to provide themselves with material goods, positive living conditions, and favourable life experiences. (201)

Life expectancy The median number of years a person can be expected to live under current mortality conditions. (373)

Looking-glass self A concept that emphasizes the self as the product of our social interactions with others. (75)

Luddites Rebellious craft workers in nineteenth-century England who destroyed new factory machinery as part of their resistance to the Industrial Revolution. (415)

M

Macrosociology Sociological investigation that concentrates on large-scale phenomena or entire civilizations. (11)

Manifest functions Open, stated, and conscious functions. (13)

Marxist feminism The stream of feminist sociological approaches that place the system of capitalism at fault for the oppression of women and hold that women are not oppressed by sexism or patriarchy, but rather by a system of economic production that is based on unequal gender relations in the capitalist economy. (15)

Mass media Print and electronic means of communication that carry messages to widespread audiences. (133)

Master status A status that dominates others and thereby determines a person's general position in society. (103)

Material culture The physical or technological aspects of our daily lives. (52)

Matriarchy A society in which women dominate in family decision making. (290)

Matrilineal descent A kinship system that favours the relatives of the mother. (289)

McDonaldization The process by which the principles of the fast-food restaurant have come to dominate more and more sectors of U.S society, as well as of the rest of the world. (120)

Mechanical solidarity A collective consciousness that emphasizes group solidarity, characteristic of societies with minimal division of labour. (113)

Media monitoring The monitoring of media content by interest groups, as well as the monitoring of individuals' media usage and choices. (138)

Medicalization of society The growing of medicine as a major institution of social control. (384)

Megachurches Large worship centres affiliated only loosely, if at all, with existing denominations. (322)

Megalopolis A densely populated area, containing two or more cities and their suburbs. (390)

Microsociology Sociological investigation that stresses study of small groups and often uses laboratory experimental studies. (11)

Minority group A subordinate group whose members have significantly less control or power over their own lives than the members of a dominant or majority group have over theirs. (235)

Modernization The far-reaching process by which periphery nations move from traditional or less-developed institutions to those characteristic of more developed societies. (217)

Modernization theory A functionalist approach that proposes that modernization and development will gradually improve the lives of people in developing nations. (217)

Monarchy A form of government headed by a single member of a royal family, usually a king, queen, or some other hereditary ruler. (350)

Monogamy A form of marriage in which one woman and one man are married only to each other. (288)

Monopoly Control of a market by a single business firm. (343)

Morbidity rate The incidence of diseases in a given population. (380)

Mores Norms deemed highly necessary to the welfare of a society. (56)

Mortality Number of deaths. (370)

Mortality rate The incidence of death in a given population. (380)

Multiculturalism A policy that promotes cultural and racial diversity, and full and equal participation of individuals and communities of all origins as a fundamental characteristic of Canadian identity. (62, 246)

Multinational corporation A commercial organization that is headquartered in one country but does business throughout the world. (219)

Multiple jeopardies Compounded effects of gender, race and ethnicity, class, age, or physical disability. (276)

Multiple-nuclei theory A response to the emergence of more than one focal point in some metropolitan areas. In this view, a metropolitan area may have many centres of development, each of which reflects a particular urban need or activity. (391)

N

Narcotizing dysfunction The phenomenon in which the media provide such massive amounts of coverage that the audience becomes numb and fails to act on the information, regardless of how compelling the issue. (137)

Narrowcasting Marketing of the media to a particular audience. (148)

Natural science The study of the physical features of nature and the ways in which they interact and change. (4)

Neo-colonialism Continuing dependence of former colonies on more industrialized foreign countries, including those that are former colonial masters. (215)

New religious movement (NRM) or **cult** A generally small, often secretive religious group that represents either a new religion or a major innovation of an existing faith. (323)

New social movement An organized collective activity that addresses values and social identities, as well as improvements in the quality of life. (410)

New urban sociology Sociologists in this field consider the interplay of local, national, and worldwide forces and their effect on local space, with special emphasis on the impact of global economic activity. (393)

Nonmaterial culture Cultural adjustments to material conditions, such as customs, beliefs, patterns of communication, and ways of using material objects. (52)

Norms Established standards of behaviour maintained by a society. (56)

Nuclear family A married couple and their unmarried children living together. (287)

O

Obedience Compliance with higher authorities in a hierarchical structure. (160)

Objective method A technique for measuring social class that assigns individuals to classes on the basis of such criteria as occupation, education, income, and place of residence. (194)

Observation A research technique in which an investigator collects information through direct participation or by closely watching a group or community. (34)

Offshoring The transfer of work to foreign contractors. (364)

Oligarchy A form of government in which a few individuals rule. (350)

Open system A social system in which the position of each individual is influenced by his or her achieved status. (202)

Operational definition An explanation of an abstract concept that is specific enough to allow a researcher to assess the concept. (29)

Opinion leader Someone who influences the opinions and decisions of others through day-to-day personal contact and communication (e.g., a film or theatre critic). (149)

Organic solidarity A collective consciousness that rests on mutual interdependence, characteristic of societies with a complex division of labour. (113)

Organized crime The work of a group that regulates relations between various criminal enterprises involved in the smuggling and sale of drugs, prostitution, gambling, and other illegal activities. (175)

Out-group A group or category to which people feel they do not belong. (107)

P

Patriarchy A society in which men dominate in family decision making. (290)

Patrilineal descent A kinship system that favours the relatives of the father. (289)

Peace The absence of war; or a proactive effort to develop cooperative relations among nations. (357)

Personality In everyday speech, a person's typical patterns of attitudes, needs, characteristics, and behaviour. (72)

Peter Principle A principle of organizational life according to which every employee within a hierarchy tends to rise to his or her level of incompetence. (119)

Play stage In interactionist theory, the second stage of Mead's three-stage model for the emergence of self. (76)

Pluralist model A view of society in which many competing groups within the community have access to government, so that no single group is dominant. (356)

Political system The social institution that is founded on a recognized set of procedures for implementing and achieving society's goals. (342)

Politics In Harold Lasswell's words, "who gets what, when, and how." (348)

Polyandry A form of polygamy in which a woman can have more than one husband at the same time. (289)

Polygamy A form of marriage in which an individual can have several husbands or wives simultaneously. (288)

Polygyny A form of polygamy in which a husband can have several wives at the same time. (289)

Population pyramid A special type of bar chart that shows the distribution of population by gender and age. (377)

Post-industrial city A city in which global finance and the electronic flow of information dominate the economy. (389)

Post-industrial society A society whose economic system is engaged primarily in the processing and control of information. (116)

Postmodern society A technologically sophisticated society that is preoccupied with consumer goods and media images. (16, 116)

Power The ability to exercise one's will over others. (192, 348)

Power elite A small group of individuals who share a common set of political and economic interests. (355)

Pre-industrial city An old city that had a few thousand people living within its borders and was also characterized by a relatively closed class system and limited mobility. (389)

Prejudice A negative attitude toward an entire category of people, such as a racial or an ethnic minority. (238)

Preoperational The second stage in Piaget's theory of cognitive development. (79)

Preparatory stage In interactionist theory, the first stage of Mead's three-stage model for the emergence of self. (76)

Prestige The respect and admiration that an occupation holds in a society. (194)

Prevalence The total number of cases of a specific disorder that exist at a given time. (380)

Primary group A small group characterized by intimate, face-to-face association and co-operation. (106)

Profane The ordinary and commonplace elements of life, as distinguished from the sacred. (314)

Professional criminal A person who pursues crime as a day-to-day occupation, developing skilled techniques and enjoying a certain degree of status among other criminals. (175)

Proletariat Karl Marx's term for the working class in a capitalist society. (191)

Protestant ethic Max Weber's term for the disciplined work ethic, worldly concerns, and rational orientation to life emphasized by John Calvin and his followers. (317)

Q

Qualitative research Research that relies on what is seen in field or naturalistic settings more than on statistical data. (34)

Quantitative research Research that collects and reports data primarily in numerical form. (34)

Questionnaire A printed or written form used to obtain desired information from a respondent. (34)

R

Racial group A group that is set apart and treated differently from others because of perceived physical attributes. (235)

Racial or **ethnic profiling** The use of a social construct of race as a consideration in suspect profiling in law enforcement and national security practices. (241)

Racialization The social processes by which people come to define a group as a "race," based in part on physical characteristics, but also on historical, cultural, and economic factors. (237)

Racism The belief that one race is supreme and all others are innately inferior. (240)

Radical feminism The stream of feminism maintaining that the root of all oppression of women is embedded in patriarchy. (15)

Random sample A sample for which every member of the entire population has the same chance of being selected. (30)

Rational-legal authority Power made legitimate by law. (349)

Reference group Any group that individuals use as a standard for evaluating themselves and their own behaviour. (107)

Relative deprivation The conscious feeling of a negative discrepancy between legitimate expectations and present actualities. (408)

Relative poverty A floating standard of deprivation by which people at the bottom of a society, whatever their lifestyles, are judged to be disadvantaged in comparison with the nation as a whole. (199)

Reliability The extent to which a measure provides consistent results. (32)

Religion A unified system of beliefs and practices relative to sacred things. (314)

Religious beliefs Statements to which members of a particular religion adhere. (319)

Religious experience The feeling or perception of being in direct contact with the ultimate reality, such as a divine being, or of being overcome with religious emotion. (320)

Religious rituals Practices required or expected of members of a faith. (319)

Representative democracy A form of government in which certain individuals are selected to speak for the people. (351)

Research design A detailed plan or method for obtaining data scientifically. (33)

Resocialization The process of discarding former behaviour patterns and accepting new ones as part of a transition in life. (92)

Resource mobilization The ways in which a social movement utilizes such resources as money, political influence, access to the media, and personnel. (409)

Rites of passage Rituals marking the symbolic transition from one social position to another. (86)

Role conflict The situation that occurs when incompatible expectations arise from two or more social positions held by the same person. (103)

Role exit The process of disengagement from a role that is central to one's self-identity in order to establish a new role and identity. (105)

Role strain The difficulty that arises when the same social position imposes conflicting demands and expectations. (105)

Role taking The process of mentally assuming the perspective of another, thereby enabling a person to respond from that imagined viewpoint. (76)

Routine activities theory The notion that criminal victimization increases when there is a convergence of motivated offenders and suitable targets. (171)

S

Sacred Elements beyond everyday life that inspire awe, respect, and even fear. (314)

Sample A selection from a larger population that is statistically representative of that population. (30)

Sanctions Penalties and rewards for conduct concerning a social norm. (57)

Sapir-Whorf hypothesis A hypothesis concerning the role of language in shaping cultures. It holds that language is culturally determined and serves to influence our mode of thought. (55)

Science The body of knowledge obtained by methods based upon systematic observation. (4)

Scientific management approach Another name for the classical theory of formal organizations. (121)

Scientific method A systematic, organized series of steps that ensures maximum objectivity and consistency in researching a problem. (28)

Secondary analysis A variety of research techniques that make use of previously existing and publicly accessible information and data. (38)

Secondary group A formal, impersonal group in which there is little social intimacy or mutual understanding. (106)

Sect A relatively small religious group that has broken away from another religious organization to renew what it views as the original vision of the faith. (322)

Secularization The process through which religion's influence on other social institutions diminishes. (312)

Segmented or **niche audience** A particular audience to which the media market themselves. (148)

Segregation The act of physically separating two groups; often imposed on a minority group by a dominant group. (245)

Self A distinct identity that sets us apart from others. (75)

Self-segregation The situation that arises when members of a minority deliberately develop residential, economic, or social network structures that are separate from those of the majority population. (246)

Sensorimotor The first stage in Piaget's theory of cognitive development. (79)

Serial monogamy A life choice in which a person can have several spouses in his or her lifetime but only one spouse at a time. (288)

Sex Biological category which distinguishes between female and male. (263)

Sexism The ideology that one sex is superior to the other. (272)

Sick role Societal expectations about the attitudes and behaviour of a person viewed as being ill. (383)

Significant others A term used by George Herbert Mead to refer to those individuals who are most important in the development of the self, such as parents, friends, and teachers. (16)

Single-parent families Families in which there is only one parent to care for children; also known as *lone-parent families.* (298)

Slavery A system of enforced servitude in which people are legally owned by others and in which enslaved status is transferred from parents to children. (187)

Social change Significant alteration over time in behaviour patterns and culture, including norms and values. (407)

Social constructionist perspective An approach to deviance that emphasizes the role of culture in the creation of the deviant identity. (173)

Social control The techniques and strategies for preventing deviant human behaviour in any society. (159)

Social epidemiology The study of the distribution of disease, impairment, and general health status across a population. (379)

Social inequality A condition in which members of a society have different amounts of wealth, prestige, or power. (186)

Social institution An organized pattern of beliefs and behaviour centred on basic social needs. (110)

Social interaction The ways in which people respond to one another. (100)

Social mobility Movement of individuals or groups from one position of a society's stratification system to another. (202)

Social movement An organized collective activity to bring about or resist fundamental change in an existing group or society. (407)

Social network A series of social relationships that link a person directly to others, and through them indirectly to still more people. (108)

Social role A set of expectations for people who occupy a given social position or status. (103)

Social science The study of various aspects of human society. (4)

Social structure The way in which a society is organized into predictable relationships. (100)

Socialism An economic system under which the means of production and distribution are collectively owned. (344)

Socialist feminism The stream of feminism that maintains gender relations are shaped by both patriarchy and capitalism, and thus equality for women implies that both the system of capitalism and the ideology of patriarchy must be challenged and eliminated. (15)

Socialization The process whereby people learn the attitudes, values, and behaviours appropriate for members of a particular culture. (72)

Societal-reaction approach Another name for **labelling theory.** (171)

Society A fairly large number of people who live in the same territory, are relatively independent of people outside it, and participate in a common culture. (49)

Sociobiology The systematic study of the biological bases of social behaviour. (75)

Socio-cultural evolution Long-term trends in societies resulting from the interplay of continuity, innovation, and selection. (113)

Sociological imagination An awareness of the relationship between an individual and the wider society. (3)

Sociology The systematic study of social behaviour and human groups. (3)

Status A term used by sociologists to refer to any of the full range of socially defined positions within a large group or society. (102)

Status group People who have the same prestige or lifestyle, independent of their class positions. (192)

Stereotype An unreliable generalization about all members of a group that does not recognize individual differences within the group. (140, 238)

Stigma A label used to devalue members of deviant social groups. (166)

Stratification A structured ranking of entire groups of people that perpetuates unequal economic rewards and power in a society. (186)

Subculture A segment of society that shares a distinctive pattern of mores, folkways, and values that differs from the pattern of the larger society. (60)

Suburb A term that generally refers to any community near a large city or any territory within a metropolitan area that is not included in the central city. (397)

Survey A study, generally in the form of interviews or questionnaires, that provides researchers with information concerning how people think and act. (33)

Symbols The gestures, objects, and language that form the basis of human communication. (76)

T

Teacher-expectancy effect The impact that a teacher's expectations about a student's performance may have on the student's actual achievements. (332)

Technology Information about how to use the material resources of the environment to satisfy human needs and desires (52); *also* according to Gerhard Lenski, "cultural information about the ways in which the material resources of the environment may be used to satisfy human needs and desires." (113)

Telecommuter An employee who work full-time or part-time at home rather than in an outside office, and who are linked to a supervisor and colleagues through computer terminals, phone lines, and fax machines. (123)

Terrorism The use or threat of violence against random or symbolic targets in pursuit of political aims. (358)

Theory A template through which to organize a way to view the world. (6)

Total fertility rate (TFR) The average number of children born alive to a woman, assuming that she conforms to current fertility rates. (372)

Total institutions Institutions that regulate all aspects of a person's life under a single authority, such as prisons, the military, mental hospitals, and convents. (92)

Totalitarianism Virtually complete government control and surveillance over all aspects of a society's social and political life. (350)

Tracking The practice of placing students in specific curriculum groups on the basis of test scores and other criteria. (331)

Traditional authority Legitimate power conferred by custom and accepted practice. (349)

Trained incapacity The tendency of workers in a bureaucracy to become so specialized that they develop blind spots and fail to notice obvious problems. (118)

Transnational   An immigrant with an allegiance to more than one nation. (425)

Transnational crime   Crime that occurs across multiple national borders. (179)

Transnational feminism   Transnational feminism recognizes that capitalism and systems of political power have severe consequences and oppress women around the world. This form of feminism embraces the multiplicity of cultures, languages, geographies, and experiences which shape the lives of women and highlights the Western/non-Western hierarchy that continues to exist in thought and practice. (15)

U

Underclass   People who are poor for the long term and who lack training and skills. (200)

Underground economy   See **informal economy.** (345)

Urban ecology   A field of study that focuses on various relationships as they emerge in urban areas; it emphasizes that different elements in urban areas contribute to stability. (390)

Urbanism   Louis Wirth's term for a distinctive pattern of behaviour emanating from a relatively large and permanently settled community. (394)

V

Validity   The degree to which a scale or measure truly reflects the phenomenon under study. (32)

Value neutrality   Objectivity of sociologists in the interpretation of data. (28)

Values   Collective conceptions of what is considered good, desirable, and proper—or bad, undesirable, and improper—in a culture. (58)

Variable   A measurable trait or characteristic that is subject to change under different conditions. (30)

Verstehen   The German word for "understanding" or "insight"; used to stress the need for sociologists to take into account people's emotions, thoughts, beliefs, and attitudes. (8)

Vertical mobility   The movement of a person from one social position to another of a different rank. (202)

Vested interests   Those people or groups who will suffer in the event of social change, and who have a stake in maintaining the status quo. (414)

Victimization surveys   Questionnaires or interviews used to determine whether people have been victims of crime. (178)

Victimless crime   A term used by sociologists to describe the willing exchange among adults of widely desired, but illegal, goods and services. (176)

Visible minority   Canadians who are non-white or are identified as being physically different from white Canadians of European descent. (235)

W

War   Conflict between organizations that possess trained combat forces equipped with deadly weapons. (357)

Wealth   An inclusive term encompassing all of a person's material assets, including land and other types of property. (186)

White-collar crime   Crimes committed by usually affluent individuals or corporations in the course of their daily business activities. (175)

Working poor   People who work a certain number of hours a year but whose family income still falls below the low-income cut-off (LICO). (200)

World systems analysis   A view of the global economic system as one divided among certain industrialized nations that control wealth and developing countries that are controlled and exploited. (215)

X

Xenocentrism   The belief that the products, styles, or ideas of our society are inferior to those that originate elsewhere. (64)

Z

Zero population growth (ZPG)   The state of a population with a growth rate of zero, achieved when the number of births plus immigrants is equal to the number of deaths plus emigrants. (378)

REFERENCES

A

ABC News. 1992. "*Primetime Live*—True Colors." Transcript of November 26 episode.

ABC Radio Australia. 2006. "China: Crackdown in Air Pollution ahead of 2008 Beijing Olympics." Accessed May 2 (www.abc.net.au).

Abercrombie, Nicholas, Bryan S. Turner, and Stephen Hill, eds. 1990. *Dominant Ideologies*. Cambridge, MA: Unwin Hyman.

Abercrombie, Nicholas, Stephen Hill, and Bryan S. Turner. 1980. *The Dominant Ideology Thesis*. London: George Allen and Unwin.

Aberle, David F., A.K. Cohen, A.K. Davis, M.J. Leng, Jr., and F.N. Sutton. 1950. "The Functional Prerequisites of a Society." *Ethics* 60 (January):100–111.

Aboriginal Healing Foundation. 2000. "The Residential School Impact." *Healing Hands* 2: 8-9.

Aboriginal Women's Health and Healing Research Group. 2007. *Annual Report: 2006–2007*. Vancouver, BC.

Abrahams, Ray G. 1968. "Reaching an Agreement over Bridewealth in Labwor, Northern Uganda: A Case Study." Pp. 202–215 in *Councils in Action*, Audrey Richards and Adam Kuer, eds. Cambridge, UK: Cambridge University Press.

Abrahamson, Mark. 1978. *Functionalism*. Englewood Cliffs, NJ: Prentice Hall.

Abu-Laban, Sharon M., and Susan A. McDaniel. 1995. "Ageing Women and Standards of Beauty." Pp. 97–122 in *Feminist Issues: Race, Class and Sexuality*, Nancy Mandell, ed. Scarborough, ON: Prentice Hall.

Acharya, Menna. 2000. *Labor Market Developments and Poverty: With Focus on Economic Opportunities for Women*. Kathmandu, Nepal: Tanka Prasad Acharya Foundation/FES.

Acosta, R. Vivian, and Linda Jean Carpenter. 2001. "Women in Intercollegiate Sport: A Longitudinal Study: 1977–1998." Pp. 302–308 in *Sport in Contemporary Society: An Anthology*. 6th ed., edited by D. Stanley Eitzen. New York:Worth.

Adam, Barry D. 1995. *The Rise of a Gay and Lesbian Movement*, rev. ed. New York: Twayne.

Adamson, Nancy, Linda Briskin, and Margaret McPhail. 1998. *Feminist Organizing for Change: The Contemporary Women's Movement in Canada*. Toronto: Oxford University Press.

Addams, Jane. 1910. *Twenty Years at Hull-House*. New York: Macmillan.

———. 1930. *The Second Twenty Years at Hull-House*. New York: Macmillan.

Adler, Patricia A., and Peter Adler. 1998. *Peer Power: Preadolescent Culture and Identity*. New Brunswick, NJ: Rutgers University Press.

Adler, Patricia A., Peter Adler, and John M. Johnson. 1992. "Street Corner Society Revisited: New Questions about Old Issues." *Journal of Contemporary Ethnography* 21(April):3–10.

Africa News Service. 1998. "CPJ's 10 Enemies of the Press." Retrieved October 8, 2000 (http://www.elibrary.com).

Agrell, Siri. 2007. "Then They Won't Get Married . . ." *The Globe and Mail*, September 13, L1.

Ahmed, Karuna Chanana. 2001. *Interrogating Women's Education : Bounded Visions, Expanding Horizons*. New Delhi: Rawat.

AIDS Alert. 1999. "AIDS Complacency Leads Back to Risk Behavior." November 14, 127–128.

Akers, Ronald L. 1997. *Criminological Theories: Introduction and Evaluation*, 2nd ed. Los Angeles, CA: Roxbury Publishing Co.

Alain, Michel. 1985. "An Empirical Validation of Relative Deprivation." *Human Relations* 38(8):739–749.

Albarracin, Dolores, Martin Fishbein, and Eva Goldstein de Muchinik. 1997. "Seeking Social Support in Old Age as a Reasoned Action: Structural and Volitional Determinants in a Middle-Aged Sample of Argentinean Women." *Journal of Applied Social Psychology* 27:463–476.

Albas, Daniel, and Cheryl Albas. 1988. "Aces and Bombers: The Post-exam Impression Management Strategies of Students." *Symbolic Interaction* 11 (Fall):289–302.

Albiniak, P. 2000. "TV's Drug Deal." *Broadcasting and Cable*, January 17, 3, 148.

Albrecht, Gary L., Katerine D. Steelman, and Michael Bury. 2001. *Handbook of Disabilities Study*. Thousand Oaks, CA: Sage.

Alfino, Mark, John S. Carpeto, and Robin Wyngard. 1998. *McDonaldization Revisited: Critical Essays on Consumer Culture*. Westport, CT: Praeger.

Allen, Bem P. 1978. *Social Behavior: Fact and Falsehood*. Chicago: Nelson-Hall.

Allen, John L. 2005. *Student Atlas of World Geography*, 4th ed. New York: McGraw-Hill Ryerson.

Allport, Gordon W. 1979. *The Nature of Prejudice*, 25th anniversary ed. Reading, MA: Addison-Wesley.

Alonzo, Angelo A. 1989. "Health and Illness and the Definition of the Situation: An Interactionist Perspective." Presented at the annual meeting of the Society for the Study of Social Problems, Berkeley, CA.

Alvord, Lori Arviso, and Elizabeth Cohen Van Pelt. 1999. *The Scalpel and the Silver Bear*. New York: Bantam.

Amato, Paul, and Alan Booth. 1997. *A Generation at Risk*. Cambridge, MA: Harvard University Press.

Amazon.com. 2001. "About Amazon.com." Retrieved September 20, 2001 (http://www. amazon.com).

Ambert, Anne-Marie. 2002. "The Changing Experience of Childhood." *Canadian Journal of Sociology* 27 (2). Retrieved February 1, 2003 (http://www.cjsonline.ca/backiss/ cjsjanfeb.03.html).

American Association of Retired Persons (AARP). 2004. *Global Report on Aging*. Washington, DC: AARP.

American Bar Association. 1999. "Commission on Domestic Violence." Retrieved July 20, 1999 (http://www.abanet.org/domviol/ stats.html).

American Humane Association. 1999. "Child Abuse and Neglect Data." Retrieved July 20, 1999 (http://www.americanhumane. org/cpfactdata.htm).

American Society of Plastic Surgeons. 2002. "National Clearinghouse of Plastic Surgery Statistics." Retrieved February 1, 2002 (http://www.plasticsurgery.org/mediactr/ stats_ncs.htm).

———. 2005. "National Plastic Surgery Statistics: Cosmetic and Reconstructive Procedure Trends." Retrieved October 23, 2005 (http://www.plasticsurgery.org/ public_education/2004Statistics.cfm).

———. 2007a. "2000/2005/2006 National Plastic Surgery Statistics: Cosmetic and Reconstructive Procedure Trends." Arlington Heights, IL: American Society of Plastic Surgeons.

———. 2007b. "2006 Gender Quick Facts: Cosmetic Plastic Surgery." Arlington Heights, IL: American Society of Plastic Surgeons.

Amnesty International. 1994. *Breaking the Silence: Human Rights Violations Based on Sexual Orientation.* New York: Amnesty International.

Amnesty International Canada. 2005. *Human Rights in Canada: Overview.* Ottawa.

Andersen, Margaret. 1997. *Thinking about Women: Sociological Perspectives on Sex and Gender,* 4th ed. Boston: Allyn and Bacon.

Anderson, Craig A., and Brad J. Bushman. 2001. "Effects of Violent Video Games on Aggressive Behavior, Aggressive Cognition, Aggressive Affect, Physiological Arousal, and Prosocial Behavior: A Meta-Analytic Review of Scientific Literature." *Psychological Science* 12(5):353–359.

Anderson, John Ward, and Molly Moore. 1993. "The Burden of Womanhood." *Washington Post National Weekly Edition* 10 (March 22–28):6–7.

Anderssen, Erin, Michael Valpy, et al. 2004. *The New Canada: A Globe and Mail Report on the Next Generation.* Toronto: McClelland & Stewart.

Andreatta, David. 2007. "First your kids won't leave . . ." *The Globe and Mail,* September 13. Retrieved August 13, 2007 (http://www.theglobeandmail.com/servlet/story/RTGAM.20070913.wlslackers13/BNStory/…)

Angier, Natalie. 1998. "Drugs, Sports, Body Image and G.I. Joe." *New York Times,* December 22, D1, D3.

AOL Time Warner. 2003. *Factbook.* New York: AOL Time Warner.

Appelbaum, Richard, and Peter Dreier. 1999. "The Campus Anti-sweatshops Movement." *The American Prospect* (September–October): 71–78.

Armer, J. Michael, and John Katsillis. 1992. "Modernization Theory." Pp. 1299–1304 in *Encyclopedia of Sociology,* Vol. 4, Edgar F. Borgatta and Marie L. Borgatta, eds. New York: Macmillan.

Armstrong, Jane. 2002. "Canada Is 30 Million, but Will That Last?" *The Globe and Mail,* March 13, A1, A7.

Aronowitz, Stanley, and William Di Fazio. 1994. *The Jobless Future: Sci-Tech and Dogma of Work.* Minneapolis, MN: University of Minneapolis.

Aronson, Elliot. 1999. *The Social Animal,* 8th ed. New York: Worth.

Ashley, David, and Michael Orenstein. 1998. *Sociological Theory,* 4th ed. Boston: Allyn and Bacon.

Associated Press. 1998. "Environmental Test Case Averted." *Christian Science Monitor,* September 21, 18.

———. 2001. "Member of the Dwindling Shaker Sect." *Chicago Tribune,* June 20, 11.

Assyrian International News Agency. 2008. "Saudi Arabia to Allow Women to Drive—With Conditions." March 20. Retrieved April 9, 2008 (http://www.aina.org/news/20080320135642.htm).

Astwood Strategy Corporation. 2003. *Results of the 2002 Canadian Police Survey on Youth Gangs.* Ottawa, ON: Public Safety and Emergency Preparedness Canada.

Atchley, Robert C. 1985. *The Social Forces in Later Life: An Introduction to Social Gerontology,* 4th ed. Belmont, CA: Wadsworth.

Augustine, Noah. 2000. "Grandfather Was a Knowing Christian." *Toronto Star,* August 9, A17.

Austin, April. 2002. "Cellphones and Strife in Congo." *Christian Science Monitor,* December 5, pp. 11.

Axtell, Roger E. 1990. *Do's and Taboos around the World,* 2nd ed. New York: John Wiley and Sons.

Azam, Sharlene. 2000. " Reality television could change rules of celebrity." *Toronto Star,* August 22.

Azumi, Koya, and Jerald Hage. 1972. *Organizational Systems.* Lexington, MA: Heath.

B

Bachrach, Christine A. 1986. "Adoption Plans, Adopted Children, and Adoptive Mothers." *Journal of Marriage and the Family* 48 (May):243–253.

Baer, Douglas, James Curtis, and Edward Grabb. 2000. "Has Voluntary Association Activity Declined? A Cross-National Perspective." Paper presented at the annual meeting of the American Sociological Association, Washington, DC.

Bainbridge, William Sims. 1999. "Cyberspace: Sociology's Natural Domain." *Contemporary Sociology* 28 (November):664–667.

Baker, Chris. 2002. "Canada After September 11th: A Public Opinion Perspective." Environics Research Group. Retrieved November 20, 2007 (http://www.yorku.ca/robarts/projects/canada-watch/conferences/conf_cnd-res/papers/cw_conf_baker.pdf).

Baker, Maureen. 2001. "The Future of Family Life." Pp. 285–302 in *Families: Changing Trends in Canada,* 4th ed., edited by Maureen Baker. Toronto: McGraw-Hill Ryerson.

Baker, Therese L. 1999. *Doing Social Research,* 3rd ed. New York: McGraw-Hill Ryerson.

Banboza, David. 2006. "Citing Public Sentiment, China Cancels Release of 'Geisha.'" *New York Times,* February 1, p. B6.

Banister, Judith. 2005. "Manufacturing earnings and compensation in China." *Monthly Labor Review,* August, 22–40.

Barbour, Rosaline S. 2007. *Introducing Qualitative Research: A Student's Guide to the Craft of Doing Qualitative Research.* London: SAGE Publications.

Barnsley, Paul. 1999. "Cree Chief Slams Gathering Strength." *Windspeaker,* January 1.

Barrett, David B., Todd M. Johnson, and Peter F. Crossing. 2005. "Worldwide Adherents of All Religions, Mid-2004" and "Religions Adherents in the United States of America 1900–2005." *Missionetric 2005: A Global Survey of World Mission.* P. 282.

Barron, Milton L. 1953. "Minority Group Characteristics of the Aged in American Society." *Journal of Gerontology* 8:477–482.

Bashevkin, Sylvia B. 2002. *Welfare Hot Buttons.* Toronto: University of Toronto Press.

Basso, Keith H. 1972. "Ice and Travel among the Fort Norman Slave: Folk Taxonomies and Cultural Rules." *Language in Society* 1 (March):31–49.

Bauerlein, Monika. 1996. "The Luddites Are Back." *Utne Reader* (March–April), 24, 26.

Bauman, Kurt J. 1999. "Extended Measures of Well-Being: Meeting Basic Needs." *Current Population Reports,* ser. P70, no. 67. Washington, DC: United States Government Printing Office.

Ba-Yunus, Ilyas, and Kassim Kone. 2004. "Muslim Americans: A Demographic Report." Pp. 299–322 in *Muslims in the American Public Square,* edited by Zahid H. Bukhari et al.Walnut Creek, CA: Alta Mira Press.

Beach, Charles M., and Christopher Worswick. 1993. "Is There a Double-Negative Effect on the Earnings of Immigrant Women?" *Canadian Public Policy* 19(1):36–53.

Beaujot, Roderic, Ellen M. Gee, Fernando Rajulton, and Zenaida R. Ravanera. 1995. *Family over the Life Course.* Ottawa: Minister of Industry.

Becker, Anne E. 1995. *Body, Self, and Society: The View from Fiji.* Philadelphia: University of Pennsylvania Press.

Becker, Anne E., and R.A. Burwell. 1999. "Acculturation and Disordered Eating in Fiji." Presented at the annual meeting of the American Psychiatric Association.

Becker, Howard S. 1952. "Social Class Variations in the Teacher–Pupil Relationship." *Journal of Educational Sociology* 25 (April):451–465.

———. 1963. *The Outsiders: Studies in the Sociology of Deviance.* New York: Free Press.

———. 1973. *The Outsiders: Studies in the Sociology of Deviance,* rev. ed. New York: Free Press.

———, ed. 1964. *The Other Side: Perspectives on Deviance.* New York: Free Press.

Beeghley, Leonard. 1978. *Social Stratification in America: A Critical Analysis of Theory and Research.* Santa Monica, CA: Goodyear Publishing.

Begley, Sharon. 1998. "Why Wilson's Wrong." *Newsweek,* June 22, 61–62.

———. 1999. "Designer Babies." *Newsweek,* November 9, 61–62.

Bell, Daniel. 1999. *The Coming of Post-industrial Society: A Venture in Social Forecasting*, with a new foreword. New York: Basic Books.

Bell, Wendell. 1981."Modernization." Pp. 186–187 in *Encyclopedia of Sociology*. Guilford, CT: DPG Publishing.

Belsie, Laurent. 1998. "Genetic Research Data Will Double Annually." *Christian Science Monitor*, July 30, B4.

———. 2000. "Strange Webfellows." *Christian Science Monitor* March 2, 15–16.

Belt, Don. 2002. "The World of Islam." *National Geographic* (January):26–85.

Bender, William, and Margaret Smith. 1997. "Population, Food, and Nutrition." *Population Bulletin* 51 (February).

Bendix, B. Reinhard. 1968. "Max Weber." Pp. 493–502 in *International Encyclopedia of the Social Sciences*, David L. Sills, ed. New York: Macmillan.

Benford, Robert D. 1992. "Social Movements." Pp. 1880–1887 in *Encyclopedia of Sociology*, Vol. 4, Edgar F. Borgatta and Marie L. Borgatta, eds. New York: Macmillan.

Berger, Peter, and Thomas Luckmann. 1966. *The Social Construction of Reality*. New York: Doubleday.

Bernstein, Anne C. 1988. "Unraveling the Tangles: Children's Understanding of Step-family Kinship." Pp. 83–111 in *Relative Strangers: Studies of Step-Family Processes*, W.R. Beer, ed. Totowa, NJ: Rowman & Littlefield.

Bernstein, Richard. 2003. "An Aging Europe May Find Itself on the Sidelines." *New York Times*, June 29, 3.

Bernstein, Sharon. 2004. "Under the Radar, HIV Worsens." *Los Angeles Times*, October 16, A1, A12.

Berlin, Brent, and Paul Kay. 1991. *Basic Color Terms: Their Universality and Evolution*. Berkeley, CA: University of California Press.

Berube, Alan. 2006. "Two Steps Back: City and Suburban Poverty Trends 1999–2005." The Brookings Institute. November 23. Retrieved November 23, 2008 (http://www.brookings.edu/reports/2006/12poverty-berube.aspx).

Best, Fred, and Ray Eberhard. 1990. "Education for the 'Era of the Adult.'" *The Futurist* 21 (May–June):23–28.

Bharadwaj, Lakshmik. 1992. "Human Ecology." Pp. 848–867 in *Encyclopedia of Sociology*, Vol. 2, Edgar F. Borgatta and Marie L. Borgatta, eds. New York: Macmillan.

Bian, Yanjie. 2002. "Chinese Social Stratification and Social Mobility." Pp. 91–116 in *Annual Review of Sociology*, edited by Karen S. Cook and John Hagan. Palo Alto, CA: Annual Reviews.

Bibby, Reginald W. 1990. *Mosaic Madness*. Toronto: Stoddart.

———. 1995. *The Bibby Report: Social Trends Canadian Style*. Toronto: Stoddart.

———. 2004. "Ethos versus Ethics: Canada and the U.S. and Homosexuality." Annual meeting of the Pacific Sociological Association, San Francisco, April 2004.

Bielby, Denise D., and William T. Bielby. 2002. "Hollywood Dreams, Harsh Realities: Writing for Film and Television." *Contexts* 1 (Fall/Winter):21–25.

Bielby, William T., and Denise D. Bielby. 1992. "I Will Follow Him: Family Ties, Gender-Role Beliefs, and Reluctance to Relocate for a Better Job." *American Journal of Sociology* 97 (March):1241–1267.

Bishop-Stall, Shaughnessy. 2004. *Down to This: Squalor and Splendour in a Big-City Shanty-town*. Toronto: Random House.

Black, Donald. 1995. "The Epistemology of Pure Sociology." *Law and Social Inquiry* 20 (Summer):829–870.

Black, Naomi. 1993. "The Canadian Women's Movement: The Second Wave." Pp. 151–176 in *Changing Patterns: Women in Canada*, 2nd ed., Sandra Burt, Lorraine Code, and Lindsay Dorney, eds. Toronto: McClelland & Stewart.

Blanchard, Fletcher A., Teri Lilly, and Leigh Ann Vaughn. 1991. "Reducing the Expression of Racial Prejudice." *Psychological Science* 2 (March):101–105.

Blanco, Robert. 1998. "The Disappearance of Mom and Dad." *USA Today*, December 17, D1.

Blau, Peter M., and Marshall W. Meyer. 1987. *Bureaucracy in Modern Society*, 3rd ed. New York: Random House.

Blauner, Robert. 1972. *Racial Oppression in America*. New York: Harper and Row.

Bluestone, Barry, and Bennett Harrison. 1982. *The Deindustrialization of America*. New York: Basic Books.

Blumer, Herbert. 1955. "Collective Behavior." Pp. 165–198 in *Principles of Sociology*, 2nd ed., Alfred McClung Lee, ed. New York: Barnes and Noble.

———. 1969. *Symbolic Interactionism: Perspective and Method*. Englewood Cliffs, NJ: Prentice Hall.

Boase, Jeffery, John B. Horrigan, Barry Wellman, and Lee Rainie. 2006. *The Strength of Internet Ties*. Washington, DC: Pew Internet and American Life Project.

Boaz, Rachel Floersheim. 1987. "Early Withdrawal from the Labor Force." *Research on Aging* 9 (December):530–547.

Bobo, Lawrence. 1991. "Social Responsibility, Individualism, and Redistribution Policies." *Sociological Forum* 6:71–92.

Bok, Sissela. 1998. *Mayhem: Violence as Public Entertainment*. Reading, MA: Addison-Wesley.

Booth, William. 2000. "Has Our Can-Do Attitude Peaked?" *Washington Post National Weekly Edition*, February 7, 29.

Bornschier, Volker, Christopher Chase-Dunn, and Richard Rubinson. 1978. "Cross-National Evidence of the Effects of Foreign Investment and Aid on Economic Growth and Inequality: A Survey of Findings and a Reanalysis." *American Journal of Sociology* 84 (November):651–683.

Boston Women's Health Book Collective. 1969. *Our Bodies, Ourselves*. Boston: New England Free Press.

———. 1992. *The New Our Bodies, Ourselves*. New York: Touchstone.

Bottomore, Tom, and Maximilien Rubel, eds. 1956. *Karl Marx: Selected Writings in Sociology and Social Philosophy*. New York: McGraw-Hill Ryerson.

Bouvier, Leon F. 1980. "America's Baby Boom Generation: The Fateful Bulge." *Population Bulletin* 35 (April).

Bowles, Samuel, and Herbert Gintis. 1976. *Schooling in Capitalist America: Educational Reforms and the Contradictions of Economic Life*. New York: Basic Books.

Bowles, Scott. 1999. "Fewer Violent Fatalities in Schools." *USA Today*, April 28, 4A.

Boyd, Monica. 1984. "At a Disadvantage: The Occupational Attainments of Foreign-Born Women in Canada." *International Migration Review* 18 (4):1091–1119.

———. 1992. "Gender, Visible Minority, and Immigrant Earnings Inequality: Reassessing Employment Equity Premise." Pp. 279–321 in *Deconstructing a Nation: Immigration, Multiculturalism and Racism in '90s Canada*, Vic Satzewch, ed. Halifax: Fernwood Publishing.

Bradsher, Keith. 2004. "Like Japan in the 1980's, China Poses Big Economic Challenge." *New York Times*, March 2, pp. A1, C2.

Brand, Dionne. 1993. "A Working Paper on Black Women in Toronto: Gender, Race, and Class." Pp. 220–241 in *Returning the Gaze: Essays on Racism, Feminism and Politics*, Himani Bannerji, ed. Toronto: Sister Vision Press.

Brandon, Karen. 1995. "Computer Scrutiny Adds to Furor over Immigrants." *Chicago Tribune*, December 5, 1, 16.

Brannigan, Augustine. 1992. "Postmodernism." Pp. 1522–1525 in *Encyclopedia of Sociology*, Vol. 3, Edgar F. Borgatta and Marie L. Borgatta, eds. New York: Macmillan.

Brannon, Robert. 1976. "Ideology, Myth, and Reality: Sex Equality in Israel." *Sex Roles: A Journal of Research* 6:403–419.

Brasfield, Charles R. 2001. "Residential School Syndrome." *BC Medical Journal* 43 (2):78–81.

Braxton, Greg, and Dana Calvo. 2002. "Networks Come under the Gun as Watchdogs Aim for Diversity." *Chicago Tribune*, June 4, sec. 5, p. 2.

Bray, James H., and John Kelly. 1999. *Stepfamilies: Love, Marriage, and Parenting in the First Decade*. New York: Broadway Books.

Brint, Steven. 1998. *Schools and Societies*. Thousand Oaks, CA: Pine Forge Press.

Brockerhoff, Martin P. 2000. "An Urbanizing World." *Population Bulletin* 55(September).

Brundtland, Gro Harlem. 2001. "Affordable AIDS Drugs Are Within Reach." *International Herald Tribune*. Retrieved March 1 (http://www.who.int/inf-pr-2001/en/note2001-02.html).

Bruni, Frank. 1998. "A Small-but-Growing Sorority Is Giving Birth to Children for Gay Men." *New York Times*, June 25, A12.

Bryant, Adam. 1999. "American Pay Rattles Foreign Partners." *New York Times*, January 17, 1, 4.

Bryant, Bunyan, and Paul Mohai, eds. 1992. *Race and the Incidence of Environmental Hazards*. Boulder, CO: Westview Press.

Buechler, Steven M. 2000. *Social Movements in Advanced Capitalism: The Political Economy and Cultural Construction of Social Activism*. New York: Oxford University Press.

Bula, Francis. 2000. "This Is an International Crisis." *Vancouver Sun*, November 21, A1, A6.

Bullard, Robert. 1990. *Dumping in Dixie: Race, Class, and Environmental Quality*. Boulder, CO: Westview Press.

Bulle, Wolfgang F. 1987. *Crossing Cultures? Southeast Asian Mainland*. Atlanta: Centers for Disease Control.

Bunzel, John H. 1992. *Race Relations on Campus: Stanford Students Speak*. Stanford, CA: Portable Stanford.

Bureau of Labor Statistics. 2004. "Current Labor Statistics." Accessed January 28 (www.bls.gov/opub/mlr/mlrhome.htm).

———. 2008. *Union Member Summary*. Press Release. Washington, DC: United States Government Printing Office.

Bureau of the Census. 1975. *Historical Statistics of the United States, Colonial Times to 1970*. Washington, DC: United States Government Printing Office.

———. 1997a. *Statistical Abstract of the United States, 1997*. Washington, DC: United States Government Printing Office.

———. 1997b. "Geographical Mobility: March 1995 to March 1996." *Current Population Reports*, ser. P-20, no. 497. Washington, DC: United States Government Printing Office.

———. 2000. "National Population Projections." Retrieved May 11, 2000 (http://www.census.gov/population/www/projection/natsum-T3html).

———. 2005. *Statistical Abstract of the United States, 2006*. Washington, DC: United States Government Printing Office.

———. 2005f. "American Fact Finder: Places with United States." Accessed December 12 (http://factfinder.census.gov).

Burgess, Ernest W. 1925. "The Growth of the City." Pp. 47–62 in *The City*, Robert E. Park, Ernest W. Burgess, and Roderick D. McKenzie, eds. Chicago: University of Chicago Press.

Butterfield, Fox. 1996. "U.S. Has Plan to Broaden Availability of DNA Testing." *New York Times*, June 14, A8.

Butler, Daniel Allen. 1998. *"Unsinkable": The Full Story*. Mechanicsburg, PA: Stackpole Books.

Butler, Robert N. 1990. "A Disease Called Ageism." *Journal of American Geriatrics Society* 38 (February):178–180.

C

Calhoun, Craig. 1998. "Community without Propinquity Revisited." *Sociological Inquiry* 68 (Summer):373–397.

———. 2003. "Belonging in the Cosmopolitan Imaginary." *Ethnicities* 3 (December): 531–553.

Calhoun, David B. 2000. "Learning at Home." P. 193 in *Yearbook of the Encyclopedia Britannica 2000*. Chicago: Encyclopedia Britannica.

Calliste, Agnes. 2001. "Black Families in Canada: Exploring the Interconnections of Race, Class and Gender." Pp. 401–419 in *Family Patterns, Gender Relations*, Bonnie J. Fox, ed. Toronto: Oxford University Press.

Campaign 2000. 2004. "Poor Jobs, Modest Social Investments Drive up Child Poverty in Canada." Retrieved November 24, 2004 (http://action.web.ca/home/c2000/alerts.shtml?x=70077).

———. 2007. *2006 Report Card on Child Poverty in Canada*. Retrieved September 2, 2007 (http://www.campaign2000.ca).

Camus, Albert. 1948. *The Plague*. New York: Random House.

Canada Citizens' Forum on Canada's Future. 1991. *Report to the People and Government of Canada*. Ottawa: Minister of Supply and Services Canada.

Canadian Association of University Teachers (CAUT). 2007. *CAUT Almanac of Post-Secondary Education in Canada*. Ottawa.

Canadian Broadcasting Corporation (CBC) News. 2000. "Stockwell Day's New Alliance." Retrieved April 5, 2002 (http://www.cbc.ca/insidecbc/newsinreview/Sep2000/stockwell/separation.htm).

———. 2004. "Voter Turnout Lowest Since Confederation." June 30. Retrieved October 26, 2007 (http://www.cbc.ca/canada/story/2004/06/29/turnout040629.html).

———. 2004. "Minorities Missing on Canadian TV." July 15. Retrieved March 8, 2007 (http://www.cbc.ca/arts/story/2004/07/15/minorityreport040715.html).

———. 2005. "Police Stop More Blacks, Ont. Study Finds." Retrieved May 27,

2005 (http://www.cbc.ca/story/canada/national/2005/05/26/race050526.html).

———. 2006a. "Gender Inequality Deals Blow to Mothers and Children: UNICEF." December 11. Retrieved December 11, 2006 (http://www.cbc.ca/world/story/2006/12/11/unicef-report.html).

———. 2006. "Indepth: Summit of the Americas: NAFTA." March 30. Retrieved June 25, 2007 (http://www.cbc.ca/news/background/summitofamericas/nafta.html).

———. 2006. "Guardian of the Airwaves." April 7. Retrieved January 24, 2008 (http://www.cbc.ca/news/background/crtc/).

———. 2007a. "Glad to be Canadian, Muslims Say." February 13. Retrieved April 21, 2008 (http://www.cbc.ca/canada/story/2007/02/12/muslim-poll.html).

———. 2007c. "Regulating 'Assisted Human Reproduction.'" April 23. Retrieved April 24, 2007 (http://www.cbc.ca/news/background/genetics_reproduction/rgtech.html).

———. 2007. "Homelessness 'Chronic' in Canada: Study." June 26. Retrieved March 28, 2008 (http://www.cbc.ca/canada/story/2007/06/26/shelter.html).

———. 2007. "Residential School Payout a 'Symbolic' Apology: Fontaine." September 19. Retrieved September 19, 2007 (http://www.cbc.ca/canada/story/2007/09/19/residential–schools.html).

———. 2007. "Vacation Nations: How Canada Compares to Other G8 Countries." Retrieved September 19, 2007 (http://www.cbc.ca/news/interactives/map-vacation-days).

———. 2008a. "CRTC imposes cross-media ownership restrictions." January 15. Retrieved December 7, 2008(http://www.cbc.ca/money/story/2008/01/15crtc.html).

———. 2008b. "Toronto Trustees Vote in Favour of Black-Focused Schools." January 29. Retrieved April 16, 2008 (http://www.cbc.ca/canada/toronto/story/2008/01/29/tto-schools.html).

———. 2008c. "Voter turnout drops to record low." October 15. Retrieved October 27, 2008 (http://www.cbc.ca/news/canadavotes/story/2008/10/15/voter-turnout.html).

Canadian Business. 2006. "Canada's Richest Families." December.

———. 2007. "Canada's Richest Families." November. (http://www.canadianbusiness.com/after-hours/article.jsp?content=20071128-205745-2952).

Canadian Centre for Policy Alternatives. 2007. "No New Year's Hangover for Top CEOs." Press Release, January 2. Retrieved September 2, 2007 (http://www.policyalternatives.ca/News/2007/01/PressRelease1523/index.cfm?pa=F4FB3E9D).

Canadian Centre for Policy Alternatives. 2008. "New Year's Party Still Going for

Top CEOs." January 1. Retrieved April 9, 2008 (http://www.growinggap.ca/node/95).

Canadian Council on Learning. 2005. "Canada's High School Dropout Rates Are Falling." Retrieved October 1, 2007 (http://www.ccl-cca.ca/CCL/Reports/LessonsInLeaning/LiL-16Dec2005.htm).

Canadian Council on Social Development. 2003. *The Personal Security Index.* Ottawa, ON.

Canadian Education Statistics Council (CESC). 2000. *Education Indicators in Canada: Report of the Pan-Canadian Education Indicators Program 1999.* Ottawa: Statistics Canada and Council of Ministers of Education Canada.

Canadian Institute for Health Information (CIHI). 1999. *Supply and Distribution of Registered Nurses in Canada.* Ottawa: Canadian Institute for Health Information.

———. 2000. *Health Care in Canada, 2000: First Annual Report.* Retrieved April 20, 2000 (http://secure.cihi.ca/cihiweb/products/Healthreport2000.pdf).

———. 2001. *Health Care in Canada, 2001.* Retrieved January 27, 2002 (http://www.cihi.ca/HealthReport2001.pdf).

———. 2005. *Health Expenditures by Source of Finance, Canada, 1975 to 2004.* Retrieved September 26, 2005 (http://secure.cihi.ca/cihiweb/en/media).

Canadian Media Research Inc. 2006. "How Many Canadians Subscribe to Cable TV or Satellite TV?" Ottawa: Canadian Radio-television and Telecommunications Commission.

Canadian Medical Association. 2007. "Percent Distribution of Physicians by Age, Sex and Province/Territory, Canada 2007." *CMA Masterfile.* Ottawa, ON.

Canadian Mental Health Association (CMHA). 2003. "Aboriginal Youth: A Manual of Promising Suicide Prevention Strategies." *Centre for Suicide Prevention.* Edmonton: CMHA.

Canadian Press. 2007. "Number of Single–Parent Families Rising: Census." September 12. Retrieved September 12, 2007 (http://www.cbc.ca/canada/story/2007/09/12/census-families.html).

Canadian Radio-television and Telecommunications Commission (CRTC). 2007. *Broadcasting Policy Monitoring Report 2006.* Ottawa.

Caplan, Ronald L. 1989. "The Commodification of American Health Care." *Social Science and Medicine* 28 (11):1139–1148.

Caplow, Theodore, and Louis Hicks. 2002. *Systems of War and Peace.* 2d ed. Lanham, MD: University Press of America.

Carey, Anne R., and Elys A. McLean. 1997. "Heard It through the Grapevine?" *USA Today,* September 15, B1.

Carey, Anne R., and Jerry Mosemak. 1999. "Big on Religion." *USA Today,* April 1, D1.

Carroll, John. 2003. "The Good Doctor." *American Way* (July 15):26–31.

Carty, Win. 1999. "Greater Dependence on Cars Leads to More Pollution in World's Cities." *Population Today* 27 (December):1–2.

Casper, Lynne M., and Loretta E. Bass. 1998. "Voting and Registration in the Election of November 1996." *Current Population Reports,* ser. P-20, no. 504. Washington, DC: United States Government Printing Office.

Castells, Manuel. 1983. *The City and the Grass Roots.* Berkeley, CA: University of California Press.

———. 1996. *The Information Age: Economy, Society and Culture.* Vol. 1 of The Rise of the Network Society. London: Blackwell.

———. 1997. *The Power of Identity.* Vol. 1 of The Information Age: Economy, Society and Culture. London: Blackwell.

———. 1998. *End of Millennium.* Vol. 3 of The Information Age: Economy, Society and Culture. London: Blackwell.

———. 2000. *The Information Age: Economy, Society and Culture* (3 vols.), 2nd. ed. Oxford, UK, and Malden, MA: Blackwell.

———. 2001. *The Internet Galaxy: Reflections on the Internet, Business, and Society.* New York: Oxford University Press.

Catalyst. 2005. *Beyond a Reasonable Doubt: Building a Business Case for Flexibility.* The Catalyst series on flexibility in Canadian law firms. Toronto.

———. 2007. "Latest count of Women in Canada's Largest Business Shows Marginal Progress." *News Release, April 4, 2007.* Toronto: Catalyst Canada.

CBS News. 1979. Transcript of *60 Minutes* segment, "I Was Only Following Orders." March 31, 2–8.

———. 1998. "Experimental Prison." *60 Minutes.* June 30.

Center for American Women and Politics. 2006. *Fact Sheet: Women in the U.S. Congress 2006 and Statewide Elective Women 2006.* Rutgers, NJ: CAWP.

Centers for Disease Control and Prevention. 2002. "Need for Sustained HIV Prevention among Men Who Have Sex with Men." Retrieved January 23, 2004 (http://www.cdc.gov/hiv/pubs/facts/msm.htm).

Central Intelligence Agency. 2007. *The World Fact Book.* Washington D.C.: Central Intelligence Agency.

Cerulo, Karen A., Janet M. Ruane, and Mary Chagko. 1992. "Technological Ties that Bind: Media Generated Primary Groups." *Communication Research* 19:109–129.

Cetron, Marvin J., and Owen Davies. 1991. "Trends Shaping the World." *Futurist* 20 (September–October):11–21.

Cha, Ariena Eunjung. 2000. "Painting a Portrait of Dot-Camaraderie." *Washington Post,* October 26, E1, E10.

Chaddock, Gail Russell. 1998. "The Challenge for Schools: Connecting Adults with Kids." *Christian Science Monitor,* August 4, B7.

Chalfant, H. Paul, Robert E. Beckley, and C. Eddie Palmer. 1994. *Religion in Contemporary Society,* 3rd ed. Itasca, IL: F.E. Peacock.

Chambliss, William. 1972. "Introduction." Pp. ix–xi in *Box Man,* by Henry King. New York: Harper and Row.

———. 1973. "The Saints and the Roughnecks." *Society* 11 (November–December):24–31.

Chan, R.W., B. Rayboy, and C.J. Patterson. 1998. "Psychological Adjustment among Children Conceived via Donor Insemination by Lesbian and Heterosexual Mothers." *Child Development* 69:443–457.

Charmaz, Kathy, and Debora A. Paterniti, eds. 1999. *Health, Illness, and Healing: Society, Social Context, and Self.* Los Angeles, CA: Roxbury.

Charter, David, and Jill Sherman. 1996. "Schools Must Teach New Code of Values." *London Times,* January 15, 1.

Chase-Dunn, Christopher, and Peter Grimes. 1995. "World-Systems Analysis." Pp. 387–417 in *Annual Review of Sociology,* 1995, John Hagan, ed. Palo Alto, CA: Annual Reviews.

Chase-Dunn, Christopher, Yukio Kawano, and Benjamin D. Brewer. 2000. "Trade Globalization Since 1795:Waves of Integration in the World System." *American Sociological Review* 65 (February):77–95.

Cheng, Wei-yuan, and Lung-li Liao. 1994. "Women Managers in Taiwan." Pp. 143–159 in *Competitive Frontiers: Women Managers in a Global Economy,* Nancy J. Adler and Dafna N. Izraeli, eds. Cambridge, MA: Blackwell Business.

Cherlin, Andrew J. 1999. *Public and Private Families: An Introduction,* 2nd ed. New York: McGraw-Hill Ryerson.

Cherlin, Andrew J., and Frank Furstenberg. 1992. *The New American Grandparent: A Place in the Family, A Life Apart.* Cambridge, MA: Harvard University Press.

Chernobyl Forum. 2005. *Chernobyl's Legacy: Health, Environmental and Socio-economic Impacts and Recommendations to the Governments of Belarus, the Russian Federation and Ukraine.* Geneva, Switzerland:International Atomic Energy Agency.

Chiang, Frances. 2001. "The Intersection of Class, Race, Ethnicity, Gender, and Migration: A Case Study of Hong Kong Chinese Immigrant Women Entrepreneurs in Richmond, British Columbia."

Unpublished Ph.D. thesis, University of British Columbia.

Chicago Tribune. 1997. "In London, Prince Meets a Pauper, an Ex-Classmate." December 5, 19.

Childcare Resource and Research Unit. 2000. *Early Childhood Care and Education in Canada, Provinces and Territories, 1998.* Toronto: Centre for Urban and Community Studies, University of Toronto.

Children Now. 2002. *Fall Colors: 2001–02 Prime Time Diversity Report.* Los Angeles: Children Now.

———. 2004. *Fall Colors: 2003–04 Prime Time Diversity Report.* Oakland, CA: Children Now.

China Daily. 2005. "'Live Life Now' is Mantra of New Rich." May 17. Retrieved March 3, 2008 (http://www.china.org.cn/english/features/fortune/129023.htm).

Christensen, Kathleen. 1990. "Bridges over Troubled Water: How Older Workers View the Labor Market." Pp. 175–207 in *Bridges to Retirement*, Peter B. Doeringer, ed. Ithaca, NY: IRL Press.

Chu, Henry. 2005. "Tractors Crush Heart of a Nation." *Los Angeles Times,* July 10, p. A9.

Citizenship and Immigration Canada. 2001. *Pursuing Canada's Commitment to Immigration: The Immigration Plan for 2002.* Cat. no. Ci51-105/2001. October. Ottawa: Minister of Works and Government Services.

Civic Ventures. 1999. *The New Face of Retirement: Older Americans, Civic Engagement, and the Longevity Revolution.* Washington, DC: Peter D. Hart Research Associates.

Clark, Andy. 2005. "Making Poverty History?" *Radio Netherlands.* Retrieved November 10, 2005 (http://www2.rnw.nl/rnw/en/features/amsterdamforum/050618af?view=standard).

Clark, Campbell. 2005. "G8 Boosts Africa Aid by $25-Billion." *The Globe and Mail,* July 9. Retrieved July 9, 2005 (http://www.theglobeandmail.com).

Clark, Thomas. 1994. "Culture and Objectivity." *The Humanist* 54 (August):38–39.

Clarke, Adele E., Janet K. Shim, Laura Maro, Jennifer Ruth Fusket, and Jennifer R. Fishman. 2003. "Bio Medicalization: Techno-scientific Transformations of Health, Illness, and U.S. Biomedicine." *American Sociological Review* 68 (April):161–194.

Cleveland, Gordon, and Michael Krashinsky. 1998. *The Benefit and Costs of Good Child Care.* Toronto: Childcare Resource and Research Unit, Univeristy of Toronto.

Cloward, Richard A. 1959. "Illegitimate Means, Anomie, and Deviant Behavior." *American Sociological Review* 24 (April):164–176.

Cockerham, William C. 1998. *Medical Sociology,* 7th ed. Upper Saddle River, NJ: Prentice Hall.

Code, Lorraine. 1993. "Feminist Theory." Pp. 19–57 in *Changing Patterns: Women in Canada*, 2nd ed., Sandra Burt, Lorraine

Code, and Lindsay Dorney, eds. Toronto: McClelland & Stewart.

Cohen, David, ed. 1991. *The Circle of Life: Ritual from the Human Family Album.* San Francisco: Harper.

Cohen, Debra Nussbaum. 2005. "Questions, Answers and Minutiae of the Faithful Can Be Found in the Blogosphere." *New York Times,* March 5, p. A13.

Cohen, Lawrence E., and Marcus Felson. 1979. "Social Change and Crime Rate Trends: A Routine Activities Approach." *American Sociological Review* 44:588–608.

Cole, Elizabeth S. 1985. "Adoption, History, Policy, and Program." Pp. 638–666 in *A Handbook of Child Welfare*, John Laird and Ann Hartman, eds. New York: Free Press.

Cole, Mike. 1988. *Bowles and Gintis Revisited: Correspondence and Contradiction in Educational Theory.* Philadelphia: Falmer.

Coleman, James William. 1985. *The Criminal Elite: Sociology of White Collar Crime.* New York: St.Martin's Press.

Collier, Gary, Henry L. Mintin, and Graham Reynolds. 1991. *Currents of Thought in American Social Psychology.* New York: Oxford University Press.

Collier, Jane, Michelle Rosaldo, and Sylvia Yanagisako. 2001. "Is There a Family? New Anthropological Views." Pp. 11–21 in *Family Patterns, Gender Relations*, 2nd ed., Bonnie J. Fox, ed. Toronto: Oxford University Press.

Collins, Gail. 1998. "Why the Women Are Fading Away." *New York Times*, October 25, 54–55.

Collins, Patricia Hill. 1998. *Fighting Words: Black Women and the Search for Justice.* Minneapolis, MN: University of Minnesota.

Collins, Randall. 1975. *Conflict Sociology: Toward an Explanatory Sociology.* New York: Academic.

———. 1980. "Weber's Last Theory of Capitalism: A Systematization." *American Sociological Review* 45 (December):925–942.

———. 1986. *Weberian Sociological Theory.* New York: Cambridge University Press.

———. 1995. "Prediction in Macrosociology: The Case of the Soviet Collapse." *American Journal of Sociology* 100 (May):1552–1593.

Commoner, Barry. 1971. *The Closing Circle.* New York: Knopf.

———. 1990. *Making Peace with the Planet.* New York: Pantheon.

Communications Canada. 2001. "Facts on Canada." Retrieved April 11, 2001 (http://www.infocan.gc.ca/facts/multi_e.html).

ComQuest Research Group. 1993. *Lifestyles Television Focus Group Report.* Vancouver: Bureau of Broadcast Measurement.

Comstock, P., and M.B. Fox. 1994. "Employer Tactics and Labor Law Reform." Pp. 90–109 in *Restoring the Promise of American*

Labor Law, S. Friedman, R.W. Hurd, R.A. Oswald, and R.L. Seeber, eds. Ithaca, NY: ILR Press.

Connidis, Ingrid A. 1989. *Family Ties and Ageing.* Toronto: Butterworths.

Conrad, Peter, ed. 1997. *The Sociology of Health and Illness: Critical Perspectives*, 5th ed. New York: St. Martin's Press.

———. 2000. *The Sociology of Health and Illness: Cultural Perspectives.* 6th ed. New York: Worth.

Conrad, Peter, and Joseph W. Schneider. 1992. *Deviance and Medicalization: From Badness to Sickness*, expanded ed. Philadelphia: Temple University Press.

Cooke, Gordon B. and Isik U. Zeytinoglu. 2006. "Females Still Face Barriers: A Commentary on the Training Gap in Canada." *The Workplace Review* 3 (1): 29–32.

Cooley, Charles H. 1902. *Human Nature and the Social Order.* New York: Scribner.

Corak, Miles, and Andrew Heisz. 1996. *The Intergenerational Income Mobility of Canadian Men.* Analytical Studies Branch no. 89. Ottawa: Statistics Canada.

Cortese, Anthony J. 1999. *Provocateur: Images of Women and Minorities in Advertising.* Lanham, MD: Rowman & Littlefield.

Coser, Lewis A. 1956. *The Functions of Social Conflict.* New York: Free Press.

———. 1977. Masters of Sociological Thought: Ideas in Historical and Social Context, 2nd ed. New York: Harcourt, Brace and Jovanovich.

Côté, James E., and Anton L. Allahar. 1994. *Generation on Hold: Coming of Age in the Late Twentieth Century.* Toronto: Stoddart.

Couch, Carl. 1996. *Information Technologies and Social Orders.* David R. Maines and Shing-Ling Chien, eds. and intro. New York: Aldine de Gruyter.

Council of Canadians. 2004. *Annual Report, 2004.* Ottawa: Council of Canadians. Retrieved January 9, 2006 (http://www.canadians.org/documents/wcp05_pg9.pdf).

Cox, Kevin. 2001. "Nova Scotia Gay Couple Given Legal Recognition." *The Globe and Mail*, June 5, A5.

Cox, Oliver I. 1948. *Caste, Class and Race: A Study in Social Dynamics.* Detroit: Wayne State University Press.

Creese, Gillian. 1999. *Contracting Masculinity: Gender, Class and Race in a White-Collar Union, 1944–1994.* Toronto: Oxford University Press.

Creese, Gillian, Neil Guppy, and Martin Meissner. 1991. *Ups and Downs on the Ladder of Success: Social Mobility in Canada.* Ottawa: Statistics Canada.

Cressey, Donald R. 1960. "Epidemiology and Individual Contact: A Case from Criminology." *Pacific Sociological Review* 3 (Fall):47–58.

Cromwell, Paul F., James N. Olson, and D'Aunn Wester Avarey. 1995. *Breaking and Entering: An Ethnographic Analysis of Burglary*. Newbury Park, CA: Sage.

Croteau, David, and William Hoynes. 2001. *The Business of the Media: Corporate Media and the Public Interest*. Thousand Oaks, CA: Pine Forge.

———. 2003. *Media/Society: Industries, Images, and Audiences*, 3rd ed. Thousand Oaks, CA: Pine Forge.

Crouse, Kelly. 1999. "Sociology of the Titanic." *Teaching Sociology Listserv*. May 24.

CTV.ca. 2007. " Canadians choosing Internet over radio." July 31, 2007. Retrieved December 7, 2008 (http://www.ctv.ca/servlet/ArticleNews/story/CTVNews/20070731/internet_crtc_070731?s…).

Cuff, E.C., W.W. Sharrock, and D.W. Francis, eds. 1990. *Perspectives in Sociology*, 3rd ed. Boston: Unwin Hyman.

Cullen, Francis T., Jr., and John B. Cullen. 1978. *Toward a Paradigm of Labeling Theory*, ser. 58. Lincoln: University of Nebraska Studies.

Cumming, Elaine, and William E. Henry. 1961. *Growing Old: The Process of Disengagement*. New York: Basic Books.

Currie, Elliot. 1985. *Confronting Crime: An American Challenge*. New York: Pantheon.

———. 1998. *Crime and Punishment in America*. New York: Metropolitan Books.

Curry, Timothy Jon. 1993. "A Little Pain Never Hurt Anyone: Athletic Career Socialization and the Normalization of Sports Injury." *Symbolic Interaction* 26 (Fall):273–290.

Cushman, John H., Jr. 1998. "Pollution Policy Is Unfair Burden, States Tell E.P.A." *New York Times*, May 10, 1, 20.

Cussins, Choris M. 1998. In *Cyborg Babies: From Techno-Sex to Techno-Tots*, Robbie Davis-Floyd and Joseph Dumit, eds. New York: Routledge.

D

Dahl, Robert A. 1961. *Who Governs?* New Haven, CT: Yale University Press.

Dahrendorf, Ralf. 1958. "Toward a Theory of Social Conflict." *Journal of Conflict Resolution* 2 (June):170–183.

———. 1959. *Class and Class Conflict in Industrial Sociology*. Stanford, CA: Stanford University Press.

Daley, Suzanne. 1999. "Doctors' Group of Volunteers Awarded Nobel." *New York Times*, October 16, A1, A6.

———. 2000. "French Couples Take Plunge That Falls Short of Marriage." *New York Times*, April 18, A1, A4.

Dalfen, Ariel, K. 2000. "Cyberaddicts in Cyberspace? Internet Addiction Disorder." *Wellness Options* (Winter):38–39.

Daniels, Arlene Kaplan. 1987. "Invisible Work." *Social Problems* 34 (December):403–415.

———. 1988. *Invisible Careers*. Chicago: University of Chicago Press.

Davies, Christie. 1989. "Goffman's Concept of the Total Institution: Criticisms and Revisions." *Human Studies* 12 (June):77–95.

Davis, Darren W. 1997. "The Direction of Race of Interviewer Effects among African-Americans: Donning the Black Mask." *American Journal of Political Science* 41 (January):309–322.

Davis, Gerald. 2003. *America's Corporate Banks Are Separated by Just Four Handshakes*. Accessed March 7 (www.bus.umich.edu/research/davis.html).

———. 2004. "American Cronyism: How Executive Networks Inflated the Corporate Bubble." *Contexts* (Summer):34–40.

Davis, James Allan, and Tom W. Smith. 1999. *General Social Surveys, 1972–1998*. Storrs, CT: The Roper Center.

———. 2001. *General Social Surveys, 1972–2000*. Storrs, CT: The Roper Center.

Davis, James A., Tom W. Smith, and Peter B. Marsden. 2003. *General Social Surveys, 1972–2002: Cumulative Codebook*. Chicago: NORC.

———. 2005. *General Social Surveys, 1972–2004: Cumulative Codebook*. Chicago: National Opinion Research Center.

Davis, Kingsley. 1937. "The Sociology of Prostitution." *American Sociological Review* 2 (October):744–755.

———. 1940. "Extreme Social Isolation of a Child." *American Journal of Sociology* 45 (January):554–565.

———. 1947. "A Final Note on a Case of Extreme Isolation." *American Journal of Sociology* 52 (March):432–437.

———. [1949] 1995. *Human Society*, reprint. New York: Macmillan.

Davis, Kingsley, and Wilbert E. Moore. 1945. "Some Principles of Stratification." *American Sociological Review* 10 (April): 242–249.

Davis, Nanette J. 1975. *Sociological Constructions of Deviance: Perspectives and Issues in the Field*. Dubuque, IA: Wm. C. Brown.

Deardorff, Kevin E., and Lisa M. Blumerman. 2001. "Evaluation Components of International Migration: Estimates of the Foreign-Born Population by Migrant States in 2000." *Working Paper Series*, No. 58. Retrieved January 8, 2002 (http://www.census.gov/population/www/documentation/twps0058.html).

Death Penalty Information Center. 2000. "The Death Penalty in 1999: Year End Report." Retrieved February 13, 2000 (http://www.essential.org/dpic/yrendrpt99.html).

Deegan, Mary Jo, ed. 1991.*Women in Sociology: A Bio-bibliographical Sourcebook*. Westport, CT: Greenwood.

Deflem, Mathieu. 2005. "'Wild Beasts Without Nationality': The Uncertain Origins of Interpol, 1898–1910." Pp. 275–285 in *Handbook of Transnational Crime and Justice,* edited by Philip Rerchel. Thousand Oaks, CA: Sage.

DeKeseredy, Walter S. 2001. "Patterns of Family Violence." Pp. 238–266 in *Families: Changing Trends in Canada*, 4th ed., Maureen Baker, ed. Toronto: McGraw-Hill Ryerson.

DeKeseredy, Walter S., and Martin D. Schwartz. 1998. *Woman Abuse on Campus: Results from the Canadian National Survey*. Thousand Oaks, CA: Sage Publications.

De Luce, Dan. 2003. "The Audrey look is very in and the mood is defiant." *Guardian,* June 12, 2003. Retrieved December 5, 2008(www.guardian.co.uk/Archive?Article/0,4373,4689096,00html).

Delaney, Kevin J. 2005. "Big Mother Is Watching." *Wall Street Journal,* November 26, pp. A1, A6.

Delawala, Imtyaz. 2002. "What Is Coltran?" January 21, 2002 (www.abcnews.com).

Della Porta, Donatella, and Sidney Tarrow, eds. 2005. *Transnational Protest and Global Activism*. Lanham, MD: Rowman & Littlefield.

Denny, Charlotte. 2004."Migration Myths Hold No Fears." *Guardian Weekly* (February 26):12.

DePalma, Anthony. 1999. "Rules to Protect a Culture Make for Confusion." *New York Times*, July 14, B1, B2.

Department of Education. 1999. *Report on State Implementation of the Gun-Free Schools Act, School Year 1997–98*. Rockville, MD: Westat.

Department of Health and Human Services. 2000. *Total Numbers of Families and Recipients for 1st Quarter FY2002*. Retrieved June 14, 2002 (http://www.acf.dhhs.gov/news/stats/tanf.htm).

———. 2002. *Percent Change in AFDC/TANF Families and Recipients, August 1996–September 2002*. Retrieved June 14, 2002 (http://www.acf.dhhs.gov/news/stats/afdc.htm).

Derné, Steve. 2003. "Schwarzenegger, McBeal and Arranged Marriages: Globalization on the Ground in India" in *Contexts, a publication of the American Sociological Association*. Berkeley, CA: University of California Press.

Derouin, Jodey Michael. 2004. "Asians and Multiculturalism in Canada's Three Major Cities: Some Evidence from the Ethnic Diversity Survey." Pp. 58–62 in *Our Diverse Cities*, number 1, Caroline Andrew, ed. Ottawa: Metropolis Project.

Desai, Manisha. 1996. "If Peasants Build Their Own Dams,What Would the State Have Left to Do?" 209–224 in *Research in Social Movements, Conflicts and Change*, vol. 19,

Michael Dobkowski and Isidor Wallimann, eds. Greenwich, CT: JAI Press.

Devine, Don. 1972. *Political Culture of the United States: The Influence of Member Values on Regime Maintenance.* Boston: Little, Brown.

Devitt, James. 1999. *Framing Gender on the Campaign Trail: Women's Executive Leadership and the Press.* New York: Women's Leadership Conference.

Diamond, Jared. 2003. "Globalization, Then." *Los Angeles Times*, September 14, M1, M3.

Diani, Marie. 2000. "Social Movement Networks: Virtual and Real." *Information, Communication and Society.* Retrieved October 14, 2001 (http://www.infosoc.co.uk).

Diebel, Linda. 2007. "McGuinty apologizes for 'ghetto dude' email." the star.com. July 23. Retrieved October 16, 2008 (http://www.thestar.com/News/Ontario/article/238744).

DiMaggio, Paul, Eszter Hargittai, W. Russell Neuman, and John P. Robinson. 2001. "Social Implications of the Internet." *Annual Review of Sociology*, vol. 27, 307–336.

Dionne, Annette, Cecile Dionne, and Yvonne Dionne. 1997. "Letter." *Time*, December 1, 39.

Directors Guild of America (DGA). 2002. *Diversity Hiring Special Report.* Los Angeles: DGA.

Doeringer, Peter B., ed. 1990. *Bridges to Retirement: Older Workers in a Changing Labor Market.* Ithaca, NY: ILR Press.

Dolbeare, Kenneth M. 1982. *American Public Policy: A Citizen's Guide.* New York: McGraw-Hill Ryerson.

Domhoff, G. William. 1978. *Who Really Rules? New Haven and Community Power Reexamined.* New Brunswick, NJ: Transaction.

———. 2001. *Who Rules America?* 4th ed. New York: McGraw-Hill Ryerson.

———. 2006. *Who Rules America?* 5th ed. New York: McGraw-Hill.

Dominick, Joseph R. 2005. *The Dynamics of Mass Communication: Media in the Digital Age*, 8th ed. New York: McGraw-Hill Ryerson.

Donohue, Elizabeth, Vincent Schiraldi, and Jason Ziedenberg. 1998. *School House Hype: School Shootings and Real Risks Kids Face in America.* New York: Justice Policy Institute.

Dorai, Frances. 1998. *Insight Guide: Singapore.* Singapore: Insight Media, APA Publications.

Doress, Irwin, and Jack Nusan Porter. 1977. *Kids in Cults: Why They Join, Why They Stay, Why They Leave.* Brookline, MA: Reconciliation Associates.

Dornbusch, Sanford M. 1989. "The Sociology of Adolescence." Pp. 233–259 in *Annual Review of Sociology, 1989*, W. Richard Scott and Judith Blake, eds. Palo Alto, CA: Annual Reviews.

Dotson, Floyd. 1991. "Community." P. 55 in *Encyclopedic Dictionary of Sociology*, 4th ed. Guilford, CT: Dushkin.

Dougherty, Kevin, and Floyd M. Hammack. 1992. "Education Organization." Pp. 535–541 in *Encyclopedia of Sociology*, vol. 2, Edgar F. Borgatta and Marie L. Borgatta, eds. New York: Macmillan.

Douglas, Jack D. 1967. *The Social Meanings of Suicide.* Princeton, NJ: Princeton University Press.

Dowd, James J. 1980. *Stratification among the Aged.* Monterey, CA: Brooks/Cole.

Downie, Andrew. 2000. "Brazilian Girls Turn to a Doll More Like Them." *Christian Science Monitor.* January 20. Retrieved January 20, 2000 (www.csmonitor.com/durable/2000/01/20/fpls3-csm.shtml).

Doyle, James A. 1995. *The Male Experience*, 3rd ed. Dubuque, IA: Brown & Benchmark.

Doyle, James A., and Michele A. Paludi. 1998. *Sex and Gender: The Human Experience*, 4th ed. New York: McGraw-Hill Ryerson.

Drache, Daniel, and Terrence J. Sullivan, eds. 1999. "Health, Health Care and Social Cohesion." *Public Success, Private Failures: Market Limits in Health Reform.* Toronto: Routledge. Retrieved August 1, 2001 (http://www.founders.ner/fn/papers).

Drucker, Peter F. 1999. "Beyond the Information Revolution." *Atlantic Monthly* 284 (October):42–57.

Dreifus, Claudia. 2006. "A Sociologist Confronts 'the Messy Stuff ' of Race, Genes and Disease." *New York Times,* October 18.

Drummond, Don, and Beata Caranci. 2007. "Markets are a Women's Best Friend." Toronto, ON: TD Economics.

Dua, Enakshi. 1999. "Introduction: Canadian Anti-racist Feminist Thought: Scratching the Surface of Racism." Pp. 7–31 in *Scratching the Surface: Canadian Anti-racist Feminist Thought*, Enakshi Dua and Angela Robertson, eds. Toronto: Women's Press.

Duberman, Lucille. 1976. *Social Inequality: Class and Caste in America.* Philadelphia: Lippincott.

Duffy, Jim, Kelly Warren, and Margaret Walsh. 2001. "Classroom Interactions: Gender of Teacher, Gender of Student, and Classroom of Subject." *Sex Roles: A Journal of Research* 45:579–593.

Dugger, Celia W. 1999. "Massacres of Low-Born Touch off a Crisis in India." *New York Times*, March 15, A3.

Duneier, Mitchell. 1994a. "On the Job, but Behind the Scenes." *Chicago Tribune*, December 26, 1, 24.

———. 1994b. "Battling for Control." *Chicago Tribune*, December 28, 1, 8.

Dunlap, Riley E. 1993. "From Environmental to Ecological Problems." Pp. 707–738 in *Introduction to Social Problems*, Craig Calhoun and George Ritzer, eds. New York: McGraw-Hill Ryerson.

Dunlap, Riley E., and William R. Catton, Jr. 1983. "What Environmental Sociologists Have in Common." *Sociological Inquiry* 53(Spring): 113–135.

Dupuis, Dave. 1998. "What Influences People's Plans to Have Children?" *Canadian Social Trends*, Spring:2–5.

Durkheim, Émile. [1893] 1933. *Division of Labor in Society*, reprint. George Simpson, transl. New York: Free Press.

———. [1912] 1947. *The Elementary Forms of the Religious Life*, reprint. Glencoe, IL: Free Press.

———. [1897] 1951. *Suicide*, reprint. John A. Spaulding and George Simpson, transl. New York: Free Press.

———. [1895] 1964. *The Rules of Sociological Method*, reprint. Sarah A. Solovay and John H. Mueller, transl. New York: Free Press.

Durrant, Joan E., and Linda Rose-Krasnor. 1995. *Corporal Punishment Research Review and Policy Development.* Ottawa: Ontario Health Canada and Department of Justice Canada.

Duster, Troy. 2002. "Sociological Stranger in the Land of the Human Genome Project." *Contexts* 1 (Fall):69–70.

Duxbury, Linda, and Chris Higgins. 2001. "Work-Life Balance in Canada: Making the Case for Change." *Asia Pacific Research.* Retrieved May 27, 2008 (http://www.asiapacificresearch.ca/caprn/cjsp_project/duxbury_final.pdf).

Dworkin, Rosalind J. 1982. "A Woman's Report: Numbers Are Not Enough." Pp. 375–400 in *The Minority Report*, Anthony Dworkin and Rosalind Dworkin, eds. New York: Holt Rinehart & Winston.

Dyck, Rand. 2006. *Canadian Politics*, 3rd ed. Scarborough, ON: Nelson.

E

Easterbrook, Gregg. 2006. "Case Closed: The Debate about Global Warning Is Over." Working paper. Washington, DC: Brookings Institution.

Eayrs, Caroline B., Nick Ellis, and Robert S. P. Jones. 1993. "Which Label? An Investigation into the Effects of Terminology on Public Perceptions of and Attitudes toward People with Learning Difficulties." *Disability, Handicap, and Society* 8 (2):111–127.

Ebaugh, Helen Rose Fuchs. 1988. *Becoming an Ex: The Process of Role Exit.* Chicago: University of Chicago Press.

Eckenwiler, Mark. 1995. "In the Eyes of the Law." *Internet World* (August):74, 76–77.

The Economist. 2003a. "Race in Brazil: Out of Eden." (July 5):31–32.

———. 2003b. "The One Where Pooh Goes to Sweden." (April 5):59.

————. 2005b. "Chasing the Dream." (August 6):53–55.

————. 2005c. "Behind the Digital Divide." (March 2):22–25.

————. 2006. "The World's Largest Economies" (March 30).

————. 2007b. "A World Awash in Heroin." (June 30):69.

————. 2007c. "Half-Measures on Poverty." (July 7):27.

Edmonton Social Planning Council. 1999. *Often Hungry, Sometimes Homeless.* Edmonton: Edmonton Social Planning Council and the Edmonton Food Bank.

Edwards, Harry. 1973. *Sociology of Sport.* Homewood, IL: Dorsey Press.

Edwards, Richard. 1979. *Contested Terrain: The Transformation of the Workplace in America.* New York: Basic Books.

Efron, Sonni. 1997. "In Japan, Even Tots Must Make the Grade." *Los Angeles Times,* February 16, A1, A17.

————. 1998. "Japanese in Quandary on Fertility." *Los Angeles Times,* July 27, A1, A6.

Ehrenreich, Barbara. 2001. *Nickel and Dimed: On (Not) Getting by in America.* New York: Metropolitan.

Ehrenreich, Barbara, and Frances Fox Piven. 2002. "Without a Safety Net." *Mother Jones* 27 (May/June):34–41.

Ehrlich Martin, Susan. 1984. "Sexual Harassment: The Link between Gender Stratification, Sexuality, and Women's Economic Status." In *Women: A Feminist Perspective,* 3rd ed. J. Freeman, ed. Palo Alto, CA: Mayfield.

Ehrlich, Paul R. 1968. *The Population Bomb.* New York: Ballantine.

————. 1997. *Family Shifts: Families, Policies, and Gender Equality.* Toronto: Oxford University Press.

————. 2001. "Biases in Family Literature." Pp. 51–66 in *Families: Changing Trends in Canada,* 4th ed. Maureen Baker, ed. Toronto: McGraw-Hill Ryerson.

Ehrlich, Paul R., and Anne H. Ehrlich. 1990. *The Population Explosion.* New York: Simon and Schuster.

Ehrlich, Paul R., and Katherine Ellison. 2002. "A Looming Threat We Won't Face." *Los Angeles Times,* January 20, M6.

Eichler, Margrit. 1984. "Sexism in Research and Its Policy Implications." Pp.17–39 in *Taking Sex into Account: The Policy Implications of Sexist Research,* edited by J. McCells Vickers. Ottawa: Carleton University Press.

————. 1997. *Family Shifts: Families, Policies, and Gender Equality.* Toronto: Oxford University Press.

————. 2001. "Biases in Family Literature." Pp. 51–66 in *Families: Changing Trends in Canada,* 4th ed. Maureen Baker, ed. Toronto: McGraw-Hill Ryerson.

Eisenberg, David M., Roger B. Davis, Susan L. Ettner, Scott Appel, Sonja Wilkey, Maria Van Rompay, Ronald C. Kessler. 1998. "Trends in Alternative Medicine Use in the United States, 1990–1997: Results of a Follow-up National Survey." *Journal of the American Medical Association* 280 (November 11):1569–1575.

Eisler, Peter. 2000. "This Is Only a Test, but Lives Are at Stake." *USA Today,* June 30, 219–220.

Eitzen, D. Stanley. 2003. *Fair and Foul: Beyond the Myths and Paradoxes of Sport.* 2d ed. Lanham, MD: Rowman and Littlefield.

Ekman, Paul, Wallace V. Friesen, and John Bear. 1984. "The International Language of Gestures." *Psychology Today* 18 (May):64–69.

Ekos Research Associates. 2001. *Canadians and Working from Home.* Retrieved November 27, 2005 (http://www.ekos.com/admin/articles/telework4.pdf).

El-Badry, Samira. 1994. "The Arab-American Market." *American Demographics* 16 (January):21–27, 30.

El Nasser, Haya. 1999. "Soaring Housing Costs Are Culprit in Suburban Poverty." *USA Today,* April 28, A1, A2.

————. 2001. "Minorities Reshape Suburbs." *USA Today,* July 9, 1A.

Elections Canada. 2003. *Explaining the Turnout Decline in Canadian Federal Elections.* Retrieved October 26, 2007 (http://www.elections.ca/content.asp?section=loi&document=index&dir=tur/tud&lang=e&textonly=false>).

————. 2005a. *Young Voters.* Retrieved September 26, 2005 (http://www.elections.ca).

————. 2005b. *Voter turnout for 2004, 2000, 1997, and 1993 General Elections,* table 4. Retrieved November 12, 2005 (http://www.elections.ca/scripts/OVR2004/23/table4.html).

————. 2007. *Voter Turnout at Federal Elections and Referendums, 1867-2006.*

Elias, Marilyn. 1996. "Researchers Fight Child Consent Bill." *USA Today,* January 2, A1.

Elliott, Barry J. 1999. "Road Rage: Media Hype or Serious Road Safety Issue?" Accessed December 14, 2005 (www.drivers.com).

Elliott, Marta, and Lauren J. Krivo. 1991. "Structural Determinants of Homelessness in the United States." *Social Problems* 38 (February):113–131.

Elliott, Michael. 1994. "Crime and Punishment." *Newsweek* 123 (April 18):18–22.

Elliot, Patricia, and Nancy Mandell. 1998. "Feminist Theories." Pp. 2–25 in *Feminist Issues: Race, Class, and Sexuality,* 2nd ed. Nancy Mandell, ed. Scarborough, ON: Allyn and Bacon.

Elmer-DeWitt, Philip. 1995. "Welcome to Cyberspace." *Time* 145 (Special Issue, Spring):4–11.

Ely, Robin J. 1995. "The Power of Demography: Women's Social Construction of Gender Identity at Work." *Academy of Management Journal* 38 (3):589–634.

Engels, Friedrich. 1884. "The Origin of the Family, Private Property and the State." Pp. 392–394 excerpt in *Marx and Engels: Basic Writings on Politics and Philosophy,* Lewis Feuer, ed. Garden City, NY: Anchor, 1959.

England, Jennifer. 2004. "Disciplining Subjectivity and Space: Representation, Film and its Material Effects." *Antipode* 36:295–321.

Entine, Jon, and Martha Nichols. 1996. "Blowing the Whistle on Meaningless 'Good Intentions.' " *Chicago Tribune,* June 20, 21.

Environics Research Group. 2007a. "Basis of Pride in Being Canadian, 2006." *Focus Canada.* Toronto: Environics.

————. 2007b. *Environics Survey of Muslims in Canada.* Toronto: Environics.

Erard, Michael. 2005 "How Linguists and Missionaries Share a Bible of 6,912 Languages." *New York Times,* July 19.

Ericson, Nels. 2001. "Substance Abuse: The Nation's Number One Health Problem." *OJJDP Fact Sheet* 17 (May):1–2.

Erikson, Kai. 1966. *Wayward Puritans: A Study in the Sociology of Deviance.* New York: John Wiley and Sons.

Etaugh, Claire. 2003. "Witches, Mothers and Others: Females in Children's Books." *Hilltopics* (Winter): 10–13.

Etzioni, Amitai. 1964. *Modern Organization.* Englewood Cliffs, NJ: Prentice Hall.

————. 1965. *Political Unification.* New York: Holt, Rinehart, and Winston.

————. 1985. "Shady Corporate Practices." *New York Times,* November 15, A35.

————. 1990. "Going Soft on Corporate Crime." *Washington Post,* April 1, C3.

————. 1996. "Why Fear Date Rape?" *USA Today,* May 20, 14A.

Eureka CountyYucca Mountain Information Office. 2006. "EPA Hears Testimony on Proposed Radiation Rule." *Nuclear Waste Office Newsletter* 11 (Winter).

Evans, Peter. 1979. *Dependent Development.* Princeton, NJ: Princeton University Press.

F

Facts on File Weekly News Report. 2001a. "Switzerland: Votes Solidly Reject E.U. Membership." Retrieved March 2 (http://www.facts.com).

————. 2001b. "Great Britain: British Elections, 1997 and 2001." Retrieved June 14 (http://www.facts.com).

Fager, Marty, Mike Bradley, Lonnie Danchik, and Tom Wodetski. 1971. *Unbecoming Men.* Washington, NJ: Times Change.

Faith, Nazila. 2005. "Iranian Cleric Turns Blogger in Campaign for Reform." *New York Times,* January 16, p. 4.

Fallows, Deborah. 2006. *Pew Internet Project Data*. Washington, DC: Pew Internet and American Life Project.

Faludi, Susan. 1999. *Stiffed: The Betrayal of the American Man*. New York: William Morrow.

Farhi, Paul, and Megan Rosenfeld. 1998. "Exporting America." *Washington Post National Weekly Edition*, November 30, 6–7.

FAIR. 2001. "Fear and Favor 2000." Accessed December 29, 2001 (www.fair.org).

Farr, Grant M. 1999. *Modern Iran*. New York: McGraw-Hill Ryerson.

Farrar, Melissa. 2005. "Road Rage and Aggressive Driving." Unpublished paper, Depaul University, Chicago.

Feagin, Joe R. 1983. *The Urban Real Estate Game: Playing Monopoly with Real Money*. Englewood Cliffs, NJ: Prentice Hall.

———. 1989. *Minority Group Issues in Higher Education: Learning from Qualitative Research*. Norman, OK: Center for Research on Minority Education, University of Oklahoma.

Feagin, Joe R., Harnán Vera, and Nikitah Imani. 1996. *The Agony of Education: Black Students at White Colleges and Universities*. New York: Routledge.

Federman, Joel. 1998. *1998 National Television Violence Study: Executive Summary*. Santa Barbara, CA: University of California, Santa Barbara.

Feketekuty, Geza. 2001. "Globalization—Why All the Fuss?" P. 191 in *2001 Britannica Book of the Year*. Chicago: Encyclopedia Britannica.

Felson, David, and Akis Kalaitzidis. 2005. "A Historical Overview of Transnational Crime." Pp. 3–19 in *Handbook of Transnational Crime and Justice,* edited by Philip Reichel. Thousand Oaks, CA: Sage.

Felson, Marcus. 1998. *Crime and Everyday Life: Insights and Implications for Society*, 2nd ed. Thousand Oaks, CA: Pine Forge Press.

Fenlon, Brodie. 2007. "More Media Consumed, More Civic Engagement: Study." *The Globe and Mail*, March 27. Retrieved March 27, 2007 (http://www.theglobeandmail.com).

Fenlon, Brodie, and Siri Agrell. 2007. "Canada's Changing Family." *The Globe and Mail*, September 12. Retrieved September 13, 2007 (http://www.theglobeandmail.com/servlet/story/RTGAM.20070912.wcensusrelease0912/BNStory/National).

Ferree, Myra Marx, and David A. Merrill. 2000. "Hot Movements, Cold Cognition: Thinking about Social Movements in Gendered Frames." *Contemporary Society* 29 (May):454–462.

Feuer, Lewis, ed. 1959. *Marx and Engels: Basic Writings on Politics and Philosophy*. Garden City, NY: Anchor Books.

———.1989. *Marx and Engels: Basic Writings on Politics and Philosophy*. New York: Anchor Books.

Fiala, Robert. 1992. "Postindustrial Society." Pp. 1512–1522 in *Encyclopedia of Sociology*, vol. 3. Edgar F. Borgatta and Marie L. Borgatta, eds. New York: Macmillan.

Fields, Jason. 2003. "Children's Living Arrangements and Characteristics: March 2002." *Current Population Reports*, ser. P-20, no. 547. Washington, DC: United States Government Printing Office.

Fin, Ed. 2007. "February 2007: When Greed Has No Limits." Ottawa: Canadian Centre for Policy Alternatives.

Fine, Gary Alan. 1984. "Negotiated Orders and Organizational Cultures." Pp. 239–262 in *Annual Review of Sociology, 1984*. Ralph Turner, ed. Palo Alto, CA: Annual Reviews.

———.1987. *With the Boys: Little League Baseball and Preadolescent Culture*. Chicago: University of Chicago Press.

Finkel, Alvin, and Margaret Conrad, with Veronica Stong-Boag. 1993. *History of the Canadian Peoples: 1867 to Present*. Toronto: Copp Clark Pitman.

Finkel, Steven E., and James B. Rule. 1987. "Relative Deprivation and Related Psychological Theories of Civil Violence: A Critical Review." *Research in Social Movements* 9:47–69.

Finnie, Ross. 1993. "Women, Men and the Economic Consequences of Divorce: Evidence from Canadian Longitudinal Data." *Canadian Review of Sociology and Anthropology* 30 (2):205–241.

Firestone, Shulamith. 1970. *The Dialectic of Sex: The Case for Feminist Revolution*. New York: Bantam.

Fisher, Ian. 1999. "Selling Sudan's Slaves into Freedom." *New York Times*, April 25, A6.

Fitzgerald, Kathleen J., and Diane M. Rodgers. 2000. "Radical Social Movement Organization: A Theoretical Model." *The Sociological Quarterly* 41 (4):573–592.

Fitzpatrick, Eleanor. 1994. *Violence Prevention: A Working Paper and Proposal for Action*. St. John's, NL: Avalon Consolidated School Board.

Fjellman, Stephen.1992. *Vinyl Leaves: Walt Disney World and America.*. Boulder CO: Westview Press.

Flanders, John. 2001. "Getting Ready for the 2001 Census." *Canadian Social Trends (Spring)*. Statistics Canada. Catalogue No. 11-008. Ottawa: Minister of Industry.

Flavin, Jeanne. 1998. "Razing the Wall: A Feminist Critique of Sentencing Theory, Research, and Policy." Pp. 145–164 in *Cutting the Edge*, Jeffrey Ross, ed. Westport, CT: Praeger.

Fleras, Augie. 2003. *Mass Communication in Canada*. Scarborough, ON: Nelson.

Fleras, Augie, and Jean Leonard Elliott. 1992. *The Nations Within: Aboriginal–State Relations in Canada, the United States, and New Zealand*. Toronto: Oxford University Press.

———. 1999. *Unequal Relations: An Introduction to Race, Ethnic and Aboriginal Dynamics*. Scarborough, ON: Prentice Hall.

———. 2003. *Unequal Relations: An Introduction to Race, Ethnic, and Aboriginal Dynamics in Canada*, 4th ed. Don Mills, ON: Prentice Hall.

Fleras, Augie, and Jean Lock Kunz. 2001. *Media and Minorities: Representing Diversity in Multicultural Canada*. Scarborough, ON: Thomson Educational Publishing.

Fletcher, Connie. 1995. "On the Line: Women Cops Speak Out." *Chicago Tribune Magazine*, February 19, 14–19.

Fong, Petti. 2001. "Brain Diseases 'Loom as Next Big Health Threat.'" *Vancouver Sun*, March 20, A3.

Foot, David K. 2002. "Boomers Blow up Census." *The Globe and Mail*, March 21, A17.

Form, William. 1992. "Labor Movements and Unions." Pp. 1054–1060 in *Encyclopedia of Sociology*, vol. 3. Edgar F. Borgatta and Marie L. Borgatta, eds. New York: Macmillan.

Fornos, Werner. 1997. *1997 World Population Overview*. Washington, DC: The Population Institute.

Fortune. 2002. "Fortune's Global 500." August 12.

———. 2005. "Fortune's Global 500." 152 (July 25), 97–142.

Fortin, Myriam, and Dominique Fleury. 2004. *A Profile of the Working Poor in Canada: Draft*. Ottawa: Social Development Canada.

Fox, Bonnie. 2001. "As Times Change: A Review of Trends in Personal and Family Life." Pp. 153–175 in *Family Patterns, Gender Relations*, 2nd ed. Edited by Bonnie J. Fox. Toronto: Oxford University Press.

Fox, John, and Michael Ornstein. 1986. "The Canadian State and Corporate Elites in the Post-war Period." *Canadian Review of Sociology and Anthropology* 23:481–506.

Fox, Jonathan. 2005. "Unpacking 'Transnational' Citizenship." Pp. 171–201 in *Annual Review of Political Science, 2005*. Palo Alto, CA: Annual Reviews.

France, David. 2000. "Slavery's New Face." *Newsweek*, December 18, 61–65.

Francis, Diane. 1986. *Controlling Interest: Who Owns Canada?* Toronto: Macmillan.

Freeman, Linton C. 1958. "Marriage without Love: Mate Selection in Non-Western Countries." Pp. 20–30 in *Mate Selection*, Robert F. Winch, ed. New York: Harper and Row.

Freeze, Colin. 2001. "Women Outwork Men by Two Weeks Every Year." *The Globe and Mail*, March 13, A1.

Freidson, Eliot. 1970. *Profession of Medicine*. New York: Dodd, Mead.

Freire, Paulo. 1970. *Pedagogy of the Oppressed*. New York: Herder and Herder.

French, Howard W. 2003a. "Insular Japan Needs, but Resists, Immigration." *New York Times*, July 24, A1, A3.

———. 2003b. "Japan's Neglected Resource: Female Workers." *New York Times,* July 25.

———. 2004. "Despite an Act of Clemency, China Has Its Eye on the Web." *New York Times*, June 27, 6.

Frey, William H. 2001. *Melting Pot Suburbs: A Census 2000 Study of Suburban Diversity*. Washington, DC: The Brookings Institution.

Fridlund, Alan. J., Paul Erkman, and Harriet Oster. 1987. "Facial Expressions of Emotion: Review of Literature 1970–1983." Pp. 143–224 in *Nonverbal Behavior and Communication*, 2nd ed., Aron W. Seigman and Stanley Feldstein, eds. Hillsdale, NJ: Lawrence Erlbaum Associates.

Friedan, Betty. 1963. *The Feminine Mystique*. New York: W.W. Norton.

Friedland, Jonathon. 2000. "An American in Mexico Champions Midwifery as a Worthy Profession." *Wall Street Monitor*, February 15, A1, A12.

Friedman, Thomas L. 2005. *The World Is Flat: A Brief History of the Twenty-first Century*. New York: Farrar, Straus and Giroux.

Friedrich, Carl J., and Zbigniew Brzezinski. 1965. *Totalitarian Dictatorship and Autocracy*. 2d ed. Cambridge, MA: Harvard University Press.

Friedrichs, David O. 1998. "New Directions in Critical Criminology and White Collar Crime." Pp. 77–91 in *Cutting the Edge*, Jeffrey Ross, ed. Westport, CT: Praeger.

Fujimoto, Kayo. 2004. "Feminine Capital: The Forms of Capital in the Female Labor Market in Japan." *Sociological Quarterly* 45 (1):91–111.

Furstenberg, Frank, and Andrew Cherlin. 1991. *Divided Families: What Happens to Children When Parents Part*. Cambridge, MA: Harvard University Press.

Fuwa, Makiko. 2004. "Macro-level Gender Inequality and the Division of Household Labor in 22 Countries." *American Sociological Review* 69 (December): 757.

G

Gabor, Andrea. 1995. "Crashing the 'Old Boy' Party." *New York Times*, January 8, 1, 6.

Gale Research Group. 2002. *Encyclopedia of Associations*. National Organizations of the U.S. Detroit: Gale Research Group.

Gallup. 2003. "The Gallup Poll of Baghdad." Retrieved November 25, 2004 (www.gallup.com).

Galt, Virginia. 1998. "Where the Boys Aren't: At the Top of the Class." *The Globe and Mail*, February 26, A6.

———. 2003. "The Future of Work." *The Globe and Mail*, September 23. Retrieved November 10, 2005 (www.suiteworks.ca/documents/GM%20Sep-23-2003.pdf).

Gamson, Josh. 1989. "Silence, Death, and the Invisible Enemy: AIDS Activism and Social Movement 'Newness.'" *Social Problems* 36 (October):351–367.

Gamson, Josh, and Pearl Latteier. 2004. "Do Media Monsters Devour Diversity?" *Contexts* (Summer):26–32.

Gans, Herbert J. 1991. *People, Plans, and Policies: Essays on Poverty, Racism, and Other National Urban Problems*. New York: Columbia University Press and Russell Sage Foundation.

———. 1995. *The War against the Poor: The Underclass and Antipoverty Policy*. New York: Basic Books.

Ganzeboom, Harry B.G., Donald J. Treiman, and Woult C. Ultee. 1991. "Comparative Intergenerational Stratification Research." Pp. 277–302 in *Annual Review of Sociology, 1991*, W. Richard Scott, ed. Palo Alto, CA: Annual Reviews.

Ganzeboom, Harry B.G., Ruud Luijkx, and Donald J. Treiman. 1989. "Intergenerational Class mobility In Comparative Perspective." *Research in Social Stratification and Mobility* 8:3–84.

Garber, Judith A., and Robyne S. Turner, eds. 1995. *Gender in Urban Research*. Thousand Oaks, CA: Sage.

Gardner, Carol Brooks. 1989. "Analyzing Gender in Public Places: Rethinking Goffman's Vision of Everyday Life." *American Sociologist* 20 (Spring):42–56.

———. 1990. "Safe Conduct: Women, Crime, and Self in Public Places." *Social Problems* 37 (August):311–328.

———. 1995. *Passing By: Gender and Public Harassment*. Berkeley, CA: University of California Press.

Gardner, Gary, Erik Assadourian, and Radhika Sarin. 2004. "The State of Consumption Today." Pp. 3–21 in *State of the World 2004*, Brian Halweil and Lisa Mastny, eds. New York: W.W. Norton.

Gardner, Marilyn. 1998. "Prime-Time TV Fare Rarely Shows Family Life as It's Really Lived." *Christian Science Monitor*, June 10, 13. Retrieved December 1, 2005 (http://csmonitor.com/cgi-bin/durableRedirect.pl?/durable/1998/06/10/p13s1.htm).

Garfinkel, Harold. 1956. "Conditions of Successful Degradation Ceremonies." *American Journal of Sociology* 61 (March):420–424.

Garner, Roberta. 1996. *Contemporary Movements and Ideologies*. New York: McGraw-Hill Ryerson.

———. 1999. "Virtual Social Movements." Presented at Zaldfest: A Conference in Honor of Mayer Zald. September 17, Ann Arbor, MI.

Garreau, Joel. 1991. *Edge City: Life on the New Frontier*. New York: Doubleday.

Gartner, Rosemary, Myrna Dawson, and Maria Crawford. 2001. "Confronting Violence in Women's Lives." Pp. 473–490 in *Family Patterns, Gender Relations*, Bonnie J. Fox, ed. Toronto: Oxford University Press.

Garza, Melita Marie. 1993. "The Cordi-Marian Annual Cotillion." *Chicago Tribune*, May 7, sec. C, 1, 5.

Gates, Henry Louis, Jr. 1999. "One Internet, Two Nations." *New York Times*, October 31, A15.

Gauette, Nicole. 1998. "Rules for Raising Japanese Kids." *Christian Science Monitor*, October 14, B1, B6.

Gearty, Robert. 1996. "Beware of Pickpockets." *Chicago Daily News*, November 19, 5.

Gecas, Viktor. 1982. "The Self-Concept." Pp. 1–33 in *Annual Review of Sociology, 1982*, Ralph H. Turner and James F. Short, Jr., eds. Palo Alto, CA: Annual Reviews.

———. 1992. "Socialization." Pp. 1863–1872 in *Encyclopedia of Sociology*, vol. 4. Edgar F. Borgatta and Marie L. Borgatta, eds. New York: Macmillan.

Geckler, Cheri. 1995. *Practice Perspectives and Medical Decision-Making in Medical Residents: Gender Differences—A Preliminary Report*. Wellesley, MA: Center for Research on Women.

Gelles, Richard J., and Claire Pedrick Cornell. 1990. *Intimate Violence in Families*, 2nd ed. Newbury Park, CA: Sage.

Gelles, Richard J., and Murray A. Straus. 1988. *Intimate Violence: The Causes and Consequences of Abuse in the American Family*. New York: Simon and Schuster.

General Accounting Office. 2000. *Women's Health: NIH Has Increased Its Efforts to Include Women in Research*. Washington, DC: United States Government Printing Office.

General Social Survey. 1998. Ottawa: Statistics Canada.

Gerbner, George, and Larry Gross. 1976. "Living With Television: The Violence Profile." *Journal of Communication* 26:172–194.

Gerth, H.H., and C. Wright Mills. 1958. *From Max Weber: Essays in Sociology*. New York: Galaxy.

Gertner, Jon. 2005. "Our Ratings, Ourselves." *New York Times Magazine*, April 10, 34–41, 56, 58, 64–65.

Geschwender, James A. 1994. "Married Women's Waged Labour and Racial/Ethnic Stratification in Canada." *Canadian Ethnic Studies* 26 (3):53–73.

Gest, Ted. 1985. "Are White-Collar Crooks Getting off Too Easy?" *U.S. News & World Report*, July 1, 43.

Gidengil, Elizabeth, Matt Hennigar, Andre Blais, Richard Nadeau and Neil Nevitte. 2003. "The Gender Gap in Support for The New Right: The Case of Canada." Paper prepared for the conference, "Populisms in North America, South America, and Europe: Comparative and Historical," Bogliasco Italy, January.

Gifford, Allen L., William E. Cunningham, Kevin C. Heslin, Ron M. Andersen, Terry Nakazono, Dale K. Lieu, Martin F. Shapiro, Samuel A. Bozzette. 2002. "Participation in Research and Access to Experimental Treatments by HIV-Infected Patients." *New England Journal of Medicine* 346 (May):1400–1402.

Gill, Rosalind, and Keith Grist, eds. 1995. *The Gender-Technology Relation: Contemporary Theory and Research*. London: Taylor and Francis.

Giroux, Henry A. 1988. *Schooling and the Struggle for Public Life: Critical Pedagogy in the Modern Age*. Minneapolis, MN: University of Minnesota Press.

Gitlin, Todd. 2002. *Media Unlimited: How the Torrent of Images and Sounds Overwhelms Our Lives*. New York: Henry Holt and Company.

Glenn, David. 2004. "A Dangerous Surplus of Sons?" *Chronicle of Higher Education* 50 (April 30): A14–A16, A18.

Global Alliance for Workers and Communities. 2001. *Workers' Voices: An Interim Report on Workers' Needs and Aspirations in Nine Nike Contract Factories in Indonesia*. Baltimore, MD: Global Alliance.

———. 2003. *About Us*. Accessed April 28 (www.theglobalalliance.org).

Global Reach. 2002. "Global Internet Statistics (by Language)." Retrieved June 24, 2002 (http://glreach.com/globstats).

———. 2004. "Global Internet Statistics (by Language)." Retrieved October 13, 2005 (http://global-reach.biz/globestats/index.php3).

Globe and Mail. 2004a. "Canada's Wealthy Not Cheapskates, Poll Finds." August 20, B5.

———. 2004b. "Education System Failing Innu, Report Says." December 14. Retrieved December 14, 2004 (www.theglobeandmail.com/servlet/stroy/RTGAM.2004.winnu1214/BNStory).

Goffman, Erving. 1959. *The Presentation of Self in Everyday Life*. New York: Doubleday.

———. 1961. *Asylums: Essays on the Social Situation of Mental Patients and Other Inmates*. Garden City, NY: Doubleday.

———. 1963a. *Stigma: Notes on Management of Spoiled Identity*. Englewood Cliffs, NJ: Prentice Hall.

———. 1963b. *Behavior in Public Places*. New York: Free Press.

———. 1967. *Interaction Ritual: Essays in Face-to-Face Behavior*. New York: Doubleday.

———. 1971. *Relations in Public*. New York: Basic Books.

———. 1979. *Gender Advertisements*. New York: Harper and Row.

Golden, Frederic. 1999. "Who's Afraid of Frankenfood?" *Time*, November 29, 49–50.

Goldman, Benjamin A., and Laura Fitton. 1994. *Toxic Wastes and Race Revisited: An Update of the 1987 Report on the Racial and Social Economic Characteristics of Communities with Hazardous Waste*. Washington, DC: Center for Policy Alternatives, United Church of Christ Commission for Racial Justice, and NAACP.

Goldman, Robert, and Stephen Papson. 1998. *Nike Culture: The Sign of the Swoosh*. London: Sage Publications.

Goldstein, Greg. 1998. "World Health Organization and Housing." Pp. 636–637 in *The Encyclopedia of Housing*, Willem van Vliet, ed. Thousand Oaks, CA: Sage Publications.

Goldstein, Melvyn C., and Cynthia M. Beall. 1981. "Modernization and Aging in the Third and Fourth World: Views from the Rural Hinterland in Nepal." *Human Organization* 40 (Spring):48–55.

Gonnut, Jean Pierre. 2001. *Interview*. June 18, 2001.

Gonzalez, David. 2003. "Latin Sweatshops Pressed by U.S. Campus Power." *New York Times*, April 4, A3.

Goode, William J. 1959. "The Theoretical Importance of Love." *American Sociological Review* 24 (February):38–47.

Goodman, Peter S., and Akiko Kashiwagi. 2002. "In Japan, Housewives No More." *Washington Post National Weekly Edition*, November 4, 18–19.

Google. 2007. "Year-End Zeitgeist." Retrieved January 21, 2008 (www.google.ca/intl/en/press/seitgeist2007).

Gordon, RaymondG., Jr., ed. 2005. *Ethnologue: Languages of the World*, 15th ed. Dallas, TX: SIL International.

Gore, Al. 2006. *An Inconvenient Truth: The Planetary Emergency of Global Warming and What We Can Do About It*. New York: Rodale Books.

Gornick, Janet C. 2001. "Cancel the Funeral." *Dissent* (Summer):13–18.

Gornick, Vivian. 1979. "Introduction" to *Gender Advertisements*. Cambridge, MA: Harvard University Press.

Gottdiener, Mark, and Joe R. Feagin. 1988. "The Paradigm Shift in Urban Sociology." *Urban Affairs Quarterly* 24(December):163–187.

Gottdiener, Mark, and Ray Hutchison. 2000. *The New Urban Sociology*, 2nd ed. New York: McGraw-Hill Ryerson.

———. 2006. *The New Urban Sociology*. 3d ed. Boulder, CO:Westview.

Gottfredson, Michael, and Travis Hirschi. 1990. *A General Theory of Crime*. Palo Alto, CA: Stanford University Press.

Gough, E. Kathleen. 1974. "Nayar: Central Kerala." Pp. 298–384 in *Matrilineal Kinship*, David Schneider and E. Kathleen Gough, eds. Berkeley, CA: University of California Press.

Gould, Larry A. 2002. "Indigenous People Policing Indigenous People: The Potential Psychological and Cultural Costs." *Social Science Journal* 39:171–188.

Gouldner, Alvin. 1960. "The Norm of Reciprocity." *American Sociological Review* 25 (April):161–177.

———. 1970. *The Coming Crisis of Western Sociology*. New York: Basic Books.

Gove, Walter R., ed. 1987. "Sociobiology Misses the Mark: An Essay on Why Biology but Not Sociobiology Is Very Relevant to Sociology." *American Sociologist* 18 (Fall):258–277.

Government of Canada. 2002. "Sustainable Development: A Canadian Perspective. Canada at the World Summit on Sustainable Development." Retrieved February 25, 2005 (http://www.sdinfo.gc.ca/canadian_perspective/pg027_e.cfm).

Gram, Karen. 2001. "Hard Times in the Good Ol' Days." *Vancouver Sun*, May 5, A21.

Gramsci, Antonio. 1929. *Selections from the Prison Notebooks*. Quintin Hoare and Geoffrey Nowell-Smith, eds and intro. London: Lawrence and Wishort.

Grant, Judith. 1993. *Fundamental Feminism: Contesting the Core Concepts of Feminist Theory*. New York and London: Routledge.

Grant, Tavia. 2007. "The Challenge for Employers." *The Globe and Mail*, July 17. Retrieved July 17, 2007 (www.reportonbusiness.com/servlet/story/RTGAM.20070717.wworkplace0717/BNStory/robNews/home).

Graydon, Shari. 2001. "The Portrayal of Women in Media: The Good, the Bad, and the Beautiful." Pp. 179–195 in *Communications in Canadian Society*, 5th ed., Craig McKie and Benjamin D. Singer, eds. Scarborough, ON: Thompson Educational Publishing.

Greaves, Lorraine. 1996. *Smoke Screen: Women's Smoking and Social Control*. Halifax: Fernwood Publishing.

Greeley, Andrew M. 1989. "Protestant and Catholic: Is the Analogical Imagination Extinct?" *American Sociological Review* 54 (August): 485–502.

Green, Joyce. 2003. "Decolonizing in the Age of Globalization." *Canadian Dimension* (March/April): 3–5.

Grewal, Inderpal. 2005. *Transnational America: Feminisms, Diasporas, Neoliberalisms*. Durham: Duke **University Press.**

Grewal, Inderpal, and Caren Kaplan, eds. 1994. *Scattered Hegemonies: Postmodernity and Transnational Feminist Practices*. Minneapolis, MN: University of Minnesota Press.

Grewal, San. 2007. "Childless Families on the Rise." *Toronto Star*, September 13. Retrieved September 24, 2007 (www.thestar.com/News/article/256083).

Grossman, David C., H.J. Neckerman, Thomas D. Koepsell, P.Y. Liu, K. Asher, Kathy Beland, Karen S. Frey, and Frederick P. Rivara. 1997. "Effectiveness of a Violence Prevention Curriculum among Children in Elementary School." *Journal of the American Medical Association* 277 (May 28):1605–1617.

Grossman, Ler, and Hannah Beech. 2006. "Google Under the Gun." *Time,* February 13, p. 53.

Groza, Victor, Daniela F. Ileana, and Ivor Irwin. 1999. *A Peacock or a Crow: Stories, Interviews, and Commentaries on Romanian Adoptions.* Euclid, OH: Williams Custom Publishing.

Guardian Unlimited. 2005. "Eight Women, One Voice." Retrieved July 9, 2005 (http://www.guardian.co.uk/africa8).

Guppy, Neil, and Scott Davies. 1998. *Education in Canada: Recent Trends and Future Challenges.* Ottawa: Statistics Canada.

Gurin, David. 2003. *Understanding Sprawl.* Vancouver: David Suzuki Foundation.

Guterman, Lila. 2000. "Why the 25-Year-Old Battle over Sociology Is More Than Just 'an Academic Sideshow.'" *Chronicle of Higher Education,* July 7, A17–A18.

Gutierrez, Gustavo. 1990. "Theology and the Social Sciences." Pp. 214–225 in *Liberation Theology at the Crossroads: Democracy or Revolution?* Paul E. Sigmund, ed. New York: Oxford University Press.

Gwynne, S.C., and John F. Dickerson. 1997. "Lost in the E-mail." *Time,* April 21, 88–90.

H

Ha, Tu Thanh. 2004. "Pregnant Woman Called Him 'Papa,' Sperm Donor's Court Petition Says." *The Globe and Mail,* September 14. Retrieved November 27, 2004 (www.theglobeandmail.com).

Haaland, Bonnie. 1993. *Emma Goldman: Sexuality and the Impurity of the State.* Montreal: Black Rose.

Haas, Michael, ed. 1999. *The Singapore Puzzle.* Westport, CT: Praeger.

Hacker, Andrew. 1964. "Power to Do What?" Pp. 134–146 in *The New Sociology,* Irving Louis Horowitz, ed. New York: Oxford University Press.

Hacker, Helen Mayer. 1951. "Women as a Minority Group." *Social Forces* 30 (October):60–69.

———. 1974. "Women as a Minority Group, Twenty Years Later." Pp. 124–134 in *Who Discriminates against Women?* Florence Denmark, ed. Beverly Hills, CA: Sage.

Hafner-Burton, Emilie M., and Kiyoteru Tsutsui. 2005. "Human Rights in a Globalizing World: The Paradox of Empty Promises." *American Journal of Sociology* 110 (March):1373–1411.

Haines, Valerie A. 1988. "Is Spencer's Theory an Evolutionary Theory?" *American Journal of Sociology* 93 (March):1200–1223.

Halbfinger, David M. 1998. "As Surveillance Cameras Peer, Some Wonder If They Also Pry." *New York Times,* February 22, A1.

Hall, Kay. 1999. "Work from Here." *Computer User* 18 (November):32.

Hall, Mimi. 1993. "Genetic-Sex-Testing a Medical Mine Field." *USA Today,* December 20, 6A.

Hall, Robert H. 1982. "The Truth about Brown Lung." *Business and Society Review* 40 (Winter 1981–82):15–20.

Haller, Max, Wolfgang Konig, Peter Krause, and Karin Kurz. 1990. "Patterns of Career Mobility and Structural Positions in Advanced Capitalist Societies: A Comparison of Men in Austria, France, and the United States." *American Sociological Review* 50 (October): 579–603

Hallinan, Maureen T. 1997. "The Sociological Study of Social Change." *American Sociological Review* 62 (February):1–11.

Hanes, Stephanie. 2005. "Woman Quota Changes Dynamics of Lesotho Vote," *USA Today,* June 10, p. 12A.

Hani, Yoko. 1998. "Hot Pots Wired to Help the Elderly." *Japan Times Weekly International Edition,* April 13, 16.

Hank, Karsten. 2001. "Changes in Child Care Could Reduce Job Options for Eastern German Mothers." *Population Today* 29 (April):3, 6.

Hanson, Ralph E. 2005. *Mass Communication: Living in a Media World.* New York: McGraw Hill Ryerson.

Harlow, Harry F. 1971. *Learning to Love.* New York: Ballantine.

Hara, Hiroko. 2000. "Homeless Desperately Want Shelter, Jobs." *Japan Times International,* January 16, 14.

Harap, Louis. 1982. "Marxism and Religion: Social Functions of Religious Belief." *Jewish Currents* 36 (January):12–17, 32–35.

Harlow, Harry F. 1971. *Learning to Love.* New York: Ballantine.

Harrington, Michael. 1980. "The New Class and the Left." Pp. 123–138 in *The New Class,* B. Bruce-Briggs, ed. New Brunswick, NJ: Transaction.

Harris, Chauncy D., and Edward Ullman. 1945. "The Nature of Cities." *Annals of the American Academy of Political and Social Science* 242 (November):7–17.

Harris, Judith Rich. 1998. *The Nurture Assumption: Why Children Turn out the Way They Do.* New York: Free Press.

Harris, Marvin. 1974. *Cows, Pigs, Wars, and Witches: The Riddles of Culture.* Toronto: Random House.

———. 1997. *Culture, People, Nature: An Introduction to General Anthropology,* 7th ed. New York: Longman.

Harris, Misty. 2007. "A Nation of Incessant Adolescents." *National Post,* May 24, B6.

Harrison, Trevor W., and John W. Friesen. 2004. *Canadian Society in the Twenty-First Century.* Don Mills, ON: Prentice Hall.

Harston, P.J. 2007. *Popularity of Telecommuting Drops.* Retrieved July 21, 2007 (http://career.jobboom.com/workplace/challenges/2007/06/27/4294385-sun.html).

Hart, Stacey. 1995. "(Re)searching Lesbian Health Care: Methodological Considerations for Future Directions." Retrieved April 18, 2002 (http://www.usc.edu/isd/archives/queerfrontiers/queer/papers/hart.html).

Hartjen, Clayton A. 1978. *Crime and Criminalization,* 2nd ed. New York: Praeger.

Hartman, Chris, and Jake Miller. 2001. *Bailouts That Work For Everyone.* Boston: United for a Fair Economy.

Harvey, Bob. 2004. "Women Poised to Match Men on the Protestant Pulpits." *National Post.* August 7.

Haub, Carl. 2001. *World Population Data Sheet.* Washington, DC: Population Reference Bureau.

———. 2003. *World Population Data Sheet, 2003.* Washington, DC: Population Reference Bureau.

———. 2004. *World Population Data Sheet, 2004.* Washington, DC: Population Reference Bureau.

———. 2005. *World Population Data Sheet 2005.* Washington, DC: Population Reference Bureau.

Haub, Carl, and Diana Cornelius. 2000. *2000 World Population Data Sheet.* Washington, DC:Population Reference Bureau.

Hauser, Robert M., and David B. Grusky. 1988. "Cross-National Variation in Occupational Distributions, Relative Mobility Chances, and Intergenerational Shifts in Occupational Distributions." *American Sociological Review* 53 (October):723–741.

Haviland, William A. 1999. *Cultural Anthropology (Case Studies in Cultural Anthropology),* 9th ed. Fort Worth, TX: Harcourt Brace.

Hayward, Mark D., William R. Grady, and Steven D. McLaughlin. 1987. "Changes in the Retirement Process." *Demography* 25 (August):371–386.

Health Canada. 1993. *Gender and Violence in the Mass Media.* Ottawa, Canada: Health Canada.

———. 2000. "The Changing Face of Heart Disease and Stroke in Canada 2000." Retrieved January 30, 2002 (http://www.hc-sc.gc.ca/hpb/lcdc/bcrdd/hdsc2000/index.html).

———. 2001. *Canada Health Act Annual Report, 1999–2000.* Ottawa: Queen's Printers.

———. 2002. "Women's Health Strategy." Ottawa: Health Canada, Women's Health Bureau. Retrieved April 4, 2002 (www.hc-sc.gc.ca/english/women/womenstrat.htm).

———. 2003a. *Acting on What We Know: Preventing Youth Suicide in First Nations.* Ottawa: Advisory Group on Suicide Prevention.

———. 2003b. *HIV and AIDS in Canada. Surveillance Report to June 30, 2003.* Ottawa: Surveillance and Risk Assessment Division, Centre for Infections, Disease Prevention and Control, Health Canada.

———. 2006. "Aboriginal Health." Retrieved October 16, 2007 (www.hc-sc.gc.ca/ahc-asc/media/nr-cp/2006/2006_118bk1_e.html).

Heckert, Druann, and Amy Best. 1997. "Ugly Duckling to Swan: Labeling Theory and the Stigmatization of Red Hair." *Symbolic Interaction* 20 (4):365–384.

Hedley, R. Alan. 1992. "Industrialization in Less Developed Countries." Pp. 914–920 in *Encyclopedia of Sociology*, vol. 2. Edgar F. Borgatta and Marie L. Borgatta, eds. New York: Macmillan.

Heilman, Madeline E. 2001. "Description and Prescription: How Gender Stereotypes Prevent Women's Ascent up the Organizational Ladder." *Journal of Social Issues* 57 (4):657–674.

Heise, Lori, M. Ellseberg, and M. Gottemuelle. 1999. "Ending Violence against Women." *Population Reports*, ser. L, no. 11. Baltimore: Johns Hopkins University School of Public Health.

Hellmich, Nanci. 2001. "TV's Reality: No Vast American Waistlines." *USA Today*, October 8, 7D.

Henley, Nancy, Mykol Hamilton, and Barrie Thorne. 1985. "Womanspeak and Manspeak: Sex Differences and Sexism in Communication, Verbal and Nonverbal." Pp. 168–185 in *Beyond Sex Roles*, 2nd ed., Alice G. Sargent, ed. St. Paul, MN: West.

Henly, Julia R. 1999. "Challenges to Finding and Keeping Jobs in the Low-Skilled Labor Market." *Poverty Research News* 3 (No. 1):3–5.

Henneberger, Melinda. 1995. "Muslims Continue to Feel Apprehensive." *New York Times*, April 14, B10.

Henry, Francis, C. Tator, W. Mattis, and T. Reese. 1995. *The Colour of Democracy: Racism in Canadian Society.* Toronto: Harcourt Brace.

Henry, Mary E. 1989. "The Function of Schooling: Perspectives from Rural Australia." *Discourse* 9 (April):1–21.

Herman, Edward S., and Noam Chomsky. 1988. *Manufacturing Consent: The Political Economy of the Mass Media.* New York: Pantheon Books.

Herman, Edward S., and Gerry O'Sullivan. 1990. *The "Terrorism" Industry: The Experts and Institutions That Shape Our View of Terror.* New York: Pantheon.

Hickman, Jonathan. 2002. "America's 50 Best Corporations for Minorities." *Fortune*, July 8, 110–120.

Hillery, George A. 1955. "Definitions of Community: Areas of Agreement." *Rural Sociology* (2):111–123.

Hirschi, Travis. 1969. *Causes of Delinquency.* Berkeley, CA: University of California Press.

Hochschild, Arlie Russell. 1973. "A Review of Sex Role Research." *American Journal of Sociology* 78 (January):1011–1029.

———. 1990. "The Second Shift: Employed Women Are Putting in Another Day of Work at Home." *Utne Reader* 38 (March–April):66–73.

———. 2005. *The Commercialization of Intimate Life: Notes from Home and Work.* Berkeley: University of California Press.

Hochschild, Arlie Russell, with Anne Machung. 1989. *The Second Shift: Working Parents and the Revolution at Home.* New York: Viking Penguin.

Hodge, Robert W., and Peter H. Rossi. 1964. "Occupational Prestige in the United States, 1925–1963." *American Journal of Sociology* 70 (November):286–302.

Hoebel, E. Adamson. 1949. *Man in the Primitive World: An Introduction to Anthropology.* New York: McGraw-Hill Ryerson.

Hoffman, Adonis. 1997. "Through an Accurate Prism." *Los Angeles Times*, August 8, M1.

Hoffman, Lois Wladis. 1985. "The Changing Genetics/Socialization Balance." *Journal of Social Issues* 41 (Spring):127–148.

Hofrichter, Richard, ed. 1993. *Toxic Struggles: The Theory and Practise of Environmental Justice.* Philadelphia: New Society.

Holden, Constance. 1980. "Identical Twins Reared Apart." *Science* 207 (March 21):1323–1328.

———. 1987. "The Genetics of Personality." *Science* 257(August 7):598–601.

Hollingshead, August B. 1975. *Elmtown's Youth and Elmtown Revisited.* New York: John Wiley and Sons.

Holmes, Steven A. 1997. "Leaving the Suburbs for Rural Areas." *New York Times*, October 19, 34.

Holmes, Tracy. 2000. "Performance Anxiety." *Peace Arch News*, February 2, 11.

Homans, George C. 1979. "Nature versus Nurture: A False Dichotomy." *Contemporary Sociology* 8 (May):345–348.

Hondagneu-Sotelo, Pierette. 2001. *Domestica: Immigrant Workers Cleaning and Caring in the Shadows of Affluence.* Berkeley, CA: University of California Press.

Horgan, John. 1993. "Eugenics Revisited." *Scientific American* 268 (June):122–128, 130–133.

Horovitz, Bruce. 2003. "Smile! You're the Stars of the Super Ad Bowl." *USA Today*, January 24, B1, B2.

Horowitz, Irving Louis. 1983. *C. Wright Mills: An American Utopia.* New York: Free Press.

Horsey, Jen. 2004. "Canada's Rich Getting Richer." *The Globe and Mail*, December 5.

Retrieved December 6, 2004 (http://www.theglobeandmail.com).

Houghton County. 2005. "MTV Student Electrifies NBC's *Fear Factor*." Accessed March 1 (www.wluctv6.com).

Howard, Judith A. 1999. "Border Crossings between Women's Studies and Sociology." *Contemporary Sociology* 28 (September):525–528.

Howard, Michael C. 1989. *Contemporary Cultural Anthropology*, 3rd ed. Glenview, IL: Scott Foresman.

Howard, Philip E., Lee Rainie, and Steve Jones. 2001. "Days and Nights on the Internet." *American Behavioral Scientist* 45 (November):383–404.

Howell, Nancy, Patricia Albanese, and Kwaku Obusu-Mensah. 2001. "Ethnic Families." Pp. 116–142 in *Families: Changing Trends in Canada*, 4th ed. Maureen Baker, ed. Toronto: McGraw-Hill Ryerson.

Hua, Anh. 2003. "Critical Race Feminism." Presented at the Canadian Critical Race Conference 2003: Pedagogy and Practice. University of British Columbia, Vancouver, May 2–4.

Huang, Gary. 1988. "Daily Addressing Ritual: A Cross-Cultural Study." Presented at the annual meeting of the American Sociological Association, Atlanta.

Huddy, Leonie, Joshua Billig, John Bracciodieta, Lois Hoeffler, Patrick J. Moynihan, and Patricia Pugliani. 1997. "The Effect of Interviewer Gender on the Survey Response." *Political Behavior* 19 (September):197–220.

Huffstutter, P.J. 2003. "See No Evil." *Los Angeles Times*, January 12, 12–15, 43–45.

Hughes, Everett. 1945. "Dilemmas and Contradictions of Status." *American Journal of Sociology* 50 (March):353–359.

Human Resources and Social Development Canada (HRSDC). 2000. "Adult Education and Training in Canada: Key Knowledge Gaps." Retrieved October 2, 2007 (http://www.hrsdc.gc.ca/en/cs/sp/hrsd/prc/publications/research/200-000122/page07/shtml).

———. 2007. "A Study of Poverty and Working Poverty Among Recent Immigrants to Canada." Retrieved September 12, 2007 (http://www.hrsdc.gc.ca/en/publications_resources/research/categories/inclusion/2007/sp_680_05_07_e/page00.shtml).

Human Rights Watch. 2007. "Darfur 2007: Chaos by Design: Peacekeeping Challenges for AMIS and UNAMID." 19:15. Retrieved January 9, 2008 (http://hrw.org/reports/2007/sudan0907).

Hunt, Darnell. 1997. *Screening the Los Angeles "Riots": Race, Seeing, and Resistance.* New York: Cambridge University Press.

Hunt, Geoffrey, Stephanie Riegel, Tomas Morales, and Dan Waldorf. 1993. "Changes in Prison Culture: Prison Gangs and the

Case of the 'Pepsi Generation.'" *Social Problems* 40 (3):398–409.

Hunter, Herbert, ed. 2000. *The Sociology of Oliver C. Cox: New Perspectives: Research in Race and Ethnic Relations*, vol. II. Stanford, CT: JAI Press.

Hurn, Christopher J. 1985. *The Limits and Possibilities of Schooling*, 2nd ed. Boston: Allyn and Bacon.

I

Ibata, David. 2001. "Greener Pastures Devoured by Sprawl." *Chicago Tribune*, March 18, 1, 18.

Inglehart, Ronald, and Wayne E. Baker. 2000."Modernization, Cultural Change, and the Persistence of Traditional Values." *American Sociological Review* 65 (February):19–51.

Ingram, Matthew. 2007. "Boosting Citizen Journalism." *The Globe and Mail,* July 30. Retrieved July 30, 2007 (www.theglobeandmail.com/servlet/story/RTGAM.20070730.wsm-0730/BNStory/International/).

Institute for Social Policy and Understanding. 2004. *The USA PATRIOT Act: Impact on the Arabs and Muslim American Community.* Clinton Township, MI: ISPU.

Institute for Social Research. 1994. *World Values Survey, 1990–1993.* Ann Arbor, MI: The Regents of the University of Michigan.

Institute of International Education. 1998. "Foreign Students in U.S. Institutions 1997–98." *Chronicle of Higher Education* 45 (December 11):A67.

Instituto del Tercer Mundo. 1999. *The World Guide 1999/2000.* Oxford, UK: New International Publications.

———. 2005. *The World Guide 2005/2006.* Oxford: New Internationalist Publications.

International Herald Tribune Europe. 2007. "Serbia Failed to Prevent Genocide, UN Court Rules." February 26. Retrieved August 25, 2007 (http://www.int.com/articles/2007/02/26/news/serb.php).

International Institute for Democracy and Electoral Assistance. 2005. "Turnout in the World—Country by Country Performance."Modified March 7, 2005. Accessed April 18, 2006 (www.idea.int).

International Monetary Fund. 2000. *World Economic Outlook: Asset Prices and the Business Cycle.* Washington, DC: International Monetary Fund.

Inter-Parliamentary Union. 2006. *Women in National Parliaments.* March 31. Retrieved March 2, 2007 (www.ipu.org/wmn-e/classif.htm).

———. 2007. "Women In Parliament in 2006: More Women Make It To The Top." Press Release, March 1, 2007. Retrieved December 9, 2008 (http://www.ipu.org/press-e/Gen264.htm).

———. 2008. *Women in National Parliaments.* October 31, 2008. Retrieved December 11, 2008 (http://www.ipu.org/wmn-e/classif.htm).

Intini, John. 2007. "When It Comes to Love, Sex Hurts." *Maclean's*, March 23. Retrieved April 17, 2008 (http://www.macleans.ca/article.jsp?content=20070323_161000_7800).

International Tanker Owners Pollution Federation (ITOPF). 2006. *Statistics: International Tanker Owners Pollution Federation Limited.* Accessed May 2 (www.itopf.com/stats.html).

Iritani, Evelyn, and Marla Dickerson. 2002. "People's Republic of Products." *Los Angeles Times,* October 20, pp. A1, A10.

J

Jackson, Elton F., Charles R. Tittle, and Mary Jean Burke. 1986. "Offense-Specific Models of the Differential Association Process." *Social Problems* 33 (April):335–356.

Jackson, Philip W. 1968. *Life in Classrooms.* New York: Holt Rinehart & Winston.

Jacobs, Charles A. 2001. "Slavery in the 21st Century." Pp. 310–311 in *Britannica Book of the Year, 2001.* Chicago: Encyclopedia Britannica.

Jacobson, Jodi. 1993. "Closing the Gender Gap in Development." Pp. 61–79 in *State of the World*, Lester R. Brown, ed. New York: Norton.

Jagger, Alison M., and Paula S. Rothenberg. 1984. *Feminist Frameworks.* 2nd ed. New York: McGraw-Hill Ryerson.

Jasper, James M. 1997. *The Art of Moral Protest: Culture, Biography, and Creativity in Social Movements.* Chicago: University of Chicago Press.

Jehl, Douglas. 1999. "The Internet's 'Open Sesame' Is Answered Warily." *New York Times*, March 18, A4.

Jenkins, Richard. 1991. "Disability and Social Stratification." *British Journal of Sociology* 42 (December):557–580.

Jennings, M. Kent, and Richard G. Niemi. 1981. *Generations and Politics.* Princeton, NJ: Princeton University Press.

Jimenez, Marina. 2007. "How Canadian are you? Visible-minority immigrants and their children identify less and less with the country, report says." *The Globe and Mail*, January 12:A1.

Jimenez, Marina, and Kim Lunmann. 2004. "Canada's Biggest Cities See Influx of New Immigrants." *The Globe and Mail*, August 19, A5.

Jobtrak.com. 2000. "79% of College Students Find the Quality of an Employer's Website Important in Deciding Whether or Not to Apply for a Job." Retrieved on June 29, 2000 (http://static.jobtrak.com/

mediacenter/press_polls/polls_061200.html).

Johanis, Paul, and Albert Meguerditchian. 1996. *A Framework for Statistics on Employment in the Services Sector.* Ottawa: Statistics Canada.

Johnson, Allan G. 2000. *The Blackwell Dictionary of Sociology.* Oxford, UK: Blackwell Publishing.

Johnson, Anne M., Jane Wadsworth, Kaye Wellings, and Julie Field. 1994. *Sexual Attitudes and Lifestyles.* Oxford, UK: Blackwell Scientific.

Johnson, Benton. 1975. *Functionalism in Modern Sociology: Understanding Talcott Parsons.* Morristown, NJ: General Learning.

Johnson, George. 1999. "It's a Fact: Faith and Theory Collide over Evolution." *New York Times*, August 15, 1, 12.

Johnson, Harry M. 1960. *Sociology: A Systematic Introduction.* New York: Harcourt, Brace and World.

Johnson, Holly. 1996. *Dangerous Domains: Violence against Women in Canada.* Scarborough, ON: Nelson Canada.

Johnson, Jeffrey, et al. 2002. "Television Viewing and Aggressive Behavior During Adolescence and Adulthood." *Science* 295 (March 29):2468–2471.

Johnson, Patrick. 1983. *Native Children and the Child Welfare System.* Toronto: Canadian Council on Social Development in association with James Lorimer Publishing.

Johnston, David Cay. 1994. "Ruling Backs Homosexuals on Asylum." *New York Times,* June 12, D1, D6.

———.1996. "The Divine Write-Off." *New York Times*, January 12, D1, D6.

Jolin, Annette. 1994. "On the Backs of Working Prostitutes: Feminist Theory and Prostitution Policy." *Crime and Delinquency* 40 (No. 2):69–83.

Jones, Charles, Lorna Marsden, and Lorne Tepperman. 1990. *Lives of Their Own: The Individualization of Women's Lives.* Toronto: Oxford University Press.

Jones, Stephen R.G. 1992. "Was There a Hawthorne Effect?" *American Journal of Sociology* 98 (November):451–568.

K

Kaiser Family Foundation. 2001. *Few Parents Use V-Chip to Block TV Sex and Violence.* Menlo Park: Kaiser Family Foundation.

———. 2005. *Sex on TV:2005.* Santa Barbara, CA: Kaiser Family Foundation.

Kahn, Joseph. 2003a."Made in China, Bought in China." *New York Times*, January 5, sec. 3, pp. 1, 10.

———. 2003b. "China's Workers Risk Limbs in Export Drive." *New York Times,* April 7, p. A3.

———. 2006. "A Sharp Debate Erupts in China over Ideologies." *New York Times*, March 12, pp. 1, 8.

Kang, Mee-Eun. 1997. "The Portrayal of Women's Images in Magazine Advertisements: Goffman's Gender Analysis Revisited." In *Sex Roles: A Journal of Research* 37 (December):979–996.

Kapur, Deutsch, and John McHale. 2003."Migration's New Payroll." *Foreign Policy* (November/December):48–57.

Katel, Peter. 2005. "Ending Poverty." *CQ Researcher* 15 (September 9):733–760.

Katovich, Michael A. 1987. Correspondence. June 1.

Kaufman, Leslie. 2000. "As Biggest Business, Wal-Mart Propels Changes Elsewhere." *New York Times*, October 27, A1, A24.

Kazemipur, Abdie. 2002. "The Intersection of Socio-Economic Status and Race/Ethnicity/ Official Language/Religion." Prepared for the Intersections of Diversity Seminar, Draft, March 8.

Keating, Noah and Brenda Munro. 1988. "Farm Women/Farm Work." *Sex Roles: A Journal of Research* 19 (August):155–168.

Kelly, Katherine, and Walter S. DeKeseredy. 1993. "The Incidence and Prevalence of Woman Abuse in Canadian University and College Dating Relationships." *Journal of Human Justice* 4 (2):25–52.

Kelsoe, John R., E.I. Ginns, J.A. Egeland, D.S. Gerhard, A.M. Goldstein, S.J. Bale, D.L. Pauls, R.T. Long, K.K. Kidd, G. Conte, D.E. Housman, and S.M. Paul. 1989. "Reevaluation of the Linkage Relationship between Chromosome 11p Loci and the Gene for Bipolar Affective Disorder in the Old Order Amish." *Nature* 342 (November 16):238–243.

Kemper, Vicki, and Viveca Novak. 1991. "Health Care Reform: Don't Hold Your Breath." *Washington Post National Weekly Edition*, October 28, 28.

Kennedy, M. Alexis, and Boris B. Gorzalka. 2002. "Asian and Non-Asian Attitudes Toward Rape, Sexual Harassment, and Sexuality." *Sex Roles: A Journal of Research* 46: 227–238.

Kent, Mary M., and Carl Haub. 2005. "Global Demographic Divide." *Population Bulletin* 60 (December).

Kent, Mary Mederios. 1999. "Shrinking Societies Favor Procreation." *Population Today* 27 (December):4–5.

Kentor, Jeffrey, and Yong Suk Jang. 2004. "Yes, There Is a (Growing) Transnational Business Community": *International Sociology* 19 (September), 355–368.

Kerbo, Harold R. 2000. *Social Stratification and Inequality: Class Conflict in Historical, Comparative, and Global Perspective*. New York: McGraw-Hill Ryerson.

———. 2003. *Social Stratification and Inequality: Class Conflict in Historical,* *Comparative, and Global Perspective*, 5th ed. New York: McGraw-Hill Ryerson.

Kilbourne, Jean. 2000a. *Can't Buy My Love: How Advertising Changes the Way We Think and Feel*. New York: Touchstone Book, Simon and Schuster.

———. 2000b. *Killing Us Softly 3*. Videorecording. Northampton, MA: Media Education Foundation (Cambridge Documentary Films).

King, Leslie. 1998. "'France Needs Children': Pronatalism, Nationalism, and Women's Equity." *Sociological Quarterly* 39 (Winter):33–52.

King, Peter H. 2004. "Their Spiritual Thirst Found a Desert Spring." *Los Angeles Times*, August 4, pp. A1, A10, A11.

Kinkade, Patrick T., and Michael A. Katovich. 1997. "The Driver Adaptations and Identities in the Urban Worlds of Pizza Delivery Employees." *Journal of Contemporary Ethnography* 25 (January):421–448.

Kinsella, Kevin, and David R. Phillips. 2005. "Global Aging: The Challenge of Success." *Population Bulletin* 60 (March).

Kinsella, Kevin and Victoria A. Velkoff. 2001. "An Aging World: 2001." *Current Population Reports*, ser. 95. no. 01-1. Washington, DC: United States Government Printing Office.

Kinsey, Alfred C., Wardell B. Pomeroy, and Clyde E. Martin. 1948. *Sexual Behavior in the Human Male*. Philadelphia: Saunders.

Kinsey, Alfred C., Wardell B. Pomeroy, and Paul H. Gebhard. 1953. *Sexual Behavior in the Human Female*. Philadelphia: Saunders.

Kirk, Margaret O. 1995. "The Temps in the Gray Flannel Suits." *New York Times*, December 17, F13.

Kiser, Edgar. 1992. "War." Pp. 2243–2247 in *Encyclopedia of Sociology*, edited by Edgar F. Borgatta and Marie L. Borgatta. New York: Macmillan.

Kitchener, Richard F. 1991. "Jean Piaget: The Unknown Sociologist." *British Journal of Sociology* 42 (September):421–442.

Klass, Perri. 2003. "This Side of Medicine." P. 319 in *This Side of Doctoring: Reflection for Women in Medicine*, edited by Eliza Lo Chin. New York: Oxford University Press.

Klein, Naomi. 1999. *No Logo: Money, Marketing, and the Growing Anti-Corporate Movement*. New York: Picador.

Kleiner, Art. 2003. "Are You In with the In Crowd?" *Harvard Business Review* 81 (July):86–92.

Klinger, Scott, Chris Hartman, Sarah Anderson, and John Cavanagh. 2002. *Executive Excess 2002: CEOs Cook the Books, Skewer the Rest of Us*. Boston, MA: Institute for Policy Studies and United for a Fair Economy.

Klug, Heinz. 2005. "Transnational Human Rights: Exploring the Persistence and Globalization of Human Rights." Pp. 85–103 in *Annual Review of Law and Social Sciences*. Palo Alto, CA: Annual Reviews.

Kohn, Alfie. 1988. "Girltalk, Guytalk." *Psychology Today* 22 (February):65–66.

Kohn, Melvin L. 1970. "The Effects of Social Class on Parental Values and Practices." Pp. 45–68 in *The American Family: Dying or Developing*, David Reiss and H.A. Hoffman, eds. New York: Plenum.

Kohn, Melvin L., Kazimierz M. Slomeznsky, and Carrie Schoenbach. 1986. "Social Stratification and the Transmission of Values in the Family: A Cross-National Assessment." *Sociological Forum* 1, 1:73–102.

Kolata, Gina. 1998. "Infertile Foreigners See Opportunity in U.S." *New York Times*, January 4, 1, 12.

———. 1999. *Clone: The Road to Dolly and the Path Beyond*. New York: William Morrow.

Koolhaas, Rem, et al. 2001. *Mutations*. Barcelona, Spain: Actar.

Korn/Ferry International. 2007. "61% of Executives Surveyed Believe Telecommuters are Less Likely to Advance Compared to Working in Traditional Office Settings" (press release). Retrieved July 21, 2007 (http://www.kornferry.com/Library/Process.asp?P=PR_Detail&CID=2766&LID=1).

Kornell, Sam. 2007. "The Pros and Cons of Fair-Trade Coffee." *The Santa Barbara Independent*, April 5. Retrieved April 9, 2008 (http://www.organicconsumers.org/articles/article_4738.cfm).

Kortenhaus, Carole M., and Jack Demarest. 1993. "Gender Role Stereotyping in Children's Literature: An Update." *Sex Roles: A Journal of Research* 28 (3–4):219–232.

Kotulak, Ronald. 2005. "Increase in Women Doctors Changing the Face of Medicine," *Chicago Tribune*, January 12, pp. 1, 4.

Kovaleski, Serge F. 1999. "Choosing Alternative Medicine by Necessity." *Washington Post National Weekly Edition*, April 5, 16.

Kral, M. 2003. *Unikkaatuit: Meanings of Well-Being, Sadness, Suicide and Change in Two Inuit Communities*. Report to Health Canada, February 2003.

Krieger, Nancy, and Elizabeth Fee. 1994. "Man-Made Medicine and Women's Health." Pp. 11–29 in *Women's Health Politics and Power: Essays on Sex/Gender, Medicine and Public Health*, Elizabeth Fee and Nancy Krieger, eds. Amityville, NY: Baywood Publications.

Kriesberg, Louis. 1992. "Peace." Pp. 1432–1436 in *Encyclopedia of Sociology*, edited by Edgar F. Borgatta and Marie L. Borgatta. New York: Macmillan.

Kristof, Nicholas D. 1998. "As Asian Economies Shrink, Women Are Squeezed Out." *New York Times*, June 11, A1, A12.

Kunkel, Dale, et al. 2001. *Sex on TV2*. Menlo Park, CA: Kaiser Family Foundation.

Kuumba, M. Bahati. 1999. "A Cross-Cultural Race/Class/Gender Critique of Contemporary Population Policy: The Impact of Globalization." *Sociological Forum* 14 (3):447–463.

Kwong, Jo. 2005. "Globalization's Effects on the Environment." *Society* 42 (January/February):21–28.

Kyodo News International. 1998. "More Japanese Believe Divorce Is Acceptable." *Japan Times,* January 12, B4.

L

Lacey, Marc. 2005. "Accents of Africa: A New Outsoaring Frontier." *New York Times,* February 2, pp. C1, C6.

Lakshimi, Rama. 2001. "Gender Prejudice in India Still against Daughters." *The Globe and Mail*, April 4, A10.

Lampkin, Lorna. 1985. *Visible Minorities in Canada.* Research paper for the Abella Royal Commission on Equality in Employment. Ottawa: Ministry of Supply and Services.

Landler, Mark. 2005."Mixed Feelings as Kyoto Pact Takes Effect." *New York Times,* February 16, pp. C1, C3.

Landtman, Gunnar. [1938] 1968. *The Origin of Inequality of the Social Class.* New York: Greenwood (original edition 1938, Chicago: University of Chicago Press).

———. 1968. *The Origin of Inequality of the Social Class.* New York: Greenwood.

Lang, Eric. 1992. "Hawthorne Effect." Pp. 793–794 in *Encyclopedia of Sociology,* Vol. 2. Edgar F. Borgatta and Marie L. Borgatta, eds. New York: Macmillan.

Langman, L. 1987. "Social Stratification." Pp. 211–249 in *Handbook of Marriage and the Family.* Marvin B. Sussman and Suzanne K. Steinmetz, eds. New York: Plenum.

Lasch, Christopher. 1977. *Haven in a Heartless World: The Family Besieged.* New York: Basic Books.

Lasn, Kalle. 2003. "Ad Spending Predicted for Steady Decline." *Adbusters* (January/February).

Lasswell, Harold D. 1936. *Politics: Who Gets What, When, How.* New York: McGraw-Hill Ryerson.

Lauer, Robert H. 1982. *Perspectives on Social Change.* 3rd ed. Boston: Allyn and Bacon.

Laumann, Edward O., John H. Gagnon, and Robert T. Michael. 1994a. "A Political History of the National Sex Survey of Adults." *Family Planning Perspectives* 26 (February):34–38.

Laumann, Edward O., John H. Gagnon, and Robert T. Michael, and Stuart Michaels. 1994b. *The Social Organization of Sexuality: Sexual Practices in the United States.* Chicago: University of Chicago Press.

Lautard, Hugh E., and Donald J. Loree. 1984. "Ethnic Stratification in Canada, 1931–1971." *Canadian Journal of Sociology* 9:333–343.

Lautard, Hugh, and Neil Guppy. 1999. "Revisiting the Vertical Mosaic: Occupational Stratification among Canadian Ethnic Groups." Pp. 219–252 in *Race and Ethnic Relations in Canada.* 2nd ed., Peter S. Li, ed. Toronto: Oxford University Press.

Lazarsfeld, Paul, and Robert K. Merton. 1948."Mass Communication, Popular Taste, and Organized Social Action." Pp. 95–118 in *The Communication of Ideas,* Lymon Bryson, ed. New York: Harper and Brothers.

Leacock, Eleanor. 2001. "Women in an Egalitarian Society: The Montagnais-Naskapi of Canada." Pp. 55–66 in *Family Patterns, Gender Relations,* 2nd ed., Bonnie J. Fox, ed. Toronto: Oxford University Press.

Leacock, Eleanor Burke. 1969. *Teaching and Learning in City Schools.* New York: Basic Books.

Leavell, Hugh R., and E. Gurney Clark. 1965. *Preventive Medicine for the Doctor in His Community: An Epidemiologic Approach,* 3rd ed. New York: McGraw-Hill Ryerson.

Lee, Alfred McClung. 1983. *Terrorism in Northern Ireland.* Bayside, NY: General Hall.

Lee, Barrett A. 1992. "Homelessness." Pp. 843–847 in *Encyclopedia of Sociology,* Vol. 2, Edgar F. Borgatta and Marie L. Borgatta, eds. New York: Macmillan.

Lee, Jennifer A. 2001. "Tracking Sales and the Cashiers." *New York Times,* June 11, C1, C6.

Lehne, Gregory K. 1995. "Homophobia among Men: Supporting and Defining the Male Role." Pp. 325–336 in *Men's Lives,* Michael S. Kimmel and Michael S. Messner, eds. Boston: Allyn and Bacon.

Lem, Sharon. 2000. "Life Expectancy Gender Gap Narrowing." *Toronto Sun,* June 7. Retrieved July 30, 2001 (http://www.canoe.ca/Health0003-6/07_men.html).

Lengermann, Patricia Madoo, and Jill Niebrugge-Brantley. 1996. "Contemporary Feminist Theory." Pp. 436–486 in *Sociological Theory,* 4th ed., George Ritzer, ed. New York: McGraw-Hill Ryerson.

———. 1998. *The Women Founders: Sociology and Social Theory, 1830–1930.* Boston: McGraw-Hill Ryerson.

———. 2008. "Contemporary Feminist Theory." Pp. 436–486 in *Sociological Theory,* 7th ed., George Ritzer, ed. New York: McGraw-Hill Ryerson.

Lenski, Gerhard. 1966. *Power and Privilege: A Theory of Social Stratification.* New York: McGraw-Hill Ryerson.

Lenski, Gerhard, Jean Lenski, and Patrick Nolan. 1995. *Human Societies: An Introduction to Macrosociology,* 7th ed. New York: McGraw-Hill Ryerson.

Leo, John. 1987. "Exploring the Traits of Twins." *Time,* January 12, p. 63.

Levin, Jack, and William C. Levin. 1980. *Ageism.* Belmont, CA: Wadsworth.

Levine, Felice. 2001. "Deja Vu All over Again—The Third Amendment." *Footnotes* 29 (May/June).

Levy, R., and J. Hawks. 1996. "Multicultural Medicine and Pharmacy Management: Part One: New Opportunities for Managed Care." *Drug Benefit Trends* 7 (3):27–30.

Lewin, Tamar. 2000. "Differences Found in Care with Stepmothers." *New York Times,* August 17, A16.

———. 2001. "Anthrax Is Familiar Threat at Nation's Abortion Clinics." *New York Times,* November 7, B7.

Lewis, Anthony. 1999. "Abroad at Home: Something Rich and Strange," *New York Times,* October 12.

Li, Peter S. 1988. *Ethnic Inequality in a Class Society.* Toronto: Wall and Thompson.

———. 1992. "Race and Gender as Bases of Class Fractions and Their Effects on Earnings." *Canadian Review of Sociology and Anthropology* 29 (4):488–510.

———. 2000. "Earning Disparities between Immigrants and Native-Born Canadians." *Canadian Review of Sociology and Anthropology* 37 (3).

———. 2003. "Social Inclusion of Visible Minorities and Newcomers: The Articulation of 'Race' and 'Racial' Difference in Canadian Society." Presented at the Conference on Social Inclusion, Ottawa, March 27–28.

Li, W. 1999. "Building Ethnoburbia: The Emergence and Manifestation of the Chinese Ethnoburb in Los Angeles's San Gabriel Valley." *Journal of Asian American Studies* 2 (1):1–28.

Lian, Jason Z., and David Ralph Matthews. 1998. "Does the Vertical Mosaic Still Exist? Ethnicity and Income in Canada, 1991." *Canadian Review of Sociology and Anthropology* 35 (4):461–481.

Liao, Youlian, Daniel L. McGee, Guichan Cao, and Richard S. Cooper. 2000. "Quality of the Last Year of Life of Older Adults: 1986–1993." *Journal of American Medical Association* 283 (January 26):512–518.

Lichtenstein, Nelson. 2005. *Wal-Mart: Template for Twenty-First Century Capitalism.* New York: New Press.

Liebow, Elliot. 1993. *Tell Them Who I Am: The Lives of Homeless Women.* New York: Free Press.

Light, Donald W. 2004. "From Migrant Enclaves to Mainstream: Reconceptualizing Informal Economic Behavior." *Theory and Society* 33:705–737.

Liker, Jeffrey K., Carol J. Hoddard, and Jennifer Karlin. 1999. "Perspectives on Technology and Work Organization." Pp. 575–596 in *Annual Review of Sociology 1999.* Karen S. Cook and John Hagen, eds. Palo Alto, CA: Annual Reviews.

Lin, Nan, and Wen Xie. 1988. "Occupational Prestige in Urban China." *American Journal of Sociology* 93 (January):793–832.

Lin, Nan. 1999. "Social Networks and Status Attainment." Pp. 467–487 in *Annual Review of Sociology 1999*, Karen S. Cook and John Hagen, eds. Palo Alto, CA: Annual Reviews.

Lindbergh, Anne Morrow. 1955. *Gift from the Sea*. Reprint. New York: Pantheon.

Lindholm, Charles. 1999. "Isn't It Romantic?" *Culture Front Online Spring*:1–5.

Lindner, Eileen, ed. 1998. *Yearbook of American and Canadian Churches, 1998*. Nashville: Abingdon Press.

———, ed. 2000. *Yearbook of American and Canadian Churches*. Nashville: Abingdon Press.

Link, Bruce G., and Jo Phelan. 1995. "Social Conditions as Fundamental Causes of Disease." *Journal of Health and Social Behaviour* (Extra Issue):80–94.

Linton, Ralph. 1936. *The Study of Man: An Introduction*. New York: Appleton-Century.

Lips, Hilary M. 1993. *Sex and Gender: An Introduction*. 2nd ed. Mountain View, CA: Mayfield.

Lipset, Seymour Martin. 1996. *American Exceptionalism: A Double-Edged Sword*. New York: Norton.

Lipson, Karen. 1994. "'Nell' Not Alone in the Wilds." *Los Angeles Times*, December 19, F1, F6.

Liska, Allen E., and Steven F. Messner. 1999. *Perspectives on Crime and Deviance*. 3rd ed. Upper Saddle River, NJ: Prentice Hall.

Little, Kenneth. 1988. "The Role of Voluntary Associations in West African Urbanization." Pp. 211–230 in *Anthropology for the Nineties: Introductory Readings*, Johnnetta B. Cole, ed. New York: Free Press.

Livernash, Robert, and Eric Rodenburg. 1998. "Population Change, Resources, and the Environment." *Population Bulletin* 53 (March).

Livingstone, David. 1999. *The Education–Jobs Gap: Underemployment or Economic Democracy?* Toronto: Garamond Press.

Livingstone, D. W., and Meg Luxton. 1989. "Gender Consciousness at Work: Modification of the Male Breadwinning Norm among Steelworkers and Their Spouses." *Canadian Review of Sociology and Anthropology* 26:240–275.

Livingstone, Sonia. 2004. "The Challenge of Changing Audiences." *European Journal of Communication* 19 (March):75–86.

Lock Kunz, Jean. 2002. "Intersections of Diversity in Labour Market and Training: A Challenge Paper." October 25. Ottawa: Metropolis Project.

Lofland, Lyn H. 1975. "The 'Thereness' of Women: A Selective Review of Urban Sociology." Pp. 144–170 in *Another Voice*, M. Millman and R.M. Kanter, ed. New York: Anchor/Doubleday.

Longman, Phillip. 2004. "The Global Baby Bust." *Foreign Affairs* 83 (May/June): 64–79.

Longworth, R.C. 1993. "UN's Relief Agendas Put Paperwork before People." *Chicago Tribune*, September 14, 1, 9.

Lorber, Judith. 1994. *Paradoxes of Gender*. New Haven, CT: Yale University Press.

Lowman, John, and Ted Palys. 2000. "Ethics and Institutional Conflict of Interest: The Research Confidentiality Controversy at Simon Fraser University." *Sociological Practice: A Journal of Clinical and Applied Sociology* 2(4):245–264.

Lu, Ming, Jianyong Fan, Shejan Liu, and Yan Yan. 2002. "Employment Restructuring During China's Economic Transition." *Monthly Labor Review* (August):25–31.

Luciw, Roma. 2007. "Overworked Before You Get to the Office? You'll Pay For It." *Globe and Mail*, April 10. Retrieved April 10, 2007 (http://www.theglobeandmail.com/servlet/story/RTGAM.20070410.wworkersfamilty0410)

Lukacs, Georg. 1923. *History and Class Consciousness*. London: Merlin.

Luker, Kristin. 1984. *Abortion and the Politics of Motherhood*. Berkeley, CA: University of California Press.

———. 1996. *Dubious Conceptions: The Politics of Teenage Pregnancy*. Cambridge, MA: Harvard University Press.

Lundy, Colleen. 1991. "Women and Alcohol: Moving Beyond Disease Theory." Pp. 57–73 in *Health Futures: Alcohol and Drugs*, Douglas J. McCready, ed. Waterloo: Interdisciplinary Research Committee, Wilfred Laurier University.

Luo, Michael. 1999. "Megachurches Search for Ideas to Grow Again." *Los Angeles Times*, June 7, B1, B3.

Lupton, Deborah. 1999. "Monster in Metal Cocoons: 'Road Rage' and Cyborg Bodies." *Body and Soul* 3 (N.1):57–92.

———. 2001. "Constructing 'Road Rage' as News: An Analysis of Two Australian Newspapers." *Australian Journal of Communication* 28 (N.3):25–36.

Luster, Tom, Kelly Rhoades, and Bruce Haas. 1989. "The Relation between Parental Values and Parenting Behavior: A Test of the Kohn Hypothesis." *Journal of Marriage and the Family* 51(February):139–147.

Luxton, Meg. 1980. *More Than a Labour of Love: Three Generations of Women's Work in the Home*. Toronto: Women's Press.

———. 2001. "Husbands and Wives." Pp. 176–198 in *Family Patterns, Gender Relations*, 2nd ed., Bonnie J. Fox, ed. Toronto: Oxford University Press.

Lyall, Sarah. 2002. "For Europeans, Love, Yes; Marriage, Maybe." *New York Times*, March 24, pp. 1–8.

Lynch, Margaret, and Richard Ferri. 1997. "Health Needs of Lesbian Women and Gay Men." *Clinicians Reviews* 7(1):85–88, 91–92, 95, 98–102, 105–107, 108–115, 117–118.

Lyotard, Jean François. 1993. *The Postmodern Explained: Correspondence, 1982–1985*. Minneapolis: University of Minnesota Press.

M

Macintyre, Sally, Kate Hunt, and Helen Sweeting. 1996. "Gender Differences in Health: Are Things Really As Simple As They Seem?" *Social Science and Medicine* 42:617–624.

Mack, Raymond W., and Calvin P. Bradford. 1979. *Transforming America: Patterns of Social Change*, 2nd ed. New York: Random House.

Mackenzie, Hugh. 2008. Canadian Centre for Policy Alternatives. "New Year's Party Still Going for Top CEOs." January 1. Retrieved April 9, 2008 (http://www.growinggap.ca/node/95).

Mackie, Richard. 2001. "Ontario Opposed School Subsidies before Courts, UN." *The Globe and Mail*, June 13. Retrieved June 15, 2001 (http://www.globeandmail.com).

MacKinnon, Catharine A. 1987. *Feminism Unmodified: Discourses on Life and Law*. Cambridge, MA: Harvard University Press.

MacLeod, Alexander. 2000. "UK Moving to Open All (E-)Mail." *Christian Science Monitor*, May 5, pp. 1, 9.

MacMillan, Angus B., David R. Offord, and Jennifer L. Dingle. 1996. "Aboriginal Health." *Canadian Medical Association Journal* 155(11):1569–78.

MacMillan, H.L., J.E. Fleming, N. Trocme, M.H. Boyle, M. Wong, Y.A. Racine, W.R. Beardslee, and D.R. Offord. 1997. "Prevalence of Child Physical and Sexual Abuse in the Community: Results from the Ontario Health Supplement." *Journal of the American Medical Association* 278:131–135.

Maguire, Brendan. 1988. "The Applied Dimension of Radical Criminology: A Survey of Prominent Radical Criminologists." *Sociological Spectrum* 8 (2):133–151.

Mah, Bill. "No Slackers, Teens Stressed Out: StatsCan." *Edmonton Journal*, May 23. Retrieved May 23, 2007 (http://www.canada.com/edmontonjournal/news).

Mahbub ul Haq Human Development Centre. 2000. *Human Development in South Asia 2000*. Oxford, England: Oxford University Press for Mahbub ul Haq Human Development Centre.

Maine Times. 2001. *Article on Wal-Mart's Plan to Build near the Penja*. January 4.

Maines, David R. 1977. "Social Organization and Social Structure in Symbolic Interactionist Thought." Pp. 235–259 in *Annual*

Review of Sociology, 1977, Alex Inkles, ed. Palo Alto, CA: Annual Reviews.

———. 1982. "In Search of Mesostructure: Studies in the Negotiated Order." *Urban Life* 11 (July):267–279.

Malcolm X, with Alex Haley. 1964. *The Autobiography of Malcolm X.* New York: Grove.

Malthus, Thomas Robert. 1798. *Essays on the Principle of Population.* New York: Augustus Kelly, Bookseller; reprinted in 1965.

Malthus, Thomas Robert, Julian Huxley, and Frederick Osborn. [1824] 1960. *Three Essays on Population.* Reprint. New York: New American Library.

Mandell, Nancy, ed. 1998. *Feminist Issues,* 2nd ed. Scarborough, ON: Prentice Hall Allyn and Bacon.

Mangham, Colin. 2007. "A Critique of Canada's INSITE Injection Site and its Parent Philosophy: Implications and Recommendations for Policy." *Journal of Global Drug Policy and Practice* 1 (2).

Manitoba Human Rights Commission. 2004. "The Fighting Spirit of Lee Williams." *Connections* 4 (2):1–2.

Mann, Jim. 2000. "India: Growing Implications for U.S." *Los Angeles Times,* May 17, A5.

Manson, Donald A. 1986. *Tracking Offenders: White-Collar Crime.* Bureau of Justice Statistics Special Report. Washington, DC: United States Government Printing Office.

Maracle, Lee. 1996. *I Am Woman: A Native Perspective on Sociology and Feminism.* Vancouver: Press Gang Publishers.

Marchak, M. Patricia. 1975. *Ideological Perspectives on Canada.* Toronto: McGraw-Hill Ryerson.

Mark, Gloria, Victor M. Gonzalez, and Justin Harris. 2005. "No Task Left Behind? Examining the Nature of Fragmented Work." Paper presented at CHI 2005, Portland, Oregon.

Marklein, Mary Beth. 1996. "Telecommuters Gain Momentum." *USA Today,* June 18, 6E.

Marmor, Theodore. 1995. P. 1505 in "Medicare 'Canada's Postwar Miracle,' U.S. Management Expert Tells CMA Conference," by J. Rafuse. *Canadian Medical Association Journal* 152 (9).

Marriott, Michel. 2004. "The Color of Mayhem, in a Wave of Urban Games." *New York Times,* August 12.

Marshall, Gordon. 1998. *Dictionary of Sociology.* Oxford: Oxford University Press.

Marshall, Kathleen. 1999. *The Gambling Industry: Raising the Stakes.* Ottawa: Minister of Industry.

Martin, P. and J. Widgren. 1996. *International Migration: A Global Challenge.* Population Bulletin 51(1). Population Reference Bureau, Washington, DC.

Martin, Philip, and Elizabeth Midgley. 1999. "Immigrants to the United States." *Population Bulletin* 54 (June):1–42.

Martin, Susan E. 1994. "Outsider within the Station House: The Impact of Race and Gender on Black Women Politics." *Social Problems* 41 (August):383–400.

Martineau, Harriet. 1896. "Introduction" to the translation of *Positive Philosophy* by Auguste Comte. London: Bell.

———. [1837] 1962. *Society in America.* Edited, abridged, with an introductory essay by Seymour Martin Lipset. Reprint, Garden City, NY: Doubleday.

Martyna, Wendy. 1983. "Beyond the He-Man Approach: The Case for Nonsexist Language." Pp. 25–37 in *Language, Gender and Society,* Barrie Thorne, Cheris Kramorae, and Nancy Henley, eds. Rowley, MA: Newly House.

Maryanski, Alexandra R. 2004. "Evaluation Theory." Pp. 257–263 in *Encyclopedia of Social Theory,* edited by George Ritzer. Thousand Oaks, CA: Sage.

Marx, Karl, and Friedrich Engels. [1847] 1955. *Selected Work in Two Volumes Reprint.* Moscow: Foreign Languages Publishing House.

———. [1848] 1969. "Communist Manifesto." Pp. 98–137 in *Selected Works,* Volume 1. Translated by Samuel Moore. Reprint. Moscow, Russia: Progress Publishers.

Masaki, Hisane. 1998. "Hashimoto Steps Down." *Japan Times,* July 20, 1–5.

Masland, Tom. 1992. "Slavery." *Newsweek,* May 4, pp. 30–32, 37–39.

Mason, J. W. 1998. "The Buses Don't Stop Here Anymore." *American Prospect* 37 (March):56–62.

Matrix.net. 2000. "State of the Internet, January 2000." *MMQ 701.* Retrieved October 14, 2001 (http://www.mids.org).

Matsushita, Yoshiko. 1999. "Japanese Kids Call for a Sympathetic Ear." *Christian Science Monitor,* January 20, p. 15.

Matthews, Beverly. 2000. "The Body Beautiful: Adolescent Girls and Images of Beauty." Pp. 208–219 in *New Perspectives on Deviance: The Construction of Deviance in Everyday Life,* Lori G. Beaman, ed. Scarborough, ON: Prentice Hall.

Matthews, Jay. 1999. "A Home Run for Home Schooling." *Washington Post National Weekly Edition,* March 29, 34.

Maugh, Thomas H., II. 2004. "AIDS Epidemic Continues to Grow, U.N. Reports." *Los Angeles Times,* July 7, p. A3.

Mayer, Karl Ulrich, and Urs Schoepflin. 1989. "The State and the Life Course." Pp. 187–209 in *Annual Review of Sociology, 1989,* W. Richard Scott and Judith Blake, eds. Palo Alto, CA: Annual Reviews.

McCloud, Aminah Beverly. 1995. *African American Islam.* New York: Routledge.

McClung, H. Juhling, Robert D. Murray, and Leo A. Heitlinger. 1998. "The Internet as a Source for Current Patient Information." *Pediatrics* 10 (June 6). Retrieved November 27, 2005 (http://pediatrics.aappublications. org/cgi/content/full/101/6/e2).

McCoy, Kevin, and Dennis Cauchon. 2001. "The Business Side of Terror." *USA Today,* October 16, 1B, 3B.

McCreary Centre Society. 2006. *No Place to Call Home.* Burnaby, BC: McCreary Centre Society.

McCreary, D. 1994. "The Male Role and Avoiding Femininity." *Sex Roles: A Journal of Research* 31:517–531.

McCright, Aaron M., and Riley E. Dunlap. 2003. "Defeating Kyoto: The Conservative Movement's Impact on U.S. Climate Change Policy." *Social Problems* 50(3):348–373.

McDonough, Peggy, and Vivienne Walters. 2000. "Gender, Work and Health: An Analysis of the 1994 National Population Health Survey." *Centres of Excellence for Women's Health Research Bulletin* 1(1):3–4.

McEwen, Andrew. 2007. "Forbidden City Told to Shut Its Gates on Starbucks." *Sunday Herald,* January 20. Retrieved March 13, 2008 (http://www.sundayherald.com/ international/shinternational/display. var.1137066.0.0.php).

McFalls, Joseph A., Jr. 1998. "Population: A Lively Introduction." *Population Bulletin* 53 (September).

McFalls, Joseph A., Jr., Brian Jones, and Bernard J. Gallegher III. 1984. "U.S. Population Growth: Prospects and Policy." *USA Today,* January, 30–34.

McGue, Matt, and Thomas J. Bouchard, Jr. 1998. "Genetic and Environmental Influence on Human Behavioral Differences." Pp. 1–24 in *Annual Review of Neurosciences.* Palo Alto, CA: Annual Reviews.

McGuire, Meredith B. 1981. *Religion: The Social Context.* Belmont, CA: Wadsworth.

———. 1992. *Religion: The Social Context.* 3rd ed. Belmont, CA: Wadsworth.

McIntosh, Peggy. 1988. "White Privilege and Male Privilege: A Personal Account of Coming to See Correspondence through Work and Women's Studies." Working Paper No. 189, Wellesley College Center for Research on Women, Wellesley, MA.

McIntyre. Lisa J. 2006. *The Practical Skeptic.* New York: McGraw-Hill Ryerson.

McKenna, Barrie. 2004. "Unions Starting to Make Inroads at Wal-Mart." *The Globe and Mail,* August 23, B1, B12.

McKinlay, John B., and Sonja M. McKinlay. 1977. "The Questionable Contribution of Medical Measures to the Decline of Mortality in the United States in the Twentieth Century." *Milbank Memorial Fund Quarterly* 55(Summer):405–428.

McKinley, James C., Jr. 1999. "In Cuba's New Dual Economy, Have-Nots Far Exceed Haves." *New York Times,* February 11, A1, A6.

McLane, Daisann. 1995. "The Cuban-American Princess." *New York Times Magazine,* February 26, pp. 42–43.

McLuhan, Marshall. 1962. *The Gutenberg Galaxy: The Making of Typographic Man.* Toronto: University of Toronto Press.

———. 1964. *Understanding Media: The Extensions of Man.* New York: New American Library.

McLuhan, Marshall, and Quentin Fiore. 1967. *The Medium Is the Message: An Inventory of Effects.* New York: Bantam Books.

McNeil, Donald G., Jr. 2004. "Plan to Battle AIDS Worldwide Is Falling Short." *New York Times*, March 28, pp. 1, 14.

McTeer, Maureen A. 1999. *Tough Choices: Living and Dying in the 21st Century.* Toronto: Irwin Law.

McVey, Wayne W., Jr., and Warren Kalbach. 1995. *Canadian Population.* Scarborough ON: Nelson Canada.

Mead, George H. 1934. *Mind, Self and Society,* Charles W. Morris, ed. Chicago: University of Chicago Press.

———. 1964a. *On Social Psychology,* Anselm Strauss, ed. Chicago: University of Chicago Press.

———. 1964b. "The Genesis of the Self and Social Control." Pp. 267–293 in *Selected Writings: George Herbert Mead,* Andrew J. Reck, ed. Indianapolis: Bobbs-Merrill.

Mead, Margaret. [1935] 1950. *Sex and Temperament in Three Primitive Societies.* Reprint, New York: Morrow.

———. [1935] 1963. *Sex and Temperament in Three Primitive Societies.* Reprint, New York: Morrow.

———. 1973. "Does the World Belong to Men— Or to Women?" *Redbook*, October, pp. 46–52.

Media Awareness Network. 2008. "Government and Industry Responses to Media and Violence." Retrieved January 23, 2008 (http://www.media-awareness.ca/english/issues/violence/govt_industry_responses.cfm).

Mehra, Bharat, Cecelia Merkel, and Ann P. Bishop. 2004. "The Internet for Empowerment of Minority and Marginalized Users." *New Media and Society* 6: 781-802.

Meisel, John. 2001. "Stroking the Airwaves: The Regulation of Broadcasting by the CRTC," Pp. 217–232 in *Communications in Canada,* 5th ed., Craig McKie and Benjamin D. Singer, eds. Scarborough, ON: Thompson Educational Publishing.

Melia, Marilyn Kennedy. 2000. "Changing Times." *Chicago Tribune*, January 2, 12–15.

Memmi, Albert. 1991 (1957). *The Colonizer and the Colonized.* Boston: Beacon.

Mendez, Jennifer Bickham. 1998. "Of Mops and Maids: Contradictions and Continuities in Bureaucratized Domestic Work." *Social Problems* 45 (February):114–135.

Mendelsohn, Matthew. 2002. *Canadian Public Opinion on Representative Democracy.* Ottawa: Canadian Centre for Management Development.

Mensah, Joseph. 2002. *Black Canadians: History, Experiences, Social Conditions.* Halifax: Fernwood.

Merton, Robert K. 1968. *Social Theory and Social Structure.* New York: Free Press.

Merton, Robert K., and Alice S. Kitt. 1950. "Contributions to the Theory of Reference Group Behavior." Pp. 40–105 in *Continuities in Social Research: Studies in the Scope and Method of the American Soldier,* Robert K. Merton and Paul L. Lazarsfeld, eds. New York: Free Press.

Messner, Michael A. 1997. *Politics of Masculinities: Men in Movements.* Thousand Oaks, CA: Sage.

Meyers, Thomas J. 1992. "Factors Affecting the Decision to Leave the Old Order Amish." Presented at the annual meeting of the American Sociological Association, Pittsburgh.

Meyerson, Harold. 2004. "Wal-Mart Loves Unions (in China)." *Washington Post*, December 1, A25.

Michels, Robert. 1915. *Political Parties.* Glencoe, IL: Free Press (reprinted 1949).

Mifflin, Lawrie. 1999. "Many Researchers Say Link Is Already Clear on Media and Youth Violence." *New York Times*, May 9, 23.

Migration News. 2003. "China: Economy, Migrants." January. Retrieved August 23, 2003 (http://migration.ucdavis.edu).

———. 2005b. "Offshoring" (January). Accessed (http://migration.ucdavis.edu).

Milgram, Stanley. 1963. "Behavioral Study of Obedience." *Journal of Abnormal and Social Psychology* 67 (October):371–378.

———. 1975. *Obedience to Authority: An Experimental View.* New York: Harper and Row.

Miller, David L. and JoAnne DeRoven Darlington. 2002. *Fearing for the Safety of Others: Disasters and the Small World Problem.* Paper presented at Midwest Sociological Society, Milwaukee, WI.

Miller, George A., and Oleg I. Gubin. 2000. "The Structure of Russian Organizations." *Sociological Inquiry* 70 (Winter):74–87.

Miller, G. Tyler, Jr. 1972. *Replenish the Earth: A Primer in Human Ecology.* Belmont, CA: Wadsworth.

Miller, Reuben. 1988. "The Literature of Terrorism." *Terrorism* 11 (1):63–87.

Millet, Kate. 1971. *Sexual Politics.* New York: Avon Books.

Mills, C. Wright. 1956. *The Power Elite.* New York: Oxford University Press.

———. [1956] 2000b. *The Power Elite.* A New Edition. Afterword by Alan Wolfe. New York: Oxford University Press.

Mills, Robert J. 2000. "Health Insurance Coverage." *Current Population Reports*, ser. P60, no. 211. Washington, DC: United States Government Printing Office.

Miner, Horace. 1956. "Body Ritual among the Nacirema." *American Anthropologist* 58 (June):503–507.

Mirapaul, Matthew. 2001. "How the Net Is Documenting a Watershed Moment." *New York Times*, October 15, E2.

Mitchell, Alanna. 1999. "Home Schooling Goes AWOL." *The Globe and Mail*, February 2, A1, A6.

Mitnick, Kevin D., and William L. Simon. 2005. *The Art of Intrusion: The Real Stories behind the Exploits of Hackers, Intruders and Deceivers.* New York: John Wiley and Sons.

Mizruchi, Mark S. 1996. "What Do Interlocks Do? An Analysis, Critique, and Assessment of Research on Interlocking Directorates." Pp. 271–298 in *Annual Review of Sociology,* 1996, edited by John Hagan and Karen Cook. Palo Alto, CA: Annual Reviews.

Mlynek, Alex, Graham Scott, Steven Dam, Joe Castaldo, Calvin Leung, and Rachel Pulfer. 2006. "The Rich 100 List: The Rich List." *Canadian Business*, Winter 2006/2007. Retrieved September 2, 2007 (http://www.canadianbusiness.com/after_hours/lifestyle_activities/article.jsp?content=20061204_83955_83955).

Moeller, Susan D. 1999. *Compassion Fatigue.* London: Routledge.

Moen, Phyllis, and Patricia Roehling. 2005. *The Career Mystique: Cracks in the American Dream.* Lanham, MD: Rowman and Littlefield.

Moffatt, Susan. 1995. "Minorities Found More Likely to Live Near Toxic Sites." *Los Angeles Times*, August 30, B1, B3.

Mogelonsky, Marcia. 1996. "The Rocky Road to Adulthood." *American Demographics* 18 (May):26–29, 32–35, 56.

Mohanty, Chandra T. 2003. *Feminism Without Borders: Decolonizing Theory, Practicing Solidarity.* Durham, NC: Duke University Press.

Monteiro, Lois A. 1998. "Ill-Defined Illnesses and Medically Unexplained Symptoms Syndrome." *Footnotes* 26 (February):3, 6.

Moore, Oliver. 2004. "Ontario Liberals Focus on School Violence." *The Globe and Mail*, December 14. Retrieved December 14, 2004 (www.theglobeandmail.com/Servlet/story/RTGAM.20041214.wskul1214/BNStory).

Moore, Wilbert E. 1967. *Order and Change: Essays in Comparative Sociology.* New York: John Wiley and Sons.

———. 1968. "Occupational Socialization." Pp. 861–883 in *Handbook of Socialization Theory and Research,* David A. Goslin, ed. Chicago: Rand McNally.

Morin, Richard. 2000. "Will Traditional Polls Go the Way of the Dinosaur?" *Washington Post National Weekly Edition*, May 15, 34.

Morris, Aldon. 2000. "Reflections on Social Movement Theory: Criticisms and Proposals." *Contemporary Sociology* 29 (May): 445–454.

Morris, Bonnie Rothman. 1999. "You've Got Romance! Seeking Love on Line." *New York Times*, August 26, D1.

Morris, Marika. 2000. "Millennium of Achievements." *CRIAW Newsletter* 20 (1). Retrieved September 30, 2007 (http://www.criaw-icref. ca/factSheets/millennium_e.htm).

Morrison, Denton E. 1971. "Some Notes toward Theory on Relative Deprivation, Social Movements, and Social Change." *American Behavioral Scientist* 14 (May–June):675–690.

Moseley, Ray. 2000. "Britons Watch Health Service Fall to Its Knees." *Chicago Tribune*, January 22, 1, 2.

Mossman, M.J. 1994. "Running Hard to Stand Still: The Paradox of Family Law Reform." *Dalhousie Law Journal* 17 (5).

Mossman, Mary Jane. 1998. "The Paradox of Feminist Engagement with Law." Pp. 180–206 in *Feminist Issues: Race, Class, and Sexuality*, 2nd ed., Nancy Mandell, ed. Scarborough, ON: Prentice Hall Allyn and Bacon Canada.

MOST. 1999. *MOST Quarterly.* Internet vol. 1. Retrieved July 19, 1999 (http://www. mostonline.org/qtrly/qtrly-index.htm).

Mueller, G.O. 2001. "Transnational Crime: Definitions and Concepts." Pp. 13–21 in *Combating Transnational Crime: Concepts, Activities, and Responses,* edited by P. Williams and D. Vlassis. London: Franklin Cass.

Murdock, George P. 1945. "The Common Denominator of Cultures." Pp. 123–142 in *The Science of Man in the World Crisis,* Ralph Linton, ed. New York: Columbia University Press.

———. 1949. *Social Structure.* New York: Macmillan.

———. 1957. "World Ethnographic Sample." *American Anthropologist* 59 (August): 664–687.

Murphy, Caryle. 1993. "Putting aside the Veil." *Washington Post National Weekly Edition*, April 12–18, 10–11.

Murphy, Dean E. 1997. "A Victim of Sweden's Pursuit of Perfection." *Los Angeles Times*, September 2, A1, A8.

N

Naiman, Joanne. 2004. *How Societies Work: Class Power and Change in the Canadian Context,* 3rd ed. Scarborough, ON: Nelson.

Nakao, Keiko, and Judith Treas. 1990. *Computing 1989 Occupational Prestige Scores.* Chicago: NORC.

———. 1994. "Updating Occupational Prestige and Socio-economic Scores: How the New Measures Measure Up." Pp. 1–72 in *Sociological Methodology, 1994,* Peter V. Marsden, ed. Oxford, UK: Basil Blackwell.

Nabalamba, Alice. 2001. *Locating Risk: A Multivariate Analysis of the Spatial and Socio-demographic Characteristics of Pollution.* Unpublished Ph.D. dissertation, University of Waterloo, Ontario.

Nanda, Serena. 1991. *Cultural Anthropology.* Belmont, CA: Wadsworth Publishing Company.

Nash, Manning. 1962. "Race and the Ideology of Race." *Current Anthropology* 3 (June):285–288.

Nass, Clifford, and Youngme Moon. 2000. "Machines and Mindlessness: Social Responses to Computers." *Journal of Social Issues* 56 (1):81–103.

National Advisory Commission on Criminal Justice. 1976. *Organized Crime.* Washington, DC: U.S. Government Printing Office.

National Center for Educational Statistics. 1999. *Digest of Education Statistics, 1998.* Washington, DC: U.S. Government Printing Office.

National Center on Elder Abuse. 1998. *The National Elder Abuse Incidence Study.* Washington, DC: American Public Human Services Association.

National Council of Welfare. 2006. *Number of People on Welfare.* August. Ottawa: National Council of Welfare.

National Geographic. 2002. "A World Transformed." *National Geographic* (September): map.

———. 2005. *Atlas of the World,* 8th ed. Washington DC: National Geographic.

National Homeschool Association. 1999. *Homeschooling Families: Ready for the Next Decade.* Retrieved November 19, 2000 (http://www.n-h-a.org/decade.htm).

National Institute on Aging. 1999. *The Declining Disability of Older Americans.* Washington, DC: United States Government Printing Office.

National Partnership for Women and Families. 1998. *Balancing Acts: Work/Family Issues on Prime-Time TV.* Executive Summary. Washington, DC: The National Partnership for Women and Families.

Navarro, Mireya. 2002. "Trying to Get Beyond the Role of the Maid." *New York Times,* May 16, E1, E4.

Neary, Ian. 2003. "Burakumin at the End of History." *Social Research* 70 (Spring):269–294.

Nelson, Adie, and Augie Fleras. 1995. *Social Problems in Canada: Issues and Challenges.* Scarborough, ON: Prentice Hall.

———. 1998. *Social Problems in Canada: Conditions and Consequences.* 2nd ed. Scarborough, ON: Prentice Hall.

Nelson, Adie, and Barrie W. Robinson. 1999. *Gender in Canada.* Scarborough, ON: Prentice Hall.

———. 2002. *Gender in Canada,* 2nd ed. Don Mills, ON: Prentice Hall.

Nelson, Emily. 2004. "Goodbye, 'Friends'; Hello, New Reality."*Wall Street Journal,* February 9, B6, B10.

Nelson, Gary. 2006. "Manitoba School Trustee Favours Tolerance." *Humanist Association of Manitoba.* Retrieved October 2, 2007 (http://www.mb.humanists.ca/manitoba_ school_trustee.html).

Nelson, Jack. 1995. "The Internet, the Virtual Community, and Those with Disabilities." *Disability Studies Quarterly* 15 (Spring):15–20.

Neuborne, Ellen. 1996. "Vigilantes Stir Firms' Ire with Cyberantics." *USA Today,* February 28, A1, A2.

Neuman, W. Lawrence. 2000. *Social Research Methods: Qualitative and Quantitative Approaches.* Boston: Allyn and Bacon.

Newman, William M. 1973. *American Pluralism: A Study of Minority Groups and Social Theory.* New York: Harper and Row.

Newport, Frank. 2004. "A Look at Americans and Religion." Accessed April 14 (www. gallup.com).

Newsday. 1997. "Japan Sterilized 16,000 Women." September 18, A19.

New York Times. 1998. "2 Gay Men Fight Town Hall for a Family Pool Pass Discount." July 14, B2.

Ng, Roxanna. 1988. *The Politics of Community Services: Immigrant Women, Class and the State.* Toronto: Garamond Press.

Nguyen, S. D. 1982. "The Psycho-social Adjustment and Mental Health Needs of Southeast Asian Refugees." *Psychiatric Journal of the University of Ottawa* 7 (1):6–34.

Nie, Norman H. 1999. "Tracking Our Techno-Future." *American Demographics* (July):50–52.

———. 2001. "Sociability, Interpersonal Relations, and the Internet." *American Behavioral Scientist* 45 (November):420–435.

Nielsen, Joyce McCarl, Glenda Walden, and Charlotte A. Kunkel. 2000. "Gendered Heteronormativity: Empirical Illustrations in Everyday Life." *Sociological Quarterly* 41 (2):283–296.

Nixon, Howard L., II. 1979. *The Small Group.* Englewood Cliffs, NJ: Prentice Hall.

Nolan, Patrick, and Gerhard Lenski. 1999. *Human Societies: An Introduction to Macrosociology.* New York: McGraw-Hill Ryerson.

———. 2006. *Human Societies: An Introduction to Macrosociology.* 10th ed. Boulder, CO: Paradigm.

Noonan, Rita K. 1995. "Women against the State: Political Opportunities and Collective Action Frames in Chile's Transition to Democracy." *Sociological Forum* 10:81–111.

NORC (National Opinion Research Center). 1994. *General Social Surveys 1972–1994.* Chicago: National Opinion Research Center.

Norris, Pippa, and Ronald Inglehart. 2004. *Sacred and Secular: Religion and Politics Worldwide.* New York: Cambridge University Press.

Nussbaum, Daniel. 1998. "Bad Air Days." *Los Angeles Times Magazine*, July 19, pp. 20–21.

O

Oberschall, Anthony. 1973. *Social Conflict and Social Movements*. Englewood Cliffs, NJ: Prentice Hall.

O'Connor, Anne-Marie. 2004. "Time of Blogs and Bombs." *Los Angeles Times,* December 27, pp. E1, E14–E15.

O'Donnell, Mike. 1992. *A New Introduction to Sociology*. Walton-on-Thames, United Kingdom: Thomas Nelson and Sons.

Office of Justice Programs. 1999. "Transnational Organized Crime." *NCJRS* Catalog 49 (November/December):21.

Ogburn, William F. 1922. *Social Change with Respect to Culture and Original Nature*. New York: Huebsch (reprinted 1966, New York: Dell).

Ogburn, William F., and Clark Tibbits. 1934. "The Family and Its Functions." Pp. 661–708 in *Recent Social Trends in the United States,* edited by Research Committee on Social Trends. New York: McGraw-Hill.

O'Hanlan, Kate. 2002. "Lesbian Health and Homophobia: Perspectives for Treating Obstetrician/Gynecologist." Retrieved April 4, 2002 (http://www.ohanlan.com/lhr.htm).

Okano, Kaori, and Motonori Tsuchiya. 1999. *Education in Contemporary Japan: Inequality and Diversity*. Cambridge, UK: Cambridge University Press.

Oliver, Melvin L., and Thomas M. Shapiro. 1995. *Black Wealth/White Wealth: New Perspectives on Racial Inequality*. New York: Routledge.

Organization for Economic Co-operation and Development (OECD). 2004. *Early Childhood Education and Care Policy: Canada Country Note October 2004*. Retrieved October 28, 2004 (www.11.sdc.go.ca/en/cs/sp/socpol/publications/reports/2004-002619/page00.shtml).

Ormond, James. 2005. "The McDonaldization of Football." Accessed January 23, 2006 (http://courses.essex.ac.uk/sc/sc111).

Ornstein, M. 2006. *Ethno-Racial Groups in Toronto, 1971-2000: A Demographic and Socio-Economic Profile*. Toronto, ON: Institute for Social Research, York University.

Orum, Anthony M. 1989. *Introduction to Political Sociology: The Social Anatomy of the Body Politic,* 3rd ed. Englewood Cliffs, NJ: Prentice Hall.

Orwell, George. 1949. *1984*. New York: Harcourt Brace Jovanovich.

Ostling, Richard N. 1993. "Religion." *Time International,* July 12, p. 38.

Ouchi, William. 1981. *Theory Z: How American Businesses Can Meet the Japanese Challenge*. Reading, MA: Addison-Wesley.

Ouellette, Laurie. 1993. "The Information Lockout." *Utne Reader,* September–October, pp. 25–26.

P

Page, Charles H. 1946. "Bureaucracy's Other Face." *Social Forces* 25 (October):89–94.

Pager, Devah. 2003. "The Mark of a Criminal Record." *American Journal of Sociology* 108 (March):937–975.

———, and Lincoln Quillian. 2005. "Walking the Talk? What Employers Say Versus What They Do." *American Sociological Review* 70 (June):355–380.

Paik, Haejung, and George Comstock. 1994. "The Effects of Television Violence on Antisocial Behavior: A Meta-analysis." *Communication Research* 21:516–546.

Paik, Nancy. 2001. *One Nation: Islam in America*. Accessed March 15 (www.channelonenews.com/special/islam/media.html).

Palmer Patterson, E. 1972. *The Canadian Indian: A History Since 1500*. New York: Collier-Macmillan of Canada Ltd.

Paquet, Laura Byrne. 2003. *The Urge to Splurge: A Social History of Shopping*. Toronto: ECW Press.

Parents Television Council. 2003. *TV Bloodbath: Violence on Prime Time Broadcast TV*. LosAngeles: PTC.

Park, Robert E. 1916. "The City: Suggestions for the Investigation of Human Behavior in the Urban Environment." *American Journal of Sociology* 20 (March):577–612.

———. 1922. *The Immigrant Press and Its Control*. New York: Harper.

———. 1936. "Succession, an Ecological Concept." *American Sociological Review* 1 (April):171–179.

Park, Steve. 1997. "In the Spirit of Jerry Maguire, I Submit This to the Hollywood Community." *Social Culture. Korean newsgroups* 48:17. Retrieved August 17, 2005 (http://www.dpg.devry.edu/ akim/sck/ho1.html).

Parker, Alison. 2004. "Inalienable Rights: Can Human-Rights Law Help to End U.S. Mistreatment of Noncitizens?" *American Prospect* (October):A11–A13.

Parsons, Talcott. 1951. *The Social System*. New York: Free Press.

———. 1966. *Societies: Evolutionary and Comparative Perspectives*. Englewood Cliffs, NJ: Prentice Hall.

———. 1972. "Definitions of Health and Illness in the Light of American Values and Social Structure." Pp. 166–187 in *Patients, Physicians and Illness*, Gartley Jaco, ed. New York: Free Press.

———. 1975. "The Sick Role and the Role of the Physician Reconsidered." *Milbank Medical Fund Quarterly, Health and Society* 53 (Summer):257–278.

Parsons, Talcott, and Robert Bales. 1955. *Family, Socialization, and Interaction Process*. Glencoe, IL: Free Press.

Passel, Jeffrey S. 2006. *The Size and Characteristics of the Unauthorized Migrant Population in the U.S. Estimates Based on the March 2005 Current Population Survey*.Washington: Pew Hispanic Center.

Pate, Antony M., and Edwin E. Hamilton. 1992. "Formal and Informal Deterrents to Domestic Violence: The Dade County Spouse Assault Experiment." *American Sociological Reviews* 57 (October):691–697.

Patton, Carl V., ed. 1988. *Spontaneous Shelter: International Perspectives and Prospects*. Philadelphia: Temple University Press.

Paulson, Amanda. 2000. "Where the School Is Home." *Christian Science Monitor,* October 10, pp. 18–21.

Pear, Robert. 1996. "Clinton Endorses the Most Radical of Welfare Trials." *New York Times,* May 19, 1, 20.

———. 1997a. "New Estimate Doubles Rate of HIV Spread." *New York Times,* November 26, A6.

———. 1997b. "Now, the Archenemies Need Each Other." *New York Times,* June 22, 1, 4.

Pearlstein, Steven. 2001. "Coming Soon (Maybe): Worldwide Recession." *Washington Post National Weekly Edition* 19 (November 12):18.

Pellow, David Naguib. 2002. *Garbage Wars: The Struggle for Environmental Justice in Chicago*. Cambridge, MA: MIT Press.

Pelton, Tom. 1994. "Hawthorne Works' Glory Now Just So Much Rubble." *Chicago Tribune,* April 18, 1, 6.

Pendakur, Krishna, and Ravi Pendakur. 1998. "The Colour of Money: Earnings Differentials across Ethnic Groups in Canada." *Canadian Journal of Economics* 31 (3):518–548.

———. 2002. "Colour My World: Have Earnings Gaps for Canadian-Born Ethnic Minorities Changed over Time?" *Canadian Public Policy* 28 (4):489–512.

Perrow, Charles. 1986. *Complex Organizations*. 3rd ed. New York: Random House.

Persad, Judy Vashti and Salone Lukacs. 2002. "No Hijab is Permitted Here—A Study on the Experiences of Muslim Women Wearing Hijab Applying for Work in the Manufacturing, Sales and Service Sectors." Windsor, ON: Women Working with Immigrant Women.

Peter, Laurence J., and Raymond Hull. 1969. *The Peter Principle: Why Things Always Go Wrong*. New York: Morrow.

Petersen, William. 1979. *Malthus*. Cambridge, MA: Harvard University Press.

Pew Global Attitudes Project. 2006. *Muslims in Europe: Economic Worries Top Concerns About Religious and Cultural Identity*. Report. Washington, DC: Pew Global Attitudes Project.

———. 2007a. *Selected Countries' Views of American Exports: 2007*. Washington, DC: Pew Global Attitudes Project.

————. 2007b. *Global Unease With Major World Powers*. Report. Washington, DC: Pew Global Attitudes Project.

Philip, Margaret. 2001. "Teens' Dilemma: Cash or Class." *The Globe and Mail*, March 27, A7.

Phillips, E. Barbara. 1996. *City Lights: Urban–Suburban Life in the Global Society*. New York: Oxford University Press.

Piaget, Jean. 1954. *The Construction of Reality in the Child*. Translated by Margaret Cook. New York: Basic Books.

Picard, André. 2007. "Sex and Age Affect Access to Critical Care." *The Globe and Mail*, November 15. Retrieved November 15, 2007 (http://www.theglobeandmail.com/servlet/story/RTGAM.20071115.wlwomen15/BNStory/specialScienceandHealth).

Piller, Charles. 2000. "Cyber-Crime Loss at Firms Doubles to $10 Billion." *Los Angeles Times*, May 22, C1, C4.

Pinderhughes, Dianne. 1987. *Race and Ethnicity in Chicago Politics: A Reexamination of Pluralist Theory*. Urbana: University of Illinois Press.

Pinkerton, James P. 2003. "Education: A Grand Compromise." *Atlantic Monthly* 291 (January/February):115–116.

Platt, Steve. 1993. "Without Walls." *Statesman and Society* 6 (April 2):5–7.

Pleck, J. H., and E. Corfman. 1979. "Married Men: Work and Family." *Families Today: A Research Sampler on Families and Children* 1:387–411.

Plomin, Robert. 1989. "Determinants of Behavior." *American Psychologist* 44 (February):105–111.

Plüss, Caroline. 2005. "Constructing Globalized Ethnicity." *International Sociology* 20 (June):201–224.

Polk, Barbara Bovee. 1974. "Male Power and the Women's Movement." *Journal of Applied Behavioral Science* 10:415–431.

Polletta, Francesca, and James M. Jasper. 2001. "Collective Identity and Social Movements." Pp. 283–305 in *Annual Review of Sociology, 2001*, Karen S. Cook and Leslie Hogan, eds. Palo Alto, CA: Annual Review of Sociology.

Pomfret, John. 2000. "A New Chinese Revolution." *Washington Post National Weekly Edition*, February 21, 17–19.

Ponczek, Ed. 1998. "Are Hiring Practices Sensitive to Persons with Disabilities?" *Footnotes* 26 (3):5.

Poniewozik, James. 2001. "What's Wrong with This Picture?" *Time* 157 (May 28):80–81.

————. 2005. "The Decency Police." *Time*, March 28.

Population Reference Bureau. 1978. "World Population: Growth on the Decline." *Interchange* 7 (May):1–3.

————. 1996. "Speaking Graphically." *Population Today* 24 (June/July).

————. 2007. "2007 World Population Data Sheet." Washington, DC: Population Reference Bureau. (www.prb.org/pdf07/07WPDS_Eng.pdf).

Porter, John. 1965. *The Vertical Mosaic: An Analysis of Social Class and Power in Canada*. Toronto: University of Toronto Press.

Power, Carla. 1998. "The New Islam." *Newsweek* 131 (March 16):34–37.

Power, Samantha. 2002. *A Problem from Hell: America and the Age of Genocide*. New York: Perennial.

Powers, Mary G., and Joan J. Holmberg. 1978. "Occupational Status Scores: Changes Introduced by the Inclusion of Women." *Demography* 15 (May):183–204.

Princeton Religion Research Center. 2000. "Nearly Half of Americans Describe Themselves as Evangelicals." *Emerging Trends* 22 (April):5.

Proctor, Bernadette D., and Joseph Dalaker. 2002. "Poverty in the United States: 2001." *Current Population Reports*, ser. P-60, no. 219. Washington, DC: United States Government Printing Office.

The Province (Vancouver). 2007. "74% of Us Want to Put Family First." May 6, A41.

Prus, Robert. 1989. *Pursuing Customers: An Ethnography of Marketing Activities*. Newbury Park, California: Sage.

————.1996. *Symbolic Interaction and Ethnographic Research: Intersubjectibility and the Study of Human Lived Experience*. Albany, NY: State University of New York Press.

Public Broadcasting Service (PBS). 2001. "Store Wars: When Wal-Mart Comes to Town." Retrieved August 24, 2001 (http://www.pbs.org).

Public Health Agency of Canada. 2006. *HIV/AIDS Epi Updates*.

————. 2006. *HIV and AIDS in Canada. Surveillance Report to June 30, 2006*. Surveillance and Risk Assessment Division, Centre for Infectious Disease Prevention and Control, 2006.

Q

Quadagno, Jill. 1999. *Aging and the Life Course: An Introduction to Social Gerontology*. New York: McGraw-Hill Ryerson.

Quart, Alissa. 2003. *Branded: The Buying and Selling of Teenagers*. New York: Perseus.

Quinney, Richard. 1970. *The Social Reality of Crime*. Boston: Little, Brown.

————. 1974. *Criminal Justice in America*. Boston: Little, Brown.

————. 1979. *Criminology*, 2nd ed. Boston: Little, Brown.

————. 1980. *Class, State and Crime*, 2nd ed. New York: Longman.

R

Rainey, Richard. 2004. "Groups Assail 'Most Violent' Video Games, Industry Rating System." *Los Angeles Times*, November 24, A34.

Rainie, Lee. 2001. *The Commons of the Tragedy*. Washington, DC: Pew Internet and American Life Project.

————. 2005. *Sports Fantasy Leagues Online*. Washington, DC: Pew Internet and American Life Project.

Rainie, Lee, and Dan Pakel. 2001. *More Online, Doing More*. Washington, DC: Pew Internet and American Life Project.

Rajan, Gita, and Shailja Sharma. 2006. *New Cosmopolitanisms: South Asians in the U.S.* Stanford, CA: Stanford University Press.

Ramet, Sabrina. 1991. *Social Currents in Eastern Europe: The Source and Meaning of the Great Transformation*. Durham, NC: Duke University Press.

Rau, William, and Ann Durand. 2000. "The Academic Ethic and College Grades: Does Hard Work Help Students to 'Make the Grade?'" *Sociology of Education* 73 (January):19–38.

Reddick, Randy, and Elliot King. 2000. *The Online Student: Making the Grade on the Internet*. Fort Worth: Harcourt Brace.

Rees, Ruth. 1990. *Women and Men in Education: A National Survey of Gender Distribution in School Systems*. Toronto: Canadian Education Association.

Reinharz, Shulamit. 1992. *Feminist Methods in Social Research*. New York: Oxford University Press.

Reitz, Jeffrey. 1980. *The Survival of Ethnic Groups*. Toronto: McClelland and Stewart.

Religion Watch. 1995. "European Dissenting Movement Grows among Laity Theologians." 10 (October):6–7.

Religious Tolerance. 2005. "Female Genital Mutilation (FGM): Informational Materials." Accessed March 15 (www.religioustolerance.org).

Remnick, David. 1998. "Bad Seeds." *New Yorker* 74 (July 20):28–33.

Rennison, Callie. 2002. *Criminal Victimization 2001*. Changes 2000–01 with Trends 1993–2001. Washington, DC: U.S. Government Printing Office.

Rennison, Callie Marie, and Sarah Welchans. 2000. *Intimate Partner Violence*. Washington, DC: United States Government Printing Office.

Repper, J., R. Perkins, S. Owen, D. Deighton, and J. Robinson. 1996. "Evaluating Services for Women with Serious and Ongoing Mental Health Problems: Developing an Appropriate Research Method." *Journal of Psychiatric and Mental Health Nursing* 3:39–46.

Rheingold, Harriet L. 1969. "The Social and Socializing Infant." Pp. 779–790 in *Handbook of Socialization Theory and Research*, David A. Goslin, ed. Chicago: Rand McNally.

Rheingold, Howard. 2003. *Smart Mobs: The Next Social Revolution*. Cambridge, MA: Perseus.

Richard, Amy O'Neill. 2000. *International Trafficking in Women to the United States: A Contemporary Manifestation of Slavery and Organized Crime*. Washington, DC: Center for the Study of Intelligence, CIA.

Richardson, James T., and Barend van Driel. 1997. "Journalists' Attitudes toward New Religious Movements." *Review of Religious Research* 39 (December):116–136.

Richtel, Matt. 2000. "www.layoffs.com." *New York Times*, June 22, C1, C12.

Riding, Alan. 1998. "Why 'Titanic' Conquered the World." *New York Times*, April 26, 1, 28, 29.

———. 2005. "Unesco Adopts New Plan Against Cultural Invasion." *New York Times*, October 21, B3.

Rifkin, Jeremy. 1995. *The End of Work: The Decline of the Global Labor Force and the Dawn of the Post-Market Era*. New York: Tarcher/Putnam.

———. 1996. "Civil Society in the Information Age." *The Nation* 262 (February 26):11–12, 14–16.

———. 1998. *The Biotech Century: Harnessing the Gene and Remaking the World*. New York: Tarcher/Putnam.

Riley, Matilda White, Robert L. Kahn, and Anne Foner. 1994a. *Age and Structural Lag*. New York: Wiley Inter-Science.

Riley, Matilda White, Robert L. Kahn, and Anne Foner, in association with Karin A. Mock. 1994b. "Introduction: The Mismatch between People and Structures." Pp. 1–36 in *Age and Structural Lag*, Matilda White Riley, Robert L. Kahn, and Ann Foner, eds. New York: Wiley Inter-Science.

Riley, Nancy E. 2004. "China's Population: New Trends and Challenges." *Population Bulletin* 59 (June).

Ritzer, George. 1995b. *The McDonaldization of Society*. Thousand Oaks, CA: Pine Forge Press.

———. 2004. *The McDonaldization of Society*. Rev. new cent. ed. Thousand Oaks, CA: Pine Forge Press.

———. 2007. *Sociological Theory*, 7th ed. New York: McGraw-Hill.

Rivoli, Pietra. 2005. *The Travels of a T-Shirt in the Global Economy: An Economist Examines the Markets, Power, and Politics of World Trade*. Hoboken, NJ: John Wiley and Sons.

Robb, N. 1993. "School of Fear." *OH&S Canada*:43–48.

Roberts, D.F., Lisa Henriksen, Peter G. Christenson, and Marcy Kelly. 1999. "Substance Abuse in Popular Movies and Music." Washington, DC: Office of Juvenile Justice. Retrieved October 19, 2000 (www.whitehousedrugpolicy.gov/news/press/042899.html).

Roberts, Keith A. 1995. *Religion in Sociological Perspective*, 3rd ed. Belmont, CA: Wadsworth.

Roberts, Lynne D., and Malcolm R. Parks. 1999. "The Social Geography of Gender-Switching in Virtual Environments on the Internet." *Information, Communication and Society* 2 (Winter).

Robertson, Grant. 2007. "Battle for Foreign Shows Hits the Bottom Line." *Vancouver Sun*, March 29, B1.

Robertson, Roland. 1988. "The Sociological Significance of Culture: Some General Considerations." *Theory, Culture, and Society* 5 (February):3–23.

Robinson, Gregory, and May Cohen. 1996. "Gay, Lesbian and Bisexual Health Care Issues and Medical Curricula." *Canadian Medical Association Journal* 155:709–711. Retrieved April 4, 2002 (http://www.cma.ca/cmaj/vol-155/issue-06/0709.htm).

Robinson, James D., and Thomas Skill. 1993. "The Invisible Generation: Portrayals of the Elderly on Television." Unpublished paper. University of Dayton.

Robinson, Thomas N., Marta L.Wilde, Lisa C. Navracruz, K. Farish Haydel, and Ann Varady. 2001. "Effects of Reducing Children's Television and Video Game Use on Aggressive Behavior." *Archives of Pediatric Adolescent Medicine* 155 (January):17–23.

Rocks, David. 1999. "Burger Giant Does as Europeans Do." *Chicago Tribune*, January 6, 1, 4.

Rodgers, M. 1993. "Helping Students, Families, and Schools of the Niagara Region Resolve Conflict." *Brock Education* 3 (1):12–14.

Rodin, Judith, and Jeanette R. Ickovics. 1990. "Women's Health: Review and Research Agenda as We Approach the 21st Century." *American Psychologist* 45:1018–1034.

Roethlisberger, Fritz J., and W.J. Dickson. 1939. *Management and the Worker*. Cambridge, MA: Harvard University Press.

Roher, Eric M. 1993. "Violence in a School Setting." *Brock Education* 3(1):1–4.

Rollins, Judith. 1985. *Between Women: Domestics and Their Employers*. Philadelphia: Temple University Press.

Rose, Arnold. 1951. *The Roots of Prejudice*. Paris: UNESCO.

Rose, Peter I., Myron Glazer, and Penina Migdal Glazer. 1979. "In Controlled Environments: Four Cases of Intense Resocialization." Pp. 320–338 in *Socialization and the Life Cycle*, Peter I. Rose, ed. New York: St. Martin's Press.

Rosen, Laurel. 2001. "If U Cn Rd Ths Msg, U Cn B Txtin W/Millions in Europe and Asia." *Los Angeles Times*, July 3, A5.

Rosenbaum, Lynn. 1996. "Gynocentric Feminism: An Affirmation of Women's Values and Experiences Leading Us toward Radical Social Change." *SSSP Newsletter* 27 (1):4–7.

Rosenberg, Douglas H. 1991. "Capitalism." Pp. 33–34 in *Encyclopedic Dictionary of Sociology*, 4th ed., Dushkin Publishing Group, ed. Guilford, CT: Dushkin.

Rosenthal, Elizabeth. 1999. "Web Sites Bloom in China, and Are Waded." *New York Times*, December 23, A1, A10.

———. 2000. "China Lists Controls to Restrict the Use of E-Mail and Web." *New York Times*, January 27, A1, A10.

———. 2001. "College Entrance in China: 'No' to the Handicapped." *New York Times*, May 23, A3.

Rosenthal, Robert, and Elisha Y. Babad, and Lenore Jacobson. 1968. *Pygmalion in the Classroom: Teacher Expectation and Pupils' Intellectual Development*. New York: Holt.

Rosman, Abraham, and Paula G. Rubel. 1994. *The Tapestry of Culture: An Introduction to Cultural Anthropology*, 5th ed. Chapter 1, Map, p. 35. New York: McGraw-Hill Ryerson.

Ross, John. 1996. "To Die in the Street: Mexico City's Homeless Population Booms as Economic Crisis Shakes Social Protections." *SSSP Newsletter* 27 (Summer):14–15.

Rossi, Alice S. 1968. "Transition to Parenthood." *Journal of Marriage and the Family* 30 (February):26–39.

———. 1984. "Gender and Parenthood." *American Sociological Review* 49 (February):1–19.

Rossi, Peter H. 1989. *Down and Out in America: The Origins of Homelessness*. Chicago: University of Chicago Press.

———. 1990. "The Politics of Homelessness." Presented at the annual meeting of the American Sociological Association, Washington, DC.

Rotella, Sebastian. 1999. "A Latin View of American-Style Violence." *Los Angeles Times*, November 25, A1.

Roter, Debra L., Judith A. Hall, and Yutaka Aoki. 2002. "Physician Gender Effects in Medical Communication: A Meta-analytic Review." *Journal of the American Medical Association* 288 (August 14): 756–764.

Royal Commission Status of Women. 1970. *Report of the Royal Commission on the Status of Women in Canada*. Ottawa: The Commission.

Russell, Cheryl. 1995. "Murder Is All-American." *American Demographics* 17 (September): 15–17.

Russo, Nancy Felipe. 1976. "The Motherhood Mandate." *Journal of Social Issues* 32:143–153.

Rutenberg, Jim. 2002. "Fewer Media Owners, More Media Choices." *New York Times*, December 2, C1, C11.

Rutten, Tim. 2008. "A grateful nation needs to do more." *Los Angeles Times*, November 19. Retrieved November 20, 2008 (http://www.latimes.com/news/opinion/sunday/la-oe-rutten19-2008nov19,1,5385587.colu…).

Ryan, William. 1976. *Blaming the Victim*. Rev. ed. New York: Random House.

S

Saad, Lydia. 2003. "What Form of Government for Iraq?" Retrieved September 26 (http://www.gallup.com).

Sachs, Jeffrey D. 2005a. *The End of Poverty: Economic Possibilities for Our Time*. New York: Penguin.

———. 2005b. "Can Extreme Poverty Be Eliminated?" 56–65.

Sadker, Myra Pollack, and David Sadker. 1985. "Sexism in the Schoolroom of the '80s." *Psychology Today* 19 (March):54–57.

———. 1994. *Failing at Fairness: How America's Schools Cheat Girls*. New York: Scribner.

———. 1995. *Failing at Fairness: How America's Schools Cheat Girls*, 2nd ed. New York: Touchstone.

Safire, William. 1996. "Downsized." *New York Times Magazine*, May 26, pp. 12, 14.

Sagarin, Edward, and Jose Sanchez. 1988. "Ideology and Deviance: The Case of the Debate over the Biological Factor." *Deviant Behavior* 9 (1):87–99.

Said, Edward W. 1978. *Orientalism*. New York: Pantheon Books.

Sale, Kirkpatrick. 1996. *Rebels against the Future: The Luddites and Their War on the Industrial Revolution* (with a new preface by the author). Reading, MA: Addison-Wesley.

Salkever, Alex. 1999. "Making Machines More Like Us," *Christian Science Monitor*, December 20.

Samuelson, Paul A., and William D. Nordhaus. 1998. *Economics*, 16th ed. New York: McGraw-Hill Ryerson.

———. 2001. *Economics*, 17th ed. New York: McGraw-Hill Ryerson.

Samuelson, Robert J. 1996a. "Are Workers Disposable?" *Newsweek* 127, February 12, 47.

———. 1996b. "Fashionable Statements," *Washington Post National Weekly Edition*, March 18, 5.

———. 2001. "The Specter of Global Aging." *Washington Post National Weekly Edition*, March 11, 27.

Sandberg, Jared. 1999. "Spinning a Web of Hate." *Newsweek*, July 19, 28–29.

Saunders, Doug. 2007. "Rift Between Old and New." *The Globe and Mail*, July 28, F4.

Sawyer, Tom. 2000. "Antiretroviral Drug Costs." Correspondence to author from Roxane Laboratories, Cincinnati, OH, January 19.

Schaefer, Peter. 1995. "Destroy Your Future." *Daily Northwestern*, November 3, 8.

Schaefer, Richard T. 2004. *Racial and Ethnic Relations*, 9th ed. Upper Saddle River, NJ: Prentice Hall.

———. 2006. *Racial and Ethnic Relations*. 10th ed. Upper Saddle River, NJ: Prentice Hall.

Schaefer, Sandy. 1996. "Peaceful Play." Presentation at the annual meeting of the Chicago Association for the Education of Young Children, Chicago.

Schaller, Lyle E. 1990. "Megachurch!" *Christianity Today* 34 (March 5):10, 20–24.

Scharf, Barbara F. 1999. "Beyond Netiquette: The Ethics of Doing Naturalistic Discourse Research on the Internet." Pp. 243–255 in *Doing Internet Research*, Steve Jones, ed. London: Sage Publishing.

Schellenberg, Grant, and Christopher Clark. 1996. *Temporary Employment in Canada: Profiles, Patterns and Policy Considerations*. Ottawa: Canadian Council on Social Development.

Schellenberg, Kathryn, ed. 1996. *Computers in Society*, 6th ed. Guilford, CT: Dushkin.

Schlenker, Barry R., ed. 1985. *The Self and Social Life*. New York: McGraw-Hill Ryerson.

Schmetzer, Uli. 1999. "Modern India Remains Shackled to Caste System." *Chicago Tribune*, December 25, 23.

Schmitz, Sonja. 1999. "Promiscuity, Pollination, and Genes." *Synthesis/Regeneration* 18 (Winter 1999). Retrieved November 25, 2008 (http://www.greens.org/s-r/18/18-13.html).

Schmid, Carol. 1980. "Sexual Antagonism: Roots of the Sex-Ordered Division of Labor." *Humanity and Society* 4 (November):243–261.

Schmidt, Sarah. 2004. "Older Men Kick Tradition, Opt for Cosmetic Surgeries." *Vancouver Sun*, October 29, A8.

Schnaiberg, Allan. 1994. *Environment and Society: The Enduring Conflict*. New York: St. Martin's.

Schoenfeld, A. Clay, Robert F. Meier, and Robert J. Griffin. 1979. "Constructing a Social Problem: The Press and the Environment." *Social Problems* 27:38–61.

Schur, Edwin M. 1965. *Crimes without Victims: Deviant Behavior and Public Policy*. Englewood Cliffs, NJ: Prentice-Hall.

———. 1968. *Law and Society: A Sociological View*. New York: Random House.

———. 1983. *Labelling Women Deviant: Gender, Stigma and Social Control*. Philadelphia: Temple University Press.

———. 1985. "'Crimes without Victims': A 20-Year Reassessment." Paper presented at the annual meeting of the Society for the Study of Social Problems.

Schulman, Andrew. 2001. *The Extent of Systematic Monitoring of Employee E-mail and Internet Users*. Denver, CO: Workplace Surveillance Project, Privacy Foundation.

Schurman, Rachel. 2004. "Fighting 'Frankenfoods': Industry Opportunity Structures and the Efficacy of the Anti-Biotech

Movement in Western Europe." *Social Problems* 51 (2):243–268.

Schwab, William A. 1993. "Recent Empirical and Theoretical Developments in Sociological Human Ecology." Pp. 29–57 in *Urban Sociology in Transition*, Ray Hutchison, ed. Greenwich, CT: JAI Press.

Schwartz, John. 2004. "Leisure Pursuits of Today's Young Man." *New York Times*, March 29.

Scott, Alan. 1990. *Ideology and the New Social Movements*. London: Unwin Hyman.

Scott, W. Richard 2003. *Organizations: Rational, Natural, and Open Systems*. 5th ed. Upper Saddle River, NJ: Prentice Hall.

———. 2004. "Reflections on a Half-Century of Organizational Sociology." Pp. 1–21 in *Annual Review of Sociology 2004*, edited by Karen S. Cook and John Hagan. Palo Alto, CA: Annual Reviews.

Segall, Alexander. 1976. "The Sick Role Concept: Understanding Illness Behavior." *Journal of Health and Social Behavior* 17 (June):163–170.

Segall, Rebecca. 1998. "Sikh and Ye Shall Find." *Village Voice* 43 (December 15):46–48, 53.

Segerstråle, Ullica. 2000. *Defense of the Truth: The Battle for Science in the Sociobiology Debate and Beyond*. New York: Oxford University Press.

Sernau, Scott. 2001. *Worlds Apart: Social Inequalities in a New Century*. Thousand Oaks, CA: Pine Forge Press.

Seidman, Steven. 1994. "Heterosexism in America: Prejudice against Gay Men and Lesbians." Pp. 578–593 in *Introduction to Social Problems*, Craig Calhoun and George Ritzer, eds. New York: McGraw-Hill Ryerson.

Sellers, Frances Stead. 2004. "Voter Globalization." *Washington Post National Weekly Edition*, November 29, 22.

Shaheen, Jack G. 1999. "Image and Identity: Screen Arabs and Muslims." In *Cultural Diversity: Curriculum, Classrooms, and Climate Issues*, J.Q. Adams and Janice R. Welsch, eds. Macomb, IL: Illinois Staff and Curriculum Development Association.

Shapiro, Joseph P. 1993. *No Pity: People with Disabilities Forging a New Civil Rights Movement*. New York: Times Books.

Sharma, Hari M., and Gerard C. Bodeker. 1998. "Alternative Medicine." Pp. 228–229 in *Britannica Book of the Year 1998*. Chicago: Encyclopaedia Britannica.

Shcherbak, Yuri M. 1996. "Ten Years of the Chernobyl Era." *Scientific American* 274 (April):44–49.

Sheehy, Gail. 1999. *Understanding Men's Passages: Discovering the New Map of Men's Lives*. New York: Ballantine Books.

Shenon, Philip. 1995. "New Zealand Seeks Causes of Suicides by Young." *New York Times*, July 15, 3.

Sherman, Lawrence W., Patrick R. Gartin, and Michael D. Buerger. 1989. "Hot Spots of Predatory Crime: Routine Activities and the Criminology of Place." *Criminology* 27:27–56.

Sherrill, Robert. 1995. "The Madness of the Market." *The Nation* 260 (January 9–16):45–72.

Shields, Rob, ed. 1996. *Cultures of Internet: Virtual Spaces, Real Histories, Living Bodies*. London: Sage.

Shinkai, Hiroguki, and Ugljesa Zvekic. 1999. "Punishment." Pp. 89–120 in *Global Report on Crime and Justice*, Graeme Newman, ed. New York: Oxford University Press.

Shostak, Arthur B. 2002. "Clinical Sociology and the Art of Peace Promotion: Earning a World Without War." Pp. 325–345 in *Using Sociology: An Introduction from the Applied and Clinical Perspectives*, edited by Roger A. Straus. Lanham, MD: Rowman and Littlefield.

Shu, Xialing, and Yanjie Bian. 2003. "Marketing Transition and Gender Gap in Earnings in Urban China." *Social Forces* 81 (4):1107–1145.

Shupe, Anson D., and David G. Bromley. 1980. "Walking a Tightrope." *Qualitative Sociology* 2:8–21.

Sigelman, Lee, Timothy Bledsoe, Susan Welch, and Michael W. Combs. 1996. "Making Contact? Black–White Social Interaction in an Urban Setting." *American Journal of Sociology* 5 (March):1306–1332.

Sierra Club of Canada. 2003. "Sierra Club Urges Canadians to Have a 'Green' Valentines Day." News Release. Retrieved September 11, 2007 (http://www.sierraclub.ca/national/media/item.shtml?x=369).

Silicon Valley Cultures Project. 1999. "The Silicon Valley Cultures Project Website." Retrieved July 30, 1990 (http://www.sjsu.edu/depts/anthropology/svcp).

Silver, Cynthia, Cara Williams, and Trish McOrmond. 2001. "Learning on Your Own." *Canadian Social Trends* (Spring). Statistics Canada. Catalogue No. 11-008. Ottawa: Minister of Industry.

Silver, Ira. 1996. "Role Transitions, Objects, and Identity." *Symbolic Interaction* 19 (1):1–20.

Simmel, Georg. 1950. *Sociology of Georg Simmel*. K. Wolff, transl. Glencoe, IL: Free Press (originally written in 1902–1917).

Simmons, Alan, Dwaine Plaza, and Victor Piché. 2005 "The Remittance Sending Practices of Haitians and Jamaicans in Canada." *Expert Group Meeting on International Migration and Development in Latin America and the Carribean*. United Nations Secretariat.

Simmons, Ann M. 1998. "Where Fat Is a Mark of Beauty." *Los Angeles Times*, September 30, A1, A12.

Simmons, Ann M., and Robin Wright. 2000. "Gender Quota Puts Uganda in Role of Rights Pioneer." *Los Angeles Times*, February 23, p. A1.

Simon, Bernard. 2001. "Canada Warms to Wal-Mart." *New York Times*, November 1, B1, B3.

Simons, Marlise. 1997. "Child Care Sacred as France Cuts Back the Welfare State." *New York Times*, December 31, A1, A6.

Simpson, Sally. 1993. "Corporate Crime." Pp. 236–256 in *Introduction to Social Problems*, Craig Calhoun and George Ritzer, eds. New York: McGraw-Hill Ryerson.

Sjoberg, Gideon. 1960. *The Preindustrial City: Past and Present*. Glencoe, IL: Free Press.

Skull Valley Band Goshutes. 2006. Homepage. Accessed May 2 (www.skullvalleygoshutes.org).

Smart, Barry. 1990. "Modernity, Postmodernity, and the Present." Pp. 14–30 in *Theories of Modernity and Postmodernity*, edited by Bryan S. Turner. Newbury Park, CA: Sage.

Smart Growth. 2001. "About Smart Growth." Retrieved August 24, 2001 (http://www.smartgrowth.org).

Smelser, Neil. 1963. *The Sociology of Economic Life*. Englewood Cliffs, NJ: Prentice Hall.

Smith, Christian. 1991. *The Emergence of Liberation Theology: Radical Religion and Social Movement Theory*. Chicago: University of Chicago Press.

Smith, Dan. 1999. *The State of the World Atlas*. 6th ed. London: Penguin.

Smith, David A. 1995. "The New Urban Sociology Meets the Old: Rereading Some Classical Human Ecology." *Urban Affairs Review* 20 (January):432–457.

Smith, David A., and Michael Timberlake. 1993. "World Cities: A Political Economy/Global Network Approach." Pp. 181–207 in *Urban Sociology in Transition*, Ray Hutchison, ed. Greenwich, CT: JAI Press.

Smith, Dorothy. 1987. *The Everyday World as Problematic: A Feminist Sociology*. Toronto: University of Toronto Press.

Smith, Kirsten. 2007. "History of the Census." *Vancouver Sun*, March 14, A6.

Smith, Kristin. 2000. "Who's Minding the Kids? Child Care Arrangements." *Current Population Reports*, ser. P-70, no. 70. Washington, DC: United States Government Printing Office.

Smith, Michael Peter. 1988. *City, State, and Market*. New York: Basil Blackwell.

Smith, Tom W. 2001. *Estimating the Muslim Population in the United States*. New York: American Jewish Committee.

Smith-Rosenburg, Carroll. 1986. *Disorderly Conduct: Visions of Gender in America*. Toronto: Oxford University Press.

Smith-Rosenberg, Carroll, and Charles Rosenberg. 1974. "The Female Animal: Medical and Biological Views of Woman and Her Role in Nineteenth-Century America." *Journal of American History* 60 (March):332–356.

Snyder, Thomas D. 1996. *Digest of Education Statistics 1996*. Washington, DC: United States Government Printing Office.

Sohoni, Neera Kuckreja. 1994. "Where Are the Girls?" *Ms.*, July–August, 96.

Song, Vivian. 2007. "Home, Sweet Home." *CNews*, June 10. Retrieved July 21, 2007 (http://cnews.canoe.ca/cnews/science/2007/06/10/4249814-sun.html).

Sørensen, Annemette. 1994. "Women, Family and Class." Pp. 27–47 in *Annual Review of Sociology, 1994*, Annemette Sørensen, ed. Palo Alto, CA: Annual Reviews.

Soriano, Cesar G. 2001. "Latino TV Roles Shrank in 2000, Report Finds." *USA Today*, August 26, 3.

Sorokin, Pitirim A. [1927] 1959. *Social and Cultural Mobility*. New York: Free Press.

Sovereign Indigenous Nations. 1991. Union of B.C. Indian Chiefs. "First Nations People of British Columbia." Published by Technical Support Section, Surveys and Resources Mapping Branch, Ministry of Environment, Lands and Parks, Victoria, British Columbia.

Spar, Debora. 2001. *Ruling the Waves: Cycles of Discovery, Chaos, and Wealth from the Compass to the Internet*. Harcourt.

Specter, Michael. 1998. "Doctors Powerless as AIDS Rakes Africa." *New York Times*, August 6, A1, A7.

Speirs, Rosemary. 1993. "Violence Affects Half of Women, Study Says." *Toronto Star*, November 19, A1, A29.

Spengler, Joseph J. 1978. *Facing Zero Population Growth: Reactions and Interpretations, Past and Present*. Durham, NC: Duke University Press.

Spielmann, Peter James. 1992. "11 Population Groups on 'Endangered' List." *Chicago Sun-Times*, November 23, 12.

Spindel, Cheywa, Elisa Levy, and Melissa Connor. 2000. *With an End in Sight*. New York: United Nations Development Fund for Women.

Spitzer, Steven. 1975. "Toward a Marxian Theory of Deviance." *Social Problems* 22 (June):641–651.

Spradley, James P., and David W. McCurdy. 1980. *Anthropology: The Cultural Perspective*, 2nd ed. New York: John Wiley and Sons.

Squires, Gregory D., ed. 2002. *Urban Sprawl: Causes, Consequences and Policy Responses*. Washington: Urban Institute.

Staggenborg, Suzanne. 1989a. "Stability and Innovation in the Women's Movement: A Comparison of Two Movement Organizations." *Social Problems* 36 (February):75–92.

———. 1989b. "Organizational and Environmental Influences on the Development of the Pro-Choice Movement." *Social Forces* 68 (September):204–240.

Stammer, Larry B. 1999. "Former Baptists Leader Seeks a Dialogue with Gay Church." *Los Angeles Times*, July 27, B1, B5.

Standing, Guy. 2004. *Economic Security for a Better World*. Geneva: International Labour Organization.

Stark, Rodney, and William Sims Bainbridge. 1979. "Of Churches, Sects, and Cults: Preliminary Concepts for a Theory of Religious Movements." *Journal for the Scientific Study of Religion* 18 (June):117–131.

———. 1985. *The Future of Religion*. Berkeley, CA: University of California Press.

Stark, Rodney, and Laurence R. Iannaccone. 1992. "Sociology of Religion." Pp. 2029–2037 in *Encyclopedia of Sociology*. Vol. 4, Edgar F. Borgatta and Marie L. Borgatta, eds. New York: Macmillan.

Starr, Kevin. 1999. "Building from Within." *Los Angeles Times*, March 7, 1.

Starr, Paul. 1982. *The Social Transformation of American Medicine*. New York: Basic Books.

Statistics Canada. 1996. "Sexual Activity and Contraceptive Use." *National Population Health Survey 1994/1995*. Retrieved February 15, 2002 (http://www.statcan.ca/english/kits/preg/preg3c.htm).

———. 1997. "Divorces, 1995." *Divorces*. Catalogue No. 84-213-XPB.

———. 1998. "1996 Census." *The Daily*, March 17. Retrieved November 27, 2005 (http://www.statcan.ca/Daily/English/980317/d980317.htm#ART2).

———. 1999b. *Overview of the Time Use of Canadians in 1998*. Catalogue No. 12F0080XIE. Ottawa: Minister of Industry. Retrieved November 27, 2005 (http://www.statcan.ca/english/freepub/12F0080XIE/12F0080XIE1999001.pdf).

———. 1999c. "Survey of Labour and Income Dynamics: The Wage Gap between Men and Women." *The Daily*, December 20. Retrieved April 21,2002 (http://www.statcan.ca/Daily/English/991220/d991220a.htm).

———. 2000a. *Women in Canada: A Gender-Based Statistical Report*. Catalogue No. 89-503-XPE. Ottawa: Ministry of Industry, p. 115.

———. 2000b. "Attending Religious Services." *The Daily*, December 12.Retrieved April 21, 2002 (http://www.statcan.ca/Daily/English/001212/d001212b.htm).

———. 2001a. *The Assets and Debts of Canadians: An Overview of the Results of the Survey of Financial Security*. Catalogue No. 13-595-XIE. Retrieved August 15, 2001 (http://www.statcan.ca/cgi_bin/downpub/research.cgi).

———. 2001b. "Crime Comparisons between Canada and the United States." *The Daily*, December 18, 2001. Retrieved December 7. 2008 (http://www.statcan.ca/Daily/English/o11218/d011218b.htm.

———.2001d. *Family Violence in Canada: A Statistical Profile*. Catalogue No. 85-224-XIE. Retrieved January 19, 2002 (http://www.statcan.ca/english/freepub/85-224-XIE/0100085-224-XIE.pdf).

———. 2002d. *A Profile of the Canadian Population: Where We Live, 2001 Census*. Catalogue No. 96F0030XIE2001001. Retrieved November 27, 2005 (http://geodepot.statcan.ca/Diss/Highlights/Index_e.cfm).

———. 2002e. "Census of Agriculture: Profile of Farm Operators." *The Daily*, November 20. Retrieved November 27, 2005 (http://www.statcan.ca/Daily/English/021120/d021120a.htm).

———. 2003a. *Family Income and Participation in Post-secondary Education*. Analytical Studies Branch Research Paper Series. Catalogue No. 11F0019M1E. Retrieved November 27, 2005 (http://www.statcan.ca/english/research/11F0019MIE/11F0019MIE2003210.pdf).

———. 2003c. *Income of Canadian Families, 2001 Census*. Catalogue No. 96F0030XIE2001014. Retrieved May 13, 2003 (http://www12.statcan.ca/english/census01/products/analytic/companion/inc/contents.cfm).

———. 2003d. *Analysis Series, Canada's Ethnocultural Portrait: The Changing Mosaic, 2001 Census*. Catalogue No. 96F0030XIE2001008. Retrieved January 21, 2003, (http://www12.statcan.ca/english/census01/products/analytic/companion/etoimm/contents.cfm).

———. 2003e. *Ethnic Diversity Survey: portrait of a multicultural society*. Catalogue No. 89-593. Retrieved September 29, 2003 (http://www.statcan.ca/english/freepub/89-593-XIE/89-593-XIE2003001.pdf).

———. 2003f. *Earnings of Canadians, 2001 Census*. Catalogue No. 96F0030. Retrieved November 27, 2005 (http://www.statcan.ca/bsolc/english/bsolc?catno=97F0019X2001057).

———. 2003g. *Women in Canada: Work Chapter Updates*. 89F0133XIE. Retrieved November 27, 2005 (http://www.statcan.ca/english/freepub/89F0133XIE/89F0133XIE00001.pdf).

———. 2003h. *Aboriginal Peoples of Canada. 2001 Census (Analysis Series)*. Retrieved September 15, 2003 (http://www12.statcan.ca/english/census01/products/analytic/companion/abor/contents.cfm). Catalogue No. 96F003XIE2001007.

———. 2003i. "Family Violence." *The Daily*, June 23. Retrieved December 1, 2005 (http://www.statcan.ca/Daily/English/030623/d030623c.htm).

———. 2003j. "Religions in Canada," *2001 Census* (Analysis Series). Catalogue No. 96F0030XIE2001015. Retrieved November 27, 2005 (http://www12.statcan.ca/english/

census01/Products/Analytic/companion/rel/canada.cfm).

———. 2003k. "University Enrolment by Age Groups." *The Daily*, April 17. Accessed September 24, 2003 (http://www.statcan.ca/daily/english/030417/d030417b.htm).

———. 2003l. "Deaths." *The Daily*, April 2. Accessed September 24, 2003 (http://www.statcan.ca/daily/english/030402/d030402b.htm).

———. 2003m. "Marriages, 2000." *The Daily*, June 2. Retrieved November 27, 2005 (http://www.statcan.ca/Daily/English/030602/d030602a.htm).

———. 2003n. *Characteristics of Household Internet Users, by Location of Access (Home)*. CANSIM tables 358-0003, 358-0004, 358-0005, and 358-0017. Retrieved November 27, 2005 (http://www40.statcan.ca/l01/cst01/comm10b.htm).

———. 2003o. *Marriages*. Retrieved Monday, June 2, 2003 (http://www.statcan.ca/Daily/English/030602/d030602a.htm).

———. 2003p. *Divorces, 2003*. Retrieved Wednesday, March 9, 2005 (http://www.statcan.ca/Daily/English/050309/d050309b.htm).

———. 2004a. "Study: The Union Movement in Transition." *The Daily*, August 31. Retrieved November 4, 2004 (http://www.statcan.ca/Daily/English/040831/d040831b.htm).

———. 2004b. *Immigrants to Canada, by Country of Last Permanent Residence, Canada*. Retrieved January 28, 2005 (http://www.statcan.ca/english/Estat/guide/track.htm).

———. 2004c. "Crime Statistics," *The Daily*, July 28. Retrieved November 27, 2005 (http://www.statcan.ca/Daily/English/040728/d040728a.htm).

———. 2004d. *Divorces, 2001 and 2002*. Retrieved May 4, 2004 (http://www.statcan.ca/Daily/English/040504/d040504a.htm).

———. 2004e. "E-commerce: Household Shopping on the Internet." *The Daily*, September 23. Retrieved September 23, 2004 (http://www.stat.ca/Daily/English/040923/d040923a.htm).

———. 2004f. "Household Internet Use Survey." *The Daily*, July 8. Retrieved February 26, 2005 (http://www.statcan.ca/Daily/English/040708/d040708a.htm).

———. 2004g. *Immigrants in Canada's Census Metropolitan Areas*. Catalogue No. 89-613-MIE. Retrieved November 27, 2005 (http://www.statcan.ca/english/research/89-613-MIE/2004003/89-613-MIE2004003.pdf).

———. 2004h. "Divorces, 2001 and 2002." *The Daily*, May 4. Retrieved November 27, 2005 (http://www.statcan.ca/Daily/English/040504/d040504a.htm).

———. 2004i. "Marriages, 2002." *The Daily*, December 21. Retrieved November 27, 2005 (http://www.statcan.ca/Daily/English/041221/d041221d.htm).

———. 2004j. "Study: Self-Employment Activity in Rural Canada." *The Daily*, July 23. Retrieved November 27, 2005 (http://www.statcan.ca/Daily/English/040723/d040723c.htm).

———. 2005a. *Health Reports* 16 (3). Catalogue No. 82-003-XIE2004003.

———. 2005b. *Population by Selected Origins, Canada, 2001 Census.* Retrieved November 25, 2005 (http://www40.statcan.ca/l01/cst01/demo26a.htm?sdi=population%20selected%20origins).

———. 2005c. "Census Family." *Definitions, Data Sources and Methods: Statistical Units.* Retrieved July 4, 2005 (http://dissemination.statcan.ca/English/concepts/definitions/cen-family.htm).

———. 2005d. "Divorce and the Mental Health of Children." *The Daily*, December 13. Retrieved September 24, 2007 (http://www.statcan.ca/Daily/English/051213/d051213c.htm).

———. 2005e. "Earnings of Temporary Versus Permanent Employees." *Perspectives on Labour and Income* 6 (1). Retrieved April 17, 2008 (http://www.statcan.ca/english/freepub/75-001-XIW/10105/art-1.htm).

———. 2005f. Family Violence in Canada: A Statistical Profile. Catalogue No. 85-224-XIE.

———. 2005g. "General Social Survey: Victimization." *The Daily*, July 7. Retrieved April 24/2008 (http://www.statcan.ca/Daily/English/050707/d050707b.htm).

———. 2005h. Participation in Post-Secondary Education in Canada: Has the Role of Parental Income and Education Changed Over the 1990s? Catalogue No. 11F0019MIE—No. 243.

———. 2005i. "Divorces, 2003" Catalogue No. 84F0213XPB.

———. 2005j. "General Social Survey: Victimization." *The Daily*, July 7. Retrieved April 24, 2008 (http://www.statcan.ca/Daily/English/050707/d050707b.htm).

———. 2006a. "Canadian Internet Use Survey." *The Daily*, August 15. Retrieved July 10, 2007 (http://www.statcan.ca/Daily/English/060815/d060815b.htm).

———. 2006b. *Characteristics of Individuals Using the Internet.* CANSIM Table 358-0125.

———. 2006c. *Low Income Cut-Offs Before Tax, 2005.* Catalogue No. 75F0002MIE.

———. 2006d. "Human Activity and The Environment: Transportation." *The Daily*, November 9. Retrieved October 16, 2007 (http://www.statcan.ca/Daily/English/061109/d061109b.htm).

———. 2006e. Measuring Violence Against Women: Statistical Trends 2006. Catalogue No. 85-570-XIE.

———. 2006f. *Sexual Offences Recorded by Police, by Sex and Age Group of Victims, 2004.* Incident-Based Uniform Crime Reporting Survey, Canadian Centre for Justice Statistics.

———. 2006g. "Study: Adult Education and Its Impact on Earnings." *The Daily*, March 24. Retrieved October 2, 2007 (http://www.statcan.ca/Daily/English/060324/d060324a.htm).

———. 2006h. "Television Viewing." *The Daily*, March 31. Retrieved January 21, 2008 (http://www.statcan.ca/Daily/English/060331/d060331b.htm).

———. 2006i. The Wealth of Canadians: An Overview of the Results of the Survey of Financial Security: 2005. Minister of Industry, Catalogue No. 13F0026MIE.

———. 2006j. "What's New in the 2006 Census Questionnaire?" Retrieved October 14, 2007 (http://www12.statcan.ca/english/census06/info/new/whatsnew.cfm).

———. 2006k. *Who's on the Internet.* CANSIM Table 358-0125.

———. 2006l. "Who's Religious?" *Canadian Social Trends*, Summer: 2-9. Catalogue No. 11-008.

———. 2006m. *Women in Canada*, 5th ed. 2006 cat. No. 89-503-XIE. Retrieved October 12, 2007 (http://www.statcan.ca/Daily/English/060307/d060307a.htm).

———. 2006n. *Youth in Transition Survey: Education and Labour Market Pathways of Young Adults, 2002.* Catalogue No. 81-595-MIE2004018.

———. 2006o. *Human Activity and the Environment; Annual Statistics, 2006.* Catalogue No. 16-201-XPE.

———. 2007a. *Births. The Daily*, September 21. Retrieved September 21, 2007 (http://www.statcan.ca/Daily/English/070921/d070921b.htm).

———. 2007b. "Crime Rates by Province, 2006." Table in *The Daily*, July 18. Retrieved July 25, 2007 (http://www.statcan.ca/Daily/English/070718/d070718b.htm).

———. 2007c. "Crime Statistics." *The Daily*, July 18. Retrieved July 25, 2007 (http://www.statcan.ca/Daily/English/070718/d070718b.htm).

———. 2007d. *Family Portrait: Continuity and Change in Canadian Families and Households in 2006.* Catalogue No. 97-553-XWE200601. Retrieved January 8, 2008 (http://www12.statcan.ca/english/census06/analysis/famhouse/charts/chart13.htm).

———. 2007f. "Foreign-Born as a Percentage of Metropolitan Population." *Immigration in Canada: A Portait of the Foreign-Born Population, 2006 Census: Data, Figures and Maps.* Retrieved January 3, 2008 (http://www12.statcan.ca/english/census06/analysis/immcit/charts/chart4.htm).

———. 2007g. Immigration in Canada: A Portait of the Foreign-Born Population, 2006 Census. Catalogue No. 557-XWE2006001.

———. 2007h. *Income in Canada: 2005.* Catalogue No. 75-202-XIE.

———. 2007i. "Marriages." *The Daily*, January 17. Retrieved September 17, 2007 (http://www.statcan.ca/Daily/English/070117/d070117a.htm).

———. 2007j. *Portrait of the Canadian Population in 2006, by Age and Sex, 2006 Census.* Catalogue No. 97-551-XWE2006001. Retrieved October 15, 2007 (http://www.statcan.ca/bsolc/enlglish/bsolc?catno=.97-551-XWE2006001).

———. 2007k. "Study, Service Offshoring and Employment." *The Daily*, May 22. Retrieved October 26, 2007 (http://www.statcan.ca/Daily/English/070522/d070522b.htm).

———. 2007l. *Union Membership in Canada, 1997–2006.* The Labour Force Survey.

———. 2007m. *Women in Canada: Work Chapter Updates: 2006.* Catalogue No. 89F0133XWE. Retrieved March 17, 2008 (http://www.statcan.ca/bsolc/enlglish/bsolc?catno=89F0133XWE).

———. 2007n. World: Place of Birth of Recent Immigrants to Canada, Census 2006. Produced by Geography Division.

———. 2007o. *The busy lives of teens. Perspectives on Labour and Income.* May 23, 2007. Statistics Canada Catalogue number 75-001-XIE.

———. 2008a. Ethnocultural Portrait of Canada Highlights, 2006 Census. Catalogue No. 97-562-WE2006002.

———. 2008b. "Aboriginal Peoples in Canada in 2006: Inuit, Métis and First Nations, 2006 Census." *The Daily*, January 15. Retrieved April 16, 2008 (http://www.statcan.ca/Daily/English/080115/d080115a.htm).

———. 2008c. "The Teaching Profession: Trends from 1999 to 2005." *Education Matters.* Catalogue No. 81-004-XIE.

Status of Women Canada. 1995. *Setting the Stage for the Next Century: The Federal Plan for Gender Equality.* Ottawa: Status of Women Canada.

———. 2002. *On Her Own: Young Women and Homelessness in Canada.* Ottawa: Status of Women Canada.

———. 2003. *Women in Non-Standard Jobs: The Public Policy Challenge.* Retrieved April 25, 2008 (http://www.swc-cfc.gc.ca/pubs/pubspr/0662334809/200303_0662334809_10_e.html).

Stearn, J. 1993. "What Crisis?" *Statesmen and Society* 6 (April 2):7–9.

Stedman, Nancy. 1998. "Learning to Put the Best Shoe Forward." *New York Times*, October 27.

Steele, Jonathan. 2005. "Annan Attacks Britain and U.S. over Erosion of Human Rights." *Guardian Weekly*, March 16, 1.

Steffenhagen, Janet. 2001. "City Streets Draw Non-B.C. Youths." *Vancouver Sun*, March 26, A3.

Stein, Leonard. 1967. "The Doctor–Nurse Game." *Archives of General Psychiatry* 16:699–703.

Steinhauer, Jennifer. 2000. "The New Landscape of AIDS." *New York Times*, June 25, 1, 15.

Stenning, Derrick J. 1958. "Household Viability among the Pastoral Fulani." Pp. 92–119 in *The Developmental Cycle in Domestic Groups*, John R. Goody, ed. Cambridge, UK: Cambridge University Press.

Sternberg, Steve. 1999. "Virus Makes Families Pay Twice." *USA Today*, May 24, 6D.

Stevenson, David, and Barbara L. Schneider. 1999. *The Ambitious Generation: America's Teenagers, Motivated but Directionless*. New Haven, CT: Yale University Press.

Stolberg, Sheryl Gay. 2000. "Alternative Care Gains a Foothold." *New York Times*, January 31, A1, A16.

Stoughton, Stephanie, and Leslie Walker. 1999. "The Merchants of Cyberspace." *Washington Post National Weekly Edition*, February 15, 18.

Stout, Madeline Dion. 1996. *Aboriginal Canada: Women and Health: A Canadian Perspective*. Paper prepared for the Canada–USA Forum on Women's Health. Ottawa: Health Canada.

Strassman, W. Paul. 1998. "Third-World Housing." Pp. 589–592 in *The Encyclopedia of Housing*, Willem van Vliet, ed. Thousand Oaks, CA: Sage.

Straus, Murray A. 1994. "State-to-State Differences in Social Inequality and Social Bonds in Relation to Assaults on Wives in the United States." *Journal of Comparative Family Studies* 25 (Spring):7–24.

Strauss, Anselm. 1977. *Negotiations: Varieties, Contexts, Processes, and Social Order*. San Francisco: Jossey Bass.

Strauss, Gary. 2002. "'Good Old Boys' Network Still Rules Corporate Boards." *USA Today*, November 1, pp. B1, B2.

Stuckey, Johanna H. 1998. "Women and Religion: Female Spirituality, Feminist Theology, and Feminist Goddess Worship." In *Feminist Issues: Race, Class, and Sexuality*, 2nd ed., Nancy Mandell, ed. Scarborough, ON: Prentice Hall.

Sugimoto, Yoshio. 1997. *An Introduction to Japanese Society*. Cambridge, UK: Cambridge University Press.

Sumner, William G. 1906. *Folkways*. New York: Ginn.

Sunstein, Cass. 2002. *Republic.com*. Rutgers, NJ: Princeton University Press.

Sutcliffe, Bob. 2002. *100 Ways of Seeing an Unequal World*. London: Zed Books.

Sutherland, Edwin H. 1937. *The Professional Thief*. Chicago: University of Chicago Press.

———. 1940. "White-Collar Criminality." *American Sociological Review* 5 (February):1–11.

———. 1949. *White Collar Crime*. New York: Dryden.

———. 1983. *White Collar Crime: The Uncut Version*. New Haven, CT: Yale University Press.

Sutherland, Edwin H., and Donald R. Cressey. 1978. *Principles of Criminology*, 10th ed. Philadelphia: Lippincott.

Suttles, Gerald D. 1972. *The Social Construction of Communities*. Chicago: University of Chicago Press.

Swatos, William H., Jr., ed. 1998. *Encyclopedia of Religion and Society*. Lanham, MD: Alta Mira.

Sweet, Kimberly. 2001. "Sex Sells a Second Time." *Chicago Journal* 93 (April):12–13.

T

Talbot, Margaret. 1998. "Attachment Theory: The Ultimate Experiment." *New York Times Magazine*, May 24, 4–30, 38, 46, 50, 54.

Tallarico, Claire M., and Deborah Gillis. 2007. "Catalyst Canada: Latest Count of Women in Canada's Largest Businesses Shows Marginal Progress." *News Release*. Toronto: Catalyst.

Tannen, Deborah. 1990. *You Just Don't Understand: Women and Men in Conversation*. New York: Ballantine.

———. 1994a. *Talking from 9 to 5*. New York: William Morris.

———. 1994b. *Gender and Discourse*. New York: Oxford University Press.

Tapscott, Don. 2009. *Grown Up Digital: How the Net Generation is Changing Your World*. New York: McGraw-Hill.

Tarrow, Sidney. 2005. *The New Transnational Activism*. Boulder, CO: Rowman and Littlefield.

Taylor, Carl S. 1990. "Gang Imperialism." In *Gangs in America*, C. Ronald Huff, ed. London: Sage Publications.

Taylor, Verta. 1995. "Watching for Vibes: Bringing Emotions into the Study of Feminist Organizations." Pp. 223–233 in *Feminist Organizations: Harvest of the New Women's Movement*, Myra Marx Ferree and Patricia Yancy Martin, eds. Philadelphia: Temple University Press.

TD Bank Financial Group. 2007. "Markets Are A Woman's Best Friend." TD Economics Special Report, September 25, 2007.

Tedeschi, Bob. 2004. "Social Networks: Will Users Pay to Get Friends?" *New York Times*, February 9, pp. C1, C3.

Terry, Sara. 2000. "Whose Family? The Revolt of the Child-Free." *Christian Science Monitor*, August 29, 1, 4.

Thomas, Jim. 1984. "Some Aspects of Negotiating Order: Loose Coupling and Meso-structure in Maximum Security Prisons." *Symbolic Interaction* 7 (Fall):213–231.

Thomas, Robert McG., Jr. 1995. "Maggie Kuhn, 89, the Founder of the Gray Panthers, Is Dead." *New York Times*, April 23, 47.

Thomas, William I. 1923. *The Unadjusted Girl*. Boston: Little, Brown.

Thompson, Clive. 2005. "Meet the Life Hackers." *New York Times Magazine*, October 16, pp. 40–45.

Thornton, Russell. 1987. *American Indians Holocaust and Survival: A Population History Since 1492*. Norman, OK: University of Oklahoma Press.

Tibbetts, Janice. 2007. "Boys Trail Girls by Age 15 in Preparing for University." *Vancouver Sun*, September 21, A10.

Tidmarsh, Lee. 2000. "If I Shouldn't Spank, What Should I Do? Behaviour Techniques for Disciplining Children." *Canadian Family Physician* 46:1119–1123.

Tierney, John. 1990. "Betting the Planet." *New York Times Magazine*, December 2, 52–53, 71, 74, 76, 78, 80–81.

Tilly, Charles. 1993. *Popular Contention in Great Britain, 1758–1834*. Cambridge, MA: Harvard University Press.

———. 2004. *Social Movements, 1768–2004*. Boulder, CO: Paradigm.

Time Warner. 2004. "America Online and AOL International: Who We Are." Accessed February 6 (www.timewarner.com).

Tolbert, Kathryn. 2000. "In Japan, Traveling Alone Begins at Age 6." *Washington Post National Weekly Edition*, May 15, 17.

Tong, Rosemary. 1989. *Feminist Theory: A Comprehensive Introduction*. Boulder, CO: Westview.

Tonkinson, Robert. 1978. *The Mardudjara Aborigines*. New York: Holt.

Tönnies, Ferdinand. [1887] 1988. *Community and Society*. Rutgers, NJ: Transaction.

Touraine, Alain. 1974. *The Academic System in American Society*. New York: McGraw-Hill Ryerson.

Treiman, Donald J. 1977. *Occupational Prestige in Comparative Perspective*. New York: Academic.

Trimble, Linda, and Jane Arscott. 2003. *Still Counting: Women in Politics across Canada*. Peterborough, ON: Broadview Press.

Tuchman, Gaye. 1992. "Feminist Theory." Pp. 695–704 in *Encyclopedia of Sociology*. Vol. 2, Edgar F. Borgatta and Marie L. Borgatta, eds. New York: Macmillan.

Tuck, Bryan, Jan Rolfe, and Vivienne Adair. 1994. "Adolescents' Attitudes toward Gender Roles within Work and Its Relationship to Gender, Personality Type and Parental Occupations." *Sex Roles: A Journal of Research* 31 (9–10):547–558.

Tuhiwai Smith, Linda. 2005. *Decolonizing Methodologies: Research and Indigenous Peoples*. New York: Zed Books.

Tumin, Melvin M. 1953. "Some Principles of Stratification: A Critical Analysis." *American Sociological Review* 18 (August):387–394.

———. 1985. *Social Stratification*, 2nd ed. Englewood Cliffs, NJ: Prentice Hall.

Turkle, Sherry. 1995. *Life on the Screen: Identity in the Age of the Internet*. New York: Simon and Schuster.

———. 1999. "Looking toward Cyberspace: Beyond Grounded Sociology." *Contemporary Sociology* 28 (November):643–654.

Turner, Bryan S., ed. 1990. *Theories of Modernity and Postmodernity*. Newbury Park, CA: Sage.

Turner, J.H. 1985. *Herbert Spencer: A Renewed Application*. Beverly Hills, CA: Sage.

Twaddle, Andrew. 1974. "The Concept of Health Status." *Social Science and Medicine* 8 (January):29–38.

U

Uchitelle, Louis. 1996. "More Downsized Workers Are Returning as Rentals." *New York Times*, December 8, 1, 34.

UNAIDS. 2004. "UNAIDS 2004 Report on the Gobal Epidemic." Retrieved November 28, 2004 (http://www.unaids.org/bangkok2004/epi_graphics.html).

———. 2006. *Report on the Global AIDS Epidemic*. Geneva, Switzerland: UNAIDS.

UNESCO. 2002. *Education for All, 2002*. Paris, France: UNESCO.

Union of B.C. Indian Chiefs. 1991. "First Nations People of British Columbia." Published by Technical Support Section, Surveys and Resources Mapping Branch, Ministry of Environment, Lands and Parks, Victoria, British Columbia.

United Nations. 1995. *The World's Women, 1995: Trends and Statistics*. New York: United Nations.

———. 2000. *Poverty Report, 2000: Overcoming Human Poverty*. Washington, DC: UNDP.

———. 2001. *Human Development Report, 2001: Making New Technologies Work for Human Development*. New York: UNDP.

———. 2001. "World Marriage Patterns 2000." Retrieved September 13, 2002 (www.undp.org/popin/wdtrends/worldmarriage.patters2000.pdf).

———. 2002. *Human Development Report, 2002: Deepening Democracy in a Fragmented World*. New York: Oxford University Press.

———. 2003. *Water For People, Water for Life: Executive Summary*. New York: United Nations World Water Assessment Programme.

———. 2004. *AIDS Epidemic Update*. New York: United Nations.

———. 2005a. *The Millennium Development Goals Report*. Washington, DC: United Nations.

———. 2005b. *In Larger Freedom: Towards Development, Security and Human Rights for All*. New York: United Nations.

———. 2006. *Human Development Report, 2006*. Retrieved September 12, 2007 (http://hdr.undp.org/hdr2006/report.cfm).

United Nations Children's Fund (UNICEF). 2004. *Report: The State of the World's Children, 2004*. New York: UNICEF.

———. 2005. *Report: Child Poverty in the Rich Countries, 2005*. New York: UNICEF.

———. 2006. *The State of the World's Children, 2007: The Double Dividend of Gender Equality*. New York: UNICEF.

United Nations Conference on Trade and Development (UNCTAD). 2006. *Information Economy Report, 2006: The Development Perspective*. New York: United Nations.

United Nations Development Programme. 1995. *Human Development Report 1995*. New York: Oxford University Press.

———. 2000. *Poverty Report 2000: Overcoming Human Poverty*. Washington, DC: UNDP.

United Nations Office on Drugs and Crime. 2005. "The United Nations Convention Against Transnational Organized Crime and Its Protocols." Accessed March 18, 2005 (www.unodc.org).

United Nations Population Division. 1998. *World Abortion Policies*. New York: Department of Economic and Social Affairs, UNPD.

———. 2004a. *World Population Monitoring 2002: Reproductive Rights and Reproductive Health*. New York: United Nations.

———. 2004. *World Fertility Report 2003*. Press release. Retrieved June 13, 2004 (www.bls.gov/news.release/union2.nrO.htm).

United States Surgeon General. 2001. *Youth Violence: A Report of the Surgeon General*. Washington, DC: United States Government Printing Office.

United States Trade Representative. 2003. *2002 Annual Report*. Washington, DC: United States Government Printing Office.

Uttley, Alison. 1993. "Who's Looking at You, Kid?" *Times Higher Education Supplement* 30 (April 30):48.

V

Valdez, Enrique. 1999. "Using Hotlines to Deal with Domestic Violence: El Salvador." Pp. 139–142 in *Too Close to Home*, Andrew R. Morrison and Maria Loreto Biehl, eds. Washington, DC: Inter-American Development Bank.

Vallas, Mary. 2005. "When Grandkids Don't Leave." *National Post*, October 8, A1.

Vallas, Steven P. 1999. "Rethinking Post-Fordism: The Meaning of Workplace Flexibility." *Sociological Theory* 17 (March):68–101.

Vancouver Sun. 2000. "Youth Violence in Canada." December 2, B4.

———. 2004a. "Smarter Doesn't Always Equal Richer." September 3, B3.

———. 2004b. "Not Enough Starbucks in the World, CEO Says." October 15, H4.

van den Berghe, Pierre. 1978. *Race and Racism: A Comparative Perspective*, 2nd ed. New York: John Wiley and Sons.

van der Gaag, Nikki. 2004. *The No-Nonsense Guide to Women's Rights*. Toronto: New International Publications.

Vanneman, Reeve, and Lynn Weber Cannon. 1987. *The American Perception of Class*. Philadelphia: Temple University Press.

Van Slambrouck, Paul. 1999. "Netting a New Sense of Connection." *Christian Science Monitor*, May 4, 1, 4.

van Vucht Tijssen, Lieteke. 1990. "Women between Modernity and Postmodernity." Pp. 147–163 in *Theories of Modernity and Postmodernity*, edited by Bryan S. Turner. London: Sage.

van Zoonen, Liesbet. 1994. *Feminist Media Studies*. London: Sage.

Vasagar, Jeeran. 2005. "'At Last Rwanda Is Known for Something Positive.'" *Guardian Weekly*, July 22, p. 18.

Vavrus, Mary D. 2002. *Postfeminist News: Political Women in Media Culture*. New York: State University of New York Press.

Veblen, Thorstein. 1919. *The Vested Interests and the State of the Industrial Arts*. New York: Huebsch.

Venkatesh, Sudhir Alladi. 2000. *American Project: The Rise and Fall of a Modern Ghetto*. Cambridge, MA: Harvard University Press.

Verhovek, Sam Howe. 1997. "Racial Tensions in Suit Slowing Drive for 'Environmental Justice,'" *New York Times*, September 7, 1, 16.

Vernon, Glenn. 1962. *Sociology and Religion*. New York: McGraw-Hill Ryerson.

Vernon, JoEtta A., Allen Williams, Terri Phillips, Janet Wilson. 1990. "Media Stereotyping: A Comparison of the Way Elderly Women and Men Are Portrayed on Prime-Time Television." *Journal of Women and Aging* 2 (4):55–68.

Vidaver, R.M., B. LaFleur, C. Tong, R. Bradshaw, and S.A. Marts. 2000. "Women Subjects in NIH-funded Clinical Research Literature: Lack of Progress in Both Representation and Analysis by Sex." *Journal of Women's Health Gender Based Medicine* 9 (June):495–504.

Vissandjee, Bilkis. 2001. "The Consequences of Cultural Diversity." *The Canadian Women's Health Network* 4 (2):3–4.

Vladimiroff, Christine. 1998. "Food for Thought." *Second Harvest Update* (Summer):2.

Vobejda, Barbara, and Judith Havenmann. 1997. "Experts Say Side Income Could Hamper Reforms." *Washington Post*, November 3, A1.

W

Wages for Housework Campaign. 1999. *Wages for Housework Campaign*. Circular. Los Angeles.

Wagley, Charles, and Marvin Harris. 1958. *Minorities in the New World: Six Case Studies*. New York: Columbia University Press.

Wahl, Andrew. 2004. "Leaders Wanted: Skills Shortage Dead Ahead." *Canadian Business*. Retrieved March 1, 2004 (http://www.canadianbusiness.com/article.jsp?content=20040301_58657_58657&page=1).

Waite, Linda. 2000. "The Family as a Social Organization: Key Ideas for the Twentieth Century." *Contemporary Sociology* 29 (May):463–469.

Wake, Bev. 2000. "Home Schooling Gets Top Marks: More Parents are Home Schooling their Children because of Better Internet Access and the Availability of Educational Material." *Ottawa Citizen*, September 7, C3.

Waldinger, Roger, and David Fitzgerald. 2004. "Transnationalism in Question." *American Journal of Sociology* 109 (March): 1177–1195.

Waldman, Amy. 2004a. "India Takes Economic Spotlight, and Critics Are Unkind." *New York Times*, March 7, p. 3.

———. 2004b. "Low-Tech or High, Jobs Are Scarce in India's Boon." *New York Times*, May 6, p. A3.

———. 2004c. "What India's Upset Vote Reveals: The High Tech Is Skin Deep." *New York Times*, May 15, p. A5.

Wallace, Ruth A., and Alison Wolf. 1980. *Contemporary Sociological Theory*. Englewood Cliffs, NJ: Prentice Hall.

Wallerstein, Immanuel. 1974. *The Modern World System*. New York: Academic Press.

———. 1979a. *Capitalist World Economy*. Cambridge, UK: Cambridge University Press.

———. 1979b. *The End of the World as We Know It: Social Science for the Twenty-First Century*. Minneapolis, MN: University of Minnesota Press.

———. 2000. *The Essential Wallerstein*. New York: The New Press.

Wallerstein, Judith S., Judith M. Lewis, and Sandra Blakeslee. 2000. *The Unexpected Legacy of Deviance*. New York: Hyperion.

Wallis, Claudia. 1987. "Is Mental Illness Inherited?" *Time*, March 9, 67.

Wal-Mart. 2001. "Wal-Mart News: Our Commitment to Communities." Retrieved August 24, 2001 (http://www.walmartstores.com).

Wal-Mart Watch. 2000. "Riverside, California Swats Wal-Mart Away." Retrieved August 24, 2001 (http://www.walmartwatch.com).

Walzer, Susan. 1996. "Thinking about the Baby: Gender and Divisions of Infant Care." *Social Problems* 43 (May):219–234.

Wanner, Richard A. 1998. "Book review of *The Vertical Mosaic Revisited* by Rick Helmes-Hayes and James Curtis." *CJS Online* (December). Retrieved May 12, 2005 (http://www.arts.ualberta.ca/cjcopy/reviews/vmrevisited.html).

Ward, Doug. 2007. "A Third of Street Kids Attend School or Have a Job, Survey Shows." *Vancouver Sun*, April 13, A1.

Watts, Duncan J. 2004. "The 'New' Science of Networks." Pp. 243–270 in *Annual Review of Sociology, 2004*, Karen S. Cook and John Hagan, eds. Palo Alto, CA: Annual Reviews.

Wax, Emily. 2005. "Where Woman Rule." *Washington Post National Weekly Edition* July 18, p. 18.

Weber, Martha L. 1998. "She Stands Alone: A Review of the Recent Literature on Women and Social Support." *Prairie Women's Health Centre of Excellence*. Winnipeg: Prairie Women's Health Centre of Excellence.

Weber, Max. [1913–1922] 1947. *The Theory of Social and Economic Organization*. Translated by A. Henderson and T. Parsons. New York: Free Press.

———. [1904] 1949. *Methodology of the Social Sciences*. Edward A. Shils and Henry A. Finch, transl. Glencoe, IL: Free Press.

———. [1904] 1958a. *The Protestant Ethic and the Spirit of Capitalism*. Talcott Parsons, transl. New York: Scribner.

———. [1916] 1958b. *The Religion of India: The Sociology of Hinduism and Buddhism*. New York: Free Press.

Weedon, Chris. 1999. *Feminism, Theory and the Politics of Difference*. Oxford, UK: Blackwell Publishers.

Weeks, Carly. 2007. "Canada's Growth Outpaces Rest of G-8." *Vancouver Sun*, March 14, A5.

Weeks, John R. 2002. *Population: An Introduction to Concepts and Issues*, 8th ed. Belmont, CA: Wadsworth.

———. 2005. *Population: An Introduction to Concepts and Issues*, 9th ed. with InfoTrac 8th ed. Belmont, CA: Wadsworth.

Wei, Minquian. 2004. "Religion and Earnings of Immigrants in Ontario." Thesis, Department of Economics, University of Ottawa, Ottawa.

Weinfeld, M. 1994. "Ethnic Assimilation and the Retention of Ethnic Cultures." Pp. 238–266 in *Ethnicity and Culture in Canada: The Research Landscape*, J.W. Berry and J.A. Laponce, eds. Toronto: University of Toronto Press.

Weinstein, Deena. 1999. *Knockin' The Rock: Defining Rock Music as a Social Problem*. New York: McGraw-Hill/Primis.

———. 2000. *Heavy Metal: The Music and Its Culture*. Cambridge, MA: Da Capo.

Weinstein, Deena, and Michael A. Weinstein. 1999. "McDonaldization Enframed." Pp. 57–69 in *Resisting McDonaldization*, Barry Smart, ed. London: Sage.

———. 2002. "Hail to the Shrub." *American Behavioral Scientist* 46 (December):566–580.

Weinstein, Henry, Michael Finnegan, and Teresa Watanabe. 2001. "Racial Profiling Gains Support as Search Tactic." *Los Angeles Times*, September 24, A1, M9.

Weisbrot, Mark, Dean Baker, and David Rusnick. 2005. *The Scorecard on Development: 25 Years of Diminished Progress*. Washington, DC: Center for Economic and Policy Research.

Weiss, Rick. 1998. "Beyond Test-Tube Babies." *Washington Post National Weekly Edition*, February 16, 6–7.

Weitz, Rose. 1996. *The Sociology of Health, Illness and Health Care: A Critical Approach*. Belmont, CA: Wadsworth.

Wellman, Barry, J. Salaff, D. Dimitrova, L. Garton, M. Gulia, and C. Haythornthwaite. 1996. "Computer Networks as Social Networks: Collaborative Work, Telework, and Virtual Community." Pp. 213–238 in *Annual Review of Sociology, 1996*, John Hagan, ed. Palo Alto, CA: Annual Reviews.

Welsh, Moira. 2008. "Is Earth Day Still Relevant 18 Years On?" *Toronto Star*, April 22. Retrieved April 24, 2008 (http://www.thestar.com/article/416854).

Wentz, Laurel, and Claire Atkinson. 2005. "'Apprentice' Translators Hope for Hits All Over Globe." *Advertising Age*, February 14, 3, 73.

West, Candace, and Don H. Zimmerman. 1983. "Small Insults: A Study of Interruptions in Cross Sex Conversations between Unacquainted Persons." Pp. 86–111 in *Language, Gender, and Society*, Barrie Thorne, Cheris Kramarae, and Nancy Henley, eds. Rowley, MA: Newbury House.

———. 1987. "Doing Gender." *Gender and Society* 1 (June):125–151.

West, William G. 1993. "Violence in the Schools/Schooling in Violence: Escalating Problem or Moral Panic? A Critical Perspective." *Orbit* 24 (1):6–7.

White, J., and N. Jodoin. 2003. *Aboriginal Youth: A Manual of Promising Suicide Prevention Strategies*. Calgary: Centre for Suicide Prevention:261-262.

Whyte, William Foote. 1981. *Street Corner Society: Social Structure of an Italian Slum*, 3rd ed. Chicago: University of Chicago Press.

Wickman, Peter M. 1991. "Deviance." Pp. 85–87 in *Encyclopedic Dictionary of Sociology*, 4th ed. Guilford, CT: Dushkin.

Wilford, John Noble. 1997. "New Clues Show Where People Made the Great Leap to Agriculture." *New York Times*, November 18, B9, B12.

Wilkinson, Tracy. 1999. "Refugees Forming Bonds on Web." *Los Angeles Times*, July 31, A2.

Willett, Jeffrey G., and Mary Jo Deegan. 2000. "Liminality and Disability: The Symbolic Rite of Passage of Individuals with Disabilities." Presented at the annual meeting of the American Sociological Association, Washington, DC.

Williams, Carol J. 1995. "Taking an Eager Step Back." *Los Angeles Times*, June 3, A1, A14.

———. 1995. *Still a Man's World: Men Who Do Women's Work*. Berkeley, CA: University of California Press.

Williams, Robin M. (in collaboration with John P. Dean and Edward A. Suchman). 1964. *Strangers Next Door: Ethnic Relations in American Communities*. Englewood Cliffs, NJ: Prentice Hall.

Williams, Simon Johnson. 1986. "Appraising Goffman." *British Journal of Sociology* 37 (September):348–369.

Williams, Wendy M. 1998. "Do Parents Matter? Scholars Need to Explain What Research Really Shows." *Chronicle of Higher Education* 45 (December 11):B6–B7.

Wilson, David. 2000. "Residential Schools: Bearing History's Burden." *The United Church Observer*. Retrieved August 16, 2005 (http://www.ucobserver.org/archives/nov00_cvst-part1.htm).

Wilson, Edward O. 1975. *Sociobiology: The New Synthesis*. Cambridge, MA: Harvard University Press.

———. 1978. *On Human Nature*. Cambridge, MA: Harvard University Press.

Wilson, Jennifer. 2007. "Faith-Based Schools." CBC News online, September 17. Retrieved October 1, 2007 (htto://www.cbc.ca/ontariovotes2007/features/features-faith.html).

Wilson, John. 1973. *Introduction to Social Movements*. New York: Basic Books.

Wilson, Jolin J. 2000. *Children as Victims*. Washington, DC: United States Government Printing Office.

Wilson, Warner, Larry Dennis, and Allen P. Wadsworth, Jr. 1976. "Authoritarianism Left and Right." *Bulletin of the Psychonomic Society* 7 (March):271–274.

Wilson, William Julius. 1980. *The Declining Significance of Race: Blacks and Changing American Institutions*, 2nd ed. Chicago: University of Chicago Press.

———. 1987. *The Truly Disadvantaged: The Inner City, the Underclass and Public Policy*. Chicago: University of Chicago Press.

———. 1996. *When Work Disappears: The World of the New Urban Poor*. New York: Knopf.

———. 1999a. *The Bridge over the Racial Divide: Rising Inequality and Coalition Politics*. Berkeley, CA: University of California Press.

———. 1999b. "Towards a Just and Livable City: The Issues of Race and Class." *Address at the Social Science Centennial Conference, April 23*. Chicago, IL: DePaul University.

———, ed. 1989. *The Ghetto Underclass: Social Science Perspectives*. Newbury Park, CA: Sage.

Winter, J. Alan. 1977. *Continuities in the Sociology of Religion*. New York: Harper and Row.

Wirth, Louis. 1928. *The Ghetto*. Chicago: University of Chicago Press.

———. 1938. "Urbanism as a Way of Life." *American Journal of Sociology* 44 (July):1–24.

Wolf, Charles, Jr. 2001. "China's Capitalists Join the Party." *New York Times*, August 13, A21.

Wolf, Naomi. 1991. *The Beauty Myth: How Images of Beauty Are Used against Women*. New York: Anchor Books.

Wolf, Richard. 1996. "States Can Expect Challenges after Taking over Welfare." *USA Today*, October 1, 8A.

Wolff, Edward N. 2002. *Top Heavy*. Updated ed. New York: New Press.

Wolinsky, Fredric P. 1980. *The Sociology of Health*. Boston: Little, Brown.

Women's International Network. 1995. "Working Women: 4 Country Comparison." *WIN News* 21 (September 9):82.

Wood, Daniel B. 2000. "Minorities Hope TV Deals Don't Just Lead to 'Tokenism.'" *Christian Science Monitor*, January 19.

Wood, Julia T. 1994. *Gendered Lives: Communication, Gender and Culture*. Belmont, CA: Wadsworth.

Woodard, Colin. 1998. "When Rate Learning Fails against the Test of Global Economy." *Christian Science Monitor*, April 15, 7.

Wooden, Wayne. 1995. *Renegade Kids, Suburban Outlaws: From Youth Culture to Delinquency*. Belmont, CA: Wadsworth.

Woolf, Virginia. 1977. *A Room of One's Own*. San Diego, CA: Harvest/HBJ.

World Bank. 1995. *World Development Report, 1994: Workers in an Integrating World*. New York: Oxford University Press.

———. 1997. *World Development Report, 1997: The State in a Changing World*. New York: Oxford University Press.

———. 2000. *World Development Report 2000/2001*. Washington, DC: World Bank.

———. 2000a. *World Development Indicators, 2000*. Washington, DC: World Bank.

———. 2001. *World Development Report 2002: Building Instructions for Markets*. New York: Oxford University Press.

———. 2002. *World Development Indicators, 2002*. Washington, DC: World Bank.

———. 2003. *World Development Report, 2003: Sustainable Development in a Dynamic World*. Washington, DC: World Bank.

———. 2004. *World Development Report 2005. A Better Investment Climate for Everyone*. Washington, DC: World Bank.

———. 2005. *World Development Indicators, 2005*. Washington, DC: World Bank.

———. 2006. *Repositioning Nutrition as Central to Development: A Strategy for Large-Scale Action*. Washington, DC: World Bank.

World Economic Forum. 2005. *The Global Information Technology Report, 2004–2005*. Davos, Switzerland: World Economic Forum.

World Fact Book. CIA. https://www.cia.gov/library/publications/the-world-factbook/print/ca.html.

World Health Organization. 2000. *The World Health Report, 2000: Health Systems: Improving Performance*. Geneva, Switzerland: WHO.

———. 2005. *AIDS Epidemic Update, December 2005*. Geneva, Switzerland: WHO.

World Resources Institute. 1998. *1998–99 World Resources: A Guide to the Global Environment*. New York: Oxford University Press.

Wresch, William. 1996. *Disconnected: Haves and Have-Nots in the Information Age*. New Brunswick, NJ: Rutgers University Press.

Wright, Charles R. 1986. *Mass Communication: A Sociological Perspective*, 3rd ed. New York: Random House.

Wright, Eric R., William P. Gronfein, and Timothy J. Owens. 2000. "Deinstitutionalization, Social Rejection, and the Self-Esteem of Former Mental Patients." *Journal of Health and Social Behavior* (March).

Wright, Erik Olin, David Hachen, Cynthia Costello, and Joy Sprague. 1982. "The American Class Structure." *American Sociological Review* 47 (December):709–726.

Wu, Zheng. 1999. "Premarital Cohabitation and the Timing of First Marriage." *Canadian Review of Sociology and Anthropology* 36 (1):109–127.

Wu, Zheng, and Michael S. Pollard. 2000. "Economic Circumstances and the Stability of Nonmarital Cohabitation." *Journal of Family Issues* 21(3):303–328.

Wurman, Richard Saul. 1989. *Information Anxiety*. New York: Doubleday.

Wuthnow, Robert. 1996. *Poor Richard's Principle: Recovering the American Dream through the Moral Dimension of Work, Business, and Money*. Princeton, N.J.: Princeton University Press.

Y

Yalnizyan, Armine. 2007. *The Rich and the Rest of Us: The Changing Face of Canada's Growing Gap*. Toronto: Canadian Centre for Policy Alternatives.

Yamagata, Hisashi, Kuang S. Yeh, Shelby Stewman, and Hiroko Dodge. 1997. "Sex Segregation and Glass Ceilings: A Comparative Statistics Model of Women's Career Opportunities in the Federal Government over a Quarter Century." *American Journal of Sociology* 103 (November):566–632.

Yardley, Jim. 2005. "Fearing Future, China Starts to Give Girls Their Due." *New York Times*, January 31, p. A3.

Yap, Kioe Sheng. 1998. "Squatter Settlements." Pp. 554–556 in *The Encyclopedia of Housing*, Willem van Vliet, ed. Thousand Oaks, CA: Sage.

Yinger, J. Milton. 1970. *The Scientific Study of Religion*. New York: Macmillan.

———. 1974. "Religion, Sociology of." Pp. 604–613 in *Encyclopaedia Britannica*, Vol. 15. Chicago: Encyclopedia Britannica.

York University. 2006. "Toronto Poverty is Highly Racialized: York University Census Study." Media Release. Retrieved January 2, 2008 (http://www.yorku.ca/mediar/archive/Release.asp).

Young, K. 1988. " The Social Relations of Gender." In *Gender in Caribbean Development*, P. Mohammed and C. Shepard, eds. Mona, Jamaica: Women and Development Studies Group.

Youth Works. 2006. "Raising the Roof Launches $1.2 million Youth Works to Combat Youth Homelessness." Press Release, January 11.

Z

Zang, Xiaowei. 2002. "Labor Market Segmentation and Income Inequality in Urban China." *Sociological Quarterly* 43 (1):27–44.

Zarembo, Alan. 2003. "Funding Studies to Suit Need." *Los Angeles Times,* December 7, pp. A1, A20.

———. 2004. "A Theater of Inquiry and Evil." *Los Angeles Times,* July 15, pp. A1, A24, A25.

Zelizer, Gerald L. 1999. "Internet Offers Only Fuzzy Cyberfaith, Not True Religious Experiences." *USA Today*, August 19, 13A.

Zellner, William M. 1978. "Vehicular Suicide: In Search of Incidence." Unpublished M.A. thesis. Western Illinois University, Macomb.

———. 1995. *Counter Cultures: A Sociological Analysis*. New York: St. Martin's Press.

———. 2001. *Extraordinary Groups: An Examination of Unconventional Lifestyles*, 7th ed. New York: Worth.

Zimbardo, Philip G. 1972. "Pathology of Imprisonment." *Society* 9 (April):4, 6, 8.

———. 2004. "Power Turns Good Soldiers into 'Bad Apples.'" *Boston Globe*, May 9.

———. 2005. "What Do You Believe Is True Even Though You Cannot Prove It?" *New York Times*, January 4, D3.

Zimbardo, Philip G., Ann L.Weber, and Robert Johnson. 2003. *Psychology: Core Concepts*. 4th ed. Boston: Allyn and Bacon.

Zimbardo, Philip G., Craig Haney, W. Curtis Banks, and David Jaffe. 1974. "The Psychology of Imprisonments: Privation, Power, and Pathology." In *Doing unto Others: Joining, Molding, Conforming, Helping, and Loving*, Zick Rubin, ed. Englewood Cliffs, NJ: Prentice Hall.

Zola, Irving K. 1972. "Medicine as an Institution of Social Control." *Sociological Review* 20 (November):487–504.

———. 1983. *Socio-Medical Inquiries*. Philadelphia: Temple University Press.

Zook, Matthew A. 1996. "The Unorganized Militia Network: Conspiracies, Computers, and Community." *Berkeley Planning Journal* 11:1–15.

Zuckerman, Laurence. 2001. "Divided, An Airline Stumbles." *New York Times*, March 14, C1, C6.

Zuckerman, M.J. 2000. "Criminals Hot on Money Trail to Cyberspace." *USA Today*, March 21, 8A.

Zweigenhaft, Richard L., and G. William Domhoff. 1998. *Diversity in the Power Elite: Have Women and Minorities Reached the Top?* New Haven, CT: Yale University Press.

———. 2006. *Diversity in the Power Elite: How It Happened, Why It Matters*. 2d ed. New York: Rowman and Littlefield.

ACKNOWLEDGEMENTS

Chapter 1

P. 2: Quotation from Paquet, Laura Byrne. *The Urge to Splurge: A Social History of Shopping.* Toronto: ECW Press, 2003.

P. 20: Quotation in Box 1-2 from Carol Brooks Gardner. 1989. "Analyzing Gender in Public Places," *American Sociologist* 20 (Spring): 42–56. Reprinted by permission of Transaction Publishers. Copyright © 1989 by Transaction Publishers.

Chapter 2

P. 25: Quotation from Sarah Schmidt. 2004. "Older Men Kick Tradition, Opt for Cosmetic Surgeries," *Vancouver Sun*, October 29: p. A8. Material reprinted with the express permission of CanWest News Service, a CanWest Partnership.

PP. 26–27: Canadian Sociology and Anthropology Association (CSAA), *Statement of Professional Ethics.* www.csaa.ca/structure/Code.htm.

P. 32: Figure 2-3: Adapted from the Statistics Canada publication, *Analytical Studies Branch Research Paper Series,* Catalogue No. 11F0019MIE, No. 243, February 2005, p. 12.

P. 36: Unnumbered figure in Box 2-2 from William Rau and Ann Durand. 2000. "The Academic Ethic and College Grades: Does Hard Work Help Students to 'Make the Grade?'" *Sociology of Education* 73(January):26. Used by permission of the American Sociological Association and the authors.

P. 41: Figure 2-4: From Henry J. Kaiser Family Foundation. February 2005. Executive Summary of Sex on TV 4:4: A Biennial Report of the Kaiser Family Foundation (#3324). This information was reprinted with permission from the Henry J. Kaiser Family Foundation. The Kaiser Family Foundation, based in Menlo Park, California, is a nonprofit, private operating foundation focusing on the major health care issues facing the nation and is not associated with Kaiser Permanente or Kaiser Industries.

P. 42: Table 2-3: Adapted from the Statistics Canada publication "Health Reports," Catalogue 82-003, Vol. 16, No. 3, May 2005.

Chapter 3

P. 48: Quotation from Horace Miner. 1956. "Body Ritual among the Nacirema." *American Anthropologist* 58(3). Reprinted by permission of the American Anthropological Association.

P. 54: Figure 3-2: From Michael Erard. 2005. "How Linguists and Missionaries Share a Bible of 6,912 Languages," *New York Times* (July 19): Dr. New York Times. Copyright © 2005 The New York Times. Reprinted by permission.

P. 57: Table 3-1: From Industry Analysis, Policy Development and Research Sector. 2007. *Television Statistical and Financial Summaries,* 2002–2006, p. 13. Reproduced with the permission of the Minister of Public Works and Government Services Canada, 2007.

P. 58: Figure 3-3: From Erin Anderssen, Michael Valpy, et al. 2004. *The New Canada: A Globe and Mail Report on the Next Generation.* Toronto: McClelland & Stewart. Used by permission of McClelland & Steward Ltd and Ipsos-Reid.

P. 61: Figure 3-4: Illustration by Jim Willis. 1996. "The Argot of Pickpockets," *New York Daily News* (November 19):5. © New York Daily News, L.P. Reprinted by permission.

P. 63: Table 3-2: Adapted from Pew Global Attitudes Project. 2007. Reprinted by permission.

Chapter 4

P. 71: Quotation from the Aboriginal Healing Foundation. 2000. "The Residential School Impact," *Healing Words 2:8–9.* Reprinted by permission.

P. 77: Quotation in Box 4-1 from Daniel Albas and Cheryl Albas. 1988. "Aces and Bombers: The Post-Exam Impression Management Strategies of Students." *Symbolic Interaction* 11(Fall):289–302. © by the Society for the Study of Symbolic Interaction.

P. 90: Unnumbered figure in Box 4-3: From Population Reference Bureau. 2007. 2007 World Population Data Sheet. www.prb.org/pdf07/07/WPDS_Eng.pdf. Reprinted by permission.

Chapter 5

P. 99: Quotation from Philip G. Zimbardo. 1972. "Pathology of Imprisonment," *Society,* 9(April):4. Copyright © 1972 by Transaction Publishers. Reprinted by permission of the publisher. Quotation from P. G. Zimbardo, C. Haney, W. C. Banks, & D. Jaffe. 1974. "The Psychology of Imprisonment: Privation, Power, and Pathology." In Z. Rubin (Ed.), *Doing Unto Others: Explorations in Social Behaviour:* 61–73. Used by permission of Philip G. Zimbardo, Inc.

P. 125: Figure 6-1: Data adapted in part from Statistics Canada, "Perspectives on Labour and Income," *The Union Movement in Transition,* Catalogue 75-001, Vol. 5, No. 8, August 2004.

Chapter 6

P. 132: Quotation from Don Tapscott. 2009. *Grown Up Digital: How the Net Generation is Changing Your World.* © 2009. Reprinted by permission of the McGraw-Hill Companies.

P. 135: Table 6-1: Google Zeitgeist. © Google Inc. Used with permission.

P. 144: Figure 6-1: Adapted from National Geographic Atlas of the World, 8e. National Geographic Society, 2005. The Fuller Projection Map design is a trademark of Buckminster Fuller Institute™. © 1938, 1967, 1992. All rights reserved. www.bfi.org. NG Maps/National Geographic Image Collection. Used by permission of National Geographic Image Sales and the Buckminster Fuller Institute.

P. 145: Figure 6-2: Adapted from Statistics Canada Web site http://www40.statcan.ca/101/cst01/comm15.htm (last modified 2006-08-15).

Chapter 7

P. 158: Quotation from "A World Awash in Heroin." *The Economist.* June 30, 2007, p. 69.

P. 168: Table 7-2: Adapted with permission of The Free Press, copyright renewed 1985 by Robert K. Merton.

P. 177: Figure 7-1: Adapted from Statistics Canada, "Crime Statistics," *The Daily,* July 18, 2007. http://www.statcan.ca/Daily/English/070718/d070718b.htm.

Chapter 8

P. 185: Quotation from Hugh Mackenzie. January 2, 2008. "New Year's Party Still Going for Top CEOs." Canadian Centre for Policy Alternatives Press Release. www.policyalternatives.ca/News/2008/01/PressRelease1791/. Reprinted by permission.

P. 188: Table 8-1: Adapted from "The Rich 100," *Canadian Business,* December 2008. www.canadianbusiness.com/rankings/rich/100/2008.

P. 195: Table 8-2: Adapted from James A. Davis, Tom W. Smith, Peter B. Marsden. 2005. *General Social Surveys, 1972–2004: Cumulative Codebook.* Chicago: National Opinion Research Center. Used by permission.

P. 196: Figure 8-1: Adapted from Statistics Canada publication, *Income in Canada,* 2005, Catalogue No. 75-202, p. 77, www.statcan.ca/bsolc/english/bsolc?catno=75-202-X; and the publication, *The Wealth of Canadians: An Overview of the Results of a Survey of Financial Security 2005,* Catalogue No. 13F0026MIE, No. 001. Release date: December 7, 2006. p. 9. www.statcan.ca/bsolc/english/bsolc?catno=13F0026MIE2006001.

P. 197: Figure 8-2: Adapted from Armine Yalnizyan. March 2007. *The Rich and the Rest of Us: The Changing Force of Canada's Growing Gap,* p. 16. Canadian Centre for Policy Alternatives. Reprinted by permission.

P. 198: Table 8-3: Adapted from Statistics Canada publication, *Income Research Paper Series,* Catalogue No. 75F0002MIE, No. 4, May 2007, p. 23. www.statcan.ca/english/bsolc?catno=75F0002M.

P. 199: Figure 8-3: United Nations *Human Development Report 2007/2008.*

P. 200: Table 8-4: Adapted from Statistics Canada publication, *Income in Canada 2005,* Catalogue No. 75-202-XIE. www.statcan.ca/bsolc/english/bsolc?catno=75-202-X.

P. 205: Quotation in Box 8-2 from "Eight Woman One Voice," a Gideon Mendel/ActionAid project. This part is spoken by Rutica Banda. Her complete part can be read at www.guardian.co.uk/africa8/0,16068, 1501265,00.html.

Chapter 9

P. 212: Quotation from Steve Derné. 2003. "Schwarzenegger, McBeal and Arranged Marriages: Globalization on the Ground in India," in *Contexts,* a publication of the American Sociological Association. © 2003 University of California Press—Journals. Used by permission of California Press—Journals, via Copyright Clearance Centre.

P. 214: Figure 9-1: Adapted from Bob Sutcliffe. 2002. *100 Ways of Seeing an Unequal World.* Fig. 1, p. 18. London: Zed Books. Reprinted by permission.

P. 216: Figure 9-2: Adapted in part from John R. Weeks. 2002, 2005. Population: *An Introduction to Concepts and Issues,* with InfoTrac, 8th ed. and 9th ed. Belmont, CA: Wadsworth. © 2002 and © 2005. Reprinted with permission of Wadsworth, a division of Thomson Learning, www.thomsonrights.com. Fax (800) 730-2215. And adapted in part from Carl Haub. 2005. *World Population Data Sheet 2005.* Used by permission of Population Reference Bureau.

P. 220: Table 9-2: Adapted in part from Fortune, 2005. FORTUNE Global 500, *Fortune*, July 25. © 2005 Time Inc. All rights reserved. And adapted in part from World Bank. 2005. *World Development Indicators 2005.* © World Bank. Used by permission of the World Bank, via Copyright Clearance Centre.

P. 222: Figure 9-4: From Chronic Poverty Research Center. 2005. Administered by the Institute for Development Policy and Management, School of Environment and Development, University of Manchester, UK. Used by permission.

P. 223: Figure 9-5: From *The Economist*, July 7, 2007; based on data from the World Bank and the UN.

P. 225: Figure 9-6: Data from the World Bank, 2005. *World Development Indicators 2005.* © World Bank. Used by permission of the World Bank, via Copyright Clearance Centre.

Chapter 10

P. 234: Excerpt and cover from *The New Canada: A Globe and Mail Report on the Next Generation* by Erin Anderssen and Michael Valpy. Used by permission of McClelland & Stewart Ltd.

P. 239: Table 10-1: From Statistics Canada, "Ethnocultural Portraits of Canada Highlights," 2006 Census. Catalogue No. 97-562-XWE2006002. www12.statcan.ca/English/census06/data/highlights/ethnic/pages/Page.cfm?Lang=Eg&Geo=PR&Code=01&Data=Count&Table=2&StartRec=1&Sort=3&Display=All&CSDFilter=5000.

P. 248: Quotation in Box 10-2: From Augie Fleras and Jean Lock Kunz. 2001. *Media and Minorities: Representing Diversity in a Multicultural Canada.* Toronto: Thompson Educational Publishing: 30–31.

P. 251: Figure 10-2: © Province of British Columbia. All rights reserved. Reprinted with permission of the Province of British Columbia. www.ipp.gov.bc.ca.

P. 254: Figure 10-3: Adapted from the Statistics Canada "Ethnic Diversity Survey: Portrait of a Multicultural Society," 2002, Catalogue 89-593, September 29, 2003, available at http://www.statcan.ca/english/freepub/89-593-XIE/89-593-XIE2003001.pdf.

P. 256: Figure 10-4: From Statistics Canada, 2006 Census of Canada. www.12.statcan.ca/english/census06/analysis/immcit/maps/world/World_RecentImmig_ec.pdf.

P. 257: Figure 10-5: Statistics Canada 2006; Australian Bureau of Statistics 2006 Census; US Census Bureau, 2005 American Community Survey.

Chapter 11

P. 262: Quotation from Janice Tibbetts. 2007. "Boys trail girls by age 15 in preparing for university," *Vancouver Sun*, September 21, 2007, A10. Material reprinted with the express permission of CanWest News Service, a CanWest Partnership.

P. 265: Table 11-1: From Joyce McCarl Nielsen, et al. 2000. "Gendered Heteronormalinity: Empirical Illustrations in Everyday Life," *Sociological Quarterly* 41 (No. 2): 287. © 2000 Blackwell Publishing. Reprinted by permission of Blackwell Publishing, via Copyright Clearance Centre.

P. 272: Table 11-3: Adapted from Statistics Canada publication, *Women in Canada: A Gender-based Statistical Report*, 2005, Catalogue No. 89-503-XPE. www.statcan.ca/bsolc/english/bsolc?catno=89-503-X.

P. 274: Figure 11-1: From Makiko Fuwa. 2004. "Macro-level Gender Inequality and the Division of Household Labor in 22 Countries." American *Sociological Review* 69: December 2004, Table 2, p. 757. Used by permission of the American Sociological Association and the author.

P. 275: Figure 11-2: Adapted from Statistics Canada publication, *Women in Canada: Work Chapter Updates*, 2006, Table 6, Catalogue No. 89F0133XIE. Release date: April 20, 2007. www.statcan.ca/english/freepub/89F0133XIE/89F0133XIE2006000.htm.

P. 275: Table 11-4: Adapted from Statistics Canada publication, Women in Canada: Work Chapter Updates, 2006, Table 11, Catalogue No. 89F01EEXIE. Release date: April 20, 2007.

www.statcan.ca/english/freepub/89F0133XIE/89F0133XIE2006000.htm.

P. 277: Figure 11-3: Adapted from Linda Duxbury and Chris Higgins. 2001. *Work–Life Balance in Canada: Making the Case for Change*, p. 22. Reprinted by permission of Linda Duxbury and Chris Higgins.

Chapter 12

P. 286: Quotation from Tu Thanh Ha. 2004. "Pregnant woman called him 'Papa,' sperm donor's court petition says," which appeared on www.globeandmail.com on September 14, 2004. Reprinted with permission from *The Globe and Mail*.

P. 288: Figure 12-1: Adapted from Statistics Canada publication, *Family portrait: Continuity and change in Canadian families and households in 2006: National portrait: Census families*, Catalogue No. 97-553-XWE2006001. www12.statcan.ca/english/census06/analysis/famhouse/cenfam1.cfm.

P. 293: Figure 12-2: From *World Fertility Report 2003.* © 2004 United Nations Population Division. Used by permission.

P. 296: Figure 12-3: Adapted from Statistics Canada publication, *Family Portrait: Continuity and Change in Canadian Families and Households in 2006, 2006 Census*, Catalogue No. 97-553-XWE2006001. www12.statcan.ca/english/census06/analysis/famhouse/charts/chart13.htm.

P. 302: Figure 12-4: Adapted from the Statistics Canada publication *The Daily*, Catalogue No. 11-001, "Divorces," Monday, December 2, 2002 and "Marriages," Monday, June 2, 2003. www.statcan.ca/Daily/English/021202/d021202f.htm and www.statcan.ca/Daily/English/030602/d030602a.htm; the Statistics Canada publication *The Daily,* "Divorces," 2001 and 2002, May 4, 2004, www.statcan.ca/Daily/English/040504/d040504a.htm; the Statistics Canada publication, *The Daily,* "Marriages," 2002, December 21, 2004, www.statcan.ca/Daily/English/041221/d041221d.htm; also from the publication entitled "Divorces," 1995, Catalogue No. 84-213, January 15, 1997; the Statistics Canada publication, *The Daily,* "Marriages," 2003, Wednesday, January 17, 2007, www.statcan.ca/Daily/English/070117/d070117a.htm; the Statistics Canada publication, *The Daily,* "Divorces," 2003, Wednesday, March 9, 2005, www.statcan.ca/Daily/English/050309/d050309b.htm.

Chapter 13

P. 311: Quotation from Noah Augustine. "Grandfather was a Knowing Christian." *Toronto Star*, August 9, 2000, A17. Reprinted with permission of Noah Augustine.

P. 313: Figure 13-1: From John L. Allen. 2003. *Student Atlas of World Geography*, 4e. Copyright © 2005 by The McGraw-Hill Companies, Inc. All rights reserved. Reprinted by permission of McGraw-Hill/Contemporary Learning Series.

P. 320: Figure 13-2: Adapted from Pippa Norris and Ronald Inglehart. 2004. *Sacred and Secular: Religion and Politics Worldwide:* Table 3.6, p. 74. Cambridge University Press © 2004. Reprinted with permission of Cambridge University Press.

P. 323: Table 13-3: Adapted from Statistics Canada publication, *2001 Census: Analysis Series, Religions in Canada*, Catalogue No. 96F0030XIE2001015, May 13, 2003. www12.statcan.ca/english/census01/products/analytic/companion/rel/contents.cfm.

Chapter 14

P. 341: Quotation from "More media consumed, more civic engagement: Study" by Brodie Fenlon, *The Globe and Mail*, March 27, 2007. Reprinted with permission from *The Globe and Mail*.

P. 346: Figure 14-1: © 2006 *The Economist Newspaper Ltd.* All rights reserved. Reprinted with permission. Further reproduction prohibited. www.economist.com.

P. 352: Figure 14-2: © International Institute for Democracy and Electoral Assistance, www.idea.int. Used by permission.

P. 353: Figure 14-3: From Inter-Parliamentary Union (IPU), 2006, *Women in National Parliaments*, www.ipu.org/wmn-e/classif.htm. Used by permission.

P. 355: Figure 14-4 (right): From G. William Domhoff. 2001. *Who Rules America*, 4th ed.:96. © 2001 by The McGraw-Hill Companies, Inc. Reproduced by permission of the publisher.

P. 358: Table 14-2: From Chris Baker. 2002. *Canada After September 11th: A Public Opinion Perspective*, Environics Research Group, a FOCUS CANADA study, 2002. Reprinted by permission.

P. 360: Figure 14-5: Adapted from the Statistics Canada publication, *Women in Canada: Work Chapter Updates*, 2006, Table 1, Catalogue No. 89F0133XIE. Released date: April 20, 2007. www.statcan.ca/english/freepub/89F0133XIE/89F0133XIE2006000.htm.

Chapter 15

P. 369: Quotation from *Down to This: Squalor and Splendor in a Big-City Shantytown* by Shaughnessy Bishop-Stall. Copyright © 2004 Shaughnessy Bishop-Stall. Reproduced by permission of Random House Canada.

P. 372: Table 15-1: Adapted from Statistics Canada publication, *Canadian Social Trends*, Catalogue No. 11-008, No. 60, Spring 2001, p. 4. www.statcan.ca/bsolc/english/bsolc?catno=11-008-X.

P. 373: Figure 15-1: From Carl Haub. 2005. *World Population Data Sheet 2005.* Used by permission of Population Reference Bureau.

P. 385: Figure 15-4: From Carl Haub. 2005. *World Population Data Sheet 2005.* Used by permission of Population Reference Bureau.

P. 390: Table 15-5: Based on Gideon Sjoberg. 1960. *The Preindustrial City: Past and Present*: 323–328. Adapted with the permission of The Free Press, a Division of Simon & Schuster Adult Learning Group. Copyright © 1960 by The Free Press. Copyright renewed 1968 by Gideon Sjoberg. All rights reserved. And based on E. Barbara Phillips. 1996. *City Lights: Urban–Suburban Life in the Global Society*, 2/e. Copyright © 1981 by E. Barbara Phillips and Richard T. LeGates, 1996 by E. Barbara Phillips. Oxford University Press. Used by permission.

P. 391: Figure 15-5: Adapted from *National Geographic Atlas of the World*, 8e. National Geographic Society, 2005. NG Maps/National Geographic Image Collection. Used by permission.

P. 392: Figure 15-6: From Chauncy Harris and Edward Ullmann. 1945. "The Nature of Cities," *Annals of the American Academy of Political and Social Science*, 242 (November):13. Reprinted by permission of the American Academy of Political and Social Science, Philadelphia.

P. 401: Figure 15-7: From UNAIDS. 2006. Adapted with permission from UNAIDS, Geneva, Switzerland. For further information, please view the 2006 Report on the global AIDS epidemic at www.unaids.org.

Chapter 16

P. 406: Quotation from Debora L. Spar. 2001. *Ruling the Waves: Cycles of Discovery, Chaos, and Wealth from the Compass to the Internet.* Copyright © 2001 by Debora L. Spar. Reprinted by permission of Harcourt, Inc. and the William Morris Agency.

P. 411: Quotation in Box 16-1: From Manisha Desai. 1996. "If Peasants Build Their Own Dams, What Would the State Have Left to Do?" *Research in Social Movements, Conflicts and Change*, 19:214, ed. Michael Dobkowski and Isidor Wallimann. Greenwich, CT: JAI Press. Used with permission from Elsevier.

P. 423: Figure 16-1: Reprinted by permission of Jerrad Pierce.

P. 425: Figure 16-2: Adapted from *National Geographic Atlas of the World*, 8e, National Geographic Society, 2005. NG Maps/National Geographic Image Collection. Used by permission.

PHOTO CREDITS

NAME INDEX

Vavrus, M.D., 143
Veblen, T., 414, 415
Velkoff, V.A., 90
Vernon, G., 326
Vernon, J.A., 91
Victor, A., 305
Vidaver, R.M., 382
Vissandjee, B., 381, 382
Vladimiroff, 4

W

Wadsworth, A.P., Jr., 64
Wages for Housework Campaign, 196
Wagley, C., 236
Waite, L., 143
Wake, B., 335
Walden, G., 265
Waldinger, R., 426
Walesa, L., 344, 404
Walker, L., 362
Wallace, R.A., 13, 412
Wallerstein, I., 215, 221, 393
Wallerstein, J.S., 303
Wallis, C., 75
Wal-Mart, 399
Walsh, K., 83
Walters, V., 381
Walton, S., 399
Walzer, S., 278
Wanner, R.A., 11
Ward, D., 160
Warren, M., 83
Watts, D.J., 108
Weber, M., 8–9, 26, 28, 42, 117, 118, 120, 121, 192, 317–18, 323, 348, 349, 409
Weber, M.L., 382
Weedon, C., 270
Weeks, C., 371, 378, 379, 397
Wei, M., 328
Weinfeld, M., 63
Weinrib, G.L., 245
Weinstein, D., 143, 417
Weinstein, M.A., 143, 417

Weisbrot, M., 224
Weiss, R., 306
Welchans, S., 301
Wells, I.B., 10
Wentz, L., 141
West, C., 264, 271
Weston, G., Sr., 188
White, J., 6
Whyte, W.F., 35
Wickman, P.M., 165
Widgren, J., 257
Wilford, J.N., 114
Wilkinson, T., 140
Willet, J.G., 104
Williams, C., 334
Williams, C.J., 293
Williams, L., 103
Williams, R.M., 330
Williams, S.J., 77
Williams, W., 80
Wilson, D., 250
Wilson, E.O., 75
Wilson, J. J., 301
Wilson, Jennifer, 337
Wilson, John, 318, 408
Wilson, W., 64
Wilson, W.J., 108, 200, 244
Winter, J.A., 317
Wirth, L., 394
Wolf, A., 13, 412
Wolf, N., 91, 165, 265
Wolff, E.N., 197
Wolinsky, F.P., 383
Wollstonecraft, M., 270
Wood, D.B., 249
Wood, J.T., 142
Woodard, C., 329
Wooden, W., 170
Woolf, V., 332
World Bank, 137, 138, 146, 190, 206, 220, 224, 227, 255, 385
World Economic Forum, 218
World Fact Book, 377

World Health Organization (WHO), 374, 379, 400, 401
World Resources Institute, 420
Worswick, C., 254
Wresch, W., 146
Wright, C.R., 134, 149
Wright, E.O., 191
Wright, E.R., 173
Wright, R., 354
Wuthnow, R., 360
Wyngard, R., 53

X

Xie, W., 195

Y

Yalnizyan, A., 197
Yamagata, H., 240
Yanagisako, S., 281
Yardley, J., 376
Yeltsin, B., 408
Yeoh, M, 141
Yinger, J.M., 317
York University, 238
Young, K., 167
Youth Works, 160
Yufe, J., 74

Z

Zang, X, 347
Zarembo, A., 100, 357
Zellner, W.M., 27, 61, 81
Zeman, Klarka, 262
Zeytinoglu, I.U., 363
Zhang, Z, 141
Zheng Wu, 303
Zimbardo, P.G., 99, 100, 357
Zimmerman, D.H., 264, 271
Zola, I.K., 384, 385
Zuckerman, L., 126
Zuckerman, M.J., 176
Zvekic, U., 179
Zweigenhaft, R.L., 356

SUBJECT INDEX